Port Cities of the Eastern Mediterranean

Eastern Mediterranean port cities, such as Constantinople, Smyrna, and Salonica, have long been sites of fascination. Known for their vibrant and diverse populations, the dynamism of their economic and cultural exchanges, and their form of relatively peaceful coexistence in a turbulent age, many would label them as models of cosmopolitanism. In this study, Malte Fuhrmann examines changes in the histories of space, consumption, and identities in the nineteenth and early twentieth centuries while the Mediterranean became a zone of influence for European powers. Giving voice to the port cities' forgotten inhabitants, Fuhrmann explores how their urban populations adapted to European practices, how entertainment became a marker of a Europeanized way of life, and how consuming beer celebrated innovation, cosmopolitanism, and mixed gender sociability. At the same time, these adaptations to a European way of life were modified according to local needs, as was the case for the new quays, streets, and buildings. Revisiting leisure practices as well as the formation of class, gender, and national identities, Fuhrmann offers an alternative view on the relationship between the Islamic World and Europe.

MALTE FUHRMANN is a research fellow at the Leibniz-Zentrum Moderner Orient (ZMO). Having spent many years doing research and teaching in Istanbul, he is the author of *Imagining a German Orient: Two German Colonies in the Ottoman Empire 1851–1918* (2006, in German) and coeditor of *The City in the Ottoman Empire: Migration and the Making of Urban Modernity* (2011) with Ulrike Freitag, Nora Lafi, and Florian Riedler.

Port Cities of the Eastern Mediterranean

Urban Culture in the Late Ottoman Empire

MALTE FUHRMANN
Leibniz-Zentrum Moderner Orient

CAMBRIDGE
UNIVERSITY PRESS

University Printing House, Cambridge CB2 8BS, United Kingdom

One Liberty Plaza, 20th Floor, New York, NY 10006, USA

477 Williamstown Road, Port Melbourne, VIC 3207, Australia

314–321, 3rd Floor, Plot 3, Splendor Forum, Jasola District Centre, New Delhi – 110025, India

79 Anson Road, #06–04/06, Singapore 079906

Cambridge University Press is part of the University of Cambridge.

It furthers the University's mission by disseminating knowledge in the pursuit of education, learning, and research at the highest international levels of excellence.

www.cambridge.org
Information on this title: www.cambridge.org/9781108477376
DOI: 10.1017/9781108769716

© Malte Fuhrmann 2020

This publication is in copyright. Subject to statutory exception and to the provisions of relevant collective licensing agreements, no reproduction of any part may take place without the written permission of Cambridge University Press.

First published 2020

A catalogue record for this publication is available from the British Library.

Library of Congress Cataloging-in-Publication Data
Names: Fuhrmann, Malte, author.
Title: Port cities of the eastern Mediterranean : urban culture in the late Ottoman Empire / Malte Fuhrmann, Leibniz-Zentrum Moderner Orient.
Other titles: Urban culture in the late Ottoman Empire
Description: Cambridge, United Kingdom ; New York, NY : Cambridge University Press, [2020] | Includes bibliographical references and index.
Identifiers: LCCN 2020012386 (print) | LCCN 2020012387 (ebook) | ISBN 9781108477376 (hardback) | ISBN 9781108708623 (paperback) | ISBN 9781108769716 (epub)
Subjects: LCSH: Turkey–Civilization–Western influences–19th century. | Turkey–Social life and customs–19th century. | Port cities–Turkey–Social life and customs–19th century. | Port cities–Mediterranean Region–Social life and customs–19th century. | Cosmopolitanism–Turkey–History–19th century. | Mediterranean Region–Civilization–19th century. | Mediterranean Region–Social life and customs–19th century.
Classification: LCC DR432 .F84 2020 (print) | LCC DR432 (ebook) | DDC 956/.015–dc23
LC record available at https://lccn.loc.gov/2020012386
LC ebook record available at https://lccn.loc.gov/2020012387

ISBN 978-1-108-47737-6 Hardback

Cambridge University Press has no responsibility for the persistence or accuracy of URLs for external or third-party internet websites referred to in this publication and does not guarantee that any content on such websites is, or will remain, accurate or appropriate.

Contents

List of Figures and Table	*page* vii
Acknowledgments	viii

	Part I Introduction	1
1	The Enigma of Eastern Mediterranean Urban Culture	3
2	A Historiography of Disentanglement: The Long Legacy of the Nineteenth Century	10
3	Culture and the Global in Mediterranean History	19
	Part II Constructing Europe: Spatial Relations of Power in Eastern Mediterranean Cities	37
4	The European Dream	43
5	The Making of a European Spatial Discourse on the Levantine City	49
6	Dreaming of a City in Stone	63
7	Reinventing the City from the Sea Inward	70
	Part III The City's New Pleasures	93
8	Visiting, Strolling, Masquerading, Dancing: The Consumers of Europeanism	99
9	Staging Europeanness: The Rise of the Eastern Mediterranean Opera	122
10	Theater, the Civilizing Mission, and Global Entertainment	138

11	The One World of Workers of the Dramatic Arts	157
12	Beer Consumption and Production on Mediterranean Shores	173
13	Beer, the Drink of a Changing World	194

Part IV Identities on the Mediterranean Shore: Between Experiment and Restriction 211

14	Educational Imperialism or Enlightenment?	219
15	The French-Language Press: A Common Forum?	234
16	Renegotiating Masculinities and Femininities at the Turn of the Century	243
17	Reining in the Free Experiment: Discourses on Class Formation	266
18	Urban Milieus vs. National Communities: The Case of the Levantines	288
19	North-to-South Migration and Its Impact on the Urban Population	302

Part V The End of the European Dream 345

20	The Lack of an Anti-European Perspective	347
21	Economies of Violence and Challenges to the Thalassocentric Order	357
22	The Anti-Western Rebellion on the Eve of the Belle Époque	364
23	Deconstructing the European Female	371
24	The "Unraveling" of Port City Society	390

Part VI Europe and the Eastern Mediterranean Revisited 405

Bibliography 417
Index 455

Figures and Table

Figures

Cover image Constantinople, Galata Bridge, 1912
1.1 The Smyrna Quays, ca. 1870s	*page* 4
1.2 The Olympia Cinema in Salonica, 1917	4
1.3 Constantinople, Galata Bridge and Karaköy Square, 1912	6
8.1 Smyrna, a coffeehouse with shishas in the bazaar area, pre-1922	100
13.1 Giannis Kakavopoulos' Viennese Beerhouse, Constantinople, ca. 1890s	197
13.2 A family gathering in the beer garden, ca. 1900s	197
13.3 A family gathering in the beer garden, ca. 1918	198
13.4 A street in Salonica, ca. 1913, with a modern-style waiter on the right	201
13.5 Patrons of a beer garden on Prinkipos Island, ca. 1900s, dressed in a style reminiscent of Bihruz Bey	203

Table

12.1 Beer production according to district, 1899–1912   *page* 190

Acknowledgments

My two terms at the Leibniz–Zentrum Moderner Orient (ZMO) in Berlin bracket my odyssey between various places of work and research. Here, the initial research for this book began and many years later, I completed my final changes. Our initial research group "Migration and Urban Institutions in the Late Ottoman Reform Period" proved to be the inspiration to delve at length into the forgotten worlds of nineteenth-century Mediterranean cities. For all I learned there I am very grateful to my fellow group members Nora Lafi, Florian Riedler, and Ulrike Freitag. My thanks go to all colleagues and former fellows, and in particular to Dana Sajdi who read and commented on one of my earliest and as yet premature papers on these matters; to Zafer Yenal who likewise commented on my work; to Kai Kresse who helped me sharpen my arguments; and to Sonja Hegasy who inspired me to relate my research more strongly to the present.

I am very grateful to Stefan Leder, Filiz Kıral, and Richard Wittmann for the chance to research and write several chapters in situ, that is, at the Orient–Institut Istanbul (OII). Many thanks to my good colleagues from that time, especially Sara Nur Yıldız, Alexandre Toumarquine, Martin Greve, and Tomas Wilkoszewski. While teaching at Ruhr University Bochum, I enjoyed the great collegial support of Manuel Borutta, Fabian Lemmes, Benjamin Flöhr, and Markus Koller, and discussions with them have decisively shaped this book. In particular, Manuel shared with me the draft of his forthcoming monograph *Mediterrane Verflechtungen* (*Mediterranean Entanglements*), allowing me to fill important missing links within my own narrative. When I returned to Istanbul after my time in Bochum, it was for a two-year term as lecturer at Istanbul Bilgi University and in particular its European Institute. I am indebted especially to Pınar Uyan Semerci, Ayhan Kaya, and my other colleagues and students for this opportunity and making it a very agreeable experience. Among the most inspiring moments at Bilgi, I remember my coffee conversations with the pioneer of Ottoman cultural history, Suraiya Faroqhi, who would effortlessly divulge countless reading suggestions on any of the points I was researching, while the student café's electronic beats boomed over our heads. Some of the chapters were written in the quarters of the former embassies in Pera, which proved highly inspirational. I have to thank Çağla Aykaç and Ayşegül Sert for this opportunity.

I am very much indebted to Patrick Bernhard, Manuel Borutta, Jasmin Daam, Fernando Esposito, Andreas Guidi, Nora Lafi, Fabian Lemmes, Esther Möller, Stefan Preiß, and Daniel Tödt, who together make up our network "The Modern Mediterranean: Dynamics of a World Region, 1800–2000," funded by the Deutsche Forschungsgemeinschaft (DFG). Our discussions have been of great help in refining and contextualizing much of what I have written here and have been exemplary in creating a solidary community of scholars of common interests.

Apart from these, I have received lots of helpful advice, suggestions for various sources and readings, and inspiring feedback from many other researchers. My thanks to the two anonymous reviewers for helping to give the book more focus. Very many thanks to Ayşe Ozil for her fantastic comments and advice on an excerpt of the book I presented. Many thanks also to Julia Hauser for her careful reading of parts of the manuscript and for being there as a friend, as well as to M. Erdem Kabadayı. Edhem Eldem, besides inspiring me and countless others to pick up the thread of urban history of the region, was a great help when I initially started to dabble in the subject, sharing important sources and creating a model for how to pursue this research both with the necessary seriousness and lightness. Conversations with Oliver J. Schmitt during my first forages into the Habsburg archives were another source of inspiration to pursue this topic further. I am indebted to Avner Wishnitzer for introducing me to the world of late Ottoman literature as sources for cultural history, and for our many inspiring conversations, late at night on the squares of medieval wine-growing towns, in the corridors of international convention hotels, or in Istanbul's taverns. Karl Kreiser has been highly supportive of my work, as has Philip Mansel who was so kind to introduce me to his research and several colleagues in the field. Sadly, some of the people who I am most obliged to for contributing to my research are no longer with us. Most of all, Vangelis Kechriotis was a great colleague and friend who helped shape my approach to Eastern Mediterranean urban history. This book owes a lot to him, to his memory, and to Ceyda and Rana.

Several other colleagues and friends drew my attention to sources that have greatly contributed to widening my perspective or drew my attention to interrelations of my findings to wider fields. In particular, I would like to thank Meropi Anastasiadou, Anna Vlachopolou, Paris Chronakis, Sakis Gekas, Ellinor Morack, Nazan Maksudyan, Rıfat Bali, Malek Sharif, Ulrike Stamm, and Dietrich Daur. Christoph Neumann helped me to refine my search strategies in the Ottoman archive catalog when I was getting started there. Sotirios Dimitriadis kindly let me read his PhD thesis for this work. The employees of the excellent Eren Bookstore in Istanbul were of invaluable help guiding me to the published sources and literature relevant to my research.

Over the years, a legion of student assistants and interns has supported my research, both at ZMO and OII, with painstaking work to process sources and edit writings. Some have become dear friends and have produced outstanding research and publications in their own right. Katja Jana especially has been an inspiration with her work and a good friend, as have Martin Joorman and Marie Charbonnier. Many thanks also for all the invaluable assistance by Desislava Hristova, Martina Naydenova, Müzehher Selçuk, Ferdinand Schlechta, David Aufsess, and Jan Tasci, as well as by Fulden Eskidelvan, Suphi Yalcın Akyol, Marina Kleymenova, Hoda Namazian, Fatma Nur Özdemir, and Lisa Schambortski.

I thank Canay Şahin for her great help in dealing with Ottoman documents and moreover, for those many shared years. Many thanks to Anne Hartmetz and Jörg Depta for putting me up upon my return from Istanbul and for those long years of friendship; to my dear friends Julia Dittmann, Sönke Guttenberg, and Jonas and Rosa for accommodating me many times; and to Marcus Tschacher, Sabine Heurs, and Alistair Noon. My mother, father, and sister have been a great source of support throughout all these years. Thanks very much to Malve, Gunther, and Arnika. Most of all, Funda Soysal has been an inspiration, a steady source of information and sources, and of invaluable help with the Ottoman documents. Moreover, I must thank her for all her love and support throughout these years.

Funding Acknowledgments

My projects at the ZMO were funded by the Deutsche Forschungsgemeinschaft (DFG) and the German Ministry of Education and Research (BMBF). The German Academic Exchange Service (DAAD) co-funded my work at Istanbul Bilgi University. In between positions, the Agentur für Arbeit was there to keep my research going. My humble thanks to all reviewers, taxpayers, and contributors who made this work possible.

Article Acknowledgments

Chapter 7 contains parts of my contribution "Staring at the Sea, Staring at the Land: Waterfront Modernization in Nineteenth Century Ottoman Cities as a Site of Cultural Change," in Carola Hein (ed.), *Port Cities: Dynamic Landscapes and Global Networks*, London: Routledge 2011, 138–154. Chapters 12 and 13 are based on my article "Beer, the Drink of a Changing World: Beer Consumption and Production on the Shores of the Aegean in the 19th Century," in *Turcica* 45 (2014), 79–123. Chapter 19 is based on my contribution "North to South Migration in the Imperial Era: Workers and Vagabonds between Vienna and Constantinople," in Ulrike Freitag and Nora Lafi (eds.), *Urban Governance under the Ottomans: Between Cosmopolitanism and Conflict*, London: Routledge 2014, 187–212, and on "'I Would Rather Be in the Orient': European Lower Class Immigrants into the Ottoman Lands," in Ulrike Freitag, Malte Fuhrmann, Nora Lafi, and Florian Riedler (eds.), *The City in the Ottoman Empire: Migration and the Making of Urban Modernity*, London: Routledge 2011, 228–241. Chapter 23 is based on "'Western Perversions' at the Threshold of Felicity: The European Prostitutes of Galata-Pera (1870–1915)," *History and Anthropology* 21 (2/2010), 159–172. However, none of the chapters in this book and the articles cited are identical. Except where the footnotes refer to an already translated text, translations into English are mine throughout the book.

PART I

Introduction

1 | The Enigma of Eastern Mediterranean Urban Culture

Photographs can give us glimpses of lost worlds. In a picture taken sometime in the last quarter of the nineteenth century, we see pedestrians rushing past each other across the tram tracks on Smyrna's (İzmir) quays, while a great number of ships with flags of various countries and steam rising from their funnels are being loaded and unloaded (Figure 1.1). We see one man wearing a fez with a kerchief wound around it, a very short jacket, a shawl with dangling coins wrapped around his waist, baggy trousers, and boots. He is followed by a man with a similar fez-kerchief combo and boots, but wrapped in a wide, flowing overcoat. They seem about to collide with a man rushing the other way with big steps, wearing a bowler hat, black jacket, needle stripe pants, and city shoes. A man with a similar bowler hat and straight cut overcoat can be seen in the background. If we took only these four pedestrians, we could muse about culture clash. However, we also see a man who, like the first two, wears a fez (albeit with no further adornment), but needle stripe pants like the third, and an overcoat somewhere in between the length and cut of those of the second and third pedestrian described. This slightly older pedestrian also carries a walking stick and wears his beard trimmed at half-length. Next to him, we see yet another man with a fez, but with his beard trimmed short, wearing an elegant tightly tailored light-colored vest and jacket over equally tight-fitting pants. Off to the left, we see the back of yet another man, apparently in military uniform, with a conical fez and half-long coat that is tight at the waist, but widens almost like a dress around his hips. Dressing up in late nineteenth-century Smyrna, one could surmise, was not a matter of choosing between East and West, city and countryside, or tradition and modernity, but of combining them in a manner that fit to one's personality or worldview.

Another picture takes us onto the quays of Salonica (Salonico/Selânik/Thessaloniki/Solun, Figure 1.2). The year is 1917, after the city has

Figure 1.1 The Smyrna Quays, ca. 1870s
Courtesy of the Ahmet Piriştina Archive, Izmir Metropolitan Municipality

Figure 1.2 The Olympia Cinema in Salonica, 1917
Public domain

been annexed from the Ottoman Empire to Greece and while it was occupied by Entente soldiers. In contrast to the earlier picture from Smyrna, the tram tracks have an electric overhead wire. A crowd is gathered outside the Olympia, a luxurious cinema built according to the recent architectural style of Art Nouveau. Again we see fezzes mingling with Western-style hats, but now also flat caps, and especially many women's hats as well as the bonnets and braids of schoolgirls, as they jostle to enter the Olympia. There are very few soldiers present, the crowd appears to be made up of mostly locals. The posters advertise the 1910 short film *Hearts of the West* as well as the more recent films *L'homme qui assassina* and *Les fiancés de 1914*. All three are only announced in their original language, with no translation of the title visible. First written as a novel by the Frenchman Claude Farrère, *L'homme qui assasina* is situated in the multicultural milieu of nearby Constantinople, as the fezzes on the posters show. Salonica, even after being taken by the Greek army, we could surmise, was far from Greek but still interested in Constantinople affairs, and also consumed American and French culture with great enthusiasm.

What of Constantinople (Istanbul/Dersaadet/i Poli/Bolis/Kushta/Tsarigrad)? A picture from 1912 shows us the downtown business district and commuter hub of Karaköy, just after the steel bridge over the Golden Horn, together with an electric-powered tram line that had been completed, and we see a crowd no less colorful than those of the two previous pictures rushing through the streets, over the bridge, and along the quays (Figure 1.3). A cacophony of advertisement in Greek, French (Latin), Armenian, and Turkish (Arabic) characters praise the quality of the department stores Stein, Tiring, and the furniture store Psalty. The dominant building on the waterside, another recent Art Nouveau creation, declares in big letters that it belongs to the *Wiener Bankenverein*, while immediately adjacent to it a small mosque stands as another experiment in twentieth-century architecture.

These are images from the city centers of some of the largest, most affluent, and most well-connected cities that existed 100 years ago on the Eastern shores of the Mediterranean. By rights, we would expect them to adorn the history text books on Middle Eastern, Southeast European, Ottoman, Turkish, or Greek modern history, as a late nineteenth-century photo image of the Champs Élysées, Piccadilly Circus, or Unter den Linden might illustrate a text book on French, British, or German history. But instead, the images of colorfully

Figure 1.3 Constantinople, Galata Bridge and Karaköy Square, 1912
Courtesy of German Archaeological Institute Istanbul

dressed pedestrians on the quays, the waiting lines for the American movie, and the multilingual advertisement billboards strike us as something exotic. They give testimony of a range of multilayered, complex, and certainly contradictory ways of engaging with overseas cultures. By and large, the master narratives for the nineteenth-century history of the region do not touch much on such realities. Instead, they have been relegated to a special interest section subsumed under the headings of either cultural or urban history.

The Europeanized culture of the modern Eastern Mediterranean therefore needs more attention in historiography. Of course one cannot claim that the West has not been a subject of research in studies of the nineteenth century around the Eastern Mediterranean. Far from it, the relationship Turks, Greeks, Arabs, Bulgarians, Armenians, and other inhabitants of the region had to the rest of Europe has been the classic subject for historians of the nineteenth century for a long time. But the framing of the questions posed in the context of Europeanization has limited the scope of phenomena that have been discussed in this context. What dominates the common narrations of the region are clear bifurcations: tradition – modernity, modern – premodern,

West – East, or along ethnic or religious lines. Standard works highlight economic upheavals that changed contemporary society, state actors' efforts to adapt to the challenges of their times, and the various struggles for national hegemony and the violence that came with it. All of these are naturally important processes to be studied, but why are they usually dissociated from the milieus in which many of these processes took place?

Are we to consider the Levant's infatuation with Western culture and the hybrid forms it produced a short and superficial aberration that we need not concern ourselves with in detail, as it had no consequences for the course of history? It seems not, as an example will show. Europe – as a paradigm and as a collective agent – was not only a distant imperial center that through its great military and economic might managed to reach out into the lives of inhabitants of the marginalized periphery. It was also an intimate part of people's everyday lives, as intimate as factors such as ethnicity or denomination. A Greek colleague once told me about her grandfather. He was suffering from dementia. Dementia is understood as the gradual erosion of an individual's personality as it has evolved throughout his or her life. By losing his memories one step at a time, from most recent to those of events long past, her grandfather was reverting, traveling back in time through his own life until he would ultimately end up in a childlike state. During his illness, two ruptures managed to particularly startle his relatives. At some point the man stopped speaking Greek and would only talk in Turkish anymore. But in a later stage, Turkish came to be replaced by the singing of French Christian and children's songs.

The initial reversion to Turkish will not come as a surprise to those who have followed critical enquiries into the history of nationalism in the Eastern Mediterranean region. Case studies have shown that the ethnic markers of a group that in theory should be clear and unchangeable in practice proved confusing and negotiable. Thus, instead of clearly outlining Greeks as subjects of the Greek-Orthodox Church and speakers of a modern Greek dialect vis-à-vis Turks as adherents of Islam and speakers of a Turkish dialect, many more confusing identities have emerged, such as the Pomaks, who as speakers of a Bulgarian dialect and adherents of Islam have been claimed to belong to the Bulgarian, Greek, and Turkish nations;[1] the Levantines, who were

---

[1] Karagiannis, "The Pomaks of Bulgaria," 143–158.

mostly Catholic but would as a rule speak a Greek idiom strongly influenced by Italian;[2] and the *Karamanlis* community to which my colleague's grandfather apparently belonged.[3] Despite being considered Greek Orthodox Christian, he had in his family spoken Turkish and had only learned Greek in a later stage of his life, possibly after he had been deported from Asia Minor to the Hellenic Kingdom in the Greco-Turkish Exchange of Populations of 1922/1923, which targeted people solely on the base of their religion without regard for their spoken language.

But the second reversion from Turkish to French seems indicative of a constellation that has not received proper attention in academic debate. If a man who grew up in the late Ottoman Empire remembers the French language after having been stripped of most of the memories of his adult life, and his active command of both Greek and Turkish, then it would seem that – besides the different elements of the Ottoman mosaic – West European culture had made a fundamental impact on him as well. This phenomenon hints at a more widespread and deeper penetration of "Europe" into nineteenth-century port city residents' identity, an "internal Europe"[4] that evolved within a constant dialogue with the rest of the continent. The photograph of the cross-dressing pedestrians alludes to the fact that there was no clash of binary opposites on the Eastern quays, but rather a wide spectrum from which individuals had to choose their own place. What amount of soul-searching, identity building, curiosity, experiment, despair, and line-drawing did interaction with "Europe" produce when local residents tried to carve out their particular place in the modern, quickly evolving world around them? Answers are best found not by assuming the port city residents' situation to be exceptional, but rather part of a European, if not global predicament of how to come to terms with a constant state of polyvalence, where a word has "a hundred meanings" and society takes on the form of a "cosmopolitan gods-, morals-, and arts-carnival," as Robert Musil and Friedrich Nietzsche characterized the predicament.

This book reconstructs, analyzes, and interprets the evolution of Eastern Mediterranean culture and the ways in which it became "Europeanized" in the course of the nineteenth century. I demonstrate how

---

[2] For more on the Levantines, see Chapter 18, pp. 288–301.
[3] Kechriotis, "Atina'da Kapadokyalı."   [4] Barak, *Egyptian Times*, 299.

for the urban residents, European culture initially stood for a curious, but distant ideal. It then became something they could become a part of, but finally evolved into a model to be rejected. What people in Smyrna, Salonica, or Constantinople considered European often followed ostensible forms from elsewhere on the continent, but these forms became suffused with meanings the local residents projected onto them: They played a very active part in determining the course of the Europeanization of their urban surroundings and their identities, blending various aspects of overseas and local culture to find a style for themselves; utilizing foreign innovations to find new and more appropriate forms for buildings and the urban public space of their choice; and determining the flow of exchange as consumers. In this way, I hope to establish this urban culture as an important element of nineteenth-century history. To explain why it has so far not been given the attention it deserves I must first discuss the predominant master narrative we have commonly employed to frame nineteenth-century Eastern Mediterranean urbanism and demonstrate its shortcomings.

2 | A Historiography of Disentanglement
The Long Legacy of the Nineteenth Century

The reason why cities have not played a central part in historiography of the Eastern Mediterranean dates back to the nineteenth century. Breaking with the Enlightenment age disenchanted approach to the history of Asia, nineteenth-century West and Central Europe attempted to find holistic answers to the study of non-European societies.[1] In fact, a rather particular division of labor developed especially from the 1830s onward: The growing number of specialists in Southeast European or West Asian societies and languages would produce valuable and voluminous research on their regions of study, but, accepting their position as specialists of a territory considered peripheral to world events, would refrain from interpreting their findings as relevant for the course of world history (with the notable exception of researchers of Greek and biblical antiquity).[2] Such interpretations were left not so much to historians of Western and Central Europe, but initially to practitioners of philosophy of history and toward the dawn of the twentieth century, to sociologists. These would harvest the aforementioned pioneering studies for material for their own reflections on world history, evoking the image of expert knowledge, but would often seek in them no more than cues and buzzwords for a narrative developed mainly by analyzing the society best known by the authors themselves. These resulted in philosophically intriguing, but in their generalizations often crude meta-explanations of the course of history: "the view to the Orient was gradually emerging as the inherent anathema to modernity and ... the sharp conceptual distinctions between Orient and Occident contributed to establishing them as representational poles of mutual self-construction ... a variety of self-reflective constructions to the Mediterranean can be observed, which

---

[1] On Enlightenment age study of the East, see Osterhammel, *Die Entzauberung Asiens*; see also Deringil, *The Well-Protected Domains*, 4.
[2] Marchand, *German Orientalism in the Age of Empire*.

are not without parallel to Orientalism."[3] As the nineteenth century progressed and the gap in living conditions between Northern Europe and other parts of the world widened, the trend to see Germany, France, or England as the pinnacle of development and other countries as lacking gained pace. Industry was believed to be the key to success and the lack thereof a stigma.

Accordingly, the Ottoman Empire was categorized as an agrarian state. Karl Marx's formulation of the "Asiatic Mode of Production" echoed this assumption, which also found its way into Max Weber's worldview, and in essence reduced socially relevant agents to the despotic ruler and his agrarian subjects.[4] The fact that in the nineteenth century the Eastern Mediterranean was host to not only a large rural population, but also to one of the only fourteen cities with over a million inhabitants in the world and one of seven in Europe qualifying for this category, and that Smyrna, Salonica, Beirut (Beyrouth), and Alexandria (al-Iskanderiya), with their respective populations of hundreds of thousands were not insignificant by the standard of the times either, did not inspire pre–World War I researchers to seriously engage with contemporary Levantine urbanity. Weber, writing at the pinnacle of European world dominance, developed parameters to gauge the progress of societies that equated being like Central or Northern Europe with being most developed. Supposedly, only the Occidental city had managed to produce a responsible, self-conscious citizen, as it had guaranteed a status of municipal autonomy that made civic action meaningful. The Asiatic city, by comparison, seemed dull, devoid of an inner ability to create and to change, a mere seat of an imperial administrator, as it had no *Bürgertum* and no municipality.[5] No wonder it was not considered worthy of analysis.

What also becomes visible in Weber's deliberations on the Asiatic city is the assumption that cultures are by and large closed off entities.

---

[3] Stauth, "Anatomies of the Mediterranean in Modern Theory," 60. See also Marchand, *German Orientalism in the Age of Empire*.
[4] Minuti, "Oriental Despotism."
[5] Weber, *Wirtschaft und Gesellschaft* I, vol. XXII/V: *Die Stadt*, 84–88, 450–453. Weber, however, slightly differentiated between Middle Eastern cities and those of the rest of Asia, as he saw some elements of the autonomous city in the former. The construction of teleological lines of thought on modernization disadvantageous to the incorporation of Mediterranean regions can also be traced from other, less Germanocentric perspectives; see for example Salzmann, *Tocqueville in the Ottoman Empire*.

This is clearly inspired by Johann Gottfried Herder's romantic worldview, according to which a distinct culture's development is determined by its innate qualities rather than through the degree of exchange it engages in.[6] Although already Nietzsche had criticized this assumption, claiming that historic great cultures had only attained their achievements by taking up elements of neighboring societies and developing them further, the idea of predominantly autochthonous development prevailed.[7] In addition, the Weberian impetus, by favoring culturally defined world regions as units of analysis, strongly blurred chronology and thus possible change: It was rather irrelevant if an argument against the Asiatic city was taken from antiquity or the Middle Ages, while Weber remains precise in terms of which period he speaks about concerning European cities.[8] Many of these assumptions were canonized in post–World War II modernization theory literature on the Eastern Mediterranean, which remained focused on a singular path to modernity determined by France and Great Britain.[9] Şerif Mardin claims that the modernization framework prevented any meaningful comparisons, let alone entangled perspectives, for decades.[10] Attempts to overcome this legacy, according to which the rest of the world would have to shrug off its traditions and embrace the model path, have taken a myriad of approaches, but more often than not, their conceptual shortcomings have become apparent soon after. In order to establish for them a proper place as objects of historical and social enquiry despite Weber's devastating remarks, historians of the second half of the twentieth century attempted to reconstruct first an Islamic, and later a specific Ottoman type of city.[11] However, already Roger Owen debunked the assumption that Middle Eastern cities were subject to a different political or economic order than the lands around them, pointing out the interdependence of cities and agricultural sites

---

[6] Herder, *Theoretische Schriften*, 2.7.1; Heckmann, "Ethnos, Demos und Nation," 23.
[7] Prange, "Cosmopolitan Roads to Culture," 284, fn. 15.
[8] Weber, *Wirtschaft und Gesellschaft* I, vol. XXII/V: *Die Stadt*, 85–89. This oversight has in more recent times even led to the claim that Islam has no concept of progress; Diner, *Lost in the Sacred*.
[9] Lewis, *The Emergence of Modern Turkey*.
[10] Mardin, "Conceptual Fracture," 7, 8.
[11] Kreiser, "Zur inneren Gliederung der osmanischen Stadt"; Hourani and Stern (eds.), *The Islamic City*; Busch-Zantner, *Agrarverfassung und Siedlung in Südosteuropa*.

and the clearly entangled nature of rural and urban political and socioeconomic rule.[12] While this assertion made in the year 1981 did not establish outright freedom from typological thinking in its time, it resonated more strongly with subsequent generations of authors.

The Estranged Elder Sister of Port City Studies: The World System School

Expanding on other approaches critical of modernization theory, such as the dependency school, and borrowing from the Annales school, Immanuel Wallerstein's world system theory aimed to critically reconstruct how regions such as the Eastern Mediterranean were integrated into an economic and social order determined by the London Stock Exchange. Adherents of this school hoped to be "'decolonizing' Ottoman history, dissociating it from the self-image of the West and restoring the Ottoman Empire its place in world history."[13] The problem with such a perspective is that especially in its initial phase, it one-sidedly highlighted world market processes, reduced local agency to little more than reactions or resistance to a nigh-omnipotent Europe, and that it marked any Western influence on or Western views of the Sultan's domains a priori as destructive, thus reinforcing a nationalist belief that the region would have been better off without its European neighbors. In addition, it focused almost exclusively on agricultural exports, in accordance with the old belief that the Eastern Mediterranean was little more than a farming entrepôt, and as this seemed to prove best the exploitative nature of the constellation, as the London capitalists drained the rural laborers' surplus. This overemphasis on agriculture once again obscured the complexity of nineteenth-century economic, financial, and social processes.

Port cities were identified as a key element in the relationship of the London city to the Balkan, Anatolian, and Middle Eastern agrarian regions, but mostly submitted to a bird's-eye view, in which local agency and shades of grey had no place. What led subsequent generations of historians to rebel were the sweeping statements especially about the port city population, which was reduced in the narrative to a few bourgeois and merchants, as if the wider population did not exist,

---

[12] Owen, *Middle East in the World Economy*, 56, 57.
[13] İslamoğlu-İnan, "'Oriental Despotism' in World-System Perspective," 2.

and a lighthearted juxtaposition of "foreign" and "local." Port cities were an "anomaly,"[14] "outposts of European bourgeoisie,"[15] "were primarily populated by men pursuing commercial interests," as "liminal spaces where Europe could expand because the state receded ... The territory around them was weakly governed ... The typical port-city(s) primary population was merchants."[16] Needless to say, such an approach cannot be the base for an enquiry of the phenomena visible in the photographs displayed. It would mean to exaggerate the bourgeois perspective on Europeanization and hybrid culture to the detriment of other social strata and to a priori assume that these cities were in principle established by an amorphous, but hostile entity called Europe, rather than to impartially look at the historical agents one encounters via the sources.

To be fair, several, but not all of the partisans of the world system theory have rephrased their stances, dropping some of the inherited baggage of the dependency school and taking a more open-minded, less determinist look at the Eastern Mediterranean and the social dynamics of port cities instead.[17] One must also concede that the world system theoreticians are the school that remains superior in contextualizing the Eastern Mediterranean in an entangled world. Faruk Tabak's final article remains unrivaled when it comes to a global perspective of

---

[14] Keyder, Özveren, and Quataert, "Port-Cities in the Ottoman Empire," 540.
[15] Kasaba, Keyder, and Tabak, "Eastern Mediterranean Port Cities and Their Bourgeoisies," 122.
[16] Keyder, "Port-Cities in the Belle Epoque," 14. Besides singling out commerce as an abnormal activity and exaggerating its role in the port cities, the fact that capitalism thrived was exactly because the Ottoman police and courts enforced the safety of capital here much more rigorously than in provincial settings; see Hanssen, Philip, and Weber, "Towards a New Paradigm," 4, 5, and Chapter 21, pp. 357–363, of this book.
[17] Already Keyder, Özveren, and Quataert, "Port-Cities in the Ottoman Empire," paints a much more differentiated picture than previous articles. The most extreme convert was possibly Donald Quataert, who changed from a very negative assessment of late Ottoman society to a positive one in his later writings; see Quataert, "Labor History and the Ottoman Empire." Others such as Cem Emrence have attempted to come up with more flexible models of world system integration for the Ottoman Empire; see Emrence, *Remapping the Ottoman Middle East*. Intriguing as his approach is, it still fails to cover the multiple interconnections between the different regions of the empire and oversimplifies what was a chaotic and multifaceted process of globalization, as will be sketched in more detail in the course of this book.

the region in the nineteenth century.[18] Overall, the world system school has proven itself something akin to the estranged elder sister of the emerging urban history approach in nineteenth-century Eastern Mediterranean studies: It had made some steps in the right direction, such as posing the question of what the region's role was in contemporary global relations; it had shifted the focus away from the palaces and ministries toward the flows of trade, and from questions of politics in the narrow sense of the word to socioeconomic processes at various levels. However, its top-down or center-periphery approach, its sweeping generalizations, and tendency to a bird's-eye view caused the younger sister to rebel.

Escape into the Microverse: Eastern Mediterranean Urban Studies

The decisive impetus to rebel against the Wallersteinian impositions that set forth a countermovement came in the late 1990s. Two collective volumes stand out as having set off the trend to counter the constant reference to a nigh-omnipotent world system by intense micro-studies. One was *The Ottoman City between East and West*, published in 1999, in which Bruce Masters, Daniel Goffman, and Edhem Eldem focused on one city respectively to demonstrate that, rather than through teleological terms such as "peripheralization," these cities were best assessed by close readings of local and external sources, not only economic ones, to then gauge the city's place on the contemporary global map. In doing so, the authors argued against the Weberian idea of the Western city as well as counter-models developed against it, pleading against typologies and for the singularity of every city.[19]

The other collective volume that marked the beginning of a new era, François Georgeon and Paul Dumont's *Vivre dans l'empire ottomane: Sociabilités et relations intercommunitaires (XVIIIe–XXe siècles)*,

---

[18] He acknowledged that a particular "epoch of cosmopolitan port-cities" had existed. However, he pleaded to see this particular culture not as a product of its internal dynamics, but rather of a fortunate conjuncture in Great Power rivalry and global financial flows; see Tabak, "Imperial Rivalry and Port-Cities."

[19] Eldem, "Istanbul: From Imperial to Peripheralized Capital," especially 138–142, and Eldem, Goffman, and Masters, "Conclusion: Contexts and Characteristics," 207.

echoed several of the concerns Goffman, Masters, and Eldem voiced. It attacked the focus predominant in Weberian studies of cities, but also among world system adherents on questions of status, and instead drew attention to practice, proposing especially "sociabilities" as an approach to make visible previously overlooked aspects of urbanism around the Eastern Mediterranean. The volume included a number of in-depth local case studies by young researchers that proved indicative of the new roads historical research would take, making creative use of Ottoman, consular, and non-state sources, mistrusting both state and foreign sources in order to come up with fiercely local perspectives.

A third volume in 2002 by Jens Hanssen, Thomas Philipp, and Stefan Weber, rejecting the modernist and world system typologies, attempted to bridge the gap between the by then already lively field of urban history and the critical study of the Empire's reforms and modernization attempts.[20] Since then, many other case studies have shown that whatever their structural position in global economics might have been, port city residents were more creative in designing their identity, their lifestyle, and their social practices. Not surprisingly, this is the strand of research that most readily accommodates the lifeworlds captured in the three pictures mentioned in the beginning, as it addresses among others questions of multilingualism, diversified culture, and agency. We know about the internal community developments of obscure ethnic and pseudo-ethnic groups, about the people who ran the cities, the changes in urban spatial practices due to the introduction of street lights, tramways, and street regulations; we know in depth what schoolbooks, magazines, erotic novels, or foreign newspapers nineteenth-century Mediterranean urbanites read; how they would or could dress up; where they would go shopping and for what; what they could do to kill time; and many things more. While few urban historians have made the effort to explicitly reject the world system approach after Eldem, Masters, and Goffman's book, it can be said that the subsequent generations of researchers have voted with their feet, choosing to investigate various facets of nineteenth-century urban life, rather than stepping in Wallerstein's footsteps. Biray Kolluoğlu and Meltem Toksöz, writing in 2010, register "an explosion of

[20] Hanssen, Philip, and Weber, "Towards a New Paradigm," 1–28. While formulating a critical assessment of the state of the art, the volume tends to lay strong emphasis on reform studies and thereby occasionally loses sight of the city.

interest in these spaces since the closing decade of the twentieth century."[21] While twentieth-century historians had been preoccupied with isolating the early strands of modernity that would develop into the nation-state, early twenty-first-century researchers and reading audiences were attracted by the prospects of finding in the nineteenth century a constellation reminiscent of contemporary processes of globalization and the concomitant rise of commercial cities. If one can notice any developments at all in this atomized field of research, besides the obvious one toward a more detailed and encompassing knowledge of the cities under study, it is in the words of Devin E. Naar from a "celebratory" to a "post-celebratory" or critical appreciation of port cities.[22] The early works, especially of the 1990s, needed to assert port cities as subjects of study independent of the Wallersteinian paradigm. Moreover, with the rise of notions of multiculturalism and cosmopolitanism, the extremely mixed port cities became subjects of interests as a "peripheral model of conviviality" in need of historical discovery.[23] Needless to say, in the course of time, the tendency to overstate the cosmopolitan nature of nineteenth-century Mediterranean society, and especially contemporary fashions of styling early twenty-first-century cities with nostalgic imagery from the Belle Epoque, were criticized and put into perspective.[24]

Kolluoğlu and Toksöz also already realize the major weakness of the urban historians: Focusing on in-depth case studies, no-one has stepped forth to tie this vast reservoir of knowledge together and explain how the various aspects combined to affect the course of history. Since their publication, this development toward specialization has only increased. The collective knowledge of nineteenth-century Eastern Mediterranean urban practices is voluminous, but its depth

---

[21] Kolluoğlu and Toksöz, "Mapping Out the Eastern Mediterranean," 2. The volume, especially the cited introduction, is one of the few exceptions that strike a dialogue between world system and urban history approaches to Eastern Mediterranean port cities. See also Fuhrmann and Kechriotis, "The Late Ottoman Port Cities and Their Inhabitants," and other articles in *Mediterranean Historical Review* 24 (2/2009), a special edition dedicated to port city history.

[22] Naar, *Jewish Salonica*; Sakis Gekas calls the "celebratory" approach the "romantic" view on port cities; Gekas, "Class and Cosmopolitanism."

[23] Ilbert and Yannakakis, *Alexandrie 1860–1960*.

[24] Mills, *Streets of Memory*; Starr, *Remembering Cosmopolitan Egypt*; Hanley, "Grieving Cosmopolitanism in Middle East Studies"; Hayden and Naumović, "Imagined Commonalities."

rarely finds any form of condensation or overarching discussion, let alone synthesis. As Kolluoğlu and Toksöz correctly state, this leaves the overall interpretation of the period to others, if not the démodé Wallersteinians, then the still vigorous state-centered study of the era.[25]

This of course begs the question why Eastern Mediterranean urban historians have by majority been too timid to enter the arena and reclaim terms such as "modernity" from the monopoly by other historiographic schools. Is the study of the region as a whole too much keyed to "big" politics as to pay attention to our subtler observations? Is this a way for urban historians to avoid the politically heavily mined fields of the history of the region? Or have we simply given up on the synthesis, preferring comfortable areas where the degree of specialization is so high few will ever rise to challenge our claims? It seems not that such a highly specialized field of research bears no relevance to larger questions per se, as many of these studies have in fact been revolutionary in their respective findings on questions such as identity, gender, or the relationship of the global to the local. A look at the comparable historiography of the cities interconnected by maritime exchange along the Indian Ocean proves that it is possible to write the history of port cities as part of a common space in which actors moved around, where knowledge, cultural practices, and commercial exchange circulated, and where residents employed similar strategies in marking out spaces as their own, to pursue common questions, and to abstract from the objects of study to more general phenomena.[26]

---

[25] Kolluoğlu and Toksöz, "Mapping Out the Eastern Mediterranean," 3; see also Fuhrmann and Kechriotis, "The Late Ottoman Port Cities and Their Inhabitants." Survey studies that dominate our perceptions of modernity or Westernization in the region include Findley, *Turkey, Islam, Nationalism, and Modernity*; Zürcher, *Turkey: A Modern History*; Ortaylı, *İmparatorluğun en uzun yüzyılı*; Deringil, *The Well-Protected Domains*; Georgeon, *Abdülhamid II*. While all these works are important contributions to the study of the nineteenth century, as a rule they do not do sufficient justice to non-statist agents.

[26] Deutsch and Reinwald, *Space on the Move*; McPherson, "Port Cities As Nodal Points of Exchange"; Rothermund and Weigelin-Schwiedrzik, *Der indische Ozean*; Simpson and Kresse, *Struggling with History*.

3 Culture and the Global in Mediterranean History

Where can researchers interested in urban cultural phenomena deemed odd by teleological narratives get inspiration in order to conceptualize them within larger frameworks? To some degree, historians of the Early Modern Ottoman world have progressed much further in tackling these issues. On the other hand, there is the growing literature at the interstices of global and cultural history that has so far mostly dealt with this world region in passing. I shall first briefly touch upon the former before focusing on the latter.

The call for a more entangled approach to the Eastern Mediterranean's modern history – whether directed against top-down theories, such as modernization or world system, naval-gazing approaches, such as many of the reform discussions, or insular research such as our field of urban history – is of course not completely unique. Recent collective volumes carry titles such as *Towards an Entangled Ottoman History* or *A Global Middle East*.[1] They represent important landmarks on the way to establish a more extroverted approach in modern history and bring together contributions that show in an exemplary way what the new approaches toward the field are capable of. However, these volumes mainly offer yet another assortment of interesting case studies. They fall short of providing a new paradigm in their rather brief introductions, as Paul Dumont and François Georgeon did in their 1997 *Vivre dans l'Empire Ottoman*, which marked the beginning of the trend toward intense microstudies of modern Ottoman urbanity. Therefore, the recent collective volumes represent something akin to manifestos, rather than constitutions for future historiography.

Surprisingly, historians of the Early Modern Ottoman Empire have often dealt with these challenges – to overcome the limitations of

---

[1] There are of course other examples of practiced global or entangled history in the field. See for example Esenbel and Chiharu, *The Rising Sun and the Turkish Crescent*.

leader-centered history and incorporate innovative cultural history perspectives; to avoid proscriptive world system or sociological schemes and instead make sense of local constellations; to use the new archival sources, but to remember their limitations and nonetheless position the region within a wider global network – in a more productive way than the modernists. The fact that global perspectives, cultural enquiries, local studies, and more systemic approaches are not incompatible is demonstrated by Suraiya Faroqhi's *The Ottoman Empire and the World around It*. It seeks to combine diplomatic history with an approach to economic questions inspired by Braudel and Wallerstein, but includes also local case studies and the history of ideas. Faroqhi stresses "how permeable the frontiers really were in many instances. Of course, this implies that the neat dichotomy between the 'house of Islam' and the 'house of war' is not very useful for the purposes of this study, as it masks the much more complicated relationships existing in the real world."[2] A similar comprehensive work for the nineteenth century has unfortunately not been written yet.

So where can historians of nineteenth-century Eastern Mediterranean urban studies turn to be inspired toward more global and comprehensive visions from authors writing about the same period? There is obviously the growing academic interest in the nineteenth century as the hitherto most globalized century. Christopher A. Bayly's and Jürgen Osterhammel's respective grandes oeuvres, published in 2004 and 2009, have both promoted a vision of the nineteenth century in which not everything originates from the French Revolution and the invention of the steam engine, but everything is in multiple ways connected to them. Osterhammel does not debunk structural approaches outright, but appeals to its partisans to reconceptualize the preexisting assumptions and adapt them to a more critical and multilocational perspective.[3] Likewise, these books have been important milestones on the way toward putting the colonial experience into perspective. Within the comprehensive global approach to the history of the nineteenth century, colonialism and several derivatives thereof (such as the center–periphery paradigm) are accepted as constituent

---

[2] Faroqhi, *The Ottoman Empire and the World around It*. For other important contributions to the early history of Euro-Ottoman relations see Aksan, *Ottomans and Europeans*; Goffman, *The Ottoman Empire and Early Modern Europe*.
[3] Osterhammel, *The Transformation of the World*, 904–906.

experiences of modernity both for the subjugated and the dominant regions of the world. However, the global interaction in the nineteenth century is no longer seen as limited to the colonial situation, nor is colonization a monolithic process. A more precise look at the result and the modalities of interactions between different parties is called for, which can however no longer be separated from the gap in access to power and resources.[4] Such a framework has inspired a number of international comparative investigations of port cities, their populations, their external networks, and their image.[5]

Nonetheless, while global or entangled histories provide an important perspective, they do not constitute a discipline or theoretical approach to history in their own right.[6] When trying to understand the cross-dressing on Smyrna's quays, the fascination for French-language drama in Salonica, or the multilingual lure of capitalist shopping on Constantinople's billboards, we must throw into our soup another ingredient, namely cultural history. In a concise definition, "culture" has been declared "the sum of all attributions of meaning and deeper dimensions which are attributed to the material world and social constellations."[7] Its study therefore occupies itself more with phenomenological questions, rather than causes, which had attracted the interest of structurally minded schools, such as the development and world system theoreticians.

Dana Sajdi states that the cultural turn has come rather belatedly to Ottoman history. The area study specialists were for a long time preoccupied with the rejection of modernization theory and its claim of decline in the region, which they fought out in discussions about the nature of the state and the socioeconomic order. The cultural dimension was dismissed outright especially by the Wallersteinians, as the Orientalist camp around Bernard Lewis had extensively dwelt on it and integrated it into a "civilizationist narrative." By turning not only against this narrative, but against cultural topics per se, historians

---

[4] Osterhammel and Conrad, "Einleitung," 7–27.
[5] Hein (ed.), *Port Cities*; Masashi (ed.), *Asian Port Cities 1600–1800*; Amenda and Fuhrmann (eds.), *Hafenstädte – Mobilität, Migration, Globalisierung*; Cerasi, Petruccioli, Sarro, and Weber (eds.), *Multicultural Urban Fabric and Types*.
[6] Conrad, *Globalgeschichte*, 9–13.
[7] Gotter, "'Akkulturation' als Methodenproblem," 373–406.

initially made little use of discursive and cultural analyses in studies of the Eastern Mediterranean.[8]

By contrast, the cultural turn and its means of reading cultural production as an expression of power relationships, social order, and to pursue phenomenological enquiries strongly impacted on the emerging urban history of the Eastern Mediterranean. However, while many have applied the possibilities of cultural enquiry, rather few have explicitly discussed it. One of the few authors to engage theoretically with the process of Euro-Ottoman acculturation is Halil İnalcık. He draws attention to the fact that for cultural elements to be successfully transferred from one culture to another (with the exception of weapons, technology, and administrative techniques), "a certain socio-cultural ambience" and "milieu" is necessary in the receiving society. As early modern Ottomans society lacked this, many transfers from Europe were not sustainable in contrast to those of the nineteenth century. While İnalcık theoretically acknowledges the importance of the transfers through port cities, his own narrative is limited to those that affected the court, the army, and the administrators. What is more, by equating Ottoman with Muslim, he blacks out large parts of the transfers. His outlook is also limited by his perspective on cultural processes: Cultures appear as distinct entities that can exchange elements, but essentially remain removed from one another.[9] Cultural theory has embraced much more dynamic models of change. The stalemate in the rather fruitless debate about whether the driving forces behind change in the Ottoman nineteenth century were exterior or domestic can be overcome by focusing on the mobility of ideas, practices, and agents between different locales, as the various case studies in this book will demonstrate.

However, the question of how to analyze cultural interaction has not been properly resolved. The basic problem that none of the newer approaches have managed to eradicate dates from the field's origin in anthropology. This science had originally, just like İnalcık, conceived of cultures as distinct entities based on closed-off societies. Contact was

---

[8] The explicit rejection of cultural topics by world system adherents refers to a statement by Huri İslamoğlu-İnan in Sajdi, "Decline," 29. For the Orientalist discussion she refers to, see Lewis, *What Went Wrong?*

[9] İnalcık, *Turkey and Europe in History*. An even more crude concept of culture can be noticed in recent writings by Ortaylı, *Avrupa ve Biz*, especially 2–4, 218–220.

believed to be the exception, rather than the norm. In situations of permanent contact and exchange however, the entities start to blur and are no longer clearly distinguishable, a situation that, rather than heightening the interest and analytic rigor of the researchers, led to their disdain toward the object of study. This was clearly echoed in François Braudel's statement on the culture of Mediterranean port cities. In his classic *La Méditerranée et le monde méditeranèen à l'époque de Philippe II*, Braudel, despite adding to our awareness of the sea's interconnectivity, vociferously denied the possibility of spontaneous cultural evolution and fusion. Rejecting the notion of a common, but multicentered Mediterranean culture championed by Gabriel Audisio, he defined it from a geographical determinist stance copied from Jovan Cvijić and Konstantin Jireček. Mediterranean culture is conceived of as the product of remote mountain villages, rather than the ports.[10] This definition has led to a general assumption of an archaic nature and uniformity of Mediterranean society that influenced subsequent generations. In such a worldview, culture is an impersonal and abstract determinant that shapes individuals.

More enlightening interpretations of recent years however have insisted on agency in the determination of culture. While culture does not change easily, it is subject to social processes and innovation produced by individuals. Cultural historians now tend to highlight the fact that cultures in contact do not manage to remain aloof from one another, but undergo fundamental change in the process, creating in-between zones and hybridity. Neither do the objects of cultural transfers remain the same throughout the process: New meanings are inscribed onto them, and often the images of the other culture prolific in the receiving society are more influential in inscribing these meanings than those originating in the society from which the cultural element came from.[11] Such an anthropo-centric concept of cultural history is not ignorant toward determinants of power, such as military might, material inequality, or discursive hegemony. Instead, it traces their repercussions into literary, academic, and artistic production as well as the question of how marginality is produced and why. However, it focuses on the windows of choice individuals and groups could

---

[10] Braudel, *The Mediterranean and the Mediterranean World*, vol. II, 743.
[11] Middell, "Transregional Studies," 5, 6. Kaelble, "Die Debatte über Vergleich und Transfer."

profit from when trying to shape their lives and the world around them in light of the mentioned determinants.

For the purpose of this book, it is not necessary to solve the basic problems of cultural history, as historians have come up with a trick to save themselves from this dilemma: the exceptional or contact zone. The third space, seascapes, frontier zones are but some of the names researchers have developed for spaces of heightened interaction, where the stability and even the very existence of cultures as distinct entities are in question. Arjun Appadurai has been the leading theoretician in developing such perspectives in the post-1989 era.[12] Especially Ulrike Freitag and Achim von Oppen have taken up his notion of Translocality and adapted it to historical scenarios, while Matthias Middell has developed this further into Transregionality.[13] In the same vein, Brigitte Reinwald's defines "maritime culture" as "the combining and overlapping of transoceanic, littoral and interior flows in the mediation of culture on the one hand, and to people's appropriation and blending of diverse cross-bordering cultural elements on the other."[14] It is this basic assumption that hopefully will take us further in the search for meaningful assessments of urban life on the shores of the Eastern Mediterranean.

In the long run, however, cultural history should do away with the equation of a culture with a particular assumedly homogenous group all together. One of the more radical departures from traditional approaches, inspired by communication studies, defines culture as

the whole ensemble of elements, i.e. of signifiers, symbols, or codes, by means of which individuals communicate, both verbally and non-verbally, in a social context and according to a certain set of rules ... The cultural ensemble can therefore, figuratively, be understood as a dynamic communicative space, in which, by establishing or rejecting elements, of signifiers, symbols, or codes – including artefacts – social lifeworlds are constructed, constituted, represented, and reproduced continuously and performatively, individual and collective identities are created, and power relations are negotiated.[15]

Such a definition has the potential to divorce the term from its categorizing, anthropological origins as well as determinist

---

[12] Appadurai, *Modernity at Large*, 44.
[13] Freitag and v. Oppen, *Translocality*; Middell, "Transregional Studies."
[14] Reinwald, "Space on the Move," 14.
[15] Csáky, *Das Gedächtnis der Städte*, 101.

interpretations and is more suited to analyses in which a common space, such as the city, is highlighted rather than common (imagined or real) origins. However, such sociological concepts have not yet gained sufficient ground in history, which as a discipline still struggles to come to terms with open or non-determinist culture(s) by labeling it/them as moments or spaces of exception.

Culture(s) in Contact, Europe and the Eastern Mediterranean

In the following, I will set out to recreate the colorful milieus that existed in port cities, such as Salonica, Smyrna, and Constantinople in the nineteenth century and in particular their relationship to European culture. In doing so, I will engage with four lines of investigation: space, entertainment, identity, and the breakdown of this particular form of culture.

Inspired by the writings of such authors as Henri Lefebvre, Pierre Bourdieu, Jürgen Habermas, or Homi Bhabha, "space" has taken on a myriad of meanings in political, sociological, and cultural research. While I occasionally will use the term in a more general sense, in this section, I will limit myself to a restrictive definition of space, in other words, the mental map of the seas, continents, empires, and cities that characterized the locations under study here. How did Great Power politics, state ideologies, intellectual trends, and technological developments together shape the nineteenth-century real and imagined environment of the city? I will begin with the mental map of European imperialist designs on the Eastern Mediterranean at the beginning of the century and the arrival of gunboat diplomacy. In the next step, I describe the discourse emerging from these politics, the "European Dream" that promised to level the geographic and power gap between the various shores of the Mediterranean. It originated to the West, but was very much shaped by agents local to the Eastern shores as well. I then go on to explain how this particular discourse informed the image of Eastern Mediterranean cities and thereafter, how this image produced visions of how to reconstruct the port cities. Taking the quays of Smyrna erected in the 1870s as a point of departure, I then study how the reshaping of the cities impacted upon and was shaped by local residents, but also how the developed parts of the cities were increasingly seen as bifurcating the urban space, along the lines of perceived tradition and modernity.

Part III will employ François Georgeon and Paul Dumont's notion of sociabilities for the study of "entertainment," focusing on variants that were relatively new to the region in the nineteenth century. By closely reading these new activities and studying both the agents who enacted and those who consumed them, I will highlight the meanings they attributed to these new forms of leisure and if, why, and how they were associated with "Europe." Sociabilities in the field of Eurocentric entertainment are particularly interesting because they were easily accessible: While transforming the Eastern Mediterranean into an economic or political peer of its European neighbors was strongly impeded by such factors as imperial and global capitalist dynamics, there were much fewer barriers to spreading leisure practices, if locals of the region or from beyond were willing to pay the price. In a first step, I focus on the consumers of entertainment and leisure practices to understand how they navigate the expanding assortment on offer. I then take theater and in particular opera in the port cities as topic. After tracing their rapid expansion, I describe how watching Verdi operas becomes a hopeful field for achieving reciprocal recognition by overseas societies, but in the end mutates more into a kind of substitute for fulfilling the European Dream. Contemporaries hoped for a single "one world of stage theater," where mutual recognition by East and West could take place despite more complicated economic and political differences. Attending the opera was in the eyes of aficionados a possibility to flaunt cultural capital and to participate in a global civilizing mission of the unenlightened masses. Throughout the century, a yearning by the Eastern Mediterranean theater audience for reciprocity in the process of cultural curiosity for overseas culture is evident. This yearning remains mostly frustrated. To a certain degree though, the flows of theater workers from West to East and the achievements by locals in the dramatic arts were seen as evidence of a single world of theater entertainment. The final two chapters in the part are dedicated to the rise of a new commodity. Beer production developed from a frowned upon activity by foreign residents and local Christians to one of the most successful industries in the empire. Consuming beer celebrated innovation, cosmopolitanism, as well as mixed gender sociability and was only challenged by the rise of nationalist consumer movements.

Part IV explores the question of identity formation in the port city. In this way, we can contradict the notion that so-called Eastern

Mediterranean cosmopolitanism was completely ephemeral and nationalism the dominant trope in determining local ideas of the self. Even critical studies of identity formation have predominantly located the process within the framework of the respective communities. I believe that by highlighting the urban and European context instead, and moreover by juxtaposing discourses on gender and class, and the more fluid practices of identity with the more rigid discourses on identity prevalent in nineteenth-century Eastern Mediterranean maritime society, we will come to different results. As a point of departure, I claim that men and women growing up on the nineteenth-century Eastern Mediterranean, overwhelmed by the wide array of choices to fashion the self, were in essence "without qualities" in the sense of Robert Musil. The section follows this theme and explores the role of press, education, gender, class, ethnicity, and migration in determining their stance as individuals. Its first chapter investigates why foreign-based schools, despite their obvious colonialist intentions, were the object of cultural capital and even appreciation in local society. The second traces the evolvement of the French-language press and its role as trendsetter, partner, and neutral platform for the shaping and voicing of local opinion. A discussion in the letters to the editor in one such newspaper is then taken as point of departure for exploring the conundrum of the men and women "without qualities" in respect to building a gendered identity believed to be appropriate for the late nineteenth century. Linking this up to the well-established discussion of class formation around the Eastern Mediterranean, I claim that class and concomitant nation-building processes, established both in accordance with and in rejection of Europe, are attempts to rein in more individualized processes of identity fashioning. Not only did the class and nation-building processes do violence to the wide array of individual identity possibilities; they also brought groups such as the Levantines to attempt to construct a rigid identity, whereas their existence was intrinsically linked not to ethnic specifics, but to the particularity of port city space. This scenario is further complicated by the presence of migrants in the port cities and their hybrid identities, as the final chapter of the section will show.

Part V deals with the end of the European Dream. Historians, especially during the "celebratory" phase of nineteenth-century port city studies, were always at somewhat of a loss to explain the "unraveling" (Reşat Kasaba) of the Thalassocentric order at the beginning of the twentieth century. Was it the end of a particular conjuncture of the global economy, imperialist meddling, or a crescendo of competing nationalisms? While all of these explanations contain some validity, they remain unsatisfactory to explain the end of an order that continued in different variations for over a century. The section will therefore combine some approaches from political culture to shed light on the collapse of this system. Contextualizing the "unraveling" of the Thalassocentric order in the "Age of Anger" (Pankaj Mishra), I will more closely examine the Ottoman elites' "reverse Orientalism" (Erdal Kaynar), the endemic "economies of violence" (Tolga Esmer), and most especially the process of marginalization of some groups of Europeans that paved the way to deconstructing the Europeanization paradigm all together. I claim that unlike some other world regions, Eastern Mediterranean urban society did not bring forth an outright autochthonous intellectual rejection of the West, as it was too closely intertwined with it. There were other forms of rejections though. This was on the one hand the endemic violence in the countryside that threatened material possessions and the well-being of foreigners. Moreover, intercommunal violence could target foreigners and especially consuls, as became evident in the St. George's Day riots of 1876. Whereas the success of such violence was limited, I claim that European dominance in the Eastern Mediterranean was not so much challenged but deconstructed. My example of such a process is the Ottoman campaign targeting the reputation of European women on moral grounds, which provokes the European-led campaigns against the "white slave trade." Finally, following the moral erosion of the dream of the port cities pertaining to Europe, I trace the steps of their violent disassociation from the Thalassocentric order and the subsequent steps of bringing them into a nation state order.

What Makes the Urban Perspective Different

I argue that this focus on spatial history in combination with histories of consumption, leisure, self-fashioning, but also antagonistic political culture, allows us to discern a more nuanced notion both of Eastern Mediterranean modernity as well as of the process of "Europeanization." Many of these interrogations are not altogether new and can actually look back on long epistemological traditions outside of cultural history. In particular, figurational or process sociology, the history of ideas, and phenomenological enquiries have in part addressed similar questions. However, I hope to come to new conclusions by operationalizing a set of assumptions based on the state of the art of global and cultural history theory as sketched, and in particular by firmly rooting these enquiries in the specific space of the city. These assumptions are as follows.

First, I will avoid as much as possible any a priori divisions of people into groups. The city is conceived of as an arena or stage upon which many different agents left their imprint. Foreigners vs. locals, Ottoman vs. non-Ottoman subjects, and Muslims vs. non-Muslims, Turks, Greeks, Arabs, Bulgarians, Armenians, Sephardim, etc. were of course important categories in the nineteenth-century mindset and when this becomes relevant, I will make these differentiations. However, I believe that much of the nineteenth century urban experience actually was shared across these dividing lines, even if certainly not univocally or to equal degrees. In this way, we can draw new results from some of the old favorite texts often cited in the literature next to others that will be introduced to the readership for the first time. More importantly, I will not a priori assume that any of these inhabitants of the urban space have a more legitimate right to the city than others. Therefore, I will whenever possible not speak of "citizens," or "subjects," but "residents," thus excluding only people present in the cities for a short duration. These are not exercises in political correctness, but attempts to mobilize the sources of a potentially larger number of participants in the port city culture (after all, this is a period of rapid urban growth, country-to-city migration, and increased circulation of people leaving their imprint on the locale), and thus to better understand what makes up the urban space and its affinity to Europeanization. Nonetheless, I do not claim to represent all port city residents equally here. The selection is obviously dictated by my language skills, my talent at reading and acquiring sources, and by their relevance to the Europeanized culture.

Second, rather than seeing the region we are concerned with here as the antithesis of Europe, I will assume it to be, in the words of one contemporary writer, Refik Halid Karay, "a corner of Europe." The grandees of social and cultural theory, from Max Weber to Edward Saïd, have focused on juxtaposing Europe and the Eastern Mediterranean. What will happen if instead we follow up the many hints that not all nineteenth-century contemporaries would have agreed with them?

Moreover, I believe that some phenomena of the modern Eastern Mediterranean can be better understood if we consider them not as exceptions, but as part of a continuity with wider repercussions. This is not to brush over existing differences, which obviously distinguish the Ottoman realm and its successor states from other parts of the continent, but then again, one would have to concede such distinguishing elements just as easily to Ireland or Portugal. It is high time we stop studying the Ottoman realm within a framework of exceptionalism. In other words, the time has come to provincialize the Ottoman Empire. Europe, as a concept and a culture, is therefore both the object and the approach of this study. What specifically Europe is, is of course not a given, but something constructed. The construction process for the greater part took place locally, albeit in an atmosphere well informed of and touched by overseas events and phenomena. As mentioned, "people's appropriation and blending of diverse cross-bordering cultural elements" is the subject of this study, port cities the space where we can observe a particular dynamic of the process, and Europe an attribution of meaning many of these elements received in their time.

Third, I will attempt to locate the cities under study here within the Mediterranean. Using "Mediterranean" in the title of books on nineteenth-century changes in the region has become trendy and is to some degree an attempt to ditch the negative connotations that the "Balkans," the "Middle East," the "Arab World," the "Muslim World" or other partially overlapping territories evoke. While obviously the Ottoman framework remains important and will find sufficient mention in the pages to come, I believe emphasizing the Mediterranean dimension lends a different perspective to the study of these cities. As mentioned, cultural history has used "contact zones" or similar constructs to avoid the problem of older, more holistic concepts of culture. If one were to simply declare the port cities themselves to be these zones, one would easily repeat the Wallersteinian fallacy of creating an exceptional status for them, divesting them of their interactions with their hinterland and the world at large. By declaring the Mediterranean to be the contact zone, we are more flexible as to how large the zones on its shore under our scrutiny can be. Such an approach, in the words of Manuel Borutta and Sakis Gekas, serves as a magnifying glass for "asymmetric relationships and shared experiences among Europe, the Maghreb and the Middle East." In this perspective, the nineteenth-century Mediterranean is "a maritime space of colonial interactions and entanglements that transcended continental and national boundaries."¹⁶ Such a post-constructivist concept of the region follows up on contemporary trends in global history and in particular on other attempts to reconceptualize seas as "seascapes," in other words as geographical entities that have been conceived and shaped by human agency. Such a historiography of the Mediterranean thus strongly differs from the Braudelian notion of a meta-region in need of comprehensive explanation. In the new conceptualization, it is no not a problem that when speaking of the Mediterranean, Julia Clancy-Smith talks about Tunis, La Valetta, and Bône, Ilham Makdisi of Cairo (al-Qâhira), Alexandria, and Beirut, and my examples refer to Salonica, Constantinople and Smyrna.¹⁷ While I can prove my statements for these three cities – the leading port cities of the northern half of the empire with predominantly Greco-Turkish cultural imprint – very similar or comparable constellations can be assumed for Beirut and Alexandria, the leading port cities of the southern, Arab-dominated half of the region, and whenever possible I will try to compare or contrast them based on recent studies. A related constellation under rather different circumstances is likely for port cities beyond the Ottoman imperial legacy, such as Trieste (Trst), while my findings will probably only be vaguely reminiscent of the situation in Algeciras and Tangiers at the time.

---

¹⁶ Borutta and Gekas, "A Colonial Sea"; see also Burke, "The Deep Structures of Mediterranean Modernity." Such a historiography is still somewhat in the making. As Manuel Borutta and Sakis Gekas have pointed out, older history of the Mediterranean was heavily influenced by colonialism, both in the Braudelian, essentialist variety, and in the cosmopolitan variety influenced by Gabriel Audisio. Furthermore, the modern historiography of the Mediterranean must struggle with the common assumption that the sea deserves to be the subject of study only until the early modern period. This is not surprising, as Peregrine Horden and Nicholas Purcell have explicitly claimed that the meta-region had lost its interconnectivity in modernity, a claim that has been widely accepted. However, as Manuel Borutta has stated, the nineteenth century saw the advent of steamships, which made the traffic of people, goods, and ideas much easier. Likewise, migration took place on a scale that had not been seen since the time of the Reconquista. It seems therefore that it was rather the hitherto most "well-connected" century for the Mediterranean. The difference lies rather in the fact that more economically and politically viable regions had arisen in the central and northern half of Europe and that from their perspective, the Mediterranean looked underdeveloped.
¹⁷ Clancy-Smith, *Mediterraneans*; Khuri-Makdisi, *Eastern Mediterranean and the Making of Global Radicalism*; see also Rothman, *Brokering Empire*.

Fourth, I will not limit my study to either actions or texts, but rather in the sense of Arlette Farge read actions as texts. In this way, I believe we can overcome some of the silences inherent in the sources. While the juxtaposition of what maritime residents had to say about themselves and their actual deeds might occasionally be enlightening, as a rule this study will not privilege one level over the other, but attempt to study them as complementary elements of maritime culture

These are the working tools I will use to analyze the Europeanized urban culture of the nineteenth century: a concept of culture that combines actions and texts; the Mediterranean as the focal point of a "maritime culture" of "appropriation and blending"; the assumption that the Eastern Mediterranean subjectivity is subject to trans-European, if not wider trends in the human condition; and to stress the port city residents' role in constructing their city and its place in the world around it.

Situating the Port City in the "Age of Revivals"

An urban history of the modern period is hardly reconcilable with the assumption of state-propelled change. Instead, the city appears as an arena in which a multitude of actors compete to influence the world around them. To do away with the primacy of politics, that is, the implicit assumption that administrative change initiated social change, it would be better to discard the term "Age of Reforms" or *Tanzimat* (reorderings) as the master narrative of mid-nineteenth-century changes. Instead, I propose to adopt and slightly abuse another term that has been used for this period: The Age of Revivals. Revival (Bulgarian *vâzraždane*, Arabic *Nahda*) has often been understood as mere foreplay of nation-state independence in nation-centered historiography of the era, interpreting the heightened sense of ethnic self produced by intellectual and cultural output among Bulgarians parallel to the *Tanzimat*, and in the Arab case in the Hamidian Era as a source of legitimacy for separatist aspirations for statehood. But more detailed studies have brought to light the multidirectional ways people would choose to think, act, and associate during the revival movements.[18]

---

[18] Mestyan, *Arab Patriotism*; Zachs, "Cultural and Conceptual Contributions"; Clayer, Grandits, and Pichler (eds.), *Conflicting Loyalties*; Vakali, "Nationalism, Justice and Taxation"; Petrov, "Everyday Forms of Compliance."

I wish to use "revivals," noticeably in the plural, not in the limited way of national historiography, but rather in the sense Gilles Veinstein has used it: to denote an unprecedented expansion in the possible ways to relate to the wider world due to intellectual processes, technological innovation, and government policies.[19] As different waves and phases of revivals followed upon each other, I will use this term broadly, for the entire period covered here. *Tanzimat* will be used to refer to government reform or as part of established compound words.

There are of course several other aspects that would deserve more clarification with regards to their relationship to previous works, theoretical stance, and terminology. In particular, the use of terms such as "modern," "modernization," and modernity"; the pros and cons of describing nineteenth-century processes of change as "modernization," "westernization," or "Europeanization"; and whether or not to depict diverse societies as "cosmopolitan," all have an ample history of debate. Rather than making an already lengthy introduction even longer I will abstain from further deliberations and simply state that I use these terms in a purely descriptive manner without trying to ascertain any kind of particular status for any phenomena, persons, or societies analyzed here. Likewise, my usage of old names for the cities under scrutiny and their residents are the product of an intense interaction with the sources and not meant to signify anything more than their former highly mixed status.

A Potpourri of Archived Voices

For my endeavor, I have retrieved contemporary voices from a myriad of materials of different origins and types. The sources employed here are of an eclectic character. Assuming that an elusive subject such as urban culture will not be revealed by reading a set of dossiers with subsequent running numbers from A to Z, nor that the relative documents could ever be studied in total, I have taken the liberty to proceed intuitively. Certain patterns of port city culture can be traced across a broad spectrum of sources. Naturally, my use of material is limited by my language skills. Utilizing sources in all relevant Eastern

---

[19] Veinstein, "Un paradoxe séculaire." This suggestion also follows up on Ortaylı's demand that a history of modernization in the Ottoman Empire should discard ethnocentricity and include for example the intellectual developments of early modern Serbia and Wallachia; Ortaylı, *İmparatorluğun en uzun yüzyılı*, 32.

Mediterranean languages can only be the aim of a collective effort.[20] The Ottoman Archives in Istanbul, often considered the high road to decipher this region's past, feature prominently in some sections, but overall appear as one set of partisan voices, both with the potential to put into perspective other views on the era and in need of correction themselves.[21] While historiography of the nineteenth century has made ample use of consular archives, only a few writers to date have studied the personal files assorted by the various consulates in the Eastern Mediterranean. The consular files stored in Berlin (PA-AA, BA, and GStA), but much more the former Habsburg embassy and consular files archived in Vienna (HHStA), have proven invaluable in widening the scope of knowledge on port city society. While their nominal topic is their respective subjects, these individuals are often involuntarily represented within a network of relationships to foreigners of other nationalities, to locals of various ethno-religious attributes, and to competing state and ecclesiastical authorities. Beyond the institutional perspective, individual petitions, forgotten private letters, and court interrogations recorded in the consular archives have also proven themselves as rich voices from the past. From among the ecclesiastical authorities, I have occasionally made use especially of the German-speaking Protestant Church archives kept in Berlin (ezab) and in situ (EGS).

A perspective inspiringly different from those mentioned previously manifests itself in the local press. While the indigenous French-language press has been used to gather information before, this book also intends to understand its position in local society, besides using it to gauge contemporary sentiment (at least on those subjects considered publishable). These are complemented by the Ottoman Turkish and the English-language press. The nineteenth century was the age of an unprecedented expansion of printing, and the numerous memoirs, travelogs, and pamphlets, but also novels in the British Library in London, the Bibliothèque Nationale in Paris, and the Staatsbibliothek in Berlin as well as a number of other places, help us to understand contemporary urban culture. Especially in today's Istanbul, Thessaloniki, and Izmir, the lively scene of printing houses, specialist bookstores,

[20] Such efforts are under way, see the project "Istanbul Memories: Personal Narratives of the Late Ottoman Empire," http://istanbulmemories.org.
[21] On the need to balance Ottoman state documents with other sources see Quataert, "Labor History and the Ottoman Empire," 98.

and municipal initiatives contribute to making nineteenth-century texts accessible. Within the framework of postcolonial criticism of Orientalism, nineteenth-century writings by Westerners on the East have become highly suspect. However, a closer look reveals that they are often not in opposition, but in congruence with what locals have to say about their society (which is not proof of their authenticity, but rather that authors from the region and from without, often inhabited interrelated discursive spaces). Following up on the critique, narrative sources, independent of their author's origin, will be used not as the product of omniscient narrators, but as the voices of partisan participants in social constellations.

These diverse sources in combination will bring forth a broad spectrum of voices of various social standing, origins, and eloquence, including newspaper critics and editors; members of merchant families; writers of anonymous letters to the editor; performers of popular music; as well as an educator and a sex worker both petitioning their consulate. However, while I develop my perspective on the port cities based on their subjective views, I do not aim to reproduce biographies here and limit my analysis to what I find relevant to the various aspects of urban culture under exploration. To use a pun, by exploiting the voices of multiple agents, I ultimately aim for the "death of the agent."

The following pages would not have been possible simply based upon my own source work. The rich field of urban history has made it possible to put into perspective or generalize or contrast many of my findings. By referring to the invaluable work of colleagues who have meticulously labored to make particular aspects of nineteenth-century life visible, I am able to describe the Europeanized urban culture in a much more congruent way than if I had solely relied on my own findings.

PART II

Constructing Europe
Spatial Relations of Power in Eastern Mediterranean Cities

On July 2, 1798, a French fleet landed near Alexandria and took the city and its surroundings with relative ease. Following the debacle, the Egyptian commanders debated who was to blame for having let the fortress at Alexandria fall into disrepair; who had understaffed the garrison; and who failed to equip it with functioning weaponry. More than neglect though, sheer disbelief had led to the loss of Egypt's main port. According to Abd al-Rahman al-Jabarti's account, the city's administrator, Muhammad Kurayyim, had renounced an offer by a British squadron to protect Alexandria, as he could not have imagined that the Ottomans' long-standing ally would attack without provocation.[1]

The French advance upon Alexandria upset a century-old equilibrium in the Mediterranean. In 1571, Ottoman pretensions toward hegemony over the entire Mediterranean were ended at the battle of Lepanto. Thereafter, the House of Osman presided over the Southern and Eastern shores of the sea, whereas the Habsburgs and other Catholic rulers essentially resigned themselves to the Northern and Western half – Veneto-Ottoman wars notwithstanding. The sultans had inherited from the Eastern Roman emperors the designation "ruler over two seas and two continents," or more precisely "the White Sea, the Black Sea, Rumelia, Anatolia," thus creating the image of a symmetrical empire centered on their palace in Istanbul. The exact meaning of "White Sea" has changed over time, but historically stood for the Aegean and adjacent parts of the Mediterranean. At the end of the eighteenth century, with Tsarist Russia capturing the Northern shore of the Black Sea and revolutionary France taking besides Egypt "Illyria" on the Eastern Adriatic coast, not only was the post-Lepanto equilibrium upset; with both alleged Ottoman *maria nostri*, the Black and White Seas, partially lost, Pax Ottomana in the entire region

[1] Al-Jabarti, *Al-Jabarti's Chronicle*, 33–37.

essentially came to an end. While the Ottoman naval defences had proven a pushover, first the French and subsequently most Great Powers learned that it was not easy to fill both the power vacuum and the ideological gap left behind after Pax Ottomana.

Muhammad Kurayyim could have known of French Mediterranean aspirations, had he followed the debates in Paris as the British Navy, but also the administration and public of Tunis, had. What did the adherents of the Revolution want in Egypt? While their new mission was ostensibly to liberate and enlighten the oppressed masses of Europe and beyond, imperialist dreams of expansion were very much present. In the latter vein, Bertrand Barère dreamed of the Mediterranean as a French *mare nostrum*: "For France, the Mediterranean is but a large navigational canal, the policing of which can and must be her responsibility."[2] Within this framework, it was important that "Turkey does not leave Europe."[3] Matteo Galdi, an Italian supporter of the revolution, by contrast promoted "regeneration for all the peoples of the Mediterranean."[4] The ambassador to the Porte, Marie Louis d'Escorches, especially, worked actively toward rapprochement, believing the Republic had "a duty to play a regulating role in this part of the world and bring it under the rule of justice, peace and harmony, for the greater happiness of the peoples."[5] Finally, it was the Foreign Minister Charles de Tallyerand who initiated the turn to a clearly imperialist agenda in the region and recommended the attack.

While the occupation of Egypt remained a short episode, shrewd power politics, dominated mostly by a changing cast of Great Powers, remained one pillar of the new order in the Eastern Mediterranean. Until World War I and its trench warfare, and for the Eastern Mediterranean most importantly until the failed Allied landing at Gallipoli, it was a common opinion that whoever ruled the waves ruled the world. With the advent of the steamer in the late 1820s and its further development, the potential for naval powers to intervene or retaliate all over the world at fairly short notice grew considerably. With unilateral aggression against the militarily weak Ottoman incumbent usually not

---

[2] Bertrand Barère, quoted from Sellaouti, "The Republic and the Muslim World," 99.
[3] Ibid.
[4] Galdi, quoted from Sellaouti, "The Republic and the Muslim World," 99.
[5] d'Escorches, quoted from Sellaouti, "The Republic and the Muslim World," 106.

an option due to Great Power rivalry, multilateral paternalism more often than not became the default option. Interventions, sometimes on the side of the Ottoman government, sometimes against it, became a common feature of most nineteenth-century wars in the Levant. Promising an intervention on behalf of the Porte against the insubordinate governor of Egypt, Muhammad Ali, Great Britain pressured the Porte into providing liberal access to the Ottoman market for British commerce in the 1838 Baltalimanı Treaty. Other countries followed suit. Lower custom tariffs and partial indemnity to Ottoman jurisdiction, as provided by the Sultanic privileges to foreign trade communities, the capitulations, gave European commerce further advantages on the Ottoman market. These treaties with the Porte, originally negotiated to facilitate trade between the Ottoman Empire and its neighbors, had been successively developed to exempt European foreigners from many taxes and in several cases provided indemnity from Ottoman executive measures and judicial prosecution, assigning this task to the respective consulates instead.[6]

That the military force was always a backdrop for this new Thalassocentric order is on the one hand illustrated by the successive occupations of Ottoman littoral provinces by other European states, but more importantly for the discussion at hand, it is necessary to recall the everyday demonstrations of naval might. During the entire century, it was common for warships to parade around Ottoman ports to remind the locals of their place. One description of such a casual display of power:

To maintain existing interests and as a threat to the Turkish government, the Great Powers sent numerous warships to Smyrna, which anchored in the outer harbor. Upon my arrival, one German, Italian, and Austrian ship each had already anchored, and one fine day around noon, four more Italians came in. I watched their arrival from the quay. These collosses seemed like mighty fortresses, they came closer at great speed, producing great masses of smoke. After anchoring, the salutes of the present flags of war began, which were greeted with varying amounts of cannon shots, depending on the rank of their commander. Since the greeted flags on the various ships reciprocated, the effect was a non-ending cannon thunder that attracted great human masses to the quay. Two days later, three Frenchmen arrived, then one

---

[6] Zarinebaf, *Mediterranean Encounters*.

Frenchmen and one Russian, and each time the shooting was repeated. All in all, twelve warships lay in the harbor.[7]

But rather than recount the well-known history of interventions or make an argument here for the colonial or semi-colonial status of the Eastern Mediterranean, I wish to draw attention to the fact that in opposition to direct colonial rule, such sporadic interventions and demonstrations could only set a general framework for the Thalassocentric order, thus leaving much of the new system to be negotiated. As Faruk Tabak puts it,

> Precisely when the colonial world was coming within the ever-tightening embrace of rival powers, with no breathing room at its disposal, the dynastic [Ottoman and Chinese, MF] empires managed to retain, if not grant, substantial room for maneuvre due in large part to the escalation of competition among the "great powers." This was, then, a latitudinarian conjuncture for dynastic polities that escaped colonization[8] ... In the absence of colonization, port-cities became nodes of political incertitude and promise, and hence a world of possibilities.[9]

Imperialist rivalry thus created this "conjuncture" for the region between the end of Pax Ottomana and the abolishment of the Ottoman Empire. I wish to draw attention here to the second pillar on which regional hegemony rested between roughly 1801 and 1911: the spread of a new formula for happiness availing itself of Enlightenment rhetoric. Talleyrand's decision to invade Egypt did not put an end to proclamations in the spirit of d'Escorches. Already while advancing towards the Nile Delta, the French commander Napoleon Bonaparte had a propaganda leaflet distributed, claiming that the invasion was not a hostile act at all. The general went out of his way to affirm that the only reason for the intervention was to end the despotic rule of the Mamluk local administrators and that the French army respected Islam, the Sultan, and the local population:

> O ye Egyptians ... tell the slanderers that I have not come to you except for the purpose of restoring your rights ... And tell them also that all people are equal in the eyes of God and the only circumstances which distinguish one from the other are reason, virtue, and knowledge.[10]

---

[7] Kauder, *Reisebilder aus Persien, Turkestan und der Türkei*, 317, 318.
[8] Keyder, *State and Class in Turkey*, 38–41 (Tabak's citation).
[9] Tabak, "Imperial Rivalry and Port-Cities," 80.
[10] Napoleon Bonaparte, quoted from al-Jabarti, *Al-Jabarti's Chronicle*, 40; Firges, *French Revolutionaries in the Ottoman Empire*, passim.

Such declarations were not simply disinformation or classic colonial claims to a civilizing mission. Instead, they reflect an ambivalence in the expansion of the Western and Central European powers into the Eastern Mediterranean that remained unresolved throughout the three-year occupation, but also the century. While gunboat policy was characteristic for the Eastern Mediterranean, the idea that the West of the continent could somehow bring about "justice, peace and harmony" as well as "greater happiness" on the shores of the Eastern Mediterranean was developed further in the course of the following decades, and gained credibility in wider society. Over time, it evolved into a notion that informed the imagination and daily lives of many residents of the region.

4 | *The European Dream*

The European Promise: To Join a World on the Move

No doubt, the threat of the Ottoman Empire's forced integration into the Western sphere of economics, aesthetics, and power politics through colonization, unequal treaties, or similar infringements was always in the air. As the Stambouliote author Stephanos Kastriotis stated in the 1840s: "Must the Western nations therefore subjugate these peoples, divide them up amongst themselves in order to, as one says, educate them? However, they are strangers to the land, and within providential harmony, the Orient must remain the Orient."[1]

Many contemporary observers concentrated more on the salutary elements of the messages they received from the West of the Mediterranean. While d'Escorches's initiatives had remained diplomatic, and French rule over Egypt was too short to establish a model – although al-Jabarti gave them some points for clean uniforms, street order, and dedication to science[2] – public elaboration on the benefits of a European "regeneration" of the Eastern Mediterranean developed over the course of the century.

What promise did Europe have in store for the locals? Pamphlets, speeches, and memorandums attempted to provide an answer. Possibly, adherents of Saint-Simonianism, the early nineteenth-century ideology that claimed technical progress would radically transform human society for the better, were the pioneers of developing Napoleon's hyperbole into a more specific vision of the future Mediterranean. The economist Michel Chevalier, writing in 1832 upon the advent of regular steamship services in the Eastern Mediterranean (and two years after the French capture of Algiers), predicted that the emerging tighter network of communication, traffic, and trade between

---

[1] Kastriotis, *Lettre*.
[2] Salama, *Orientalism and Intellectual History*, 148–162; al-Jabarti, *Al-Jabarti's Chronicle*.

Europe and the far shores of the Mediterranean would transform the region from the site where world civilizations clashed into a "wedding bed" for Orient and Occident. Steamers, railways, and telegraphs would combine to produce a severe space-time contraction of the region, rendering smaller entities such as the nation redundant in the process and setting the prerequisites for perpetual peace. France would be reduced to a province within a Euro-Mediterranean super-state governed from the North.[3] We know precious little about the direct diffusion of such visions in the Eastern Mediterranean at the time, but the appearance of images of West-Eastern harmonization by local authors, as shown later, clearly demonstrates that the idea was not alien to the region. A close reading of Chevalier's vision reveals that the "wedding" was not conceived as a union of equals, but rather as a paternalistic guardianship;[4] nonetheless, the Eastern Mediterranean authors apparently concentrated on the opportunities rather than the pitfalls of pan-Mediterranean unity. Or more precisely: Authors from the Eastern shores of the sea appropriated the "wedding" theme, used it to demand and effect change to conditions in their immediate surroundings that they were not satisfied with, and over time changed the narrative from paternalistic guardianship to one of harmonization and mutual respect.

In the course of the following decades, the European promise was reiterated and commented upon repeatedly, with shifting geographical stress and by a changing array of West and Central European actors. The longtime British ambassador Stratford Canning, who had exacted vital influence on both Ottoman foreign and internal politics, spoke at the laying of the cornerstone to Smyrna's first railway station at La Punta (now Alsancak) in 1858. He summed up his vision as "the consolidation of European interests with those of Turkey ... a progressive diminution of abuses, prejudices and national animosities."[5] A few years later, when in 1862 the railway had reached Ayasoluk (now Selçuk) near Ephesus, Hyde Clark, chairman of the Smyrna-Aydın Railway, described the European Dream in even more detail. He claimed that the country's best prospects for development were "in direct relations with the Capitalists of London." The resident foreigners should do "our duty as Europeans for the advancement of the

---

[3] Borutta, *Mediterrane Verflechtungen*, II.1.   [4] Ibid.
[5] Stratford Canning, quoted from Mansel, *Levant*, 161.

people ... [and] contribute to the prosperity of this flourishing country ... and before ten years the population and commerce would double." Mehmed Reşid Pasha, governor of the province of Aydın, also at the inauguration in Ayasoluk, explicitly raised the issue of "the prosperity and civilization of the empire."[6]

The vague prospects Stratford Canning had evoked in an almost literal quotation from d'Escorches thus finds a more pronounced elaboration. Work, commercial exchange, and following imported tastes were the keys to finding happiness. By accepting the world rule of the London capitalists and the superiority of European ways, and by participating in the commerce based in London or Marseille, the Smyrniotes would attain a better standard of living. Besides the promise of riches, it was presumed that somehow peace with the European Great Powers and with the local neighbors as well as good governance would trickle down.

This vision continued to have an influence roughly until the eve of World War I. It was further elaborated on by the orientalist Martin Hartmann. In the introduction to the account of his journey to Salonica and Constantinople, he states,

My attitude towards all people, apart from those who reveal themselves to be vermin, is friendship and good will. I feel these emotions also for the Ottoman Turks, in fact to a very high degree. And because of that my words against them often sound harsh. I see them on paths that do not lead up but down, while I wish for them what one must wish for every people and every individual: progress towards the only decent goal, the development and useful employment of all forces, fulfillment in the limits of nationhood and the great community of cultured nations ... I have proven that two heavy loads weigh this people down, so it cannot get up and merrily join in advising and doing with the hoard of nations in Southeastern Europe and West Asia who are rising in force and willingly following the call of the cultured nations: towards a union of all parts of the whole Western Eurasia, from the Atlantic Ocean to the mountain cordon of the Tienshan, towards the union that will bring to this tremendous economic zone the blessings of a magnanimous economic policy impregnating even the most remote corner of the individual parts, the union that will lead the freely inundating hosts of

---

[6] *Smyrna Mail*, 23 Sept. 1862, 2–3.

culture through the tight network of roads into regions that momentarily still turn their heads in disdain.[7]

The Dream's promise has not changed since the earlier quotations at the railway inaugurations: peaceful coexistence, prosperity, productivity, and a higher state of culture. Hartmann is however more precise (or more threatening) in spelling out that these promises are dependent on certain conditions. First, it is paramount that those who wish to profit from this dream must embrace it willingly: Belief in the superiority of the European model is a precondition for joining the community of European nations. Second, unlike in more rigid notions of Orientalism, in this vision, which localities and which people could be included in the greater community of Europe is not a foregone conclusion. While Europe is not a completely open-ended category, its delimitations are subject to negotiation (the furthest conceivable border being the Tienshan). This negotiation process depends less on convincing geographic or genealogic arguments, but rather on performance: Those who due to tradition, lack of will, or lack of desire to reform are not productive in this global capitalist, future-oriented, and Eurocentric world are threatened with exclusion. While Hartmann is not explicit as to what consequences exclusion from the "community of cultured nations" will have, we can assume that the result is the loss of the right to subjecthood and thus of political rights, implying the need for others, be it competing national movements or imperial states, to assume a mandate to "educate/subjugate" the immature creatures, as Kastriotis put it.[8]

Thus a peripheral integration not only into a Eurocentric economy, but also into a Eurocentric cultural order became characteristic of this era. As this was an ongoing process of negotiation, residents of the Eastern Mediterranean littoral were motivated by the hope that integration would get the upper hand over peripheralization and would one day once again lead to the equal status they had enjoyed in previous centuries. This is why the quoted governor Mehmed Reşid

---

[7] He continues, "Those two loads are the Sharia, the 'Holy Law,' and xenophilia (Fremdländerei)." Hartmann, *Der islamische Orient*, vol. III, pp. V, VI.

[8] Hobsbawm, *Nations and Nationalism since 1780*, 32. Thomas Mann explicitly states that some nations, despite their political awareness, are destined to never achieve statehood due to their "inability in matters of power and state." He explicitly mentions the Irish and the Poles, proving his lack of talent as a political oracle; Mann, *Betrachtungen eines Unpolitischen*, XXXIII.

calls for "civilization" of the empire. As Birgit Schäbler writes, "Until about the end of the 1860s/1870s, civilization was a universal concept of which Islamic societies perceived themselves to be a part."[9] It is in this vein that we must understand Khedive Ismail of Egypt's famous 1871 statement that Egypt no longer lay in Africa, but in Europe.[10] This was not simply the audacity of a faltering monarch, but a historical player from the Eastern Mediterranean insisting that since Egypt had shown considerable administrative, economic, and cultural progress, it was now the turn for the West to deliver on its share in a common bargain, a promise, that is, the European Dream.

Not only government representatives called for integration into the Thalassocentric order. A significant part of the Ottoman urban public embraced the same path. Contemporaries who made use of this discourse framed their exposal to Europe not as an act of submission, but as an end to provincialism, a lesson to be learned, a gap to be bridged. For the late nineteenth-century generation, it was the choice between the wide world (or rather what could be glimpsed of it from the quays on the Marmara or Aegean coast) or the parochialism of the respective *mahalla* (neighborhood) and religious group.

For, as commercial intercourse had increased between Salonica, the natural outlet of the Balkans, and the West, so had the need for a better understanding of that world in whose hands our destinies seemed to be evolving. And aside from this purely economic necessity, there was also the thirst for a broader culture, an unconscious drive toward a larger world than our own with which we unwittingly sought identification. The visits of foreign travellers, the casual contact with Western institutions, the foreign language schools, the occasional trip abroad, these were making the people conscious of their provincialism, a provincialism the more oppressive since it derived its own particular narrowness from within each national group.[11]

In this description by the contemporary observer Leon Sciaky, exposure to the West no longer serves the purpose of delivering the empire or the province from gunboat politics and rapacious creditors, but the innate desires of the maritime residents. It has become a new

---

[9] Schäbler, "Civilizing Others," 23. Even after that point in time, a reciprocal interest to include the Ottomans in the civilized world occasionally resurfaces; see for example the description of Ubeydullah Effendi's transatlantic voyage in 1893 in Deringil, "The West within and the West Without," 112–115.
[10] Khedive Ismail, quoted from Barring, *Modern Egypt*, 48.
[11] Sciaky, *Farewell to Ottoman Salonica*, 84.

décloisonnement (to borrow a term Shirine Hamadeh has coined for eighteenth-century innovations in urban culture).[12] People managed to move both within their own city and beyond at much accelerated speeds, industrial products as well as newspapers from France, Germany, or England reached the local shops within a matter of days, thus facilitating the exchange.

In definitions by Ottoman subjects, Westernization is always described as a dynamic process; while Sciaky in the quote associates it with commodity transport, travel, and learning, another common association is construction. Ahmed Cevad (Emre), in his definition of Westernization, paints a picture of the buildings and structures he deems necessary in this process. While Sciaky's personal horror is the constraints within a too small part of the world, Ahmed Cevad's opposition is against a lack of movement.

The word Westernization has in our language taken on the permanent meaning to transfer the West's social and economic life as much as possible to the East, i.e. to make the East engage in science, technology, and industry just like the West, to revitalize it by means of universities, factories, parks (large municipal gardens), operas, big observatories, in short to save society from indifference and immobility by orienting them towards knowledge and the arts.[13]

While such explicit renderings of what a Europeanized Eastern Mediterranean should look like are the products of literati, administrative, or social elites, we will later find ample proof that non-elite residents could just as well carve out their own little "corners of Europe." Both Sciaky's and Ahmed Cevad's ideas of Westernization are intimately tied to an urban and maritime context. We must therefore turn to the port cities and determine their place on the map of the Thalassocentric order.

---

[12] Hamadeh, *The City's Pleasures*.
[13] Ahmed Cevad (Emre), quoted from Tüccarzade, *Avrupalılaşmak*, 58.

5 | *The Making of a European Spatial Discourse on the Levantine City*

What vision of the cities on the Eastern Mediterranean shores did the European Dream entail? This was not clear from the outset, as we can notice a rather long hiatus between the Napoleonic occupation and the hardening of a discourse on the Levantine city. This new trope was shaped in a dialogical process by agents from the west and east of the Mediterranean. While commentators from the Western shores set the general framework, many Easterners, rather than revoking the outsiders' framework outright, affirmed it in order to enrich it with their own nuances. This process only gathered full force once the initial hiatus had passed.

In early nineteenth-century travelogs by European travelers to the Ottoman lands, the descriptions of cities mostly do not reveal supremacism, but rather great reverence for the places they see. Heinrich von Moltke, reaching Constantinople on horseback after a ride in freezing weather through Southeast Europe in November 1835, felt both relieved and moved:

> on the tenth morning after leaving Rusçuk, we saw the sun rise behind a distant mountain range, with a silver lining at its feet – it was Asia, the cradle of peoples, snow-covered Olympus and the clear Propontis, on whose deep blue surface a few sails shimmered like swans. Soon a forest of minarets, of masts, and cypress trees shone up from the sea – it was Constantinople.[1]

Approaching the city from the sea, Anna Forneris, sailing from Corfu in 1826 and having experienced a pirate raid, detention at the hands of the Greek navy, and a fire, exclaims, "When one sees this giant city extending so wonderfully along the seashore, one honestly believes to have reached paradise."[2]

---

[1] Moltke, *Briefe über Zustände*, 19; Propontis = Marmara Sea; Olympus = Uludağ, visible from Constantinople on particularly clear days.
[2] Forneris, *Schicksale und Erlebnisse einer Kärtnerin*, 35–39.

In the first half of the nineteenth century, reaching the cities on the Aegean and Marmara shores was still a feat of hardship. Traveling in a part of the world without rudimentary infrastructure proved a trial, if not purgatory, for individuals accustomed to the comforts of urban life (and possibly this trial was augmented by culturalist fears of the East). Legends of the Orient, the high esteem for classical Greece, and the region's role as site of biblical exploits combined to imbue the northeastern Mediterranean region with a special role in the Western imaginary. To experience this hypertrophic land first hand in an era that prided itself for its romanticism, that is, deeply emotional reactions to experiences of nature, foreign cultures, and cosmologies, provoked strong responses. Henry Formby's prologue to entering the Bosporus by sea from 1843 begins:

Some such train of thought as this, I am perfectly assured, can never fail to arise naturally to every right-minded man, on his coming in view of any of the regions which are well known in the early legends of mankind; and they will be found to convey to the heart, rather than the mind, an overwhelming feeling that life is, after all, but a passenger-sort of thing, a mere shadow.[3]

Such reactions were not limited to visitors who were complete strangers to the Eastern Mediterranean. Paul Calligas visited Constantinople in 1844. A native of Smyrna, he had fled to Trieste in 1825 due to the danger of massacres, as many Ottoman subjects suspected the Greek population of supporting the war of secession in Morea. Following his studies in Berlin and Heidelberg, where he had completed a dissertation in law in 1837,[4] he moved to the Hellenic Kingdom to work at the Court of Appeals. Upon his visit to the Ottoman capital, he climbed Çamlica Hill, the highest peak in the vicinity, which commands a spectacular view of the Bosporus and the Marmara Sea. Overwhelmed by the view, Calligas writes, "The Golden Horn separates two great cities: Pera and Byzantium, the city of commerce and the one of power ... It is here, says the observer despite himself, it is here we find the universal passageway."[5] In his vision, the city morphs into

---

[3] Formby, *A Visit to the East*, 36, 37. Even Jakob Philipp Fallmerayer, who is remembered more for his destructive criticism of the Greek nation, would feel overwhelmed by the impressions of the Greco-Ottoman landscape; Fallmerayer, *Fragmente aus dem Orient*.

[4] *Heidelberger Jahrbücher der Literatur* 30 (2/1837), 1229.

[5] Calligas, *Voyage à Syros, Smyrne et Constantinople*, 161.

a meeting place of Mesopotamians with Rhinelanders, Persians and Tibetans with Englishmen and Americans. This gateway between Orient and Occident, he concludes, should be open to all save Ares, god of war. He envisions Constantinople as a peaceful site of exchange between Europeans and Asians, free of violence. Not only goods, but also ideas, such as the initial concepts of the great religions, had been and still were exchanged as well as transformed here in this city between the continents.

Calligas' vision presents a number of discursive novelties. At the height of their power, in the fifteenth and sixteenth century, the Ottoman sultans had constructed the palace and the city into "a world with a center from which increasingly heterogeneous centralities proliferate, referencing at every remove the transcendent site, sight, and oversight of the sultan."[6] A premodern version of Bentham's Panopticon, the Tower of Justice within the imperial palace symbolized the invisible ruler's power to see all, as he strove to maintain imperial justice throughout his realm,[7] while the palace as a whole stood for divine grace: "The Sultanic Fortress with its central palace, kiosks, and gardens constituted a quasi-sacred city, totally separate from the city of Istanbul" and was supposedly "believed to be the locus where God's grace or Good Fortune (sa'āda or kut) manifested itself."[8] It is debatable to what degree such discourses ever managed to convince wider society and especially if they continued to hold sway during the more unruly and hedonistic seventeenth and eighteenth centuries. What is noticeable though is that it had completely disappeared by the end of Pax Ottomana.

In Calligas' vision, the city on the Straits is no longer a harmonious center of the universe, but its gateway, connecting some of the planet's more obscure corners, such as Tibet and America, regions that were not actually in close exchange with Istanbul. Any port city functions as a gateway. In this city, the Sultan's throne seems empty, and the freely flooding movements of commercial and intercultural exchange dominate. It is in this role that Calligas wishes to preserve it: His plea against Ares must be read as a plea against Great Power or irredentist attempts to take the city.

---

[6] Andrews, "Speaking of Power," 286, 287.
[7] Necipoğlu, *Architecture, Ceremonial, and Power*. On the Panopticon see Foucault, *Discipline and Punish*.
[8] İnalcık, "Istanbul: An Islamic City," 22, 23.

Nonetheless the Smyrna-born and Western-educated author reproduces some of the common characteristics of imperialist discourse. He thinks in binaries: Rather than a heterogeneous and self-contradictory whole, as the Ottoman space had been conceived of by the court, it is now seen as a borderland between civilizations, that is, Europe and Asia. Binaries also affect Calligas' vision of the urban space. The district of Galata-Pera to the north of the Golden Horn was juxtaposed to *intra muros* Istanbul with its Muslim predominance and the ministries, despite the fact that in daily practice, the two complemented each other, and were far from neatly functionally divided.

The difference between the two peninsulas would however come to play a major role in the city's image in the decades to come. How had the northern peninsula, which had once only housed Galata, the small faubourg founded by the Genoese, evolved into the rival of the ancient city to its south? The area was known as Pera, "beyond" in Greek, signifying its location across the Golden Horn from the city proper. From the seventeenth century onward, the ambassadors to the Sublime Porte one after the other were granted permission to erect their own embassies there. They concentrated in the space outside Galata, not on the steep coast, but among the vineyards surrounding the ridgeway heading north. Around the embassies, settlements of countrymen, new *han*s (inn or commercial center), churches, and hospitals developed.[9] However, these developments prior to the nineteenth century were minimal compared to the growth of other areas around the capital and its environs.

Salonica and Smyrna: New Jerusalem by the Grace of the Sultan and the City without History

If the new vision of the Levantine city focused primarily on commercial and cultural exchange, what legacy did the other two major ports of the Northeastern Mediterranean harbor? Were they better prepared to become gateways between supposedly distinct continents and cultures?

Not necessarily. The Balkan port city Salonica, having been almost completely depopulated after the 1430 capture of the city by the Ottomans, had been the object of a decisive policy of repopulation

---

[9] Başdaş, *Old Buildings/New Faces*, 2; Eldem, "Istanbul, from Imperial to Peripheralized Capital," 150.

and creation of industries. The settlement of immigrant Spanish-speaking Jews and the development of a textile industry were predominantly the result of state policy. The greater degree of freedom these Jews enjoyed in comparison to those living under West and Central European Catholicism and the fact that they numerically dominated the city, even led Saloniqueno writers to make active propaganda for emigration among the Jews of other countries, while praising the Sultan for laying the foundation for this "Madre de Israel" in Macedonia.[10] Although Salonica was a port city, the port facilities were not in the center, but *extra muros* until the mid- nineteenth century. Keeping the port apart and limiting access to the city proper was considered necessary for fear of unruly sailors from overseas and from the port workers, who in part were also considered strangers due to their origins in the hinterland, as well as to minimize the risk of contagious infections.[11] Resident European foreigners, by contrast, were allowed to settle *intra muros*, but were relegated to a peripheral and inhospitable corner of the city, just across from the tower where the gunpowder was stored.[12]

However, Salonica's textile industry had suffered a severe decline since the end of the classic age due to the systemic crisis in state finance and decay in order. Trade with other European markets grew in importance. After 1720 several consulates opened in the city. While bakeries, taverns, and a tailor shop operated by non-Ottomans were noticed by the mid-eighteenth century, cultural liberties were restricted, as a clampdown on an illegal Jesuit church illustrates.[13]

By contrast, Smyrna had never enjoyed a strong development strategy during the classic age: "what the Ottomans inherited in Izmir and its surroundings in the 1420s was a land without much manifest history ... For the rulers of this new world state, western Anatolia was a region to be absorbed and exploited, not reserved or restored or improved."[14]

---

[10] Veinstein, "Un paradoxe séculaire," 48; Mazower, *Salonica: City of Ghosts*, 46–66.
[11] Ginio, "Migrants and Workers," 126–148.
[12] Brunau, *Deutschtum in Mazedonien*, 55.
[13] Veinstein, "Un paradoxe séculaire," 55–58; Mazower, *Salonica: City of Ghosts*, 120–131.
[14] Goffman, "Izmir: From Village to Colonial Port City," 82, 86.

According to Daniel Goffman, from the mid-seventeenth century onward Smyrna evolved from a neglected village to a colonial port city. Imperial neglect offered local actors, such as state officials, warlords, and incoming merchants from Venice, the Netherlands, England, France and other parts of the empire, the opportunity to create a "pocket of *laissez-faire*ism within the strictly statist Ottoman economy and society."[15] The combination of a calm natural harbor with a convergence of river valleys was ideal as caravan routes facilitated the establishment of trade patterns in which the agricultural products of Western Anatolia were sold to the evolving markets around the Western Mediterranean and the North Sea.[16] The 1784 trade statistics show Smyrna as having by far the largest share in imports and exports with Marseille. Despite the capital's much larger size, Constantinople only figured as Marseille's second largest partner, its and Salonica's imports and exports together amounting to the same size as Smyrna's. Salonica only figured as fifth-largest port of the Levant after Alexandria and Alexandretta (İskenderun).[17] The Napoleonic wars, the English blockade of Mediterranean trade, the Greek war of secession, local xenophobic riots, and fire dealt Smyrna and all Eastern Mediterranean ports a strong blow, but when trade improved from about 1830 onward, the West Anatolian port once again assumed supremacy.

It is in Smyrna that we can first notice a strongly developed open space allowing for "the combining and overlapping of transoceanic, littoral and interior flows in the mediation of culture on the one hand, and to people's appropriation and blending of diverse cross-bordering cultural elements on the other." These processes crystalized in the *Frangomahalla*. "Frankish Quarters," that is, neighborhoods inhabited by significant numbers of people originating from Central or Western Europe, had been a mainstay of Eastern Mediterranean cities since the medieval period. Their reappearance in Smyrna in the mid-seventeenth century signaled the revival of long-distance movements of persons and commodities beyond the Eastern Mediterranean. In this initial phase the *Frangomahalla* of Smyrna was a sphere apart from the city proper: located outside the walled city; created in a haphazard manner that served the business interests of the merchants, the practicalities of shipping, and converging around the so-called Frank Street. But the relative seclusion had its benefits for the residents:

[15] Ibid, 90. [16] Ibid, 87–93. [17] *Courrier de Smyrne*, 14 March 1830.

There was a large amount of freedom for the pursuit both of ecclesiastical and mundane paths to happiness. Beyond accommodation and warehouses, the quarter housed inns, possibly even theaters, and despite the general Ottoman ban on new places of non-Muslim worship, several representative churches.[18]

The Smyrna waterfront was also a site for intellectual exchange: Supposedly the German-Danish Protestant pastor of the city between 1783 and 1805, Johannes Usko, in his second function as librarian of the British Levant Company, imported Enlightenment literature, and had amicable discussions with the local writer and later celebrated intellectual Admantios Korais.[19] Smyrna's significance as an interface between the Ottoman world and its Western neighbors in the premodern era should not be exaggerated. However the conditions sketched made it the foremost site of Westernization in the mid- nineteenth century.

1850: The Return of the Panopticon

The binary difference came to dominate European visitors' accounts not long after Calligas' visit. Timothy Mitchell sees the 1850s as the turning point in depictions of Eastern cities by visiting Europeans. Romanticism was démodé: Emotionality was now replaced by a new desire to remain objective, that is, to distance oneself from what one observed. The visitors would still seek out places opening up onto impressive vistas, but unlike Calligas and Formby not to let themselves be overwhelmed, but to have a vantage point from where to perceive the city without having to interact with it, as interaction would undo their objective sobriety.

Among European writers who travelled to the Middle East in the middle and latter part of the nineteenth century, one very frequently finds the experience of its strangeness expressed in terms of the problem of forming a picture. It was as though to make sense of it meant to stand back and make a drawing or take a photograph of it; which for many of them actually it did ... Bentham can remind us of one more similarity between writer and camera, and of what it meant, therefore, to grasp the world as though it were a

---

[18] Goffman, "Izmir: From Village to Colonial Port City," 93–95.
[19] Seetzen, "Reise-Nachrichten;" Center for Asia Minor Studies (ed.), *Smyrna Metropolis*.

picture or exhibition. The point of view was not just a place set apart, outside the world or above it. It was ideally a position from where, like the authorities in the panopticon, one could see and yet not be seen.[20]

Although Timothy Mitchell argues that the objective view of the unseen observer creates a knowledge that translates into power as described by Michel Foucault's interpretation of Bentham's Panopticon to be a European nineteenth-century innovation, an obvious analogy to the unseen Sultan in his Tower of Justice in Topkapı Sarayı comes to mind. This technique of power therefore unknowingly reproduced the Ottoman imperial cosmology, albeit imbibed with Western notions of binary divides and spatial delineations between Orient and Occident.

While in Cairo, Damascus, or Aleppo, these vantage points to observe and objectify the city had to be hills, rooftops, or minarets, Istanbul and other ports offered the simpler solution of surveying the city from the deck of a ship. Three factors – the end of the romantic fashion and its replacement by a new belief in progress; the search for a vantage point to see the city from a distance; and the end of trying forms of travel to the Ottoman lands (all against the background of the growing political and economic dependency of the Ottoman Empire) – converged in a single vehicle that came to serve more than anything else the hardening of a European discourse on the Ottoman city: the steamship. The local and the European concepts of the Ottoman cities had developed only through a rather mediated interdependence before 1854. This however changed dramatically in the age of the steamship.

The Steamship Revolution of Perception 1: Staring at the Land

The *Swift* is acclaimed to be the first steam-propelled vessel to arrive in Constantinople. It immediately attracted great attention. A passenger, Charles MacFarlane, describes its arrival in 1827:

The combination of a violent contrary wind and a rapid current in a narrow strait was admirably calculated to give the Turks an advantageous idea of steam. Immense crowds gathered on the shores of the promontory on which Constantinople stands to gaze in astonishment as we passed, for this was the first steam-boat seen in these parts. The evidence of their senses told them

---

[20] Mitchell, *Colonising Egypt*, 22, 24.

that the wind was blowing hard from the Black Sea – that the current was running with its eternal violence, yet they saw the ship rapidly advancing. Several parties threw up their arms and hailed us, whilst others on horseback cantering along the beach kept up with us to learn in what this miracle should end. At some batteries along the coast as we were afterwards informed, we were well nigh receiving less agreeable signs of wonder, – the cannoniers, in their ignorance, had conceived the vessel must be some extraordinary *brulot*, and had proposed firing into us.[21]

MacFarlane's feeling of superiority toward those watching from the shore already foreshadows the general trend in travelogs from this point onward. Within a few years of the arrival of the *Swift*, the experience of travel from Western or Central Europe to the Ottoman lands changed dramatically. The suppression of piracy, the establishment of quarantines in the Ottoman ports, and most especially the new regular services by steamer from the mid-1830s onward combined to make the sea passages much safer, more reliable, and more comfortable. A traveler could now normally avoid having strange people, the elements, and fate overwhelm her- or himself and thus also avoid disorientation. Boarding a ship (or from 1883 onward even a train) from the Western Mediterranean, one could enter a fairly sterile world that would allow one to travel to the Eastern Mediterranean without much unexpected sensory input until the first port, except for the changing vistas. In combination with the intellectual trend toward postromantic objective sobriety, this led to a new way of seeing the other. It is telling that 1833, the year that regular scheduled steamer voyages between the Central and Eastern Mediterranean commenced, also witnessed the first pre-organized package tour and the first guidebook of the Levant.[22]

Offering a different kind of beauty to that earlier favourite – the sublime – the picturesque prompted not terror or a sense of insignificance but rather delicate musings on the harmonious interplay of nature and civilisation, of a kind evoked by gentle inclines, graduated tones, and ruins.[23]

The moment of culture shock was therefore delayed until one reached the port of disembarkation, bypassing grueling horseback

---

[21] MacFarlane, *Constantinople in 1828*, vol. I, 490, 491; see also Müller-Wiener, *Die Häfen*, 70, 71.
[22] Kontente, *Smyrne et l'occident*, 459.
[23] Mazower, *Salonica: City of Ghosts*, 190.

rides and stomach-wrenching sailboats. Passengers traveled "intercity" and according to the binary East-West opposition previously established, interculturally at the same time. Unlike Moltke or Forneris, they would no longer compare the civilization of the urban with the barbarity of the rural, but the degree of civilization in one city with that in another. Without the elemental experiences of the past and with the growing economic and military preponderance of the West, judgments on the ports at the east end of the Mediterranean became increasingly arrogant.

Travelers arriving in Smyrna would write eulogies about the view from deck:

> Smyrna's location has often been compared to that of Naples, and truly, the volcanic cones of the "two brothers" surpass even the Vesuvius in height ... The mountain ranges of Tahtalı and Sypilus, rising up to 6,000 feet, enchain the sea from all sides, only the latter opens onto the wide valley of the Hermus River, flowing down from Sardes and Magnesia to run through a narrow but fruitful delta into the gulf. In general, the shores are covered by thick, plentiful vegetation up to the first heights ... The city with its 180,000 inhabitants has a massive circumference, as, due to the earthquakes, most houses only have two stories and are as a rule only inhabited by one family. The Frank, Greek, and Armenian quarters are situated on the plain ending in a cape; the Jewish and Turkish cities climb up Mount Pagos in terraces, delimited by cypress forests, with the ruins of the old Acropolis jutting out ... Coming from Europe, the Orient presents itself in front of one's eyes here for the first time in all its originality and the encounter from a distance is one that enchants the senses.[24]

"Enchants the senses" sounds harmless compared to the overwhelming experience Formby had a mere twenty years before, and the neat, orderly dissection of the city into ethnic zones presupposed the distant vantage point. But the "delicate musings" are shattered upon entering the city: After hurriedly passing by boat to the piers and the narrow wharfs, the passengers would find themselves cut off from the sea and abruptly hurled into street scenes they found hard to cope with.

Those well versed in promenades would find rich bounty for their desire to see in Smyrna. There is no mention of elegant shops, galleries, and passages à

---

[24] Scherer, *Reisen in der Levante 1859–1865*, 91–92. While Pagos was originally the locus of the acropolis, the visible ruin is actually a fortress dating back to Genoese settlement.

la parisienne of course, there are no interesting little ladies to be followed, with tiny feet and flirtatiously high dresses, there are no carriages rolling through the street and if one tires, there are no omnibuses or coaches to lend a hand ... There is no chance of a sidewalk during the excursion, the pavement has holes the police would not allow and in some places resembles ours back home after the barricade fights of 1848. No peace for dreamy thoughts! Two fiery eyes glow brightly through a loose window grid towards you, you raise your head to see better, but a camel, approaching silently from behind with its soft steps, pushes your hat onto the nose. Having escaped this Charybdis, you fall into the Scylla of a Turkish hamal (porter) who is carrying on his broad, flatly bent back weights of up to ten hundredweights and pushes you with it onto the wall, leaving you to thank the heavens for the thin waist it has granted you.[25]

The moment of culture shock thus no longer occurred when a Tatar guide rushed the traveler through the icy Thracian countryside, nor when the Greek pirates boarded the sailing ship, but after disembarkation in the relatively safe port city. It was delayed to the moment when the travelers had to abandon their aloof vantage point and descend into the streets. In this way, the steamer served as a shelter for prefabricated concepts of the other that were not upset by existential experiences on the way, as a Panopticon-style focal point to survey the city as an object, and as the vehicle to transport Western weapons and goods into the region. The travelers arriving from the metropolis thus saw themselves at the center of contemporary aesthetics and believed the Ottoman realm to be subordinated to the same set of tastes. If the city where they went ashore did not reveal itself to the traveler, they did not conclude that they themselves had not made a sufficient effort to understand the other; instead, they assumed that the city had failed to meet the supposedly universal aesthetical criteria, such as easy access, regularity, cleanliness, easily discoverable visual highlights. Foreign travelogs almost invariably began their impressions of a given city with the favorable impression the Ottoman conglomeration gave from the sea, then contrasted this first impression with negative

---

[25] Scherer, *Reisen in der Levante 1859–1865*, 94. The physical limits of hamals should also be corrected slightly. According to the strict regulations of the Constantinople port guilds, hamals only carried burdens of less than one hundredweight (50 kg) single-handedly. Accounts of arrival by train after the beginning of direct services from Central and Western Europe also reveal culture shock upon leaving the train; see for example Klötzel, *In Saloniki*, 13–19.

remarks about the city from up close. These impressions had none of the elemental awe of Formby's or Calligas' impressions and the desire to keep the city at a distance, that is, as an object of contemplation from deck rather than as a maze of streets to wander about in, is obvious in most such descriptions.[26]

The Steamship Revolution of Perception 2: Staring at the Sea

If steamers changed European foreigners' perceptions, the locals' perceptions suffered an equally dramatic shift. With the arrival of the steamer, the older patterns of configuring space in Constantinople and the Ottoman port cities were finally disrupted. From the Topkapı Tower of Justice the Sultan could only have seen the foreign gunboats that would remind him of his faded potency. In the pleasure gardens and seaside villas of the eighteenth century, the Istanbul residents would have been disturbed in their pleasant contemplation of the sea by the heavy smoke of the steamers, and their kayaks would have been upset by the heavy waves created by the engines.

When the *Swift* had arrived in Constantinople, it had been immediately bought and presented to Sultan Mahmud. This was an attempt to keep the old order in place, the idea that innovation, physical power, and the power to attract and direct the gazes of the masses should be the privilege of the ruler. Mahmud played along and took the steamer on a tour to inspect the fortifications in Rodosto (now Tekirdağ), Gallipoli (Gelibolu), and the Dardanelles (Çanakkale), thus linking imperial presence, military might, and speed and technical innovation.[27] This rule persisted for a short while: When in 1829 Niven Kerr Black came with another steamer, the head of the mint bought it and again sold it to the Sultan.[28] But with the growing proliferation of both military and commercial steamers, a handful of ships in the possession of the Sultan could not hope to compete with this onslaught of the new era.[29] Regular steamer connections around the Eastern

---

[26] For a prototypical account see Jahn, "Reise von Mainz nach Egypten," 33.
[27] *Courrier de Smyrne*, 22 Feb. 1829.   [28] *Courrier de Smyrne*, 14 June 1829.
[29] See also Mansel, *Constantinople*, 255. By 1836 the Austrian Lloyd, initially sponsored by the Austrian government, was offering regular passenger and freight services from Trieste to all major ports of the Levant. The Marseille-based Messageries Maritimes followed soon after; Scherzer, Humann, and Stöckel, *Smyrna*, 85, 86.

Mediterranean (in combination with free trade treaties) greatly increased the volume of goods passing through the Ottoman ports. Together with the more intense exchange and the aforementioned self-referential perspective transported by the steamships came the demand for standardized structures and procedures. Also, demographical changes in other parts of the continent led to a large number of lower class subjects moving around the continent in search of work opportunities, including the Eastern and Southern Mediterranean.[30]

A secondhand description exists of the first arrival of a steamship in Salonica. Leon Sciaky, growing up in Salonica in the late nineteenth century, claims that his father as a child witnessed the first steamship to enter the city's harbor. The impact on the local public was no less impressive than in the capital.

> The news of a burning clipper had spread rapidly through the city and throngs had ascended the stone steps leading to the parapet. There was no mistake. A great cloud of smoke hung close to the water, not far from Küchük Karaburun, the Small Black Cape. As the excited crowd watched, the smoke came nearer and nearer, until they could distinguish a black hull surmounted by a black smokestack. They stood aghast as the first ship without sails, the first vessel mysteriously propelled by fire, dropped anchor before our shores.[31]

The steamer and the Constantinopolitan and Salonician public's reaction to it set a pattern that preconfigured much of public behavior in Ottoman port cities for the next three quarters of a century. Roughly from the advent of regular commercial steamer traffic in the Mediterranean in the mid-1830s until World War I, the port city residents would turn their heads to the sea to find the new, innovative, modern, thus returning the Western gaze searching for the exotic, the picturesque, the Oriental. The Saloniquenos expected the modern to originate from overseas, from "Europe." If their gazes now turned to the sea, it is not a trivial matter, but an indicator that a certain "morphology of

---

[30] See Chapter 19, pp. 302–343.
[31] Sciaky, *Farewell to Ottoman Salonica*, 30. It seems unlikely that Leon Sciaky's (born 1893) father was old enough to witness the first steamer in Salonica, as the *Levant* in 1836 is claimed to be the first to reach Salonica (Mazower, *City of Ghosts*, 225). Probably Leon Sciaky is recounting the testimony of his grandfather.

domination," a specific mechanism for the "concerted positioning of bodies, surfaces, lights, and gazes"[32] had gained ascendancy.

It is telling that MacFarlane, who describes the arrival of the *Swift*, recounts that the steamer had first called at Smyrna, but makes no mention of such a spectacular reception there, as it was possibly not the very first steamer in this much busier port. Already by 1833, Smyrna was connected to Trieste by regular scheduled steamer.[33] Thus another new pattern emerged: No longer would the imperial capital be the trendsetter for the era of nineteenth-century global capitalism; instead the Anatolian port city with its closer integration into West European commerce played the part. Smyrna was experiencing a phase of rapid growth following the post-Napoleonic revival of Mediterranean commerce, the end of the Greek war of secession, and more vigorously after the introduction of regular steamer services. The main artery of the *Frangomahalla*, Frank Street, had expanded and become the hub of maritime commerce: The merchant villas known as *frenkhane*s had made way for narrow elongated houses that offered landing space to a larger number of entrepreneurs as well as accommodation, storage, and offices.[34] These trends would radiate outward both to Istanbul and to Salonica.

---

[32] Michel Foucault, quoted in Lüdtke, "Einleitung," 11.
[33] Kontente, *Smyrne et l'occident*, 458.
[34] Zandi-Sayek, *Ottoman Izmir*, 16, 17.

6 | Dreaming of a City in Stone

With the urban aesthetics from both sides of the Mediterranean in more immediate contact than ever before, commentators criticized what they saw on the Eastern shores. The foreign, landward gaze and the local, seaward perspective came to the same assessment when scrutinizing the Ottoman port cities' streets. Streets were a constant object of complaint. As early as 1826, the German traveler August M. Jahn wrote about Constantinople, "The streets are mostly narrow, actually paved, but badly maintained, stinking, and disgusting. The so-called houses are without relation to one another, without proportion, without order, yes, without any architecture."[1]

This complaint was echoed by the locals. The nineteenth century was also a century of recurring campaigns to ameliorate the streets. In 1834, the chief of police Hacı Bey, on orders of the *vali* (governor general) of Smyrna, had all merchandise blocking the narrow main artery of Frank Street removed, including freely roaming pigs owned by the vendors of livestock. The local press lauded the authorities.[2] The same preoccupation was still evident in January 1873: The newly arrived *vali* in Smyrna immediately ordered the city's streets to be cleaned and swept (and incidentally "cleansed" of street vendors).[3] The matter was obviously a populist measure to cater to local public opinion and its preoccupation with street filthiness.

One source of concern was the huge packs of dogs that roamed the inner cities and could even be seen to gather on the Grand Rue de Pera. While these packs were a source of danger especially for pedestrians wandering around the city by night, their sight by day tarnished the image of a city free of dangers and serving as a source of pleasure and aesthetics. Nonetheless, a long tradition of respect for animals stopped

---

[1] Jahn, "Reise von Mainz nach Egypten," 33.
[2] *Journal de Smyrne*, 11 Oct. 1834. A mere rumor that urban "beautification" was planned was considered worth reporting; *Journal de Smyrne*, 5 Jan., 2 Feb. 1834.
[3] *Levant Herald*, 3 Jan. 1873.

the eradication of these unruly dogs. Passersby would even feed them a particular cheap sort of bread baked from waste in the city's bakeries.[4] Supposedly a French advisor to Mustafa Reşid Pasha during his grand-vizirate, Dr. Barachin, who had in turn brought a score of countrymen with Saint-Simonist inclinations to support the reforms, was the first to come up with the plan to catch all dogs and bring them to the island of Tavşan Adası in the Marmara Sea, where according to the plan they were to be slaughtered and their hides, fat, and meat processed. While Abdülmecid refused to have the protected albatrosses and dolphins of the Bosporus slaughtered, he let Barachin's committees of French advisors go ahead with the dog extermination. Despite catching and deporting hundreds of dogs to the island, the slaughter plans could not be carried out due to the fierce opposition of the dogs. When the unsuccessful committee members and butchers returned to town, the general embarrassment led to their dismissal.[5] It was not until the Young Turks came to power in 1908 that such drastic measures to cleanse the city's streets were attempted again.

Not only what was to be found on or in the streets mattered, the streets themselves and the way they were constructed were the subject of much debate. Pavements, one commentator claimed, were as vital to streets as skirts for women.[6] Accordingly, the Istanbul newspaper *Le Matin* in 1879 commended the municipality of Galata-Pera's attempts to pave the district's streets with granite, but admonished it for carrying out the works poorly; the new pavement, the paper claimed, had already sagged due to bad substructure and carriages had been banned from using them.[7] Still, in 1895 the *Journal de Salonique* commented in a satirical fashion that the recent rains had turned the city into a copy of Venice as the flooded streets now had to be crossed by boat. The paper admonished the municipality for its neglect of the area of Unkapanı, where the rains had exacerbated the pollution by the nearby fish market and *han*s, and for its failure to erect and maintain enough pissoirs.[8]

Within the discussions on street politics, the invocation of Europe became an increasingly powerful rhetorical tool, even if there were no

---

[4] *Revue commerciale du Levant* 99 (June 1895), 146.
[5] Wanda, *Souvenirs Anecdotiques sur la Turquie 1820–1870*, 176–180.
[6] *Journal de Salonique*, 5 Jan. 1903. On the contemporary obsession with pavement see also the debate in Alexandria in Barak, "Scraping the Surface."
[7] *Le Matin*, 2, 5 July 1879.   [8] *Journal de Salonique*, 14, 28 Nov., 9 Dec. 1895.

European foreigners immediately involved and the debate was being led between bureaucrats and local residents. (Koca) Mustafa Reşid Pasha (1800–1858), an Ottoman ambassador to Paris, Vienna, and London, grand vizier and coauthor of the 1838 Reform Charter, advocated a rectangular and "scientific" street layout. Zeynep Çelik cites him as an example of the dichotomy of Westernization by agents not of Western origin: "As was typical of nineteenth-century Ottoman bureaucrats, he justified his own ideas by passing them through a Western filter. He quoted articles published in European newspapers."[9]

Streets were not only an end in itself, but stood for an alternative worldview. Mitchell describes Ali Pasha Mubarak (1824–1893), Egyptian Minister for Education and Public Services, who wrote a fictionalized account of his journey to France, praising the industriousness and the spirit of serious business he experienced in Marseille, as well as the discipline the Marseillians exercised while moving through public space. He believed this discipline to be the result of the regularity of the streets. Concerning Paris, he lauded the width of the streets and boulevards, its trade, and the elegance and cleanliness of the public space.[10]

Utilizing the discourse of Europe was not restricted to bureaucrats with educational or professional experience abroad. In support of an 1859 petition by 200 Smyrna residents demanding the establishment of a municipality based on local support, the newspaper *L'Impartial* declared that by addressing "a myriad of issues associated with urban improvement and beautification, which are beyond the responsibility of the central government," the new local council would place Smyrna "among the most beautiful cities of Europe."[11] This remained the recurrent model for all cities under study here for at least half a century: Even in 1903 the *Journal de Salonique* claimed that if the city's mayor Hulusi Bey continued his good work embellishing Salonica, the Macedonian port would rival "the great provincial cities of Europe."[12]

---

[9] Çelik, *Remaking of Istanbul*, 49, 50.
[10] Ali Pasha Mubarak later played an important role in constructing and reforming schools in Egypt; Mitchell, *Colonising Egypt*, 63, 64.
[11] *L'Impartial*, quoted from Zandi-Sayek, *Ottoman Izmir*, 94.
[12] *Journal de Salonique*, 5 Jan. 1903.

This new consensus – the negative assessment of the street and Europeanization as its panacea – has been concisely summed up by Mitchell:

> The "disorder" of Cairo and other cities had suddenly become visible. The urban space in which Egyptians moved had become a political matter, material to be "organised" by the construction of great thoroughfares radiating out from the geographical and political centre. At the same moment Egyptians themselves, as they moved through this space, became similarly material, their minds and bodies thought to need discipline and training. The space, the minds, and the bodies all materialized at the same moment, in a common economy of order and discipline.[13]

It is important to add that these radical transformations extended not only to cities in peripheral locations, but under different circumstances also to other European cities. The European city of the nineteenth century was at the time still an ongoing project. The contemporary Western mind frame, while confident in declaring the inadequacy of "Oriental" cities vis-à-vis European ones, was just as confident in declaring cities at home as "material to be 'organised,'" ridding them of their medieval legacy, changing them according to the aesthetics of regularity, easy access, the desires of the bourgeoisie, and the needs of industry and the masses. Thus throughout the nineteenth century, medieval or early modern city walls were being demolished to make way for wide ring roads or railway tracks; ancient buildings were cleared of medieval additions in order to let the beholder witness their original symmetry; and streets were widened.

Thus, when the inhabitants of Smyrna, Salonica, and Constantinople began to see their cities as "material to be 'organised,'" they were not acting simply out of a colonial inferiority complex, performing an unfortunate form of mimicry. Instead they could claim that through their actions, their struggle for progress, and the betterment of humankind, they were entitled to be treated as peers of their counterparts in distant areas of the continent.

A Dream of Symmetry

According to the majority of historians, the story of the Westernization of Ottoman cities begins in 1836 with a memorandum. The

---

[13] Mitchell, *Colonising Egypt*, 68.

aforementioned Reşid Pasha, in a letter from London concerning a recent fire in Constantinople, addresses Sultan Mahmud to explain his ideas about how the city had to change. The buildings should be built out of nonflammable material, that is, stone; the streets should not follow an organic pattern, but should be drawn according to preplanned rectangular shapes. Knowledgeable engineers and architects from Europe should be invited to erect exemplary buildings in the new style in vogue in their home countries. However, he also felt the need for distinction from Europe at large: Reşid Pasha warned of the Parisian apartment houses, as mass housing would not allow for the Muslim notion of family privacy, propagating London row houses instead. The author assumed his plans would be met with ignorance by the masses. He suggested that an avant-garde recruited from among rich private individuals and enlightened state actors should be the first to implement them and only later expected the wider populace to see their advantages. Money for his designs, he claimed, would have to be raised by credit. Fulfilling public services by loan according to the author was nothing dubious, as it was now an established practice in Europe.[14]

The memo in a nutshell features several elements that would become integral to urban change in the mid- to late nineteenth-century port cities: the desire for radical change, for a utopia of rectangular shapes to replace the grown city; a state bureaucracy that considered itself an elite best equipped to steer the city into the modern era; the reliance on an oligarchy in the implementation of urban change; the constant evocation of an almost mythical Europe; foreign models, expertise, and capital; distrust of popular politics; but also, more like an afterthought, a search for how to distinguish the self while following foreign models. These elements would resurface in different constellations throughout the process.

Three years after the memo, the vision of a Constantinople with orderly streets and houses found its way into official planning. A document Murat Gül describes as a development plan from 1839 resurfaced in the archives decades later. After the creation of a detailed map of the city, the plan imagined large thoroughfares of 15 meters' width that would allow for the passage of horse-drawn

---

[14] Yerasimos, "A propos des réformes urbaines," 20, fn. 7, 9; Yerolympos, *Urban Transformations in the Balkans*, 68.

carriages neatly separated from the pedestrians on the sidewalk; trees to embellish the streets; large squares in front of public buildings; no more dead-end streets; and as a rule, masonry houses erected according to architectural planning and on geometrically shaped plots with substructure aligned by engineering works assigned by the authorities, rather than the previously predominant wooden buildings constructed by improvisation and often infringing upon public space.[15] The maximum height of the future buildings, 15 meters, corresponded with the ideal width of the streets, a correlation that was throughout Europe widely believed to permit for a sufficient amount of ventilation and sunlight in the quarters. Incidentally it would open the city up to carriages, which previously had been unpractical due to the lack of regular pavement, narrowness of the streets, and the nongeometric grid. This scenario was to be realized by expropriation and demolishing as well as by creating new faubourgs beyond the previous city limits. The plan also mentioned regularized masonry wharves to replace the improvised wooden jetties along the shoreline. As this document remains isolated, it is unclear whether it is to be regarded as part of a coordinated effort of urban renewal, a guideline for future development, or a mere declaration of intent. The plan however remained a utopia at a time shortly after Jahn's disgusted remarks about Istanbul streets and with orderlies chasing pigs through Smyrna's Frank Street; there is no sign of its implementation. Galata-Pera suffered a devastating fire in 1841, but during the reconstruction the directive was not applied.[16]

Smyrna also suffered serious fires in 1841 in the Jewish quarters and in 1845 in the Christian quarters. After the latter, reconstruction actually created in part a rectangular block grid replacing the prior topographic course of the streets and the numerous dead-end alleyways. This reconstruction for the first time applied new central government legislation for post–fire zones on minimum widths of streets, restrictions on balcony and bay window sizes, and firewalls. Streets of less than 4 meters width were to be widened to between 4.5 and 6 meters width. Also, the preexisting streets were punctured by new thoroughfares. In addition, the reconstructed space saw new landmark

---

[15] Gül, *Emergence of Modern Istanbul*, 28–30.
[16] Tekeli, "Nineteenth Century Transformation," 38–40; Rosenthal, "Foreigners and Municipal Reform," 227–245.

churches dominating the public space rather than the organically integrated places of worship that had existed before.[17]

In the capital's surroundings, the central government first tried to create a new type of neighborhood 1.5 kilometers north of Taksim, across from the military school (Harbiye). The new quarter of Pangaltı was to have ten avenues. Each of them was to be 15 meters wide, with 2.3 meters on each side set aside for sidewalks. The avenues were to be linked by 6.8-meter wide secondary streets. All buildings were to consist of stone. Implementation of the plan, however, was slow.[18] Whether based on the 1839 directive or on these first examples of a new type of street grid, the central administration in 1849 reissued a guideline for street development, albeit a more moderate one: The minimum street width had been reduced to a realistic 9 meters, and in some cases 7.5 or even 4.5 meters, and these rules were to apply only to Constantinople.[19] Nonetheless, these visions, plans, and early attempts at rearranging public space had an important function: They made it clear that street disorder was no longer simply an issue for disgruntled travelog writers and casual conversation in the coffeehouses. Improving Ottoman cities to meet nineteenth-century demands was now a public obligation both for the administration and residents. Also, the plans had set the priorities for how to achieve amelioration: stone, symmetry, and abundant space.

---

[17] Zandi-Sayek, *Ottoman Izmir*, 79–83.
[18] Çelik, *The Remaking of Istanbul*, 68.
[19] Gül, *The Emergence of Modern Istanbul*, 34.

7 Reinventing the City from the Sea Inward

Thus, a hegemonic discourse on what the city should look like was established. Change began in several places at once. The gradual reconstruction of burnt neighborhoods was too peripheral to the city as a whole to change its image. What was to have more of an effect on at least Constantinople's skyline was the mid-nineteenth-century representational arms race between the Great Powers and the Sultan. After the 1831 Pera fire that ruined most embassies, Russia was the first to rebuild what had been a countryside villa into a "permanent world exhibition"[1] to promote Russia's influence with the help of the St. Petersburg court architect of Swiss origin, Gaspare Fossati (thus unwittingly fulfilling one of the desiderata of Mustafa Reşid's memorandum). While the Netherlands and the Habsburg Empire, as well as the Sublime Porte and several local parishes also made use of Fossati's services, France and the United Kingdom commissioned new embassies from architects in their respective motherlands.[2] These neoclassical buildings aimed to impress through their monumentality and symmetry. They also were to serve as the nucleus of a wider ensemble, with churches, dragoman offices, consular courts, but also nunneries and masonic lodges clustering around them.

Possibly as a reaction to the "embassy seraglios," Abdülmecid ordered the construction of Dolmabahçe Palace. With a seaside façade of 600 meters length, a total size of 45,000 square meters on grounds covering 250,000 square meters, Dolmabahçe was the representational overkill nobody could contend with.[3] It was complemented by a number of military, infrastructural, and representational buildings scattered around adjacent Maçka Gorge, which thus took on the character of a showcase of Ottoman state-propelled modernity, a

---

[1] Girardelli, "In & Around Lord Elgin's Palace."
[2] Köprülü, *İstanbul'daki Yabancı Saraylar*.
[3] Tuğlacı, *Balyan Ailesi*, 29–40, 46, 58–59.

"Tanzimat Valley."[4] Abdülmecid's vision of a Europeanized Ottoman state and its symbolic inscription into Constantinople's silhouette however failed to develop social breadth. Instead of seriously engaging with civil society, he had intended to redraw the chaotic onslaught of modernity unfolding in the streets of his port cities into a well-ordered, nicely decorated stage play with himself and his court at the center. Across Europe, absolutist rulers increasingly failed to hold onto the reins of social developments, and the well-intentioned reformist sultans were no exception.

Creating a New Urban Agenda: The Quays

When an urban reordering set in that managed to act as a game changer, it was very much due to civil initiative and capitalist preoccupations. In mid-century, Smyrna's long-established commercial exchange with the European ports was thriving,[5] and the increasing turnover in the city's bazaars seemed to justify investments to facilitate growth. Although the Gulf had in previous times been considered a good natural harbor, the higher standards of the steamship era made it appear inadequate to load and unload ships in due time.[6] Also the old narrow and winding Frank Street seemed insufficient in the face of European supremacy in technology and culture, as did the ramshackle quays. Frank Street ran parallel to the sea, the houses' rear side made up the waterfront. This was not a singular, but more a chaotic and uneven structure. Each owner of a plot had individually adopted it to his or her needs. Many warehouses had back doors with private piers, which were convenient for the evasion of customs duties. Apart from them, one could only reach the sea through some short alleyways. Only at two points did the waterfront expand to a publicly accessible wharf. The growing sprawl stopped the mass of the Smyrniotes from enjoying the sea. As early as 1829, the *Courrier de Smyrne* lamented the fact that spring was approaching but the waterfront was in such deplorable shape – large sections fenced off and the remainder stacked with all kinds of goods – that taking a stroll there was almost unthinkable.[7] Over the course of the next decades, the situation worsened as the

---

[4] Belge, "Istanbul Past and Future," 161, 162.
[5] Frangakis-Syrett, *Commerce of Smyrna*.
[6] Oberling, "The Quays of Izmir," 316.
[7] *Courrier de Smyrne*, 29 March 1829.

Ministry of Pious Endowments auctioned off long-term entitlement deeds to the bay that was, in theory, owned by the Sultan. The deeds obliged their owners to develop the waterfront, leading to several extremely narrow private piers, rather than public port facilities.[8] As part of this privatization of space *avant la lettre*, cafés were erected on haphazard platforms of wooden poles stuck in the sea. They were routinely slandered by middle-class Smyrniotes, both because of their cheap, unaesthetic character and because of the occasionally serious accidents occurring there due to construction faults or fire.[9] Debates about reshaping the waterfront set in around 1850. Already by 1862, descriptions of this future project were euphoric:

> To say nothing of the doing away with those loathsome Coffee Houses built along the marina, Smyrna will possess a Quay second to none in the World, exceeding a mile in length, an ornament to the City and a place of recreation for all classes, so much needed in this Country.[10]

Through the long-lasting debate, the new quays evolved into a panacea to cure all the city's economic, fiscal, social, recreational, and image deficits. It is not surprising that accordingly, the proposed construction plans increased in dimension as the debate continued.[11] Finally in 1867 three holders of British passports residing in Smyrna acquired a concession to construct new port facilities. Their plans reflected the high hopes in the city: The new quays were to stretch from Punta past the *Frangomahalla*, the bazaar area, and the *Konak* (governor general's office) up to the Amber Barracks, taking up practically all the seafront of the city proper. With 3.5 kilometer length and 19 meters width, the new quays were to dominate Smyrna. They were designed to allow up to 300 ships to dock immediately on the waterfront and unload their cargo without the use of tenders. A rail line along the quays was to serve both for transporting goods to and from the city's stations as well as people by means of a tram. Later a 900-meter long jetty was added to protect part of the quays from stormy weather. But the construction project was not only meant to

---

[8] Zandi-Sayek, *Ottoman Izmir*, 119–126.
[9] E. Goad Insurance Plan (June 1905), reproduced in Atay, *İzmir Planları*, 108–113; Zandi-Sayek, "Struggles over the Shore," 60–62; Fröbel, *Ein Lebenslauf*, vol. II, 579; Calligas, *Voyage à Syros*, 57–65.
[10] *Smyrna Mail*, 28 Oct. 1862.
[11] Zandi-Seyek, "Struggles over the Shore," 64, 65.

make transport easier. The Société des Quais intended to fill 146,000 square meters of sea, creating a whole new part of town. In order to do this, they constructed one broad road along the quays and another one between them and the old waterfront, both of them running the full length of 3.5 kilometers.[12]

Not surprisingly, this building endeavor, hitherto the largest in the city, did not evoke unmitigated support. Envy toward the concession owners was one factor. Those who had owned precious seaside territory were to find themselves stranded two blocks away from the water. The planned port fees did not appeal to the shipping companies. The gradual process of filling in the sea covered the city with stagnant pools. The original stockholders could not manage the 6 million Francs project, so eventually the Marseille-based construction company Frères Dussaud took over from the bankrupt Société des Quais.[13]

Despite financial difficulties, civic opposition, and the interference of the British consul, the project was completed after only eight years (1868–1875). Toward the end of this time, opposition decidedly weakened, as it became obvious that the newly erected quarters would soon become the city center. A last-minute scramble for buying property on the quays or at least on the second new street, Rue Parallèle, set in, so that upon completion of the works there was no sizable free lot to be found.[14]

So while a passenger entering Constantinople from the sea and eager to take in a panoptical view of the city was greeted by Abdülmecid's brave new world of mighty palaces, barracks, and mosques, those arriving by ship in Smyrna now first set eyes on a miniature version of what lay behind them on the shores of France, Italy, or South Russia. This monument to progress and the European way of life was soon to be copied elsewhere. In 1870 Salonica, similarly located at an intersection between land and sea routes and experiencing an increase in Mediterranean trade,[15] construction of a new, 1,650 meter

---

[12] Oberling, "The Quays of Izmir," 316–319.

[13] The opposition against the quays has been discussed in Oberling, "The Quays of Izmir," 317–320; Zandi-Seyek, "Struggles over the Shore"; Frangakis-Syrett, "The Making of an Ottoman Port," 23–46. For a typical complaint see *Levant Herald*, 4 Jan. 1873.

[14] Federal Archives, Berlin Branch (BA Berlin), R 901/39576, 107: Griesebach (Consulate) to German Foreign Office (AA), Smyrna 25 June 1875 (confidential).

[15] Berov, "The Course of Commodity Turnover," 76.

long waterfront began, which was to serve simultaneously as port and fancy new center of town. Here the symbolism of the act is interesting: *Vali* Sabri Pasha struck several blows with a golden hammer against the sea wall. Thereafter, the seaside part of the Roman city walls was torn down and the debris used to fill in the space for the new quays, streets, and buildings. This was meant to illustrate that the city, having remained closed off and locked in its "mediaeval" ways, was now opening itself to the fresh sea breeze, the influences blowing in from across the sea, intending to take in without hesitation European philosophies, fashions, and commodities. The *vilayet* (governorate general) undertook the construction directly, without giving concessions or hiring foreign firms, to avoid complications as in Smyrna, but was faced with problems of its own, such as embezzlement and lack of funding, which resulted in several delays and the selling of all new land intended for public buildings to finance the remaining works. Unlike Smyrna, where the port had one small pier for passport controls and a larger one for customs, construction in Salonica concentrated on the establishment of a new section of town and regularized quays; port facilities remained very limited. A new port adjacent to the quays was constructed only in 1896–1902 by concession to the French citizen Edmond Bartissol.[16] Once again, the local press rejoiced, "Let us hope that we will finally be provided a port and that under the glorious reign of Sultan Abdul Hamid II, our dear Salonica will become one of the most important cities of Europe."[17] As the problem of inclement weather interfering with the reliability of communications and the passengers' comfort would thus be solved, the *Journal de Salonique* even predicted that Salonica would become the preferred port for dispatching the British mail to Egypt and for passengers to India.

Interestingly, the reconstruction of the Constantinople quays was realized much later than in the two Aegean port cities, in 1890–1895/ 1899.[18] This delay can partly be explained by the size and

---

[16] Anastassiadou, *Salonique 1830–1912*, 140–150; Dumont, "Le français d'abord," 208; Yerolympos, *Urban Transformations in the Balkans*, 62–67.

[17] *Journal de Salonique*, 14 Nov. 1895.

[18] Earlier suggestions to undertake construction in Constantinople are numerous, see for example *Smyrna Mail*, 28 Oct. 1862; *Le Matin*, 1 July 1879. An initial concession for the construction of regular quays had been issued as early as 1879 but never put into action; see Çelik, *Remaking of Istanbul*, 73–76. In contrast to the two Aegean towns, this plan like the one implemented later never

multicentered character of the city. While the wharf area in Galata and Eminönü, located on both sides of the mouth of the Golden Horn, was the commercial heart of the city, the adjacent lower-class residential areas prevented the transformation of the area into a zone for upper-class leisure and shopping. The stage for such social activities was set in the streets around the Great Powers' embassies in Pera, a fifteen-minute steep uphill walk from Galata. Thus, while the Constantinople quays contributed to the transformation of working practises, it did not take part in rearranging leisure and free-time activities to the same extent, except perhaps for sailors, port workers, and some white-collar workers. Like its counterparts though, it became a site for extended controversies.[19]

The New Waterfront Order and Ways of Working

When turning the gaze from the sea to the land in Smyrna, while standing on evenly paved quays that stretched for a considerable distance to either side, one could no longer spot cafés on poles extending into the sea, private piers, or sheds or warehouses extending across the wharf. For the first time a considerable section of the city that was frequented by large numbers of residents and visitors met the aesthetical tenets of the time, that is, regularity, accessibility, and ordering of the sensual input. It was no longer difficult to "form a picture" of the town, as the regularized quays allowed for vistas of the waterside buildings and the gulf from practically every point. This new center of town would now increasingly bring changes to everyday life. On the one hand, the quays changed the rhythm of the working day. Arrival and departure of the steamers dictated the movements of many white-collar employees of companies involved in trade, as they depended on the postal service. The German E. Kauder recounts his impressions from a business trip to Smyrna:

In any case, the Austrian Post is the institution that has the liveliest traffic. One has to see the shoving, yelling, and pushing in front of the pickup

---

intended to fill in land from the sea and sell it for the erection of houses. This had been the most profitable part of the construction in Smyrna and Salonica.

[19] The controversies continued over other Constantinople points of disembarkation, such as the quays in Anatolian Kadıköy; *Stamboul*, 6 Jan. 1911.

counter after the arrival of a postal steamer to have an understanding of the enormous business life that vibrates in Smyrna. All the day's activities are regulated according to postal matters. In the morning, one first takes a walk to the blackboard to see if and when a ship to Europe departs and at what time the deadline is for postal deliveries for this shipment (usually one hour before the steamer's departure).[20]

What impressed the German visitor was seen as a cause of stress by locals. Ernest Giraud, entrepreneur and later president of the French Chamber of Commerce in Constantinople, satirically reflected on the change at the time of the completion of the Galata quays. Life in the old days had been a pleasant equilibrium of work and relaxation. There would be one steamer for France on Wednesdays, so the correspondence would have to be done on Tuesdays and finished and sent Wednesdays before departure. Thursdays and Fridays would be spent recovering in the countryside. Saturdays, the arrival of the next steamship from Marseille with mail would bring new work, which in turn would be followed by another two days of recreation. But now eight steamers departed from Constantinople per week for Marseille, not counting the passenger service of the Messageries Maritimes. The correspondents' eyes were used up from all the writing, country trips had become a matter of the past, and the employees developed a belly.[21]

While the white-collar workers suffered from burnout and the messengers had to race to the post offices around Smyrna's and Salonica's quays or Galata's Voyvoda Caddesi several times a day, the consequences were more drastic for the manual laborers in the port. The new facilities that made direct unloading from ship to the quays possible threatened the existence of boatmen operating the tenders. The railways on the quays, designed to transport goods between ships and train stations, were serious competition for the porters. As these workers' interests coincided with those of many businessmen, who opposed the stiff tariffs imposed by the new port authorities, and as porters and lighter boatmen were organized in tightly controlled

---

[20] Kauder, *Reisebilder*, 319. Under the capitulations system, the Great Powers maintained their own national post offices in the Ottoman Empire that attracted the lion's share of international mail. The 1900 delivery time for letters was far superior to today's air mail delivery. A letter from Smyrna would reach Central Germany in four to six days.
[21] *Revue commerciale du Levant* 102 (Sept. 1895), 93.

guilds, they were in a position to take collective action against the reorganization of port activities. In Constantinople it delayed the full imposition of modern port technology for several years. When the port facilities in Galata started operations in 1894, lighter men prevented a steamer from docking directly on the quays. In 1895, when a further section of the quays was inaugurated, they set the floating docks that were to replace their lighters adrift. The French company operating the port had to submit to the guilds' Luddite resistance, and for several months, Constantinople saw the spectacle of lighters unloading ships in front of an unused port infrastructure built to more quickly complete the process. While the port company succeeded in gradually suppressing the guilds' monopoly, the conflict violently resurfaced in the short summer of Ottoman labor radicalism following the Young Turk Revolution of 1908.[22]

The New Waterfront Order and Ways of Moving

While the new quays were primarily designed for intercity and international ships, they soon also evolved into the hub of a new way of traveling around town. Even before their establishment, local steamers had become a common site in Constantinople. A short-lived company began offering commutes from the upper-class suburbs along the Bosporus to Istanbul in 1850 on a single steamer. In the following year the Şirket-i Hayriye was founded as an Ottoman shareholder company with the purpose of providing more regular connections. Among the major stockholders were well-known members of the court, the bureaucracy, and the banking sector. The pleasant, speedy, and reliable way to travel was thus to a certain extent democratized: It was no longer the privilege of the few intercity travelers, but a fairly large part of middle-class commuters who could join in the contemplative gaze upon their own city. Local steamer traffic increased considerably in the

---

[22] The conflict is described in detail in Quataert, *Social Disintegration and Popular Resistance*, 95–120, and can also be traced in the issues of *Revue commerciale du Levant* 1895–1908. While the resistance of the porters and boatmen in Smyrna and Salonica certainly played a role, it has not received detailed analysis; see Quataert, "The Industrial Working Class," 194–197; Frangakis-Syrett, "Making of an Ottoman Port," 31, 32; BA-MA Imperial Navy Files (Reichsmarine, RM) 40/565, 274 (black numbers): Philipp Goeben to Mediterranean Division, Military Political Report, Smyrna Christmas 1913 (written Piraeus 9 Jan. 1914).

course of the second half of the nineteenth century, extended to more destinations, and also became more comfortable over time.[23] Steamers across the Gulfs of Smyrna and Salonica soon followed.

While the streets' narrowness had previously prohibited horse-drawn carriages from most of the city, the regular quays and the thoroughfares that radiated inward led to the possibility of horse-drawn carriages servicing the city, both in private possession and as taxi services. Rails were first laid out on the Smyrna quays to facilitate the transport of goods between the ships and the railway stations. They were also used for horse-drawn trams that served a network slowly extending into the city, as was the case for Salonica from its quays and from the Eminönü and Galata waterfronts of Constantinople. Trams with their greater capacity, seating space, and more regular movement in comparison to ordinary carriages were considered another revolution in an aesthetic and carefree way of moving through the enlarged streets of the city. After the turn of the century, electrically operated trams became common on main routes.

Railways also alleviated commuting. The Smyrniotes were the first and foremost to profit from them, as the lines established since the 1850s here also led to several popular upper-class country settlements, such as Burnabad and Buca. In Constantinople, once the city had its railway links, the two lines along the Sea of Marmara made suburban life on this sea an alternative to the Bosporus fishing villages and saw the development of more suburban housing. Only in Salonica there was no link between suburbanization and the railways, as these mainly served the new industrial zones in the swampy land to the west of the city, while upper-class housing spread to the East. All of these settlements far from the city did not decrease the importance of the center, but further elevated it. The suburban retreats were not settlements by themselves, but depended on the combination with downtown business, entertainment, and commerce, which appeared easily accessible due to the comfortable traffic links.

Steam power also alleviated a short but important part of movement in Constantinople from the Galata waterfront to uptown Pera. Created in 1875 by Eugène Henri Gavand and a company based on English capital, the steam-driven underground funicular, known in Turkish simply as the "Tünel," helped to overcome the steep incline of

[23] Çelik, *Remaking of Istanbul*, 82–87.

60 meters between the business district near the port and the glamor zone around the embassies, thus relieving residents of the necessity to trudge uphill on a sweaty fifteen-minute walk.[24] This underground funicular was among the first such lines in Europe.

Modern commuter traffic infrastructure enabled those with the necessary loose change to experience their city as an aesthetically pleasurable one. However, in none of the three cities did the new modes of transport manage to erase aspects of hardships and repugnance. Old modes of transport coincided with the new, be it to cater to those who could not afford modern modes of transportation, distrusted them, or to provide it in places where infrastructure was inadequate. Reflecting on the state of progress in 1896, the Constantinople resident Ernest Giraud concluded that the sedan chair had almost completely disappeared since carriages had become the more widespread and faster mode of transport. However, women still occasionally made use of them in order to protect a particularly important dress, such as for balls, from street dirt. The more robust *talika*s or *voitures de muhacirs* were still common instead of the more refined carriages when one came to less well-off suburbs with their more difficult roads. The country roads, such as the one down to Kağıthane still needed to be served by oxen carts. He had less understanding for the remaining *kayık*s. While middle-class passengers used the scheduled ferries, those who needed to travel economically would wait a considerable time for a rowing boat to fill up, then spend thirty to sixty minutes being bounced and splashed by the waves in order to save little in comparison to the comfortable steamer passage.[25] Thus, modern transport possibilities, while in part closing the gap between the Aegean and Marmara seaports and Western Europe, widened the gaps in the cities themselves. They caused their residents to realize the differences between one another due to their respective incomes, their access to infrastructure, and their attitudes

The New Waterfront and Ways of Living

But the quays were not simply a means to transform economic processes and commuting. Soon after their inauguration in 1875, the Smyrna quays became, just like their Salonica counterpart, a stage

[24] Ibid., 96–98.   [25] *Revue commerciale du Levant* 108 (March 1896), 143 ff.

where the city could be reinvented according to the newly revered culture from across the sea. Here all attributes of modern Europe were to be embraced and enacted with vigor. The large shipping companies had their offices here, the main offices of the important banks erected impressive buildings, and the consulates of most major European countries moved to the quays. Large, representative, and comfortable hotels with adjacent luxurious cafés established themselves. The cafés served Pilsener beer.[26]

These edifices and their users did not only intend to impose their interpretation of European-style modernity upon the Smyrna populace, but also to placate the critical gaze of the arriving visitors, demonstrating that this version of modernity had already been successfully adapted and that Smyrna was under full European cultural hegemony. In the latter scheme, they mostly succeeded. Travelers' comments, especially about Smyrna, now came to much friendlier conclusions than earlier, especially when comparing the towns to other Ottoman coastal regions. Paul Lindenberg, arriving from Palestine, commented,

The next morning led us back into the world of modern life, when we anchored before Smyrna at the seventh hour ... In some streets the Orient has been almost totally forced to retreat. One European shop is followed by the next, and the thousand-fold choice of all European articles possible (and impossible) at comparatively cheap prices is on offer, next to Japanese and Chinese products. Even the big Parisian department stores have opened outlets here and find much interest.[27]

Less impressionable travelers at least remarked upon the better state of streets and sidewalks in Smyrna compared to Constantinople,[28] but the more critical noticed that this regularity ended at the point where one entered the older streets.[29] Now the older parts of the city were a reminder of times gone by, and their very presence seemed a lingering resistance to the application of Western paradigms of order.

---

[26] See Chapter 12, pp. 173–193.
[27] Lindenberg, *Auf deutschen Pfaden im Orient*, 113. Lindenberg is probably fooled by a local store adapting the name of a Parisian department store without license; see Köse, *Westlicher Konsum am Bosporus*, 202.
[28] Schulz-Labischin, *Die Sängerreise der Berliner Liedertafel*, 179.
[29] Barth, *Unter südlichem Himmel*, 3–24.

The Smyrniote and Salonician waterside building development did not end with the completion of the quays in the 1870s, but continued throughout the following decades of the Belle Époque. A look around the Smyrna quays after the turn of the century aptly illustrates its European facade. Offices of the German, Austrian, Russian, French, and British post clustered around. Shopping passages, named after their Levantine owners or just copying French and English names, such as "Kraemer," "Hönischer," and "Bon Marché" ran from the quays to the Rue Parallèle, from there to the Quais Anglais (which had retained its name despite the construction of the new quays leaving it landlocked) and finally to Frank Street. To eat out, one could choose between the restaurants "République Française" and "Grande Bretagne"; for a Western-style coffee or a pint of beer, there was the choice between "Café Parisien," "Brasserie Strasbourg," or "Brasserie Puntingam." If one fell ill, one could find remedies at such trustworthy institutions as the "Royal English Pharmacy" or "Perini's Great Britain Pharmacy."[30] The Kraemer brothers, Smyrniotes of Trieste origin, were leading entrepreneurs in the field of European-style amenities. Besides having introduced the first major beer garden on the quays, they had also set up a bank, a theater, and the city's first cinema.[31] Opened in 1908, the Grand Hotel Kraemer Palace, with its lifts and permanent electric light, made the 1870s Grand Hotel Huck look third-rate.[32]

Entrance to or membership in the Club des Chasseurs, the Cercle de Smyrne, or the Cercle des Européens was deemed the pinnacle of social success.[33] The most prestigious of them was the Sporting Club with an extensive garden, salons with high roofs, its own theater, and a terrace overlooking the quays.[34] Salonica's waterfront luxury was more limited in size, but followed the same basic patterns. First-class accommodation and cuisine were available in Olympos Palace, Hotel Royal, Hotel Imperial, or Splendid Palace; high society congregated in the Cercle de Salonique.[35]

---

[30] Meyers Reisebücher, *Griechenland und Kleinasien*, 282–284.
[31] Makal, "İzmir Sinemaları," 390, 391; Atay, *19. Yüzyıl İzmir Fotoğrafları*, 59, 198.
[32] Meyers Reisebücher, *Balkanstaaten und Konstantinopel*, 37.
[33] Pınar, "Retrospektif bir Gezi Denemesi," 159.
[34] Lindau, *An der Westküste Klein-Asiens*, 82–91.
[35] Meyers Reisebücher, *Balkanstaaten und Konstantinopel*, 121–123.

Corso, Smyrneiko, and Nude Bathing: Lower-Class Appropriation of the Quays

Before their completion, the quays and the port had been lauded as the ticket to put the respective port cities back onto the map of Europe. Once they were completed however, locals did not simply mimic the inhabitants of Marseille, Genoa, or other Western Mediterranean port cities. The majority might have made use of the modern amenities, but did not see them as incompatible with the life they had led until the completion of the quays. Rather than mimicry, one should speak of appropriation: The Smyrniotes and Saloniquenos adapted the Europeanized public space to their lifeworlds, not the other way around. The old and the new often happily intermingled here. However, what the mix should look like and where exactly the limits to "non-European" behavior lay were questions that everyone answered differently.

As the photograph at the beginning of the book illustrates, men rushing past one another on the waterside wore bowler hats, turbans, or fez and baggy pants and wide coats as well as short jackets and vests. The resistance against the modern port operations did not make the Christian port workers in Constantinople outright conservative. They are reported to have been the first to adopt the classical working-class flat cap, presumably directly from their colleagues on incoming ships.[36] From even before construction was over, the quays were a great attraction. The common practice was to get dressed up as well as one could, and then as a couple or as a family go for an evening stroll along the waterfront, enjoying the fresh breeze coming from the sea, and happily intermingling with the neighbors, relatives, and friends one would inevitably run into every few meters. Sitting down in one of the expensive beer houses along the quays was financially out of the question for most, but this did not seem to discourage the strollers participating in the "corso" of Smyrna or the "volta" of Salonica.[37]

For most European observers, walking up and down the promenade was in principle in adherence to "civilized" behavior. Some of the

---

[36] *Revue commerciale du Levant* 212 (Nov. 1904), 633.
[37] While the evening stroll along the quays existed in Constantinople, it was not the singular most important site of leisure activities; *Revue commerciale du Levant* 109 (April 1896), 123. On the impact of the "corso" and its claim to modernity, see Vučinić-Nešković and Miloradović, "Corso As a Total Social Phenomenon," 229–250; Gavrilova, "Historische Anthropologie der Stadt," 269–289.

occurrences accompanying it, however, were not. The German Consul to Smyrna during the completion of the quays, Julius Fröbel, particularly deplored the practice of many male youths who used the promenade for diving into the sea and would then climb back out and stand naked and soaking wet among the Smyrniote ladies in their Sunday best. Other under-class practices that spoiled the elegant atmosphere of the waterfront appeared more like curiosities to him, such as fishing or especially the gathering of clams from the quay walls. At one point though the German Consul became romantic. He felt touched by the Greek songs he heard along the promenade:

> coming from little orchestras in front of improvised coffee houses,[38] the wonderful sounds of Greek music boomed in the mild air. I regret the fact that I can only speak of it theoretically. I can only say that an emotionality alien to our education seizes our spirits. In these sounds produced by the singing of an improviser, and the free accompaniment of a few string instruments and a dulcimer, sentimentality and a burning passion combine to produce an effect which wakes in us, the children of a conventional culture, dormant feelings not experienced before, while reason poses to the thinking listener the question as to who and what these people are, whose innermost emotionality shows itself in such a way? – The singer, his head sideways inclined in hands, staring at the sky, sitting amidst the instrumental musicians, emits long, wailing sounds. The accompanying string instruments give these sounds, depending on the words' contents, sometimes a soft, sometimes a harsh, even screaming note, while the dulcimer most effectively decorates, varies, and interprets the simple theme. In a moonshine night under the stars, this gave the impression of a fairy tale come to life.[39]

This romantic music, he assumed, would soon have to make way for waltz music and operetta songs, which could increasingly be heard in the simpler coffeehouses of Smyrna. But fortunately, Fröbel underestimated the resilience of Anatolian popular music. Although so-called Bohemian Orchestras composed of Austrian musicians as well as French and Italian singers now toured the Eastern Mediterranean cities,[40] this did not cause local music to disappear. Instead it adapted elements of waltz and operetta to its songs.[41]

---

[38] The lower-class improvised coffee houses had to make way once the quay construction was finished.
[39] Fröbel, *Ein Lebenslauf*, vol. II, 617, 618.   [40] See Chapter 19, pp. 314–320.
[41] Giannatou, "Smyrneiko Minore," sleeve notes.

Bringing the State Back In

The roles of residents and private capital in the construction and appropriation of the quays were highlighted in the previous section. This is of course not to say that the state did not have its place in the nineteenth-century Thalassocentric rearrangement of urban space. The Ottoman state was no passive spectator to the emergence of new forms or representation in the major provincial ports. As during Abdülmecid's construction projects, it was not alone, but always acting in a dialectic relation to the Great Powers. The demonstrative presence of foreign diplomatic representations spurred the Sublime State and its satraps to show themselves more prominently. The most obvious clash took place in Alexandria, where the first public square on the waterfront had been laid out and named Place des Consuls. In 1873 an equestrian statue of Muhammad Ali was placed on the square by Khedive Ismail and it was renamed Place Muhammad Ali. The Ottoman dynasty itself shied away from the practice of erecting monuments to its own members in public, as it was scorned in Islam.[42] Instead, clock towers and other buildings fulfilling practical modern functions were to symbolize the penetration of urban society by the state.

In Smyrna, the reformist state amassed its modern institutions and their heavy buildings around Konak Square at the southern end of the quays. The oldest but also by far the most massive state building there was the Amber Barracks (Sarıkışla), erected in 1829 under Mahmud to signify the installation of his new army to replace the janissary corps. It occupied much of the waterfront, as did the adjacent maneuver grounds. Its simple classicist facade was intended to symbolize order (and thus contrast to the defunct janissary corps known for its disorder). In Abdülmecid's reign, a public, nondenominational hospital was added at the far hand corner beyond the barracks in the 1850s. Combining these and other institutions into a coherent public space did not happen until the later years of Abdülaziz's reign, contemporaneously with the construction of Smyrna's quays. The desire to match this mercantile and civil infrastructure with a regularity and monumentality of one's own and to outshine the German, Russian, and French consulates, which had in part taken residence along the Quays,

---

[42] Kreiser, "Public Monuments," 103–117; Mansel, *Levant*, 68, 69, 112, 113.

seems apparent.⁴³ In place of the wooden *Konak*, a new brick building with long classicist facade now faced the sea. Other buildings in front of it had been cleared to create a minor park with greenery and to thus enlarge Konak Square (which was in addition extended to the sea by the quays' construction), now delimited on the south side by the barracks, on the eastern side by the *Konak*, to the north by warehouses, and to the west by the sea. The state had thus taken up the rules of symmetry and presented itself as a mighty part of the urban ensemble, just as Dolmabahçe showed its facade defiantly to the incoming ships. However, unlike in the capital, the state institutions complemented the commercial infrastructure, rather than competing with it. From the square a regularized street led inland toward the bazaar while another ran parallel to the sea, away from the *Konak* and behind the barracks, cutting across land taken from the maneuver grounds. Further inland from that road, also on land taken from the maneuver grounds, was the massive city prison, laid out in modern, star shape according to the Panoptikon principle, adjacent to the hospital.⁴⁴ Abdülhamid's reign made little change to this ensemble. Only the clock tower erected for the twenty-fifth anniversary of his ascendance to the throne in the middle of Konak Square added an eye-catcher to the showcase of late Ottoman statehood in Smyrna. A school for the arts and handicrafts adjacent to the *Konak* also dates to his reign.⁴⁵ Konak Square was not a counter-model to the quays; rather it was the state inscribing itself in a marked way onto the new urban fabric with institutions that were at the time invariably the privilege of statehood.

By contrast, the state did not manage to erect anything comparable to Smyrna's Konak Square in Salonica. While originally public buildings were intended for the Macedonian port city's waterfront, the financial troubles experienced during the building of the quays, including incidents of embezzlement, led to increasing expenses, so that all public property along the quays had to be sold.⁴⁶ New public buildings therefore had to be built far inland and uphill from the water, or along

---

⁴³ "Plan de la ville de Smyrne," reproduced in Georgelin, *La fin de Smyrne*, after p. 128.

⁴⁴ Tekeli, *Anadolu'da Yerleşme Sistemi*, 318–321; Zandi-Sayek, *Ottoman Izmir*, 35–40.

⁴⁵ Berkant, *İzmirli bir Mimar*, 34–41; E. Goad Insurance Plan (June 1905), reproduced in Atay, *İzmir Planları*, 51–56.

⁴⁶ Yerolympos, *Urban Transformations in the Balkans*, 66, 67.

the roads leading to the suburbs. Although isolated and erected at a comparatively late date, during Abdülhamid's reign, these new edifices nevertheless made their mark. One of the first symbolic monuments of this kind was the Hamidiye Fountain in 1889. While donating for new fountains was a traditional way the ruler or the well-off could show their presence in the city, Abdülhamid's fountain nonetheless tried to tie together this practice with modernity, as the fountain was erected at the intersection of two boulevards built just beyond the eastern city walls to highlight a model settlement featuring wide roads, sidewalks, trees, and houses set back from the road.[47] Already in 1887, a public preparatory high school for state service and higher learning, the *İdadiye*, had been founded.[48] Its neoclassicist buildings were located outside the eastern gate of the old city, between the boulevard running to the suburb of Kalamaria and the Jewish cemetery. Even further up the slope and away from the sea was the *Hamidiye* or public hospital, founded in 1903.[49] Slightly downhill from the *İdadiye* but set further along the road to the suburbs were the army barracks and military hospital, also established in 1903.[50] Of all major state institutions, only the large governor general's office took seat in the old city, in the place where the *Konak* had stood for centuries. However, its location was as far inland as the *Hamidiye* Hospital, on the steep slope, far removed from the bazaar and quays area, but joined to them by a new boulevard through the city's heart, Sabri Pasha Boulevard.[51] In Salonica therefore, rather than being met by a coherent ensemble on the waterside, one could run into new state institutions at various odd places around the wider city.

The Making of a New Other: The Anti-Quays

Thus, a decisive discursive shift had taken place. While before Mustafa Reşid Pasha or the journalists of Smyrna had clamored for an as yet unrealized utopia of symmetry, this space was now real. The quays had become the decisive "showcase of modernity" of the Anatolian and Balkan major ports. They aimed to placate both the foreigners' critical gaze arriving and assessing the city's qualities as well as the locals' desire for state-of-the-art public spaces. But the Europeanizing

---

[47] Anastassiadou, *Salonique 1830–1912*, 155, 156. [48] Ibid., 181, 182.
[49] Ibid., 111. [50] Colonas, "Vitaliano Poselli," 162–171. [51] Ibid.

paradigm had a bifurcating effect on the urban space: Seeing the starkly distinct new quays in correlation to the older, more inland parts of town or, in the case of Constantinople, Pera with its embassies, churches, and businesses vs. the old city with its palaces, mosques, and bazaars led most outside observers to compare and judge both localities and people.

It would be wrong to see in the quays as the fulfillment of Paul Calligas' vision of a peaceful interface between north and south, east and west. Different people might have access according to the European nineteenth-century bourgeois norm prescribing free circulation within the city. However, their specific use was subject to the unwritten rules of global capitalism and upper-class bias. As a result, encounters could encourage othering rather than class-transgressing solidarity. In Salonica, the Greek-language newspaper *Hermes* polemically deplored the fact that some citizens came to the quays dressed in pajamas.[52] This attack was aimed at those who declined to get dressed up in suit and tie, preferring more comfortable or traditional dress. This comment demonstrates a social rift that had a cultural, social, but also spatial dimension. This rift features prominently in many contemporary publications. *La revue commerciale du Levant*, a monthly digest of business activities and opportunities published by the French Chamber of Commerce in Constantinople, featured a column called *La Rue*. In it, the editor Ernest Giraud narrates how a recent arrival from France and a long-established French Stambouliote walk Pera's streets together. The newcomer asks all sorts of naive questions to which the local has humoristic answers. When walking the Galata quays, the newbie believes that somebody is crying "Murder!" at the top of his lungs, but the local reassures him that this is only a porter calling in Judeo-Spanish "Guarda!" for people to get out of his way. He describes the porters as camels with only two legs, two hooves, and one hump, thus biologizing the cultural and social divide between the French businessmen and the Eastern Anatolian laborers.[53] The presence of traditional dress, technically obsolete professions, irregular street grids, and encroaching upon the street was now increasingly seen as a resistance against the Europeanizing paradigm per se.

---

[52] Yerolympos, "Conscience citadine et intérêt municipal," 137, 138.
[53] *Revue commerciale du Levant* 109 (April 1896), 116.

Toward the end of Abdülhamid's reign, the local debate on urbanity was haunted by the idea that perhaps the residents had not done enough to "merrily join in advising and doing," as Martin Hartmann phrased it, that perhaps the city's waterfront might be judged a superficial varnish of modernity camouflaging its older face. A Salonician visitor to Niš in 1907 was embarrassed when he found out that the Serbian city would soon have electric streetlights and that automobiles had already become fairly common there, while neither innovation was common to his hometown.[54] "On the whole Salonica appeared less Westernized [than Beirut, MF]. Around 1900, observed from the sea, the capital city of Rumelia still looked like a typical Turkish town, with its landscape dotted with white minarets."[55] Due to this continuous comparison not only with Western, but increasingly also with cities of the region, the urban beautification debate had lost none of its vivacity. In 1903 the *Journal de Salonique* had lots of unsolicited advice for the mayor or Hulusi Bey: Raise new credits for more street widening projects, especially Sabri Pasha Boulevard, as a true metropolis needed at least three to four major thoroughfares; buy up private land around the White Tower to create a public garden there; extend the gas pipes to the suburbs, as the city needed more illumination; increase paving activities, perhaps build some urban squares in the center, more hotels, two to three theaters, a museum, ten public monuments, etc.[56] In Salonica, especially the old Muslim Quarter on the hill with its winding, haphazard streets, closed off courtyards and simple coffeehouses appeared like a bastion of defiance against the clear ordered lines, big windows, and flashy lights along the quays. The governors and municipal administrations began a process of extending the quayside urban forms into the old city, building wide and even boulevards into areas they had cleared by demolition (or arson, as some rumors charged). They built the Hamidiye Boulevard from the White Tower up the hill to the Hamidiye Hospital. They also built the main thoroughfares of Sabri Pasha and Midhat Pasha Boulevards. Besides creating thoroughfares of 15 meters in tune with the new ideas of streets, their agenda involved gas illumination of major roads, piped water, horse trams, and public parks.

[54] *Journal de Salonique*, 2 Dec. 1907. The construction of an electric power plant in Salonica was still in the planning phase at the time; *Journal de Salonique*, 5 Dec. 1907. Constantinople did not have one until 1913.
[55] Dumont, "Salonica and Beirut," 195.   [56] *Journal de Salonique*, 5 Jan. 1903.

Not even Smyrna's urban renewal could be considered a fait accompli. While its northern waterfront was a uniform structure of cafés and hotels, already the parallel street and the Quais Anglais behind were a much more mixed case. When gazing over the 1905 Insurance Map, one notices next to the *Passage de Hönischer* a large vacant lot occupied by construction materials and a brick depot. The whole area saw many warehouses and depots of firewood, coal, and granaries. Factories for drying and processing fruits as well as distilleries were sure to produce smells that would not be fancied in the upper market hotels nearby.[57] Taken together these gave the impression of a neighborhood in transition.

In Constantinople, the comparison was not only between the new city that had sprung up around the embassies and its periphery, but also between the new city and the old one south of the Golden Horn, which Calligas had evoked in mid-century. As Byzantium's role as city of power was fading, many European observers poured derision on the old city. Eduardo de Amicis stated how strange it was to see signs of modernity south of the Golden Horn, such as a tram bringing speed, noise, and orderliness in the shape of uniforms and printed tariffs into the otherwise Oriental old city.[58] But de Amicis' judgment was unjust. Constantinople's historic center was far from the sleepy, mostly residential uptown areas of Salonica or Smyrna.[59] It remained an important site for commerce and politics and developed new roles in the fields of communication and even entertainment. The Sublime Porte had its seat there, as did other ministries. The Public Debt Administration took its seat within the immediate vicinity of the Sublime Porte, and several major banks had branch offices or even their headquarters in or around the port area of Eminönü. For communications, going to Eminönü could prove inevitable, either for the Ottoman Post, or more likely for the telegraph office; Sirkeci Station was the terminus of the Oriental Railways to the Balkan provinces and the remainder of Europe beyond. Nor was commerce in the old city restricted to the ageless tradition of the bazaar: Between 1883 and 1921, thirteen department stores existed in the old city, while Galata-Pera boasted fourteen.[60] The problem therefore with the old city was not that there

[57] E. Goad Insurance Plan (June 1905), reproduced in Atay, *İzmir Planları*, 51–56.
[58] Çelik, *The Remaking of Istanbul*, 56.
[59] Girardelli, "Levantine Architecture in Late Ottoman Istanbul," 118.
[60] Köse, *Westlicher Konsum am Bosporus*, 278.

was no sign of modernity. Unlike Pera, this modernity was not integrated into signs of a Western presence (the embassies and later the increasing number of oversized churches); the historic peninsula continued to be dominated by the large mosques of the sixteenth and seventeenth centuries, the extensive bazaar area, and a predominantly, though nowhere nearly homogenous Muslim population. One could not negate or belittle the presence of a Muslim state and society here. But the historic peninsula also found appreciation among European foreigners with a tendency to exoticism. Pierre Loti described Pera as a "lamentable pastiche," that is, denounced it for its hybridity, while lauding old Istanbul for its oriental sagacity.[61] Locals could also find the contrast between the old city and Pera to work to the detriment of the latter. Next to the miraculous and ancient edifices of the imperial capital, this upstart city, even its imperial palace and show-off embassies, and its most splendid hotels, paled to insignificance, could seem like a distorted image of a faraway Europe:

Leaving this still somewhat fantastic Stamboul where I live, when I once again see Pera and its "refinements," I actually have the impression of observing our Europe in one of these distorting mirrors, some concave, some convex, which twist the images and increase their ridiculousness in order to make the crowd laugh.[62]

While Pera could not outshine Stamboul in everyone's opinion, it fared much better in competition with other parts of the city. Talat Dura for example remembers the contrast between the Kasımpaşa neighborhood that had once been the proud seat of the Ottoman Navy and its extensive docks, where he grew up during the 1920s and 1930s, and the nearby Voyvoda Caddesi in lower Galata, where the most important banks had their headquarters:

We would walk up the hill from Kasımpaşa. There were pools along that slope – I can't remember its name. Next to it was Lovers' Cemetery. And there were tombs of saints and all. So we would go up that slope or through Lovers' Cemetery, by foot, and would go down to Banks Street ... Now we were very much impressed by the neighborhood when we came here because where we lived and played, all the houses were wooden houses. Stone and brick buildings started later. So when we came down from Şişhane and saw

---

[61] Hughes, "Exotic Drift," 252, 253.
[62] Willy Sperco, quoted in Pannuti, *Les italiens d'Istanbul*, 247.

all these huge stone buildings, our world would change ... I mean, when I was a kid, this was an extraordinary sight.[63]

Yet another step up the social ladder was to go to the very top of the hill, to the flashy commerce of the Grande Rue de Pera. Halid Ziya (Uşaklıgil), while working as a modest clerk for the Tobacco Régie in Galata around the turn of the century, would marvel at the displays of the Pera department stores:

I would take the *tünel* up and then slowly proceed to Taksim, passing in front of the shop windows, hanging around for a long time, never gathering the courage to enter, if only to satisfy my curiosity by asking the price. I would return home, with a tight heart due to the discrepancy between my tight budget and my long list of desires.[64]

Downtown residents who would wander into the marginal districts felt the contrast no less, and it was not restricted to the appearance of buildings; it encompassed the way people dressed, what they used to cover their heads, or how people cut their hair and beard. Leon Sciaky remembers following his grandfather into uptown Salonica as a disorientating experience: "Children would sometimes run over from the near-by fountain to stand shyly before our table and look at the little boy in Western clothes, their eyes full of wonder."[65]

But for Western travelers these remote uptown regions could become the last reserve of the classic Orient, places they sought out to experience what in their eyes was authentic and exotic, such as drinking coffee local style or smoking *shisha*. Many visiting photographers would seek out the hillside quarters of Salonica or Smyrna to capture this world that was seemingly retreating from the flashy hotels, banks, and clubs near the waterfront in order to upkeep the dichotomy of Occident and Orient, modern and traditional, innovation and tradition that was no longer self-evident on the quays, where wearers of the fez or turban would intermingle with others preferring bowler hats and where advertisement would praise Nestlé, Singer, or other international brands in French, Greek, Turkish, and Armenian simultaneously.[66]

---

[63] Talat Dura, Interview in Eldem, *Bankalar Caddesi*, 257–259, 267–269.
[64] Halid Ziya Uşaklıgil, quoted in Köse, *Westlicher Konsum am Bosporus*, 448.
[65] Sciaky, *Farewell to Ottoman Salonica*, 46.
[66] See for example Hauts-de-Seine Open Data, "Archives de la Planète," or Kerr, *Die Welt im Licht*, vol. II, 212–217.

And yet, the contrast was never perfect. Even the most aloof upper-class districts could not shield themselves completely from the hardships and squalor the lower-class districts experienced on a more regular basis. Alka Nestorova, the Croatian-born wife of a Bulgarian diplomat, in her letters to her parents narrates her family's arrival to her husband's post in Constantinople and their apartment in Nişantaşı near the military school at Maçka, one of the best addresses in town. After only a few days, a leprous beggar had slipped past the doorman to ask her for alms, ragged Jewish scavengers from Galata toured the neighborhood in search of clothes, the servants had to regularly feed the street dogs in their vicinity to keep them quiet at night, and a neighbor in the same building was afflicted by Asian cholera.[67]

Conclusion

The creation of new spatial patterns in the Ottoman maritime city was the result of complex interactions that are only insufficiently described if they are reduced to their semi-colonial aspects. The huge gap between Western gunboat politics and an actual Western ability to rule the Eastern Mediterranean; the creation and constant reinterpretation of a promise of a West-Eastern reconciliation under Western cultural supremacy; the creative appropriation of this promise for purposes of urban renewal; local and overseas state representation; new infrastructure; the fusion of the remodeled urban space with various local practices, both time-honored and new, but also a heightened sense of cultural bifurcation between home and overseas, uptown and downtown, old and new, winners and denialists of contemporary change all together characterize the upheavals of the time. Contemporaries experienced these changes as a restless process of unending transition. Even when the pace seemed to slow down at the beginning of the twentieth century, this was only interpreted as a growing lag and need to speed up further. Together, these changes in spatial practices set the stage for new forms of sociabilities and quests for identities.

[67] Nestoroff, *Istanbul Letters*, 33–35.

PART III

The City's New Pleasures

Europe now made up part of the Eastern Mediterranean port cities, its quays, main streets, and buildings. It was a vague ideal and the object of discussions about urban beautification. It was a general threat that hovered over the cities concerned, where foreign gunboats could make their states' political interests felt. It had also captured a prominent place in economics; to ignore it could lead to ruin.

Nonetheless, what made the European Dream more than a distant, despised semi-colonial order that one sought to have contact with only on minimalist terms, is its integration into Eastern Mediterranean port city social practice. "Sociabilities," understood not as a coherent social counter-space vis-à-vis the state, but rather as a myriad of multidirectional practices that significant parts of society engaged in in order to communicate, fraternize, and enjoy themselves, has become the often implicitly used concept to shed a more intense light on late imperial Eastern Mediterranean society ever since it was promulgated by François Georgeon as a means to overcome the more narrow statuary and structural perspectives formerly common to the field.[1] While sociabilities as a concept can entail many forms of exchange, participation, and negotiation, the following section will concentrate on those collective practices that at first glance cannot be associated with an economic, spiritual, or political aim, but must be labeled as pursuits of leisure. Marios Sarigiannis has identified Ottoman leisure practices and concepts as an area in need of further research.[2] This particularly pertains to the nineteenth century, not only because members of the middle class had by our standards a large amount of time on their hands.[3] While nineteenth-century practices and concepts are more well documented than those of former centuries, they have received

---

[1] Georgeon, "Présentation," 5–20.
[2] Sariyannis, "Time, Work, and Leisure"; MacArthur-Seal, "Intoxication and Imperialism"; Wishnitzer, "Eyes in the Dark."
[3] Georgeon, "Le ramadan à Istanbul," 37.

empirical, but little analytic research. From our present day perspective, the long-established Ottoman forms of sociabilities revolving around imperial spectacles, the coffeehouse, or the baths (*hamam*) seem to warrant more explanation,[4] as their social role has been lost and replaced by new ones, whereas the social importance of an opera visit, participating in a ball, or having a beer at the pub, practices particular to the nineteenth century, still seem significant for us today. However, despite these superficial continuities, this fails to shed light on the significance these activities had for a nineteenth-century inhabitant of the Eastern Mediterranean shoreline, who most likely had grown up with shadow theater (*karagöz*) performances, cafés for *nargile* (*shisha*) smoking, and gatherings of religious associations. For such a person, operas, balls, and beer were novelties, and it would not do them justice to simply study their presence in port city society as part of a teleology of transition toward European or global uniform practices. Instead, they must be seen as a search for the satisfaction of contemporary desires. The nineteenth-century sociocultural order developed sociabilities, self-expression, and a culture that people deemed appropriate for their lives and times.

New forms of entertainment were a low-threshold possibility of familiarizing oneself with or appropriating the new, so-called Western ways. Conspicuous consumption became a mode of demonstrating one's progressiveness, but also to show ways of combining tradition and the modern, or rejecting the West. While many of these new forms revolved around commodities or activities that also existed in Central and Western Europe, it would be wrong to see in them simply a carbon copy or mimicry of those regions' culture. Though it used forms that could be recognized in other parts of the Westernized world, a closer look at Eastern Mediterranean port city culture reveals that it was very much the product of local aspirations, innovations, and blends. What is more, it was not exclusively performed by a limited circle in possession of extraordinary wealth, education, and power, but came in several varieties, including some that were affordable for the lower middle classes; some forms of culture could even be enjoyed without money. Entertainment was not only a high-end, happy few sector, but also had low-end as well as non-commodified varieties.

---

[4] Wishnitzer, "Shedding New Light"; Kırlı, "Coffeehouses"; Macaraig, *Çemberlitaş Hamamı in Istanbul*.

One cannot say that these new cultural forms all served one purpose. As they soon formed important parts of everyday life, their purposes were multilayered, as will become apparent in the following chapters. While establishing new modes of entertainment, arts, and consumption patterns no doubt served the curiosity and interests of the Eastern Mediterranean port residents, they also functioned as a rite of passage, a performance one had to undertake in order to prove one's ability to enter the brave new world that was waiting for all. It was a playful, but not innocent way to demonstrate one's language skills, refined manners, and knowledge; in short, one's cultural capital depended on it. Port city residents consumed and performed according to the newly established norms of Western-centered, but not exclusively Western ways, and observers would differentiate between people who possessed the proper cultural capital for the nineteenth century, those who were getting there, and those who had no place in it.[5]

Nonetheless, the spread of Occidentocentric leisure practices also had a utopian or carnivalesque element to it. While education, urban renewal, political, economic, or social attempts at overcoming the dividing lines between the more prosperous and prestigious Western parts of the continent and their Eastern neighbors could only prove possible in the long run, if at all, a night at the society ball, the theater, a concert, or even the beer garden offered the possibility to imagine a world where the rules of exclusion were less severe or overcome. This act of inversion, short and limited as it might be, constitutes the moment when "a subaltern or emergent culture and its modes of production enter the visibility of participation and documentation within those of a dominant culture."[6] Port city culture had to become something that strongly resembled overseas culture in order for it to be recognized as a legitimate form of expression.

What did the sociabilities nineteenth-century Eastern Mediterranean residents engaged in look like? A list of all innovations is neither within the scope of this book, nor would such an empirical work contribute to the overall question of what was characteristic of the times. One

---

[5] In this respect, the new practices served as a cultural capital in the sense of Bourdieu; Bourdieu, "Forms of Capital." Other relevant works to understand the nineteenth-century process of cultural revolution around the Eastern Mediterranean are Thurston, *Popular Theatre Movement in Russia*, and Elias, *On the Process of Civilisation*.

[6] Henri Lefebvre, quoted in Grindon, "Revolutionary Romanticism," 216.

common characteristic perhaps is that nineteenth-century port city culture was much more commodified than in previous times. The following chapter will therefore focus on the consumers of this culture and how they navigated their respective experiences of Eurocentric leisure practices. The chapters thereafter will trace one leisure pursuit in particular that like no other stood for enacting and celebrating the new nineteenth-century culture: the dramatic arts and opera. I will first roughly trace the creation of major theater venues in the three cities under study here. This endeavor however can only be dealt with in a cursory manner, as more exhaustive local studies have already in part investigated the question of when and where modern theater institutions in the Eastern Mediterranean cities had been created. What symbolic content and appeal drama and opera had over the Eastern Mediterranean audiences is a matter for the chapter thereafter. I will therefore concentrate on these attitudes and in particular why port city residents identified the theater with the European Dream. Thirdly, I will take a look at the people who created or shaped the particular blend of theater that succeeded on the Eastern Mediterranean stages and inquire whether they successfully promoted the vision of blending the European Dream with Eastern Mediterranean realities. Globally oriented entertainment in the nineteenth century was not like that of the twenty-first, where we have a myriad of possibilities from all corners of the earth at our disposal through the tap of a finger without the need for further social interaction. While it did involve the movement of ideas and objects, a massive movement of people was necessary to upkeep the rapid cultural exchange in the entertainment sector. The following chapter will therefore provide some insights into the milieus of foreign European but also Ottoman actresses and actors, musicians as well as entertainment entrepreneurs or impresarios and their role in creating new sociabilities and a particular culture. But besides expensive highbrow entertainment such as at the opera, the European Dream was also exemplified in more easily accessed commodities, such as the hitherto practically unknown beverage beer. Its rise and the sociabilities (as well as the lack thereof), challenges, and promises associated with it, will be the subjects of the final chapters in this section.

A disclaimer pertaining to this section is called for. Much of preexisting research on the leisure practices dealt with here has focused on empirical matters, such as the question of origins. When did the first opera troupe from Italy perform on the Eastern Mediterranean shores? Where was the first proper theater house in a Levantine port city? Who was the first person to brew beer for the markets of Smyrna, Salonica, and Constantinople? This section does not promise to give the ultimate answers to these questions. While the following chapters can only either reiterate the results of previous research on these questions or in some cases refute them for my own findings, it should be stated clearly that my aim is not to provide a history of institutions, but to reconstruct how residents as well as recent arrivals helped to establish certain new cultural forms, how they were experienced, and what vision of contemporary society and the future they pertained to.

8 | Visiting, Strolling, Masquerading, Dancing
The Consumers of Europeanism

What did a social life by port city residents attempting to be modern and open to new influences look like? Would we find a local society clinging to the heels of the foreigners, ready to mimic every move they make and pass off as one of them? It seems not. Overseas fashions often blended with long-established traditions. Smyrniote, Salonician, and Perote entertainment culture was local, having taken up impulses both from Anatolian Greek, Turkish, or Armenian sources as well as from overseas, especially of Italian provenance.

One should also not fall for the fallacy that, as some sources and literature might suggest, it was the West that taught the Eastern Mediterranean port cities how to enjoy life. There were many pastimes that had existed in the Levant for some time and that the locals as well as newcomers continued to enjoy throughout the nineteenth century. The Mediterranean had been a two-way route of exchange for cultural goods and phenomena long before the nineteenth century. Novelties from the respective other side were noticed and, in many cases, adopted. Coffee spread westward and northward from Egypt, just as New World agricultural products such as tobacco or tomatoes spread eastward. Oriental carpets and Italian clocks were much desired luxury products on the respective far side of the Mediterranean. However, speed and intensity were far from that of the modern age. The coffeehouse continued to play an important part in casual and semi-formal social interaction. In these coffeehouses, there was a variety of ways of killing time, which included besides the obvious consumption of coffee also *shishas* and games. More formal entertainment could also take place there or in other public, easily accessed places. Popular were traditional storytellers (*meddâh*) and shadow theater with its classic burlesque stories. Also, a variety of local music and dance styles existed. Religious holidays were among the largest public events, especially Ramadan, Easter, and certain popular saints' days that could be accompanied by fairs. The Italian tradition of Carnival had already

Figure 8.1 Smyrna, a coffeehouse with shishas in the bazaar area, pre-1922
Courtesy of Pierre Gigord/public domain

gained its place among Eastern Mediterranean practices, but was to grow in importance during the nineteenth century, as will become apparent later.

Even once Western forms of entertainment had become common and objects of social prestige, locals saw no necessity to do away with time-honored practices. A famous late nineteenth-century photograph of two men dressed in *alla franga* clothes, possibly local residents with foreign passports, shows them sitting at ease in the Smyrna bazaar while reading newspapers and smoking *shisha* among an otherwise Muslim crowd (Figure 8.1). By the turn of the century, entertainment possibilities had multiplied and become socially more widespread, more varied, and in its upmarket varieties more luxurious. While earlier observers had feared that the imported varieties of leisure pursuits would completely extinguish the longer established forms, this was not the case. In some cases, older traditions even saw a revival, as people became aware of new possibilities of enriching them with modern techniques and customs. Hybrid forms of cultural expression had become established, and moreover, consumers of culture often did not see the necessity to choose sides, but rather enjoyed the rich palette on offer.

Not Modernized: The Classic House Visit

Besides the institutions that have found a certain degree of academic attention, some more low-key activities have largely been left unconsidered, as their existence was considered self-evident. Nonetheless they constitute important elements of Eastern Mediterranean culture and social exchange and continued to remain important throughout the nineteenth century. The least spectacular activity, which was however perhaps also the most widespread, was the home visit between neighbors, families, and friends. It remained rather immune against Western fashions and followed locally established rituals and tastes.[1] While visits were certainly not exclusive to this part of the world, the account of a German woman who migrated to Smyrna can give us an impression of how unusual some of the conventions around the local form must have seemed to a Central European. Marie Louise Werwer, a native of the Ruhr region, married the representative of the Berlin Museums in West Asia, Carl Humann, and moved to Smyrna in the mid-1870s. Several of the local habits she describes to her German friends as unusual, either excessive or overly moderate according to her standards:

one is never without visits for more than three days.

These are not coffee visits as with us, people come, stay for an hour, if one is intimate, even longer; and one presents only a small cup of Turkish coffee with a little pastry and does not sit down at a table, but takes it in hand and drinks it up immediately. The servant waits with tray in hand until everyone has drunk up and receives the cups. In summer, only sweet pickles, all kinds of preserves are offered with water.

Another habit is to make visits in the evenings after dinner and to stay together until midnight – and even then, either coffee or water are offered – the local men do not fancy wine, only the Germans. But these visits are repeated so often that overall it runs up expenses.[2]

The nigh continuous presence of neighbors and family friends in the house; the duration and repetitiveness of the visits; the rather limited choice of food and drinks served and the haste with which they were consumed; reservations on drinking alcohol in family circles; and

---

[1] Couroucli, "Se rendrer chez l'autre."
[2] L. Humann to Marie Pöppinghaus, Smyrna 7 Dec. 1876, in Schulte, *Carl Humann*, 49.

different rules as to when to sit and when to stand – these conventions might not have universally unnerved all visitors from the far side of the Mediterranean, as the rules varied and continue to do so greatly in Europe, but they did not fit into what was considered common courtesy in Werwer's local Westphalia. Nonetheless, rather than imposing imported rules, she adapted to local expectations of sociability, as later sources reveal. Overall it seems the institution of home visits was not much affected by trends from abroad, although the furniture considered appropriate for guests changed.[3] The spread of urban infrastructure worked in its favor; gaslights at least on the major roads and more well paved streets worked to facilitate late night visits even beyond the immediate neighborhood. On the other hand, more attractive streets invited the port city residents not only to pass longer distances for visits, but especially to forsake the visits altogether for the sake of strolling around in the evening.

Celebrating the City and the Countryside: The Corso and the Picnic

Another leisure practice that continued to exist but decisively changed character was the picnic. With the coming of railways, excursions could have a wider radius and accommodate more participants and also less mobile ones who would have shied away from a long ride on horseback. The urban notables with large lands in the countryside sometimes opened their estates to groups or school classes. Major and semi-formal excursions were announced in newspapers. The *Smyrna Mail* of 1862, for example, reported on the picnic excursions of both the Buca and the Burnabad communities, before they returned to the city for the winter season, when indoor theater and opera resumed. The Buca residents traveled together by train to Cumaovası, which would also be the destination of the upcoming excursion from Seydiköy (now Gaziemir).[4] By undertaking picnic tours by train, the day-trippers could also demonstrate their modernity and show that it was not simply an economic necessity, but also allowed for the enjoyment of landscapes previously beyond easy access.

In the chapter on the quays, the widespread habit of strolling up and down the main street together with family or friends, dressed as well as

[3] See Chapter 17, pp. 276–281.   [4] *Smyrna Mail*, 7 Oct. 1862.

one can, stopping to greet neighbors and colleagues along the way, or to consume or observe something, has already been mentioned. The tradition's names of "corso" or "volta" mark it as an adaption from the Italian shore of the Mediterranean. While promenades were not an invention of the nineteenth century, they for a long time lacked a proper stage. An area wide enough to avoid having constantly to watch one's step, without too much uneven or dirty ground that could unpleasantly interrupt one's preoccupations, but with enough movement to not get bored, and offering a number of different vistas – such a place was rare in the cramped and hilly port cities before urban renewal began. And yet, the concept existed from early on, as already one of the earliest Smyrniote newspapers complains of the bad condition of the quays, which does not allow for casual strolls.[5] The locals nonetheless made do with the Quais Anglais, as the only slightly longer, regularized, and public section of the waterfront, despite the many impositions on it by commerce and the waterside coffeehouses on stilts. Galata-Pera society meanwhile chose to stroll in the company of the dead: The small Muslim graveyard off the Grande Rue overlooking the Golden Horn (Petit Champ des Morts or Tepebaşı) or the large Christian graveyards at the end of the Grande Rue (Grand Champ des Morts or Taksim) were the main strolling grounds even before the municipality had the gravestones removed and the respective areas officially turned into municipal parks in 1879. Together they made up the only larger green areas within easy walking distance that did not necessitate a steep downhill climb from Pera. While a *corso* did take place on the Galata quays once they had been paved and widened around the turn of the century, the preferred upper-class promenades remained the two former graveyards on top of the hill.

In Smyrna and soon after in Salonica, the quays offered the preferred sites for promenades, as they combined spaciousness, regularity, length, evenness, solidity, relative cleanliness, a fresh breeze, and varying vistas of the ships docked or anchored. They thus provided the seemingly perfect stage for this highly diverse popular spectacle, allowed for it to grow to a new dimension, and thus propelled it into modernity. With the addition of gas streetlights, the *corso* extended into the late hours, although after a certain time, families disappeared

---

[5] *Courrier de Smyrne*, 29 March 1829.

and the quays were then dominated by men in search of nightlife pleasure.[6]

The *corso* was the most urban pursuit among all the different pastimes. It could be enjoyed independently of income and personal relations, as it simply made use of the city's public space, but cultural capital of various forms helped participants make the most of it. Well-connected members of urban society could display their fortunes through expensive dress; their fortuitous family situation by showing off spouse and children; their role in society by public conversations and interactions; or their wit and sociability by entertaining others. The *corso* was also not simply a means to itself. If it enjoyed broad participation, the location did not impose too drastic limitations, and its participants used their imagination, it could serve as a platform from which to start all kinds of activities. The aforementioned clam-diving off of Smyrna's quays may serve as one of the most creative examples. The more obvious concomitant activities entailed flirting (as this was, just as the previously popular excursions to the Sweet Waters of Asia and Europe, an occasion to meet members of the opposite sex beyond family contacts), eating, drinking, and enjoying music. All of these were possible either through street vendors and musicians or by entering a café in the vicinity of the *corso* parcours.

The character of the *corso* varied greatly over time. It could be anything from a rather boring tour around town to the beginning of a long and exhausting nightlife escapade. Initially the stroll around the large graveyard beyond Pera seems to have offered access only to a limited number of related activities. Even after the Crimean War had led to more intense movement of people and cultural exchange with oversea locales, social life possibilities seem only to have diversified slowly in the capital. Jean Henri Abdolonim Ubicini complained about his stay in Constantinople in the 1850s:

There is not much variety of amusement. In winter three days a week theater, occasionally a dinner or ball to which only the most accomplished merchants and bankers are invited, occasionally soirées are held at home. On summer evenings, one goes out to the Grand Champ to eat an ice cream while listening to Tyrolean or Hungarian music. Unlike Smyrna, there are no

---

[6] *Journal de Salonique*, 18 Dec. 1902.

casinos, literary societies, concerts and society balls, not even a simple reading salon exists.⁷

Thus Ubicini only undertook the walk faute de mieux, wishing himself away from what in his opinion was banal and boring popular culture, and hoped for more prestigious or intellectually challenging activities, but did not find them in 1850s Pera in contrast to Smyrna. Thus the latter was not only on the forefront of commercial integration into the West, but also into its consumption patterns.

The situation for Pera seems to only have decisively changed toward the 1870s. Edmondo de Amicis' description of the Grand Champ shows quite a different picture from that traced by Ubicini twenty years earlier. He speaks of a "human flood" pouring out over the Grand Champ on Sunday evenings and heading for the coffeehouses, beerhouses, and gardens across from the Taksim Barracks.⁸ What de Amicis observes here is the formation of a middle-class leisure culture that is quite distinct from earlier more down-to-earth pubs catering to sailors or workers. In his description, the *corso* has become little more than a feeder for the beer gardens awaiting customers, which will be dealt with in later chapters. The embassies remained important sites, especially for the high society balls and gossip about them, but the middle classes could now enjoy themselves independently of them.⁹

But despite its name, there was nothing that necessarily limited the *corso* to the immigrants, the Christians, or their quarters. Théophile Gautier mentions Beyazıt Square as a site of strolling and flirtation in the 1830s and Direklerarası, also at the heart of the old city, evolved in a similar way and at roughly the same time as Taksim. As one of the wider roads in good condition even before the *Tanzimat*, it attracted large crowds for strolls. Little by little, the surroundings filled up with coffeehouses and subsequently more elaborate forms of entertainment.¹⁰

Following the growth of the cities, suburbanization seriously threatened the *corso* as a single space for all social classes. The *Journal de Salonique* of 1902 for example recommended the avenue from the

---

⁷ Jean Henri Abdolonim Ubicini, quoted from Cezar, *XIX. Yüzyıl Beyoğlusu*, 410. For similar laments from foreigners visiting Constantinople in the first half of the nineteenth century, see Mestyan, "A Garden with Mellow Fruits," 104 fn. 3.
⁸ Cezar, *XIX. Yüzyıl Beyoğlusu*, 410–411.   ⁹ *Levant Herald*, 13 Jan. 1873.
¹⁰ Georgeon, "Le ramadan à Istanbul," 70–79.

White Tower, where the quays strollers would turn back, toward the suburbs of Campagna and Kalamaria, although the author admitted it was too bright in summer and too slippery in winter. Concerning the crowded quays, where in the writer's words elegance rubbed shoulders with sloppiness, the strollers did not undertake their outing out of conviction, but out of ennui, rather constantly looked at passersby or the arriving ships. The pleasure of walking here was also restrained due to the odor of the nearby fish market hall. A quick drink at the northern or southern end of the quays was usually followed by the family's return home. The journalist thus also hinted at the idea that this ritual, which had had its heyday in the 1870s as a celebration of a nascent outdoor culture, had maybe lost its function and significance.[11]

The Greatest Party of the Century

Despite the longevity of older pastimes and the high popularity of the *corso*, the nineteenth century and especially its second half brought an unprecedented expansion in entertainment possibilities. The Paris Commune of 1871 has been claimed to be the biggest party of the nineteenth century.[12] And yet, when one delves into the plethora of memoirs, letters, and newspaper columns from Smyrna, Salonica, and Constantinople, one is tempted to challenge the Parisians' claim as geographically biased. One reads over and over about the countless balls on the shores of the Eastern Mediterranean that lasted into the morning; the theaters crowded so badly they came close to collapse (or occasionally did); and of the social vices performed there that threatened the future of entire generations. The Levant was of course no social utopia, but it was more culturally diverse than even Paris. Entertainment practices could both mitigate or stress preexisting divides.

As already mentioned, Smyrna spearheaded the development. The West Anatolian city and especially its *Frangomahalla* had already had a hedonist reputation in earlier centuries. The nineteenth-century practices and places of pleasure however were different, because they no longer resembled introverted or semi-open community institutions.

---

[11] *Journal de Salonique*, 18 Dec. 1902.
[12] Karl Marx, quoted in Grindon, "Revolutionary Romanticism," 216.

They unabashedly marked the public space and most importantly stood in constant dialogue and exchange with other parts of the Mediterranean, Europe, and occasionally beyond.

After the Eastern Mediterranean had recovered from the violence, economic depression, and natural disasters that had marked the end of the eighteenth century and after Constantinople-centered hegemony had become eclipsed in the age of the gunboat, it seems the Smyrniotes were among the first not only to adapt to the new paradigms of the nineteenth century, but also to embrace them. Travelers of the first half of the nineteenth century such as Anton von Prokesch Osten and J. O. Hanson, when contrasting the social atmosphere of Constantinople and Smyrna almost always favored the latter for its egalitarian, open, and pleasure-oriented forms of communications, whereas the imperial center came across as hierarchical, scheming, and stiff.[13] One typical remark, establishing the Western Anatolian city's reputation as Paris of the Levant: "What one finds at Smyrna is all the appeal of the Orient and the comfort of Europe, the varying spectacle of Muslim populations and the salons of Paris."[14] Salonica's social life would find mention only much later.

Immediately after Smyrna's disaster of 1797, when a brawl between janissaries and Cephalonians – who had tried to enter an acrobats' performance without paying – had sparked off major riots, the upper-class residents of foreign origin had founded the European Casino as a place of entertainment. While it excluded people of local origin, sailors, and soldiers, for its limited audience it became the site of festive social occasions. It encompassed several smaller conversation rooms, salons for newspaper reading and billiards, and a 250 square meter ballroom that could house 500 or according to another account even 1,000 guests in the 1820s and 1830s. It patronized a local amateur theater group in another building. It was soon copied by the Greek Casino and the Cercle Levantin.[15]

Why did Smyrniotes turn to Western-style entertainment and in particular to the ball and the theater already at the beginning of the century, even before steamships facilitated exchange; before the urban environment contained any modern Occidentalist forms; and before

---

[13] Schmitt, *Levantiner*, 81; Mansel, *Levant*, 42–44.
[14] *L'Illustration*, Dec. 1852, quoted in Kontente, *Smyrne et l'occident*, 493.
[15] Kontente, *Smyrne et l'occident*, 45; Schmitt, *Levantiner*, 422, 423; Mansel, *Levant*, 43–44.

the economic relations had become significant? It can only be explained by a strong desire to embrace what was considered to be progressive in that day and age. A letter to the editor from 1829 affirms this. Defending the Buca amateur theater group against condescending remarks by the *Courrier de Smyrne* in its previous edition, the letter writer, who partook in amateur performances himself, claimed that in a city without public schools, libraries, literary cabinets, or any other form of free public education, one should be thankful if the local youths chose to study and perform enlightened dramas (rather than partake in local contemporary Greek music and dance).[16] In other words, the letter writer and others of his mentality desired a much stronger immersion into Western European intellectual activity, but made do with what was on offer and what was easier to realize, that is, a few dilettante attempts to perform grand theater.

The *Courrier* had claimed that the Buca company members had played two French plays, *Mme Bertrand* and *Merlin*, without being able to understand or pronounce French, as they were obviously Grecophone.[17] However when they next played a tragedy, *Artaxerxes*, the newspaper found the translation into modern Greek vulgar.[18] But exactly this kind of amateurish experimentation despite upper society's highbrow snobbish criticism set the stage for the Eastern Mediterranean's century-long experiment into Western ways. Things were tried out and if need be adapted; mastery of languages, trends, and the necessary technical infrastructure often did not match up to the standards of observers who would compare the local drama performances with those in France or Italy. Due to their zest for things from beyond, the consumers and amateur activists of Western leisure persevered nonetheless. As in the initial dispute about the Buca theater group, the audience could be pleased by the best one could get, even though many had a sense there could better. Several (though far from all) commentators, both from abroad and from the region stated that local musicians, theaters, and the technicians and actors they attracted were not quite up to the standard of the times.[19] In fact, far from specializing on drama, they often kept up other skills, such as ventriloquism and

---

[16] *Courrier de Smyrne*, 12 July 1829. Beyru argues that performing in the Buca suburb in summer picked up on the ancient Greek tradition of open-air performances; Beyru, *19. Yüzyılda İzmir'de Yaşam*, 234.

[17] *Courrier de Smyrne*, 5 July 1829.   [18] *Courrier de Smyrne*, 19 July 1829.

[19] Alpargın, *Istanbuls theatralische Wendezeit*, 34.

magic, or even services outside the entertainment business, in order to make a living.[20] This however did not diminish the audience's interest.

It is perhaps no coincidence that Buca is one of the first places mentioned where locals engage with overseas culture despite an obvious language gap. While downtown Smyrna might have seemed liberal to arrivals from Constantinople, the Casino reveals its obvious ethnic and social dividing lines. During the summer months, possibly as long as from May to October, well-to-do families would retreat to their country houses in the rural suburbs. Within the smaller population and the more informal atmosphere of village life and without institutions such as the consulates and the casinos, social and ethnic borders were not as stiffly observed. In the other prominent village cum summer resort, Burnabad, Paul Calligas, visiting his place of birth in 1844, observed how in local festivities the musicians would play both Greek *Syrtos* dances and pieces from other parts of Europe, an interaction that obviously was only possible in a place where the residents were more relaxed about cultural hybridization then at the European Casino.[21]

With the growing population and rising commercial exchange by the mid-nineteenth century, entertainment possibilities both multiplied and diversified. While the social balls remained the backbone binding middle and upper classes together, there were now more institutionalized highbrow forms of distraction as well. The *Smyrna Mail* of 1864 lists them for the benefit of the British subjects recently settled due to the newly established railway: See the "head of the Amazon in the Barrack"; visit the Opera at Place d'Opéra; visit the Theatro Evterpo on Rose Street; "participate in the German Singing Society that meet at the English Club on Frank St."; inspect the "Cabinet of Medals of Louis Meyer," "Svoboda's Photo Gallery," or the "Gallery of Count Bentiviglio d'Aragon" at the French Consulate; go to the racecourse out of town; help at the institution of the Deaconesses, "a celebrated school for Young Ladies"; become a member of the

---

[20] Beyru, *19. Yüzyılda İzmir'de Yaşam*, 232.
[21] Kontente, *Smyrne et l'occident*, 479. Local Greek music apparently did not have a good reputation in the Francophone public. The letter writer mentioned believed he could convince the newspaper readers by claiming that the youths, if forbidden to pursue dramatic arts, would go for Greek whirling dances and the "discordant harmony of nasal voices of our Greek singers"; *Courrier de Smyrne*, 12 July 1829.

Masonic lodges, the English Club, the Smyrna Literary and Scientific Institute, the European Casino, the Cercle Levantine, the Greek Casino, Library and Reading Room, etc.[22] Pastimes thus included some that the letter writer had demanded some thirty-five years earlier: The Literary and Scientific Institute on 19 Frank Street for example was open every day from 9 a.m. to 10 p.m., offering English and local papers, and occasionally hosting lectures and classes. There was also a self-proclaimed Academy of Anatolia for Archaeology and Geology, and a Literary Repository at Han Barbaresque (Cezayir Hanı), which imported French and English books, newspapers, and other related objects. These were just the initiatives aiming at the Anglophone public, ignoring the much broader activities of for example the Greek-, French-, and Italian-speaking community. Such projects could obviously be short-lived, especially as they often relied on the initiative of a select few. Nonetheless they give an impression of what was possible and often continued to exist in different incarnations.

Compared to these lively and after 1797 usually peaceful pursuits in Smyrna (except perhaps at major holidays such as Easter, when the local media complained of drunken and aggressive lower-class Greek men in the streets),[23] the Constantinople leisure activities were much less inventive. The ambassadors did host balls, including masked balls for Carnival.[24] But J. M. Tancoigne reported in the early 1810s that these took place outside the embassies (which had not yet been rebuilt as stone seraglios) in rented houses of Franks. It was necessary to have janissaries stationed at these occasions, as even these upper-class festivities could degenerate into drunken brawls, an embarrassment for the Westerners, as Tancoigne stated. There was also not much original input yet by the residents of overseas origin into the coffeehouse culture. According to Tancoigne, one had the choice of either visiting the Greek- or Armenian-run sleazy bars frequented by Ionian Islands sailors or, as most upper-class Perotes preferred to do, stick to the classic Muslim-run coffeehouses, where drinking local-style coffee, sherbet, or smoking a *shisha* were the choices.[25] The great fascination the Naum Theater enjoined around the middle of the century can perhaps be better understood in light of the dearth of other

---

[22] *Smyrna Mail*, 23 Sept. 1862.   [23] *Courrier de Smyrne*, 23. Apr. 1830.
[24] *Courrier de Smyrne*, 29 March 1829.
[25] Tancoigne, *Voyage à Smyrne*, 89–96.

entertainment possibilities. Constantinople leisure practices only seriously changed in the second half and especially the last quarter of the century. Until then Smyrna remained the trendsetter.

The Season and Its Festivities As Interethnic Site

For members of the middle to upper levels of the Smyrniote, Salonician, and Constantinople bourgeoisie, both attending and organizing large-scale gatherings were serious obligations during the "season." The season extended from Christmas until Lent, coming to a finale in the Carnival Week. As the dates for Lent in all cities under study here were observed by the majority according to the Eastern rules, all of January, February, March, and sometimes even all of April could be the "season." While activities could be various, except that they were restricted to indoors due to the climate and time of year, most attention focused on the balls. Balls, both masked and open, were central events for the big clubs or casinos as well as middle- and upper-class families.[26] There was a hierarchy among the different events. A successful ball had to be exclusive and open, hierarchical and egalitarian at the same time. A ball had to attract noticeable crowds, but also had to lend its participants the feeling of taking part in an event limited to an elite they formed a part of. It had to create opportunities beyond usual social, ethnic, and gender stratification, but needed to avoid transgressions considered unpleasant or in violation of social, ethnic, and gender status. Besides these there were numerous more exclusive gatherings. Carl Humann, husband of the wife cited earlier and as museum director a member of Smyrna's high society, relates to a German colleague his social obligations on a typical week at the end of January:

Yesterday night there was big dinner at France's. Today 6 to 9 dance soirée in the club, day after Emperor's Birthday, Saturday dinner at Salzani's, in the evening dance at Weber's, Wednesday dinner at Clemm's etc. My wife and I today set up the list of four dinners for 12 people (each), that is beyond innocent fun![27]

---

[26] Dimitriadis, "Making of an Ottoman Port-City," 161; Schwan, *Erinnerungen eines Konsuls*, 52, 53.

[27] France = the French consul general's; club = Sporting Club; Salzanis = long-established Smyrniote businessmen family of Napolitan origin and French nationality; Weber = probably the director of the Smyrna branch of the Ottoman

Social obligations were multiple, both national and cosmopolitan. One of the Humann's four dinners was for the German community, another for the consular corps. Such social obligations were time consuming, possibly excessive, and far from uniform. Carl Humann states that his family's first dinner of the season a week later was followed by singing, dancing, and merrymaking until 2:30 at night.[28] Giving a private ball, as Humanns did when German warships anchored in Smyrna for a month, could easily inflate the number of guests to 180.[29] The various social skills one had to master, depending on the occasion, included dining, small talk, but also stiff representation.[30] Young people were expected to pass through dance schools to prepare themselves for such occasions, and these were in turn judged on whether their teachers, often of Italian or other overseas origins, could transmit the latest fashionable dances from abroad.[31]

By contrast, once the summer had begun, downtown entertainment activities practically came to a standstill. Social life then concentrated around the villages where the middle- and upper-class city dwellers had their summer residences or rented rooms for the hot months, that is, in Smyrna's Burnabad or Buca, Salonica's Kalamaria, or Constantinople's upper Bosporus or Islands. Not even a concert by a world star such as Friedrich Liszt could attract more than a rudimentary audience in this period.[32]

Toward the end of the century, such practices were firmly established and widespread in all cities under study here. An important site of semi-open social intercourse was the diverse clubs. In Salonica, some of the more elitist organizations one could aspire to were the Cercle de Salonique, the Cercle des Négociants, the Club des Intimes, also the Salonica Lawn Tennis and Croquet Club and the local Sporting Club, elitist associations dominated by Franks, but also by several Sephardic names, including the richest families, the Modianos and the Allatinis.[33] There were numerous organizations for different welfare purposes, associations of former students of different high schools and other

---

Bank; Friedrich Clemm = merchant and consul of Denmark and Sweden; Carl Humann to Kern, Smyrna 25 Jan. 1893, in Schulte, *Carl Humann*, 178.
[28] Carl Humann to Hiller, Smyrna 1 Feb. 1893, in Schulte, *Carl Humann*, 178.
[29] Carl Humann to Kern, Smyrna, 16 May 1895, in Schulte, *Carl Humann*, 181.
[30] Carl Humann to Kern, Smyrna 9 Feb. 1893, in Schulte, *Carl Humann*, 178.
[31] *Stamboul*, 7 Jan. 1890.   [32] *Österreichische Zuschauer*, 28 July 1847.
[33] Anastassiadou, "Sports d'élite et élites sportives," 146, 147.

organizations that seemingly brought people together for a specific purpose, but lent plenty of opportunities for social gatherings.

Despite the increase in public venues, the most prestigious social events were still society balls. The *Journal de Salonique* gives an impression of what the city's middle and upper classes could expect from the festive winter season of 1895/1896: the Italian Charity Ball at Hotel Olympia, which was draped in "the colors of all nations," in the presence of Italian Navy officers, visited by the *vali*, several other Ottoman officials, an Italian counter-admiral, and most of the Salonica rich families; an amateur theater performance by the officers of a British Navy ship with several different consuls and their wives, leading foreign employees and major businessmen and families present; a celebration by the young ladies of the Allatini family for their friends, also visited by many officers; the welfare ball by La Charité, an association headed by several women of Jewish background, which witnessed dancing until five in the morning; a farewell dinner by the Habsburg community for the Austro-Hungarian navy squadron in a large room at La Turquie; La Fraternité's ball at Hotel Imperial, which was considered a success; the Serbian School charity ball held on St. Sava's Day, honored by a donation of 70 Turkish liras by the Sultan for its needy students and attended by the *vali*'s son, the chief of police, and several of the upper-class families of Salonica; a Bulgarian theater event as fundraiser for Bulgarian primary schools, during which the Bulgarian schoolchildren led the present Ottoman military officers, the consuls, and the city's oligarchs to tears; a successful great masked ball by the city's major families at Olympia; a charity lottery organized by the Soeurs de la Charité for St. Vincent de Paul's.[34] Naturally the paper would only list the biggest or most prestigious, so one must add to these listed events a multitude of others of a more private or more middle-class nature.

The capital had definitively shed its earlier reluctance to embrace the new forms of socializing. The season was now also an intense, sometimes excessive, and diverse experience. The year 1900 for example opened with various New Year's parties, including the one by the Union Française, which witnessed dancing until three o'clock in the morning and more socializing until seven. The Société de Bienfaisance des Adolescentes israélites organized a charity concert in the Union

---

[34] *Journal de Salonique*, 9 Dec. 1895 until 13 Feb. 1896.

Française, supposedly visited by "800 people of the finest families." It began with the French and Ottoman national anthem, followed by a German and a French comedy, piano music, and dance. La Società Operaia di Mutuo Soccorso, the leading organization catering to patriotic Italians, hosted an evening of theater, music, and dance by its philodramatic society. The Société musicale de Constantinople or Association for Chamber Music performed at the German social club, the Teutonia, as did a renowned pianist; a Greek theater company was to enact Bergère at the Odeon; the Cirque de Péra vaudeville troupe would replace for one month the circus of Pierantoni, while at the Théâtre de Petit Champ a Viennese operetta troupe was visiting. The dance teacher Psalty held a children's ball at the Union, the Café concert du Commerce announced a concert by the sisters Lindau and the extravagant Hedwig Zunkel; the Dutch ambassador took the musician Elise Peschken to a reception by the Sultan; the second grand orchestra concert of the year would be performed by the aforementioned Société musicale, while the Pera Palace Hotel was refurbishing its basement floor in expectation of the traditional supper after the grand balls that the season would soon bring to its halls.[35] In addition to organizations similar to those listed for Salonica, various Masonic lodges and the Maccabi Association would be among those hosting major balls.[36]

If one only studied the news of these social events, one would be led to believe that the Sultan, the Ottoman bureaucracy, the various organized ethnic communities, the oligarchic families, and the foreign military and consular representatives were all united via an endless dance, showing mutual respect for, and solidarity with one another. Nonetheless, in the development from the times of the European Casino, the aim of which had been to isolate the Europeans from a distrusted larger society, we see that a definite transformation had taken place not only in size and number of occasions and venues to celebrate *alla franga*. Celebrations and events were more transparent and it seems that part of their very purpose was now to bridge the national and ethnic divides within the city. Going through both the Humanns' representational activities and the events listed for Salonica, we see the immense effort all sides must undertake to balance out and not discriminate against any relevant party. The Humanns must cater

[35] *Stamboul*, 1 until 8 Jan. 1900.   [36] *Stamboul*, 15 Jan. 1890, 5 Jan. 1911.

to the German community of Smyrna, besides accepting invitations by and inviting all major consul families, but also other important families such as the Salzanis. The Salonica local state dignitaries, such as the *vali* and his major officials must appear at practically every school ball, even of smaller communities such as the Serbs and Bulgarians, and even if those communities were often considered potential separatists. Foreign and Christian institutions were also obliged to show their respects to Ottoman state and Muslim representatives. When in 1903, (Gregorian) New Year and the first day of Ramadan coincided, the newspapers commented that this was fortunate, as New Year and Ramadan congratulatory visits between the consulates and local institutions could be paid reciprocally.[37] It is noteworthy that a large number of these social events were charity events and fundraisers. Most balls and some concerts and plays would serve some philanthropic purpose, every school and welfare organisation would organize one, and even visiting musicians and theater troupes were often obliged to give one performance for the benefit of a local orphanage, school, or other.[38]

For celebrations and events to serve as rituals of intercommunal reciprocity and respect, the growing proliferation of a common set of cultural forms was a prerequisite: Port city residents, no matter whether of Italian, Greek, Judeo-Spanish, Bulgarian, Armenian, French, or English background had in large numbers learned to dance the waltz, to follow theater developments, or to play instruments such as the piano. This common knowledge helped to bridge gaps, including those dictated by lacking language skills, for example if one did not understand the Italian or French theater plays, but also if one had difficulty finding a common language with one's dance partner, who could after all be a foreign naval officer only briefly in town.

The Muslim Role in the Great Party

Did Muslims form part of this colorful, but Occidentophile crowd? Yes and no. Some port city historians have marked the exclusion of

---

[37] *Journal de Salonique*, 1 Jan. 1903.
[38] Beyru, *19. Yüzyılda İzmir'de Yaşam*, 247–256. In Constantinople, both Ottoman and foreign theater troupes were obliged to donate a substantial portion of their returns to the imperial almhouse *Darülaceze*; see ZB 603/35, in *Arşiv Belgelerine göre Osmanlı'da Gösteri Sanatları*, 276–278.

Muslims as the racist, dark side of the late nineteenth-century order, and especially Alexandria with its British colonial rule and its traditional bias against the rural population seems to offer plenty of examples of such discrimination.[39] Such a systematic discrimination of Muslims is not visible in the regions still de facto ruled by the Ottomans. Muslims were certainly underrepresented as active and passive participants in the leisure activities based on Western models; however there were no principle rules against Muslims joining in. Occidentocentric pastimes were based on acquired cultural capital: One had to take dancing lessons, waste precious hours reading imported or translated literature in order to grasp what was happening on the theater stage, and learn how to behave, move, and make conversation, possibly from an educator one's family had arranged from abroad. These were efforts Muslims could undertake as well, but did not always choose, or only to some degree.

As an example of a Muslim's role in the great party, we can turn to the journals and household registers of Said Bey, which we know of thanks to the studies of Paul Dumont and François Georgeon. Said was a member of the High Council of Sanitation and in addition translated for the palace, taught French at the School of Economics, and Ottoman Turkish at the Imperial School. The upper-scale bureaucrat lived together with a family of six and several servants in the heart of the old city. During the week of February 11–17 1902, his routine included the following pastimes:

Monday 11 – Lunch in the bazaar, a desert of muhallebi; a shisha at Direklerarası; visiting neighbors in the evening, a *meddâh*'s performance
Tuesday 12 – Lunch at Gianni's [the Viennese Beerhouse on Grand Rue de Pera, MF]; Rakı at Sirkeci [the Train Station Quarter near the Bazaar, MF]
Wednesday 13 – Lunch at Tokatliyan [the Grand Hotel on Grand Rue de Pera, MF]; in the evening visiting neighbors
Thursday 14 – Lunch at Gianni's; in the evening Karagöz
Friday 15 – at Çalgılı Casino [café chantant, MF]
Saturday 16 – Pastry shop in Pera; Rakı at Tokatliyan's; Rakı elsewhere; visited Seyfeddin Bey; Greek Carnival in Pera
Sunday 17 – in Arifi's Kıraathane [a literary café on Divan Yolu, MF]; Arab music, in the evening Karagöz.[40]

---

[39] Mansel, *Levant*, 127–147.
[40] Dumont and Georgeon, "Un bourgeois d'Istanbul," 133.

Any attempts at pegging down Said Bey's cultural practices along the political dividing lines we are accustomed to in the study of late Ottoman history seem futile. Was he a traditionalist for listening to Arab music? But then what was he doing munching on a French-style pastry in the Frangomahalla? Was he perhaps a populist nationalist, as he went to see the lower-class popular shows of *karagöz*? In this case, why would he hang out among the elitist and international circles at Hotel Tokatliyan or visit the Christians' Carnival? If he was an Ottomanist modernizer or from among the super-Westernized deifying Parisian culture, why would he waste his time on storytellers and smoking *shisha* in the old city? While Said might well have embraced one of the popular worldviews of his time, his practices show that he managed to make use of a number of different social, ethnic, culinary, and linguistic registers. He also failed to conform to the grand opposition of old Istanbul as the seat of timeless tradition and Pera as the abode of progress. Instead, his work and leisure schedule show Said Bey's private carriage rushing back and forth across the bridges over the Golden Horn on an almost daily basis. His visit to the Greek Carnival in Pera shows that he is in principal open to the "season's" particular activities, although not as intimately integrated into them as the non-Muslim upper class was. The celebrations of the Muslim calendar took precedence, such as the outdoor evening entertainment during the month of Ramadan, Eid ul-Fitr at the end of Ramadan, Eid al-Adha (the Feast of Sacrifice), Ashure, but also the regional spring holiday of Hıdrellez (Ederlezi/St. George's Day). Said Bey's socializing is for the larger part male-centered, except for occasional exceptions, when he joins his wife and her visitors at home, or when his wife accompanies him to public events.[41] His reading expenses show him to equally enjoy French- and Turkish-language publications, the French local paper *Stamboul* as well as the Turkish *Sabah*, a *Grande Encyclopédie* ordered from France as well as many contemporary Turkish novels and some educational tracts, nothing particularly radical, but with a general curiosity to learn of the world and its affairs, without actually leaving Constantinople to travel.[42] The one thing we can state for sure from his records is that he was not a man of abstention or an ascetic, but someone who aimed to enjoy the myriad possibilities of

---

[41] Ibid, 138–143.
[42] Ibid, 127–181; see also Zerman, *Studying an Ottoman "Bourgeois" Family*.

Constantinople life at the beginning of the twentieth century. Overall, he personifies an attitude to readily engage with new influences without relinquishing what one is used to through tradition and sees no need to replace.[43]

One social occasion sticks out that saw a decisively different degree of participation according to religion: the social ball. While balls met opposition by some Christian clergy and laymen and laywomen due to too liberal mingling of the sexes, Muslims not so much opposed but by majority abstained from this activity. The ball was however not a bastion of Christians or non-Muslims. It was expected of high representatives such as governors to show themselves on such occasions, but not necessarily dance. We find only sparse mention of Muslim women ever attending such occasions. Said Bey's wife accompanying him to some embassy balls is one of those exceptions.[44]

But beyond mere presiding and representing, balls offered the possibility to transgress against prescribed ethnic rolls and limitations. For example, after the masked ball hosted by the Austrian ambassador for Carnival 1829, gossip abounded on the subject of two masked men in Arabic gowns who were rumored to be high members of the court.[45] Muslim notables were not limited to visiting balls; in some cases they also hosted them. An 1862 newspaper announcement records Yusuf Pasha's upcoming great ball at his residence in Burnabad.[46] Beyond such prestigious officeholders, Muslim men's way into the balls was more difficult. Refik Halid, growing up in Constantinople after the turn of the century, recounts how he was one of the few Muslim men among the 500 guests of the popular ball. He relates that this was less an event in itself, but rather a stepping-stone where adolescents premiered on the public stage hoping to find their way to the more elitist balls, to master dancing and social skills before moving up the social ladder.[47]

One is generally tempted to narrate the nineteenth century as an age of rising nationalist and imperialist attitudes, but studying leisure practices in the Eastern Mediterranean port cities does not confirm this. While the beginning of the century saw some extreme arrogance and intolerance against both overseas and local cultures respectively – one

---

[43] This attitude and its significance will receive more in-depth treatment in Part IV.
[44] Dumont and Georgeon, "Un bourgeois d'Istanbul," 143.
[45] *Courrier de Smyrne*, 29 March 1829. [46] *Smyrna Mail*, 28 Oct. 1862.
[47] Gülersoy, *Tepebaşı*, 58.

needs only to recall the statement that even bad performances of French theater plays are better than Greek dance – the fin-de-siècle port city residents seem to have been much more at ease with the manifest hybridity of their culture. *Intra muros* Constantinople during Ramadan had in the course of the nineteenth century mutated from a place where infidels were warned not to go, to a tourist attraction.[48] Both Pera's Odeon and Smyrna's Sporting Club, besides receiving French itinerant theater troupes, would also house performances of Dikran Çuhacıyan's Turkish-language operetta classic *Leblebici Horhor Ağa* by the Benliyan operetta group.[49] The prestigious Salonica Café Cristal saw a Turkish orchestra perform Oriental music during Ramadan 1902 that supposedly received much applause even by the non-Muslim customers.[50] Faiz Efendi Kapıcı was purportedly equally well received when his compositions, including waltzes, Oriental pieces, and Mazurka were performed in Salonica's prestigious Olympia.[51]

While ethnic prejudice will have lingered on, it must be noted that within the nineteenth century, a transformation had taken place from the semi-apartheid house rules of Smyrna's European Casino, which had banned all but those of European descent from entering, past a fairly liberal mixing of non-Muslims from the middle of the century onward, until both elite and middle class Muslims participated in this central ritual of urban society.

From Kahvehane to Highlife

In the century after Tancoigne's and the half-century after Ubicini's visit, entertainment habits in the Eastern Mediterranean world and Constantinople in particular had changed dramatically. Going out no longer had the air of seedy, morally questionable, and potentially dangerous activity, but was increasingly believed to be one of the quintessential means of joy in the modern urban world not only for seamen and simple laborers, but also for the port cities' middle and upper classes. The waterside institutions were no longer restricted to

---

[48] Georgeon, "Le ramadan à Istanbul," 87.
[49] *Stamboul*, 4 Jan. 1911; Beyru, *19. Yüzyılda İzmir'de Yaşam*, 250.
[50] *Journal de Salonique*, 11 Dec. 1902. See also Dimitriadis, "Making of an Ottoman Port-City," 166.
[51] *Journal de Salonique*, 6 Feb. 1896.

frowned-upon watering holes for Ionian islanders, but had become the site of the respective cities' foremost social clubs, hotels, and restaurants. The theater and the ball had evolved from quaint activities by people of foreign origin or with exotic tastes to activities indispensable for the acquirement and maintenance of social and cultural capital. At the beginning of the twentieth century, a further step in the evolvement of the entertainment sector was underway. Going out to dance, drink, and socialize was increasingly detached from the social restraints of family, community, and the urban public. Instead of the seasonal, extremely ritualized, and socially normed balls, individuals and their chosen acquaintances would expect the opportunity for hedonistic, self-fulfilling, and unlimited enjoyment whenever they felt like it. Precursors of the more excessive entertainment culture of the 1920s can be noticed as early as the zero years.

Several establishments, such as the Brasserie Aleko, the Ice Skating Palace, or the Winter Garden at the Petit Champ advertised their performances as "highlife." Highlife has been defined as a new, distinctly urban, and metropolitan form of entertainment emerging at the beginning of the twentieth century, encompassing a new, more lively tempo: "The modern world had moved from the sense of rationalized restraint to a quest for experience which could be found only in an exciting urban world. The sense of liberation emerged from and in conflict with organization and efficient production."[52] One would have to investigate in some more detail whether in a city with little heavy industry such as Constantinople, expectations toward the stage were really the same as toward an "assembly line" of various interchangeable forms of spectacle, or whether the Perote audience had a different understanding of the term. If the program is any indication, the *Mandolinata* performed at Aleko's and the purportedly Viennese (but possibly Bohemian) orchestra playing at the Winter Garden from 4 to 7 p.m. and from 9 p.m. to midnight, off hand do not seem too different from what one could have heard there twenty years earlier. But the local press promised, very much in the wording of the overseas trend, that at the Winter Garden one would forget to eat and drink because of all the excitement (including pieces from *Mme Butterfly*). The length of performances possibly indicates new expectations by the audience. The Ice Skating Palace promised that its band would play

[52] Erenberg, *Steppin' Out*, 209.

three sets of three hours. Other possibilities of paid entertainment included the cinema in the adjacent amphitheater, the Variété offering Greek theater, and the Kataklum Variété on Hamalbaşı Avenue, just outside the British Embassy, where supposedly Montmartre-based musicians performed.[53] Individualist hedonism and excess were on the rise on the eve of the Ottoman long decade of war and dissolution.

[53] *Stamboul*, 2, 3, 5 Jan. 1911.

9 | Staging Europeanness
The Rise of the Eastern Mediterranean Opera

Of all the new or changing possibilities to pass time, one activity stands out because of its particular claim to represent Western civilizational progress: theater and especially opera.

Smyrna and the Beginning of Opera and Modern Theater in the Levant

The emergence of opera had been noticed in the Eastern Mediterranean from the beginning onward. In 1675, the genre, popular in Italy and other countries since around 1600, had caught the attention of Mehmed IV. For his sons' circumcision ceremony, he inquired in Venice whether it would be possible to send an opera company for the occasion. At the time, the plan failed, as transporting a whole opera troupe plus equipment by sea over such a long distance was considered logistically too challenging.[1] But even in this early period, the Smyrna theater aficionados were more flexible and creative than the Constantinople court in bringing Western dramas to their shore. As early as 1654 or 1657, theater plays were regularly enacted during the winter season. Among them was Pierre Corneille's *Nicomède* that premiered in 1651 within the French consulate, an ancient story situated in nearby Anatolia. Such performances behind consulate walls as well as open air performances by the waterside, presumably by amateurs, continued into the next century.[2]

By then, the court undertook a more serious attempt at inviting a professional opera troupe. Selim III had received regular reports about opera from his ambassadors. His representative to London was honored by a special composition dedicated to him. In 1793 Selim managed to have an opera performed at the court. Nonetheless at least

---

[1] Aracı, *Naum Tiyatrosu*, 32.
[2] Beyru, *19. Yüzyılda İzmir'de Yaşam*, 232; Sevinçli, *İzmir'de Tiyatro*, 9.

one court scribe complained about the new style of music, claiming that it gave him a headache.[3] But just as with urban renewal, changes at the court were rather a reaction to what was happening in wider circles of society than part of an avant-garde. Granted, at least since Abdülmecid and his newly built Dolmabahçe Theater, all sultans had custom-built theater stages, including at Abdülhamid's preferred palace Yıldız, even though performances were not public and limited to some court dignitaries, the imperial family, or even the Sultan alone. But rather than fostering a development from which society at large could benefit, quite often the sultans simply invited renowned touring musicians and drama troupes that were in town anyway to their court theater for a special performance. In this way, they sanctioned the consumption of the imported styles, but rather than actively promoting it, simply fed off what local urban society's demand and the musicians' and dramatists' readiness to get on the road provided.[4] In 1856, when in need of a new head of the *Mızıka-yı Hümayun* (imperial military music band and school), Abdülmecid simply snatched the Pera Naum Theater's music director. Some later stages, such as the Gedikpaşa or the Petit Champ Theaters, were founded by court musicians or dramatists, but these did not bring unique skills unavailable outside the court to a wider audience. Instead, the court bureaucracy supported these entrepreneurs against competitors from the local urban society, as they knew, trusted, and favored them.

Tours by foreign professional drama groups catering to commoner audiences are attested from roughly the same time as Selim's court premiere. For example, the Austrian theater company Rebellio is mentioned to have enacted a pantomime in March 1797 in Smyrna.[5] What is more, even without foreign professionals, Smyrniotes continued for quite some time to be self-sufficient in drama. While it is difficult to say anything more precise on the seventeenth-century opera performers, we know an amateur troupe had formed in Smyrna in 1775 and even possessed its own venue that was outfitted as a proper theater, including boxes for the audience, until the building burned down in 1797. However their performances were not always convincing, nor did the audience always appreciate their efforts. Following the fire, the Smyrna amateurs refurbished a large room in the so-called Madama Hanı

[3] Aracı, *Naum Tiyatrosu*, 31–34. [4] Sevengil, *Türk Tiyatrosu Tarihi*, vol. III, 3.
[5] Sevinçli, *İzmir'de Tiyatro*, 10.

(the han owned by the widowed Baroness de Hochepied) under the patronage of the European Casino. In 1824 a new generation of amateur theater performers opened their own proper theater building. They generally received good reviews by locals and visitors.[6]

The professionalization however began more through supply than demand, as sources attest that Italian touring actors and actresses became increasingly common from the 1830s onward. An initiative for a theater building for professionals in Smyrna began in 1834, as foreign drama troupes found no appropriate venue and came to the conclusion they had best build one themselves. From among them, Tobias Quagliardi claimed in the local papers that he would build a dedicated building on Frank Street for visiting Italian troupes at his own expenses, but asked for subscriptions to future performances in his house to support the initiative. Whether this attempt was frowned on by the authorities, was simply mismanaged, or an outright scam is not clear, however Quagliardi's theater was never realized.[7] The Euterpe Theater was the first professional, state-of-the-art theater. It opened the same year as Constantinople's Naum Theater in 1841, even some weeks earlier, and had 300 or according to other claims 400 seats and two rows of boxes.[8] It focused on Italian opera and French drama, but intermittently also opened its stage to magicians, ventriloquists, or solo music performances. Hans Christian Andersen, arriving in Smyrna in 1841, commented positively on the performances of *La Reine du seize ans* and *Les premiers amours* in the Euterpe Theater, as did Gérard de Nerval two years later, who watched a Donizetti opera by Italian performers. Gustave Flaubert echoed their impressions nine years later when seeing the French-language dramas *Passé Minuit*, *La Seconde Année*, *Indiana*, and *Charlemagne* performed there. However, some locals complained that the boxes were not comfortable enough and the Italian engineer Luigi Storari even claimed that the Smyrniotes were ashamed of their theater.[9]

By 1862, the Euterpe had been joined by the Italian Melodrama Theater and more importantly, by what the *Smyrna Mail* a bit presumptuously called the Opera, but was otherwise mostly referred to simply as the Grand Theater or more precisely as the Cammarano

---

[6] Beyru, *19. Yüzyılda İzmir'de Yaşam*, 230–235.   [7] Ibid., 236.
[8] Ibid., 238; Sevinçli, *İzmir'de Tiyatro*, 10.
[9] Beyru, *19. Yüzyılda İzmir'de Yaşam*, 237–240; Sevinçli, *İzmir'de Tiyatro*, 6.

Theater. Cammarano had been the name of the entrepreneur who had collected donations from the local oligarchs in order to build a venue that could outshine the Euterpe. The engineer responsible for the construction was a certain Barbieri. From its opening on November 31, 1861 until February of the coming year, Verdi's *Macbeth* could be seen at the Cammarano. Situated on a lot adjacent to the British Consulate, it was three stories high, and contained seventeen boxes alone. This supposedly made it the largest theater in the Eastern Mediterranean region with the exception of Cairo. However, it remained mostly empty until 1864, when Adelaide Ristori came from Alexandria to play *Medea*. In the following years, the venue's impresario changed often. Names known are Rival, Parmeggani, and Lebruns, which indicate that the theater remained dominated by arrivals from overseas. Besides mostly Italian traveling troupes, it also featured some from the Kingdom of Greece. A plan for a rival opera building by an impresario called M. Labruna who had arrived from Egypt failed to materialize in 1877–1879, even though performers had already arrived in town.[10]

This establishment of elegant theaters seemed at first to coincide with the end of large-scale performances in coffeehouses. The Kivotos Café or Theater, which according to many contemporary descriptions was a haphazard construction built on stilts into the sea, in 1873 collapsed due to overcrowding during a performance. While the acrobats' show had sold 100 tickets, it was later assumed that twice as many people had been present. At 10 p.m. the building literally dissolved in less than five minutes, crushing and drowning at least eighty people, with another fifty reported missing. Among the dead were four men and three women of the eight-member acrobat troupe.[11] The finishing of the quays and a ban put an end to coffeehouses on stilts. However, the more glamorous theater venues did not fare much better. In 1884 the Cammarano Theater burned down after a performance, never to be restored again. While it did not claim any lives, the fire ruined not only the theater, but also the decor, instruments, and costumes, especially of M. Tavilari's troupe from Greece that had performed there hours before.[12]

[10] *Smyrna Mail*, 23 Sept. 1862; Beyru, *19. Yüzyılda İzmir'de Yaşam*, 240–244; Sevinçli, *İzmir'de Tiyatro*, 10.
[11] Beyru, *19. Yüzyılda İzmir'de Yaşam*, 241, 242.
[12] Ibid, 244; Sevinçli, *İzmir'de Tiyatro*, 11, 16.

The Age of the Café Chantant

Even after 1884, with no longer a prestigious venue in the West Anatolian port city, contemporaries who knew both cities well, such as Halid Ziya, considered the standard of the performing arts in Smyrna on a par with the capital, if not better. On any night, so he claims, one could choose between at least one Italian opera and one French operetta performed by natives of those countries in the theaters and cafés with stages on the quays.[13] This was the age of the *café chantant* as ubiquitous and versatile site of Mediterranean entertainment. After the opera fire, there were numerous places for entertainment and drama, mostly extended coffeehouses, among them the Eksaristeron Theater (to become the Cinema Pathé in 1909); next to it the Café de Paris, Nea Skene, Kraemer's Theater (a theater separate from the hotel cum brasserie, also located on the quays), Olympia, the Brasserie Alhambra, the Concordia, which unlike many of these other quayside establishments had a winter stage; the Kukuli or Quays Theater, Monaco Palais de Cristal; the Théâtre de Marseille across from Passport Pier; the Café de la Pointe or Lunapark; and further afield, Paradisos near the ancient aqueduct, and the Eden Garden Theater, which advertised its "indoor horse competitions."[14] While even the Cammarano had opened its stage to acrobats and magicians, these coffeehouses cum stage were even less intent on sticking to highbrow entertainment only. Exhibiting a dwarf, an albino, a giant, performing vivisection, weight lifting or wrestling could easily mingle with drama or orchestra music. In Captain Paolo's *café chantant*, claimed to be one of the oldest in town by 1878, billiard tables, orchestras in summer, and small Italian drama troupes were among the attractions. The Apollon café-cum-stage attracted vaudeville performances. Many of these places only had a sufficient stage for summer performances. The Luka Casino after the end of the Cammarano appropriated for itself the title Théâtre de Smyrne.[15]

This certainly fulfilled classic Ottoman expectations, as the coffeehouse had been the established site for many forms of entertainment

---

[13] Sevinçli, *İzmir'de Tiyatro*, 7.
[14] Ibid, 11, 12; Yeğin, *Evvel Zaman içinde ... İzmir*, 115–124; Beyru, *19. Yüzyılda İzmir'de Yaşam*, 248.
[15] Beyru, *19. Yüzyılda İzmir'de Yaşam*, 239–245. See also the impression from fin-de-siècle Smyrna night life in Deschamps, *Sur les routes d'Asie*.

since the sixteenth century. It was also a practical answer to the fact that there was no professional training for performers to the east of the Mediterranean and Ottoman entertainment venues, even the Cammarano or the Naum, usually did not have a set theater or musician troupe, but relied on changing impresarios and traveling troupes or recruitment from overseas on an annual basis. These post-1870s sites could serve as cafés or restaurants to pay their bills and when the opportunity arose could host major drama or music events. Or, as an in between variety, a less prestigious band could play while people continued to make use of the gastronomy and socialized. This flexible arrangement existed for a variety of stages, from some that rivaled the winter theaters' prestige, past some that were a second-class version of the first, up to institutions catering to lower-class customers that the middle classes considered to be of bad taste and ill repute.

A new proper dedicated theater venue took a long time to emerge. Already in 1886 the entrepreneur Terrassor Davernon had claimed he could build as a copy of the newer French theaters, a round building completely out of stone with a 250-seat-orchestra, three stories of boxes (fifty-eight in total), and eight exits for security. When the initiative failed to come up with enough money, the newspaper *Smyrni* even suggested a municipal tax to raise the necessary funds, but was ridiculed for this by the *Stamboul*: How could a few hundred drama fans extort money for their pastimes from a population of 180,000? Another initiative that was humbler in its goals but important for Smyrna's diversity came to fruition in 1888. An Ottoman Theater focusing on Turkish-language productions opened on the quays near the telegraph office as part of an ensemble including a newspaper reading room and restaurant. This was made possible by an interest-free loan by some anonymous local oligarchs to the municipality.[16]

In 1891, there was once again a renowned stage as part of the Sporting Club, the most prestigious social club in town. Located in an impressive building that also included reading rooms, a bar with terrace, and a garden, the 600-seat theater room was upon its inauguration the pride of the town. Performances there could host acrobatic horse shows, concerts by the Greek Philharmonic Association of Smyrna, and of course theater plays by traveling French, Italian, or

---

[16] Beyru, *19. Yüzyılda İzmir'de Yaşam*, 245–248.

Turkish Armenian troupes.[17] As no commercial initiative succeeded to come up with a dedicated theater venue, the municipality stepped in. As of 1889, it undertook a series of lotteries to raise the sufficient money for a prestigious theater building, but the construction did not start for several years. The building that was finally opened in 1894 at least outwardly met the standards of the time: The opulent Smyrna Theater had 784 seats, lay at the most prominent location in town, adjacent to the French Consulate in the middle of the quays. Its facade was decorated richly in fin de siècle style.[18]

Pera and the Mid-century Splendor of the Naum Theater

It was no far-sighted plan, but one of the ubiquitous fires that paved the way for the first prominent stage in the capital. The 1831 Pera fire devastated the house of Michel Naum Duhani, a prominent Maronite dragoman, which was located just across from the entrance to the imperial school (later known as Galatasaray). For want of any other immediate solution for the plot, Naum rented it out to visiting circuses and touring foreign acrobats, tightrope walkers, and the like. This intersection was one of the most prominent addresses of emerging Pera and was thus ideal as a site of spectacle. Supposedly, it was a troupe of Italians who in 1838 took the first steps toward an improvised stage. Having arrived via Greece, they found in Constantinople only three professional actors, while all other performers were multitalented and more often appeared as acrobats, clowns, or dancers. For their performances, they relied on rented rooms that however were not well suited. Also, such rooms could only house a limited number of guests, so the turnover was disappointing for the performers. So with an imperial *ferman* (concession) the newly arrived Italians undertook the construction of a sizable wooden temporary stage. For the first time in front of a large crowd in Pera, the company enacted *Aristodemo* and *Marco Bozzari*. The latter was actually one of the numerous Philhellene contemporary dramas that had been written overseas during the Greek War of Secession of the 1820s, focusing on the life and death of a volunteer fighter for the Hellenic cause. Nonetheless, this stage could not survive on drama alone and was frequently rented out for circus

---

[17] Mansel, *Levant*, 165; Beyru, *19. Yüzyılda İzmir'de Yaşam*, 250.
[18] Yeğin, *Evvel Zaman içinde ... İzmir*, 125; Sevinçli, *İzmir'de Tiyatro*, 15.

performances. Its rustic feel, far from the ceremonious pomp of theaters proper, is according to Emre Aracı, exemplified by the fact that one evening some women of the imperial harem rode up to the theater in an ox cart, parked it in front of the ordinary seat rows, and watched the entire performance directly from the cart.[19]

Attempts at a permanent indoor stage for the capital that, besides being available all year round, would also cater to contemporary tastes and a sense of grandeur, date back to the early decades of the nineteenth century, but were not crowned by success. According to Aracı one such attempt was undertaken by the entertainment entrepreneur Gaetano Mele before 1838. Having invested both his own assets and that of local theater aficionados, Mele began to build a five-story theater building in the Taksim Gardens in order to stage grand opera and French theater. Upon the end of construction however, the building fell victim to one of Pera's frequent fires.[20]

A more fortunate attempt was made around the same time by Giovanni Bartholomeo Bosco, a magician who had also performed for the imperial family. It was Bosco who began a construction on the grounds of the Naum property across from the imperial school for a theater that was to stage serious drama, ban smoking in the audience, assign seats according to numbers (rather than the usual free seating), and feature a buffet for the breaks. This theater, later unanimously dubbed Naum Theater, was in its first years called Bosco Theater or simply "the theater across from the imperial medical school." As far as can be reconstructed, the first opera performed there was Bellini's *Norma* on November 18, 1841. Paris newspapers criticized the musicians and the stage decor as lacking, but nonetheless they took notice of this development in the dramatic arts at the far end of the continent.[21]

After its initiator Bosco had absconded from the Ottoman capital, the Bosco Theater was actually opened and managed by Basilio Sansoni, who was quickly replaced by Papa Nicola as impresario. They offered the audience a steady mix of Italian opera, focusing on works

---

[19] Aracı, *Naum Tiyatrosu*, 47–51.
[20] Ibid, 51, 52. There are several more ephemeral and contradictory hints at theater activities in this time both in contemporary newspapers, travelogs, and Ottoman official sources. For a criticial discussion of these, see Mestyan, "A Garden with Mellow Fruits," 106–109.
[21] Aracı, *Naum Tiyatrosu*, 52–61.

by Gaetano Donizetti. Despite the glamorous beginning and the prominent place the Naum Theater takes up in public memory, its success at the time was far from clear. Two years after its opening, the local newspapers were still discussing whether the theater could commercially survive or whether its engagement policy had been too poor to keep up the audience's attention for long. None of the impresarios had led the theater to lasting fame. Instead, the local newspapers claimed that they had been out of their league and failed at producing grand theater.[22]

But the theater proved more resilient than contemporaries had expected. In 1844 Michel Naum personally took over the management of the theater on his property. The local feuilleton writers applauded the move, as they were convinced that Naum had a more lasting interest in the theater's operations than the recently arrived Italians. In fact, Naum first invested into refurbishing the place before the season. Despite lacking any training in the stage sector, the son of a Maronite *dragoman* dynasty led the theater into its glory years. Adam Mestyan argues that for want of a national theater proper, the Naum became a semi-imperial institution during Abdülmecid's reign. Although it was private, it operated on an imperial concession with several privileges. The Sultan would occasionally attend, as would visiting heads of state sometimes, or Abdülmecid would call the Naum's actors and actresses to his court for a private performance, and would sometimes donate to cover some of the theater's expenses. After it burned down in 1848, it was completely rebuilt as a stone building by William Smith, the British Embassy's architect. It now offered an elegant interior design and approximately 1,000 seats, which was impressive by the standards of the Eastern Mediterranean, but medium when compared to other European capitals. The Paris opera had 1,800 seats, while Covent Garden could house up to 5,000. As the theater had not succeeded in securing a larger plot of land for itself, it was restricted to the limits set out by Naum's former family villa. The reopening in 1848 set the beginning for Naum's golden years according to Aracı. Although the Sultan had only supported the reconstruction by a minor subsidy, the theater now added the prefix "imperial" to its name. Furthermore, it could benefit from the 1848 turmoil in other parts of the continent and attract a larger number of talented

---

[22] Ibid, 70.

actors and actresses. After fire damage in 1853, it was restored. Its slow fall from grace began in the 1860s, when Naum once again rented out the theater to impresarios and when the war in Italy made it harder to recruit musicians from there. Nonetheless, the theater remained the capital's foremost grand theater for three decades until 1870, when it burned down and was replaced by the Cité de Pera, leaving other drama venues to take its place.[23]

After Naum: More Coffeehouses and Theater in the Presence of the Dead

The last quarter of the nineteenth century knew a number of less prestigious venues that struggled to fill the gap the Naum Theater left behind. The Rumeli Theater had no stake in this, as it lasted for only a year after its 1861 inauguration. The Café des Fleurs, an early *café chantant* founded the same year, closed soon after Naum in 1871. The third theater founded in 1861, the Alcazar de Byzance (known in Turkish as Şark Tiyatrosu) lasted until 1876. The Concordia was founded as a *café chantant* but later aimed for the highbrow entertainment market. Nonetheless it was demolished in 1906. The main serious theater to emerge and fill the gap the Naum Theater had left behind was the French Theater. It had been founded in 1862 in a building owned by the banker Bartholomeo Giustiniani. Originally it had housed a casino with space for large social occasions such as balls run by Edouard Salla, before a part of the building was converted into a theater proper with the help of the architect Barborini.[24] One of the difficulties in tracing its history is its frequent change of names. It was also known by the name of the building as Palais de Cristal, as the Verdi Theater, the Variété Theater, and since the 1890s as the Odeon, and finally as the Alhambra Cinema.[25] One other theater of prominence in the post-Naum phase was the New French Theater. Performance places multiplied, but as late as 1886, following a general fire inspection by the police inspector Bonin together with the head of the fire department, Count Széchenyi, the authorities stated that even the large theaters had some construction flaws, while most did not deserve

---

[23] Ibid, 101–113; Cezar, *XIX. Yüzyıl Beyoğlusu*, 386; Mestyan, "*A Garden with Mellow Fruits*," 361.
[24] Mestyan, "*A Garden with Mellow Fruits*."
[25] Cezar, *XIX. Yüzyıl Beyoğlusu*, 386, 387.

the name "theater," and some were to their horror situated above distilleries in Galata.²⁶

Even beyond coffeehouse stages, it seems that Pera in the post-Naum years could make use of quite a number of multipurpose stages that housed drama performances without dedicating themselves to that exclusive purpose. There were the embassies, inclined to show off prestigious culture workers as representatives of their empire's superiority. Especially since the construction of embassy seraglios at the middle of the century, these had rooms allowing for big cultural events as part of the aforementioned "permanent world exhibition" for the various Great Powers. There were the various organized societies of foreign nationals, either motivated by the same need to show off cultural superiority, or sometimes using the cultural events to foster a sense of diaspora and belonging, or simply providing convenient venues without such motivation. From the late nineteenth century onward, most of these had prestigious buildings including stages and/ or ballrooms. In Constantinople, these included the Società operaia Italiana di Mutuo Soccorso, the Union Française, and the Germans' Teutonia, all located near to the Grand Rue de Pera. In addition to these national societies, the prestigious social clubs such as the Cercle d'Orient mostly distinguished themselves by having state of the art premises, including in some cases the best stages with the most extensive indoor seating in town. The various national, ethnocentric, or cosmopolitan welfare societies that used benefit concerts, theater performances, and balls to collect donations and foster a sense of cultural elitism at the same time usually had to depend on using the rooms of other institutions for their events. Likewise, these stages could provide an appropriate venue for local amateur musicians. With the frequent arrival of traveling troupes, amateur societies faded somewhat from the public interest, but did not disappear completely. Constantinople for example saw the founding of a Société Musicale de Constantinople in 1898. The society brought together musicians with the aim of performing symphonic music, something more rarely heard on the Eastern Mediterranean shores, where operetta prevailed. According to one critic, after an initial phase of trial and error, the society achieved a degree of surety under the direction of M. Nava and had

---

²⁶ Y.PRK.ZB 3/73, in *Arşiv Belgelerine göre Osmanlı'da Gösteri Sanatları*, 174, 175.

successfully familiarized the local public with both the classics and the more innovative recent compositions.[27]

Despite the gap of almost ten years, the actual successor of the Naum was the Petit Champ Theater. As mentioned, the Petit Champ des Morts was originally a Muslim graveyard at today's Tepebaşı, one of Pera's few open spaces and used as a promenade. A theater was first based here as early as the Crimean War, but it was a temporary outdoor summer stage erected by the traveling company of the French subject Louis Persoviz for just two months.[28] The municipality was petitioned to convert the area into "a European-style park." When inner-city graveyards were removed in the 1870s, the district municipality used the area first to dump the debris from building the Tünel and then constructed a park on the thus evened ground in 1871.

The court bandmaster Guatelli Pasha had seized the opportunity posed by the fact that the Naum Theater had burned down in 1870 and the construction for the Petit Champ Park was about to begin. He demanded and received a concession for an opera building with a similar repertoire as Naum's but grander, and suggested the new park as the location.[29] He assigned the construction to the ubiquitous architect Barborini. It took until 1880 for the theater to begin operating. A summer stage, possibly originally as an impromptu response to the delay of the indoor venue, began operating around the same time and later on became a permanent second stage in the park. The opera, that is, the winter stage, in the initial years saw a Boston-based theater company headed by a Ms. Byron as long-term act. Their rivals were an Italian troupe headed by Lenora Monte, but Monte left town due to her debts, leaving the field to Byron and a visiting French vaudeville group. A fire devastated the summer theater in 1889, but its longtime impresario Claudius and the dramatists and musicians used the winter stage until the outdoor venue was restored in 1892 with the aid of the French Embassy. Also called the amphitheater, the summer theater was

---

[27] Çayan, "La musique à Constantinople," 329–331.
[28] İ.MVL, 324/13828_2,5, in *Arşiv Belgelerine göre Osmanlı'da Gösteri Sanatları*, 98, 99. The regulation is a contract with the police to establish the theater in such a way that it would not hinder traffic or residents, as apparently there had been some prior complaints; see also Mestyan, "A Garden with Mellow Fruits," 390.
[29] Ş.D 2394/47_1, 2, 3 – 2870/50_7, in *Arşiv Belgelerine göre Osmanlı'da Gösteri Sanatları*, 146–149.

reconstructed using Parisian seats and decor by the architect Kampanaki. In the process, the theater received a roof and walls and could host 1,200 spectators throughout the year.[30]

Pera was the liveliest, but by no means the only city district hosting theaters. Contemporaneous Greek-language theaters showed dramas in various places, and a Turkish-language drama scene was established in the old city in 1860 at Gedikpasa near Beyazıt, which later migrated to Direklerarası in front of Şehzade Mosque.[31] The final years of the monarchy saw a diversification of venues, with more locations spread out around town: the Apollon Theaters in Kadıköy and Beşiktaş; the Orient Theater, the National Theater, the Ferah Theater in Direklerarası; and the Pangalti Theater.[32]

It seems that the World War interrupted a steady growth and institutionalisation process on the part of the Constantinople drama scene. In 1914 a conservatory (*Darülbedayi-i Osmani*) was founded that was to ensure both the recruitment of professional new actors and actresses and regular performances. While this new institution obviously faced difficulties due to the outbreak of the war, such as its designated artistic director André Antoine having to leave the country at the outbreak of hostilities, it managed to begin performances by 1916. Other wartime initiatives attempted to found an Ottoman anonymous share company for the theater and cinema sector and a company for the founding of fine arts academies. Following the cessation of hostilities, a Turkish national Grand Theater in Constantinople's Moda was to be founded by several Turkish nationalist activists. Despite the massive loss of life on the battleground, in genocide, due to famine; despite the countless deportations and flight; and despite the bleak economic prospects, the postwar years were the absolute boom time of popular entertainment in all cities under study here. According to a census by the Ministry of the Interior, Pera accommodated the Schettini Theater, the Variéte at Taksim, the Chantant Claire Theater, the Petit Champ Winter Theater, the Petit Champ Garden Theater, the Britannia, the Olympia, as well as the Variété Theater. In addition there were sixteen cinemas (which in this time often doubled as

---

[30] Cezar, *XIX. Yüzyıl Beyoğlusu*, 388; Gülersoy, *Tepebaşı*, 28–58.
[31] *Arşiv Belgelerine göre Osmanlı'da Gösteri Sanatları*, passim, esp. 311–337.
More on the Turkish-language theater scene in Chapters 10, pp. 138–142, and 11, pp. 165–172.
[32] Alpargın, *Istanbuls theatralische Wendezeit*, 20.

theaters) and several other places of public entertainment. Of all thirty-seven sites of entertainment within the district, a staggering twenty-five at least were run by foreigners, among whom one could now also find Americans and Russians. Another forty-nine sites of entertainment (not counting Ramadan-only sites) pervaded the old city, both Bosporus shores, Galata, and Makriköy. It was also the time when Muslim actresses, among them the famous graduate of Darülbedayı, Afife Jale, debuted on stage, resulting in a conflict with religious authorities and the police.[33]

Salonica's Late Blossom

The origins of nineteenth-century theater in Salonica still warrant more research. Possibly the city was converted to join the cult of opera via Smyrna. In 1862, not long after the founding of Smyrna's Grand Theater that served as the stage for such performances, the impresario Signor G. Malpassuto and the prima donna Signora Lisa Malpassuto, who had resided for a considerable time in Smyrna, were reported to be leaving for Salonica to establish an opera there, leaving their countryman Cammarano in charge of the Smyrna opera.[34] Whether or not the Malpassutos were involved, it seems the Concordia Theater with its roughly 600 seats was the leading theater for serious opera and drama since the 1860s. Rather than meet with a fiery death like its contemporaries in Constantinople and Smyrna, it was simply judged outdated and unsafe by the audience twenty years later.

In correlation to Smyrna and Constantinople, Salonica witnessed a growing number of cafés with incorporated stages from the 1870s onward, often as part of a hotel complex. Among those prestigious enough for their stage acts to be mentioned in the press were the cafés of the Hotel Colombo, the Étranger, the Imperial, and the Salon de Variété.[35] A former chief cook of the Oriental Railways, Giacomo Colombo, founded the Hotel Colombo adjacent to the Ottoman Bank. Another important site of nightlife was the Hotel Royal on the quays founded by the Ottoman subject Antonis Trakalis. After a fire in 1890, it was replaced by İsmail İpekçi Efendi, who built the Hotel Splendid in

[33] İ.DUİT, 120/31-120/32 İ.DUİT, 122/34;DH. EUM. AYŞ, 38/53; DH.EUM. AYŞ, 76/46; DH. UMVM, 117/45; DH.EUM:AYŞ, 38/53 in *Arşiv Belgelerine göre Osmanlı'da Gösteri Sanatları*, 310–317, 322–333.
[34] *Smyrna Mail*, 23 Sept., 7 Oct. 1862.   [35] *Journal de Salonique*, 22 Dec. 1902.

its place.[36] They later received competition through the Olympos Palace, the Hotel d'Angleterre, and the café at the White Tower. The Eden, the Odeon, and the White Tower were judged to be theaters proper, besides the aforementioned Concordia, the New French and Italian Theater.[37] Salonica had its outdoor park and entertainment area at Beşçınar, on the Western end of the quays near the port and the train station, officially dedicated as a people's park by *vali* Sabri Pasha. But as early as 1902 locals complained that it had lost its appeal and was no longer up to the standards of the time.[38] The park around the White Tower at the far end of the quays, where the aforementioned theater was located, served as a much smaller alternative.[39]

The inability to establish a theater that would permanently guarantee high-quality performances was a source of embarrassment and lament for the local educated bourgeoisie. The *Journal de Salonique* for example in its very first edition in late 1895 stated that previously theater troupes in the Eastern Mediterranean had only repeated well-known theater pieces. Since the founding of the Eden Theater, Saloniquenos finally had the opportunity to see the latest pieces and even actors straight from Paris. However, only an elite audience chose to make use of it. The newspaper, believing in the good taste of the Salonica public against all odds, blamed this on the economy, as several local businessmen were badly affected by the stock market crash in Galata.[40] A few issues later, the theater correspondent had changed his mind. He now claimed it was not the Saloniquenos' financial dire straits, nor their disinterest in theater, but rather the fact that they had hitherto not been offered true high quality. The highly successful performance by Philippe Garnier from Paris at the Eden had proven that Salonica was able to entertain a high-quality theater troupe in town for several weeks.[41] Otherwise the Eden Theater hosted drama performances such as Verdi's *Othello* opera performed by an Italian company.[42]

[36] Dimitriadis, "The Making of an Ottoman Port-City," 168.
[37] Ibid, 168–170; Meyers Reisebücher, *Balkanstaaten und Konstantinopel*, 121–123.
[38] Dimitriadis, "Making of an Ottoman Port-City," 175; *Journal de Salonique*, 18 Dec. 1902.
[39] *Journal de Salonique*, 28 Nov. 1907.
[40] *Journal de Salonique*, 7, 28 Nov. 1895.
[41] *Journal de Salonique*, 5 Dec. 1895.   [42] *Journal de Salonique*, 22 Nov. 1902.

The most prestigious winter stage to emerge in turn-of-the-century Salonica was the Olympia, also a brasserie, established at the turn of the century and later to be succeeded by the Olympia Cinema, a pompous structure in floral Art Nouveau. However it possibly failed to cater to the audience sufficiently. The local press felt it necessary to start a campaign calling for the audience to visit the Olympia more often, fearing that it might otherwise close.[43]

[43] *Journal de Salonique*, 22 Dec. 1902.

10 Theater, the Civilizing Mission, and Global Entertainment

While the three cities mentioned embraced the dramatic arts at different points in time, by the mid-nineteenth century going to the theater and especially to see operas had become an important and prestigious part of leisure activities and despite fires, little public funding, and the volatility of artistic and theater entrepreneurial careers, several theater venues or mixed stages were established. The question that remains, however, is why opera and drama conquered the hearts of the Eastern Mediterranean public. What kind of attitudes persisted at the court, among the administration, in the embassies, and among the widely mixed population of the Eastern Mediterranean port cities? Attitudes varied extremely, but were not simply transferable from the Western part of the continent.

A Source of Enlightenment or Harmless Pastime? Contemporary Attitudes toward Theater

Especially in the first half of the century, the dramatic arts were sold as a rather harmless amusement that would have no further consequences for local society. Indicative of contemporary attitudes among the Constantinople authorities toward the emerging genre is the 1840 file related to the petition by several French dramatists in Constantinople who together applied for a permit to perform comedy and opera in the Pera-based Odeon Theater. Although the troupe under the leadership of a Monsieur Filleulle (?) in true French rhetoric of the times wanted to be "beneficial to education and civilization," the Ministries of Trade and Foreign Affairs recommended granting the license simply on the grounds that the theater would only appeal to the limited number of speakers of French and that its rejection could lead to malicious rumors and unrest among the foreign residents.[1]

---

[1] İ.HR, 6/292_1,2, in *Arşiv Belgelerine göre Osmanlı'da Gösteri Sanatları*, 76, 77. There are few other sources on the Odeon Theater from these times, so it can be assumed that it did not survive long.

The files concerning Basilio Sansoni's demand for a permit to take over, extend, and supply the Bosco Theater prior to the opening relate a similar mentality. The Austrian Embassy, writing in support of its subject Sansoni's plans, felt the need to explain to its counterpart what opera is: "a variety of theater called opera which according to European tradition is commonly performed in the evening" would be enacted at the new stage. This could serve to enlighten the resident foreigners, the ambassador went on to elaborate. "Performance of such fine plays" would be "extremely pleasing to all kinds of resident foreigners at the Threshold to Felicity and moreover, it would provide a good alternative to keep hot-blooded youths away from indulging in gambling and other improper activities." The Ottoman Foreign Minister, rather than seconding the notion of a salutary nature of opera, described it as a harmless upper-class Western pastime: "Some stories and some songs without any indecency" would be consumed by an "audience that will not include people lacking propriety, but ambassadors and honorable merchants." He also referred to precedence cases of licensing theater in the years before. Abdülmecid complied with the demand, but made it clear that the license would not become a customary right, but could be revoked after a due set of time.[2] The careful wording and maneuvering on all sides is indicative of the first few years of Abdülmecid's reign, when it was as yet unclear whether the factions favoring a direct influence by foreigners would win the battle over the young sultan's policy or whether a more cautious approach would gain the upper hand. No one dared suggest that the opera could be enjoyed by, let alone change the lives of wider sections of society, including the Muslims. And yet, Abdülmecid's restrictive attitude became a pattern that was observed throughout the last century of the empire. Theaters and their impresarios could only apply for a permit for a limited duration. An extension was always subject to prior compliance with the rules.

But as the Age of Revivals and its spirit of encouraging experiments based on Western models took shape, the sultans and their administrators showed themselves more appreciative of theater and opera in particular. When the Naum Theater had suffered fire damage and was petitioning the Sultan for an interest-free loan of 250,000 Kuruş to rebuild in a more resilient way, the newly formed *Meclis-i Vâlâ-yı*

---

[2] İ.HR, 12/609, in *Arşiv Belgelerine göre Osmanlı'da Gösteri Sanatları*, 78, 79.

Ahkâm-ı Adliyye (Supreme Council of Judicial Ordinances) suggested the Sultan should rather support the reconstruction with a grant of 60,000 Kuruş, as the existence of a prominent, well-built opera in the capital would improve the Sultan's reputation abroad.[3] Permits for foreign language theaters in Pera were now generally treated benevolently.[4] However when finally an entertainment investor intended to bridge the divide between foreigners and Christians on the one hand and Muslims and locals on the other, the administration reacted defensively.

Henri Houquet stated in his petition directly to Grand Vizier Mustafa Reşid Pasha that while Pera already had an established theater "that leaves nothing to be desired in comparison to other countries," Houquet wanted "to open a theater in Istanbul (*intra muros*, MF), so drama will make its entrance to the old city as well." As he knew that Italian- and French-language drama might have a difficulty or could be frowned on by the authorities there, he proposed a program of "pantomime mixing musical instruments and dance without spoken word and combat, intermingled with noteworthy stories from the history of the Ottoman Empire, which could increase and entice the will and bravery of the imperial military and moreover increase the people's love for virtue and educate them to appreciate people of talent and education." Such a kitschy mix of acrobatics, nationalist history romance, and music was declared by Houquet to be "a big step forward for civilization." However it was apparently a well thought up plan that neither amounted to outright exporting of Western drama without adaptation, nor to well-intended, but Orientalizing treatment of the other. In fact, it apparently attempted to combine traditional popular acrobatic performances with current nationalist romantic currents as they were en vogue around 1850. Nonetheless the Supreme Council believed it better to draw a thick line and once again restrict theater to Pera, which they characterized as a foreigners' ghetto. Rather than blame the need for separation on the outsiders, they blamed the assumed ignorance of their coreligionists and fellow countrymen:

As it is superfluous to state, this thing called theater is a form of entertainment for the people, and its way of performance is based on the Frankish

---

[3] İ.MVL, 90/1830_3, in *Arşiv Belgelerine göre Osmanlı'da Gösteri Sanatları*, 84–86.
[4] İ.HR, 42/1971, in *Arşiv Belgelerine göre Osmanlı'da Gösteri Sanatları*, 88–90.

way of doing things. As such, it exists in all foreign countries ... Since Galata is a center of foreigners, and since most of the spectators are foreigners and people who have become accustomed to such things in their respective home regions, there is no harm there. But such a performance in Istanbul is likely to create all kinds of harm. In Istanbul most residents do not know foreign languages, the establishment will therefore not be profitable. Moreover it is in principle something that takes place late at night and most people there do not know the proper behavior, they will go there simply due to word-of-mouth, and this is likely to produce all kinds of improprieties. This could create problems for urban security.[5]

It is hard to understand why in the 1850s, when Western and Central European fashions had become mainstream, the authorities still decided to act so restrictively toward the theater. We know that the statement "most of the spectators are foreigners" was not true at the time. From the published results of a lottery for early reservation of boxes and seats for the entire season 1851/1852 at the Naum Theater, we see among the five winners of an entire box two Italian names, two Turco-Armenian names, and one of a Muslim Turk. Of the twelve winners of half a box, we see one Frenchman, Englishman, Dutchman, and Italian each, but three Armenians, two Greeks, one Romanian, one possibly Christian Arab winner, and one Muslim Turk. Of the ten winners of seats, we see two seats held by an Italian society, one Greek, one Armenian, one Judeo-Spanish, one Dalmatian, one Montenegrin, one Italian, and one Turkish Muslim name.[6] Although people of foreign origin were overrepresented, all local communities with a sizable middle class including Muslims had been afflicted by operamania by the middle of the century. Yet the authorities acted as if it was still a foreigners' ghetto culture.

Ten years later however, the authorities were happy to finally accept a theater founding in the old city. By then, they claimed, this was a much demanded institution. Perhaps they were also less cautious as the licensed impresario would be Yaver Bey, who had served with the *Mızıka-yı Hümâyun*. Nonetheless they spent considerable energy in designing this first licensed *intra muros* theater in such a way that it

---

[5] A.DVN 57/82 – A.MKT.MVL 26/33, in *Arşiv Belgelerine göre Osmanlı'da Gösteri Sanatları*, 94, 95. This is the deliberation based on the original petition cited in Mestyan, "A Garden with Mellow Fruits," 94, 95.
[6] *Journal de Constantinople*, 23 Nov. 1851, reprinted in Aracı, *Naum Tiyatrosu*, 221.

could not be confused with or degenerate into one of the sleazy places traditionally associated with entertainment in the old town. It should be off limits for women. It should not settle within the vicinity of a restaurant, only a theater buffet for refreshments in the break was permissible. Furthermore, there should be no rentable rooms around, nor alcohol sales. Under these stipulations, Yaver Bey received a fifteen-year monopoly on theater *intra muros* and thus laid the founding stone for Gedikpaşa and its vital contributions to Turcophone drama.[7]

The authorities had for Constantinople issued exclusive, monopolistic concessions. Naum had a similar monopoly in Pera to Yaver's in the old city. While this might have been intended to prevent a ruinous competition, as many early theaters had come and gone quickly, a few years later, the authorities had to concede that they had underestimated the dynamics and vitality of the drama scene. For example, the French Theater's director Seraphine Manasse had to pay a huge annual sum (200 Turkish lira) to Michel Naum and in addition had to reserve a private box and other amenities for him in order for Naum to grant the French Theater a sub-concession. Slowly the government started to limit and rescind previous exclusive concessions. Whereas Michel Naum's heirs protested this development and the fact that the government considered their monopoly null and void once the fire had destroyed their theater, Güllü Agop, the dramatist and impresario who after many short-lived interim solutions in 1867 had taken over and led Gedikpaşa to success, shifted into other parts of the city with new venues.[8]

Opera and the Civilizing Mission?

Why did watching the reenactment of fictitious historical plots in combination with singing and orchestral music take such a prominent place among mid-nineteenth-century Eastern Mediterranean urban residents? How did it compare to other regions? In this context, it is

---

[7] İ.MMS 16/691_2, in *Arşiv Belgelerine göre Osmanlı'da Gösteri Sanatları*, 110, 111.
[8] *Arşiv Belgelerine göre Osmanlı'da Gösteri Sanatları*, passim, especially 128–134, 140–146, and 150, 151. For more on the controversy between the French and the Naum Theater, see Mestyan, "A Garden with Mellow Fruits," 167, and Aracı, *Naum Tiyatrosu*, 305, 306.

useful to recall Norbert Elias' *Civilizing Process*. Elias stated that self-restraint and self-refinement in Western and Central Europe, initially termed *courtoisie*, began in sixteenth- and seventeenth-century court circles as a sign of distinction. It was adopted and transformed by the bourgeoisie, which in the eighteenth century embraced *civilité* as the correct form of refinement and restraint. After *civilité* had effectively transformed bourgeois society, its proponents now called for *civilization*. Civilization however differed from its predecessors insofar as it was no longer a matter of self-refinement, but a mission: to transform the unenlightened masses, the peasantry, the lower classes, or the colonial Other. While theater and opera are not central to Elias' argument, they fit very well to the trajectory he suggests.[9] The dramatic arts in Western Europe had emerged as a form of aristocratic and monarchic representation and amusement that were intended to demonstrate a sophisticated but nonetheless luxurious and enjoyable spectacle. Bourgeois circles appropriated the genre in the name of Enlightenment. A visit to the theater or opera was henceforth like going to school, a lesson in history, morals, aesthetics all rolled into one. What can also be noticed is the turn toward civilizing the others in mid-nineteenth century. The colonialist arrogance and the disregard for all non-Western forms of entertainment become apparent for example in a foreign press report commenting on the establishment of a permanent theater at the Ottoman court in 1858 with the words, "nothing is missing now for Turkish civilization."[10] More telling even is a police agent report by an anonymous, presumably non-Arab police informant from Cairo 1871 stating:

Nothing is more moral than to dissuade the indigenous population from entering these coffeehouses in which they sing obscene songs in the evening, where singing and music are at the mercy of pedants, where decent behavior is banished; nothing could be more moral than to dissuade the indigenous population from their obscene dances. The theater will have the double aim of curing this social plague while also inspiring men to morality and good behavior; it will also arouse civil virtues in which a nation takes pride.[11]

---

[9] Thurston, *Popular Theatre Movement in Russia*, 283, 284.
[10] *Le Ménestrel*, 31 Jan. 1858, quoted in Mestyan, "*A Garden with Mellow Fruits*," 24.
[11] Agent Z to Police Inspector Nardi, Cairo 27 Jan. 1871, reproduced in Mestyan, "*A Garden with Mellow Fruits*," 482.

What did the objects of this patronizing attitude expect from the theater and opera? If one believes their own statements, they were ready and even eager to be civilized by means of drama. In a very similar vein to the Cairo police agent, the letter writer in *Journal de Smyrne* in 1829 cited earlier expressed that theater would be an efficient way of deterring the Smyrna youth from Greek dancing. Local feuilleton articles, petitions, and aficionados reiterated the dramatic arts' civilizing mission ad nauseam. The *Journal de Constantinople* for example claimed that "theater is one of the most effective means of civilization" and that Muslims would soon begin to find it both pleasant and instructive.[12] Perhaps the most eloquent preacher of the theater's civilizing mission to the Eastern Mediterranean was the Egyptian opera director Sulayman Qardahi, who wrote in a petition for public funding from the Egyptian nationalist government in 1882:

[Theatrical plays] contain a knowledge that counts among the causes of progress and means of civilization since these plays are mirrors of various matters, and help us become familiar with ideas. These plays are a school for the people to learn what cannot be learned from the [old] education. From these plays seriousness derives in the form of entertainment. Indeed, the plays – and I do not exaggerate their definition – are one of the most important channels to educate the minds. These are the kindest teachers and the best scholars; they are a garden with mellow fruits of refinement that can be harvested by anyone.[13]

But Eastern Mediterranean theater observers did not only repeat and expound the stage's civilizing mission. They also participated in discussions about how to refine it. Writing in 1900, the theater critic Ahmed Şuayip argued against the Schiller-style sense of aesthetics (to inspire to moral conduct by aesthetic example) that had inspired much of nineteenth-century theater. He promoted French realist drama instead:

if one accepts the theater's right and duty, alongside nature and the arts, to participate in the permanent interrogation of the nature of humanity in a perfectly free and audacious manner, why should one forbid it to openly discuss and describe the horror of love's most serious, most agonizing aspects?[14]

[12] *Journal de Constantinople*, quoted in Aracı, *Naum Tiyatrosu*, 120.
[13] Sulayman Qardahi, quoted in Mestyan, "A Garden with Mellow Fruits," 9.
[14] *Servet-i Fünun*, 23 Kanunevvel 1315 (4 Jan. 1900).

But although some segments of Eastern Mediterranean society readily acquiesced to the dramatic arts' civilizing mission, one should not take their statements at face value. Did thousands of opera aficionados frequent the port cities' lavish theaters for no other purpose than additional education? Was their purpose and their utility no more than that of an evening class in accounting? Indeed, this was not the case. In the following, I will show that, just as to the west of the Mediterranean, the civilizing mission in Eastern Mediterranean theaters was intended not for the refining of the self, but to indoctrinate the Other, that is, the less-enlightened masses. Second, I will demonstrate that theater and opera mainly served as an imagined shortcut toward Europeanization.

The Civilizing Mission toward the Audience

To what degree theater spread self-refinement, whether the spectators at the port city theaters actually derived inspiration, knowledge, and aesthetic impetuses from watching operas in languages some of them did not or only partially understand, would require further and very nuanced research. What stands out is the fact that the educated middle classes saw it as their duty to discipline their fellow residents until they behaved at theaters, balls, or concerts just as good Viennese or Parisian bourgeois would. Thus, the entertainment sector mutated into a stage for the local urban society to prove its civilizing achievements in relationship to the West. Early foreign visitors were put off by the fact that while the Perotes had no inhibitions to waste away the night at the theater, they had to make their way home by the light of a lantern afterward, as if they were inhabitants of a forlorn village and not the proud residents of a world capital. Moreover, commenting on the opening of the Naum Theater, the Parisian press had noticed that unfortunately despite the smoking ban, some visitors, accustomed to mixing narrative entertainment with coffeehouse pleasures, had lit their *shisha* during the performance.[15] However, annoying behavior was not limited to locals. During the Crimean War, foreign officers proved to be so disrespectful toward women in the audience that local women soon refrained from going to the opera.[16]

---

[15] Aracı, *Naum Tiyatrosu*, 59, 66.   [16] Willson, "Operatic Battlefields," 186.

The local critic Tigran Çayan sought to explain the Constantinople audience's behavior to the international *Revue Musicale* journal. He claimed that the majority of the audience somehow believed that to visit a classical Western-style concert was an act of self-refinement or of status, but then once at the concert they were hard-pressed not to distract themselves, as the deeper meaning of the performance eluded them. After such an act of critique of his co-citizens however, Çayan changed from defensive to offensive. After all, most all over the world, the masses could not grasp art and if the Perote (i.e. the elite) audience was served really high class performances, they understood that they had witnessed something special and answered with standing ovations.[17] In a similar vein, the *Journal de Salonique* felt the need to publicly chastise the drunkards who had been noisy during a theater performance.[18]

However, often the problem was not that the audience had forgotten that they were at a theater and therefore behaved out of place. The most severe scenes destroying the middle-class sense of tranquility and progressive evolution toward a higher form of being actually derived from the audience's overidentification with the play or the actors and especially actresses involved. In November 1848, some visitors to the Naum Theater insulted the leading actress Giuseppina Vilmot-Medori, resulting in a fight that disrupted the show for one hour. In May 1851, during the final applause for the prima donna Marcella Lotti, a violent fight erupted among the Naum Theater's audience between Lotti's fans and a supposedly hired mob that booed her. The combatants used batons and knifes, thus fatally injuring a local Greek shoemaker (who according to one version was of Ottoman nationality, but was later claimed to be registered as a Cephalonian and thus under British protection). In 1861, two spectators refusing to take off their hats sparked off a riot in the Naum that could only be stopped by massive police intervention. These were only the most spectacular events in the auditorium itself, disregarding shootouts in the foyer and a hand grenade attack on the theater café.[19] In Salonica, even the use of guns during theater performances is reported, in one case even as an active intervention by a spectator who took the side of some characters in the

---

[17] Çayan, "La musique à Constantinople."
[18] *Journal de Salonique*, 14 Nov. 1895.
[19] Aracı, *Naum Tiyatrosu*, 121–124, 182–184, and passim.

plot.[20] Violent disruptions of performances continued until after the World War.[21]

Despite these serious excesses by opera aficionados, the blame was always directed at the audience, never at the institution itself. On the other hand, when crime happened in lower-class sites of entertainment, the media did not hesitate to call for them to be closed down. When in 1896 gambling dens had sprung up in a burnt down part of Salonica and the robbery of a coat as well as a knife fight were reported in the area, the local press appealed to the chief of police, Musa Bey. Cabarets seemed to hold an in between position on the ladder of social acceptance. When a theft for example took place in a cabaret, this was explicitly stated, but also that the cabaret staff helped to arrest the criminal.[22]

As early as 1856, the police had gotten involved in maintaining order at the Naum Theater, as some people in the audience had "ridiculed the actors and actresses, had whistled, thrown inappropriate objects, taken uncouth actions, and practiced other improprieties." To protect the "very respected and honorable families" that would frequent the Naum, the police believed it was called for to intervene, reprimand, and if necessary, remove the unruly spectators and report them to their embassies.[23] As of the same year, internal regulations of the Naum and Gedikpaşa Theaters banned arms, canes, and umbrellas from the building. They explicitly forbade smoking, throwing things, whistling, shouting, and insulting. A *chef de surveillance* appointed by the municipality would be on site to decide what kind of action would be appropriate against those that transgressed against the house rules.[24]

Moreover the port city intelligentsia was puzzled not only about how to assess the bourgeois mass audience's volatile behavior, but also that of the working class. While a 1909 article in the Committee of Union and Progress newspaper *İttihad* claimed that in the West even

---

[20] Dimitriadis, "Making of an Ottoman Port-City", 177, 178.
[21] In 1919, an Azeri theater company was abused by the audience, including a drunkard demanding dance as part of the performance; Alpargın, *Istanbuls theatralische Wendezeit*, 28.
[22] *Journal de Salonique*, 23, 30 Jan. 1896; *Progrès d'Orient*, 24 Aug. 1874.
[23] HR.MKT 170/32, in *Arşiv Belgelerine göre Osmanlı'da Gösteri Sanatları*, 102, 103.
[24] HR.TO 472/21_1,2,4, and İ.MVL, 430/18931,1,2,4, in *Arşiv Belgelerine göre Osmanlı'da Gösteri Sanatları*, 112–122.

the proletarians would save until they could afford a theater ticket, and that unfortunately the local lower classes had no such aspirations, a writer for *Servet-i Fünun* who in 1898 actually ventured into the Yenibahçe neighborhood in the old city noted that the local theater was frequented by children and apprentices, who saved the entrance fee from their meager wages (although the low ticket prices made this possible). However the kids jeered and clapped out of place, behaving very much as at a *karagöz* show, while the grownups smoked *shisha*, which had been successfully banned from the more prestigious theaters years ago.[25]

While smoking might have disappeared from the downtown theaters, eating was still very common. At the Theatre de Petit Champ, plum stones were supposedly tossed from the boxes to fall on the audience's heads below; sandwich and water vendors, chewing noises, and nuts were a constant distraction. Also the audience would feel too much at home, discarding headgear, coats, vests, and stretch out to sleep. The papers criticized that this was due to the fact that the theater issued tickets without assigned seats, so aficionados would arrive early to get a good seat, but would then have to wait a long time and grow hungry and tired in the process.[26]

It is against such a background that we must read the occasional laudations for the audience, such as Said Naum Duhani's, who wrote about the Petit Champ Winter Theater that spectators would usually have read the plays beforehand or would bring the script to the performance.[27] Overall, the theater directors, the newspaper critics, and the intelligentsia were at a loss how to successfully preach self-refinement to the wider segment of the audience; how to impose pacifism, abstention from tobacco, food, drink; a restriction of bodily movements; how to prevent untimely noise; and how to prompt proper and timely acknowledgment of the performers. In tackling violent partisanship for actors and actresses, consumption and noise during the performances, they were however far from alone. Similar outbreaks were still ongoing for example in London, and the intelligentsia elsewhere also struggled to educate the wider audience to observe plays in silence.[28] These habits were probably nuisances in themselves to

---

[25] Alpargın, *Istanbuls theatralische Wendezeit*, 27, 28; Sevinçli, *İzmir'de Tiyatro*, 19.
[26] Alpargın, *Istanbuls theatralische Wendezeit*, 2013, 29.
[27] Gülersoy, *Tepebaşı*, 53.   [28] Willson, "Operatic Battlefields," 183, 184.

other spectators of the Eastern Mediterranean, but they also stood in the way of another mission theatergoers had: the shortcut to Europe.

Confessions of an Opera Addict

To understand the success of the theater and especially opera around the Eastern Mediterranean, one should look more closely at the consumers of the product. One source sticks out due to its sincerity and self-criticism and is therefore particularly enlightening. *Servet-i Fünun*'s pioneering literature critic and proponent of realism, the aforementioned Ahmed Şuayip, in one of his first articles, published a section one could dub "Confessions of an Opera Addict." As a teenager visiting the military middle school (*Rüştiye*) in old Istanbul, a fellow student who was the son of a theater director would offer his classmates discounted tickets. Ahmed Şuayip thus began visiting theaters in the outskirts of the old city, such as Yenibahçe or near Edirnekapı. While he laughed and cried through all the classic Turkish-language plays and operas of the day there, by the time he was a seventeen-year-old, third-year *İdadiye* high school student, he looked down on this base entertainment and set his sights on higher things. Pera's French Theater and operas and operettas powerfully attracted him despite the fact that his pocket money hardly allowed for the price of a ticket, let alone the fare for getting home from Pera, so he would have to walk across the bridge in any weather. As an opera buff, it was also quintessential to follow the libretto, so a hunt through the French bookstores preceded an actual opera visit, although usually he would have to settle for checking out a book from the Depasta Brothers' library. Also he would keep records, note down the life stories and careers of the composers from the then classic Verdi to the more recent Wagner, illustrate them, sing duets in the quiet of his room, etc.

His dramamania reached its apogee when he read that Sarah Bernhardt would come to town. He counted the months, the weeks, days, hours, until the day finally came and he went to high school immaculately dressed and received words of admiration from his classmates. After that, the addiction began to lose its hold on him. He started studying at law school and reprimanded himself for all the lost time, the unproductive idleness of his obsession, which he could have used to advance his personal development or that of Ottomanism. But was French theater not an oeuvre of eternal art, rather than the pursuit of base pleasures? Harshly, he comes to the conclusion that going to Pera's theaters amounts to nothing else but a waste of time for someone of his class. He then describes himself cured of his addiction, immune to the lure of the colorful posters advertising the arrival of Italian traveling operetta troupes or nigh salacious depictions of the leading actresses. His methadone therapy for overcoming his earlier addiction is to follow Paris theater by reading the reviews of performances and developments there, which he assumes to be on a higher level, and to relate these developments to the readers of *Servet-i Fünun*.[29]

Ahmed Şuayip's confession is in part very self-critical, but also in part very condescending and elitist. He leaves no doubt that theater is not per se educative, as many contemporary tropes still made it out to be. It was most of all a site of escapism. Laughing and crying to the run-of-the-mill Turkish operettas in the old city outskirts was already such an outlet into a parallel world, but one that proved too vulgar for an *İdadiye* student. Following the French and Italian theater seemed more of a challenge to an intellectually talented teenager. It also seemed to bring the promise of social distinction based on a rarer form of social capital that not everyone could acquire, as the scene shows in which his fellow students compliment him for going to Sarah Bernhardt's performance. Nonetheless, Ahmed Şuayip makes it clear that his operamania was not limited to superficial motives, but amounted to a real obsession, including the pursuit of trivial knowledge about the composers and repeating parts of the score to himself. These are signs of fetishism and escapism, not unlike the cases of football fans, philatelists, or hobby gardeners, but as in all cases, they speak to a specific cultural climate of emotional hope and lack.

In the microcosm of the Eastern Mediterranean port cities, it seems the opera stage appeared as a door to the European Dream. To follow the call to "merrily join in advising and doing" was to lead to peaceful coexistence, prosperity, productivity, a higher state of culture, and moreover establish the port city inhabitants as equals among the "cultured nations." Obviously, this was not a reality to be experienced in the everyday life of a lower middle-class student from the Fatih neighborhood, but rather a utopia that could maybe be achieved in the course of several decades. The opera ticket bought such a person

---

[29] *Servet-i Fünun*, 7 Teşrinevvel 1315 (449/19 Oct. 1899).

not only a window unto the wider world, but an entrance into an imagined space where the Dream was already reality. If one could at the Naum Theater enjoy the same opera plays that moved Milan, Paris, or Vienna to tears, laughter, and catharsis, and if one studied the librettos and the artistic vogues of the drama field, was one not already part of that greater community of the "cultured nations?"

However, the plethora of activities Ahmed Şuayip undertook also reveals that the feeling of happiness that should have set in remained evasive. Like many other teenagers obsessed with a music star, games, or some hobby, he one day discovered the limits of his activities and attempted to move on. This once again coincided with an advance in cultural capital due to his joining law school, an advance that called for greater social distinction and intellectual challenge, which he then sought by following Parisian theater, if only from a distance. The language of utilitarianism, patriotism, and pedagogy served to mark the distinction. It remains to be seen how widespread Şuayip's case was, however the opera stage as the shortcut to the European Dream and equality to other European people, at least in cultural consumption, seems a helpful explanation to the new art's great popularity.

The Elusive One World of Drama Writing

Historically speaking, residents of the Eastern Mediterranean regions had good reason to expect something like a global village to emerge from stage entertainment. On the one hand, the Eastern Mediterranean was its birthplace: Theater, as well as tragedy and comedy are all Greek words, Drama a small town to the east of Salonica. Ancient open-air theaters had been a mainstay of all major cities in the region. On the steep slope below the castle on Mount Pagos (Kadifekale), ancient Smyrna's amphitheater was still visible in the early twentieth century. Only from the fourteenth century onward did people at the western end of the European continent turn to these ancient plays for inspiration once more. While the East may have dreamt of Western dramas coming to its shores by the mid-nineteenth century, for a long period of time the West wished for dramatic interaction with the East all the same. Such longing is evident as of the seventeenth century. According to Larry Wolff, the fascination with especially Turkish motifs in operas emerged in the late seventeenth century and lasted one and a half centuries.[30] However, initially, ideas of the Other were still vague and not based on concise information. In 1638 five anonymous authors published in France *L'aveugle de Smyrne*, a tragicomedy set in ancient Smyrna. As Rauf Beyru states, the story displayed absolutely no local knowledge of the city, believing it to lie on an island, thus lumping together information bits on the Eastern Mediterranean as it was imagined in distant regions.[31]

It seems in the course of the following century, knowledge of the other improved. Sébastien-Roch Chamfort in 1770 created *Le Marchand de Smyrne*, in which French and Smyrniote Muslim characters are united irrespective of religion by their common belief in humanity's inherent goodness, true love, and the fight against slavery.[32] In sum, the play reflected the openness toward Eastern Mediterranean cultures characteristic of Enlightenment and is highly politically correct, but fails to impress as a story. By contrast, Carlo Goldoni in 1759 brought his *L'impresario delle Smirne* to the Venetian stage. In the comedy, a Smyrniote merchant by the name of Ali seeks to recruit actors in Venice for the opera he wants to found back home. Ali is ignorant of the genre and not too serious in his venture, but causes the theater actors, full of vanity, but actually living from hand to mouth, to intrigue against one another for what they believe to be a good opportunity. The play rightfully states that contemporary Smyrna was a large port with many Brits, Italians, and others who might be inclined toward opera, but did not have a proper venue or professional actors or actresses for it, while the Italian port cities were rich in unemployed stage performers who might be inclined to travel far beyond the peninsula if the price was right. Goldoni had thus rightfully identified a way to overcome both Italian and Ottoman problems concerning the opera, but imagined the attempt to resolve them comical to impossible. But by 1830 at the latest, Italian opera performers had become a mainstay of the Eastern Mediterranean cities.

But by then, this earlier interest if not fascination for Muslim and Turkish culture had been eclipsed. Culture workers in other European countries had turned decisively anti-Ottoman during the decade-long Greek War of Secession. Between 1820 and 1830, a flurry of poems,

---

[30] Wolff, *The Singing Turk*, 360.
[31] Les cinq auteurs, *L'aveugle de Smyrne*; Beyru, 19. *Yüzyılda İzmir'de Yaşam*, 229.
[32] Chamfort, *Der Kaufmann von Smyrna*.

operas, and dramas had been produced that celebrated Greek independence and denounced Ottoman despotism, often projected onto historical events. George G. Lord Byron wrote several poems and prose texts calling for support to Greek secession. Gioachino Rossini, who before had in the vein of Mozart used Turkish oriental motives for operatic discussions on the possibilities and limits of love beyond Catholic restraints, composed his opera *Maometto II* in 1820, lauding the Venetian war party in its fifteenth-century resistance against the Ottoman expansion, and in 1826 adapted this to the Greco-Turkish conflict as *Le siège de Corinthe*. By contrast, Rossini's friend Giacomo Meyerbeer in his 1824 *Il crociato in Egitto*, projecting the conflict into crusader times, still hoped for reconciliation between Christians and Muslims. While these operas, just as Beethoven's contemporary Ninth Symphony, had made ample citation of janissary music, Turkish instruments and characters were no longer popular in new operas once the Greek War of Secession was over.[33] Philhellenism did not fare much better, as its adherents had hoped for a democratic state to emerge from the war, but were disappointed by the Hellenic Kingdom created by the grace of Europe's absolutist monarchies instead. Disappointment even led Jakob Philipp Fallmerayer to disclaim nineteenth-century Greeks' heritage completely due to the fact that they were by majority the descendants of medieval migrants from beyond the Mediterranean basin.[34]

The dearth of serious musical and dramatic exchange with the East after the 1820s continues almost uninterrupted throughout the nineteenth century. The Crimean War, during which the Ottoman Empire found itself on the same side with Great Britain, France, and Sardinia-Piedmont and at the center of those countries' media attention, and with many foreign officers among the Naum's audience, seemed to be a moment when a rapprochement in operatic matters could have been reestablished. In fact, the Naum Theater impresario's brother, Gabriel Naum, collaborated with the prominent Italian composer Giacomo Panizza to write *L'Assedio di Silistria* (The Siege of Silistra), an opera that could appeal to both Ottoman and other European viewers. Based on the Crimean War events of winter 1853/1854, Naum created a nationalist-romantic libretto focusing on the Silistra Fortress

---

[33] Wolff, *The Singing Turk*, 343–360.
[34] Fallmerayer, *Geschichte der Halbinsel Morea*.

commander Musa Pasha. To give the scenario a more European dimension and to allow for some amorous intricacies, a Prussian colonel in Ottoman service and his daughter were added to the story, which otherwise focused on Ottoman patriotism and military gung ho attitude. Nonetheless, the opera does not seem to have had any impact or caused any inspiration for further Crimean War stage plays in other countries.[35]

Unilateral Dependency and Imperialist Competition in the Operatic Field

With reciprocity and exchange dwindling, the Eastern Mediterranean opera enthusiasts had little choice but to unilaterally closely follow the overseas development. Toward mid-century, it is astounding to see how despite the still difficult travel conditions, Italian operas would quickly find their way to the Aegean and Bosporus shores. Purportedly, the Eastern Mediterranean stages had a greater affinity to Verdi than any other place outside of Italy, showing his plays before they made it to Paris or Vienna.[36] Jean Henri Abdolonim Ubicini claimed that the Eastern Mediterranean audience was biased to constantly demand music and opera by Gaetano Donizetti (because of his brotherly connections to Constantinople) as well as Verdi.[37] A look into a number of local newspapers and the music theaters' programs confirms this for the early period, and Verdi remained a mainstay even in the twentieth century.[38] When Richard Wagner, whose music was believed by some to have revolutionized the field, was first performed in Constantinople in the 1860s, the critics disapproved and called for a return to classics such as Rossini and Meyerbeer.[39] But just as the time of theater monopolies was coming to an end, the singular fixation on Italian opera gave way to a more diversified relationship to European stage activities. Adam Mestyan argues that the establishment of Seraphine

---

[35] Aracı, *Naum Tiyatrosu*, 227–232. It may well be assumed that Namık Kemal was aware of this opera when writing his own *Vatan yahut Silistre* in 1873. See also Mestyan, "A Garden with Mellow Fruits," 343.
[36] Eğecioğlu, "The Liszt-Listmann Incident," 2–3, fn. 2.
[37] Jean Henri Abdolonim Ubicini, quoted in Cezar, *XIX. Yüzyıl Beyoğlusu*, 383.
[38] *Progrès d'Orient*, 25 Aug. 1874; *Le Matin*, 1 July 1879; *Journal de Salonique*, 22 Dec. 1902.
[39] Aracı, *Naum Tiyatrosu*, 296.

Menasse's French Theater in rivalry to the Naum that predominantly played Italian opera reflects the rivalry between the two imperialist centers and their attempts at cultural influence.[40]

France definitely grew in theatrical prestige in the last quarter of the nineteenth century. It is telling that when a direct railway link was established between Salonica and the Central and Western European network, some locals did not so much ponder the possibilities or dangers this posed for commerce, diplomacy, or morals, but rather its meaning for theater aficionados: "We will all be able, three nights after our departure, to be in the audience of the *Paris Grand Opera*, attending the finest musicians."[41] Likewise, the drama critique Ahmed Şuayip almost exclusively refers to the Parisian stage. Thus the hopes in the unilateral following of foreign stage developments shifted, but also diversified. As time progressed, the Eastern Mediterranean residents apparently overcame their conservatism and were more open to new trends and composers of various origins.[42]

Talking about a Revolution: 1908 on the International Stage

1908 not only brought a revolution to political institutions, but also to the usage of public space. As people took to the streets, they also gathered in the coffeehouse and spoke without the fear of informants. Political events of a mass scale became possible. The Committee of Union and Progress for example convened in Salonica's Eden Theater.[43] Moreover it also saw a brief rekindling of the West's interest in the East in the dramatic field. While the nineteenth century had not seen a repetition of the *Merchant of Smyrna* or the *Impresario of Smyrna*, in 1908 the French author Léon Crétot felt inspired by the Ottoman revolutionary events. Crétot, otherwise an author of kitschy French patriotic pieces, wrote a theater play called *Union et Progrès ou La Nouvelle Turquie*. In it, a Young Turk embodying progress and dressed in superb fashion debates with an Old Turk, who defends tradition. Many locals of the Eastern Mediterranean port cities felt flattered that their affairs once again found the attention of Parisian

---

[40] Mestyan, "*A Garden with Mellow Fruits*," 331, 332.
[41] *Faros tis Makedonias*, 16 Jan. [28], 1886, quoted from Dimitriadis, "Making of an Ottoman Port-City," 156, 157.
[42] Lindau, *An der Westküste Klein-Asiens*, 82; *Stamboul*, 2 Jan. 1900.
[43] *Journal de Salonique*, 22 Nov. 1908.

literati (even if of doubtful standing). The play was performed by a French troupe in Salonica and Constantinople.[44] More importantly, Paris's Odeon Theater decided to enact a play by the Ottoman Khalil Ghanem Effendi. Even the Minister of Foreign Affairs Rifat enthusiastically spoke of a new era for Ottoman literature.[45] However, just as on the domestic stage, international infatuation with the 1908 revolution did not last long and soon gave way to new skepticism about the future of the region.

[44] *Journal de Salonique*, 26 Nov. 1908.
[45] İ.TAL, 464/12, in *Arşiv Belgelerine göre Osmanlı'da Gösteri Sanatları*, 286–288.

11 The One World of Workers of the Dramatic Arts

The One World of Music at the Court

With foreign composers' and playwrights' interest in Eastern Mediterranean societies dwindling, local opera aficionados' only choice was to act as consumers and order the exchange. Countless music teachers, musicians, actors and actresses, directors, impresarios, and even composers were lured from abroad to work on the Eastern shores. Their stays could last for just a few gigs or a lifetime. While demand might have been large, this would not have resulted in more than the aforementioned local amateur groups had there not been a readiness on the part of musicians, actresses, and entertainment entrepreneurs from abroad to tour or even settle in the Levant.

The most long-term engagements of overseas musicians came about through the court. While some recruitments took place out of the preexisting Italian music scene in Constantinople and not all positions were occupied for a lifetime, a position at the court was prestigious enough that the foreign musicians could survive afterward as much sought after music teachers and performers. Sultan Mahmud initiated this new form of ordered exchange. As if to rekindle the dialogue between Western and Eastern dramatists, composers, and musicians, Mahmud had in 1826 together with the Janissary Corps also disbanded their music bands and formed the *Mızıka-yı Hümâyun*. Its music directors were also charged with training the royal family members to play Western instruments, as all future sultans and many members of the imperial harem did. The desire not only for a one-sided pursuit of foreign styles, but to reenter a dialogue is apparent in this royal interest in classic music. One expression of this need for reciprocity is that Mahmud's son Abdülmecid, after listening to performances by foreign virtuosos passing through town, made them listen to members of the royal family and court.[1]

---

[1] *Vossiche Zeitung*, 28 Jan. 1848, quoted in Eğecioğlu, "The Liszt-Listmann Incident," 10, 11; Sevengil, *Türk Tiyatrosu Tarihi*, vol. III, 4.

Italians commandeered a major place among the musicians prominent in the Levant in general and at the court in particular from early on, and purportedly even represented a sizable portion of the large Italian community in the port cities. The most well-known is (Giuseppe) Donizetti Pasha, who was appointed head of the military marching bands in 1828 and head of the *Mızıka-yı Hümâyun* by Mahmud II. He was known for adding instruments such as oboes and clarinets to the marching bands, for introducing the Western note system for Ottoman music as developed by Guido d'Arezzo, but also for promoting Western classical music beyond the court walls in local society, for example as advisor to the Naum Theater.[2] While such a career is without doubt exceptional, we can safely assume that it inspired other less fortunate Italian musicians to also try their luck to the east of the Mediterranean.

Callisto Guatelli from Parma succeeded Donizetti as court music director. His position was short-lived, so his biography shows some elements that he could have in common with less noted Italians in the East. Guatelli entered Parma's music school at the age of twelve, learned to play contrabass, and graduated at the age of nineteen in 1837. After working in an orchestra for eight years, he arrived in Constantinople together with an orchestra that was scheduled to perform at the Naum in 1845. He later served as musical director to the Naum and was in 1856, upon Donizetti Pasha's death, appointed to the Sultan's state orchestra and made director of the *Mızıka-yı Hümâyun*. However following a fallout with the court, possibly because of a love scandal, he was replaced by Bartolomeo Pisani, but was later reinstated as court bandmaster and music instructor to the royal family. He was in his times criticized for not having had a thorough conservatory education or similar position that would have qualified him for his high post. Nonetheless, Guatelli fulfilled the royal family's expectation to engage with Oriental music. Twenty-six of his compositions have been preserved for posterity. Some of them managed to successfully adapt Eastern music to Western orchestra

---

[2] Aracı, *Naum tiyatrosu*, 66; Pannuti, *Les italiens d'Istanbul*, 567; Sevengil, *Türk Tiyatrosu Tarihi*, vol. III, 3. By contrast, see the badly informed reference by Bernard Lewis to Donizetti Pasha, believing that he lived until the end of the nineteenth century (and not until 1856) and that Donizetti had remained the only musician at the court or in Constantinople society, a claim so obviously ignorant or deceptive of the now well-established state of the art in the study of nineteenth-century Ottoman music history; Lewis, *What Went Wrong?*, 133–136.

arrangements and often had explicitly Oriental names. He composed several marches for official occasions, such as the *Marche de l'Exposition Ottomane* and perhaps the most peaceful national anthem ever, the *Marche Impériale*, also known as *Azizye*, as it was dedicated to Abdülaziz.[3] Besides initiating the founding of the Petit Champ Theater, Guatelli in his later years still worked in Constantinople as a music teacher. Many musicians doubled as music teachers, as the local middle and upper classes were eager to learn or make their offspring learn Western music.[4] The work of these resident Italian musicians leant new hope to the goal of the Eastern Mediterranean appearing on the international map of music and drama. For example, local newspapers announced happily that the aforementioned Bartolomeo Pisani had in 1873 completed his five-act opera *La Gitana* and that it was supposedly about to premiere in "one of the principal theatres in Italy."[5] Italians were no less present in other services related to the theater. The Italian Alessandro Marlo is claimed to have painted the stage sets of many early major Constantinople theaters, including the one at Dolmabahçe.[6]

The One World of Stage Workers: The Ottoman Stage As Career Step

But these court bandmasters and instructors were obviously only a select few from among a larger community. With the lack of any public institutions of training until the eve of the Great War, professional classical music, opera, and modern drama were to a large extent maintained by import. While the great demand has been mentioned, there also needed to be a sufficiently high number of musicians, theater actresses and actors, and circus artists, both from without the region and within, who could offer entertainment in the new style for the audiences of Smyrna, Salonica, and Constantinople and were willing to travel in between these cities (and/or to there from other parts of the

---

[3] Aracı, *Naum Tiyatrosu*, 86, 87, 242, 243.
[4] Pannuti, *Les italiens d'Istanbul*, 567; *Journal de Salonique*, 21 Dec. 1895.
[5] *Levant Herald*, 11 Jan. 1873. Pisani, although largely forgotten today, continued to have success in Florence, Milan, Venice, Paris, and other places abroad; Aracı, *Naum Tiyatrosu*, 304, 305. He was an offspring of one of the old Dragoman families of Constantinople; Schmitt, *Levantiner*, 128–130.
[6] Alpargın, *Istanbuls theatralische Wendezeit*, 37, 38; Aracı, *Naum Tiyatrosu*, 122.

world). In the words of Adam Mestyan, such efforts entailed "an enormous amount of traffic between different geographical locations within the late Ottoman Empire and between Western European cities, transporting literally hundreds of people from city to city, knowledges, tastes, languages, using new techniques to organize and manage their troupes with incredible financial and physical effort."[7]

The Levant tour was not a way out for losers who had failed to make it in Milan, Paris, or elsewhere. Especially around 1848, Constantinople could be a career springboard, from which young talents could take off to more esteemed venues. Angelo Mariani, who was later to become Verdi's assistant and was a composer, director, and orchestra conductor of his own right, left the Italian lands due to Habsburg persecution and the ongoing upheaval to take up a position as orchestra conductor at the Naum. Although shocked by the ongoing cholera epidemic and one of the ubiquitous Pera fires upon his arrival and prevented from fleeing only by Naum's intervention with the authorities, Mariani finally remained in Constantinople for four years and became a much requested guest and instructor in many upper-class salons.[8] Likewise the previously mentioned Giuseppina Vilmot-Medori, a Belgian-born soprano performing in Constantinople at the age of twenty-one, would later make it to Milan, Venice, Paris, New York, and Montevideo.[9]

Touring stars from overseas were instrumental in establishing fixed local troupes and venues, as the account in the previous chapters show. Many port city residents turned to the Western Mediterranean for highbrow entertainment, but more down-to-earth forms were also welcomed. Vaudeville troupes from France and elsewhere as well as dancers, magicians, and solo entertainers toured the Levant.[10] Except for world stars, such tours did not happen in a hurry. Both theater troupes and orchestras would get engagements for several months. In order to attract the same spectators more than once, they had a large repertoire of pieces to perform and could vary them with little preparation.[11]

---

[7] Mestyan, "*A Garden with Mellow Fruits*," 264.
[8] Aracı, *Naum Tiyatrosu*, 135–140. [9] Aracı, *Naum Tiyatrosu*, 122.
[10] *Levant Herald*, 4 Jan. 1873; *Le Matin*, 11 July 1879.
[11] See for example Mrs. Lindsey's troupe in *Journal de Salonique*, 14, 21 Nov., 15 Dec. 1895, 13 Feb. 1896.

Performers originating from Central and Western Europe and performing on the shores of the Eastern Mediterranean seem to have been well aware of their audience's desire for reciprocity and a Western interest in the East. From among the few pieces available, foreign performers would often enact works with a connection to an Eastern theme. Several of the earliest performances in Pera in the 1840s attest to this. An Italian troupe enacted a play on the life of Justinian for which translations of the script were made available in a local bookstore. Likewise the opera *Belisario* by Gaetano Donizetti focused on the life of a Byzantine general.[12] When the visiting English pianist Leopold de Meyer, a guest of the British ambassador Stratford Canning, performed, he included two Turkish melodies arranged for him by Donizetti Pasha, which was very much appreciated by the audience.[13]

The Eastern Mediterranean public was soon accustomed to these touring musicians and actors from overseas, closely followed their coming and going, and commented on and discussed their performances. An internationally active artist could for example announce her or his upcoming engagement in a Constantinople café to a newspaper at the site of her or his present performances, say, in Odessa, and this would make the newspaper editions of the Ottoman capital a few days later. Likewise, a Parisian star's intent to tour the Levant, but also an incoming Athenian or Russian artist, was worth an early announcement. The announcement of Parisian stars such as the comedian Armand Duterte from that city's Odeon to plan a concert at Constantinople's Petit Champ was major news.[14] The fact that the coming of an Italian theater company had to be canceled after the agent's negotiation for renting a stage in Constantinople had failed and that the company members were thus stranded in Alexandria could be the subject both of newspaper reports and letters to the editor.[15] But such incidents are also reminders that the Levant tour could bring unpleasant surprises and perils far from home. An Italian comedian troupe that was scheduled to play in Salonica's Jupiter Theater in 1895 unexpectedly fled the town on an overnight boat to Kavalla, as it had amassed too much debt in town.[16] Performances or entire tours could

---

[12] Aracı, *Naum Tiyatrosu*, 67.   [13] Ibid, 68.
[14] *Le Matin*, 11 July 1879; *Journal de Salonique*, 20 Jan. 1896; *Stamboul*, 7 Jan. 1890, 4 Jan. 1911.
[15] *Stamboul*, 4 Jan. 1890.   [16] *Journal de Salonique*, 7 Nov. 1895.

also be ruined by the periodic epidemics that continued to haunt the Eastern Mediterranean and that led the urban residents to avoid crowded places such as theaters.[17]

What made these foreign stars and starlets so attractive for the Salonician, Smyrniote, and Stambouliote public? Foreign theater and nonlocal music were obviously ways of dreaming oneself away from the Eastern Mediterranean, making believe that one was in Milan, Paris, or Vienna, at the heart of what was considered sublime culture at the time, rather than somewhere on its fringe. Or one might say, it was a way of finding approval for the "fringe" localities: Did the fact that Parisian stars chose to bless the Eastern Mediterranean with their presence not prove that this was not such a forsaken backwater after all? That even Salonica was part of a wider international community of music and theater aficionados?

We can hope to find some answers to the question of the foreign stars' cultural role for local society by analyzing what it had to say about them. We often find admiration as well as protectiveness in the press. For example, when the prima donna of the troupe at the Concordia Theater was molested by district municipal orderlies who had come to collect the Concordia's overdue municipal dues, the *Levant Herald* declared this a scandalous treatment of an important international star.[18] Upon the departure of the bass singer Conti to take up a new assignment in Italy, the Constantinople press sent him off with a warm goodbye, promising to keep him in good memory.[19] As far as the critiques of performances are concerned, we find an overall tendency to laud the artists; claiming that foreign troupes performed well served a double purpose. On the one hand, it suggested to the general public that the level of art in the respective town was high and the city's reputation should thus stand in good esteem. On the other hand, a good reception by the local public also pacified the touring troupes, made them extend their stays, and attracted new performers. Every so often though, a theater piece would have to be trashed, in order to prove that the local theater enthusiasts were not too easy to please but discerning critics.[20] While the public in general wooed the foreign performers, woe befell those who showed themselves

---

[17] *Stamboul*, 10 Jan. 1890.
[18] *Levant Herald*, 17 Jan. 1873; see also *Journal de Salonique*, 4 Dec. 1902.
[19] *Stamboul*, 2 Jan. 1900.
[20] Çayan, "La musique à Constantinople;" *Le Matin*, 2 July 1879.

ungrateful. The Naum's prima donna in the 1845–1846 season, Madalena Emilia Cominotti, had been lauded by the *Journal de Constantinople*'s theater critic, calling for her to be "smothered in flowers and jewels." When Cominotti took off for Milan the next year however, the *Journal* maliciously commented that she apparently preferred a mediocre role there to the great affection the audience had shown her in Constantinople.[21] When in 1879 a tenor singer who had just arrived for a longer duration of stage performances prematurely and unexpectedly returned to Italy, the newspapers were full of scorn. Had this man expected the Croissant to be a Grand Opera or the Sultan's court? Whatever the case, Constantinople could do without him.[22]

The One World of Entertainment: Paris in Constantinople, Salonica in Paris

The steady flow of actresses and actors touring the Eastern Mediterranean main cities lent the residents of those places the impression they were not forgotten by the metropolis. The greatest prospect for a *fin de siècle* drama fan however, as Ahmed Şuayip had stated, was to see the contemporary world star Sarah Bernhardt. In a world before radio and television, the fame of the Parisian actress relied to a large extent on her many European and world tours. Four of those took her to Constantinople: In 1883 she played in the Tokatliyan Hotel's Nova Theater, a large venue, but not the largest at the time. In 1888 she supposedly had several concerts in houses that offered 700 seats, but were sold out every evening, relieving the audience of 17,000 Franks in the process. The special performance for the Sultan at Yıldız was canceled however.[23] Her 1893 tour took her to the French Theater. According to an urban legend, the district mayor did not permit the performance, until he was convinced that the building had been reinforced to cope with the expected crowds. In 1904, already a legend, Bernhardt performed in the Petit Champ's Winter Theater, and was supposedly constantly followed and besieged by her numerous fans.[24] The craze for Bernhardt, while essentially not too different from what she experienced in other parts of the world, gave the Stambouliotes a certain opportunity. As in today's mass consumer and entertainment culture, taking part in

---

[21] Aracı, *Naum Tiyatrosu*, 87–95.   [22] *Le Matin*, 5 July 1879.
[23] And, "Eski İstanbul'da Fransız Sahnesi."   [24] Gülersoy, *Tepebaşı*, 28, 53–55.

and reenacting a fan culture that is shared with other people around the globe gives one the feeling of being connected to a wider world, even if one just went to the theater down the street. In this way, Sarah Bernhardt gave the Stambouliotes the feeling of being on the global map, just as to her venues in the United States or other parts of Europe.

Could there be more gratitude, more appreciation for the Eastern Mediterranean, a bigger sign of acceptance than the presence of Sarah Bernhardt in the Petit Champ? There could. While it is rarely explicitly mentioned, a fervent but repressed hope by many fans of European entertainment was for reciprocity, for the more western regions of the continent and especially the hallowed halls of Paris theaters to show recognition to artists from the Eastern Mediterranean port cities.

It is in this vein that we must understand the excitement in a review by Vitalis Cohen, former editor in chief and at the time Parisian correspondent of the *Journal de Salonique*, when in 1907 reciprocity finally seemed to set in. While Cohen had often satirized his hometown's provinciality, he now became an ardent local patriot. The reason was the stage success of the twenty-year-old Paul Ardot. Despite this inconspicuous stage name, Cohen knew the actor to be the grandson of the Saloniqueno Han Youssé Cohen and as if to dispel his own disbelief, cited the Salonica downtown districts the young actor could have grown up in, evoking the image of crowded and ancient streets with a definite Ottoman imprint: "Roghos, Las Encantadas, Unkapanı, Meydan, Noubé." According to the correspondent, these clashed with the locale where he witnessed Ardot's success, namely in Cluny, Paris, not far from the Pantheon or Notre Dame. He lauded the young actor for his chansonettes and claimed the Parisian upper classes would reassemble day after day to hear Ardot. Cohen closed his review with the enthusiastic claim that an artist was slumbering in the heart of every Saloniqueno, probably less an observation than the product of wishful thinking.[25]

The fascination for the Parisian stage, its writers, composers, actresses, actors, musicians, and *mise-en-scène* prevailed. It is only on the eve of the Great War, in 1911, that we find a rather marginal slight against Paris in the *Stamboul*, chastizing "ultra-modern" theater, which is defined by actresses changing their costumes up to six times in a play and elaborate stage sets as well as stagings.[26] Perhaps even

[25] *Journal de Salonique*, 25 Nov. 1907.   [26] *Stamboul*, 6 Jan. 1911.

this affront was less a conceptual challenge to Parisian theater, but rather a line of defense for the Constantinople theaters, as a contemporary article in *Servet-i Fünun* lamented the fact that they technically lagged behind the West European venues. While conventional (hydraulic) stage mechanisms and decor of most Ottoman venues had not been state of the art, by that point in time electricity had revolutionized these technical aspects, while the Eastern Mediterranean cities were only in the early stages of introducing electricity.[27] Thus, throughout most of the long nineteenth century, with small exceptions, the Eastern Mediterranean remained unilaterally dependent on artistic development to the west and north of it.

Going Local: The Turcophone Composers, Actors, and Impresarios

Nonetheless, in the course of the nineteenth century, an active scene formed that even without much recognition on the international stage, strove to adapt the foreign forms of entertainment to local content, and local melodies to the assumed international standard. Even more than the consumption of the Italian and French performances, this endeavor must be seen not as an import, nor as following the narratives of "Westernization" or "national cultural awakening." Instead they represent the longing for reciprocity and to legitimately be "in between," that is, of the East, but in dialogue with the West.

The history of modern theater and highbrow music in the former Ottoman Empire (as that of many other aspects of nineteenth-century social life the world over) has traditionally been written with a nationalist teleologos. The fact that foreign traveling theater companies and musicians were essential in bringing these pastimes to the Aegean shores is considered a sign of lack or lag, as is the fact that Armenian actresses and actors were the pioneers of Turkish-language dramatic arts. Therefore, most classic works on theater and music as well as some to the present day, include the foreign and Armenian artists rather unwillingly in their narrative. The information on them is sparse, and as soon as Turkish-language theater begins to establish itself, the subject of foreign troupes is dropped, and once again, as soon as Muslim actors make it to the stage, the Armenians are only treated

[27] Alpargın, *Istanbuls theatralische Wendezeit*, 34, 35.

in passing.[28] Such a perception is ahistorical. While many Eastern Mediterranean residents found the proliferation of theater and music in local languages and local compositions desirable, the foreign artists were seen as a source of pride and fruitful exchange with the world at large. As becomes most evident in the example of Ahmed Şuayip, the port city residents closely followed artistic developments abroad and viewed music and theater as international arenas to which they did not seek to be accepted via hermetically sealed off national schools, but through open exchange, access, and reciprocity. The tours by foreign performers did not diminish with the rise of domestic acting scenes, but were judged part of a colorful mosaic that included local or regional performers, but did not necessarily juxtapose them. Regarding the question whether the development of autochthonous theater must be considered an adaption by Ottoman intelligentsia trained in the West or a truly local development, a comparison of some of its main agent's life trajectories shows that it was an amalgam of both.

The first original stage play in the modern sense in Turkish is claimed to have been written after the Crimean War in 1858. İbrahim Şinasi, a scribe at the Tophane armory, raised on Boğazkesen Street, between the armory and the embassies, who later studied in Paris under the influence of Samuel (Ustazade) Silvestre de Sacy, returned to Constantinople to translate foreign literature, publish cheap popular editions, edit a Turkish-language newspaper, and write *kaside*s (poems) in a style influenced by his Parisian times. His comedy *The Poet's Marriage* (Şair Evlenmesi) was printed in 1860, but did not make it to the stage in its time and only premiered in 1910, when a more nationalist-minded audience was eager to celebrate the first Turkish comedy and especially the first one written by a Muslim.[29]

The person who had had much more of an impact on the development of Turcophone drama in his time was Dikran Çuhacıyan. Born in 1837 as the son of a court clockmaker, he studied music in Milan and upon his return in the late 1860s composed music for dramas and operettas, including *Arshak II*, an opera about a historical Armenian king. Such works followed the vein of mid-nineteenth-century romantic nationalism, but the libretto was originally in Italian, to comply

---

[28] Sevengil, *Türk Tiyatrosu Tarihi*, vol. III; Sevinçli, *İzmir'de Tiyatro*; Alpargın, *Istanbuls theatralische Wendezeit*.
[29] Sevengil, *Türk Tiyatrosu Tarihi*, vol. III, 11–17.

with international taste. He acted in Güllü Agop's theater company and gave piano lessons until composing Turkish-language operettas with much more success. *Arif'in Hilesi* (*Arif's Trick*) premiered in 1872 at Gedikpaşa and was purportedly composed t together with A. Sebastiano, of whom we know nothing more. Subsequently Çuhacıyan broke with Güllü Agop in 1874 and formed his own theater troupe, the Opera Theater. In 1876, his self-composed *Leblebici Horhor Ağa* (*Horhor Ağa, the Chickpea Seller*) premiered in the French Theater. In this piece, Çuhacıyan is said to have adapted Turkish melodies to Western harmony. It was to become a classic and his greatest success. Soon after however, he turned over the troupe's leadership to Benliyan. Çuhacıyan went on to compose Ottoman national hymns, including one to the new sultan, Abdülhamid. After a long period of relatively low productivity, a new comical opera called *Zemire* premiered in 1891 in the New French Theater. For the premiere, the text was translated from Armenian to French, as the singers engaged for the occasion were from France. Unlike his earlier plays, by then all banned, but popular and in Turkish, *Zemire* was noticed and widely lauded by the Constantinople Francophone press.

Although he had begun his career with an Armenian historical opera and worked mainly as part of the Armenian Turcophone theater, Çuhacıyan proved himself pro-Ottoman in the tumultuous years of the Russo-Turkish War of 1876, but composed for Armenian-language theater again later and also a hymn on the occasion of the Armenian patriarch's death. He collaborated with less well-known artists as well as with the aforementioned local celebrity Bartolomeo Pisani. After a fire had destroyed his house in the Bosporus suburb of Ortaköy, he received broad solidarity in the form of a charity concert organized in the German Club Teutonia and attended by several high-ranking Turkish members of the bureaucracy, with musical contributions by several Italians. As a French newspaper wrote in his obituary, he was "the Verdi of the Orient." And yet, Mestyan claims, the fact that Çuhacıyan "embodied so well the European ideal of the lonely genius-composer" is also the reason why despite success he never attained personal commercial success in the Eastern Mediterranean music and drama environment, as this was traditionally based on collaborative efforts.[30]

---

[30] Mestyan, "*A Garden with Mellow Fruits*," 289–311, 339.

The same can be said of Seraphine Manasse. He is another case of a Western-educated Ottoman Stambouliote who left his impact on the development of the local drama scene. The son of an Ottoman Armenian translator bureaucrat born in 1837 received his higher education in Paris and spent a year in Milan around 1860, an experience that inspired him to write and publish a novel in French. Back in Constantinople, he refused to follow his father's advice for a career in the bureaucracy and became part of the Hekimyan theater group playing in diverse *cafés chantants* around town. He wrote a play called *The Miller's Daughter* in Armenian that premiered in Naum and that according to Mestyan is best characterized as "an experimental musical." In 1863 he returned to Paris in order to recruit actors for what was to become the French Theater. He repeated such summer tours for recruiting both renowned and new actors and actresses in the following years and the Ottoman feuilleton followed his activities. Nonetheless, despite his upper middle-class background and being able to negotiate with serious investors into the drama business, Manasse's career as a theater director and manager had numerous turbulent moments, including vicious critiques in the local press and quarrels with the actresses and actors that had to be resolved in court.[31] After a spectacular turn as the viceroy of Egypt's theater director and a failed attempt as impresario in Paris, Manasse returned to Constantinople in 1872 to once again take over the French Theater, but as he could not successfully manage it, tried smaller stages, tried again to find a foothold in Alexandria in Egypt, before reappearing as manager of the New French Theater in Pera as of 1886 and dying of stroke in 1889. Both his work as impresario and as composer (or possibly rather loose translator and adaptor) of operettas was soon forgotten.[32]

None of the three intellectuals lend themselves to an easy modernist or nationalist trajectory. İbrahim Şinasi had popularized French thought through publication and had experimented with various styles influenced both by traditional regional literature and French styles. Both Çuhacıyan and Manasse had moved from Armenian into Italian, Turkish, French, and back again. Çuhacıyan had written a hymn to the Sultan, while Manasse had worked for the Egyptian Khedive.

---

[31] Ibid, 165–169.   [32] Ibid, 170–188.

The World of the Grassroots Stage Workers

But as mentioned, such foreign-trained dramatists were only one side of the mix essential in the creation of the local drama scene. Initially, the translation of foreign pieces into local languages was the way in which non-French and non-Italian-speaking port city residents were confronted with the emerging new popular field. Translations of plays performed in Italian or French were sometimes available from local bookstores in time for aficionados to grab a copy and either study it before the performance or read along. Also at least since after the Crimean War, troupes of Armenian actresses and actors performed foreign pieces in Turkish translation on renowned stages, such as the Naum. Famous in these earlier years were Bedros Magakyan and the Orient Theater. They often performed translations of classics such as Molière.[33] As of the 1860s, Turkish-language drama concentrated on Gedikpaşa. This was the period when Güllü Agop dominated Turkish-language theater. Known in Armenian as Agop Vartovyan, originally an official at the fisheries, he started acting first in the evolving scene of local actors in the Café Oriental of Pera in plays translated from French into Turkish. Then he formed his own company of young amateur Armenians while in Smyrna from 1862 to 1864 and returned to the capital; after several other attempts, he finally took over the Gedikpaşa Theater from the Italian Razi and with his Ottoman Theater Company turned it into the center of Turkish-language drama.

After Güllü Agop had returned to the capital, Smyrniotes interested in Turkish drama mostly had to wait for the Ottoman Theater Company, now under the direction of Serovpe Benliyan, to come to town during a tour, which much like foreign troupes passed repeatedly from Constantinople to Cairo via Western Anatolia. However, according to Halid Ziya, their performances were nothing special, just uninspired repetitions of the contemporary canon of Turkish plays – *Leblebci Horhor*, *Arif'in Hilesi*, *Köse Kahya*, all composed by Çuhacıyan – as well as a number of French operettas, such as *Giroflé-Girofla* or *Orphée aux enfers*. However he (like many others) worshipped their star actress, Virginia Karakaşyan.[34]

---

[33] Sevengil, *Türk Tiyatrosu Tarihi*, vol. III, 4–18.
[34] Beyru, *19. yüzyılda İzmir'de Yaşam*, 246; Sevinçli, *İzmir'de Tiyatro*, 8.

While writing dramas or music was prestigious even at the court and with the higher classes, acting was not. Many of the Turcophone actors, both Armenian and Muslim, came from simple backgrounds, but managed to achieve recognition nonetheless. Bedros Magakyan (1826–1891) had been a shoemaker who only started acting at the age of thirty, but later became director; Ahmed Fehim (1857–1930) had originally been a turner and began performing during the Russo-Turkish War as a twenty-year-old; Serovpe Benliyan (1835–1900) had been an artisan and a shop clerk, before discovering theater at the age of twenty-two.[35] Until the inauguration of the conservatory on the eve of World War I, the recruitment of new actors and actresses took place through impromptu auditions for the respective companies. Stage directors had no formal training either, but were often retired actors who could only base their knowledge on their years of experience, rather than bringing new impulses through a formal education of techniques.[36] These theater companies were rather unstable, with actors and actresses often joining and soon leaving again. Some only formed for Ramadan, when the demand for Turkish-language performances was highest, and disbanded right after.[37] Not surprisingly, as the acting troupes had little institutional or material security to offer, there was little to discipline its members into sticking together if personal differences, vanity, or the stress of performing together got in the way.

Turkish intellectuals often did not hold back with their criticism of these upstarts. The aforementioned Yenibahçe Theater was criticized for the fact that its actors were ice cream vendors, shoe shiners, and shoemakers from Pera and could therefore not successfully act. Mardiros Mınakyan, director of the Oriental Theater Company, was blamed for enacting a play set in Louis XIV's time in contemporary dress, out of pure ignorance, the journalist seemed to imply.[38] The actors' and actresses' language skills were also the subject of much contempt. In May 1869, Güllü Agop was apparently aware of this criticism, as he advertised in newspapers that he was looking for Turkish mother language actors or actors that spoke and read Turkish well.[39] Not only that the Armenian accent annoyed the feuilleton

---

[35] For a detailed description of Benliyan's life, see Mestyan, "A Garden with Mellow Fruits," 245–262.
[36] Alpargın, *Istanbuls theatralische Wendezeit*, 50, 57, 63, 69.   [37] Ibid., 63–69.
[38] Ibid., 44.   [39] Ibid., 60.

critics. They also deplored the fact that the actors and actresses were illiterate, therefore could not study their scripts properly, had to rely on the prompter throughout the play, and often ended up confusing his words and using nonsensical and uncouth language.[40] While one is tempted to write off such comments as outright racism against the Armenian actresses and actors, one must see that there is a clash of different norms at work here. The theater critics, in order to attain world-class status, dreamed of a pristine language standard in which all important cultural contributions had to be performed. In this ideal, they followed the French model, according to which a state allowed for one standard language and allocated to deviations and minority languages a peripheral status. The intelligentsia, just as its Greek or Serbian counterparts, was divided over the question of whether this language should be based on classical or vernacular Turkish, and gradually the partisans of the latter were gaining the upper hand, but the point remained moot as long as the number of original plays in Turkish remained limited.[41] Nonetheless the single-language doctrine strongly contrasted with late Ottoman port city realities, where several languages existed side by side and almost everyone spoke more than one, but could not necessarily write in them, or possibly only in nonstandard scripts. By the beginning of the twentieth century, many port city residents were no longer apologetic for their hybrid character. A Greek or Armenian accent in Turkish, or a Sephardic or Levantine accent in French were not considered a source for shame, but natural.[42]

Is it equally safe to dismiss nationalist paradigms for the lower-class actresses and actors? There is no easy answer to this. Those active in these professions no doubt needed a high level of intercultural competence to navigate the necessary interaction with impresarios, fellow musicians and actors or actresses, the audience, and the authorities. There is evidence that in some cases the highly mobile entertainment performers did form a supernational network of friendships, intermarriage, collaboration, and entrepreneurship, as the case of Amanda

---

[40] Alpargın, *Istanbuls theatralische Wendezeit*, 53–57.
[41] Ibid., 58. Italian theater and opera culture in the Eastern Mediterranean port cities was more flexible than its French counterpart. There were for example comedies in Venetian dialect performed in the Naum Theater; Aracı, *Naum Tiyatrosu*, 295.
[42] *Journal de Salonique*, 22 and 24 Nov. 1908 (letters to the editor).

Lüttgens described later in this book illustrates.[43] There is however also evidence to the contrary. Ahmed Fehim for example recalls playing in the Kukuli Theater on Smyrna's quay. The Kukuli had a rich program: A matinee would be a performance by French actors, the *avant supé* another one by foreign Greeks; the soiree would then be in the hands of the local Turkish-language troop. Ahmed Fehim made malicious comments about the theater owner whom he believed to be spoiled due to the abundance of theater companies. The owner supposedly favored the performers from France and the Greek Kingdom and would cancel the Turks' performance if a foreign group turned up.[44] Not surprisingly, the stage was subject to rivalry at the workplace, which, just as in other sections of the Ottoman labor world, could divide people along ethnic lines. The fact that theater employees had been denied the opportunity of forming a guild to collectively assert their rights added to the instability and rivalry in the scene.[45]

For consumers at the Eastern end of the Mediterranean, theater became a highly popular, but elusive gateway onto the rest of Europe. While for centuries, Western Europeans had striven to learn from classical Greek drama and janissary music to improve their dramatical and musical arts, this interest waned just as the Ottoman urban population began to take a lively interest in drama and especially opera as of the 1830s. Occasional interest in librettos and actors from the Eastern Mediterranean notwithstanding, exchange by and large took on the form of one-sided consumption by Eastern opera and drama aficionados. This led to a noticeable migration especially of trained Italian actors and actresses across the Mediterranean, to locals attempting to keep up with dramatic developments by writing or translating their own pieces, but also brought about the formation of an initially very rustic class of local performers. The development of a drama scene on the Eastern shores of the Mediterranean was far from balanced and suffered from material and technical disadvantages, but developed in a sphere of transregional curiosity, improvisation and interaction, rather than in neat national schools of drama.

---

[43] See Chapter 16, pp. 259–260.   [44] Sevinçli, *İzmir'de Tiyatro*, 17.
[45] BEO 1277/95735, in *Arşiv Belgelerine göre Osmanlı'da Gösteri Sanatları*, 220, 221. Guilds were the only legal form of worker representation in late Ottoman times, as trade unions were banned.

12 Beer Consumption and Production on Mediterranean Shores

In the final two chapters of this section on entertainment, a more widespread and easier to access commodity of Westernization than the theater will be the object of study. This object is beer. Practically nonexistent at the dawn of the nineteenth century, the beverage was produced on an industrial scale 100 years later and was widely available. This transformation warrants a closer look. Once again, one should warn against an anachronistic notion when approaching the subject, such as a trajectory of secularization. While beer has been the object of social and cultural struggles in its short history in Turkey and the Ottoman Empire, the conflicts did not at all resemble today's secular vs. Islamic lifestyle struggle. Rather, the specific meaning beer assumed changed according to time periods and their fashions, ideological shifts, local context, and the size and the modes of production. While in the early twenty-first century, religion is seen as a prime factor for explaining social and cultural conflict, it was not the dominant trope for discussing the role of beer in the period from 1830 to 1920. Other studies have already established that religion was not the context for discussing alcohol, or at best, religious authorities adopted arguments of safeguarding public health, and even this mostly toward the end of the period under discussion here.[1]

These chapters will therefore highlight the frameworks contemporaries used to reflect upon the beverage in the first ninety years of its existence in the Eastern Mediterranean. These will be integrated into a picture of spatial practices that enables us to judge the beverage's role in the respective cities. However, such a history of changing attitudes and dissemination must be set against a history of the production of beer, as widespread production and distribution presupposed lenient attitudes toward the beverage, and on the other hand easy availability

---

[1] Georgeon, "Ottomans and Drinkers," 31–52; Matthee, "Ambiguities of Alcohol in Iranian History."

furthered both positive and negative reactions. Despite some very labor-intensive pioneering work, we cannot consider the history of beer production in the nineteenth century sufficiently studied. Therefore this chapter will proceed by outlining production and distribution patterns, while the following chapter will contrast these with the various attitudes and spatial practices assumed vis-à-vis beer. This chapter will proceed in a chronological matter, whereas the next will discuss more intensely the question of which images different milieus projected onto beer within the framework of the highly diverse urban society. A history of beer, its diffusion, and the attitudes attached to it must bring together a variety of different sources. So far, research has relied heavily on anecdotal material in contemporary literature, travelogs and travel guides, memoirs, and historical works based on oral tradition. This remains the most informative and significant material and is of prime importance, especially for a study concerned with the subjective dimension. However, a problem arises if this material is used alone and at face value. Some individual subjective impressions or statements out of context have been canonized by historians who do not contrast them with material of a different quality. Luckily Ercan Eren has already reconstructed the legal and institutional framework that was used to control the production of beer.[2] Valuable quantifiable sources are insurance maps, business directories, and statistical material, which are however available only for limited periods of the era under discussion. For other periods we have some estimates by well-informed merchants, but the exact object of study varies from observer to observer so that no continuous quantifiable results can be found. Lastly, the chapter makes use of official documents of the Ottoman Archives. These are mostly either applications, for the founding of breweries, or police reports about incidents believed to affect the public order in the widest sense. The applications give us an impression of the expectations toward the market and the institutional difficulties (or non-difficulties) applicants could face in a particular period. The police reports would ideally be our key to the fear, apprehension, anxiety, and disorder provoked by beer, that is, all the dark emotions that do not find their way into dry statistics, formal applications, or whitewashed memoirs or guidebooks. However, as their style for this period is extremely terse, many just consisting of a single sentence, the insights

---

[2] Eren, *Geçmişten Günümüze Anadolu'da Bira*.

they provide are limited. To utilize these sources – beyond those that warranted in-depth scrutiny and will find more detailed discussion – they have been used for a statistical survey based on the catalog entries that in many cases sampled were identical with the whole length of the source. The survey's purpose is to roughly quantify trends of sociocultural change that are evident from the sources discussed in more detail. For the sake of statistic comparability I have divided the time under scrutiny into four periods of equal length (except the first, as it has been lengthened to include the early years for which we have narrative documents, but no archival material).

Between 1830 and 1922, the proliferation and cultural role of beer changed repeatedly. The years demarcating the beginning and end of one of the four phases I have divided the process into are not to be taken as harsh cleavages, but simply as markers of a very gradual process. The initial phase between 1830 and 1868 can be characterized as the times of gold rush and chaos; the second phase between 1869 and 1886 I would describe as the period of beer's slow and quiet ascent to popularity; the third phase from 1887 to 1904 is the age of unchallenged mass production and consumption; the fourth phase between 1905 and 1922 is the apogee of the drink's success, as it becomes a target of agitation. In these four phases, beer to a certain degree reflects the cycles of the acceptance of Europeanization around the Eastern Mediterranean.

Phase 1: The Coming of Beer to the Ottoman Empire (1830–1868)

Beer in its modern incarnation was a novelty introduced from the more western parts of Europe into the Ottoman domains.[3] While it had found its definite composition due to technical developments and legal enforcement in the Holy Roman Empire in the late Middle Ages, it was

---

[3] Strictly speaking beer is of course not a European invention. The Middle East had known different forms of the beverage since prehistorical times, and these survived into Ottoman times in the form of *boza*. It was apparently served either as sweet *boza*, which has survived until today, sour *boza*, which resembles beer, and Tatar *boza*, which is laced with opium. For reasons that cannot be clarified, possibly because of different spells of prohibition, it seems sour or alcoholic *boza* had lost popularity by the early nineteenth century; Eren, *Geçmişten Günümüze Anadolu'da Bira*, 44–59.

not until later revolutions in production in the mid-nineteenth century that beer could be stored for extended periods of time under artificially cool and sustainable conditions, and thus was produced in large quantities and shipped over long distances regardless of the season.[4] These developments were the prerequisites for beer to become the beverage of the industrial age: mass production technology, easy availability almost everywhere, and affordable prices for the (more or less) common people.

It seems the first contact with the beverage by the residents of the Aegean region was established by Italians, as the word for beer in Turkish, Greek, and Bulgarian is pronounced identically to the Italian word "birra" and not "beer," "bière" (French), "Bier" (German), or "pivo" (Russian and other Slavonic languages). In Turkish, the word "arpa suyu" (barley juice) existed as an alternative term for the beverage in the nineteenth century, but was soon eclipsed by the pan-Ottoman "bira."

In the field of Turkish beer history, writers have competed to find the first Ottoman beerhouse, importer, and the first Ottoman beer producer. There are different stories about the establishment of the first beerhouse in Constantinople. Rejecting other claims by Said Duhani and Reşad Ekrem Koçu, which will be addressed shortly, Ercan Eren in his extensive compilation on the history of beer in Turkey claims to pinpoint the earliest pioneers of the beer business. According to Eren, the actual presence of beer in the Ottoman Empire began in the late 1840s in Smyrna with a German immigrant, Prokopp. Eren states that the first beerhouse in Constantinople was established in the suburb of Şişli, under the name of Kosmos in 1850.[5] Of Kosmos, we know little except for some anecdotal notes by his grandnephew Hristo Brâzitsov. Following this author, Kosmos was a Bulgarophone migrant to Constantinople from the region of Panagjurište (Otlukköy). Kosmos is said to have been an informal elder of the Constantinople Bulgarian community and to have possessed many buildings on the then still mostly empty land between Şişli and Tatavla. His decision to begin beer production here set a pattern, which turned the area into the foremost site of beer production in the city for over a century.[6]

---

[4] Eren, *Geçmişten Günümüze Anadolu'da Bira*, 12–18, 26. [5] Ibid., 64.
[6] Brızitsov, *İstanbul'dan Mektuplar*, 72, 83.

Phase 1: The Coming of Beer to the Ottoman Empire (1830–1868)

While Constantinople's beer production origins remain somewhat in obscurity, Smyrna had by 1862 already at least two semi-industrial breweries. One advertisement in the English-language *Smyrna Mail* of 1862 praises "Smyrna Beer. German Brewery, near the Smyrna and Aydın Railway Station. Price 2 ½ Piastres per bottle." This brewery in the district of Punta was the one founded by Prokopp. Another brewery in the countryside at Cumaovası also produced for the Smyrna market.[7]

Prokopp is mentioned in several accounts independently of each other; however no state archival material, only entries in his children's church records have been found. Gottfried Prokopp migrated from southern Germany (some claim from the principality of Württemberg, others Bavaria) to Smyrna. He married the widow Clara Stengel née Pohl around 1842 and together they started producing beer in 1845. The Prokopp family's production over time took on a large output. Writing in the 1890s, Hans Barth calls Prokopp's brewery, which had moved to the suburb of Diana's Bath (Halkapınar), an "adequate temple" to Gambrinus, the patron saint of beer, and mentions the pleasant adjacent garden. He claims that Prokopp had made the whole province of Aydın dependent on him. When Prokopp died (in the 1860s or later), first his widow carried on the business until her death in 1898 (the beer was identified with her, as one can find bottles labeled "Veuve Prokopp") and after her three children until purportedly World War I, when the family sons were drafted and production was discontinued and never resumed after the end of hostilities.[8]

---

[7] The settlement at the former Genoese castle of Cumaovası, according to one source founded by a Swiss resident of the Ottoman lands, according to another by a Prussian subject, comes across as a sleepy agricultural enterprise in German sources; Bülow, "Eine Konsular-Reise," 207; Barth, *Unter südlichem Himmel*, 39–40. The *Smyrna Mail* however makes the Cumaovası brewery appear like a serious business with close links to the city. It produced both barreled and bottled beer and therefore must have supplied bars in Smyrna. It attracted excursionists coming from Smyrna by rail. Its manager was "Mr. Richard Lohmann, late of the British Club Coffeehouse" and its owner "Mr. Cramer." *Smyrna Mail*, 7 Oct. 1862. The name could refer to a member of the Smyrniote entrepreneur family of Austrian nationality Krämer. Nonetheless the Cumaovası brewery was not to survive for long; Barth, *Unter südlichem Himmel*.

[8] Levantine Heritage, "Prokopp"; a contradicting view exists stating that Prokopp merely took over the business started by his wife and her first husband, but this is not likely; Levantine Heritage, "Walker"; Eren, *Geçmişten Günümüze Anadolu'da Bira*, 64–70; Barth, *Unter südlichem Himmel*, 92–93; Sandalcı, "Interview"; see also Gürsoy, *Harcıâlem İçki Bira*, 42, 43.

However, the Prokopp family's role as the pioneer of Ottoman beer must be put into perspective on two grounds. On the one hand his production, while possibly impressive by the standards of the mid-nineteenth century, could not compete with the industrial output that emerged from the 1890s onward, as will be shown later. The other reason is that they were not the original producers on Ottoman soil either. They only distinguish themselves by having established a business that managed to survive for seventy years while early rivals opened and closed up shop frequently.

Based on the documents and literature used here, the quest for origins seems futile. Beer consumption, import, and production started in a decentralized, chaotic, unregulated, and small-scale manner, on the margins of local society. Many small businesses will have taken up the import, production, and sale of beer, but will have given up, moved, or found no heirs to take up the business. Beer had been produced in small quantities by non-Ottoman residents or imported for quick consumption by ambassadors since the eighteenth century. We know of an increased presence of beer in the Well-Protected Domains from the 1830s onward. According to Yavuz Köse's study on Ottoman consumption habits, French and British beer was imported into the Ottoman Empire at the time in small quantities, catering mostly to expatriate communities.[9] It can be assumed that the beer was transported by steamer, as the technical revolution in beer durability had not yet taken place. Even then, it probably had to be consumed within a few days after arrival. A more viable way of bringing beer to the consumers on the Aegean and Marmara shores was local production. Apparently in the 1830s, it was not too difficult to acquire in Constantinople or Smyrna the necessary technology for this production.[10]

Anna Forneris, born in Carinthia, Austria, in 1789, recounts in the memoirs of her long stays in Persia and the Ottoman Empire that she ran a small brewery cum bar in Galata in the late 1830s. Together with her Sardinian husband, she had bought the necessary technology and ran a business that according to her account was very popular with

---

[9] Köse, *Westlicher Konsum am Bosporus*, 151, 170.
[10] We know that by 1856 ferment for producing beer was imported into the Ottoman Empire; BOA, HR. MKT. 148/61, 14 L 1272 (18 June 1856).

local Germans.[11] However, several incidents led them to finally abandon their enterprise and relocate to Persia. Their first business was forced to close down by the police when a row between their German customers and those of a wine bar frequented by Greeks resulted in a fatality among the Germans. Their second bar was evicted by court order because of complaints by an Armenian neighbor about the brewery's smell. When they had bought their own house with a garden to operate as home, brewery, bar, and beer garden, the *kadı* forced them to close down, as the lot had been determined to be the burial ground of a saint and thus their establishment to be impious. In addition, several foreign customers slipped away without settling their bills.[12]

Hostility toward beer production could even result in outright violence, as the event that took place in Constantinople's Bosporus suburb of Kuruçeşme shows. Two Frenchmen by the names of de Gallier and Tokas had been operating a small brewery in the village until in late 1855 both of them and de Gallier's wife were physically attacked and injured. They claimed that the attacker had acted in order to collect a watch as bounty that someone in the Ministry of War had promised to the assailant for assaulting the brewers.[13] Thus the reasons why small-scale enterprises in Constantinople in the last years of Mahmud's and especially the first years of Abdülmecid's reign did not reach any formidable size or durability were neighborhood pressure and legal insecurity.

There was however also a positive side to legal uncertainties. Immigrants from the German lands, many of whom in this period were partisans to the idea of market liberalism, were amazed at the unregulated state of semi-industrial production in the early Age of Revivals. A German who had set up his brewery in the Bosporus suburb of Bebek in early 1847 described his working conditions as full of

---

[11] Unfortunately we do not have any detailed description of sailors' drinking habits, but it is safe to assume that with the growing turnover in the Aegean ports and the capital, the number of sailors who sought distraction in the port vicinity rose and that at least among other options, these sailors will have looked for beer. On *baloz* as a typical institution visited by sailors, see Sakaoğlu and Akbayar, *Binbir Gün Binbir Gece*, 239–241.
[12] Forneris, *Schicksale und Erlebnisse einer Kärtnerin*, 56–64.
[13] The French victims demanded compensation from the Ottoman state. BOA DH. MKT. 134/13, 16 Ca 1272 (25 Jan. 1856); HR. MKT. 131/36, 23 R 1272 (2 Jan. 1856).

"extraordinary advantages." There were no particular taxes or imposts on beer production and the natural ingredients were 25 percent cheaper. The price of a bottle of beer however was double the price in Germany. The brewer noted "a half dozen" breweries already on the market, but hoped to compete against them with good quality wheat beer, porter, and ale.[14]

Besides the lack of special imposts, the absence of any licensing system was another advantage. This becomes apparent in an attempt to construct a brewery in Bosnia. An application by the Habsburg subject Jakob Elyahari in 1856 for erecting a large-scale brewery in Sarajevo (Saraybosna) was simply ignored by the local governor so that Elyahari needed to urge the local Austrian Consul to intervene. Forced to respond, Governor Hurşid Pasha granted permission but at the same time appealed to the Ministry of Public Works, inquiring whether Elyahari would need a license from the central authorities. The officials at the ministry claimed that there was no precedence for such a case and they needed instructions on how to proceed. They later opposed the entrepreneur on the ground that Elyahari would acquire real estate in order to construct the brewery, which was illegal for foreigners in the Ottoman Empire. A brewery on rented ground, however, would not even need any license by the center.[15] Soon after an application for the construction of an industrial-size brewery in Monastir (Manastır/Bitola) by the former officer of the Rumelian Army Kanczesky was received.[16]

Prompted by such applications, the state sought in 1861 to regulate the alcohol sector, introducing a law that prescribed a tax of 10 percent on all alcohol produced in the Well-Protected Domains. However it allowed a slight reduction for beer because of the higher losses incurred by beer going bad compared to wine or hard liquor (once again this is before the revolution in storage technology).[17]

Imperial documents are sparse on this early period, but reflect this ambiguity between lack of regulation and local contention. The Ottoman Archives show catalog entries for beer, casino (*gazino*), and related terms only from 1851 onward, which reflects the largely

---

[14] *Morgenblatt für gebildete Leser* 141 (14 June 1847), 561, 562.
[15] BOA HR. MKT. 159/39, 14 M 1273 (15 Sept. 1856); HR. MKT. 165/16, 29 S 1273 (30 Oct. 1856).
[16] BOA A.} MKT. NZD. 425/81, 20 Z 1278 (18 June 1862).
[17] Eren, *Geçmişten Günümüze Anadolu'da Bira*, 201.

unregulated origins of beer production and consumption in the 1830s and 1840s. The sources reveal the difficulties beer producers would experience even between 1851 and 1868. Of the only thirty-one documents, 32.26 percent deal with applications for licenses for beer production or for serving it, a notable 19.35 percent deal with protest against places of beer consumption or production, 12.9 percent address transgressions against the public order, and 6.45 percent voice moral concerns associated with such places. Other documents are concerned with matters of finances, taxes, or ownership (12.9 percent), construction (9.68 percent), employment (3.23 percent), or other (3.23 percent).[18]

Based on these examples, we can gather that the initial phase of beer in the empire was one of "anything goes." Legal and judicial nonregulation opened up opportunities and profit margins, but also chances for foul play and abuse. Moreover the lack of state regulation was balanced by what might be termed local self-regulation, or more precisely by what is known in modern Turkey as *mahalle baskısı*, neighborhood pressure, that is, by NIMBY (not in my backyard) style protests. This is best exemplified by the vigilante attack on Tokas and the de Galliers, but also by the opportunist evictions by the police or the *kadı* following pressure by competitors or neighbors against Forneris. Religion cannot be seen as the sole reason for this unforthcoming attitude to beer producers, as two evictions were based on conflicts arising with Christians. The third eviction was based on arguments of impiousness, but Forneris claimed these to be a pretext, as the deed had originally been approved, then modified, and only then annulled. Overall these extreme reactions to an as yet young production and consumption industry reflect that beer still remained in a state of marginalization in general society.

Phase 2: The Silent Rise of Beer (1869–1886)

The following period was characterized by four significant changes: the disappearance of protests, the invention of pasteurization and as a consequence the end of spatial marginalization, and finally the introduction of the Public Debt Administration.

---

[18] For a list of the documents used see the Bibliography.

As a result of the revolution in storage technology by Louis Pasteur, a new market for imported beer evolved. Early travel guidebooks and nostalgic memoirs meticulously cite the beers that were on offer at the large cafés in the respective quarters of the Ottoman port cities. Accordingly we can assume that the local production in this phase catered to the lower price segments of the market, the sailors' and corner bars, whereas imported beers served the middle and affluent segments of society. Following Koçu's meticulous accounting of beer brands, Jagodina from Belgrade (Beograd) was originally a market leader, which then had to make way for Grazer Export, Pilsner from Pilsen (Plzň), Dreher from Vienna or Trieste; these in turn later had to make way for Hacker, Pschorr, and Spaten from Munich.[19]

The greater availability both of imported and locally manufactured beer corresponded to an evolving new leisure culture that quickly became an essential part of the urban public sphere. As mentioned earlier, this was the period when Edmondo de Amicis describes a new middle-class going out culture that starkly contrasts to earlier descriptions such as the one by Ubicini.

This new leisure culture generated its own founding myths of the first beerhouse in Constantinople. While it is impossible to verify, Said Duhani's account nonetheless brings together several elements that were characteristic of this period, as other sources confirm, and can thus at least be deemed a realistic view of how things could have been. Duhani refers to a German named Bruchs who had opened the first beer pub in the place of what later became the London Beerhouse at the end of a dead-end street in Galata. He trained several waiters from the Hellenic Kingdom in his trade, and as he had to retreat from the business after having contracted syphilis, these young men established their own as Gianni's (Giannis Kakavopoulos' Viennese Beerhouse) and Nikoli's (Nikolaos Lalos' Swiss Beerhouse), leading to the Greek predominance in Perote beer enterprises.[20] These

---

[19] Meyers, *Griechenland und Kleinasien*, 283; Baedeker, *Konstantinopel, Balkanstaaten, Kleinasien, Archipel, Cypern*, 194; Koçu, "Bira, Birahane," 2805–2806. Dreher even had their own representative in Constantinople and printed special etiquettes for the Ottoman market; Sandalcı, "Interview."

[20] Duhani, *Quand Beyoğlu s'appelait Pera*, 52–54; Sakaoğlu and Akbayar, *Binbir Gün Binbir Gece*, 252–253; *Revue commerciale du Levant* 86 (May 1894), 3. The founding myth reported by Koçu on the other hand can be dismissed as anachronistic at the least. Koçu's *İstanbul Ansiklopedisi* claims that the Bosporus Beerhouse, or Niko's, operating from 1885 to 1910 was the first true *birahane*, serving not only drinks but also a great variety of different *meze* (appetizers). Supposedly Niko's was the blueprint that all later Galata

two establishments were located on the Grand Rue de Pera and in the adjacent Testa Passage. The move from back alleys onto the fashionable main road signified the end of beer's spatial marginalization, while the collaboration and competition of speakers of German and of Greek in the business is also documented.

The 1883 *Indicateur Ottoman Illustré* almanac advertises brasseries in the prestigious location of the Grand Rue and around the intersection of Galata Sarayı. Beer was, among others, on tap at the Hotel cum Restaurant Sponek and the Viennese Beerhouse on the Grand Rue, at the Brasseries Panagioti Spanelis in the Hazzopoulo Passage, and at the Swiss Beerhouse in the Testa Passage. All in all, the *Indicateur* mentions twenty-five brasseries, mostly with similarly prestigious addresses. Of their twenty-six proprietors, eight have German names, three have Slavonic names in German spelling, eight have Greek names, and Arab, French, and Italian names are two each. While names should not be equated with nationality, the preponderance of people of German and Greek background is striking, even more so among the four listed small brewers: Cosma (Kosmos), Grein, and Schaffer all produced beer in the Şişli suburb of Feriköy, while Scherrer was located at Zincirlikuyu.[21]

The Austrian Schweigel in 1873 claims that these four local breweries produced poor quality, but at 40 percent of the price of imported beer. Schweigel considered the local beer market to be still in its infancy, but to have great potential and growth rates. He makes no mention of discriminatory measures.[22] The security situation apparently had changed in the new era of active encouragement of Western ways, and greater guarantees for the right to property and foreign investments. As is well known, this is the period when following the

---

beerhouses tried but failed to imitate. It also offered outstanding service through the great number of purportedly beautiful fifteen- and sixteen-year old Rumelian waiters; Mimaroğlu, "Bosfor Birahanesi." However by 1885 there were already many established middle-class beerhouses. Even Koçu lists the much older Caucasian Beerhouse (founded ca. 1860) in Sirkeci that catered in the beginning mostly to Muslim refugees from the Caucasus; Koçu, *Eski İstanbul'da Meyhaneler ve Meyhane Köçekleri*, 133-135.

[21] Cervati, *Indicateur Oriental* 1887; see also Köse, *Westlicher Konsum am Bosporus*, 163. By 1894 another brewer in Dolmabahçe had joined them; Eren, *Geçmişten Günümüze Anadolu'da Bira*, 71; see also Gürsoy, *Harcıâlem İçki Bira*, 94.

[22] Köse, *Westlıcher Konsum am Bosporus*, 156.

Ottoman state bankruptcy, foreign powers intervened to enforce the safety of capital in the Ottoman economy. In 1881 beer together with all other alcohol production was transferred to the Public Debt Administration. Thus collecting taxes in this sector was now a task for the Debt administrators and the revenue was used to pay the state's foreign debts.[23] An era of legality, tolerance, but also emerging control set in.

The authorities now sanctioned beer drinking places by providing licenses for them, but were wary of them and feared them as places of improper conduct. In 1874, the central municipality of Constantinople, based on a report it had received, urged the Sixth District (Pera-Galata) to take action against the ten *meyhanes* (*rakı* taverns) and *gazinos* it had recently licensed, as "some individuals were violating the applicable rules" by "acts that were most improper and disgusting and should be prevented."[24] Unfortunately for the historian, the officers instructed the bearer to make a verbal report on the precise nature of the violation, as it was considered too improper to mention in writing.

Both in archival and narrative sources, the period between 1869 and 1886 is rather quiet on the subject of beer consumption. Of only twenty-six relevant documents that can be traced through the catalog in the Ottoman Archives, a staggering 69.23 percent deal with construction issues, while 15.38 percent concern licenses; 3.85 percent deal with questions of taxes, finances, or ownership; another 3.85 percent address transgressions against the public order; and 3.85 percent are concerned with moral issues.[25] These cases illustrate a rather relaxed attitude toward the beverage, but the really astonishing development is, in contrast to the previous decades, the complete silence concerning public protest against beer production and consumption. However, the documents remain sparse.

Phase 3: The Age of Unchallenged Mass Consumption and Production (1887–1904)

At the turn of the century, beer had finally arrived in Ottoman society. François Rougon in the 1890s still considered Smyrna's beer consumption to be insignificant, but others contradicted him.[26] In 1893 the

---

[23] Eren, *Geçmişten Günümüze Anadolu'da Bira*, 201.
[24] BOA A.} MKT. MHM. 473/60, 17 Z 1290 (5 Feb. 1874).
[25] See Bibliography.   [26] Köse, *Westlicher Konsum am Bosporus*, 161, 163.

journalist Hans Barth saw Smyrna as the most developed beer market in the Orient and describes the wide and growing acceptance the beverage enjoyed in different parts of society.[27] The 1890s were the breakwater when beer consumption in the Eastern Mediterranean had reached the critical mass that warranted large-scale investments into mass production in order to conquer the markets that had been established by the local producers and the importers. A number of schemes are recorded from the period, most of which never materialized. Bellas Effendi petitioned the Ottoman government and explained his plans for setting up a network of breweries that would cater to the needs of every province with a noticeable demand, including İzmit, Hüdavendigar (Bursa and environs), Adrianople (Edirne), and Salonica.[28] Charles Bolland intended to set up a factory in Constantinople.[29] An application for constructing an industrial brewery in Üsküp (Skopje/Shkup) was rejected.[30]

The ones that actually managed to erect and maintain a factory-size brewery were on the one hand Swiss nationals under German capitulary protection, the Bomonti Brothers, on the edge of Constantinople, and a consortium founded by Saloniqueno oligarchic families. The Bomontis acquired land in Feriköy, where, as mentioned, proto-industrial brewing was already taking place for their factory that started operating in 1893.[31] As Bomonti later became the Turkish Republic's state monopoly producer, this is the brewery that is most prominent in today's collective memory. In Salonica around the same time, Modiano, Fernandez, and Co. seized the opportunity to establish the Olympos Brewery in the suburb of Beşpınar.[32] Foreign observers

---

[27] Barth, *Unter südlichem Himmel*, 91. He also mentions three Athenian breweries founded by Germans that shared most of the domestic market, as Greek import duties on foreign products were prohibitive. The oldest and most established brewery was Fix, which had been established during the Bavarian monarchy; ibid., 89–90.
[28] BOA ŞD. 1190/19, 19 C. 1309 (19 Jan. 1892).
[29] BOA Y. PRK. MYD. 9/105, 3 R. 1308 (13 Nov. 1890).
[30] BOA A.} MKT. MHM. 533/8, 16 Ra 1312 (16 Sept. 1894).
[31] Eren, *Geçmişten Günümüze Anadolu'da Bira*, 90–91; Koçu, "Bira, Birahane," 2805–2806. The neighborhood is still named after the brothers until today. It developed into one of Constantinople's foremost industrial sites of its time.
[32] Quataert, "The Industrial Working Class," 203, 204.

discredited the small-scale breweries, but had to admit that Bomonti and Olympos produced good quality beer that was competitive to the imported products. As the local products were much cheaper than the beer that had traveled over 1,000 kilometers, Bomonti and Olympos managed to take over large segments of the market and the market for imported beer shrank. Those that still stubbornly insisted on high quality products from abroad were apparently affluent and/or willing to pay any price. Thus after the turn of the century a rather small high-end quality market for imported beer existed (which could only be satisfied with the best or most prestigious on offer, i.e. Munich products).[33]

The trend of beer consumption occupying the most prominent spaces of the cities continued. In Smyrna the most prestigious place was undisputedly in Levantine hands: The Smyrniote local business family of Trieste origin and Austrian nationality, the Kraemers, operated from the turn of the century onward not only the best hotel in town, located at the center of the waterfront, but also on its ground floor and in the adjacent gardens the Café Kraemer with imported beer from Pilsen, Munich, and Strasbourg.[34] The other brasseries include the Brasserie Graz or Puntingam and Brasserie Budapest, later joined by the Alhambra, all invoking distant place names to sell themselves as genuinely European.[35]

Beer also literally had its "coming out": consumption under the open sky and in front of the passersby was now an important part of its social prestige. The aforementioned Kraemers operated a beer garden adjacent to its hotel brasserie, as was common practice also in Salonica. Prominent beer gardens were those of the Hotel Olympos Palace serving Munich Spatenbräu while the Brasserie Pentzikis with one branch in the Hotel d'Angleterre and one near the White Tower was provisioned by Pschorr from the same city.[36] In Pera the prestigious place for outdoor consumption was the Petit Champ where many of the best hotels and theaters were located.

---

[33] *Revue commerciale du Levant* 86 (31 May 1894), 3.
[34] *Meyers Reisebücher, Griechenland und Kleinasien*, 283.
[35] Baedeker, *Konstantinopel*, 330–333; Gürsoy, *Harcıâlem İçki Bira*, 14.
[36] Baedeker, *Konstantinopel*, 121.

Phase 3: Age of Unchallenged Mass Consumption & Production   187

Considerably later than in Central Europe, beer consumption on the cities' outskirts became a mainstay of middle-class excursions. The Bomonti Brewery became a destination for Sunday trips where beer was served in a "factory outlet" manner. Beyond the factory, beer was consumed in the public garden on top of Çamlıca, the highest hill in the surroundings of Constantinople. In Smyrna, Diana's Bath became a popular beer garden, as it combined a green location on the riverside with vicinity to the Prokopp brewery. Another destination was the Athanassoula Beer Garden in the suburb of Kokaryalı (now Güzelyalı).[37]

In this phase, the coming of beer mass production and its wider dissemination were lauded by the public. Ottoman urban residents finally had their own beer brand, locally made, distributed, and enjoyed in the new premises. The *Servet-i Fünun* newspaper advised its readers to head out to the suburbs to enjoy the Bomonti Beer Garden, as both the ice produced by the factory as well as the constant cool breeze were a relief in the hot summer months.[38] The garden was depicted as a genuine and enjoyable part of the city and no mention was made of the fact that beer as a product was a novelty that had not been available prior to the Age of Revivals, that the owners of the factory were Swiss, or that they had established their business with the help of German diplomacy.

Likewise Barth in his description of Smyrna mentions the wide acceptance of the beverage in this time as reflected by the customers of the prestigious Café Kraemer who included young lieutenants of the Ottoman army (who under the influence of their German instructors, might have been more prone to engage in beer drinking), but also a member of the Ulema, besides Greeks and Levantines.[39] The enjoyment of beer did not preclude nationalists. Purportedly Mustafa Kemal followed his fellow officers in training to the Perote Deutsche Bierhalle managed by the German subject Zowe while attending the military academy of Harbiye.[40] Later he is reported to have visited the

---

[37] Eren, *Geçmişten Günümüze Anadolu'da Bira*, 94; Yeğin, *Evvel Zaman içinde ... İzmir*, 124.
[38] *Servet-i Fünun* 244, 2 Teşrinisani 1311 (14 Nov. 1895).
[39] Barth, *Unter südlichem Himmel*, 91–92.
[40] Eren, *Geçmişten Günümüze Anadolu'da Bira*, 63, 68.

Olympos Palace Hotel, which served Spatenbräu on its premises in his hometown Salonica together with Ali Fuad (Cebesoy) and Ali Fethi (Okyar).[41]

Mass production eventually saw more rigorous control. A new law from the year 1904 foresaw an official of the Public Debt issuing banderoles for all produced beer barrels and bottles as well as serial numbers for all barrels and an unlimited inspection right for beer pipes to prevent untaxed production or uncontrolled movement of any beer in the country.[42]

As many as 110 relevant documents of the imperial center could be identified in the archive for 1887–1904. The larger number of documents reflects a growth of the market, but also the fact that it had become more controllable due to changes in the production structure and patterns of consumption. As in the period before, their subject matters indicate a relatively conflict-free environment; 28.18 percent are concerned with construction; 14.55 percent with matters of ownership, finances, or taxes; 14.55 percent address various issues revolving around the public order (including hygiene and accidents); 10 percent are on general or unspecified matters; 10.91 percent deal with licenses for alcoholic beverages; 6.36 percent concern licenses for gambling; while only 4.55 percent address moral concerns. Minor matters are politics and censorship (2.73 percent); popular protest (2.73 percent); export (2.73 percent); and opening hours (1.82 percent).[43] This relatively stable situation, beer being controlled but not inhibited, was to change in the last years of the empire.

Phase 4: Beer at Its Apogee (1905–1922)

Without doubt beer was, by the time of the introduction of popular government in the Ottoman Empire, a success story. The representative of the Constantinople French Chamber of Commerce, Ernest Giraud, writes in his 1908 study that despite its favorable conditions for wine the Ottoman Empire produced only 600,000 to 700,000 hectoliters per year, of which approximately 100,000 were exported. He considered the 500,000 to 600,000 hectoliters for the domestic market

---

[41] Ibid., 82.   [42] Ibid., 201–203.   [43] See Bibliography.

negligible for a country of 20 million inhabitants, and claimed that wine had a limited popularity among Greeks, but not among the other large ethnic groups. Giraud demonstrated the large popularity of *rakı* among all parts of society by referring to the import of 14,182,420 kilograms of alcohol for its production.[44] Beer by contrast was conquering for itself a growing market segment and ranked third in popularity.[45] In 1901/1902 the state began to encourage domestic industrial beer production by lowering the tax on beer production from 100 Kuruş per 100 kilogram of produced beer to 71 Kuruş. The intention was to make the price of local beer more competitive and thus to lower the Ottoman economy's dependency on imports.[46] Production in the following years developed exponentially. From 1,741,404 kilograms output in the year 1318 (1902–1903), it grew eightfold to 14,481,729 kilograms in 1327 (1911–1912).[47] While Olympos in Salonica and Prokopp at Smyrna profited from this growth, Bomonti seized the lion's share. In 1318 (1902–1903) Constantinople produced 57.8 percent of all Ottoman beer; Salonica 33.6 percent; and Smyrna 7.51 percent. By 1327 (1911–1912) the respective shares were 76 percent for Constantinople; 19.62 percent for Salonica; and 4.1 percent for Smyrna. Thus, the capital now produced eleven times as much as eight years before; the Macedonian port 4.85 times as much; and the West Anatolian center 4.54 times its former output (see Table 12.1).[48] Government officials showed themselves content with the success of their policy of import substitution.[49] It can be assumed that much of the expansion went to the detriment of the 882,500 kilograms of imported beer in barrels and 81,716 bottles that the Austrian author Joseph Grunzel had noted in 1903, but the overall increase must also be attributed to a spectacular expansion of consumption.[50]

Investors hoped to grab their share of the market for beer made in the Well-Protected Domains. In 1908 construction began in Bahçeköy

---

[44] *Revue commerciale du Levant* 256 (July 1908), 807.
[45] *Revue commerciale du Levant* 294 (Sept. 1911), 412.
[46] BOA DH. İD. 70 –1/28, 03 Z 1329 (25 Nov. 1911).
[47] Eldem, "A French View of the Ottoman-Turkish Wine Market."
[48] *Revue commerciale du Levant* 199 (Oct. 1903), 571, and 306 (Sept. 1912), 382.
[49] BOA DH. İD. 70 –1/28, 03 Z 1329 (25 Nov. 1911).
[50] Köse, *Westlicher Konsum am Bosporus*, 170.

Table 12.1 Beer production according to district, 1899–1912

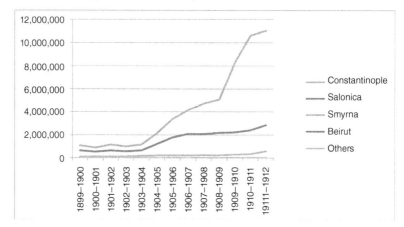

Courtesy of Malte Fuhrmann, Marina Kleymenova

near Constantinople for a brewery that probably never entered operation.[51] A serious but short-lived competitor to Bomonti was the Nektar Brewery in Çayırbaşı on the upper Bosporus. Founded in 1909 as a London-based stock company, it merged with Bomonti in 1912 and in 1914 all production was concentrated on the Feriköy site.[52] The Bomonti-Nektar Company founded a third factory in Smyrna in 1912 under the name of Aydın Brewery at the source of Diana's Bath.[53]

These actually constructed breweries were far surpassed by those that were still on the drawing board on the eve of the Balkan Wars. In 1911 A. Duchaine (?) and the banker Kostaki Papadopoulos introduced their plan of a National Brewery Ottoman Joint-Stock Company located in central Constantinople with 100,000 Turkish lira as capital.[54] Founded in the same year, the Ottoman Brewery Company never managed to erect the planned factories in Smyrna and Beirut,[55]

[51] BOA BEO 3434/257508, 19 L 1326 (14 Nov. 1908).
[52] Eren, *Geçmişten Günümüze Anadolu'da Bira*, 92–94. The Nektar Brewery later became a match factory and lies dormant today.
[53] Eren, *Geçmişten Günümüze Anadolu'da Bira*, 94.
[54] Eren, 96-98; BOA BEO 3933/294913, 5 N 1329 (30 Aug. 1911).
[55] BOA ŞD. 1235/12, 13 Za 1329 (5 Nov. 1911).

Phase 4: Beer at Its Apogee (1905–1922) 191

nor did the Büyük Sulh (Grand Peace) Brewery Ottoman Joint-Stock Company that tried to repeat the plans of Papadopoulos and Duchaine in 1919.[56] Despite beer becoming big business, small-scale production continued, at least in the Constantinople suburbs: The Catholic monks of Makriköyü asked for permission for beer production in 1912.[57]

The tremendous growth of the beer market notwithstanding, consumption was spread unevenly, reflecting the deep economic, social, and cultural divides that had emerged in Ottoman society. In general beer distribution concentrated around the Marmara, Aegean, and Mediterranean littoral and the Balkans. The cultural and consumption practices in the empire increasingly diverged, and beer is a good example, as the statistics will illustrate.

Some contemporary observers believed the split geography of beer production and consumption would be overcome soon. According to Giraud, beer had penetrated into the hinterland where it could now be found and consumed at village grocery-stores.[58] But the geography of the recorded or attempted places of beer production cited, widespread though it is, shows clear demarcations. All four statistically relevant production sites lay in the large port cities, that is, Constantinople, Salonica, Smyrna, and Beirut. For the first decade of the twentieth century, for which we have the Public Debt's statistics, we see minor production in Trabzon, Manastır, Sivas, Aleppo (Halep), Adrianople, Adana, Lesbos, Benghazi, and Durrazzo (Durrës), which either popped up and disappeared again within four to five years or reported ridiculously low quantities, such as six liters in Yemen in the year 1315 (1899–1900) and three in Bursa in 1323 (1907–1908).[59] The archival documents on *gazinos* as potential places for the proliferation of beer also show a preponderance of the large port cities, a lesser presence of Rumelia and an almost negligible presence of Anatolia and especially Arabia. Of the fifty-two relevant documents in the Ottoman Archives explicitly mentioning places outside of Constantinople, an overwhelm-

---

[56] Eren, *Geçmişten Günümüze Anadolu'da Bira*, 97–98; BOA ŞD. 1266/22, 7 R 1338 (30 Dec. 1919); MV. 254/32, 20 R 1338 (12 Jan. 1920).
[57] BOA DH. İD. 117/20, 6 M 1329 (8 Jan. 1911).
[58] Köse, *Westlicher Konsum am Bosporus*, 164; *Revue commerciale du Levant* 86 (May 1894), 3.
[59] *Revue commerciale du Levant* 1900 to 1912.

ing 30 percent refer to Salonica; another 27 percent refer to large ports or trade centers on or close to the Aegean or Mediterranean (in the order of frequency of mentions: Smyrna, Beirut, Bursa, and İzmit); 23 percent to other Balkan cities and islands of the Aegean Archipelago (Adrianople, Rodosto, Üsküp, Sarajevo, Dedeağaç (now Alexandroupoli), Sarantakilise [now Kırklareli], Kos, and Lesbos); a mere 15 percent to other Anatolian cities (Ankara, Amasya, Kastamonu, Trabzon, Niğde, Silifke, and Maraş); and a single source (2 percent) to Arabia outside of Beirut (Yemen).[60]

It would be a simple mistake to try to translate the geographic discrepancy into a religious one – to assume that Christians would consume all kinds of alcohol and Muslims would not. However, the split ran between partisans and opponents of innovation on the drinking market, for this was in fact the meaning Ottoman contemporaries ascribed to beer: It was the drink of a changing world. Individuals had different reasons to defend or oppose this change, as will become apparent from the examples to follow.

The relatively peaceful coexistence of different power networks, channels of economic distribution, and cultural codes was drawing to a close in the first two decades of the twentieth century. While production was soaring, the statistics of relevant materials from the archives for this period affirm that beer had once more become an object of contention, but more due to state measures than to individual protest. Of the 138 documents, license matters amounted to 23.19 percent, while transgressions against the public order had risen considerably to 20.29 percent, and moral misconduct had also risen to now 10.87 percent of the subject matters. Other minor but critical issues addressed protest (1.45 percent); political violence, politics and

---

[60] See Bibliography. Another eighty-five documents are of a general nature or do not make clear geographic indications. The much larger segment of documents referring to the capital reflects a more even distribution of drinking places across the city, although with certain centers. Of 178 documents on Constantinople, 9% do not give a more precise location; 22% mention the territory of the Sixth District; 16% report on the upper Bosporus suburbs; 14% mention *intra muros* Istanbul; 10% Beşiktaş or the adjacent areas of Ihlamur and Yıldız; 7% the western suburbs; 6% Üsküdar; 6% the Kadıköy and adjacent Haydarpaşa region; 4% Şişli and Feriköy; 3% the Princes Islands; and 2% the eastern suburbs and the Golden Horn, respectively.

Phase 4: Beer at Its Apogee (1905–1922)

espionage (2.9 percent); censorship (0.72 percent); accidents (0.72 percent); and prices (0.72 percent). Of a more neutral matter were subjects such as construction (16.67 percent); general and unspecific matters (11.6 percent); taxes, finances, and ownership matters (6.52 percent); export, the media, statistics, and land surveying (0.72 percent each).[61]

---

[61] See Bibliography.

13 Beer, the Drink of a Changing World

The more vociferous material for the later period lets us describe the various attitudes people attached to the beverage more closely. In Constantinople nationalism impinged on beer, targeting it as foreign and attempting to replace it with an invented tradition of an authentically national drinking culture (*rakı*). In Salonica by contrast, beer became an object of contention: Access to and profits from the beverage were redistributed along social and ethnic divides. Smyrna remains silent on beer matters in these years, until the Turkification of the city, which is celebrated as the triumph of the national drinking culture over everything foreign.[1]

The Pros of Beer: Sexy, Cosmopolitan, and Modern

Despite the occasional police concerns about drinking places, the Ottoman *ancien régime* had overall provided amicable conditions to beer producers and consumers. The government had in collaboration with the Debt Administration initiated the aforementioned tax cut of 1901/1902. Abdülhamid II appointed the Bomonti Brewery as the supplier of the imperial court.[2] According to Giraud, a *fatwa* by the Şeyh-ül islam of the times had decreed that despite the Koranic prohibition on wine, its consumption could be acceptable if considered to be of medical use. The household heads should decide for their families and guests if and how much of it was to be consumed. But as the statistics showed, still more people chose to transgress by *rakı* consumption. As for beer, it was claimed that Muslims under Abdülhamid approached it according to the legal principal of *nulla puena sine lege*: As it had not existed at the time of the Prophet and he had thus not banned it, there were no restrictions.[3]

---

[1] See pp. 398–400. [2] Eren, *Geçmişten Günümüze Anadolu'da Bira*, 91.
[3] *Revue commerciale du Levant* 256 (July 1908), 806–807; Köse, *Westlicher Konsum am Bosporus*, 170.

But we can assume that such dogmatic reasoning only played a minor part in everyday decisions to enjoy or abstain from the beverage. Like any other commodity in the capitalist era, beer in the port cities did not just sell because of its innate qualities but because of a plethora of both material and immaterial benefits the consumer associated with the product. In the late nineteenth century, beer was sexy (it did not reek of the exclusively male sociabilities of many other beverages); cosmopolitan (it was consumed across ethnic boundaries, as no locals could lay claim to its tradition); and it signified that its consumers were one step ahead on the road to modernity compared to their contemporaries.

The attractiveness of the beer gardens is probably best summarized in one memoir where the Muslim author depicts his reasons for going to Pera's Petit Champ des Morts as a mixture of voyeurism and love of cosmopolitanism. After describing the multitude of different visitors, Europeans, Levantines, local wearers of the fez, he summarizes,

> Why did we come to the Petit Champ and did not hang around at the Küllük Coffeehouse? The first reason which comes to our minds is "libido."
> Over there was a place where men and women sat side by side, could be found together, turning and walking around; it was full of women. Wearing no veil, headscarf, but tailored suits or dresses, on their heads they were wearing straw hats with bands and flowers held in place by long needles, women, woman types we watched with amazement which reminded us of the illustrations from French novels ...
> ... A corner of Europe![4]

While Ottoman popular drink consumption, both alcoholic and nonalcoholic, took place as a rule in establishments that were strictly male, the new Western-style cafés, brasseries, and casinos allowed for male-centered but mixed forms of socializing in public. Those like the quoted author who did not find themselves in mixed company could at least watch.

Besides mixed gender sociability, mixed origins played a large role in the appeal of beerhouses. The distant place names evoked in café names, such as London, Strasbourg, or Vienna, intended to give beer consumers the impression they could participate in a wider, European,

---

[4] Refik Halid Karay, quoted from Eren, *Geçmişten Günümüze Anadolu'da Bira*, 62–63. Küllük = a famous coffeehouse and newspaper reading room on Beyazit Square, with predominantly Muslim male customers.

cosmopolitan culture without leaving the town. European foreigners played an important role in this. They implied an authentically "European" form of sociability in that locale. Kraemer's even employed a Viennese as headwaiter to give the customers a more genuinely "European" feel of their beer experience.[5] Max Brunau recounts that in the late nineteenth century, Germans and Austrians would gather in the restaurant of Salonica's Hotel Colombo, which imported Munich beer.[6] For Pera, we have a detailed description of ethnocentric (but by no means ethnically homogenous) beer-centered fraternization by Said Duhani. The Swiss citizens of the Ottoman capital would gather at Nikoli's, known officially as the Swiss Beerhouse, where Chevalier was served. The most well-known customer was Alfred Huguenin, director general of the Anatolian Railways. German, Austrian, and Hungarian subjects frequented the city's most prestigious institution, known to regulars as Gianni's the First and otherwise as the Viennese Beerhouse. Photographs show opulent Empire-style interior decoration, high, intricately curved ceilings, and tables set at a distance to each other (see Figure 13.1). A favorite for consumption was the high-percentage Bock beer, which according to Duhani was consumed in large quantities by the commissioned Prussian military officers before they returned to the Ottoman High Command. Gianni's the Second was the preferred name for the Strasbourg Beerhouse popular among French citizens of intellectual background.[7] Thus everyone could invent their particular "corner of Europe" according to their desires.

Despite its sexiness, beer as a drink often remained a men's drink. From among the photographs of private outings to beer gardens gathered by Tarih Vakfı for its 2005 exhibition on beer in Turkish history, we see predominantly tables of men-only companies (who dress in anything from classic *Tanzimat* fez and coat to *allafranga* fashion and several shades in between), but also for example a family gathering (presumably non-Muslim) where three men with fez sit at a garden table with beer bottles set in front of them. The women with summer hats to both sides of them however have no drink (see Figure 13.2). It seems they were either not given beer, did not want it, or at least found it improper to be photographed with it. However

---

[5] Barth, *Unter südlichem Himmel*, 91.
[6] Brunau, *Deutschtum in Mazedonien*, 51–52.
[7] Duhani, *Quand Beyoğlu s'appelait Pera*, 52–54.

The Pros of Beer: Sexy, Cosmopolitan, and Modern   197

Figure 13.1 Giannis Kakavopoulos' Viennese Beerhouse, Constantinople, ca. 1890s
Courtesy of the History Foundation of Turkey

Figure 13.2 A family gathering in the beer garden, ca. 1900s
Courtesy of the History Foundation of Turkey

Figure 13.3 A family gathering in the beer garden, ca. 1918
Courtesy of the History Foundation of Turkey

such modesty was not universal and often probably just for show. A more intriguing picture shows a group of women with three infants and an adolescent boy sitting in a beer garden. Besides the one older woman dressed in black *Chador*, the four younger women's tailored coats and the rather scanty headscarves indicate that the photo was most probably taken around 1918. The adolescent boy and three of the four middle-aged to young women have a beer glass in front of them (see Figure 13.3). Besides such overt demonstrations of Muslim female alcohol consumption, we are safe to assume that already before this date much happened behind closed doors. Michael Talbot has for example drawn our attention to a postcard dating from 1910 in which a man and a woman living in Beşiktaş poke fun at Bedriye, who lives with (and is possibly married to) Cevahircizade Abdülkerim in uphill Şişli. The two who are either her siblings or intimate friends make tongue-in-cheek remarks about her drinking and especially her female friends who supposedly drink up Bedriye's supplies (of champagne?) as soon as they are replenished.[8] Drinking by upper-class Muslim women, while possibly only rarely exercised in plain sight of the

---

[8] Talbot, "Hanımefendis Just Wanna Have Fun."

neighborhood or the city's public, was far from a shameful secretive act and could be jested about on a publicly visible postcard.

It would be wrong to associate *alla franga* drinks and especially beer only with the upper classes and those who envied them. It was a part of working-class life as well. Courtesy of a lawsuit for payment of rent arrears, we know of Necep bin Ali, thirty years old in 1904, a brakeman on the Salonica–Dedeağaç railway line, who apparently was a regular at Adele Feuer's coffeehouse in the Salonica district of Bara. He would come to the Austrian woman's coffeehouse for a beer and apparently had a good standing with Feuer, as according to the court case she had entrusted the counting of the money for the rent payment to him.[9] While we have no record of Necep bin Ali's worldview, we can reconstruct from the little information we have that his lifestyle forms part of the changing world the customers and voyeurs at Petit Champ celebrated. He worked in a specialized profession that had not existed in Salonica a generation ago. His company was owned by French investors; the labor force he was part of was highly cosmopolitan. Railway workers in Macedonia could be Austrian, Italian, Greek, Sephardic, Bulgarian, German, or Turkish, thus necessitating communication in several languages or pidgin versions thereof. Even in his leisure time, Necep apparently saw no necessity to immediately retreat to his fellow Turks, but would enjoy a beer at Feuer's coffeehouse first. Thus, Necep actively participated in the cosmopolitan, intergender, and innovative practices that were epitomized by beer drinking places.

The Cons of Beer: Bitter, Foreign, and Lonely

However, after the turn of the century a vociferous movement against beer arose.[10] This movement was nurtured by a vague conservative disdain for innovation comparable to the NIMBY protests around the mid-nineteenth century, but soon took an aggressive national turn. The Armenian labor migrant Hagop Mintzuri, who had come to

---

[9] HHStA Consulate General Salonica (GK Sal) 433: Zafiriou Marcandonaki/Adele Feuer, 13 Oct. 1904.

[10] The first isolated modern anti-beer statements can be found as early as the mid-1890s. In 1896 the *Servet-i Fünun* urged an investigation of Bomonti on charges that they were polluting the drink; *Servet-i Fünun* 274, 30 May 1312 (11 June 1896). In the same year the novel *Araba Sevdası*, which will be discussed shortly, was published.

Constantinople from his Eastern Anatolian village to work in a bakery as a child, describes in his memoirs a less pleasant experience with beer. He recalls following his colleagues to the Bomonti Beer Garden at the age of fourteen. When the glasses are set in front of them, he believes the clear golden beverage to be a honey drink, but is shocked by its bitter taste and declares to his colleagues that he cannot drink it. The others reply,

"But it is a nice thing, you will get used to it, it gives you strength."
"I am already strong, what do I need strength for?"
The people at the next table were also Armenians. They looked at me. Let them stare, I thought.[11]

Mintzuri defends his countryside instinct that it is undesirable to drink something not sweet but bitter. The reference to the Armenians at the next table who find his behavior strange is not only for the reader to understand that they could eavesdrop on the conversation of the laborers. It implies that these are established urban Armenians from the nearby neighborhood of Pangaltı, who had Westernized to such a degree that they no longer followed their basic instinct that a bitter drink cannot be enjoyable, an implicit class critique.

In his relation to beer, Mintzuri stands in stark contrast to Necep bin Ali, a contrast that can best be explained through their different lifeworlds. Mintzuri came from a predominantly Armenian village in Eastern Anatolia and while in Constantinople as an apprentice at the bakery, he remained within the ethnically and socially restricted world of his peers. The village in Mintzuri's idealized view is the embodiment of an unchanging social and cultural order that provides guidance through the disorienting experience of a lower-class existence in the big city.[12] Thus, the Christian baker apprentice was not part of the changing world that beer was associated with, whereas the Muslim brakeman was.

What Mintzuri describes as a gut reaction toward the blind embrace of Western ways was utilized for nationalist distinction vis-à-vis Europe. François Georgeon believes that the progressive Ottoman bureaucracy and the anti-Hamidian intellectual opposition embraced *rakı* as a marker of difference: Good Ottoman patriots should not be hindered by overcome reservations against alcohol, but they should

[11] Mintzuri, *İstanbul Anıları*, 20–21.   [12] Riedler, "Hagop Mintzuri," 11–12.

Figure 13.4 A street in Salonica, ca. 1913, with a modern-style waiter on the right
Courtesy of Malte Fuhrmann

aim at national consumer distinction through their traditional alcoholic beverage rather than *alla franga* fashions such as wine or beer.[13]

The juxtaposition of *rakı* as an indigenous, patriotically acceptable drink and beer as an alien, colonialist, and thus unacceptable beverage is made explicit by Ahmed Rasim Bey. He ends a long eulogy to the Istanbul *meyhanes* with the sentence, "Frankish beerhouses and casinos will always remain foreign to me."[14]

Reşad Ekrem Koçu goes into detail explaining what turned contemporaries off by describing the Gambrinos Beerhouse that opened in 1898 in Pera (Figure 13.4).

Not a conversion from a former meyhane, it was an *alla franga* beerhouse from the start. Its owner Dimitri Gambrinos was a sailing boat captain who named the place after himself and who had opened it for a Chiote effeminate character named Andrea who had been traveling on boats since being a little kid. Around 1898–1900 Andrea was around thirty. He walked around in the over-decorated clothes of a European youth. Having lived for years on a

---

[13] Georgeon, "Ottomans and Drinkers," 31–52.
[14] Ahmed Rasim Bey, quoted in Koçu, *Eski İstanbul'da Meyhaneler*, 19.

sailing ship naked except for his underpants and having worked as a server of alcohol in the sailors' milieu, he took the red pirate's bandana off his head and his naked feet had forgotten the times he had awakened to an infidel's oboe and the harmony of a violin and danced to them; he always spoke French, if patrons addressed him as "effendi," "barba," "mastori," "kir," or "çelebi," he would not turn his head, it had to be "Mösyö", not even "Mösyö Andrea," "Mösyö André!"

In Beyoğlu, waiters with white jackets, white starched shirts, black bow ties, black pants, black socks and black shoes, their heads bare, their long-grown hair parted at the side or in the middle and smelling of lavender were for the first time seen in the Gambrinos Beerhouse ... They knew a few sentences of French which they had memorized by heart and used self-chosen French names: Jacques, Jean, Michel, Maurice, Alfred, Paul. They were all local stock, *pedimu*s or *ahbar*s gathered from Tatavla, Galata, Kumkapı, Hasköy.[15]

Thus to Koçu the denial of one's heritage and the faux Europeanness of such institutions is what turns the patrons off. He quotes a mocking song to back up his story.[16] However by reading Koçu's and other sources against the grain, we find that by the time of Ahmed Rasim's polemic and the derision against the Gambrinos Beerhouse, the neat distinction between *birahane* here and *meyhane* there was already a thing of the past. The conflict reflects more its authors' nostalgia and intent to create an invented tradition than the contemporary alternatives on the drinking market.

Besides targeting the drinking institutions as without heritage, the beer drinker himself was declared antisocial. Yavuz Köse has observed that Ottoman opponents of imported consumption products successfully created a "we" identity centered on local production and that they contrasted this not to "them," but to "him," the individual,

---

[15] Koçu, *Eski İstanbul'da Meyhaneler*, 129–131. Effendi, barba, mastori, kir, çelebi = titles addressed to proprietors of meyhanes; pedimu, ahbar = slang expressions for children originating from the Greek and Hebrew language.

[16] Koçu does not pour such derision on bars actually operated by foreigners, but mentions rather neutrally one run by an Ashkenazi woman originating from Poland, and lauds the Caucasian Beerhouse that Greek entrepreneurs had opened in the 1860s in Sirkeci to cater to nostalgic Muslim refugees from Russia, which later became popular among travelers on their way to the adjacent European railway terminus, when it was operated by the Ashkenazi Steinbruch between ca. 1900 to 1945, serving Munich Salvator Beer and renovating the grounds to imitate a German beerhouse. Koçu, *Eski İstanbul'da Meyhaneler*, 131–135.

Figure 13.5 Patrons of a beer garden on Prinkipos Island, ca. 1900s, dressed in a style reminiscent of Bihruz Bey
Courtesy of the History Foundation of Turkey

narcissistic Europeanized consumer who did not form part of any larger collective.[17] This also holds true for the nationalist rejection of beer. In his novel *Araba Sevdası* Recaizade Mahmut Ekrem describes in the opening scene Bihruz Bey, the personification of superficial and xenophile modernization. Bihruz is seated at an outside coffee table of the casino in Çamlıca Park. His summer coat is placed on the adjacent seat in such a way that the Terzi Mir trademark is visible. On the table in front of him a glass of beer stays untouched on the tray. His silver-topped walking cane exhibits the Latin letters M. B., while he constantly takes his pocket watch out of his white vest, then takes five to ten steps toward the exit only to turn back and sink into his chair again (see Figure 13.5).[18] The beer is a key element of conspicuous consumption that characterizes the young Europeanized dandy: There is no pleasure in the consumption, in fact there is no consumption proper (the beer is not touched), only outward appearance.

---

[17] Köse, *Westlicher Konsum am Bosporus*, 446, 447.
[18] Recaizade Mahmut Ekrem, *Araba Sevdası*, 15.

The dispassionate consumption or nonconsumption of beer and Bihruz's individualist narcissism starkly contrasts to the sociability that was seen as characteristic of *rakı*. Ahmed Midhat Effendi, for example, describes in a novel the consumption of *rakı* as something embedded in society and for which strict local traditions applied. By contrast beer is associated with a somber member of the underworld sitting and drinking by himself in a bar until an acquaintance asks him to reveal his next victim. The criminal insists on another beer as compensation, then almost empties it in one revolting gulp, before continuing the conversation.[19]

The trope of the listless and antisocial consumption of beer seems to some degree to have reflected an actual practice. Ernest Giraud could not but wonder about the dispassionate way in which he saw locals consume it. He described it as a common habit for white-collar workers to have a pint or two after the end of the working day.[20] However, they seemed to him to be forcing themselves to empty their consecutive glasses, without passion, but out of habit, to kill time, or for lack of alternative beverages.[21] It is a question of the hen and the egg what had been there first: the stigma of anti-socialness against beer consumers that prevented them from finding adequate social forms, or the awkward drinking habits. It seems the beverage still exuded an aura of novelty and foreignness, and the drinkers' inexperience was aggravated by the propagandists claiming that these upstarts did not form part of local society anyway.

Negative attitudes toward beer and beerhouses did not remain literary. After the Young Turk Revolution especially they more often informed the authorities' attitudes. In November 1908, six Austro-Hungarian Navy soldiers and consulate members had got into a bar

---

[19] Ahmet Mithat, *Bütün Eserleri*, vol. VIII, 546–552. Claims to the antisocial nature of beer consumption was not limited to Muslims or Turkish nationalists. It also showed in the lines of a *Smyrneika* song: "You stay up all night at the *cafés chantants*, drinking beer, Oh! / And the rest of us you are treating as green caviare." Quoted from Mansel, *Levant*, 158.

[20] Probably he is referring to employees of the banking district in Galata just next to where his office lay. The pub mentioned could be *Bizans Birahanesi*, which operated from 1897 to 1908 around the corner from Galata's Bank Street. It served lunch for the local employees during the day and converted into a beerhouse at night; see Koçu, "Bizans Birahanesi," 2805–2806.

[21] Köse, *Westlicher Konsum am Bosporus*, 164; see also *Revue commerciale du Levant* 86 (31 May 1894), 3.

fight in a Galata beerhouse and in the course of the confrontation, the Ottoman flag hanging there had been disgraced. The initial investigation remained inconclusive as the bar owner could not identify the culprit, and due to the capitulations, the investigation had to be left to the Habsburg officers and consulate. The report speaks in a matter-of-fact tone about the event, as if it seemed natural that Austrians (the public enemy number one at the time due to the annexation of Bosnia and Herzegovina) would have brawls in the port vicinity, that they would at such occasion disgrace the flag, and that the perpetrator would go unpunished, but lays blame on the beerhouse as an institution.

However, to unfurl a flag is not permissible in beerhouses and in similar places which are not dignified enough for the glory and great reputation of the Ottoman flag; thus the unfurling of the flag in such places causes a certain grievous situation.[22]

The author of the document then remembered that hoisting the flag was obligatory on official holidays, but urged general action to be taken to prevent its presence there on other days.

The Role of Beer in Strife-Torn Salonica

While patriots in the capital tried to show their rejection of the West by abstaining from beer to the benefit of *rakı* or by aiming to remove the national flag from beerhouses, beer had assumed a completely different status in Salonica. Here the question was not whether or not to drink beer, but rather who should profit from its consumption. For example, the newspaper *Zaman* commented on the takeover of the Brasserie d'Angleterre by the Pentziki Brothers in late 1908 that this was a positive development, as the brasserie was now run by Ottoman subjects who were also good patriots.[23] This was to some degree a more "European" struggle. Working-class men in Central and Western Europe had adapted the bourgeois ritual of fraternization with beer in hand. Thus, beer was a central object for recreation, socializing, associating, and claiming one's rights, and a perspective for quality of

---

[22] BOA BEO 3434/257482, 20 L 1326 (15 Nov. 1908).
[23] *Journal de Salonique*, 24, 26 Nov. 1908.

life.[24] Beer in Salonica was like in Central Europe an object over which to negotiate social inclusion and exclusion: the threat of withholding the product or making it unacceptably expensive was deemed a threat to one's rights to sociability and happiness. However this did not mean that the conflicts in Macedonia could abstain from nationalism any more than the pro-*rakı* movement could.

The milieus of laborers, retailers, and owners of beer in Salonica were actually too complicated to easily translate into ethnic divisions. Although the owners of the leading brewery, the Modiano, Fernandez, and later also Misrachi families, were Sephardim, they had no particular preference for Jewish workers. Perhaps being Jewish was even a disadvantage for employment, as capitalists had to fear the rigid observance of the Sabbath that was common in Salonica as an obstacle to optimal revenue. The workforce of eighty at the Olympos Brewery saw a predominance of Greeks in the machine departments, Bulgarians in the malting and brewing sections, and both Bulgarians and Jews in bottling. The casino and *meyhane* owners were by majority local Bulgarians and Greeks. A second Salonica brewery owned by four Greeks that had opened in 1908 apparently tried to conquer parts of the market by appealing to the nationalist solidarity of their fellow Greeks.[25]

With the reinstitution of the constitution and the rise of popular movements, the local monopolist, the Olympos Brewery, came under pressure from two sides: Its workers considered their wages too low and the casino owners the price per barrel too high. One conflict was suppressed with a show of arms, while the other ended as one of the many moments of interethnic strife in late Ottoman Macedonia.

When the Greek casino and *meyhane* owners decided to collectively boycott Olympos beer because of its price policy and import Serbian beer instead, some of the customers, especially of the city's Jewish majority population, complained and demanded the return of Olympos beer. As a reaction, some entrepreneurs wanted to end the boycott to appease their customers, but were threatened by the Greek boycott

---

[24] Teich, *Bier, Wissenschaft und Wirtschaft in Deutschland*, 329–340; Kaschuba, *Lebenswelt und Kultur*, 21–23, 110–112, 115–117; Machtan and Ott, "Batzebier!" *Demokratische Zeitung*, 30 July 1872.

[25] Quataert, "The Industrial Working Class," 204–207.

supporters. By June 1, 1908, the situation had become so tense that the state authorities urged an investigation into the conflict.[26]

Having just escaped this predicament with the customers, the Olympos Brewery's production was endangered next. As the Ottoman Empire entered its short but intense summer of labor radicalism, the brewery workers joined in the struggle for better living conditions. At the same time as the workers on the railway lines from Salonica to Manastır, and to (Kosovska) Mitrovica and in many other branches of labor, the brewery workers went on strike demanding a wage increase of 30 percent. As the participants prevented beer and coffeehouse employees arriving with horse carts from collecting beer and ice and as they had also erected a picket line, the authorities deemed it necessary to intervene. To strike was legal, they argued, but to picket and to obstruct sales was deemed a rebellious act against the public order. The strike was ended when 500 soldiers gathered first at the railway station and then at the brewery, leading the laborers to return to work.[27] Nonetheless it led to a significant increase in wages: They were raised from 7–8 to 10–11 Piasters.[28]

Having received state protection in these two conflicts, the Modiano, Fernandez, and Misrachi-owned company had to deal with a more hostile state in the following years. Beer was now associated with the ethnic strife and political violence that became an increasingly prominent part of Macedonian public life. An informer, Abraham Effendi, reported that under the protection of Greek-Orthodox priests, beer and cognac barrels were being used to smuggle weapons into the countryside. While this announcement has all the earmarks of a conspiracy rumor, the authorities took it seriously.[29] A decision that more materially threatened the families' profits was an increase in tax. The Salonica municipality in 1911 decided to arbitrarily increase the tax on the produce from 71 to 130 Kuruş per 100 kilograms of beer. Only after the factory director's protest against the nigh doubling of the tax, the governor's administrative council together with experts from the Public Debt Administration convened and, calling into memory the

---

[26] Eren, *Geçmişten Günümüze Anadolu'da Bira*, 76–77; BOA TFR.I.SL 185/18430, 2 Ca 1326 (1 June 1908).
[27] BOA TFR.I.M. 22/2117, 24 B 1326 (21 Aug. 1908); TFR.I.SL 194/19391, 24 B 1326 (21 Aug. 1908); TFR.I.SL. 195/19410, 27 B 1326 (24 Aug. 1908).
[28] Quataert, "The Industrial Working Class," 209.
[29] BOA TFR.I.SL. 213/21269, 28 C 1327 (17 July 1909).

earlier decision to abstain from heavy taxing on local beer production in order to substitute imports, decided to limit the increase to 78.5 Kuruş, reflecting the Olympos Brewery's increase of retail prices by 10 percent.[30]

The initial protests from the 1830s to the 1850s against an as yet new and unusual branch of production and entertainment were widespread and not limited to Muslims, but played out on the local level. They should therefore be seen instead as reactions against innovations that threaten to bring change and unrest to the neighborhood. This unstable time of little security but also little regulation for beer producers and consumers contrasts to a nigh half century of the undisturbed ascension of beer to a status symbol of modernity and cosmopolitanism to be displayed in the prestigious parts of town and to mass production, which coincides with state supervision of the production and distribution process. The social and ethnic unrest visible since the turn of the century impacted on beer in regionally different ways. While in Salonica beer and its profits were contested between socially and ethnically determined groups, Constantinople saw a prominent movement targeting beer in order to homogenize the country as a national space, a space that was later extended to Smyrna and the rest of the country.

Conclusion

Leisure practices, from the casual stroll along the waterfront in the evening to all-night dancing at the seasonal ball, from an opera performance to a visit to the beer garden, together make up a field that was thoroughly revolutionized in nineteenth-century Eastern Mediterranean port cities. Entertainment in this time created new industries, led to international migration and investments, and provoked long societal and governmental discussions about what was desirable, permissible, or dangerous. Despite initial and especially early twentieth-century resistance, a large portion of port city society readily embraced innovation. The new pastimes were opportunities to show off social and cultural capital, displaying how well attuned one was to the imported knowledge and tastes, but soon evolved into more. In their respective ways, both opera and beer appeared as tickets to a wider

---

[30] BOA DH. İD. 70 –1/28, 03 Z 1329 (25 Nov. 1911).

world, as shortcuts to or dream worlds of Europeanization, where the differences between the Ottoman lands and their European peers in military might, rule of law, public infrastructure, and standard of living were eclipsed by the common veneration of international performers or visiting the cosmopolitan beer gardens or bars. And yet, the port city residents' attitude must be seen more as a hope for reciprocity, for being recognized as equal participants in a dialogue of different parts of the continent or world moving closer together. This becomes apparent in the local pride in the few internationally successful stage writers and performers, or also in the first local beer factory and its premises. Frustration and nationalist backlash including criticizing the inadequate local stage performers were some of the reactions to reciprocity not setting in, but more commonly, port city residents took refuge in simply consuming what they could not gain through mutual exchange. And yet, both the denial by state institutions of the degree of permeation the new cultural practices such as the opera had reached, as well as the discrepancies between new practices and their lack of societal integration – exemplified by the isolated beer consumer – produced challenges for collectives and individuals. It is therefore necessary to take a look at the redefinition processes of the self and the group next.

PART IV

Identities on the Mediterranean Shore
Between Experiment and Restriction

He: *Dhe mu les kale kira mu Turka ise ya Romia*
        Ya Engleza ya Françeza k'ehis tosi emorfia
She: *Ke ti se meli esenane apo pu'me ego*
        Yapti Menemeni yapto Kordhelio
        Ke ti se meli esenane ya to salvari mu
        Ya kondo mu ya makri mu ya karari mu

In a popular Greek song from Smyrna of the nineteenth century, a male youth brazenly makes a pass at a young woman in the street. He asks her, "Dear woman, tell me, are you Turkish or Greek? Or maybe English or French? You are so beautiful!" The girl answers, in a both mocking and enticing reply, "What is it to you where I am from? Whether I am from Menemen or Kordelio? And my *shalvar* I will wear as I please, whether short or long or black."[1]

The passage in a nutshell demonstrates some of the aspects of how the seaside residents framed their identities within the multifaceted cities. The young man's question is of course not to be taken at face value. Before World War I, most women could still be identified with a distinct ethnic group by the way they dressed in public. A Muslim Turkish woman would rarely be seen not wearing at least a thin muslin or silk veil, and an English or French woman would (in contrast to previous centuries) hardly be caught wearing a *shalvar* (traditional baggy pants), except when posing in an exoticist photograph or visiting a costume party. Nonetheless the male youth asks her, "English or French? You are so beautiful!" which could be understood as flattery ("You are as beautiful as an English or French woman, who are of course more attractive than most locals"). But besides such a xenophile hierarchy of aesthetics, the young man's question displays an excitement for the fact that on the streets of Smyrna, he could run into

---

[1] Ketencioğlu, *İzmir Hatırası*, sleeve notes.

French and English women just as easily as into Greek or Turkish ones. The fact that English and French people are not beings from beyond, but very much part of the local fabric is further attested to by the woman's answer. Instead of discussing ethnic tags, she responds with different suburbs. These suburbs do not stand for a contrast between local belonging and exotic Western European nationalities; instead, neighborhood affiliation corresponds to some degree to the options listed by the man (Menemen being a town with a larger Turkish population, while Kordelio was a suburb with a strong Greek and smaller expatriate presence).

This playful interchange displays a certain degree of pleasure in the indeterminate state of identity in the cosmopolitan city on both sides. In fact, it seems both man and woman enjoy the ambivalence of the situation. While we know that de facto social pressure severely limited relationships between people of the opposite sex over ethnic and especially religious boundaries, the ambivalent space gives both speakers the opportunity to chat with and tease the other without ever actually resolving the question under debate. What ethnic identity does the woman have? Is she turned off or on by the man's advances? What actual expectations do the two have toward the other sex? Will they come closer? We do not know.

The history of identities in Southeast Europe and West Asia before World War I has often been written according to a teleological narrative. Identity was a priori premodern, following the categories defined by the early Ottoman state, or by the various religious leaders: One was either a true believer or a Reaya, or more specifically a Sunni Muslim or a Greek-Orthodox Christian, a Jew of Spanish origin, etc. This form of identity gave way, under Western and Central European influence, to the modern category of "nation," understood as a group of common origin and more or less speaking the same language and/or of the same religious denomination. People were now divided into Turks, Greeks, Sephardim, etc. Other layers of identity were subordinate to the national one: Issues of class and gender were determined by the respective national groups and the discourses they controlled.[2] Whether one was a bourgeois or a proletarian, a man or a woman,

---

[2] The debate on Southeast European nation building cannot be reproduced here. Just to list some key and exemplary publications: Ersoy, Gorny, Kechriotis, *Discourses of Collective Identity*, vol. I; Zelepos, *Die Ethnisierung griechischer Identität*; Müller, *Staatsbürger auf Widerruf*.

one was first of all a Greek or a Turkish bourgeois, a Sephardic or an Armenian woman, etc.³

While one should not belittle the influence of nationalist discourse in the nineteenth century, I wish to claim here that identity issues in the late Ottoman sphere appear much more in flux when viewed from a synchronic and not a teleological perspective. Between the end of Ottoman state–determined identities, if they were ever as clear-cut as they appear to be,⁴ and the triumph of the new nation states, many shades, blends, and experiments in describing the self, entered and exited the stage. One must characterize the era between the disintegration of the traditional *millet* and the final wars of the Ottoman Empire as one of subsequent openings and closings of windows of opportunity to style the self. In this respect, we might generalize Ilham Makdisi's statement on Eastern Mediterranean radicalism, which stresses

> the lack of orthodoxy and rigid boundaries that was a key characteristic of the fin de siècle, whether intellectually, culturally, or socially. It suggests a Weltanschauung taking shape during a period of flux, in which different groups of actors in the non-Western world felt confident they could assemble their own visions of social and world order, borrowing, adapting, synthesizing perhaps plundering ideas from 'the west and the rest' and melding them with local practices and ideas to produce what might strike us today as a radical package marked by contradictions and limitations.⁵

Such a desire for experiment can also be witnessed in the late nineteenth- and early twentieth-century practices of cross-naming. For example, Fanny Bertha Prokopp, daughter of the German Smyrna brewery founders Clara and Gottfried Prokopp, married the Italian Carlo Crespi and gave two of her children mixed Italian Arabic names, Giovanni Kiamil and Nicolas Firuz.⁶ The Üsküp-based engineer Friedrich R. Walthard and his wife Hedwig, both German Protestants, named their son Gustav Rudolf Hermann Macedonius, while the Habsburg consular official of the same town Tibor Plathy of Nagypalugyar and Turoczdivek and his wife Maria named their son Loerinz

---

³ See the critique of the historiography of Ottoman bourgeoisie(s) in Eldem, "The Bourgeoisie of Istanbul."
⁴ Masters, "Millet."
⁵ Khuri-Makdisi, *Eastern Mediterranean and Global Radicalism*, 12.
⁶ Levantine Heritage, "Prokopp."

Joseph Peter Mehmed. By contrast, the son of Mahmud Kadri, a former official of Yıldız Palace, and his wife Elisabeth (née Hillebrandt) had their son baptized as Richard Gustav Kadri.[7]

Ambivalence and unresolved issues are in fact the main characteristics of how the semi-open space in the Ottoman port-cities affected people's identities from the mid-nineteenth century until World War I. Obviously there was a myriad of different influences and contemporaries were often hard pressed to come to grips with them. Whether they were considered a source of pleasure, as in the song, or a cause of disorientation depended on the point of view. Linguistic confusion can be one result. Characteristic of this scenario is the Greek citizen originally from Constantinople I mentioned in the introduction of this book, who, after lapsing into Turkish due to his Alzheimer condition, reverted to singing French children's songs he presumably had learned in school. We can see therefore that both concerning popular awareness among contemporaries and long-term effects, identities were unstable, subject to change, and could be arrested in an in-between state. This is characteristic of maritime society, and while it has been the subject of debate many times, some reconsiderations are in order.

The Man without Qualities on the Bosporus

The discussion of an identity split in late Ottoman society is not new. It has been a recurrent theme, already prominent in contemporary literature, that men and women of that period had to face the challenge of amalgamating tradition and modernity, Orient and Occident, or Europe and Asia. Many contemporaries, especially men of letters, conceptualized this in-betweenness as a failure to master the modern world. Şerif Mardin claims that the archetype character of in-betweenness in late Ottoman literature is Bihruz Bey, the already mentioned main character of *Araba Sevdası* (*Love of Carriages*) by Recaizade Mahmut Ekrem.[8] This representative of a *jeunesse dorée* in the 1870s attempts to compose love letters first by translating from French modern poetry, then from classical Persian verse, but is not capable of understanding or paraphrasing in Turkish either one of them.

---

[7] Evangelical Parish Thessaloniki, Old Baptism Register, 1913–1916, 1917, and 1919.
[8] Mardin, "Super-Westernisation," 135–163.

However unlike previous discussions, which have focused on the particularities of the Ottoman condition in between East and West, I wish to change the perspective slightly. The dilemma the late Ottoman urban residents faced was in my view not unique vis-à-vis Europe; it was part of the general dilemma all over the continent. And it was not simply a matter of managing or not managing to cope with modernity. Moritz Csáky claims that destabilized identities are actually characteristic of nineteenth-century European cities, as was reflected in the writings of Robert Musil, Friedrich Nietzsche, or Hugo von Hofmannsthal.

These [examples from works of the aforementioned authors, MF] are all together mentions of the crisis symptoms of fragmentation, of lack of orientation, of a decentering of the ego in Robert Musil's sense of "lack of qualities." All of these owed their existence to the modernization-induced inner *vertical differentiation* of society in process and were to become defining criteria of modernity. Vertical differentiation demarks the social strata and groups a society produces; in the context of my deliberations, it is especially a sign of the progressing social permeability and is related in particular to the accelerated differentiation of traditional social formations into numerous synchronous new social strata and groups: "This is the particular people," claims Musil, "that the present has produced." He then continues, almost paraphrasing Nietzsche, "The same thing has a hundred pages, the page a hundred meanings, and to each are attached different feelings. The human brain therefore has managed to divide these things; but the things have divided the human heart."[9]

Two things from Csáky's framing of the late nineteenth-century predicament can help us reconsider the Eastern Mediterranean situation. First of all, if the dilemma individuals of the period faced is really one of multiple differentiation and polyvalence ("a hundred meanings"), then it seems an oversimplification to reduce the dilemma to one of tradition vs. modernity. Although such framing is widespread in the later literature on the period and even in memoirs by contemporaries, one cannot simply subsume the multiple challenges to clear-cut identities under a binary opposition, and if we look at the particularities of each individual situation, we will find that they are rather a multitude of identity conflicts that intertwine, but are not monolithic. They are too manifold to simply be reduced to the scheme

---

[9] Csáky, *Das Gedächtnis der Städte*, 32.

"old" vs. "new." The particularity of nineteenth-century modernity is not so much that it offers two clear answers as to how one should organize one's life (according to the modern or against the modern), but rather that it confronts individuals and groups with an unprecedented amount of impressions as possible points of reference. "Modern" and "traditional" should rather be seen as terms that some contemporaries and mostly retrospective observers use to reduce the complexity of the challenge. In doing so, they adapt a colonizing, bifurcated logic that is related to the divisive, symbolically violent gaze we have already witnessed in the earlier chapters on spatial patterns, first introduced by Calligas and later adopted widely.

Secondly, the malaise described earlier to a certain degree is universal, but it has its hot spots and multiple local particularities. The human condition around 1900 (which later resurfaced in the age of globalization), according to Csáky, is not exclusive to big heterogeneous cities; however polyethnic and socially diverse agglomerations such as the cities of the Habsburg Empire and the French, British, and German imperial metropolises were its privileged sites:

The city of modernity has both an integrative and a differentiating function. Its residents, who belong to various heterogeneous socio-cultural strata, i.e. different cultural communicative spaces, especially if they have newly migrated, are forced to adapt to their urban situation, i.e. to appropriate (new) identities, among other reasons in order to deal with the social, economic, cultural, linguistic, or intellectual differences they are now confronted with.[10]

The peculiarities of big city life had an even stronger effect if they were not mitigated by identification with a state that led its subjects to believe they were represented equally. The Habsburg Empire proved incapable of developing such a modern, comprehensive sense of belonging for its highly diverse population, either through a sense of allegiance to the dynasty or through patriotism for state institutions.[11] Despite the many outward differences, this also holds true for the Ottoman Empire, which, by attempting to erect a modern statehood and demanding a uniform loyalty from its subjects, managed more to

---

[10] Csáky, *Das Gedächtnis der Städte*, 24.
[11] Franz Kafka describes the sense of alienation of the Habsburg subjects with the dynasty and empire in "The Great Wall of China"; see Lemon, "Eastern Empires and Middle Kingdoms."

destroy preexisting loyalties and arrangements than to create a new sense of belonging.[12] By consequence, its subjects as well as all others residing within the Well-Protected Domains had to face the task of defining their proper place in the modern world without relying on the empire. Applying Csáky's scenario to the Ottoman sphere, I believe that it describes rather aptly the late nineteenth-century process of soul-searching, identity building, curiosity, experiment, despair, and line-drawing that prevailed in the port cities. In this light, Bihruz Bey appears to be an earlier version of Musil's *Man without Qualities*, unable to make use of the multiple registers at his disposal, fixated on Western status symbols, deriding the local lower classes, and without a safe home to return to. Already Şerif Mardin likened Bihruz to Ivan Goncharov's *Oblomov*, hinting at the trans-European dimension of the predicament. But as Mardin states, while both Oblomov and Bihruz (and Musil's *Man without Qualities*) suffer from a condition contemporaries described as a malaise, the exact framing of their dilemma varies greatly from one literary canon to another.[13]

In the following chapters I will explore some of the particularities of Eastern Mediterranean port city identity. As this section cannot fully take into account the whole range of influences prevalent in the nineteenth century on this complex topic, I will limit myself to the channels through which the lively exchange with other parts of Europe influenced the way people saw themselves as parts of wider collectives. I will first look at the most direct and potentially most substantial source of influence, that is, foreign schools. Then I will touch upon the space created by foreign-language newspapers. The third chapter of this section will discuss gender roles. After that, I will investigate how the creation of local bourgeoisie(s) occurred in a dialogue with Westerners. Finally I will look at the two major categories of urban residents that could at the time lay claim to (Western) European origins, the Levantines and immigrants, and will try to outline their particular positions within the urban fabric.

---

[12] Reinkowski, "Hapless Imperialists."
[13] Mardin, "Super-Westernisation," 140, 143. The literary character of the unsuccessfully super-Westernized fop exists also in Ottoman Arab literature; see Zachs, "Under Eastern Eyes," 175–180.

14 Educational Imperialism or Enlightenment?

All nineteenth-century Great Powers witnessed a tremendous expansion of spreading their worldview abroad through the means of education. Some states invested heavily from their own budget into this endeavor, others relied on private initiative. Education was believed to pave the way to stronger influence in the spheres of commerce as well as cultural and military cooperation. In the colonies, it was deemed the long-term solution for installing loyalty to the metropole among the subjugated peoples. Especially toward the end of large-scale colonization, progressive intellectuals condemned this educational policy. In 1943, Simone Weil, reflecting on German occupying practices during World War II, commented critically on France's educational policy during the era of high imperialism.

> The loss of the past is the collapse into colonial slavery. We have inflicted on others this damage which Germany intended to inflict on us without success. Because of our culpability, little Polynesians declaim in school, "Our ancestors, the Gauls, had blond hair and blue eyes." In books, which had many readers but no impact, Alain Gerbault described how we literally made these people die of grief, by prohibiting their customs, traditions and feasts, their zest for life.[1]

Undoubtedly some of the Eastern Mediterranean seaside residents shared Weil's position on educational imperialism. Salomon Reinach quotes a Sephardic family father from Salonica in 1882 as criticizing the foreign school system with the words, "So you want to turn our sons into Francs?"[2] But the overall assessment is that Eurocentric education, despite its indelible marks of mission and imperialism, were well received by a sizable number of the urban population. Schools staffed by teachers of foreign origin or founded by organizations from

---

[1] Weil, *Simone Weil on Colonialism*, 112 (my partially diverging translation).
[2] Dumont, "Le français d'abord," 208.

abroad were ample in the port cities.[3] While a few had existed for longer times, catering to the children of expatriates, the initial expansion came during the reign of Sultan Mahmud, when the empire not only founded its own schools of intermediate and higher learning based on French models, but also allowed or tolerated new foreign schools to be opened. The Sultan created the *Rüşdiye* as preparatory secondary schools for higher state schools and founded or revived three higher schools for the bureaucracy, two military engineering schools, three medicinal higher schools, and one each for music and the military. The medicinal education was to be in French in order to benefit from recent international developments in the field, and the aforementioned Imperial School of Music was in the initial decades headed by Italians.[4] Mahmud also began a program of sending promising young members of the public service to France for their studies.

These examples inspired an even larger number of schools to be founded by foreigners. Missionary institutions dominated these initial new places of learning. The American Board of Foreign Missions, staffed by Baptists and Methodists, the Anglican Church Mission Society, and a Scottish Mission to the Jews were among the first Protestant organizations to establish schools on Ottoman soil.[5] While converting Muslims was a long-term goal for these organizations, their priorities were competing with the already existing Catholic schools and influencing the Greek-Orthodox and Jewish population. Beyond tactical considerations, a great source of inspiration for the missionaries was to mark the spaces that were imbibed with great mythical importance due to the Bible or church history: Constantinople, the seat of the Greek-Orthodox Patriarch and imagined last important bastion to fall to Islam; Thessalonica, one of the early Christian parishes addressed by Paul; and Smyrna, mentioned both by Paul and in the Revelations.[6]

---

[3] For more detailed studies of schools of this era, see for example Fortna, *Imperial Classroom*; Somel, *The Modernization of Public Education*; Ertuğrul, *Azınlık ve Yabancı Okulları*; Haydaroğlu, *Osmanlı İmparatorluğunda Yabancı Okullar*; Roche, *Education, assistance et culture françaises*.

[4] Shaw and Shaw, *History of the Ottoman Empire and Modern Turkey*, vol. II, 47–48; Mansel, *Constantinople*, 255.

[5] Özcan and Buzpınar, "Tanzimat, Islahat ve Misyonerlik."

[6] Fuhrmann, *Der Traum vom Orient*, 111–118.

The relationship between schools based on foreign organizations and local ones was often a dialectical one. For example, the deaconesses, a German Protestant women's charitable organization, expanded into the Ottoman sphere during the 1850s with the personal support of the Prussian king Friedrich Wilhelm IV. They settled in Jerusalem, Constantinople, Smyrna, Alexandria, Bucharest (Bucureşti/Bükreş), and Beirut. In Smyrna they quickly decided to expand into the education sector to cross-finance their more philanthropist endeavors. While a school for girls already existed under the auspices of the Catholic Sœurs de la Charité, this was a mass institution catering to 550 often poor students, as the Sœurs did not demand tuition fees. The deaconesses offered education for girls of higher social standing and by 1861 had 220 students. This was possible because Eurocentric education for upper-class girls in Smyrna was a niche the deaconesses identified and shrewdly exploited. However, successful business models are often copied by the competition: An Italian girls' school opened, followed by the Catholic Notre Dame de Sion in 1875 and the Greek-Orthodox Homirion school for girls in 1881. The deaconesses, often criticized for their too strongly proselytizing ways, lost decisive shares of the market they could never regain. However without their efforts, the Catholic and Greek-Orthodox communities would not have as quickly woken up to the fact that upper-class female education was in demand in Smyrna and that if they did not provide it, due to ideological reasons or due to sheer lack of effort, girls would get their education elsewhere.[7]

Following the turn to a more secular policy in France and the newly founded states of Germany and Italy during the 1870s,[8] Christian schools under their protection in the Ottoman Empire were not closed down, but the window of opportunity decisively widened for secular institutions; this was the moment for Italian national schools, the *Alliance Isréalite Universelle*, and other successful institutions. It was also a moment for local community schools following Western examples to expand. A survey on Smyrna published 1873 lists twenty-four Muslim primary schools, and a number of *Rüşdiye* and *Medrese* schools, none of which according to the Austrian and German authors had embraced a modern curriculum, but reforms to install

---

[7] Fuhrmann, *Der Traum vom Orient*, 118–126, 145–147.
[8] Borutta, *Antikatholizismus*.

modern schools were supposedly underway. The Jewish community schools were also described as antiquated, with the exception of some small private institutions, while the *Alliance Israélite Universelle* had not yet succeeded in installing a branch in the city. The authors otherwise laud the contribution by the Greek Evangelical School in Smyrna, serving 2,500 students and a small number of Greek private schools catering to the elites. They also mention an Armenian school catering to 350–400 male students and another with 250–300 female students, and a Mechitarist school, active since 1845, with sixty-seven students receiving subsidies from Vienna. The deaconess girls' school, whose main language of instruction was French, had 220 enrolled at the time. France supported the Lazarist order that staffed the College of the Propaganda, founded 1845, with seventy students; the Frères Ignorantins, who catered to an unspecified number of poor students; and Vincent de Paul's girls' school for 130 students. Private institutions called Burnabat English College, British College, and English Commercial School represented English education. In addition there was an English primary school catering to the railway worker families; a Scottish missionary school; and an Italian national school.[9] The size of the city and its educational sector were yet to grow decisively. By 1913, there were seven Catholic and French-speaking boys' schools alone and another four in the various suburbs that had developed around the city proper.[10]

A survey of Salonica schools in 1908 shows a similar variety of foreign-based education, although Salonica's population never reached half the size of Smyrna's. It mentions forty-eight Jewish schools; thirty-two Turkish ones; twenty Greek-Orthodox institutions; seven French ones; six Italian places of learning; and a small number of Bulgarian, Romanian, and Serbian schools, plus the Oriental Railways' school and one private institution that both taught in German. Approximately 6,000 students visiting the institutions took French lessons. Institutions teaching completely or mostly in French were the Catholic Frères de Saint-Jean-Baptiste-de-la-Salle (227 students); Filles de la Charité (220); the Sœurs de Kalamaria (119); the orphanage school in Zeytinlik (27); and three schools by the Mission laïque française (410).[11] The

---

[9] Scherzer, Humann, and Stöckel, *Smyrna*, 60–77.
[10] Georgelin, *La fin de Smyrne*, 56.
[11] Dumont, "Le français d'abord," 208–225.

Mission laïque was at the time a newly founded institution that formed part of a third wave of Eurocentric education imperialism. Following the 1898 Fashoda incident in Sudan, where French and British troops had almost entered into hostilities over an utterly remote and unexploitable region, younger colonial activists believed the age of belligerent expansion over the globe had come to an end. As of now, "peaceful penetration," that is, influencing the elites in nominally independent countries such as the Ottoman Empire, China, Japan, or Siam, would play a much more important role. Education was believed to be an important factor in this new Great Game.[12] The Mission laïque chose Salonica as its first field of action in 1905–1906, followed by Beirut. The most important institution for teaching French to the Saloniquenos was however the *Alliance Isréalite Universelle*. While the organization might have failed to have an impact among the fairly destitute and small Jewish community of Smyrna in the early 1870s, its first school in Salonica opened in 1873 under the patronage of the local industrialist Moishe Allatini, who became head of the *Alliance*'s local branch.[13] In 1899, the *Alliance* sponsored the education of 1,209 male and female students at primary and secondary schools, both under their own administration and outside, as well as vocational training. The numbers were even more impressive in larger cities: 1,570 students and apprentices in Smyrna profited from the *Alliance*, and more than 3,102 in Constantinople.[14] By 1908, the AIU had 2,132 students taught by 55 teachers in Salonica alone. Its ambitious rival was to be the school of the *Hilfsverein der deutschen Juden* (German Jews' Aid Society), founded in 1911 and teaching exclusively in Hebrew.[15]

The AIU is a good example of the two-faced nature of imperialism in the Ottoman theater. Both contemporary and present day accounts of its founding narrate that some philanthropists of the metropole gathered together to alleviate the dire social, political, and educational situation of their coreligionists in less enlightened and less fortunate parts of Europe, the Middle East, and the Mediterranean, and liberally invested their fortunes in the endeavor. This might be true, but one should remember that the organization's main sponsor in its initial years was Baron Moritz de Hirsch, who had made his fortune by a

[12] Kloosterhuis, "*Friedliche Imperialisten.*" Missionaries adjusted their focus accordingly; see Huber, "Education and Mobility."
[13] Rekanati, *Memory of Saloniki*.   [14] Bigart, "Alliance Isréalite Universelle."
[15] Fuhrmann, *Der Traum vom Orient*, 218–222.

highly speculative deal with the Porte for constructing its European railway network. Hirsch managed to secure millions for himself, while leaving both the shareholders and the Ottoman government dissatisfied.[16] He and later his widow spent large amounts on charitable activity that Saloniquenos would profit from, including besides the AIU a social housing project and hospital for Salonica as well as a fund for destitute railway workers and families. However this does not change the fact that these funds and those for the AIU activities had been extracted from the Ottoman sphere before. By the early twentieth century, as the education sector in Salonica grew and the Parisian central committee grew stingier, the AIU's subsidy quota was reduced from 35 to 21 percent.[17] Therefore, while no doubt the foreign-based schools provided an intellectual transfer from West to East, one cannot claim that this took place in the framework of a Western benevolent enlightened mission. The Ottoman-based middle classes paid to receive good education for their children, by means of tuition fees, taxes, and railway tickets, and got what they ordered.

But what was the motivation for residents of the port cities to send their children to schools staffed in part by religious fanatics, foreigners convinced of their superiority, and teaching matters that often had little relationship to their direct surroundings? Hervé Georgelin reads into this preference an idealization of the West paired with a certain degree of self-hatred. Nonetheless, French was the language of social distinction and foreign schools the best places to learn it fluently. What is more, it opened the door to job opportunities.[18] Julia Hauser, studying the deaconess school in Beirut, believes it was an act of flaunting cultural capital within local society; and an elitist school could also offer the opportunity for children to make contact with other members of their social stratum at an early age, which might prove beneficial later.[19] These are of course valid points, but do not yet explain why this high cultural capital was predominantly identified with schools of foreign origin.

It seems that the foreign schools and most especially the French language managed to create a new space beyond Ottoman traditional conventions, where communication was not automatically geared to

---

[16] Allfrey, *Edward VII and His Jewish Court*, 91–92.
[17] *Journal de Salonique*, 25 Nov. 1907.
[18] Georgelin, *La fin de Smyrne*, 57–59, 68.
[19] Hauser, *German Religious Women*, 205.

the existing factions and ethnic/national loyalty patterns. Leon Sciaky, growing up in a Sephardic merchant family in Salonica around the turn of the twentieth century, began to visit the newly founded Petit Lycée in 1904 when eleven years old. In his memoirs, he states that despite his young age, he understood the school staffed by teachers from France to be a deliverance from the stifling, unenlightened practices of the traditional Shalom School he had visited previously. In retrospect, the author believes the reasons for the strong impact the school made on him to be the teachers' progressiveness and openness on the one hand, and the Ottoman state's failure to provide an identity that included the non-Muslim subjects on the other. The students were

> intellectual waifs, unclaimed and uncared for by our country of birth. And in no one nationality was this truer than in the case of the Spanish Jews, who, having already been reawakened to the world by the *Alliance Isréalite Universelle*, were much like a palimpsest on which French culture and thought were superimposed upon a tongue and customs of a dim past, now bereft of intellectual content.[20]

He claims he shared this feeling of liberation (or *décloisonnement*) from the confines of religious or community-based schools with the other students, who were of French, Greek, Serbian, Dönme, Armenian, Turkish, Montenegrin, or also Sephardic background. According to Sciaky, the classroom became a place not only to access the discourses of the world beyond the local perimeter, but also one of interaction and better understanding for the young boys who had until then not had much knowledge of the rites and customs of the other communities of Salonica and the central Balkans.[21] His feeling of deliverance was shared by Halid Ziya, who was happy to leave the *Rüşdiye* school that due to its outdated curriculum had not managed to promote his talents and enter a French-language Catholic school that taught modern sciences and introduced him to French literature, inspiring his later literary works.[22]

Nevile Henderson, acting High Commissioner of Egypt in 1927, realized this widespread feeling around the Eastern Mediterranean. In an internal British document, which nonetheless reads like a direct rebuttal of Simone Weil, he claims,

---

[20] Sciaky, *Farewell to Ottoman Salonica*, 96.   [21] Ibid., 90–95.
[22] Mansel, *Levant*, 163, 164.

However purely nationalist the motive of French policy may be in this respect, it has yet created numerous educational opportunities for Eastern youth hungering for education. In a sense therefore, French cultural predominance in these countries has been earned.[23]

Even when based on modern educational systems, the schools founded by the local denominational groups or by the Ottoman state could never figure as such a third space, a neutral ground outside of their respective ethnocentric norms. Sam Levy describes in his memoirs that he visited the *İdadiye* of Salonica, a preparatory *lycée* for students intending to continue their studies in higher schools, such as the *Mekteb-i Sultânî* (Imperial School) at Galatasaray in Constantinople. Theoretically the *İdadiye* was open to all, but de facto it was visited by several hundred Muslim students and only five Jews. Due to Levy's good performance in Turkish literature and his appreciation of calligraphy, the inspector general Abdullah Effendi proposed to him to convert. As Levy rejected the offer outright, he allegedly became the object of libel under the charge of blasphemy, was punished by detention, and finally forced to quit the school.[24]

Mastery of French was the ultimate prerequisite to enter the semi-elitist space within Ottoman urban society, and schools were judged on their ability to teach it thoroughly. The following sarcastic remarks (in French) in the *Levant Herald* were obviously intended to ward off potential students of the Imperial School, implying that the study of French makes a good school, whereas the thorough study of Turkish is superfluous:

> The College of Galata-Séraï ascends the rose of fortune with great steps. Perhaps it has already reached the apogee of its glory ... French itself, a frivolous and vivacious language, was correctly considered to be lacking in seriousness, which is required for the disciples of science; it has therefore been diminished and only figures as the dessert to the meal offered to the boarders by the administration, whereas the main course is made up of plenty of Turkish, a handful of English, half a portion of German, and a pinch of Italian.[25]

---

[23] Nevile Henderson, quoted from Huber, "Education and Mobility," 97.
[24] Lévy, *Salonique à la fin du XIXe siècle*, 46–52; see also Georgelin, *La fin de Smyrne*, 93–95, on Greek nationalist attempts to monopolize the space of the cosmopolitan city.
[25] *Levant Herald*, 18 Jan. 1873. In a similar vein, a character in a contemporary novel is discredited in his social standing with the phrase, "Having learnt his

While structurally the foreign schools were based on an implicit "self-hatred" and served as a neutral meeting ground, one should not idealize their neutrality. Students were taught cosmopolitan skills there, that is, how to navigate and negotiate the different languages, etiquettes, and techniques necessary to be successful in the modern, ethnically mixed regions of the Empire under strong Western European influence. These skills did not however automatically lead to a cosmopolitan outlook on life. Such skills were also of benefit to those pursuing modern nationalist worldviews. Also, the foreign schools were by no means equidistant in nurturing the spirit of "self-hatred" among their students. One point that led to many debates was which local languages should be taught in these schools and how many hours should be devoted to each. For example, any foreign-based school in early twentieth-century Smyrna was prone to teach at least some modern Greek, as this was becoming the lingua franca of the city, despite the still high social status of French. In the same period, the Ottoman state increasingly enforced the legal stipulation for mandatory Turkish lessons in foreign-based schools, but these continued to have leverage in the rule's application.[26]

If a school taught only Greek and not Turkish or devoted much less hours to the latter, it could be seen as a political statement in favor of Greek irredentism. Especially Protestant schools were suspected of favoring the nationalist aspirations of their Christian students, and the suspicion was often not unfounded. A case in point was Robert College, established by American Protestants on the outskirts of Constantinople. While Grand Vizier Âli Pasha had favored its founding in the 1860s, the Ottoman state took a more cautious stance toward the school after some of its former students had played an active part in the Bulgarian uprising of 1876. Following the 1894–1896 crisis, the state suspected the school of promoting Armenian separatism, as it hosted a large number of students of Armenian origin, and the *New York Tribune* had written in the summer of 1896, "Considering that Bulgaria attained independence through the American school Robert College in Istanbul ... it is hoped that the School for Girls will also serve

---

French from the beer pubs on the Salonica quays"; Uşaklıgil, *Aşk-ı Memnu*, 30. *Journal de Salonique* (21 July 1896) likewise stresses the importance of learning French even for blue-collar jobs.

[26] *Journal de Salonique*, 23. Jan. 1896; Soysal, "The Ottoman Period of Robert College," 69, 70.

the same function [for Armenians, MF]."[27] The state attempted to pursue a firmer stance, as its leading officials believed that "the minds of children are poisoned in such schools."[28] However the state's possibilities were limited to denying property expansion and construction and minor bureaucratic hassles.[29] In practice, schools were far from unequivocal indoctrination centers for one cause or the other. Robert College faculty and administration was divided over supporting separatism or not.[30] In other cases too, students could turn against their institution's politics. After the Young Turk Revolution for example, Muslim students demonstrated against the Syrian Protestant College in Beirut, demanding exemption from its religious services.[31]

Even if schools did not "poison children's minds" with the seeds of separatist nationalism, they still contributed to their students' further alienation from their "uncaring country of birth." The objects of study at schools such as Sciaky's Petit Lycée, which began operating independently, but was soon taken over by the Mission Laïque Française, were French literature, culture, and worldview, not Ottoman. Sciaky describes how his childhood games and reveries were inspired by the legends of *The Song of Roland* and *Charlemagne*, by reading Victor Hugo, and by learning to glorify the French Revolution. The literature, history, and worldview of Sephardic, Balkan, or other Ottoman origins did not figure. In the greater scheme of educational imperialism, this sense of loyalty to a foreign imperialist power ideally became self-reproductive, most visibly in the efforts of alumni associations that reiterated the belief in the civilizing mission of their patron countries. Leon Modiano, a member of the *Alliance Isréalite Universelle*'s alumni association, for example, declared at its 1909 convention: "France, that generous nation, did not content itself to setting a vivid example for the world, of liberty, equality, and fraternity. She has also, she has especially contributed, arms in hand, to set free the nations that groan under the yoke of slavery."[32]

If France led to such adoration by those who had experienced it mostly from the blackboard, a higher degree of exposure had even stronger effects. For those who managed through family assets or

---

[27] Soysal, "The Ottoman Period of Robert College," 58, 59. See also Makdisi, *Artillery of Heaven*; Deringil, *Conversion and Apostasy*.
[28] Soysal, "The Ottoman Period of Robert College," 64.   [29] Ibid., 95–97.
[30] Ibid., 55–57,   [31] Hauser, *German Religious Women*, 243–271.
[32] Dumont, "Le français d'abord," 212.

government sponsorship to study in France and especially Paris, identification with the foreign culture could go even further. Especially students who had been sent abroad to acquire some technical know-how, but were more attracted by Paris as a site of literature and the fine arts, could go so far as to renounce their origins completely, as to them the business-minded port cities of Salonica and Smyrna and the inherently conservative Constantinople bureaucracy seemed to stifle any intellectual development. While İbrahim Edhem (Pasha) had been one of the first to profit from Mahmud's program of sponsoring Ottoman subjects' higher education in France in 1831 and had returned with a degree in mining engineering from the École nationale supérieure des mines to then begin a career in the state service that led him to become grand vizier,[33] his son Osman Hamdi (Bey) neglected his studies of law in Paris (1860–1868) in order to pursue painting with Jean-Léon Gérôme and Gustave Boulanger. Already the letters shortly after his arrival in Paris demonstrate a high degree of anxiety on the part of İbrahim Edhem and the educators that the young Osman Hamdi would forfeit his national and religious allegiance in the alien surroundings. Seemingly trivial matters, such as whether Osman Hamdi was wearing his fez or not, were the object of their scrutiny. Indeed, his alienation from his origins seems to have progressed considerably, as by 1868 he frankly wrote to his father that he was "incapable of ever seeing my country again elsewhere than in an embassy," apparently a plea for his father to secure for Osman Hamdi a diplomatic post in Paris or Florence.[34] When İbrahim Edhem insisted on his son's return, the latter complied only under protest and with the firm intention of finding a later possibility to return and continue his studies of painting, which he believed to be impossible in Constantinople.[35]

But over-identification was not limited to Ottoman expats on the Seine. Sciaky describes how in his teenage years as a student of the Petit Lycée, he believed in France so much he began to hoist the French flag from the family's house in the predominantly Muslim quarter of Çingene Mahallesi in Salonica. When his father forced him to quit this habit, as the neighbors now speculated that the family had taken on French nationality, Leon Sciaky went to see the French Consul, Camille Louis Steeg, who happened to be the father of his school

[33] Eldem, "Bir Biyografi üzerine Düşünceler," 22–32.
[34] Eldem, "An Ottoman Archaeologist," 126.   [35] Ibid.

friend, and asked him outright to be granted French citizenship. The Consul General in a very diplomatic manner was appreciative of Sciaky's demand, but asked him to wait until maturity, because only grown-ups could legally apply.[36]

As a matter of fact, what Sciaky had asked for, to become a national of a Western country, was in principle not even unusual under the conditions of the late Ottoman port cities. The capitulatory powers had for centuries granted the status of protégé to Ottoman subjects – originally to consular employees – but later also to anyone they considered of value for their country's interests (or their own pockets, as some have alleged). Once the practice was abolished due to the Ottomans' insistence, the Great Powers granted citizenship rather liberally to locals they considered of value. The Habsburg Consulate in Constantinople for example granted Austrian nationality to the head of its telegraph office in 1913.[37] The same country's representatives in Salonica in the same year nationalized the local jeweler Aaron Mollah as a citizen of Olmütz (Olumouc), even though Mollah had never set foot in the Moravian city.[38] The Salonica consular files contain seven more cases of naturalization under the same last name, including the merchant Abraham Mollah. As a reason, the consular officials write simply, "The individual mentioned above imports mainly Austrian industrial products and has such lively intercourse with Austrian factories that his naturalization as an Austrian can be recommended in the interests of promoting exports."[39]

In the face of blatant cases of over-identification with overseas great powers and alienation from one's religion, state, and even neighbors, how could the spreading of Western supremacist notions through education be judged favorably? Did the urban residents not realize that the educational efforts supported by the imperialist states formed part of a larger attempt to reshape the earth according to agendas of world domination? How could what Simone Weil described as cultural genocide against the Polynesians be considered intellectual salvation by

---

[36] Sciaky, *Farewell to Ottoman Salonica*, 97–98.
[37] HHStA Embassy and Consulate Constantinople (BK Kpl) 115: Einbürgerung Moschopoulos.
[38] HHStA GK Sal 433: Einbürgerung Aaron Mollah.
[39] HHStA GK Sal 433: Einbürgerung Abraham Mollah. Similar cases of casual naturalization can be found concerning the families Beusussau, Beneviste, and Beraha; see HHStA GK Sal 433: passim.

middle-class Ottoman Sephardic youngsters? There are two answers to these questions, one on a more practical level, the other of more abstract nature.

On the practical level, one must consider that unlike the Polynesian school children, the Ottoman maritime residents were not confronted by a monolithic foreign school system; the market in these cities, as mentioned, was diverse. Therefore the students and especially the parents had considerable bargaining power: If schools became too religiously sectarian, if their teaching methods and equipment no longer met the standards of the time, or if the tuition fees were excessive, parents could threaten to withdraw their children and could easily find other education possibilities. The Western institutions' ethnocentrism, national biases, and aesthetic preoccupations were more rarely a concern than their missionary agenda.[40] Julia Hauser, Christine B. Lindner, and Esther Möller state with regard to schools in Greater Syria:

Foreign civilizing pretensions, Ottoman imperial endeavours, and diverse local visions stood in a complex, mutual relation of transfer, rejection, and appropriation ... However, many of these [Western, MF] organizations were structurally, politically, and economically vulnerable, and exerted much less control over their schools, students, and teachers than they feigned to exercise. Their schools were carefully monitored by the Ottoman state, which granted (or denied) licenses to foreign institutions and which created its own schools to compete with them. They negotiated with the local clientele, who brought with them their own history and expectations of education, and who played a far more influential role in shaping the environment of education than has been credited to them. Lastly, foreign schools competed with each other for resources, locations, students, and teachers. Thus, the agendas developed in the metropole(s) were almost never fully implemented on the peripheral grounds, but were subject to continuous negotiation and transformation.[41]

Therefore a school with French colonialist intentions, such as the one described by Sciaky, could be experienced as a source of *décloisonnement* rather than limitation. Its education took place in a heterogeneous sphere where it could not limit its effects to its desired intentions. French not only gave access to a particular national canon

---

[40] Fuhrmann, *Der Traum vom Orient*, 121–125.
[41] Hauser, Lindner, Möller, "Introduction," 15.

of literature, it also served as a lingua franca the educated classes could utilize to communicate and exchange views. The urban communicative space(s) saw imperialist and nationalist institutions as strong players, but not as hegemonic ones. While over-identification might have been the temporary result for Leon Sciaky during his high school and for Osman Hamdi during his studies, both managed to pass this point and to more productively combine their occidental education with their original environment. Toward the end of the Ottoman era, more skeptical attitudes toward French-language education even found their way into the French-language press. While *Journal de Salonique*'s edition from November 22, 1908 lauded both Committee of Union and Progress efforts at improving higher education and Bulgaria's success in mass education, a letter to the editor from the same day pleaded to spare Salonica more French-language schools. According to the letter writer, these schools would not manage to teach anything beyond a thoroughly Levantine French, the type he himself claimed to speak. Another letter writer in the following issue seconded the criticism of local French schools, but by contrast took offense to their spreading of a universal standard for French, as he believed that accents should be seen as natural, and Levantine French a variety of the standard, just as other variants in France.[42] Blending of identities, rather than blind adherence or a mere instrumental usage of intercultural skills and eventually even pride in the difference to the metropole, became a major characteristic of the education process.

The more abstract answer as to why foreign-based schools found acceptance may lie in the way residents of the port cities in close contact with Western Europe saw themselves. While the Great Power gunboats calling in the ports; the infringements on budgetary sovereignty through the Public Debt Administration, setting aside much of the Ottoman taxpayers' payments for the voracity of foreign creditors; and the marking of the capital's public space by embassy seraglios clearly showed the West's colonialist aspirations in the Eastern Mediterranean, many urban residents nonetheless interacted with foreigners from more western parts of Europe on a nonhostile basis. As stated in the previous chapters, locals considered Eurocentric cultural activities as an offer to join "a world on the move," be part of a European dream of economic, aesthetic, and political progress, that is, to end up among

[42] *Journal de Salonique*, 22, 24 Nov. 1908.

the winners of the late nineteenth and early twentieth centuries. When letting their children recite in school, "Our ancestors, the Gauls, had blond hair and blue eyes," the port city residents did not see themselves on a par with the French colonial subjects of Polynesia, but believed themselves to be part of the family of nations, where, after a little bit of schooling, no one would recognize the difference between a resident of the Aegean shores and a French citizen or consider it a civilizational gap. This is because identities, before the crises of the final years of the Ottoman Empire, were not considered to be primordial, but as works in progress, subject to negotiation, refinement, and adaptation. What we learn from the case of Habsburg naturalization of members of the Mollah family is not so much that the capitulatory powers were liberal about granting citizenship. The point is rather that the indeterminate political status the port cities enjoyed and especially the diversity of lifestyles visible to all, prompted their residents to absorb a variety of influences beyond the ethnic paradigm. Worldviews, enjoying literature, or role models as men/women, as proletarian/bourgeois, were inspired by a number of different sources and left their mark on individuals.

And yet, from a nationalist and statist view, such a free market system of education had to be seen as impediment. If one sees society as something that should be under state control and if one believes that states should force their worldview on the polity, rather than win their allegiance through outreach, the Eastern Mediterranean scenario could not please. For reasons very different from Weil's, Turkish nationalism's chief ideologist Ziya Gökalp lamented the split character of Constantinople's education sector, featuring a traditional Arab- and Persian-focused *Medrese* education on the one hand, the Western languages taught in the foreign-based schools on the other, and the *Tanzimat* state schools as an unfortunate hybrid, selling off bad translations and plagiarisms as their own.[43]

---

[43] Ziya Gökalp, quoted from Altın, "Ziya Gökalp'in Eğitim Tarihimiz Açısından Önemi," 498.

15 The French-Language Press
A Common Forum?

While the schools themselves were to some extent meeting grounds for local residents of different denominations, they also produced new divides according to institutional loyalties. However, their language education gave the students access to another means of communication: the French-language press. Here there was potentially another third space for communicating with fellow inhabitants of the city. These newspapers, if they managed to guard a certain degree of neutrality, could serve as forums of discussion among people of different linguistic or religious background. Moreover, they could function as mouthpieces to inform the world beyond the empire of one's point of view from the quays of Smyrna, Salonica, or Constantinople.

The Ottoman press has long been considered a source base of lesser value: censorship, self-censorship, and bans were too frequent; influence and sponsorship by the Ottoman government as well as foreign states too widespread for anyone to assume that the printed word approximately reflected the political spectrum of the country. While the press certainly never reached the freedom of expression that was possible at the time in Italy, Germany, or nearby British-occupied Egypt, it would be throwing out the baby with the bathwater to ignore it completely. The Ottoman press in its initial decades did intervene and make statements that did not please the officials. The fact that bans were fairly frequent only proves this. For example, the satirical magazine published in Greek, Turkish, and French *Diogenis* (*Diogène*), published by Teodor Kasap and including contributions by Namik Kemal, hit a nerve and was closed in early 1873, supposedly for using bad language and false signatures, or, according to another opinion, because subaltern bureaucrats used it to satirize their superiors.[1] Only once Abdülhamid II had established power did the press become truly docile. Nonetheless, debates pertaining to municipal politics and

---

[1] *Levant Herald*, 13, 16 Jan. 1873.

cultural and social affairs were not as tightly controlled and managed to uphold a certain degree of freedom of expression in matters that were not considered essential to state interests.

French-language newspapers are not an exotic offspring of the wider Ottoman publishing sphere: They are at the very origins of journalistic activity in the empire. Seza Sinanlar Uslu claims the very first newspapers to have been published on Ottoman soil to be the *Gazette Française de Constantinople* and *Bulletin des nouvelles*, both published 1795–1797 by the French Embassy as propaganda for the promulgation of the revolution (which faced some fierce opposition among the French Stambouliote residents).[2] Newspapers published on private initiative made their appearance in the 1820s and once again, Smyrna took the lead over the capital. According to Melih Gürsoy, discontent with Western European publishers about their one-sided pro-Hellenic position in the Greek war of secession in the 1820s led Smyrna foreign residents to take the initiative. At the beginning of 1824, *Smyrneea* was published by the French subject Charles Tricon, but Tricon soon after in October of that year turned the paper over to a M. Roux, who renamed it *Spectateur Oriental*. Roux in turn was followed as publisher by the French subject Alexandre Blacque.[3] In Blacque the newspaper had found an eloquent and fearless champion of an Ottoman statist worldview. Having studied law in France, Blacque had settled in Smyrna to engage in commerce, but got carried away by journalism. As the main purpose of the paper was the defense of the Ottoman side in the Greek separatist war being waged in Morea (Peloponnese) and attacking Russia and the breakaway Greek government, Blacque did not run into problems with the Ottoman authorities, but with the French government. According to Blacque's petition, following a critical comment on French policy in the Levant,[4] the Consul had Blacque arrested, chained, and put onto a corvette due to head to Marseille. His printing house was to be seized and taken to France as well. After the intervention of some French merchants, Blaque was released upon the condition that he stopped publishing the *Spectateur Oriental*.[5]

---

[2] Sinanlar Uslu, "Apparition et développement de la presse francophone," 147–156.
[3] Gürsoy, *Bizim İzmirimiz*, 216–217.   [4] *Spectateur Oriental*, 29 Dec. 1827.
[5] BnF: *Petition du Sieur Alexandre Blacque*, undated (early Jan. 1828).

Blacque founded the *Courrier de Smyrne* instead, which was just as outspoken in defending the Ottoman Empire. When the *Constitutionnel* from France criticized the *Courrier* for this, the Smyrna-based newspaper retaliated with a harsh counterattack under the guise of a letter to the editor by the self-proclaimed "Recluse of Bournabat." He rejected Western claims of Enlightenment outright, reminding the *Constitutionnel*'s readership in France of the Inquisition, and claimed the Orient to be a place of peace (despite the atrocities committed during the Greek war of secession). A short extract: "your civilization is no longer that beneficent goddess who spreads everywhere the mild light of her torch; it is a wild bacchante that runs, torch in hand, incinerating all the places that in her shortsightedness she does not perceive."[6] Such attacks served to formulate an independent stance of residents of the Ottoman lands vis-à-vis what seemed an overwhelmingly negative attitude toward the region in the Western press. Nonetheless Blacque's attacks against the Philhellenes were not disinterested either. One of the leading financial stakeholders in the *Courrier de Smyrne* and frequent contributor from the day of its founding was the Austrian officer Anton Prokesch von Osten. Prokesch, who was based in Smyrna at the time and looked down on the newly established French institutions of freedom of press and democracy, saw it as his mission to hinder the growth of Russian influence in the region. A Hellenic state, he believed, would end up a Russian satrapy. He was close with Blacque and handed him his contributions personally. Both of them disregarded cautionary warnings from Constantinople to be more circumspect in criticizing the Great Powers. The *Courrier* could be subscribed from France and Austria, testifying further to its role as international propagandist organ.[7]

Blacque's pro-Ottoman and anti-Great Powers agitation was amply rewarded: He was invited by Sultan Mahmud to publish the first official newspaper in Ottoman and French from 1831 onward, the *Takvim-i Vekayi* or *Moniteur Oriental*. Blacque's son Edouard later continued the family tradition by publishing the *Courrier de*

---

[6] *Courrier de Smyrne*, 15 March 1829. Daniel Bertsch assumes the "Solitaire de Bournabat" to be Anton Prokesch von Osten; Bertsch, *Anton Prokesch von Osten*, 108 fn. 193.

[7] Bertsch, *Anton Prokesch von Osten*, 106–111. In fact, the Russian ambassador had urged the Porte to ban Blacque's publishing activities; Lewis, *The Muslim Discovery of Europe*, 304, 305.

Constantinople before becoming mayor of the city's Sixth District. The second important publisher to emerge from Smyrna was Bousquet-Deschamps. He had been the main stakeholder in the *Courrier de Smyrne*.[8] Beginning his publishing career in the 1830s by taking over the *Courrier*, which he renamed *Journal de Smyrne*, he moved on to the *Journal de Constantinople* in 1843, which subsequently merged with the *Echo de l'Orient* and yet later became *La Turquie*.[9] Upon the merger with the *Echo*, at the time of the Crimean War, the paper pompously claimed its aim was to further progress, independence, and civilization in the Orient as well as justice, tolerance, state security, and to combat barbarity, invasions, and oppression.[10]

The advent of French-language newspapers triggered publishing activities in other local languages. The first Ottoman Greek-language newspaper *Amaltheia* (with the exception of a short-lived youth magazine five years earlier) was founded in Smyrna in 1838 and managed to survive until 1922. 1840 saw the first newspaper in Armenian, *Archaloys Araradian*, to round off the lively Western Anatolian press scene, while the capital knew no other newspaper yet than the *Moniteur Oriental*.[11]

The 1850s were a watershed in the internationalization of the port cities. The decision to allow more printers, newspapers, and books was apparently not entirely the result of liberal policy, but rather of pressure: As the market for non-Turkish publications increased, it seemed more reasonable to allow for newspapers, school books, and other reading to be published on Ottoman soil, where censorship and pressure could be exacted against writers, editors, and printers, rather than to watch foreign printed matter to spread, which could only be controlled through pressure on retailers and consumers.[12] While a large number of other newspapers appeared (and often quickly disappeared) in the decades to come, *Stamboul,* founded by the Irishman John L. Hanly, was to be the longest running of the French newspapers of the capital. Hanly, a former editor of the English-language *Levant*

---

[8] Bousquet-Deschamps had acquired 8 of the 30 shares of the *Courrier de Smyrne* in the founding meeting, Blacque 4, Borrell 4, and Prokesch 3; Bertsch, *Anton Prokesch von Osten*, 107, 108 fn. 190.
[9] Bertsch, *Anton Prokesch von Osten*, 109 fn. 196.
[10] *Journal de Constantinople*, 4 Jan. 1855.
[11] Kontente, *Smyrne et l'occident*, 466.
[12] Vakali, "A Christian Printer in Selanik," 23–38.

Herald, had first founded the bilingual French and English *Levant Times and Shipping Gazette*, which became (following a ban of the *Levant Times*)[13] purely French *Progrès d'Orient,* before adopting the name *Stamboul*. *Stamboul* was published from 1875 until 1934 despite some sporadic bans, such as in 1879, when Hanly published a similar paper under the name of *Le Matin* instead that did not fail to mention uncomfortable news such as Christian-Jewish riots in Kuzguncuk; the suspending of the *Phare du Bosphore* as well as of the Arab-language Constantinople newspaper *al-Jawa'ib*; or the three-month prison sentence against the editor of *Vakit*.[14] While frontal attacks against high office holders, such as governors, were taboo, critique of lower level functionaries was not unheard of. For example the *Levant Herald* reported on an excess of violence by *zaptiye* (policemen) against a foreign couple that had entered a road where the Sultan was due to pass; or, as mentioned earlier, of constables verbally abusing the prima donna of the Concordia Theater.[15] Private enterprises could also face the brunt of the press's wrath: In 1874 newspapers had a heated dispute over the question of whether the planned water supply from Lake Terkos by the Compagnie des Eaux de Constantinople, founded by Kâmil Bey, the Master of Ceremonies at the Palace, and Ternau Bey, an engineer, would relieve the capital's need of water or would only supply a source of contamination.[16] Another favorite target of the press was the municipality, which was considered fair game. French-language papers were read not only to follow domestic issues, but to allow for a window onto the wider world. It was not uncommon for an edition in the late nineteenth century to begin with the Jameson Raid in Transvaal or the Cuban War of Independence.[17]

While French-language newspapers were now no longer the only ones on the market, they still made up a disproportionally high segment of the Ottoman press: In 1876, there were purportedly forty-seven newspapers in Constantinople alone, thirteen Turkish ones, nine Greek, nine Armenian, seven French, three Bulgarian, two English, two

---

[13] *Progrès d'Orient*, 15 Aug. 1874.   [14] *Le Matin*, 1, 4, 7, 15 July 1879.
[15] *Levant Herald*, 16, 17 Jan. 1873.
[16] *Progrès d'Orient*, 27 Aug. 1874. The company finally started supplying water in 1891, but remained the object of public criticism; see Geyikdağı, *Foreign Investment in the Ottoman Empire*, 111.
[17] *Journal de Salonique*, 27 Oct., 2 Nov. 1895.

Hebrew, one German, and one Arabic one.[18] Smyrna in 1890 is listed as having four Greek, three Turkish, three Armenian, three Ladino, and three French-language papers.[19] No other Western language could compete with the semi-official status of French. As of 1862, when some believed that the new railway companies serving Smyrna would lead to local British dominance, there had been the experiment of a purely English newspaper in form of the *Smyrna Mail*, which tried to transport a sentiment of common progress for the region and the two empires. It closed down however after only two years. Of later newspapers, the *Levant Herald* and the *Osmanische Lloyd* had to appear bilingually, in English and French and German and French respectively, to have an impact on local readership.[20] While the number of copies in the 1870s were usually not too impressive, the impact per copy is believed to be high, as papers were not so much an object of private consumption, but very much present in the salons, coffeehouses, and gatherings of neighbors, where they would also be read out loud to the benefit of illiterates.[21]

The French-language press did not operate aloof from the papers in local languages, but took part in the common struggle against the infringements on their liberties and discussed the competition's articles in Turkish, Greek, or Armenian.[22] However as Hamidian censorship became more institutionalized, the *Stamboul* increasingly shied away from controversial politics, focusing mainly on Pera's contemporary art and theater scene as well as events in local upper society, thus setting a trend for the apolitical press of the *fin de siècle*.[23]

Salonica's longest-running newspaper in French was the *Journal de Salonique*, founded in 1895 by Saadi Levy, who had been publishing the Ladino journal *La Epoca* since 1875. The Levys were, according to their family legend, the offsprings of an immigrant printer who had arrived in 1731 from Amsterdam. Supposedly the art of printing had

---

[18] Köse, *Westlicher Konsum am Bosporus*, 187, 188. It is safe to assume that the Hebrew-language publications mentioned in the statistics compiled by Ahmed Emin [Yalman] were actually Ladino newspapers in Hebrew script.
[19] Mansel, *Levant*, 164, 165.
[20] Farah, *Die deutsche Pressepolitik und Propagandatätigkeit*.
[21] Köse, *Westlicher Konsum am Bosporus*, 187, 188.
[22] See for example, *Journal de Salonique*, 3 Feb. 1896. Likewise, the French-language press was acknowledged by the other local papers; *Journal de Salonique*, 1 Nov. 1896.
[23] Sinanlar Uslu, "Apparition et développement de la presse francophone," 149.

been passed on from father to son. In his publishing activities, Saadi Levy had enjoyed the support of the oligarch Moishe Allatini.[24] In its first issue, the *Journal de Salonique* proclaimed as its mission to further the development of the Salonica region.[25] Far from seeing itself as a Jewish community paper, an interest better served by the publishing house's other paper, *La Epoca*, the *Journal* initially printed the Gregorian, Julian, and Hicri dates on its cover, but not the Jewish date, and proclaimed it as auspicious that the first issue appeared on the day of Saint Demetrius, Thessalonica's patron saint.[26] Initially Vitalis Cohen was editor-in-chief of *Journal de Salonique*, followed by the owner's son, Sam Levy. Both Cohen and Levy had studied in Paris and especially Cohen was supposed to have acted as a dilettante of French poetry during his studies.[27] The paper developed what might be described as a success formula for late Hamidian, post-political times. Under both editors in chief, the *Journal de Salonique* did not only report on grand politics, but commented on the municipality's activities, treated French and local literature, and especially engaged with urban society. Small town gossip, Levy later admitted, was a surefire method to draw the readers' attention, cause them to flood the paper with letters to the editor, and become the talk of the salons.[28] Another mainstay of the journal was French novels published as serials. However, despite the editor in chief's reputation as Parisian literati, the feuilleton was anything but innovative by French standards. Cohen and Levy published works by authors that were by majority of an older generation, well established, and mainstream, rather than avant-garde, both in style and in worldview. Such novels warned of the dangers of the big city, of female passion unleashed, and in particular pregnancy out of wedlock. Hélène Guillon therefore claims that it was the newspaper's aim to guide the Salonician bourgeoisie toward the tastes of its Parisian counterpart. Of all authors published until 1910, only three were not French: the Greek Kostis Palamas, the Pole Henryk Sienkiewicz, and the Austrian Leopold Sacher-Masoch.[29]

---

[24] *Journal de Salonique*, 15 Jan. 1903.   [25] *Journal de Salonique*, 27 Oct. 1895.
[26] Ibid.
[27] Lévy, *Salonique à la fin du XIXe siècle*, 74–80; Dumont, "Le français d'abord," 217–219; Ur, "We Speak and Write This Language," 141–142.
[28] Lévy, *Salonique à la fin du XIXe siècle*, 74–80.
[29] Guillon, *Le Journal de Salonique*, 169–177.

Limited as the Ottoman French-language press' perspectives might seem, especially in face of the political and social constraints, it could nonetheless offer a platform for locals of the cities under scrutiny here to express their views, enter into exchange with others beyond their immediate circles, and also to realize differences to the empire-wide and international interpretations of events that might arise from their local perspective.[30] The French-language press thus offered a platform that was accessible to all who had enjoyed high school education. Its readership was not limited to those who knew Greek, Turkish, Ladino, or Armenian, but was potentially much wider. Throughout its metamorphosis from outspokenly anti-Western and pro-Ottoman in the 1820s and 1830s; past a more critical position toward local politics in the 1870s to the post-political attitude of late Hamidianism, focusing on municipal affairs, local society, and cultural events; it was an essential part of Ottoman society. Just as education in foreign-model schools, by foreign tutors, or abroad, the French-language press was a mark of distinction, of "cultural capital" that played a part in the construction of contemporary gender and class identities. Its role however decreased during the Second Constitutional Period. The higher degree of literacy in the wider population; a surge of nationalisms; more professional publicists from all ethnic communities; plus the new but short-lived freedom of expression led to a surge of publications, many of which soon disappeared. Between 1908 and 1913, supposedly 389 different newspapers tried their luck on the Ottoman market, including 161 Turkish, 118 Arabic, 42 Armenian, 38 Greek, 18 French, 10 Hebrew, 1 German, 1 English, 1 Persian.[31] Of these, 353 had existed in the fiscal year 1908–1909, as there was a dramatic flare-up of new papers with the end of Hamidian absolutism. Many did not survive the initial months of revolutionary enthusiasm.[32] The Smyrna market purportedly was served by 11 Greek, 7 Turkish, 5 Armenian, 5 Hebrew, and 4 French local newspapers.[33] Salonica with its large Judeo-Spanish-speaking population saw a rather late, but impressive boom in French-language publications. It had, according to Maniolis Kandilakis, three French-language papers before 1908: the

---

[30] See Chapter 16, pp. 243–249.
[31] Köse, *Westlicher Konsum am Bosporus*, 188, 189. On Hebrew newspapers, see the remark in fn. 18 of this chapter.
[32] Schick, "Print Capitalism and Women's Sexual Agency," 200.
[33] Milton, *Paradise Lost*, 7.

oldest being *Journal de Salonique*, plus since 1900 *Le Progrès de Salonique*, and the magazine *École et famille*. The revolutionary period of 1908–1909 and later saw the founding of a staggering eleven additional French-language papers and the demise of the prerevolutionary papers. Of all Salonician French newspapers founded in Ottoman times, *L'Indépendant* was the longest running, published from 1909 to 1940.[34]

---

[34] For a list of non-Greek newspapers of Salonica, see Kandilakis, "Xenoglosses efimerides tis Thessalonikis," 153–165.

16 | *Renegotiating Masculinities and Femininities at the Turn of the Century*

Love must be reinvented, as one knows.

Arthur Rimbaud, *Une Saison en Enfer*, 1873

In late 1895 and early 1896, the Ottoman Empire was in the throes of its worst crisis in twenty years. Unrest and massacres plagued the provinces with Armenian populations; reprisals against a demonstration by Armenians in Constantinople had left eighty dead; Great Britain threatened to intervene; the Galata stock market was in free fall.[1] And yet, if we look at the *Journal de Salonique* in these days, a completely different matter seems to occupy the readers' passions. The editor in chief Vitalis Cohen, writing under his pen name "Sheridan," had succeeded in one of his well-calculated provocations to stir up the readers' emotions. In an article entitled "Les filles à marier" (Girls to Be Married Off), he ridiculed the young women of Salonica and their supposedly incessant search for a future husband. He writes about them, "Eleventh plague which Moses forgot to smite Egypt with, they stalk our streets, hair in the wind and suggestive expressions from which one can read the violence of suppressed impulses and the despair of unfulfilled dreams." He considered it a phenomenon that predominantly afflicted petit bourgeois women, as upper class women could find other ways to evade the predicaments of bachelor life and poor women were mostly pushed by circumstances not to linger on such issues. In his satire, he suggested to export the excess of Salonician brunettes to the Mormons in Salt Lake City, as they were allowed to have fifty women according to their beliefs.[2] The clearly satirical and openly sexist article sparked an intense and serious debate among the readers. During the weeks to come, both male and female readers sent in dozens of contributions, either defending or attacking "Sheridan's" point of

---

[1] Soysal, *Ottoman Empire in the Age of Global Financial Capitalism*.
[2] *Journal de Salonique*, 18/30 Dec. 1895.

view and commenting on the failures or merits of the other sex in Salonica, reflecting on their expectations toward contemporary gender roles in the process.

The *Journal* soon after ran a similarly stinging satire of Salonician wannabe Don Juans, describing their pitiful attempts to woo the female musicians playing in the city's cafés, but being put off by the expense of buying them a drink.[3] But the debate concentrated on the original defamation of the city's young women. The first to enter the ring was the "young lady" (again a pseudonym) who in her letter rebutted the general insult "Sheridan" had lavished against the Saloniquenas. She inquired what the gist of his criticism was. Had they not married quickly enough to leave the poor bachelors alone? Or were there just too many of them? Did they seem to lack intelligence according to the arrogant editor in chief? She not only criticized Cohen, but Salonician men in general. The reason for the Saloniquenas to delay marriage and inspect the potential candidates thoroughly was the lack of quality of what was on offer for them on the local marriage bazaar. The young men of the city had precious little to appeal to the opposite sex. They were "businessmen without poetry or ideals"; the business mentality of the successful port city suppressed all other activities. According to the letter writer, the Saloniquenos had no idea what to do with their spare time beyond having a glass of *mastika* (*rakı/ouzo*) with their buddies. They were too avaricious to engage either in the pursuit of literature or sports, thus neither developing their bodies, nor their intellect into a form that would prove desirable by the standards of the soon to begin twentieth century. Instead, when the Salonician women encountered them at balls or receptions, these men would bore them with superficial talk and the elegant tail coats could not hide the plum, uncultivated bodies beneath. They would not dance very much due to lack of bodily endurance and danced badly when they did, for lack of training.[4]

A general critique of the young generation of females was thus retorted by a similar attack on the men of the town. Nonetheless it becomes obvious by the venomous tone of the counterattack that the "young lady" also knew her bargaining position was a lot weaker than the men's. While a Salonician businessman's son could most probably

---

[3] *Journal de Salonique*, 7 Jan. 1896/26 Dec. 1895.
[4] *Journal de Salonique*, 21 Dec. 1895.

ignore incitement to marry for years; get sexual fulfillment through prostitute services (a fact never stated but implicit in the discussion and also implicit in "Sheridan's" original article); enjoy relative freedom of movement around town while avoiding the responsibilities of a household head; and even when older and past his physical prime probably still score to marry a younger and attractive wife if his family's fortunes were in order, the Saloniquenas did not have these options. Sexual gratification for unmarried women was not publicly or even semi-publicly acceptable, let alone on large-scale offer for rent. Much of the public sphere was occupied by male exclusive or male-centered sociability. An unmarried middle-class woman would as a rule still be expected to closely engage with her family. Aging decisively diminished the chances on the marriage bazaar. A sense of anxiety among the female letter writers over the male contenders' lack of earnestness or even outright refusal toward the marriage bazaar is therefore understandable.

Undoubtedly the venomous attack hit a nerve, as the letter by "a young man" the next week showed. He agreed with her rebuttal of "Sheridan's" sarcasm, but found the attack on the Saloniquenos in general unfair, as, so he seemed to agree, the commercial atmosphere of the town smothered all attempts at intellectual activity. The whole education, he claimed, was intended to exorcise any ideals beyond pure moneymaking; any idealist pursuits were slandered as unrealistic. And how could one ride a bicycle in this town when in winter it would get stuck in the mud and in summer the streets would disintegrate into dust? He attempted to underline the dire picture by throwing in the phrase "struggle for life" (using the Darwinian phrase in English original) to describe the bleak prospects of a Salonica businessman.[5]

By contrast, the male letter writer "Protis" was more offensive in his deliberation on the "struggle for life," countering the "young lady's" derision of his sex by similar attacks against the Saloniquenas. Every woman these days was in possession of a piano; even servants dressed like duchesses; but no woman actually had any skill using her own fingers. This is why some Salonician men including himself preferred to remain single ("célibataire") and enjoy their freedom without having to submit to the restraints of marriage. Nonetheless he also conceded that the major hurdle to marriage was actually the wealth expected of a

---

[5] *Journal de Salonique*, 6 Jan. 1896.

husband to sustain a family. In order to clarify that his point of view was not completely misogynous, he added that single men could aid their mothers and sisters.[6]

The debate continued for months. Some readers even gathered together to send off a common reply to the allegations of the opposite sex. The editors had to reject anonymous letters for legal reasons, as the law prescribed that the real name of the letter writer be known to the editorial board, if the writer chose a pseudonym.[7] The debate, although initiated as one of the calculated provocations against the reading audience the editors regularly undertook to raise the *Journal de Salonique*'s sales, hit a nerve and is symptomatic for the theoretically broad but in practice often rather limited frameworks for fashioning the gendered self. It illustrates that young Salonician men and women of the middle classes had much in common with the *Man without Qualities* and with Bihruz Bey. They were well aware of the possibilities the wider world offered them. Through the prism of the French language, a language that all debate participants had an excellent active command of, they followed international literary, scientific, artistic, and sport developments. And yet, when it came to adapting these to enrich their own lifeworlds, they did not know how to go about the task. A tail coat was easily tailored and pianos had become ubiquitous pieces of furniture in bourgeois homes; the men's families, schools, and workplaces would quickly acquaint them with emerging ways of earning money. But beyond such simple material pursuits, they were at a loss. Could one really ride a bicycle around town when the mud and dust on one's clothes would run contrary to middle-class etiquette? Was it desirable to sweat and suffer physically in a gym rather than to let the body go limp hanging around the tavern with one's buddies? What activities could one undertake as a young woman besides the bland and predictable excursions to other families' houses, chaperoned by one's family members? What point was there in learning to play the piano or reading contemporary literature if one's surroundings were not appreciative of it? The attacks against the other sex are in large part caused by frustration with one's own inaptitude in mastering the possibilities of the modern world. If a dazzling husband

---

[6] *Journal de Salonique*, 13 Feb. 1896.
[7] *Journal de Salonique*, 16 Jan., 6 Feb. 1896. A return of the subject can be noticed in *Journal de Salonique*, 5, 18 Dec. 1907.

or wife would appear who was well adapted to the chances turn-of-the-century life offered, one could still make one's dreams come true, according to the logic of the argument. But unfortunately the liberator from the materialist boredom of Salonician middle-class life remained out of sight.

In addition, some attempted to break out of the constraints of port city middle-class life, but were frustrated easily. One writer of a letter to the editor of *Journal de Salonique* describes how she undertook an excursion by bicycle, apparently on her own. Unlike the male letter writer mentioned, she was not put off by the winter mud, and chose to finish off her tour with a café visit, reading the newspaper and enjoying something to drink. She believed the high prices would guarantee her privacy while in the café, but was soon disappointed. In turn, a peddler of armbands, then a vendor of the local delicacy of *huevos enhaminados*, followed by a salesman of Chinese imports with a Chinese peasant's hat huge enough to loom over the top of her newspaper, and lastly a match seller followed by several beggars disturbed her solitude. When she finally got up to escape the incessant annoyances, she was hindered from leaving the café by vendors of salted fish, *Bottarga*, and almonds.[8]

While the incident seems too trivial even for a local newspaper, it becomes more understandable in the context of the ongoing debate in the letters column. The writer attempted to carve her own individual space out of the otherwise male-centered urban space, and to enjoy it. The positive image of physical activity in modern times apparently enabled her to pass her bicycle excursion without molestation, although female cyclists at the time caused quite a stir in Salonica.[9] However, the second part of her plan failed due to the café's inability to protect her from the underclass street environment. Her insisting on the café's duty to ward off these annoyances becomes more understandable when one regards a 1921 survey of cafés in Smyrna that states that of the 495 coffeehouses in town, there were 13 elitist cafés and even of those, only 6 were frequented by women.[10]

Nonetheless, not all inhabitants of Salonica or the other major port cities were so easily defeated when it came to enriching their individual

---

[8] *Journal de Salonique*, 13 Feb. 1896.
[9] Anastassiadou, "Sports d'élites et élites sportives," 154.
[10] Bali (ed.), *A Survey of Some Social Conditions in Smyrna*, 106–113.

lives. As far as "idealist" activities were concerned, there were a half-dozen different nationalist projects to choose from: Bulgarian, Greek, or Armenian irredentism, Turkish nationalism, Zionism, or Levantine community politics. For the more hot-blooded, angry young men or women, these could be pursued through underground networks with radical and partly militant groups. For those more accustomed to the easy life, activities could be pursued through legit channels of philanthropy, furthering educational, artistic, or social infrastructure of the respective communities. Idealist activities were not per se bound to ethnic groups. For example, M. Faraggi and Fuad Effendi from Constantinople, both alumni of a Parisian school for the deaf and blind, campaigned for a similar institution in Salonica.[11] It might be true that literary activity was prominent only in Constantinople and neither Salonica nor Smyrna had much of a literati scene, but nonetheless, there was some activity. For example the Saloniqueno Osman Tevfik Bey in 1896 founded the literary magazine *Mütalaa* (point of view).[12] Nor did cycling remain an exotic, frowned-upon activity. Already in 1900, four years after the letter column debate, a permanent velodrome was established in Beşçınar Gardens. Bicycle races became a favorite pastime in the initial decade of the new century.[13] Not only regarding sports, but also emancipatory movements, the city diversified. In 1907, there was a report on the foundation of a "female club" by both young and senior women.[14] Once the constitution was restored in 1908, Salonica also became a hot spot of the labor movement and accompanying publications and activities.[15]

Thus there were cultural and sport activities that the Ottoman port city residents could and did pursue. Music performances were a mainstay of the port city salons. As some contemporary observers attest, it went beyond the demonstration of female finesse for the marriage bazaar and entailed a serious pursuit of modern composers and their latest pieces. Some men chose to dedicate their free time to gymnastics, as will be discussed later. However the mere existence of such activities

[11] *Journal de Salonique*, 6 Feb. 1896.
[12] *Journal de Salonique*, 6 Feb. 1896. The weekly in Ottoman Turkish existed for roughly two years.
[13] Anastassiadou, "Sports d'élites et élites sportives," 151–155.
[14] *Journal de Salonique*, 16 Dec. 1907.
[15] Quataert, "The Industrial Working Class," 194–211.

does not contradict the general feeling that obviously prevailed among many of the young men and women of the time: There was a strong discrepancy between the state of knowledge of the wider world and the possibilities they provided locally for the port city residents. To better understand them and the awkward debate turn-of-the-century Salonician readers embarked on and why it is fitting to interpret them according to Musil and the Bihruz Bey Syndrome, it is necessary to take a look at the wider field of gender norms in late Ottoman urban society.

Possibilities to fashion the gendered self were often suppressed not so much by explicit restrictions, but because of the normative discourse that tried to rein in the possibilities young people had at their disposal. Revolts against norms of gendered behavior were for the larger part relocated to the imagination and literary writing and even then symbolically vanquished in the novels on the Ottoman market. Divergent lifestyles certainly existed, but were difficult to maintain in face of the highly normative atmosphere of late Ottoman society. In the following pages, the topic of gender norms will first be traced through the pages of advice literature. The focus then shifts to erotic novels as the main repository of transgression against these norms. In a third step, we will investigate examples of divergent lifestyles and see whether they managed to overcome the Bihruz Bey Syndrome that apparently plagued the younger generation.

Smothering the Gendered Ego: Industriousness, Companionship, Nation

The Salonica public was not alone in engaging in controversies over the role of marriage and the relationship between the two sexes, nor was the debate or recourse to Darwinism restricted to non-Muslims. In 1899 for example, Mahmud Esad published a defense of polygyny, as it was supposedly licensed both by Islam and nature. He claimed the sole purpose of marriage was species reproduction, and as women were limited in their sexual activities due to the time they had to dedicate to pregnancy, nursing, and menstruation, it was natural that men had intercourse with, and children from, several women. In a reply, Fatma Aliye claimed that Mahmud Esad's argument was illogical, as mere reproduction without commitment was possible without wedlock, and pleaded for the family as an institution of companionship instead. Both pamphlets were published by the same printing house, which shows that publishers were well aware of the selling power of such controversies.[16]

When looking for advice literature on male and female behavior, the Ottoman market was not lacking. İrvin Cemil Schick counts 150 nonfiction publications in Ottoman Turkish on the topic of female gender roles alone between 1875 and 1907.[17] Unlike the discussion in the *Journal de Salonique* however, they were highly normative and had more of a prescriptive character than that of an immediate discussion between those directly affected by societal gender roles trying to find their own place. Classic authors of the Age of Revivals such as Namık Kemal, Şemseddin Sami, or Ahmed Midhat had mused about how to modify gender roles, mostly by attacking excesses of the patriarchal system, such as violence against women, polygyny, and lack of education.[18] When it came to even moderate modifications of classic gender limits, the response was negative. Even the hesitant adaptation of more androgynous styles of dress in Ottoman society at the dawn of the twentieth century was the subject of public ridicule.[19]

As in other matters concerning Ottoman urban society's search for its role in modernity, the soul-searching process was framed in a dialogue with Europe. The director of an elementary school in Salonica, Benghiat, gave a lecture on feminism in 1907. While he used feminist critique to ridicule and denounce the Western model of patriarchy and was willing to concede women the right to work, he warned against free marriage and reconfirmed the (not only Ottoman) contemporary ideals of women as mothers, householders, and beauties.[20] Fatma Aliye wrote *Nisvan-ı İslâm* (*Women of Islam*) in the form of a dialogue with three foreigners in order to explain to them institutions such as polygyny and veiling. Published in 1892 in Turkish, it was of course addressed to a local Muslim audience.[21] Europe once again served as a passe-partout: It could be the source of Enlightenment and a model to imitate or the source of all vice from which one could differentiate the innate qualities of one's own group. The Greek-

---

[16] Schick, "Print Capitalism and Women's Sexual Agency," 204–205.
[17] Ibid, 201.
[18] Enis, *Everyday Lives of Ottoman Muslim Women*, 36–39; Lewis, *What Went Wrong?*, 69–73.
[19] *Stamboul*, 4 Jan. 1911.   [20] *Journal de Salonique*, 9 Dec. 1907.
[21] Schick, "Print Capitalism and Women's Sexual Agency," 205. It was translated into French four years later.

language *Evridiki* warned its readers of coquetry: "This corrupting illness is not ours. Europe has given it to us."[22] Other authors on the contrary believed that coquetry and flirtation were originally of the East. In fact, older Ottoman, Persian, and Indian literature had celebrated romantic infatuation based on short encounters, passion, and sex. Some of it valued sexual fulfillment highly, both for men and women, and had judged it compatible both with social and divine order. Celâl Nûri Bey and Ahmed Cevad however favored the late nineteenth-century ideal of companion relationships between husbands and wives, which they identified with Europe. Both argued that with the West Asian traditional ideal of bodily pleasure and infatuation in marriage, coquetry had been the most successful strategy to make oneself attractive to a prospective husband. They believed that instead of the rather short windows of opportunity that Eastern society permitted for contact between the two sexes, during which one could not accomplish more than to infatuate the other, young men and women should be permitted to form acquaintances and thus sobermindedly verify whether they would work out as a couple.[23] Even erotic literature before World War I needed the comparison with Europe. Arguing along a line that agreed with Celâl Nûri and Ahmed Cevad in identifying emotionally restrained contact between the sexes with the West and passionate encounters with the East, but judging them differently, Mehmed Rauf writes, "Thank God we are innocent of this torment [of small talk, MF], because either the women into whose presence we are admitted are our relatives or there is license to love and lust as soon as we come face-to-face."[24]

Such bold statements however had no place in nonfiction publications. These almost uniformly believed their mission to be the education of the female sex (and much more rarely of males) toward productivity, moderation, and empathy. Newspapers by women for women were important tools in this process. They were established at very different points in time in the various local languages of the

---

[22] Sappho Leontias quoted from Falierou, "Enlightened Mothers and Scientific Housewives," 217.
[23] Schick, "Print Capitalism and Women's Sexual Agency," 209–211. On positive identification with European models, see also Türesay, "An Almanac for Ottoman Women," 225–248.
[24] Mehmed Rauf, *Bir Zambağın Hikâyesi*, quoted in Schick, "Print Capitalism and Women's Sexual Agency," 214.

Empire: *Kypseli* by Euphrosyne Samartzidou already in 1845 addressed women understanding Greek; the Armenian-language paper *Gitar* was the first produced by women in 1862, whereas *Terakki* in 1869 targeted Turkish female readers, and *Şükufezar* in 1887 was the first one run by a Turkish female editor.[25] Among a number of competitors, one of the longest running newspapers specifically targeting women was *Hanımlara Mahsûs Gazete* (1895–1908). Although founded in the very year the Saloniquenas were engaged in the "bachelor" debate, the Turkish-language paper appears ignorant of the gender roles discussed there and instead intends to transform Ottoman women "into productive, educated, healthy and moral citizens of the Empire." In doing so it followed the model of Hamidian conservative "state feminism" and modernization that was conceived of as a process of increasing effectiveness, but hardly differed from patriotic Greek or Armenian papers. This model shied away from a principle revision of hierarchies and established societal roles. It followed the mission to promulgate the ideal (upper-class) woman and support her by practical everyday advice. In doing so, it followed the tendency to overburden this woman with a myriad of tasks: efficiently managing the household, educating the children according to enlightened models, providing loving assistance to the husband, etc. These were not prerequisites to establishing one's own rights and moving on to other, possibly more egocentric activities; the ideal woman was to find her full fulfillment in them.[26] In following this path, *Hanımlara Mahsûs Gazete* attempted a feat of education that very closely resembled what Protestant girls' schools had been following since almost fifty years in the Ottoman port cities: the forging of the female body and mind according to industrial age norms of productivity in combination with piety and self-restraint.

Such sterile concepts were worlds apart from the realities the readers of the *Journal de Salonique* were grappling with: how a lone female cyclist could have her peace in the garden of the White Tower, or how not to be bored stiff by the business small talk of your dance partner at the charity ball. In fact, the world of *Hanımlara Mahsûs Gazete* only reflected the realities of rather few women in late Ottoman urban society. The need to warn against a long list of vices to be

[25] Falierou, "Enlightened Mothers and Scientific Housewives," 208.
[26] Enis, *Everyday Lives of Ottoman Muslim Women*, 17.

avoided – alcohol, tobacco, theaters, novels, bicycles – shows that they had found their way into the Ottoman and Muslim home.[27] Moreover, most women were not as secluded as the narrative of *Hanımlara Mahsûs Gazete* leads one to believe. Women had entered mixed sociabilities such as balls or salons (if of the middle and upper classes) and/ or worked outside the home (if of the lower classes).

When viewed exclusively through the prism of advice literature, the range of options late Ottoman contemporaries discussed as appropriate gender roles was fairly limited. It was perhaps more limited than in previous times: The late eighteenth-century author Enderûnlu Fâzıl had polemicized against marriage in his *Book of Women* (*Zenannâme*). It was only in 1837, at the dawn of the *Tanzimat*, that the book was banned.[28] The fixation on orderly marriage and companionship seems to speak against the argument that late Ottoman port city identities were multifold to the point that they "divided the human heart" and created "men and women without qualities." However, normative discourses made up only one part of the picture. In fiction writing, more radical concepts of gender relations were possible than those voiced by conservative women's papers. The *Journal de Salonique* had reprinted Leopold von Sacher-Masoch, who had rejected the contemporary dominant ideal of a bourgeois man–woman companion relationship, stressing the antagonistic character of gender relations instead:

That woman, as nature has made her, and as man at present educates her, is his enemy and can only be his slave or his despot, however never his companion. This she can only be once she has been granted equal rights to him, when she will be his equal in education and work. For now, we only have the choice to be hammer or anvil.[29]

Could this radical rhetoric be translated into the world of Eastern Mediterranean port city society? We find little evidence of it making any advances into late Ottoman discourse, not even once Hamidian censorship had been lifted. If one wishes to identify any influence, it would seem Ottoman writers saw the statement by *Venus in Furs*' main character Severin not as an invitation to Masochist pleasure, but as a warning to always end up hammer instead of anvil, despot

---

[27] Enis, *Everyday Lives of Ottoman Muslim Women*, 391–411.
[28] Schick, "Print Capitalism and Women's Sexual Agency," 211.
[29] Sacher-Masoch, *Venus im Pelz*, 90.

and not slave. For example, in the aforementioned novel *Araba Sevdası*, Bihruz Bey's unhappy and unrequited love is depicted not as a romantic pursuit, nor as socially inevitable and possibly pleasant as in *Venus in Furs*, but as a sign of character failure on behalf of the protagonist.

The dilemma especially young and middle-aged women found themselves in by having to conform to a limiting societal role with little self-fulfillment, let alone pleasure, became the subject of novels such as *Aşk-ı memnu* (Forbidden Love). The novel focuses on the great age difference deemed acceptable in late Ottoman marriages, unfulfilled female desire, and child rearing and material status as the limits of female pursuits. However the resulting catastrophe of adultery, suicide, and destroyed family harmony indicates that the female dilemma could not be resolved in contemporary society.[30]

The erotic revolution in post-1908 literature changed the picture. Reviewing the new novels, Schick sees in them "the sexes intermingling freely, women aware and in control of their bodies taking initiative for their own sexual gratification, and couples enjoying sexual relations outside the confines of marriage."[31] And yet only few of these novels would actually propagate a revolution of gender relations as Sacher-Masoch had. Most novels broached the issue of unfulfilled desires and expectations, but many would end by reconciling the rebel with the patriarchal system or as in *Aşk-ı memnu* by demonstrating that the road to self-fulfillment was also the road to perdition.

This is most obvious in the case of the 1910 novel *Bir Zambağın Hikâyesi*. The writer Mehmed Rauf wrote this story based on the 1883 decadent *Roman de Violette* by Madame de Mannoury d'Ectot. In the French original, two women and a man have a sexual relationship. Several statements claim that women need men neither for sexual satisfaction nor for defloration. In a key scene, the man joins the two women in bed, but agrees to leave the dominant masculine role to the elder upper-class woman. In *Bir Zambağın Hikâyesi* by contrast, the male protagonist uses the younger and lower-class woman to lure the upper-class woman, who had previously turned down his courtly

---

[30] Uşaklıgil, *Aşk-ı Memnu*.
[31] Schick, "Print Capitalism and Women's Sexual Agency," 212.

letters on account of her dislike for men, and to force himself onto her.³² Not only does he reassert the male monopoly on sex with women and the male position as hammer in this way; the protagonist's behavior must also be seen in the context of reformist debates calling for a partner-like relationship between men and women. The main character is liberated from such obligations that would include the education of his partner and monogamous fidelity, asserting his role by sheer masculine force.³³ Written in a more conciliatory tone, in *Zifaf Hâtırası* (*Memento of a Wedding Night*) the main character rebels against her arranged marriage, but in the wedding night reconciles herself to finding pleasure despite her previous reservations.³⁴

New Avenues of Escape: The Male Body and Paid Sex

The discourse on gender roles in the Ottoman port cities at the beginning of the twentieth century was thus divided. On the one hand, there was a broad literature on how women should become good mothers, householders, supporters of their respective patriotic cause, etc. On the other hand, sexual fantasies with much less idealist and more pleasure-seeking women and men appeared, although few authors could resist the temptation to end their books by reasserting the dominant trope. However, Ottoman maritime urban gender realities were more varied than the discourses accompanying them.

One case in point is that men attempted to gain a more immediate, physical sense of themselves and their bodies. In doing so, they adapted the modern idea of transforming the body along the lines of industriousness and productivity. The image of the bicycle race champion of Salonica, Mustafa Bey, in sweat-drenched tights on the podium waiting to receive his prize in front of a cheering crowd, dressed in the classic Ottoman *stambouline* or frock coats, demarks a revolution of the public display of physicality and its social acceptance.³⁵ However the focus on one's own physicality in the Ottoman context could also be a means to reject the norm of companion-based family

---

³² Karahan, "Repressed in Translation," 30–45.
³³ After the founding of the Turkish Republic, the official ideology reverted to the concept of woman as companion and assistant to man; Türe, "New Woman in Erotic Popular Literature," 175, 176.
³⁴ Schick, "Print Capitalism and Women's Sexual Agency," 210–211.
³⁵ Anastassiadou, "Sports d'élite et élites sportives," 153.

relationships, to opt for a new form of male exclusive sociability, and disregard restrictions on exhibiting the body. The new, but growing presence of gymnastic clubs gave men this opportunity. Breaking with older traditions stipulating that physical exertion was a sign of lacking social capital and being overweight a sign of wealth, the gymnastics movement promoted the ideal of the muscular man. While many institutions of the nineteenth century had produced inter-gender sociabilities, the gymnastic clubs were sites for a new male social interaction. What is more, the fashion of proudly exhibiting the muscular male body also offered the opportunity to flout established dress codes, both the more traditional and corporal attire and the post-Mahmudian dress of moderation, semi-Western and semi-Oriental at the same time, close fitting, but not too close. Instead, photographs of muscular men in the nude (except for their boxer shorts), demonstrated a new masculinity that (unlike a gender identity based on clothes) derived only indirectly from their social status and challenged bourgeois morality.[36] As the gymnastics paper *Marmnamarz* told critics of the pictures it published, "Things that are considered impure and ugly should be covered and condemned by trial permanently, but the human body is not impure ... Nudity in *Marmnamarz* should be considered art and compared to statues. Men should marvel over beautiful bodies."[37]

And yet, to a certain degree the bodybuilders were only reinventing the wheel. After all, the Mediterranean and most especially Southeast Europe had retained an ancient cult of the nigh naked male body through the art of oil wrestling. This sport had been institutionalized among Ottomans through special *tekke*s dedicated to it as well as competitions to entertain the court. And even though by the late nineteenth century, some Ottoman wrestlers had made it to international competitions – the wrestler Kara Ahmed actually being declared world champion of *alla franga* wrestling – oil wrestling in the late nineteenth century was already regarded "as rural and backward, old-fashioned and anti-modern, something that has to do with repetitive stories of grandfathers and uncles."[38] However, another factor was vital in making bodybuilding an integral part of modern

---

[36] Yıldız, "What Is a Beautiful Body?," 192–214.
[37] *Marmnamarz*, Feb. 1911, 28, quoted from Yıldız, "'What Is a Beautiful Body?'," 211.
[38] Krawietz, "Sportification and Heritagisation," 2145–2161; Anastassiadou, "Sports d'élite et élites sportives," 156, 157.

male body politics, while oil wrestling failed to be integrated. The *pehlivan* (wrestler) adhered to a specific subculture, was dependent on a patriarchic clientele-sponsoring system. By contrast, the bodybuilders believed themselves to be self-made men, dedicated only a set part of their leisure time to the cultivation of their bodies, and could otherwise live a nondescript bourgeois life.

One other factor that had evolved into a mainstay of Ottoman port city society also contributed to rearranging gender roles, improving the bargaining position of males. As hinted at in the "bachelor" discussion in *Journal de Salonique*, with the proliferation of prostitution, men were less dependent on marital arrangements for sexual fulfillment, a position they could exploit. According to the contemporary commentator Ahmed Cevad, the spread of prostitution especially in predominantly non-Muslim Pera had also led to a decrease among Muslim men of other forms of sex, such as homosexuality or pederasty.[39]

But while using sex services could be experienced as liberating, it entailed dangers that could jeopardize the male advantage. Syphilis, traditionally called the Frankish disease in the Ottoman realm, had become a serious threat to the general population by the late nineteenth century. Medicinal discourse identified soldiers and migrant workers as primarily responsible for its proliferation. Unlike with some other sexually transmitted diseases, the discourse concentrated on the male body, as it would be more conspicuously marked by the symptoms. While during the first decades of the Age of Revivals, the Ottoman government attempted to fight the disease just as it had other epidemics through authoritarian means of population policy, a shift toward a focus on the individual, hygiene, and responsible behavior set in near the end of the nineteenth century. Pamphlets instructing men how to avoid or treat syphilis and other prevalent sexual infections abounded.

While under normal circumstances, tolerance of paid sex was widespread, syphilis could turn the tables and stigmatize the affected male individual. It prompted a transformation from semi-public immorality to personal shame, thus highlighting the inherent conflict between male sexual liberation via the brothel and family honor. Seçil Yılmaz cites the case of Hüsnü Bey, a military officer who shot himself and was

---

[39] Schick, "Print Capitalism and Women's Sexual Agency," 209. Likewise, formal brothels for gay sex that according to Joseph von Hammer Purgstall's testimony had still existed at the beginning of the nineteenth century disappeared; see Schmitt, *Levantiner*, 292.

found dead in his home in Constantinople on February 27, 1894. In his farewell note, he states that he decided to end his life because of his syphilis infection. Even for posterity, Hüsnü Bey found it important to state that he had never visited a brothel, but had supposedly been infected by a syphilitic soldier serving water to him and asked for his family to be looked after.[40]

The disease thus forced a confrontation between the otherwise neatly separated spheres of semi-public immoral conduct and the respectable family. While in Hüsnü's case, its stigma invaded and destroyed the latter to the point that he found living unbearable, others drew the opposite consequence: Talking about escapades in paid sex and its dangers had to be liberated from its ban in proper society. A case of a very outspoken author in this matter is the doctor at the Gülhane Military Hospital Rıza Nur, who in his pamphlets admitted having enjoyed as a graduate of the Imperial School of Medicine the nightlife of Galata, including taverns and brothels. He describes in detail his own precautions at the time – disinfecting his penis in a solution of mercuric chloride after intercourse – and despite this, having been infected with gonorrhea.[41]

Women on Stage: A Milieu of Its Own

While veneration of the physical body, rented sex, and the dangers and opportunities it posed played major roles for maritime urban men, partaking in public life for women was a major issue at stake. Despite the conservative discourse associating women with the home, many women worked outside the house. However, despite economic necessities, paid work for women was often seen as a disgrace, even if in prestigious professions such as practicing law, as an ideal family was expected to provide its women a leisurely life that could, but would not have to, be used for charitable or idealist work.[42] As in other debates about the right way of living in the twentieth century, Europe once again was constructed as the Other of local society, serving some as role model, while others saw in it a path to be avoided at all costs. Either European women were shown as evidence that female labor was compatible with civilization or as proof that traditions in the Ottoman

---

[40] Yılmaz, "Threats to Public Order and Health," 222–243. [41] Ibid.
[42] Khalapyan, "Theater As Career for Ottoman Armenian Women," 37.

sphere were different and necessitated women's abstention from paid work.[43]

And yet, the European female served not only as a distant site for positive and negative projections. One could encounter women of European origin, as the Smyrna song mentioned earlier illustrates, on the port city streets and other public and semi-public locales around town, most especially in the entertainment and arts sector. Foreign women were certainly prominent in carving out new gender roles in the Mediterranean public, not so much because these roles were automatically more varied in Central and Western Europe, but rather because due to the nature of their work and due to the distance from their places of origin, they by necessity had to find new roles and strategies to successfully promote themselves and to cope with their quickly changing surroundings and personal constellations. These did not necessarily lead to constellations in which women had a larger degree of agency. However in some instances, we know of gender constellations and networks that seem extraordinary for the early twentieth century.

This is the case for Amanda Lüttgens, known to her audience as Aimée Lorraine, a native of Alsace, who died unexpectedly of peritonitis in a Salonica pension in 1910. She left behind an impressive wardrobe, jewelry, and bonds issued by the Cairo branch of Credit Lyonnais, all together worth about 1,500 German Marks. This sum shows that Lüttgens lived a much more affluent life than other entertainers. However, compared to a foreign Salonica railway employee for example, it is still fairly little and does not provide sufficient security against sickness or for old age. She had lost parts of her assets due to a theft in Trieste. Her tour revolved around the cities of the Levant, as did those of many musicians.

Her personal letters from her mother, which are enclosed in her consular file, reveal a network of communication, professional and personal ties with other performers and café owners throughout Europe. Amanda had grown up in a family of stage performers. That family was composed of women only: Amanda's mother had never married but had raised her daughter with the aid of several aunts. Her mother Anna Lüttgens headed an "English song and dance quintet"

---

[43] Ibid., 38; Biçer-Deveci, "The Movement of Feminist Ideas," 347–355.

performing mostly in German music halls and like her daughter lived a life on the road. Amanda's aunt Louise Donaty was in Bucharest at the time of Amanda's death. Besides Germany, Austria-Hungary, Romania, Egypt, and the Ottoman Empire, both mother and daughter apparently had ties to Italy and a number of performers with Italian names. The gossip revolves around new love affairs, prospects of marriage, etc. The letters show a high level of disrespect for contemporary morale in sexual relations and seem completely unbiased with regard to ethnicity, judging by the mix of names mentioned. We can speak of a self-confident subculture living outside society's norms in a space where transgression was permitted.

However, both mother and daughter were apparently plagued by the question of how to make a living once stage life was over. Amanda had considered settling down in Cairo during an extensive stay there, but now entertained the thought of taking over a pension business run by an apparently German woman in Salonica, where she had been staying and performing as a singer and artist for several months. She had felt happy in Salonica, believing herself to be among good people. She was suffering from bulimia and taking diet pills to keep in shape.[44]

Other archival mentions of foreign women in the entertainment sector are unfortunately too terse to more than speculate about the roles and gender relations women created for themselves. Adele Feuer for example ran a coffeehouse in the Salonica district of Bara, while living herself in Çayır. Feuer not only ran a coffeehouse attracting lower-class customers including railway workers and Muslims as an independent woman, but also did not keep an aloof distance to her customers. However, that is all we learn from her consular files.[45] The evidence is even more ephemeral in the case of the female musicians of the so-called Bohemian Orchestras. While many travelogs and memoirs claim them to be ubiquitous along the Eastern Mediterranean quays and consular registers confirm their nigh-constant presence, they hardly ever appear as individuals, let alone express their agency.[46] Martha Fehnl from the Ore Mountains is an exception. A member of an established musicians' family, she started going on tour to the

---

[44] PA-AA Consulate General Salonica (GK Sal) 32: Nachlaß Lüttgens.
[45] We know of her courtesy of a lawsuit for payment of rent arrears. The landlady Markandonaki terminated the bar's contract; HHStA GK Sal 433: Zafiriou Marcandonaki/Adele Feuer.
[46] See Chapter 19, pp. 314–320.

German and Habsburg countries at the age of fifteen. At the age of twenty-four, she embarked with her group on the Levant tour, first to Salonica, then Monastir, and four years later to Constantinople. There in 1904 at the age of twenty-nine, she met the army major İsmail Hakkı Effendi, and the Ottoman officer and the blond and blue-eyed Austrian married according to Muslim ritual and Ottoman legislation.[47] But how is one to interpret this marriage? Some more patronizing contemporaries considered such liaisons the result of modern slave trade, arranged by the bandmaster, disregarding the musician's wishes. While there is no conclusive evidence to support such a claim, we have no statement by Fehnl on her assessment of her situation that could aid us in more closely framing the marriage. One can only state that it could have been in part motivated by the hope for upward social mobility. As a musician of a Bohemian Orchestra, women earned little despite spending long hours on stage. Under such circumstances, the prospect of finding a middle- or upper-class husband from among the audience ready to flaunt the imperative of social and ethnic endogamy must have seemed attractive.

Except for foreigners, the only women one was likely to see on stage were Armenian actresses, as acting was still considered unacceptable among the other *millet*s. In practice, many of them embarked upon unorthodox lifestyles similar to Amanda Lüttgens'. The role as actress doubtlessly allowed for some freedoms from conventions: Earning their own money, they were not as dependent on the family as other women were. Some actresses thus chose to live in a relationship out of wedlock. However their rhetoric was defensive. Especially in retrospect, actresses stressed the hardships they suffered, supposedly for the sake of patriotism and progress. They complained about men not

---

[47] HHStA BK Kpl 115: Martha Fehnl, Heirath mit einem Mohamedaner. "Marrying a Muslim" is the header of the file, which should ordinarily depict whether it refers to a criminal offense, a lawsuit, or a bureaucratic act. Another case of possible "defection" from a band was even filed under prostitution. In 1885, Marie Reichmann from Sonnenberg (Výsluní), hometown to several "real" Bohemian musicians touring the East, was requested to be forcibly returned home by her parents. The Habsburg consulate in Bucharest found her living out of wedlock together with a Romanian journalist in Galați; HHStA Administrative Registratur (Adm. Reg.) F 52 – 46: Sicherheit/Prostitution, 1) Maria Reichmann, Consulate General to Foreign Ministry, Bucharest 13 June 1885. As Reichmann had not broken the law, the Romanian authorities refused to extradite her.

accepting their role and their exclusion from respectable bourgeois society, in particular families not accepting their son to be married to an actress.[48] This feeling of being ostracized was undoubtedly aggravated by the lack of security in higher age that all women on stage faced. Unlike foreign women however, the Armenian actresses remained in interaction with their community of origin and were thus more dependant on its acceptance.

Apart, but Not Aloof: Independent Women from Upper-Class Families

A combination of an open-minded family, a degree of wealth, talent, and boldness allowed some women to carve out roles beyond the stale prescriptions of the reformers and the Hamidianists. Mihri (Müşfik) Hanım, for example, born 1886, daughter of a senior instructor at the Imperial School of Medicine, received painting lessons by the court painter Fausto Zonaro and decided to embark on an artistic career. She subsequently moved to Rome and then Paris, where she made a living from portrait painting and subletting. She returned to Constantinople in 1913 to take up a position as art teacher at the Teachers' Training School for Girls and soon after to become the director of the School of Fine Arts for Girls.[49] Constantinople upper-class artistic circles were far from gender-segregated, as the note by Şair Nigar Hanım about a salon meeting involving Mihri Hanım shows:

Last night I was invited to visit my dear prince. It was an art soirée. (Prince) Burhaneddin Effendi was playing the cello, and Vildan Hanım, the daughter of Celaleddin Paşa, was playing the piano, while the painter Mihri Hanım was painting her portrait.[50]

Mihri Hanım was also self-assertive about her choice of partners and successive husbands. However more importantly for the matter discussed here, she produced a different discourse on Ottoman women. According to Burcu Pelvanoğlu's interpretation, her portraits of women, both veiled and open, depict "strong personalities who meet

---

[48] Khalapyan, "Theater As Career for Ottoman Armenian Women," 40.
[49] Pelvanoğlu, "Painting the Late Ottoman Woman," 155–169.
[50] Şair Nigar Hanım, quoted from Pelvanoğlu, "Painting the Late Ottoman Woman," 164.

the observer's eye with their own."⁵¹ And yet, such achievements had their toll. Mihri Hanım's retrospective assessment of her role echoes the Armenian actresses' lament: "There is no road as difficult as that of the artist in a country like ours, which is underdeveloped compared to Europe. Ours is a profession that demands too much sacrifice."⁵²

Individual liberation had its limits, as Duygu Köksal states in her study of Demetra Vaka. Born into Phanariot elitist and conservative circles, Vaka had been exposed in her youth both to Victorian concepts and the Greek Enlightenment. In an act of rebellion against the social norms of Mediterranean bourgeois society, she emigrated to the United States, claiming individualism and anti-class sentiment as her motives and the American Dream as her assumed solution: "America beckoned me more than any other country, perhaps because I thought there were no classes there, and that everyone met on an equal footing and worked out his own salvation."⁵³ Eventually she managed to establish herself as writer and journalist specialized on the Balkans and the Middle East. However, Vaka finds much in her new home to be a disappointment: The evident class structure and capitalist exploitation of early twentieth-century America in combination with the more blatant attempts of the Great Powers to influence the Eastern Mediterranean for their respective interests, rather than for the sake of civilization, led her to rediscover the qualities of Ottoman social life in her writings, even reinvesting the harem, the epitome of Western tropes of non-Enlightenment, with a partially positive aura of female agency. According to Köksal, Vaka redirects her social critique from the Orient to a general critique of modernity. In Vaka's words:

I realized that I was only one of the victims of that terrible disease, Restlessness, which has taken hold of women the world over. We are dissatisfied with the lines of development and action imposed by our sex ... The terrible fact remains that in our discontent we rush from this to that remedy, hoping vainly that each new one will lead to peace. We have even come to believe that political equality is the remedy for our disease. Very soon, let us hope, we shall possess that nostrum, too. When we find ourselves politically equal with men, and on a par with them in the area of economics, we may discover

---

⁵¹ Pelvanoğlu, "Painting the Late Ottoman Woman," 164.
⁵² Mihri (Müşfik) Hanım, quoted from Pelvanoğlu, "Painting the Late Ottoman Woman," 168.
⁵³ Demetra Vaka, quoted in Köksal, "From a Critique of the Orient to a Critique of Modernity," 290.

that these extraneous changes are not what we need. We may then ... see whether, as women, we have really done the best we could by ourselves ... and devote ourselves to developing that greater efficiency in ourselves along our lines, which is the only remedy for our present restlessness.[54]

In light of this statement, Vaka's predicament appears as a female and real-life variety of the Bihruz Bey Syndrome. Vaka did not fail, as Bihruz had, to achieve what she had set out to accomplish; nor did she content herself to simply imagine a course of action without undertaking any steps toward it, as Musil's Ulrich had; or like the Salonician bicycle rider become frustrated by the first confrontation with reality. From an outward perspective, her attempt at individual liberation is a success. However, as becomes apparent from the statement, individual liberation simply serves as an eye-opener for the general, deeper predicament of modern individuals. This predicament cannot be solved by simply returning to the flock one had strayed from, nor by eliminating outward constraints. The modern malaise, which is understood to be universal, limited neither to the West, nor to the Orient, needs a new, more creative kind of response, which can only be developed in time.

Gender ideals and gender realities in nineteenth-century maritime society were in flux. Both through translation and French-language originals, young men and women were aware of a myriad of gender roles and models debated around the continent and around the globe. The dominant trope for bringing them to conform to local sociopolitical ideology was to integrate them into traditional hierarchies of the family, allowing for a limited reform by tempering some excesses of preexisting patriarchy and enhancing women's roles along the line of education, industriousness, and family affairs. The new ideal of companionship was to bring fulfillment within the framework of the soberminded marital partnership. And yet, this normative trope fell far short of satisfying either sex. On the one hand, it overburdened modern men and women with additional duties heaped on top of old ones. On the other, it had raised expectations toward the other sex and led to frustration if its members fell short of mastering the new ways of styling the self or opted for more limited versions of them. To make matters worse, classic ways of transgressing patriarchic hierarchies through infatuation and romance were now considered passé, while

---

[54] Vaka, quoted in Köksal, "From a Critique of the Orient to a Critique of Modernity," 294.

leaving the hierarchies practically untouched (except for some minor reforms along the lines of Protestant-style moderation). New avenues of escape had to be sought. For men these were the easily available outlet of rented sex (with its dangers and anxieties due to venereal disease) or an intensified focus on the male body. For women, literature provided a world that at least accepted the existence of female desire and hopes for egoistic self-fulfillment, but one that often enough warned women of dramatic consequences. Nonetheless, alternative forms of self-fulfillment existed, especially for women and men of the arts and entertainment scenes and the elites, but even then the permanent threat of being ostracized prevailed. Individual gender roles, so the predominant logic in the final years of the Empire, were expected to be forged in accordance with the assumed greater benefit of the class and the nation.

17 Reining in the Free Experiment
Discourses on Class Formation

The local schools following Western models and studies abroad produced cases of over-identification with the other Great Powers, but could also develop into third spaces for the mixed urban population if the students learned to take the schools' missionary and imperialist zeal with a pinch of salt, or their parents used their negotiating powers to rein them in. The French-language newspapers, even though often founded by immigrants or their descendants, could serve as genuine third spaces for the articulation of local points of view or discussing local points of interest, although their focus had to be moderated greatly to adapt to the Hamidian era. Gender norms were in flux, hampered by the dilemma between knowledge of the wider world, the prevalence of hierarchies, and the resulting frustration and search for new forms of escape.

When addressing the question of class formation in Eastern Mediterranean port cities, one can reach two very different assessments on the role of the West, depending on whether one focuses on practices or discourse. If one observes the practices, we witness a rather liberal blending of identities. However, when we study the discourse contemporaries use to describe this process, we find that a bifurcated view takes precedence. Concerning the formation of a bourgeois stratum in the port cities, there is plenty of evidence of new work ethics, leisure pursuits, and consumption that were in tune with or at least effected by the prerogatives in the rest of Europe. As shown in the reactions to the new quays, the waterfront especially became the space to demonstrate one's social and cultural capital.[1] Photographs show men dressed in alla franga clothes (see Figures 1.1–13.5). As stages of typically bourgeois sociability, I have mentioned the social clubs, where elitism and exclusivity was celebrated. Theaters with plays and music from Italy and France; balls that most major schools and secular associations

---

[1] See Chapter 7, pp. 77–86.

would organize; and restaurants were other places to see and be seen. Imported clothes, drinks, and furniture were the objects of conspicuous consumption in order to flaunt one's cultural capital. And yet, when we study what Ottoman residents and other Europeans had to say about the proliferation of Western ways in the port cities, this does not reflect the apparent ease with which markers of international class practices were adapted. When considering the discourses on the bourgeois class(es), one is confronted with a much more dichotic relationship that resembles the gaze from the steamship to the port cities and the gaze of port city residents from the waterfront toward the steamers: European foreign observers of the local bourgeoisie(s) passed derogatory judgments, often resorting to an array of Orientalist images, whereas local observers felt obliged to formulate their own points of view as partial affirmation or rejection of Western discourses when producing their narratives on the bourgeoisie(s). Thus, the relationship of these discourses to the practices of dressing up, engaging in new forms of sociabilities, or utilizing the French language can best be described as a new *cloisonnement*: Western observers sought to limit the free and experimental styling of the self in order to maintain their superior place in defining progress and superiority vs. backwardness, whereas local elites sought to discipline the urban population into the ethnic, class, and gender roles they prescribed.[2] From both perspectives, men and women "without qualities," who would publicly joke and tease about whether they are English, French, Greek, or Turkish and who would wear their *shalvar* (or for that matter, their bowler hats or fezzes) according to their individual taste had to be taught the error of their ways.

The Making of Internationally Standardized Bourgeoisies

Traditionally the economic and structural components of class formation as well as their ramifications for politics and especially the nation construction process have been at the center of debate in Ottoman

---

[2] Such restraining discourses already existed at the time within French society, through a differentiation between civilization and "fausse civilization," based on the mimesis of outer forms without inner conviction. This served "a kind of inner pacification of France herself under the guidance of reformist intellectuals" that are identified with "the rising bourgeoisie"; see Schäbler, "Civilizing Others," 9.

social history.[3] As is the trend in the global study of class, the cultural component has in recent decades received much more attention.[4] But while the subjective aspects of making a national bourgeoisie are increasingly being taken into account in newer research,[5] it is the dialectic relationship between Ottoman residents and other Europeans on this matter that I believe needs more emphasis. Defining one's collective role as a class or national group was not a bottom-up process; it was a top-down endeavor. Western explicit or implicit views were taken as a point of departure to be refuted or affirmed, while in a second step this position was imposed on nonconformists within one's own ranks.

In the following I will first sketch the European input on the debate and then the local dimension. This division is not meant to imply that the power of definition lay with the Europeans alone, nor that Ottomans merely reacted to parameters from outside. We can assume that the construction process of bourgeoisie(s) actually had more of a dialogical nature. However local authors were well aware of the stronger leverage Western authors had and that complying to or appropriating their discourses was a more successful strategy to make their voices heard, even if it pertained to genuinely local matters such as the state of the bourgeoisie in the Eastern Mediterranean.[6]

The nineteenth-century mind frame conceived of nations as organized on the assumption that their members have certain traits in common, such as language, religion, race, or origin. A state was believed to be the natural expression of a nation's productivity. Since

---

[3] Kasaba, Keyder, and Tabak, "Eastern Mediterranean Port Cities and Their Bourgeoisies," 121–135. A similar functionalist narrowness can be found in Göçek, *Rise of the Bourgeoisie*. For a critique of these positions, see Eldem, "The Bourgeoisie of Istanbul," 159–186.

[4] In this vein, the bourgeoisie has been defined as a "community of sentiment." For a catalog of criteria based on both "hard" and "soft" aspects, see Kocka, "Das europäische Muster." The general discussion about the limits and challenges of the term "bourgeois" beyond the confines of its origin in Western continental Europe is widespread and cannot even be touched upon here; see Pernau, *Bürger im Turban*. For a short discussion of the applicability of Kocka's assumptions to the late Ottoman context, see Schmitt, *Levantiner*, 228–231. Another approach combining objective and subjective criteria for the formation of an Ottoman bourgeoisie is Eldem, "The Bourgeoisie of Istanbul."

[5] Exertzoglou, "The Cultural Uses of Consumption"; Kechriotis, "Civilization and Order."

[6] *Nahda* authors also created their visions of modernity by juxtaposing it to a European Other; Zachs, "Under Eastern Eyes," 159–162.

most of the Eastern Mediterranean was not organized as nation-states, but as polyethnic empire, nation building necessitated the division of the residents along ethnic lines and their competition for the previously shared space of the empire. We can therefore speak of competitive internationally standardized nations: Competitive, because the contested space is too small for all contenders to have their demands satisfied; internationally standardized, because their recognition depends upon the approval of the West.

So who was eligible to be part of civilized, bourgeois Europe and who was damned to be underclass, colonized periphery? It is helpful to recall here Martin Hartmann's position on the European Dream. Membership among "the great community of cultured nations" and "fulfillment in the limits of nationhood" had to be earned by performance, by "merrily join[ing] in advising and doing" as part of the modern world.[7] While recent historiography of nationalism has concentrated on deconstructing the myths of the nations' claim to ancient origin,[8] the nineteenth-century public was well aware that nations were not given, but depended on performance and a construction process.

However, who represented the "community of cultured nations" toward those on the threshold? As can be seen from Hartmann's statement: Any educated visitor from the West almost automatically felt invested with the power to pass judgment on the locals. In consequence, we find numerous Western visitors or functionaries of the nineteenth century observing in the major Aegean cities the Turks, Greeks, Armenians, (the mostly Sephardic) Jews, and (the predominantly Catholic) Levantines. Other ethnic groups are exempt from this particular form of scrutiny: Yürüks, Roma, and Blacks find only interest as objects of exotic ethnography, and Kurds and Albanians are only included in the evaluation if they are assumed to be a part of the Turkish nation. At first look, the exclusion of the aforementioned groups could be excused on the basis that they are either not participating in modernity enough or that they are numerically too

---

[7] See Chapter 4, pp. 45–46.
[8] The intellectual development from nascent to full-fledged nationalism in nineteenth-century Europe has been described several times in recent decades. The classics of this field of research are Anderson, *Imagined Communities*; Hobsbawm, *Nations and Nationalism since 1780*; Gellner, *Nations and Nationalism*.

insignificant; however, looking at Salonica we find that Bulgarians (or Slavic Macedonians) find hardly any mention, although they are demographically and militarily the "element" that stands a good chance of incorporating the region into their nation-state.[9] On the other hand, Levantines and Jews are often discussed, although their numbers outside the cities are fleeting and they stand no chance of dominating anything beyond the cities of their residence, let alone forming a nation-state. The reason for these priorities lies in another presupposition, one that neither Hartmann nor the other commentators on the late Ottoman competitive internationally standardized nations make explicit. In the nineteenth-century mind frame, it is automatically assumed that the nation is only viable if a national bourgeoisie exists. The bourgeoisie not only takes on a leading role in forming the nation; it is equated with the nation, and lower strata of society are implicitly degraded to foot soldiers, following the dominant class' prerogatives. If the sub-bourgeois members of the ethnic group, mostly depicted as adherents of the *Lumpenproletariat*, are allowed to take influence on the emerging national culture, it is detrimental to the accession process to cultured nation-states. We can therefore say that the objects of scrutiny of the European observers were actually competitive, internationally standardized national bourgeoisies.

The Acquis Communautaire of Nineteenth-Century Europeanization

But what are the actual criteria by which the European observers judged the degree of progress toward Europeanness? Like Hartmann, they often combined comparatively clear criteria, such as rule of law, corruption, productivity, and literacy, with other more random elements. A look at a number of examples will help to highlight some key aspects, but will be far from comprehensive.

While Hartmann in 1910 chastises the Turks for lagging behind the other Southeast Europeans, Julius Fröbel, a former German Consul in Smyrna, in the 1890s proved incapable of deciding whether the Turks or the Greeks were the better candidates for accession to European

---

[9] The noted exception is the "progressive" Martin Hartmann who had contact with Bulgarian workers organized as the *Club des Ouvriers* and comments positively on them; Hartmann, *Der islamische Orient*, vol. III, 18–21.

civilization. Would a philanthropic and cultured commercial bourgeoisie (the Greeks) emerge victorious or would their lack of discipline and lack of distance to the *Lumpenproletariat* prove their undoing? Would a military-bureaucratic bourgeoisie (the Turks), although less enlightened than their competitors, win the race in the end because of their discipline? The following totally contradictory remarks are selected from his memoirs.

In the Levantine racial mixture, the Greek element is the preponderant intelligence, and in the transformations, which are underway in the territory of the current Turkish Empire, it has an important culture-historical mission ...

The dominant motive for taking sides for thieves is the vigorous and concomitantly raw national sentiment which ... especially binds the Greeks together ... A victorious democracy would without doubt in all innocence erect a cleptocracy here ...

Despite this, the judicial exterritoriality of strangers in Turkey cannot be lifted in the short run, and the secularization of the law must still make great progress in this land, before the powers of Christian civilization can justifiably relinquish it. In principal, it is not likely that the Empire will survive the process of this transition, which is what the Turkish reforms are basically about ... It is touching to see how much good will there is among the Turks and how little ability to do any good with it ...

Incidentally, politically the Turkish ethnic element remains the most useful material, because it is more capable of discipline than the other elements of the population. In the last instance, great political successes are based on the capability to command and to obey, basically military features, and the Greeks possess this ability to a lesser degree than the Turks.[10]

As we can see, in the Western arrogant attitude, judgment was passed on any individuals encountered and their education, discipline, and talent were considered as possible ingredients for future state building. Every casual conversation partner on a steamship became a representative of his or her respective ethnic group. Also, while matters of good governance, due process of the law, corruption, human rights, and women's emancipation played a role, such as in Fröbel's comments, the observers compiling their travelogs included far more aspects in their scrutiny. They peeked into living rooms, onto bookshelves, and listened to conversations, songs, and musical

---

[10] Fröbel, *Ein Lebenslauf,* vol. II, 600, 603, 604, 626, 631.

performances. These latter elements show how self-confidently European authors assumed that an emerging national bourgeoisie must belong to a wider transnational "community of sentiment," echoing the behavioral patterns of the more established national bourgeoisies of the European West.

Discipline of the body to function as part of an industrialized mass and thus to efficiently make use of production and conform to urban life has been pointed out by Michel Foucault as one of the key factors in creating modern society.[11] The lack of corporal discipline in non-Western societies is one of the constant tropes of colonialist discourse. The "white man's burden" is in part justified by his obligation to bring discipline and productivity to the rest of the world. In this regard also, the view of Eastern Mediterranean society is ambivalent. While industrial work did not attract much interest by the Europeans, observations on the discipline of port city residents focused on discipline in condensed urban space: Notably, the ability to navigate the crowded inner city streets and particularly to use the sparse vehicles of mass urban transit are studied for their compatibility with the cultured nations. Commenting on the passengers of the 500-meter underground funicular railway between Galata and Pera, Ernest Giraud issues a mixed verdict. The passengers are identified as predominantly Armenian petit bourgeois, white-collar workers from the Galata banking district. On the negative side, he noticed the passengers' eagerness to conquer a seat or crowd onto an already taken seat despite the trivial traveling time of merely one and a half minutes and the pushing and shoving to get out once the "tünel" reached the other end, some men even jumping off the train before it had come to a standstill. On the other hand, he lauded the gallantry of men who stood up to offer women their seat.[12]

Foremost among the "soft" criteria for being accepted on a par with "European" bourgeois is appearance, and most notably dress. Far from demanding nationally typical dress, the expectation was that the late Ottoman bourgeois should adopt the tastes from abroad. The changes in dress in Ottoman urban centers, starting from the times of Sultan Mahmud II, have recurrently been the subject of research.[13] The shift from more oriental or local varieties of men's dress to

---

[11] Foucault, *Discipline and Punish*.
[12] *Revue Commerciale du Levant* 101 (Aug. 1895), 144.
[13] For a recent study and a discussion of the state of research, see Jana, "*Behind the Hat There Are Warships.*"

European designs or compromises between the two is one of the most thorough changes in Eastern Mediterranean material culture. It is not surprising that because of the speed at which European dress was adopted, the foreign observers soon declared it an insufficient criterion for admission to the bourgeois classes. Smyrna's European Casino mentioned earlier restricted admission to those of European descent and appearance. While European dress and etiquette became increasingly popular around the middle of the nineteenth century, the Casino continued to insist on descent. Assimilation to Western ways by Greeks or Armenians was considered a skin-deep affair: "What – admit a man, who only a few years ago wore a calpac and long robes?"[14]

The author of this statement apparently wanted the local population to prove itself by wearing Western clothes without any immediate gain for a probationary period. Others followed a different logic of argumentation in discrediting the locals in *alla franga* clothes:

In toilet matters, the Levantine woman lags behind her idol, the Parisian, only by a matter of six to eight days, depending on the arrival of the Messageries steamers. Her self-indulgence with a luxury lacking all "chic" and of indescribable bad taste concerning the choice of combinations though makes one pity the poor husband.[15]

Levantine women thus got the ingredients right, but were incapable of combining them. Their men were supposedly no less excessive in their mimicry of the European. Ernest Giraud observed that they had a semi-religious obsession with fashionable dress. A number of them would wear a cylinder at all times, no matter whether the situation was festive, casual, or mundane. They would spend excessively on good clothes and have their shoes shined daily, thus transgressing against the post-protestant paradigm of self-moderation that Max Weber highlighted as a key element in producing modernity.[16]

The borders between intimacy and publicity were also subject to discussion in the context of Europeanization. While observers often scorned the Orientals for their reluctance to open their streets, their houses, and their wives' faces to the public, there were other aspects, particularly those pertaining to personal hygiene and bare skin, that

---

[14] Quoted in Schmitt, *Levantiner*, 422–424.
[15] Barth, *Unter südlichem Himmel*, 65, 66.
[16] *Revue Commerciale du Levant* 212 (Nov. 1904), 633 ff.; 274 (Jan. 1910), 116; Weber, "Askese und kapitalistischer Geist," 166 ff.

the Europeans found too intimate while the Eastern Mediterranean locals were more free-minded about them. One Western taboo that was transgressed against was bare feet. More than by administrative incompetence Julius Fröbel was convinced of the non-Europeanness of Turks by the following incident:

> The fact that the Turks are not considered part of society in the European sense of the word needs no special mention. Individual men of the higher classes do not lack the refinement which makes their natural dignity delightful for the casual intercourse of the salon, and Esad Pasha was a man who knew how to move in salons. About one Old Turk dignitary ... I was told – I did not witness it myself – that during the Casino ball, on the sofa of a sideroom, in the presence of elegant gentlemen and ladies, he had taken off his shoes and socks and operated on his corns.[17]

While the veil is a recurrent object of criticism for some, too much bare skin also threatens the status of Europeanness. Much frowned on were Salonician Jewish women in traditional dress, supposedly revealing their breasts.[18] Hans Barth (actually a native of the Eastern Mediterranean, born in Smyrna who had only later moved to Switzerland and Germany for education)[19] on his journey to Athens, poured derision on the local practice of going to the beach and bathing nude without gender segregation.[20]

However, during other social occasions, gender segregation would be treated with scorn. During the balls, receptions, and dinner invitations that were the dominant forms of sociability among the port city bourgeois class, Muslim men who would appear without the company of their wives were pitied. This was not so much out of a genuine interest for emancipation. In the nineteenth-century bourgeois mind frame, wives were an asset, a kind of capital to invest into. A well-chosen wife could alleviate the burden of managing the household and direct the tasks of representation and socializing.[21] In mixed sex societies, a wife that managed to prove her beauty, education, and social

---

[17] Fröbel, *Ein Lebenslauf*, vol. II, 610. See also *Revue Commerciale du Levant* 101 (Aug. 1895), 144.
[18] Grothe, *Auf türkischer Erde*, 320. It is safe to assume that the observer thus exaggerated a wide décolleté.
[19] *Neue Zürcher Zeitung*, 13 July 1919.
[20] Barth, *Unter südlichem Himmel*, 80; see also Fröbel's remarks about nude bathing off the Smyrna Quays, Chapter 7, p. 83.
[21] Theweleit, *Objektwahl*.

competence could more directly raise the esteem of her husband than his wealth, networks, or descent. While the upper-class men of Jewish and Christian religion had mostly caught on to the game, the stronger reservations among Muslims against mixed sex sociability often led men to appear alone in public.[22] The German Consul in Smyrna Gustav Humbert (1910–1915) reports,

> As governor general (vali) we had Mahmud Muhtar Pasha whom we had already acquainted in Constantinople and who, due to his service with the Berlin Second Guard Regiment not only spoke fluent German, but was also uncompromisingly Germanophile. My wife and I were also invited to his private villa for dinner, where something impossible by European standards occurred: the lady of the house was condemned to stay in her private chambers, while the lord of the house laughed and jested with the invited guests and their ladies.[23]

Mahmud Muhtar's fluency in German and political orientation is thwarted in the final assessment of Europeanness by his inability to show off his wife. But making the wife visible was not an achievement per se. The wife had to convince by beauty, charm, social competence, and education. The French diplomat Bertrand Bareilles describes in his memoirs a visit to his neighbor in the suburb of Bebek, a Greek middle-class man. While the man is described as competent, learned, and aware of international constellations, Bareilles uses the description of his wife to undermine the overall impression. One of her opening comments is, "Your homeland is Europe, isn't it?" which Bareilles interprets as insufficient geographical knowledge. Surprised that Bareilles is carrying a book that he had been reading on the steamer coming back from work, the lady of the house asks him whether he is studying to become a priest or teacher. The husband is forced to intervene to enlighten his wife about the European custom of pursuit of knowledge for its own sake. In Bareilles' narrative, the Greek bourgeois has to admit defeat in front of his guest, stating that the "*horianis*" (peasants) were ignorant of this Western habit. So while the man has reached credibility in the Western eye, the inability to transform

---

[22] On the politics of female seclusion in colonial and semi-colonial societies, see Yeğenoğlu, *Colonial Fantasies*.
[23] Humbert, *Konstantinopel-London-Smyrna*, 58; see also Bareilles, *Constantinople*, 106.

the female sex according to the same prerequisites amounts to a failure in the making of a national bourgeoisie.[24]

Reading and knowledge of literature figures heavily in the nineteenth-century idea of internationally standardized national bourgeoisies. But reading according to international tastes itself was not enough: The literature read and the opinions expressed had to conform to the rules of the West or Central European salon. Friedrich Schwan, Austrian diplomat to Salonica in the 1870s, relates to his readers that he was impressed when meeting a young Greek high school student who had read Homer. However when she casually added, "It's very nicely written," Schwan was shocked over such irreverence for what he must have considered the founding work of poetry.[25] In another instance, Bareilles criticizes a Perote Levantine family for their naive and undiscerning trust in Western literature. The daughter avidly reads French literature without the reservations of his Bebek neighbor, but he finds among her books such morally corrosive and pornographic works as Emile Zola's *Rougon-Macquart*. Not sharing Bareilles' reservations against radical literature is seen as a failure: "These ignorant fools believe that a French book could only contain serious and instructive stuff."[26]

Music was seen as another quintessential ingredient of becoming a modern cultured person. Preferably, a young man should be knowledgeable in this field, have a piano at home, and his wife should know how to play it. Gérard de Nerval was impressed when he was invited to an Armenian home in Constantinople and a female visitor, apparently a Levantine, sat down at the piano to play a piece that had just recently come out in Paris.[27] Similarly, Paul Lindau lauded the Smyrniotes for the music they played in their salons, including Brahms and Moskowski.[28] But Hans Barth stated that the Smyrniote Levantines had not learned more than "a little bit of piano forte torture."[29]

Besides a wife's conversation skills, the piano sounds, and the contents of the bookshelves, the furniture and its usage were objects of the critical gaze of the Europeans. Bareilles on his visit to the

---

[24] Bareilles, *Constantinople*, 212–214.
[25] Schwan, *Erinnerungen eines Konsuls*, 51, 52.
[26] Bareilles, *Constantinople*, 114 ff.; for his opinions on women see also 264 ff.
[27] Gérard de Nerval, quoted in Bareilles, *Constantinople*, 337.
[28] Lindau, *An der Westküste Klein-Asiens*, 82.
[29] Barth, *Unter südlichem Himmel*, 64.

aforementioned upper-class family of "X Effendi," a former *saraf* (moneylender) turned capitalist, also observed the interior decor. The dinner reception took place around representative Western-style furniture, instead of a divan there was a canapé, the small round stuffed cushions for sitting had been replaced by chairs. However, Occidental habits seemed to be a skin-deep matter, hiding the Oriental mores underneath: The French diplomat reported that the Oriental furniture had been removed into the more private quarters of the family where they were still in use. The *saraf* would retire for his siesta to the divan wearing a nightcap and his wife would massage him until he fell asleep, to awaken to coffee, marmalade, and water.[30]

Internalizing the Europeanization Prerequisite: The Port City Bourgeois Obsession

The minute observations on the details of the Ottoman bourgeoisie by diplomats, businessmen, journalists, and travel writers from Western and Central Europe might seem at first glance comical, if not inconsequential. However, they are remarkably close to the standards local bourgeois would judge themselves and others by. The middle-class residents of Ottoman port cities saw themselves as competitive internationally standardized national bourgeois: Nationalist discourse had spread to most communities of the empire. In the spirit of competition and contemporaneous great power interference, conforming to the international standards set out by a handful of foreign visitors, no matter how ridiculous or wanton they might seem, became of great importance. However to be national, that is, not to be part of an undifferentiated international mass, there was also the necessity not so much to be different, but to distinguish oneself by some minute traits that could be identified as particular. This need to distinguish oneself together with conformity to the international tastes as set out by foreign visitors became the formula most chose to adopt in making their variant of a bourgeoisie.

In stating their progress but also their failures to comply with the international standards, Ottoman voices show remarkable resemblance to the outsiders quoted. The embarrassment of failing to produce a wife apparently lay heavily on some Muslim notables. When

---

[30] Bareilles, *Constantinople*, 114 ff.

addressing Wanda von Wenck, the newly appointed head mistress of the local girls' high school in 1916, the successor of Mahmud Muhtar as *vali* in Smyrna, Rahmi Bey, informed Wenck of his main concerns.

His Excellency wished the often neglected (rather sissifying) upbringing of Turkish upper class daughters to be replaced with European education not only of the mind, but also of manners, so someday Turkish ladies could also move about securely in European company.[31]

Apparently Rahmi thought mainly of the banquets and dinner parties he had been invited to and where he had to appear alone among consuls and merchants showing off the beauty, good manners, and conversational skills of their wives.

The aforementioned Leon Sciaky in his memoirs ponders his youth in Ottoman Salonica and his feeling at the time of being torn between embracing the West or sticking to the locally established lifestyle. Reflecting on the furniture in his family's house, he confirms Bareilles' suspicions.

The two antipodal tendencies which were to leave an indelible stamp on my life were already foreshadowed by the admixture of east and west which characterised the furnishings of the house. And nowhere did these two meet in as conspicuous incongruity as in the living hall upstairs, the *varandado*, where they glared uneasily at each other. One end of the uncommonly large room was distinctly Occidental. The massive walnut table, the elegantly upholstered easy chairs and sofas, the console with the gilt-framed mirror and the elaborately carved grandfather's clock might well have graced a tastefully appointed living room in Vienna or in Paris, where the furniture had been made. The other end was almost bare in its simplicity. Two low, wide divans bearing a profusion of brightly coloured downy pillows lined the wall. To this side, with its proffered hedonic comfort of the East, would the family gravitate instinctively ... The beautiful but unbending Louis XIV salon on the north side of the house was rarely used.[32]

---

[31] Wenck, "Erfahrungen im türkischen Schuldienst," 97.
[32] Sciaky, *Farewell to Ottoman Salonica*, 11. Ahmed Midhat confirms the verdict of "admixture" and vainly attempts to instruct his contemporaries how to arrange a salon according to Western rules. He insists for example that no possibility to recline should exist there; Zerman, *Studying an Ottoman "Bourgeois" Family*, 53. See also Dumont and Georgeon, "Un bourgeois d'Istanbul," 143–147.

No less than with the furniture, adaptation of Western fashions of dress could prove superficial. The Allatinis, the Salonica oligarch family often praised for furthering modern Enlightenment in their city, ordered their suits from two different tailors, one for producing *alla franga* and one for *alla turca* clothes. The former were for business and formal social life, but were discarded as soon as the businessmen reached their homes, where they would prefer the wider and more comfortable robes.[33]

The construction of national bourgeoisies also made an impact on educational pamphlets. The publisher Tüccarzâde İbrahim Hilmi in 1916 described to his readers what the ideal Europeanized Turkish family would look like.

They live in a big apartment building or in a small villa in Erenköy.[34] They consist of an older mother and father, a young woman, a cleanly and properly dressed man, three children and one servant; they of course have some relatives and close friends.

The young man is well-educated, well-read, smart and knowledgeable, entrepreneuring and bold. He works in a state office during the day. In the evenings, he constantly reads his newspapers and books. He gets up early in the morning, showers, shaves, changes his collar everyday. His underwear and shirts are spotless, he puts on an ironed suit, then goes to the dining room. The children have gotten up as well, their mother has combed her hair cleanly, the older mother and father are dressed in a plain fashion. They gather around a white tablecloth. They have their breakfast with milk coffee and hot chocolate ...

Having returned from a day of hard work and having enjoyed a hygienic family dinner, the family again spends time together.

The night time call for prayer sounds. The old man and the grandmother pray together. Afterwards, the lady of the house goes to the piano and plays a few national and patriotic pieces. The children listen lovingly ... The young woman knows French well. She is also not excessively covered. Among relatives and close friends, she behaves freely, within the framework of everyday ethics. On Fridays, the man and the woman always go on outings together.

---

[33] Molho, *The Memoirs of Doctor Meir Yoel*.
[34] Erenköy: predominantly Muslim middle class suburb of Constantinople along the Anatolian Railway.

Tüccarzâde İbrahim Hilmi then contrasts this sanitized and enlightened family life that includes the stereotypical gender ideals of productivity and education with the traditional Oriental family. They live in a cramped street in old Istanbul and hold dirty animals in the pittance they call a garden. The children are sent to the neighborhood *Medrese*, and they cannot even memorize the simple things they get to read there. The kids, dirty from playing in the street and hungry, wait with their mother for the family father, but even long after dark he does not show up, because he went out after work for drinks with his friends. When finally he comes and dinner is served, all eat in haste to then get up and let themselves fall on the more comfortable small cushions, where they begin to gossip about their neighbors.[35]

This 1916 pamphlet propagating Europeanization brings together several aspects mentioned. İbrahim Hilmi throughout his text is silent on the issue of class, although the comparison of the Europeanized and the Oriental family is obviously more reflective of their respective material situation (the first a high rank public employee, if not representative of the intelligentsia, the second urban poor or Lumpenproletariat) and their class-based resources and does not constitute a comparison of two equal parties with mere different cultural role models.[36] Thus, he follows the dominant trend to describe the social transformation at stake as a process of nation building and Europeanization rather than explicitly defining it as the building of a nationally homogenous bourgeoisie. Secondly, he aims to please all the criteria the foreign observers have compiled in their observation of the Ottoman middle classes. The young man shows exemplary discipline of the body expressed in his personal hygiene and his hard working attitude. His clothes are neat and in European style, but the family also avoids the show-off attitude of the Levantines, as is shown by the recurrent reference to plain-style dress. Education and especially reading are taken very seriously, the children are sent to school, the husband spends every moment of his free time catching up on newspapers and

---

[35] Tüccarzâde İbrahim Hilmi, *Avrupalılaşmak*, 64–71.
[36] For similar exoticizing descriptions of the non-Westernized sections of society, see Osman Hamdi Bey, quoted in Deringil, "The West within and the West Without," 109, 110. For a favorable description of the anti-Western but modern Turkish bourgeoisie see the letters of Hans Humann in the Ernst Jäckh Papers, Yale University Library, especially Box 1, Folder 3: H. Humann to Jäckh, Constantinople, 22 Dec. 1913.

books. He can boast a wife who is equally educated, speaking fluent French, and can be publicly displayed. The piano is important, as is other furniture: The model family has adopted a high wooden table for its gatherings, while the anti-model family still laze around on small sitting cushions.

The contempt against lower-class deviance from bourgeois norms, as expressed here by İbrahim Hilmi, did not stop at symbolic violence against the deviants. Even the state's authority could be employed to "better" their ways. Philip Mansel claims that the Smyrna governors general between 1894 and 1905 had men wearing baggy pants in the *zeybek* country style banned from entering the city center, forcing them to rent pants when entering the city at the railway stations.[37]

The Quest for the Self: Distinguishability in Bourgeois Class Formation

Nonetheless, İbrahim Hilmi tries to add a little local color to the ideal Turkish family. The wife plays national and patriotic songs; she should not completely uncover herself or intermingle too freely to please the local codes of decency. In doing so he honors the second strand in the making of the competitive internationally standardized national bourgeoisies: The model family must be the same as its counterparts all over the continent, but simultaneously distinguishable. This element had been part of Eastern Mediterranean local responses to European challenges from the start: In 1829, following some previous reforms, Sultan Mahmud prescribed a new dress code for state officials and officers. The long flowing robes that had been the hallmark of Ottoman dignitaries for centuries had to make way for pants and more tightly fitting coats, as had become fashionable due to imports from other European countries since the eighteenth century. In this respect, the Ottomans followed the general European trend to shed flamboyance in dress and shift to tighter fitting garments that accentuated the male body beneath it and that distinguished the wearers according to the quality of material.[38] This was however combined with a headgear that had existed, but was far from ubiquitous around the Eastern Mediterranean: the fez, a conical, brimless hat. This combination soon

---

[37] Mansel, *Levant*, 173.
[38] Jana, *"Behind the Hat there Are Warships,"* chapter 5.

caught on and was used not only by officials, but also by wider society, including non-Muslims. The imperial decree, without mentioning the obvious similarity of the combination to military uniforms of Central or Western Europe, claimed that the new dress code would abolish the embellishment that had begun to spread and that it constituted a return to the simplicity at the roots of Islam that would "shine" more strongly than the exuberant dress now common in the administration and society.[39]

This set a pattern that would become the standard for approaches to modernization of identities and the formation of bourgeois class(es) as mentioned: One should for the larger part follow standards as they had been set in the Western part of the continent, but simultaneously set some small marker of difference, of identity that could not be subsumed under Western tastes. One perfect illustration of this can be seen in the music program the Serbian High School of Salonica chose for its 1896 school ball to celebrate the day of St. Sava, the Serbian national patron saint. The orchestra always performed a *narodno kolo* (national dance) alternating with a European dance.[40] This was to signify to the polyethnic local notables that the Serbs were familiar both with the international bourgeois standard and their tradition.

Only very few authors, such as the Syrian Yaqub Sharuf, framed this process in a positive vein as an act of hybridization.[41] How exactly the balance should be kept between complying with international tastes and inventing particular identities was a matter of much debate. In the discussion, the West was omnipresent, both as a positive as well as a negative example and as an interlocutor. For example, a Dr. Misrachi chastised his fellow "Orientals" for adopting from Western civilization the worst and most despicable elements, such as the *cafés chantants*, alcohol, and wastefulness, rather than the universal ideals of hygiene, morals, and social justice.[42] In a similar vein, the Bulgarian-language

---

[39] Jana, "*Behind the Hat there Are Warships*," chapter 3.
[40] *Journal de Salonique*, 27 Jan. 1896.
[41] "There is no real future for Syria or for its civilization unless it is interwoven with the threads of tamaddun (civilization, MF) and can integrate aspects of European culture, sowing them in the ground, and watering them with the sweat of its toilers." Yaqub Sharuf (1884) quoted in Zachs, "Under Eastern Eyes," 160.
[42] *Journal de Salonique*, 16 Dec. 1907. See also Mehmet Namık Kemal's and Ahmed Midhat's critique of the *Tanzimat* generation of reformers; Aydın, *The Politics of Anti-Westernism in Asia*, 36, 42.

comedy *The Misunderstood Civilization* by Dobri Vojnikov, performed in 1871 in Constantinople as well as several towns in the Danube Province and Wallachia, shows Hadži Kosta, an established and pious businessman losing hegemony over his family, as his wife, daughter, and son have fallen for *alla franga* fashions. They identify Europe exclusively with a certain way of dress, foreign dances, speaking French (even if their grasp of the language is limited), men and women walking arm in arm, and denying one's heritage. The play seeks to expose the super-Westernized as deceived or deceivers, admonishing its viewers to remain true to their heritage.[43]

As Haris Exertzoglou has pointed out, the West mattered, but it was not a simple question of choosing between West or East, modernity or tradition, or Europe or Asia. The question was rather how to combine the various ingredients properly. New Ottoman middle class(es) in the making, whether Greek, Turkish, or other, for the larger part embraced the prospect of innovation. Unlike Sciaky and Yaqub Sharuf, they often did not frame this as overcoming tradition, but rather as a return to the roots of their own group's identity, be it the founding fathers of Islam or Greek antiquity.[44] Therefore, according to contemporary voices, innovation could lead the way to "authenticity"; one had to however guard oneself (and especially one's wives, children, and fellow community members) against "mimesis."[45] In conformity with Orientalism, most participants in the discussion did not reject Western notions of Eastern backwardness; they simply argued that the group in whose favor they were speaking did not form part of the detestable Orient, but was exempt due to racial origins, religion, convictions, etc.[46] Likewise Şerif Mardin states that the Turkish men and women of letters of the time did not attack the adaptation of modern lifestyles per se; their criticism focused on locals who copied from the West without restraint and without a sense of community values. This is

---

[43] Staitscheva, "Zum Europa-Diskurs in Bulgarien."
[44] Christoph Herzog speaks of "indigenous fiction" in such cases; Herzog, *Geschichte und Ideologie*, 4.
[45] Exertzoglou, "The Cultural Uses of Consumption," 90, 91. It is interesting to note that contemporaries defined the difference in terms similar to the anticolonial author Frantz Fanon seventy-five years later ("mimétisme" or "mimicry" in Fanon, *Black Skin White Masks*).
[46] Exertzoglou, "The Cultural Uses of Consumption," 90, 91.

associated with excessive materialism, hedonism, and loss of self-orientation.[47] Halide Edip claimed, "May Allah protect youths who like us live according to our own ways from women who greet their husbands saying 'Bon jour!', who go to Pera to shop in French, and who teach their children to say 'Maman' before they teach them 'Anne!'"[48] The discussion reveals much about anxieties prevalent in late Ottoman society over the challenge of joining a "world on the move" without ending up with the Bihruz Bey Syndrome, that is, in arrested development between the old and the new, and Salonica, Smyrna, and Constantinople seem to have lent plenty of bad examples to these elites.

In fact, as Exertzoglou states, despite conforming to outward standards of the Western bourgeoisie, many members of the Ottoman middle classes chose to distinguish themselves from the West, but most especially from the super-Westernized. A mainstream current in Greek Orthodox society for example chastised "luxury," which was associated with *alla franga* fashions in flashy clothing, excessively sized residences, imported furniture, or exotic food. While Max Weber assumed that only Protestantism produced the ethics for combining productivity of the mind and body with modesty in lifestyle, Ottoman Muslims and Orthodox Christians (besides many other religious communities around the globe) did not hesitate to phrase similar values as the expression of their autochthonous culture, as Mahmud's clothing decree and İbrahim Hilmi's model family show. Besides modesty, other central tenets of the discourse against super-Westernization were morality and family values. Patriarch Grigorios VI of Constantinople in 1869 denounced the use of schools to stage balls and theater plays, as these were considered incompatible with Christian Orthodox morality.[49] In the vein of Bareilles, another campaign targeted the imported European novel that imposed upon the mind of the middle-class girl a "world of phantasms and harmful feelings, caring only for the satisfaction of her dreaming."[50] To a certain extent, this discourse against the hedonist preoccupation prevalent in the Ottoman port cities mirrored similar discussions in Central Europe on the hegemony of

---

[47] Mardin, "Super-Westernisation," 138–145.
[48] Halide Edip, quoted in Önertoy, "Halide Edip Adıvar'ın Romanlarında Toplumsal Eleştiri," 39; anne = mother in Turkish.
[49] Exertzoglou, "The Cultural Uses of Consumption," 84.
[50] Kalliopi Kehagia, quoted in Exertzoglou, "The Cultural Uses of Consumption," 93.

the clergy over social space versus the attempt of parts of the middle classes to emancipate themselves from it.[51] It was also a tool for the rank-and-file bourgeois to close the distance between themselves and the haute bourgeoisie by declaring their public displays of wealth immoral. This became most explicit in the criticism of private tutors (mostly from France, Switzerland, or Germany) in upper-class families, teaching the family's young girls to play the piano, dance, and to speak French and other widespread languages. Middle-class criticism attacked this practice not only because of its luxury status or because it encouraged young girls' immoral behavior, but also because the education was considered skin-deep, just to impress the salons, and not to embrace knowledge for its own sake.[52]

Such discourse, affirming one's own modernity, but defining oneself in contrast to the materialist pitfalls of the West and the super-Westernized within one's own ranks, was widespread in late nineteenth-century debates.[53] However, the need to remind both the excessive upper classes and the unruly lower classes of their place within the community reveals the fact that the restraining bourgeoisie might have attained hegemony over the written word in this matter, but was apparently far from dictating social behavior. One cannot quantify how many people pertained to the respective camps, as only few super-Westernized wrote back. Osman Hamdi was one of those who gave voice to his contempt for having to observe the fine lines his more tenacious fellow citizens would draw and the need for distinction from the international standard. Even though he had returned to his homeland in 1868 and had become convinced of Ottoman patriotism and joined the administration, he still flaunted local conventions. He had married a French woman he met during his studies abroad, ate pork and drank alcohol, and in private went bareheaded, all habits some of his contemporaries frowned upon. Together with Marie de Launay he composed the official Ottoman costume book for the World Fair in Vienna. Although unusual for a costume book, Osman Hamdi felt the need to comment on individuals who had forfeited their

---

[51] Borutta, *Antikatholizismus*, 402–406; Kechriotis, "Civilization and Order."
[52] Exertzoglou, "The Cultural Uses of Consumption," 93, 94. And yet, it would be an oversimplification to reduce all opponents of super-Westernization to jealous petits bourgeois with limited knowledge of the world, as the case of Nicolae Iorga, expert on Eastern Roman and Ottoman history from a *boyar* family, shows; Dahmen, "Pro- und antiwestliche Strömungen," 71.
[53] Zachs, "Under Eastern Eyes," 162–173.

particular local dress completely for the sake of international fashion. In his description of the port city "'advanced' bourgeois types of exquisite taste," he defends his own behavior while studying in Paris, during which he had worn the fez only when visiting the ambassador or members of the Ottoman community and had otherwise worn a hat.

... the "Europeanized." He is of all religions and nationalities of the Ottoman Empire, and from all classes of society.

His costume on our illustration is the outfit rigorously adopted from the government officers. It is also the ceremonial costume, the "black coat" of the progressives. It consists, as everyone knows, of the red *fez*, the black *setri* and black trousers; but the excessively Europeanized type, very common among the rich classes, pushes things much further ... In Constantinople, Smyrna and most other large cities of the empire, one comes across "advanced" bourgeois types of exquisite taste who are not afraid to replace their fez with that marvel of elegance, the top-hat. At all times, they take care to carry a fez in their pockets, in case they need to present themselves to a backward-minded authority.[54]

Osman Hamdi was not exaggerating in stating that when covering one's head, one had to keep in mind state power, as Katja Jana's exploration of the Mehmed Effendi Affair shows. Mehmed, a forestry department secretary, on a summer night of the year 1907 in the small town of Ezine near the Dardanelles, left his room in a local *han* to watch the theater play in the *han*'s courtyard, dressed in a traditional gown (*antari*) and wearing a *Homburg* (or *Fedora*) hat. The other local dignitaries present did not take issue with his all-too-casual nightgown, but with the hat. The case was subjected to the grand vizier and the Minister of the Interior, who following the statements of a half dozen witnesses decided to have the secretary dismissed.[55]

Halil Halid, in his memoirs, like Osman Hamdi outs himself as super-Westernized. While he finds the need to distinguish oneself from the masses of one's compatriots by dress awkward in retrospect, he still justifies it. On his purchase of a cheap ready-to-wear suit from a Pera department store in 1903, he remarks,

But bad though they were, I was well content with my new clothes, as this was a step forward in satisfaction of my craze to dress as the Europeans did.

[54] Osman Hamdi and de Launay, quoted in Jana, "*Behind the Hat There Are Warships*" (my partially diverging translation).
[55] Jana, "*Behind the Hat There Are Warships*," chapter 4.

It is a fact that most people who adopt this form of dress in the nearer East look upon those who have not adopted it, or do not desire to adopt it, as incapable of acquiring "civilised" habits. Snobbish as it is, no doubt, this idea is not without reason.[56]

Sam Levy, the aforementioned editor of the *Journal de Salonique*, also walked the streets of the Macedonian port city with a French-style hat and trimmed mustache, preferred to be called "Monsieur Lévy," and his satires reveal he shared the contempt for local society.[57] Such elitism could work in two ways. Osman Hamdi was often lauded by foreign visitors for his unreservedly Occidentalist household.[58] However others, such as the overdressed Levantines Barth and Bareilles mention, could earn derision for getting the ingredients right, but failing to come up with a convincing composition. Overall, few Ottoman urbanites declared themselves publicly super-Westernized like the young Osman Hamdi or the older Halil Halid. However by the proliferation of balls in schools and other respected public institutions listed in newspapers, the widespread practice of private education for upper-class girls as evident in family histories, and contemporary photographs showing the liberal adoption of foreign fashions, we can safely assume that the super-Westernized were not of insignificant number.

Class formation was framed by contemporaries within several binaries. This included rivalry between different ethno-linguistic or religious groups. However, positioning one's group, characterized by national and class distinction vis-à-vis Europe, was another important ingredient. This included the demonstration of compliance with international standards as well as distinguishing traits. The super-Westernized from within one's own ranks were a negative trope to distance oneself from in order to define the national bourgeoisie's innate qualities. They also served to discipline those deviating from the norms prescribed by the group's dominant forces. And yet, super-Westernization continued to exist, often demonstrated not so much in words, but rather behavior. For a select few, it even served as a legitimizing discourse to strengthen one's position aloof and apart from the dominant group by taking recourse to an idealized Europe. How to define this Europe and where to draw the line between authentic innovation and blind mimesis was the difficult task facing all involved and continued to pose a challenge throughout society.

[56] Halil Halid, quoted in Köse, *Westlicher Konsum am Bosporus*, 450.
[57] Lévy, *Salonique à la fin du XIXe siècle*, 135.
[58] Alexander Conze, in Schulte (ed.), *Carl Humann*, 198, 199.

18 | Urban Milieus vs. National Communities

The Case of the Levantines

The construction of clear-cut national identities required a good degree of symbolic violence no matter what group within the urban order (and no less in the countryside) was concerned. It becomes even more complicated when extended to milieus that offer neither the potential to define them as a linguistic group, nor a clear-cut religious group with an official status (*millet*), nor even like the Dönme as a group with a common (real or imagined) origin.[1] The nineteenth-century so-called Levantines constitute such a case. More than any other part of urban society, they were a product of the circumstances that made the Eastern Mediterranean port cities and they ceased to function as major players once the port cities lost their status.

What makes up nineteenth-century Levantine identity? A question that at first glance seems simple proves difficult to answer, as this identity is rather elusive. I will therefore refrain here from big claims and limit myself to a criticism of existing hypotheses and assumptions, while only indicating the direction where I believe answers should be sought.

The existence of Levantines was intimately entwined with the Ottomans' rather liberal practice in dealing with international maritime trade. While for example China and Japan before the mid-nineteenth century were extremely cautious and restrictive in granting foreign merchants access to their soil, the Ottomans in some cases encouraged international trade and in others simply failed to enforce restrictions on the duration of foreigners' stays, their access to real estate, limits on

---

[1] The Dönme, Sabbateans, or Ma'amin, are another group where the debate is ongoing whether to consider them an ethnic group in their own right or whether external discourse on them is actually all that keeps the group together. In this case, Marc Baer has embraced a constructivist approach, whereas Dilek Akyalçın Kaya has adhered to a more deconstructivist approach that seems appropriate when discussing them in the framework of port city society; Baer, *The Dönme*; Akyalçın Kaya, *Les Sabbatéens saloniciens*.

exportable goods, or the extension of consular protection to local residents.[2]

This considerable leverage allowed the group to develop in a way that transcended the state-imposed concepts of Christian Ottoman subject or member of a national colony of temporary foreign residents. Neither language, nor denomination, nor territory, nor origin could prove them a clearly distinctive group;[3] however their role in late Ottoman urban society cannot simply be subsumed under some wider category, such as "Catholics," "foreigners," or "Europeans." A definition can only be based on the combination of some rather malleable criteria.

Levantines, as the name implies, are residents of the Eastern Mediterranean coastline who are either native to the area or have through long-term residence adapted to local conditions. The second, more closely defining criterion is that either they or an earlier generation of their family were traditionally affiliated with the Roman Catholic Church or alternatively another church based in Western or Central Europe. As Oliver Schmitt has shown, these criteria combined people from a great variety of geographic origins: Arabic-speaking Maronites from Lebanon (as the Maronite Church accepts the supremacy of the Pope); Greek-speaking Catholics from the Aegean Islands whose ancestors had been catholicized under medieval crusader rule; families descending from the original residents of the Genoese settlement at Galata across from Constantinople before the city was annexed to the Ottoman Empire; and people of Venetian or French origin who had settled in a Levantine port for commercial reasons under Ottoman rule. In the more mobile nineteenth century, their ranks grew considerably, especially due to Maltese and Dalmatians, but also Italians, Austrians,

---

[2] Eldem, "Foreigners at the Threshold of Felicity." For a detail study of how foreigners circumvented existing restrictions, see Aymes, "Port-City in the Fields." On how foreigners would circumvent the residence restrictions imposed by their home countries see Smyrnelis, *Une société hors de soi*. For a comparison with other Asian emigration practices see Masashi (ed.), *Asian Port Cities 1600–1800*.

[3] Due to the impossibility of finding fixed criteria to define Levantines, Oliver J. Schmitt calls them an "ethno-confessional group" (Schmitt, *Levantiner*), stating that they were unable to develop the criteria for an ethnic group in the strict sense.

and Germans who moved around the Eastern Mediterranean basin in search for a higher quality of life.[4]

But the Levantines did not only speak a number of different languages and had different regions they considered their homestead; they also held all kinds of different legal statuses. Whereas a considerable number because of their family's extraterritorial origins laid claim to foreign nationality and thus capitulatory rights, others despite a similar background were not foreign subjects outright, but still enjoyed consular protection as *beraatlı*. Yet others, both from among the groups of indigenous origins, but also among recent immigrants, had no official status with the consulates and were thus considered Ottoman subjects. Micro-historical studies have revealed a considerable fluctuation between these different statuses. Moreover, individuals and families would shop around and attempt to gain passports of the country that had the best relations to the Ottoman Empire and would prove most beneficial to the individuals concerned, thus further obscuring any relationship between their nominal place of origin and their nationality.

Thanks especially to Marie-Carmen Smyrnelis' and Oliver J. Schmitt's studies, we now know a lot about the origins and the practices of nineteenth-century Levantines, although there is still some margin to debate who should be counted as part of the group and who should not. The question that has however not been answered satisfactorily is how the members of this group saw themselves: Did they have a sense of community, despite the differences in language, origins, and legal status? Did more particular identities, such as adherence to their nationalities, dominate? Did they identify with the city they lived in? Was there a sense of belonging to some grander category, such as Europe, and if so, was this interpreted as a unifying factor or a sign of distinction from the rest of the local population? And was the ambivalence in Levantine identity considered a failure to develop according to the standards described in the previous chapter or as the reason for pride, that is, a cosmopolitan sense of self?

The lack of evidence to answer these questions has led to two opposing interpretations. According to Schmitt, the Levantines' collective self-positioning was determined primarily by a sense of local

---

[4] Clancy-Smith, *Mediterraneans*; Schmitt, *Levantiner*; Smith, *Colonial Memory and Postcolonial Europe*.

belonging and secondly adherence to Catholicism. He believes both to be pivotal for their sense of identity. He admits however that he comes to this conclusion based on circumstantial evidence and sources by outsiders, and regrets that his study failed to locate sufficient self-narrative sources to base these claims on.[5]

The opposing view is held by Edhem Eldem. Following a more hermeneutic approach, Eldem discusses the usage of the term "Levantine" in historical sources. He comes to the conclusion that in the nineteenth century the term never existed outside of the negative trope others employed to slander people who had developed a degree of ambivalence in between local Ottoman and other European conditions. He therefore rejects its usage as a category in modern historical research. However he offers no alternative categories for people who are neither simply European foreigners nor members of the more established groups in Ottoman society.[6]

There is much incidental evidence to back up Schmitt. His claim of Catholicism as a defining characteristic holds true for a large number of the Levantines, but cannot be seen as exclusive. For example, the Smyrniote merchant dynasty of Dutch origin, the Van Lenneps, remained Protestants despite several centuries of residence in Smyrna, where Lutheran churches catered to only a tiny minority.[7] By contrast the Salonician merchant family of English origin, the Abbots, had adapted Greek Orthodoxy as their denomination.[8] His other claim of identification with the locals seems more verifiable. The large communities of Levantines appeared especially in Constantinople and Smyrna. In personal histories, we can reconstruct that several families grew to play major roles in the local economy, social life, and occasionally municipal politics as well. Less eased members of the group still played significant roles, for example by importing new trades and businesses that were vital for shaping nineteenth-century portside Ottoman life. Thus, an assumption that Levantines identified with the city they lived in seems logical, even if not verifiable in all cases. Nonetheless this in itself is not enough to falsify Eldem's thesis that there is no positive claim to Levantine collective identity.

---

[5] Schmitt, *Levantiner*, 40.   [6] Eldem, "'Levanten' Kelimesi Üzerine."
[7] *Levantine Heritage*, "The van Lennep Genealogy."
[8] Mazower, *Salonica: City of Ghosts*, 147–149.

There is no real middle ground to negotiate between these two stances, as they are based on entirely different approaches. The only legitimate way to overcome the stalemate would be to search for a third approach by hearing the historical agents' voices. The relative obscurity of Levantine identity – divided by nationality, status, language, origins, and *ancienneté* of residence in the Levant – makes the use of self-narratives a desideratum. Unfortunately, many people of the nineteenth century spoke about the Levantines, but hardly anyone spoke for them. With extensive research, we could hope to decide whether the group had a cohesive sense of identity and rootedness in their place of residence or whether "Levantine" is no more than a pejorative exonym homogenizing a class of people who have no common denominator. There are however several pitfalls involved in such a quest and they are not only due to the dearth of known sources.

Research on Levantines: Rich in the Periphery, Weak in the Capital

The most thorough study about a Levantine family is from a fairly exotic location. Based on the Poche-Marcopoli archive, purportedly the largest private archive in the Middle East, Mafalda Ade has painted a thick description of the Poche family originating from Bohemia and settled in Aleppo since the early nineteenth century. Based on both private letters and commercial and consular correspondence, Ade traces the family's positioning in between a real or imagined overseas Europe, their integration into the diverse local society, commercial network ties, and financial practices. Josephe Poche, born in Northern Bohemia, came to Aleppo as a trade representative in 1819. His sons Frédéric and Adolphe founded a long lasting company in the middle of the nineteenth century. Already the second generation was no longer fluent in German, but more versed in Italian and French, and later Arabic. Most family members intermarried with other local families of foreign origin, but some also wed Arab Christians from among the local business families. In continuation of a century-old tradition, they lived in a *han*, but had adapted its interior to European design. Ade summarizes that the Poches became a classic representative of "Levantine" society: Although only vaguely connected to their region of origin, they understood themselves to be Europeans and simultaneously strongly identified with their place of residence and were locally well connected. Their local business partners appear rather diverse, most often Muslims, Armenian Christians, or foreign traders; it seems the Poches preferred whoever proved most efficient in serving their interests. However, we find that the Levantine family did not shy away from mobilizing communalist ties and even outright racism: When vying for the post of Austrian Honorary Consul in Aleppo against Moïse Picciotto in 1858, the Poche-Marcopoli family appealed to Catholic solidarity and utilized anti-Semitic slander against their rival (without success).[9]

While it seems probable the Poche-Marcopoli family's peculiar mix of cosmopolitan, local, and sectarian attitudes and practices could have also informed the lifeworlds of comparable Levantine families in the northern half of the Eastern Mediterranean, there is no comparable in-depth study to base this assumption on. Nonetheless, some dilettante research (in the positive sense of the word) provides some insights into the world of the nineteenth-century Smyrna Levantines.[10] It is striking that there is as yet little known about the Stambouliote Levantines. This can in part be explained by the fact that Smyrna's commerce and upper-class sociability was to a large extent dominated by Levantines, whereas in Constantinople, they formed only part of a larger and more varied upper class. Nonetheless, one cannot claim that there is no known memoir of pre-republican Levantine life in Constantinople, far from it. Said Naum Duhani's (1892–1970) partially autobiographical works are well-known. Born into a Maronite family originating from Mount Lebanon, his father served as an Ottoman diplomat and at one point as the ambassador in Paris. Said Naum Duhani grew up within the Ottoman bureaucratic elite and was well integrated into the upper-class social life of Pera. He was also the nephew of the aforementioned director of the Naum Theater, Michel Naum. Publishing his two books at the age of fifty-five and sixty-four respectively, Said recounts the time of his youth, before the First World War destroyed the peaceful coexistence of different nationalities and communities in the Europeanized parts of Istanbul. The life as seen from the elitist club Cercle d'Orient, where Ottoman dignitaries, embassy staff, officers, and bankers would mingle, is portrayed. *Vieilles gens, vieilles demeures: topographie sociale de Beyoğlu au*

---

[9] Ade, *Picknick mit den Paschas*.
[10] *Levantine Heritage*; Milton, *Paradise Lost*.

19ème siécle (first published in 1947, first Turkish edition in 1982) and more so *Quand Beyoğlu s'appelait Pera: les temps qui ne reviendront plus* (first published in 1956, first Turkish edition in 1992) are rich with details of everyday life and have therefore been consulted by scores of historians who are interested in aspects beyond "big" history.

The usage of this fascinating account has however been problematic, as much of Duhani's writing is taken as historical evidence without questioning. An account written over thirty years after the period described can hardly serve as an immediate firsthand account, and more often than not, archival or printed sources can unsettle claims based on Duhani's account.[11] The naive reception of Duhani's writings is due in part to its political correctness in the postmodern era. Their translation into Turkish and thus popularization in Turkey coincided with the rediscovery and subsequent revival of Beyoğlu and with the renewed worldwide interest in inner-city districts dating from the nineteenth century. Duhani all of a sudden seemed to be the authentic voice that could narrate to the postmodernist era the glory of this particular past. This has led to an overemphasis on these two books, which should be seen in a more limited scope: a particular man's views, informed by his particular class (high society, too high to reflect on the fate of more ordinary men and women) and gender (a man in a man's world), explaining his particular experiences with Pera life as interpreted from a particular moment (in between midlife and higher age, with nostalgia for his youth).[12]

The Making of a Twentieth-Century Master Narrative on the Nineteenth-Century Golden Age

Duhani's imprint is not only visible on the perception in Turkish society of what nineteenth-century Levantine life must have been like; it also constitutes one element of a dominant paradigm on Levantine society in the nineteenth century as employed by twentieth-century Levantine writers. However, there are also some significant shifts in

---

[11] See Chapter 12, pp. 176–182.
[12] In an ongoing project entitled *Levantine Narratives*, Ülker Gökberk attempts to read Duhani and Giovanni Scognamillo not as crown-witnesses, but as producers of a certain nostalgic space informed by a sense of former grandeur, loss, and cosmopolitanism.

the narration, as will become evident by looking at some other early to mid-twentieth-century authors.

Duhani's contemporary Willi Sperco (1887–1978), journalist, novelist, and prominent Stambouliote socializer, likewise laments the decline of Pera. While he remembers the early postwar years as the climax of the district's cosmopolitan existence, the closing of major sites of entertainment from the 1930s onward mark the end of an era for him. Yet as Alessandro E. Pannuti remarks, it would be wrong to peg down Sperco as a Levantine community writer. Pannuti in his extensive study of Sperco's many and diverse writings finds only an occasional use of the word "we" or "our" in relationship to Catholics or the French- and Italian-speaking population of the city; therefore it becomes evident that this is not his main perspective. More telling is his description of space:

Here, like in all Perote dancehalls, full of lost and lonely souls begging for tenderness mixed with alcohol and smoke, the fatalist casualness of the Orient and the negligence of Eastern cities hang heavily in the air ... the splendor of the illuminated holy mosques grabs hold of you and drags you outdoors, into the vast silence of sleeping Stamboul, where the minarets appear like fingers with heavy rings pointing to the sky.[13]

The dancehalls of Pera do not exist in isolation, in a closed-off world of "Little Paris," where everything and everyone passes as inconspicuous Europeans; despite the international music being played there, the people appear as "Orientals" instead. The splendor of Pera nights owes to the presence of the magnificent minarets from the old city as part of the skyline. As Pannuti shows, Sperco's nostalgia is not so much for a particular neighborhood, nor for a community; it is for a space that allowed for identity ambivalence, multidirectional communication, or, if one prefers the term, cosmopolitanism. One could surmise the same for Duhani.

Although only a few years younger than these two bons vivants, Angèle Loreley (1894–1975) has a different outlook. In the introduction of her 1930s manuscript for the novel *Les derniers Levantins*, Angéline Loreley attempts a definition of the term.

To the pious memory of my mother, a hundred percent Levantine ...

---

[13] Willy Sperco, quoted in Pannuti, *Les italiens d'Istanbul*, 262.

Mediterranean by race, by birth, in spirit, the author takes pride in originating from Istanbul, Chio, Naples, in belonging to three great Mediterranean nations, namely Italy, France, Turkey.[14]

The short statement seems a good illustration of Musil's claim that in the complex early twentieth-century urban fabric, everything had "a hundred meanings." While Loreley lays claim to an authenticity of identity that does not lag behind a nationalist's tone of conviction ("one hundred percent Levantine"), when trying to elaborate what makes up that identity, it becomes threefold, to be then divided again by three according to a different principle. "Race, birth, and spirit" are terms amply used in nationalist rhetoric, only that there they are usually projected onto a land, rather than a sea. While land in the collective imagination of the late nineteenth and early twentieth century could be associated with an unchanging, eternal landscape divided from the rest of the world and birthplace to a race, a sea suggests movement, change, and connection with overseas. Within such a framework a purity of race seems impossible and in her follow-up, Loreley reveals that her race would conventionally be considered hybrid. She suggests three Mediterranean ports and three (nonmatching) nations as other sources of her family's 100 percent identity.

Loreley's attempt to create a Mediterranean identity was not an isolated case in the interwar period. At the western end of the sea, Gabriel Audisio pleaded for the Mediterranean to be recognized as a "liquid continent." According to the Algerian of European settler origin, circulation around the sea had resulted in a great mixture of races, from which a common Mediterranean race including Languedociens and Berbers had evolved. In a statement that echoes Loreley's, he declared, "If France is my nation and Marseille my city, then the sea is my fatherland, the Mediterranean from one end to another."[15] Such statements might seem absurd from today's point of view. In the interwar period, with the extreme rise in the popularity of eugenics,

---

[14] Angèle Loreley, quoted in Pannuti, *Les italiens d'Istanbul*, 326, 328. The entire statement is much longer and even more contradictory. A dictionary-style definition ("Strictly speaking, Levantines are natives of the Levant of European origin, Christians having lost contact with their country of origin, or simply upholding the nationality of a country of the West even over longtime") is followed by the claim that all Christians of the Eastern Mediterranean qualify; ibid.

[15] Gabriel Audisio, quoted from Borutta, *Mediterrane Verflechtungen*, III.4.d.

they must be seen as a struggle for legitimacy for identities that do not neatly fit into the worldview of clash of races.

The following generation of purely twentieth-century Levantine writers conserved Duhani's and Sperco's trope of loss, contrasting a prewar Belle Epoque with the cultural decline of the twentieth century. They combined it however with a sense of identity that, while still impossible to categorize in the 1930s, now seems a given. The pejorative exonym "Levantine," appropriated by Loreley, is now proudly displayed in the title of works by Giovanni Scognamillo or Rinaldo Marmara. Their usage of the term and the seeming simplicity of the ethnic category implied therefore appears as an invention of tradition, that is, an invented rather than an authentic dialogue with the way nineteenth-century contemporaries saw their times. Duhani's and Sperco's claim for ambivalence rather than binding identity, as well as Loreley's multidirectional definitions, are lost in these texts. In the zeitgeist of the later decades of the twentieth century, the writers take pride not so much in a fluid identity, but rather in forming a clear-cut minority group.[16]

Other Paths to Recreating Levantine Identity: The Classic Memoir?

Research into identity questions concerning the Levantine society of the nineteenth century must therefore explore new ways. With the relative size and wealth of the Levantine society in Constantinople, should we not assume some members chose to inform the world and posterity of their worldviews before Duhani and Sperco? We should, but such sources pose another difficulty. The difficulty lies within the very question a self-narrative-based analysis should ideally clarify – to

---

[16] Pannuti, *Les italiens d'Istanbul*, 26–34. We can find parallels with the reinterpretation of Sciaky's Salonica memoirs as a tribute to a Sephardic city, rather than as an open space, as well as to the recoding of pre-1923 Smyrna as an exclusively Greek city; Naar, *Jewish Salonica*, 279, 280; Georgelin, *Fin de Smyrne*. By contrast the Smyrniote businessman Frederick de Cramer stands most firmly in the Duhani tradition. He feels uneasiness toward the term "Levantine" as well as toward Turkish (and the family's originally Austrian) national identity, concluding that his family through its mixed background, while not considered local to any place, was better suited to adapt to a number of places around the globe. *Levantine Heritage*, "Frederick de Cramer"; see also ibid., "Osman Streater."

what degree should Levantines be seen as "European" or "foreign" and to what degree as "local?"

Following the cleavage erupting around the First World War, twentieth-century historiography has spent considerable energy rewriting the complex and paradoxical entanglements within late Ottoman society into a simpler story of "us" and "them": the Turks, that is, rightful heirs of the land, versus "foreigners." Motivated originally by the attempt to create a master narrative legitimizing the Turkish Republic, this strain of interpretation grew in acceptance through a temporary trend in world system theory identifying nineteenth-century non-Muslim middle classes as a "compradore bourgeoisie," that is, a social stratum oriented solely toward Europe and the world market's demands, and ignorant of the public good of their place of residence.[17] Many printed sources will at first glance even support such a bifurcated view on foreign nationals residing in port cities, but the main reason for this lies in the genre of writing in combination with the pressure a nineteenth-century Levantine would find him- or herself under when writing.

At the time, "Levantine" and "European" in the Mediterranean context were often seen as opposites. Levantines became a projection from which "real Europeans" could distinguish themselves. Europeans were recent arrivals, "uncontaminated" by the cultural influences of the Orient, whereas Levantines were either locals who had some obscure connection to the West, or Westerners who had experienced a high degree of acculturation to local conditions and customs.[18] Obviously this is a fine and highly subjective line. When writing a work intended for publication, there was no cultural capital to be gained by identifying oneself as "Levantine," as this could provoke negative stereotypes among the readers. Writers of the period accentuated their "Europeanness" in order to participate in the discursive hegemony Western writers held over Eastern things and camouflaged any possible hint at their Levantine identity.

So how can we discern "true" Europeans from Levantines who, while posing as Westerners, could possibly still voice more informed accounts of their society than the recent arrivals? There is no easy

---

[17] For a discussion of the compradore bourgeoisie debate, see Fuhrmann and Kechriotis, "The Late Ottoman Port Cities," and other contributions in the same volume, especially Gekas, "Class and Cosmopolitanism."
[18] Şeni, "Les Levantins d'Istanbul," 161–169.

answer. Whether or not an immigrant from Central or Western Europe has become Levantine can hardly be judged by hard criteria. But what of immigrants from the West who stayed in the region for considerable lengths of time, sometimes decades? We have a wealth of memoirs in English, French, and sometimes German with titles such as *Forty Years in Constantinople, Constantinople and Istanbul: 72 Years of Life in Turkey,* or *Thirty Years in Constantinople and the Levant.* The predicament here is that these memoirs are often written for an audience in the countries of origin and thus may aim to explain the unknown mores of the Easterners to a middle-class audience in their rocking chairs in Leicester, Avignon, or Salzburg. Due to the narrative logic, the author will portray him- or herself as knowing about the Orient, but not being of the Orient. What Giovanni Scognamillo says of Willy Sperco could be generalized for most writers: "it is very Levantine of Sperco not to write for the Turks, as publishing in Istanbul cannot compare with the prestige of a Paris or Rome publication."[19]

The Western target audiences lead to another aspect of the problem in publications by Levantines following the nineteenth-century Orientalist narrative: In order to gain credibility, the author must write him- or herself out of the context, as invisibility is seen as a sign of objective knowledge in the nineteenth-century exotic explorer mentality (and double so if portraying one's personal involvement would reveal that one has a family history of several decades or centuries in the East). Accordingly Sperco writes about himself and his family in the third person singular in his chapter on non-Muslims in *Turcs d'hier et d'aujourd'hui.*[20] There are plenty of other examples, and authors who themselves migrated to Constantinople identify even less with the local milieu and knowledge.[21] On the other hand, one should not

---

[19] Giovanni Scognamillo, paraphrased in Pannuti, *Les italiens d'Istanbul,* 235, as well as similar remarks in the same section.

[20] Pannuti, *Les italiens d'Istanbul,* 239–240. In principal on the invisibility of the Orientalist observer see Chapter 5, pp. 55–56.

[21] Edwin Pears' *Forty Years in Constantinople* is intended not so much as a personal memoir but rather as an insider's account of politics, based on his journalistic work. Accordingly the actors in his book are mostly the diplomatic and political players of the Ottoman capital. Nonetheless, in a chapter entitled "Short and Personal," he briefly states that he had been "president of the Prinkipo Yachting Club," an organization made up of wealthy members of all major ethnic groups of Istanbul as well as many foreign Istanbul residents. He also mentions a dinner in his honor jointly organized by the Ottoman and European Bars of the city, as Pears' main profession in Istanbul had been lawyer.

completely disregard memoirs by twentieth-century authors, as they occasionally display remarkable excerpts from family archives of earlier times and, with the people concerned long deceased, might be more willing to include the less glamorous aspects of their lives.[22]

And yet, there is one explicit and even very early defense of Levantinism, albeit a very half-hearted one. Alexandre Blacque, the first enduring publisher of a commercial newspaper in French in 1820s Smyrna, when being called a Levantine by the Paris-based *Constitutionnel*, retorted, "The publisher of the *Courrier de Smyrne* is not a Levantine, although he finds this title nothing but honorable."[23] While he claimed not to find the label derogatory, the publisher went out of his way to prove his genuine Frenchness, mentioning his birth in Paris, his studies, and his belief in French freedom. Despite the newspaper's laudation of the East and harsh words for Western Europe, the author could not bring himself to fully identify with the East and renounce the necessity to prove to his Parisian readers that he was one of them.

To summarize, while we find with two of the prominent authors who still remember the Ottoman era firsthand a nostalgia for a lost space rather than a lost community, and the third author's group self-definition is so multidirectional it reads like a description of "men and women without qualities," the later generation of authors condensed these tension-filled discourses in order to follow a narration of the glory of the past and a more or less stringent community identity.

He consciously omitted all mention of his judicial work, although this and a less guarded approach to his private contacts could have told us much about the functioning of nineteenth-century society; Pears, *Forty Years in Constantinople*, 366–368.

[22] Sidney E. P. Nowill for example published his *Constantinople and Istanbul: 72 Years of Life in Turkey* in 2011. While Nowill, just as Scognamillo or Frederick Cramer, is a twentieth-century contemporary and knows of the nineteenth century more by family tradition than by personal experience, he manages to produce personal letters and other archival artifacts documenting the family's history in the Levant. However, they do not amount to an entire family history. His paternal grandfather had come to Istanbul in 1874 to set up a small import-export business together with his brother in Galata. While they apparently reached a noticeable social standing, scandals and suicides as well as confiscation during World War I combined to ruin the family fortunes. Nowill's mother on the other hand was from the long-standing Smyrna family of business oligarchs, the Whitalls. The richer history of the Smyrna Levantines takes precedence over the more humble story of the Galata businessmen; Nowill, *Constantinople and Istanbul*.

[23] *Courrier de Smyrne*, 15 Feb. 1829.

However, these tropes can only be identified definitely from the mid-twentieth century onward. Therefore we should clearly divide them from what Levantines might have said or written about themselves prior to this date. Our questions remain unanswered: Did a section of nineteenth-century urban society identify itself as a Levantine community? Or would they have claimed to be Europeans or adherent to more disparate identities? Was national identity really as ephemeral among them as Schmitt would claim? And how would their in-between status reflect on sociabilities, business practices, and other aspects of everyday life? It stands to reason that these questions can possibly be resolved in future research, but only if the pitfalls of projecting a twentieth-century retrospective identity-making onto the earlier past can be avoided. For the moment, one can assume by abstraction from the Poche-Marcopoli family, that Europe-wide connectedness, a strong role in local society, paired with some degree of sectarian sentiment could well be the base of at least the upper-class Levantines' identity. The ambivalent space allowing them to access these three different, seemingly contradictory sources of identity and cultural capital is only truly appreciated once it is gone.

19 North-to-South Migration and Its Impact on the Urban Population

The malleable character of Levantine identity is reason enough not to see in them a fixed group. There is yet another reason though. The nineteenth-century Ottoman port cities grew strongly and mostly due to migration. It would therefore be wrong to consider the Greeks, the Turks, the Levantines, or the Europeans of Smyrna static groups that only evolved slowly according to lifecycles. Instead we must think that many of these groups changed their social makeup, their degree of cohesion, and their place in urban society within mere decades. While internal and regional migration might have been dominant, as nodes of exchange, port cities attracted more long-distance migration than other places within the empire. A few outstanding individuals among these immigrants, most notably men of letters and major officeholders, have received posthumous attention, either through biographical studies or republishing of their writings.[1] However, European arrivals to the Ottoman Empire were for the larger part not explorers, bankers, or military drill inspectors. The vast majority came from more ordinary walks of life. The exclusive association of the Europeans of Smyrna, Salonica, and Constantinople with the haute bourgeoisie is another fallacy of later ideology and historiography that is in need of revision.[2] As this assumption is still rather deep-rooted, I must discuss in some detail the social profile, origins, and changes over time of these immigrants. In the following, I will describe where the European migrants came from, who they were, and why they came, before addressing the question of how these elements impacted on their sense of identity within urban society. Work opportunities in or around the large

---

[1] See for example Richmond, *Voice of England in the East*.

[2] The concentration on these upper-class representatives of Europe in the Ottoman sphere resulted from the preoccupation in the history of European-Ottoman relations with trade; see for example Kasaba, Keyder, and Tabak, "Eastern Mediterranean Port Cities and their Bourgeoisies"; Kössler, *Aktionsfeld Osmanisches Reich*; Anastassiadou, "Les Occidentaux de la place."

infrastructure projects; the desire of upper-class families in the Levant to educate their children and run the household in Western manners and languages; the economic stagnation of some rural areas in the European states; a desire to see more of the world than the West as well as many other disparate factors, all combined to create a "European" migrant population in the Ottoman lands of presumably several tens of thousands. While this cannot compete with other mass migratory phenomena of the period, such as the countless movements to the Americas, these Europeans were numerous enough to make an impact in the towns and cities where they concentrated and occasionally were the subject of diplomatic, political, and social debate. Thanks to a growing number of mostly recent case studies, we now know that workers and providers of low-key services originating from Italy, Malta, Spain, and France, migrated to the south and to the east of the Mediterranean throughout the long nineteenth century.[3] I will therefore in the following remarks take as a case study the diverse experiences of Habsburg and German subjects in the Mediterranean port cities.

The experiences subsumed under the heading of "Central European migration to the Ottoman lands" are highly diverse. In addition to war and political emigration, we find agrarian settlers, itinerant artisans, skilled workers, and a group called *Orientbummler*, or "Orient drifters," in their time. Time and space allowing, many other types of migrants could be discussed. Pauperized but well-educated subjects of the Hohenzollerns and the Habsburgs sought employment as tour guides for upper-class tourists in the large ports. Mostly German-speaking women served as educators in local middle- or upper-class families. Female singers and so-called Bohemian Orchestras toured the Eastern Mediterranean cities. Last but not least, women served as sometimes forced, but more often as voluntary sex workers in Constantinople and some provincial towns, with Habsburg pimps and human traffickers.[4] These diverse experiences created rather distinct social practices, which managed to various degrees to integrate aspects of the "home" cultures with those of the new

---

[3] For Istanbul and Anatolia, see Quataert, *Social Disintegration and Popular Resistance*; for Algeria, see Smith, *Colonial Memory and Postcolonial Europe*; for Tunis, see Clancy-Smith, *Mediterraneans*; for Cairo and Alexandria, see Gorman, "Foreign Workers in Egypt 1882–1914"; for Port Said, see Huber, *Channelling Mobilities*.

[4] See Chapter 23, pp. 371–389. For more information on the worldwide impact of Austrian prostitute emigration, see Ringdal, *Love for Sale*, 313–319; Fischer-Tiné, "White Women Degrading Themselves."

surroundings. The only common denominator of these groups is that they all theoretically had access to capitulatory protection by the same "mother countries." I will restrict myself here to a few remarks on war and political emigration to then concentrate on artisans and workers, as they can be traced fairly well in registers throughout most of the period, make up a substantial group among the immigrants, are occasionally subject of debate by contemporaries, and have in a few cases left some personal traces in the archives. I will proceed chronologically, as the reasons for migrating, regions of origin, and the political circumstances show four distinct phases between approximately 1820 and 1918. As the focus and quality of documentation throughout these 100 years vary greatly, no strictly systematic description can be provided, and the emphasis lies on the fairly well-documented second half of the period, after approximately 1878.

Desperate Times: Separatists, Artisans, and Farmers in Flight (1820–1856)

It seems a paradox that nineteenth-century members of lower classes emigrated to countries whose macroeconomics appeared far less favorable than those of their own countries of origin: The meta-narratives of "Oriental Decline" and the "Rise of the West" have led to the general assumption that from the eighteenth century onward, the Ottoman Empire held no promise for a Europe undergoing a process of constant progress.[5] What is forgotten in this perspective is that the "Rise of the West," far from following a steady predetermined course, was rather a consecutive series of improvisations in reaction to recurrent crises. The period spanning from the 1820s to the 1840s witnessed grand-scale poverty in Central Europe. Contemporaries coined the phrase "pauperism" to describe a situation in which population growth, peasant emancipation under unfavorable conditions, and the abolishment of guild-based professional restrictions combined to create an uprooted population seeking to find employment as artisans or affordable land as farmers. Estimates believe that up to 60 percent of the urban and a large but not quantifiable part of the rural population lived borderline existences. The low wages at the height of the crisis, rather than offering a base for the expansion of production, led to a decrease in demand and consequently to mass layoffs in the early

---

[5] See Chapter 2, pp. 10–18.

industry. Between 1820 and 1850, an estimated number of 740,000 Germans emigrated, but the majority of the pauperized population did not have the resources to pursue this path.[6] Moving southeastward was an alternative for the almost destitute for obvious reasons. The Ottoman domains appealed because of their proximity. If things did not work out as planned, one could return home and, more importantly, the journey was much cheaper than a transatlantic voyage; if need be, the path to Constantinople could be pursued on foot. Also, a parameter that is difficult to gauge undoubtedly played an important role: the proliferation of positive Orientalism among the lower classes. As early as the 1820s, German intellectuals promoted lower-class emigration to Ottoman territories because they believed that unlike in the Americas, German settlers in the Southeast would not lose their identity and could be useful in case of Germany's future imperialist expansion. They promoted the East as a land of rich soil and ample opportunities, and while the breadth of dissemination of such images cannot be ascertained, there is evidence that these descriptions directly or indirectly led many lower class members to seek a better life there.[7] Unlike migration to the Americas, however, this form of mobility was most often not recorded as migration, since it was either considered a temporary and nonessential form of displacement or happened without governmental knowledge. Accordingly, no numbers can be produced, beyond the simple observation that several thousand people were involved.

At the dawn of the nineteenth century, itinerant artisans traveled individually or in small groups.[8] But with freedom of profession and the accompanying pauperism setting in after 1800, the long-established institution of journeying artisans deteriorated to a desperate search for employment anywhere. Since little consular documentation from this period has survived, only incidental material indicates the dimension of artisans' migration to the Ottoman Empire, but all records document horrific material conditions.[9]

---

[6] Weis, *Der Durchbruch des Bürgertums*, 403–408.
[7] Fuhrmann, *Traum vom deutschen Orient*, 42–47; Fuhrmann, "Visions of Germany in Turkey."
[8] Stoklásková, "Wandernde Handwerksgesellen als privilegierte Gruppe."
[9] GStA Ministry of Foreign Affairs (MdA) III. HA II 758, 61: M. Pezzer to Ministry of Foreign Affairs, Smyrna 8 March 1845; Nahmer, "Deutsche Kolonisationspläne und –erfolge," 935; Dietrich, *Deutschsein in İstanbul*, 85–93.

The Central European crisis climaxed in the middle of the century and finally resulted in political upheaval. After successive failed crops, 1847 saw a bread revolt, followed by the uprisings across the continent in 1848 that temporarily seemed to overthrow the autocratic rule of the Habsburgs and the Hohenzollerns. The existential crisis further accelerated emigration. In the years of 1848/1849, the envoy of Hamburg in Constantinople registered numerous ships of destitute Germans entering the Bosporus.[10] But the situation did not improve upon the restoration of autocratic rule. The armed democratic and secessionist movements within the Habsburg Monarchy were defeated by autumn 1849. A large number of combatants fled across the border onto Ottoman soil. Pressure by Vienna and St. Petersburg prompted the Porte to detain them. Initially, Hungarians were restricted to Adrianople, Poles to Šumla and Silistra, and Italians to Gallipoli.[11] Thereafter their fate varied, depending on the refugees' willingness to repent, on diplomatic or personal protection, and on individual resourcefulness. Apparently many German-speaking rebels who had crossed over to Vidin were willing to return, hoping for an imperial pardon.[12] The Sardinian government managed to negotiate the release and free passage of 250 Italian rebels.[13] In accordance with the negotiations between the Porte and St. Petersburg, the almost 1,000 remaining refugees were ordered to be detained in the Anatolian town of Kütahya and in Aleppo in Syria. Although Great Britain had offered to accept some refugees in Malta, this proposal received little interest while many rebels entertained thoughts of returning home, a possibility that according to Austrian intelligence reports was mainly impeded by their destituteness.[14] A notable percentage of the refugees sought to establish a future for themselves in the port cities. They fled the camps and made their way to Constantinople, establishing small businesses such as inns or receiving help from local supporters.[15] Polish refugees

---

[10] Dietrich, *Deutschsein in İstanbul*, 67, fn. 115.
[11] HHStA Political Archive (PA) XXXVIII 92/Constantinople: Mihanovich to Schwarzenberg, Constantinople 21 Nov. 1849.
[12] HHStA PA XXXVIII 92/Rusçuk/Vidin.
[13] HHStA PA XXXVIII 93/Constantinople: Mihanovich to Schwarzenberg, Constantinople 19 March 1850.
[14] HHStA PA XXXVIII 93/Constantinople: Mihanovich to Schwarzenberg, Constantinople 19 March and 14 Aug. 1850.
[15] HHStA PA XXXVIII 93/Constantinople: Mihanovich to Schwarzenberg, Constantinople 2 Oct. 1850.

especially were anxious to enter the Ottoman armed services, motivated by the prospect of fighting against Russia, as the Crimean War drew closer.[16] Initially a group of fifty to sixty Polish refugees were sheltered by the minister Ahmed Fatih on his country estate near Constantinople. They, as well as other rebels, joined the commune-like Adampol settlers colony founded in 1842 by exiled Poles in the hinterland of the Bosporus.[17] The residents of this estate, known until today as Polonezköy (Polish Village), were still in part descendants of the 1848 rebels, when they requested Austro-Hungarian passports in 1906.[18]

Independently of the fugitive combatants, a number of disappointed democrats from the Habsburg Monarchy and the German states made their way to the East in a less spectacular manner.[19] Until the 1870s their presence gave the resident Austrian and German expatriate communities a strongly dissident character.[20] Not surprisingly, the early immigrants from among the artisans felt as unpatriotic as these political exiles, but rather than voicing dissent, they simply chose to forget about their heritage. In many but not all cases, they retained their country of origin's passport, but otherwise did not maintain close ties with their "motherland" and assimilated rather unreservedly to the mixed culture of the port cities, that is, they were "levantinized."

An indicator of how negligent this group initially was in documenting their nationality, but also of how important nationality later became, is the case of the Tošić family. In 1902, Jovan Tošić appealed to the Austro-Hungarian Consulate of Salonica for his son Georg to be taken to an insane asylum in the Monarchy, because he and his daughter could no longer handle Georg's violent tendencies. However, as residents of Salonica for generations, the Tošićs only held the status of "de-facto-subjects" of the Monarchy. This category comprised several different kinds of persons: those who had previously enjoyed the status of consular protégés despite being Ottoman subjects, although

---

[16] Dominik, "From the Polish Times of Pera"; Raschdau, *Ein sinkendes Reich*, 30, 31.
[17] Antonwicz-Bauer, *Polonezköyü-Adampol*; HHStA PA XXXVIII 93/Constantinople: Mihanovich to Schwarzenberg, Constantinople 9 Feb. 1850.
[18] HHStA Embassy/Consulate (BK) Constantinople 115/Kolonie Adampol.
[19] HHStA PA XXXVIII 92/Smyrna: Cischini to Schwarzenberg, Smyrna 5 Feb. 1850.
[20] Fuhrmann, *Traum vom deutschen Orient*, 281–291.

the practice of granting protégé status had been abandoned in the 1870s; former citizens of countries annexed by Austria who had never applied for Austrian nationality (Venetians); and Austrians, Hungarians, or their descendants who despite living in the Ottoman Empire had not registered with a consulate for a long period of time and thus had forfeited their nationality status. Because of the de facto status, the consulates only protected their rights as Habsburg subjects against the Ottoman authorities, but considered them foreigners if they touched Austrian or Hungarian soil. Accordingly, Georg Tošić was not entitled to public support for medical treatment "at home." However, there was no institution for the mentally ill in Salonica, and the Constantinople Austro-Hungarian hospital could not treat Georg either. The family could not afford the Athens institution or Constantinople's Hôpital de la Paix. The Consulate decided to investigate the family's history to prove that they originated from the Monarchy and were entitled to medical support. But unfortunately, when Jovan Tošić found his father's 1859 passport, the Consulate had just eliminated its older records five years earlier and was not able to verify it. They inquired to Castelnuovo near Catarro (now Herceg Novi near Kotor) for an emigrant named Đuro Tošić, and finally managed to find that a man by this name was reported to have left Castelnuovo for Salonica around 1820 and to have settled there.[21]

North-to-South Migration As a Peripheral Phenomenon (1856–1878)

The restoration of autocratic rule throughout the German states and the Habsburg dominions in 1849 marks the beginning of the industrial revolution in Central Europe and the subsequent rise in prosperity and work opportunities. But from the perspective of the Ottoman fringe, this assessment seems only partially correct. Prosperity was far from geographically balanced. The heart of European industrialization has been identified in the rather narrow belt stretching from Milan past the Rhineland and northern France to southern England, with some scattered outer centers.[22] Both Prussia's eastern provinces and the eastern and southern Habsburg territories played a rather peripheral role in this. In the two decades following the restoration, migration from these

[21] HHStA GK Sal 443/Tossich. [22] Hobsbawm, *On History*, 2–3.

border zones to the new industrial heartlands did not exhaust their labor reserves. Movements toward the Ottoman Empire continued, albeit mostly in a more orderly and less desperate manner. Also, the Crimean War had drawn an unprecedented number of foreign soldiers into the country, especially to Constantinople – a fact that the numerous graves in the Catholic and English cemeteries attest to – and a number of these chose to be discharged and remain in the "East." One remarkable source testifies to the fact that the Crimean War opened the door to upward social mobility, but moreover to a life of adventure, danger, and occasional glory for people who would otherwise have lived and died in the Western or Central European metropolis without having experienced much of the world. Ludwig Witt had been born in Plön in Holstein, Denmark. He had been a teenage housepainter apprentice in Hamburg when in 1853 British recruiters were searching the city for volunteers for the campaign against Russia in the Black Sea. He enlisted and at war's end, was resolved to stay in the "Orient." After serving as private secretary to a former general, he proved resourceful at finding other job opportunities, developing his language skills, and working as a dragoman, both in the sense of freelance interpreter and later consular employee. In the following two decades, he traveled or stayed in Egypt, Palestine, the Aegean Islands, Greece, Macedonia, Thrace, Constantinople, Asia Minor, Armenia, and Wallachia. At his best, he was interpreting for well-known Orient travelers such as Ernest Renan, but he also suffered a number of tragedies along the way, such as the cholera epidemic that killed his family in Cairo.[23]

As a result of preserved consular registers and reports from this period, itinerant artisans become more easily visible than in previous times. These documents record the peripheral origins of the new arrivals. The 1863 and 1872 Salonica registers of itinerant Habsburg subjects describe almost all persons with an artisan profession as originating from the Adriatic littoral or its hinterland. From among those whose listed occupations could be identified as working class, Dalmatians, that is, the inhabitants of Ragusa (Dubrovnik) and its surroundings, have the most uniform profession: Practically all of them were sailors, a document to Ragusa's long-standing overseas relations.[24] To the north, Istria and the ports of Fiume (Rijeka) and Trieste

---

[23] BA Berlin R 901/52413, 29 ff.: Ludwig Witt, CV undated (Trapezunt 1877).
[24] Palairet, *The Balkan Economies c. 1800–1914*, 19–22.

saw a number of migrants to Salonica. They were registered mostly as sailors, but also as carpenters or day laborers. Fiume's reputation as a maritime city even led the Foreign Ministry to lament the fact that the majority of its young men dispersed across the seas, thus evading or at least delaying the draft.[25] Surprisingly, the other Adriatic urban center with sheer cliffs as its hinterland, Cattaro, did not figure in the Salonica statistics as a home of seamen, but rather of day laborers and farmers. Apparently, because of the relative proximity of Cattaro to the Ottoman core regions and the great distance from other Habsburg territories, these workers were partially integrated into the Balkan tradition of landlocked itinerant labor.[26] Rather surprising is the overwhelming number of workers from distant Tyrol, especially from Trento and practically all with Italian last names, who were registered as passing through Salonica. They mostly qualified as lumbermen or day laborers (possibly pursuing the same occupation), and some as carpenters or smiths. Besides these places of origin, a scattering of other underclass professionals (workers, servants, tailors) originated from several other Habsburg provinces (Galicia, Silesia, Transylvania, and Croatia proper). Workers seem only to have left the relatively prosperous provinces of Upper and Lower Austria, Moravia, and Bohemia for the Aegean shores if they were specialists, such as railway workers with a high likelihood of finding a well-paid job. In addition, there were a number of Habsburg subjects who already in 1872 indicate Ottoman towns such as Salonica, Smyrna, or Serres (Serez/Sjar) as places of residence.[27] In his 1866/1867 report, the Austrian Consul General for Macedonia and Thessaly counted three artisan families in Salonica, two in Serres, and one in Volos; however, all twenty Habsburg subjects residing in Monastir were considered artisans.[28]

---

[25] HHStA Adm. Reg. F 47 – 31, Circulare: Ministry of Foreign Affairs, Vienna 19 March 1873.

[26] One file documents a group of eight Cattarians who set out together on foot in the summer of 1872 to seek employment in Constantinople. The group disbanded in Northern Macedonia, however, with some members returning and several staying in Üsküp and Köprülü (Veles). The only Cattarian who continued was allegedly arrested, manhandled, and deported after reaching Dupnica near Sofia; HHStA Adm. Reg. F 52 – 105/Misshandlungen: Governor-General Prizren 28 Nov. 1872; Đuro Nikov Subotić, Petition, Glavati 21 Nov. 1875. On the gurbet/pečalba tradition, see Pichler, "Hirten, Söldner und Wanderarbeiter."

[27] HHStA GK Sal 108.   [28] HHStA GK Sal 393: Handelsstatistik 1866/67.

The life worlds of the Habsburg and Hohenzollern subjects of lower-class origin in the port cities were, as in the previous period when flight from destitution had dominated, still not closely integrated into the official mechanisms of their states of origin. Some had started out as outright rebels against the absolutist regimes in their mother countries: The German, Austrian, Polish, and Hungarian communities of Constantinople and Smyrna were gathering points for frustrated former 1848 expatriates (who, in the German case, mostly changed their attitudes after German unification in 1871) and others who had integrated into local society. The majority of the new arrivals from the Adriatic littoral and beyond had left their homes because they could not find there the living conditions or job opportunities that they desired. The expatriate Habsburg subjects mostly originated from parts of the Monarchy that were located on its periphery and did not share the economic prosperity of the core regions. Moreover, as predominant speakers of Italian, Serbo-Croatian, and occasionally Polish, they did not participate in its German and Hungarian dominant cultures.

The Grand Days of Europeans in the Ottoman Empire (1878–1908)

1878 proved a watershed for lower-class migrants from Central Europe in the Southeast. After the Berlin Congress, the Ottoman state's bankruptcy was used to further install an open-door economic system. As in other cases, the open door that capital demanded for itself was exploited also by laborers, job seekers, and adventurers.

The legal framework prompted Central Europeans to uphold their temporary status even when their actual residence or migration patterns no longer showed movements outside of the Ottoman borders. As becomes apparent especially from other records, the actual number of de facto German or Austrian and Hungarian residents in a particular consular district was much higher than the number registered and the consulates had no clear knowledge of it.[29] Clear indications can be found in the records on deaths of Austrians and Hungarians, where

---

[29] The number of 18,000 German workers alone reproduced in Özgürel, "Almanya'dan işçi getirtmiştik" does not refer to a source and is doubtful at best.

innumerable remarks allege that the deceased had neglected to renew his or her registration with the consulate, was completely unknown to its employees, or even that the deceased was rumored to be Austro-Hungarian but no evidence to confirm or refute this could be found.[30] Informal immigration became too widespread for the diplomats to keep an overview. In 1892 the Dual Monarchy's Consulate in Belgrade counted no less than 450 passports that its subjects had abandoned there in order to avoid paying fees, apparently hoping to pick up new passports at another consulate. They estimated the number of passports that were destroyed by their owners to be even higher.[31] Accordingly, most European consulates no longer produced regular statistics of their subjects.[32]

The situation of labor migration however changed slowly after 1878. Young men from the Adriatic littoral at first continued to provide the mainstay of new arrivals. The files on deceased Habsburg subjects allow for a snapshot of their material circumstances and family situations. Many died in relative anonymity and alone, especially those who worked in the countryside in railway construction or in mines.[33]

By contrast, the Malfer family from Trento had established itself locally. When the day laborer Natale Malfer died in the Catholic hospital in Salonica in 1889 aged just twenty-three, he owned no other valuables than his golden watch. The watch was inherited by his brother Antonio who advanced to the position of head worker on

---

[30] HHStA GK Sal 420 to 450 give ample evidence of such cases.

[31] HHStA Adm. Reg. F 47 – 31.

[32] Schmitt, *Levantiner*, 186. Paul Lindau lists 1,800 Austro-Hungarian and 500 German subjects residing in Smyrna at the end of the nineteenth century, while other authors usually believe the respective communities to be only one third of that; Lindau, *An der Westküste Klein-Asiens*, 102.

[33] Jovan Benčić was working in a mine in rural Macedonia, when he contracted typhus. The 375 Piasters in his possession was strangely not enough to pay for his burial in the local Bulgarian-Orthodox cemetery, so the mine owner paid the rest. When Savo Đuro Mačić from Cattaro did not renew his resident registration with the Salonica consulate, a consulate employee investigated. He found out that Mačić had been working in a quarry on the Salonica-Constantinople railway in Serres province and living in a nearby village, but had recently died of pneumonia. The fifty-year-old experienced quarry worker had left behind just 250 Piasters and no valuables. He was known to have a wife in his home village on the Adriatic, but despite investigations, her exact name could not be determined; HHStA GK Sal 420/Nachlässe Baretich, Bencich; 433/ Nachlässe Macich, Malfer.

the railways before he also met an early death at the age of thirty-nine in 1894. His sole heir was his wife Elvira, daughter of Jacob Sent'Agata from Trento and a Greek mother, Maria, née Kostopolou. When Elvira died at the age of fifty-four in 1909, she owned the noteworthy sum of 11,358 Piasters, mostly in savings and partially in jewels. Her heir was her sister who lived in Pera in Constantinople.[34]

The predominance of Austrians from the Adriatic littoral among the itinerant lower-class travelers or unregistered residents of the Ottoman Empire seems to have persisted at least into the 1890s. The Austro-Hungarian hospital in Constantinople, when treating Habsburg subjects who could not afford to pay their own bill and were not registered as local residents, was entitled to charge the home municipalities of its patients. In 1895, the Dalmatian diet protested that this regulation had cost its municipalities 7,095 Gold Pounds from 1892 to 1894 alone. To the Foreign Ministry officials, this was just an indicator that Dalmatians made most use of its services.[35]

In comparison to 1872, a look into the 1906 consular register presents a rather changed picture. Sailors had disappeared, as Austrian sailing boats had been replaced by steamships that did not usually hire and fire along the way (crew members did not have to register). Thirty years of industrialization had drastically reduced the percentage of itinerant artisans. In fact, classic professions such as shoemaker, bricklayer, or carpenter had almost completely disappeared. The other striking change was that large numbers of the smiths and day laborers who still figured in the statistics were of high age. It is hard to imagine that the fifty-eight-year-old smith Franz Petek from Savenstein (Boštanj) or the day laborer, Anton Potokar from Stein, of the same age, were very successful in finding employment. While a number of unskilled or badly paid professions – such as tailors, seamstresses, painters, decorators, and day laborers – still figure in the register, and their places of origin in the Habsburg Empire are more evenly distributed (with a slight overrepresentation of Cattaro), many more "modern" professions such as mechanic, railway worker, and locksmith now appear.[36] The development and operation of the large infrastructural projects of the Ottoman Empire, such as railways,

---

[34] HHStA GK Sal 433/Nachlässe Macich, Malfer.
[35] HHStA BK Constantinople 115: Ministry of Foreign Affairs to Calice, Vienna 28 Dec. 1895.
[36] HHStA GK Sal 117/Passprotokoll 1906.

ports, roads, but also mines, created a need for workers with training or experience that the local labor market alone could not satisfy. As a consequence, infrastructure companies offered working conditions and wages that attracted candidates from Italy, Austria-Hungary, and Germany. Some companies – such as the Oriental Railway Company that operated most of the Balkan lines – made the preferential employment of foreigners their policy, because they considered these more skilled or aimed to please the foreign governments backing the company.[37]

A job around the Eastern Mediterranean was an opportunity for upward mobility for skilled workers. Moritz Müller, born in Leipzig in 1857, for example, came to Üsküp as a train engineer. In 1895 he became a railway official in Salonica. Upon his death in 1913, his Greek Orthodox wife and their five children inherited four houses in the city.[38] Georg Sörgel, born 1842 in Fischbrunn, Bavaria, had been recommended as a worker to the same company and was assured that he would earn twice his German salary and that the cost of living in Salonica was not high. When he had advanced to the position of foreman, he seemed pleased to have escaped the lot of his family members in Germany, many of whom had died, gone missing, ended up in insane asylums, or were simply earning much less. On one of the letters written by his brother, Georg Sörgel noted, "This is the man who earns 1 ½ Mecidiye per window."[39] Sörgel apparently attempted to augment his earnings by lending money to colleagues, a potentially profitable but risky business, if debtors were unwilling to pay. When he died in 1894, he was living with his wife and three daughters in the railway company's housing. They had four sheep, two pigs, chickens, ducks, and pigeons. His assets amounted to the not unsubstantial total of 35,000 Gold Piasters, but were partly in form of IOUs.[40]

Female Mobility: The Bohemian Orchestras

The narrative of this chapter on immigration has so far focused on men and their ability to contribute to socially recognized notions of labor. Ideally, this should be contrasted with an equally broad take on

---

[37] Brunau, *Das Deutschtum in Mazedonien*, 18.
[38] Vourou, "Interview Thessaloniki 1985."
[39] PA-AA GK Sal 49/Briefe des Bahnmeisters Sörgel.
[40] PA-AA GK Sal 32/Vormundschaft Sörgels Kinder.

women's paths into the Ottoman lands, as we know that there were plenty of ways women reached the Well-Protected Domains independently of the previously described paths. Unfortunately however, these are not nearly as well documented. Especially the widespread practice of taking on jobs as instructors, nannies, or householders in local families is not sufficiently documented for us to make more general statements on these women. While they played an important role in familiarizing especially youth with the languages and expected behavior of the West, they do not figure prominently in consular documentation, as such women, tightly integrated into their host families, rarely became conspicuous for their compatriots. However, for chroniclers of Eastern Mediterranean family life, they were mostly not considered important enough to comment on, nor have self-narrative documents by this group so far become widely available. The following passages will therefore restrict themselves to a particular group of women that do figure prominently in contemporary documentation and publications. This takes us back to the subject of entertainment.

The entertainment sector employees and entrepreneurs were highly visible to the general public. While Italian and French professionals dominated opera and highbrow drama, Austrians and Germans also figured prominently. Their high visibility to the public and to the consular bureaucracy makes a thick description possible, especially for the so-called Bohemian Orchestras. They would play on the streets along the quay, but also in the big restaurants and cafés. Their repertoire focused on internationally well-known operetta and waltz pieces. Travelogs and newspapers mention their nigh omnipresence in Levantine towns: "As a maritime city, Smyrna of course witnesses a constant influx of female singers, Bohemian Ladies' Orchestras, etc. The latter dominate here, as they animate all quays from Smyrna to Alexandria and Calcutta."[41]

Bohemian Orchestras originated from the Ore Mountains (Erzgebirge/Krušné Hory) in Northwestern Bohemia. Orchestras had formed part of the representation, entertainment, and bonding framework of the local mines. When these mining sites declined and employment thinned out, more miners started joining the bands and these in turn looked further away for engagements, particularly to neighboring

---

[41] Barth, *Unter südlichem Himmel*, 5, 6, 76; see also Anastassiadou, *Salonique*, 190; Fröbel, *Ein Lebenslauf*, vol. II, 617, 618.

Saxony and more northern destinations. They impressed their audiences on the one hand by their apparent exoticness but also by their ability to quickly adopt more widely spread tunes.[42] In the last quarter of the nineteenth century, the Bohemian Orchestra depicted a somewhat different institution. While before they had been an exclusively male formation – miners and sons of miners – they were now female by majority, in one recorded case ten women to five men.[43] Especially the women in these groups were strikingly young – between sixteen and twenty-five, sometimes traveling with their young children. They were headed by an older man, and the group was usually named after this bandmaster. While some bands centered on families, they were not exclusive clan projects, but enlisted members from different backgrounds, and some musicians moved around alone or in smaller groups seeking to join a band. A typical tour would run from Salonica, past Constantinople, Smyrna, Alexandria, and Cairo back to Trieste, but would also include smaller towns. It would last for five years or more, as the bands usually stayed several months or even years in one city. As they traveled with valid papers, their movements are reflected in the consular registers. While the Salonician Habsburg Consulate's 1863 passport register makes no mention of traveling musicians, already the 1872 register counts one group of six on the way to Volos and another of thirteen on the way to Constantinople, as well as several musicians traveling individually or in smaller groups. While all of the 1872 traveling musicians come from classical hometowns of such bands in the Ore Mountains, their numbers as well as their places of origin had shifted by the turn of the century. Other formations using the etiquette came from Northeastern Bohemia and a large number from the Far East of the Monarchy, from Galicia and Bukovina, in particular from Czernowitz (Černovci/Cernăuți). Bands usually had a clear predominance, either Bohemian or Eastern, but musicians of other backgrounds appeared in some lineups. The names of musicians from Bohemia were predominantly Christian German, whereas those from Galicia had German Jewish names. The passport register for 1906 shows three big orchestras moving completely out of Salonica in different directions. The Rosenkranz Orchestra from Czernowitz,

---

[42] Müns, "Migrationsstrategien der böhmischen Musikanten," 63–80.
[43] HHStA Adm. Reg. F 52 – 46 (Prostitution Türkei): "Menschenfreund" to Foreign Ministry, 20 May 1896.

recorded to have already played in the Grande Bretagne in Salonica in 1904, was moving upcountry to Monastir where they stayed for the following months. Likewise, the Ehrlich Orchestra from Stanislau (now Ivano-Frankivsk) quit Salonica for Üsküp for an extended engagement. A third group based in Czernowitz left Macedonia altogether for Smyrna.[44]

Despite performing in major locations such as the Grande Bretagne, the Olympia, and the Teatro Opera Italiana, starting to play in the afternoon at 4 p.m. and continuing until late at night, the individual band member did not earn much or carry many possessions. When the musician Rudolf Mareček in a quarrel killed another Austrian by hitting him on the head with a chair and was due to be escorted to his hometown to be tried there, the consular employee found as his personal belongings only three or four changes of clothes (but elegant, as they were intended for the stage), a box with post cards, letters, some photos, a picture of Jerusalem, a silver watch, and a gas cooker.[45]

A group including several very young and poor women, headed by men, performing in public until the early morning seems prone to raise questions about morality, protection of minors' rights, and proximity to prostitution. One anonymous petitioner, identifying himself as a Habsburg long-term resident on the Mediterranean shores, drew such conclusions and tried to draw the diplomats' attention to them. Blaming the Liebermann Orchestra in particular, the man writing under the pseudonym of "Philanthropist" calculated that the musicians could not hope to live off of what they earned on stage, but were wearing expensive jewelry and particularly the bandmaster was living a plentiful life. He could only do so because he occasionally sold some of the musicians to a harem or into prostitution. Furthermore, the young girls were playing to an audience of lusty, drunken Turkish men. They were expected to keep close contact with their customers in between pieces, according to the "Philanthropist."

Interestingly, the Consul defended Moses Liebermann against unfounded charges. The Liebermann Orchestra was not playing in a den of Muslim drunkards, but in front of a predominantly European audience in the best house in town. The members of this band and also

---

[44] HHStA GK Sal 108, 117: Paßprotokoll 1863, 1872, 1906; PA-AA GK Sal 22, Auskunftsgesuche, 253: Paula Stark to Consulate Salonica, 16 Apr. 1904.
[45] HHStA GK Sal 433: Strafsache Rudolf Marecek.

all truly Bohemian ones had never given cause for moral concern, unlike some others from Galicia or Bukovina, according to the Consul.[46] Official discourse thus left the Bohemian and pseudo-Bohemian musicians in a liminal space. They were essentially of good moral conduct so that they did not warrant intense concern and intervention on the part of the diplomats (although the governor in Prague/Praha in 1906 warned that minors were being forced to play in these bands and sought their return).[47] On the other hand, they were considered an inferior element of Central European culture and were thus not integrated into the Dual Monarchy's self-representation.

Going on tour in the Levant was not an adventure, but a business venture following tight networks established by other orchestras from the same towns. Experiences could partially be handed on from generation to generation, as often children took up the same occupation as their parents. On tour, the orchestras, at least their male leaders, were well connected among each other. They would visit the same *bakkal* (grocery store), have a glass of *mastika* there together, discuss business and possibly have arguments, as one charge of insult from 1880 shows.[48] Not all musicians returned from the tour, and obviously not all were completely secluded from Muslim men, as the earlier example of Martha Fehnl shows.[49]

But despite this comparatively thick description that allows us to construct the movements, material assets, and some networks of the Bohemian Orchestras, the lack of testimony leaves us unable to say anything substantial about the musicians' subjective view. Should we follow the self-declared "Philanthropist's" opinion that this institution was akin to modern slavery, young girls being dragged off against their will to perform in foreign lands? We do not have direct information on the degree of constraint exercised within the orchestras, but the isolation of the "Philanthropist's" claims and the lack of "deserters" in official documentation – although the bands did not always travel as

---

[46] HHStA Adm. Reg. F 52 – 46 (Prostitution Türkei): "Menschenfreund" to Foreign Ministry, 20 May 1896; Consulate General to Foreign Ministry, 17 June 1896.

[47] HHStA BK Kpl 107: Müller (Foreign Ministry, MdA) to Calice, 19 July 1906; Adm Reg. F 52 – 46 (Prostitution): Ministry of Interior to Foreign Ministry, Vienna 2 Aug. 1886; Consul Galați to Foreign Ministry, Galați 13 Aug. 1886.

[48] HHStA GK Sal 420: Strafprozeß Josef Bach/Josef Tauber.

[49] See Chapter 16, pp. 260–261.

Female Mobility: The Bohemian Orchestras 319

one compact group – speak against interpreting Bohemian Orchestras as forced labor, as does the fact that individual musicians would join bands of their own accord. But, more to the point, we end up in the classical dilemma of migration studies. Should we opt for a "happy" or "sad" interpretation of this form of lower-class mobility? Should we highlight the economic depravity of life in rural or small-town Bohemia and especially in the Eastern Habsburg domains as creating an inevitable push factor, which forced the musicians to search for employment far away, despite the limited material gain in Ottoman music halls (and, as this narrative implies, despite a "natural" desire to stay at home)? Or should we follow the adverse narrative that highlights the pull factor, the chances of mobility – the possibility to escape from the tight social constraints of rural Austria into the more multifaceted Ottoman towns, the thrill of the stage, and the social recognition of the audience? Were the Bohemian Orchestras a poor woman's possibility to escape contemporary moral constraints and the hardships of rural life? Or are they more to be read as a story of suffering and limitations? There is ample evidence for both interpretations. Without sources of a different quality, we can only guess at the subjective view of the musicians themselves.

Interestingly, the impasse this examination of the orchestras has reached is mirrored by contemporary observations. Vitalis Cohen describes one concert at the Olympia, possibly by the Liebermann Orchestra, in the false belief that the musicians were from Germany. Far from being seductive, as the "Philanthropist" petitioner claims, or morally impeccable as the Consul describes them, the young musicians just seem tired and detached from their surroundings. With no real explanation, Cohen opts for a narrative of "sad" migration, of homesickness,

> The agony of the music ceases, that of the collection commences. Holding the plate in a mechanical and fatigued way and with a similarly nonchalant and unbalanced appearance, the eyes dull and expressionless, the collector wanders around the consumers. And the *metalliks* dive underneath the napkin folded discreetly, which this pale child of Germania had wisely arranged over the plate. Every *metallik* represents five *pfennigs* of her nebulous country ... The collection over, her face reconverts to its usual calm and by the same tired gesture, the same nonchalant appearance, she reaches the stage once more, where her bored companions are presently yawning in perfect harmony. What do these young girls dream of? Probably of the

Werthers and Fritzes they left behind ... They are not pretty despite being blond.⁵⁰

European Lower-Class Immigrants' Feelings of Belonging

At this point, I take up the questions posed earlier for the case of the Levantines and pose them concerning the Central European immigrants. Can we reconstruct how the lower class "Europeans" in the Eastern Mediterranean port cities during the Hamidian period related to the country they had left and the one they now found themselves in? Did they create for themselves a clear-cut identity or was their self-image in constant flux? If the European recent arrivals had a more complex identity, did this echo local patterns of in-betweenness or was it different? If their sense of self was clear-cut, how was it integrated into the otherwise complex and fluid identity patterns present in Ottoman maritime culture?

The feasibility of such an endeavor naturally hinges on its sources. Lower class agents are less likely to have recorded their views in memoirs or travelogs, nor are their personal letters likely to have survived in an accessible form. However, in the case of the large Ottoman cities, this is more than compensated by the rich documentation in consular and church archives. But can such documents lend insight into the subjective views of the people they were written about? It seems that such insights are rare but not impossible to find. But before I discuss four examples I have chosen in detail, I must first sketch the identities that "Europeans" in the Levant were offered. While this community-based approach once again will highlight the male and actively working segments of the non-Ottoman residents, the four examples will more evenly reflect both genders, and working and nonworking segments of urban society.

The Ottoman state was not truly hospitable to its new residents. It was traditionally suspicious of people moving of their own accord and upheld a system of internal passports long after other European states, believing in the capitalist benefits of freedom of movement, had abandoned them.⁵¹ The state institutions registered with unease that the number of de facto inhabitants with foreign passports was growing

---

⁵⁰ Vitalis Cohen, quoted from Anastassiadou, *Salonique*, 190.
⁵¹ Herzog, "Migration and the State."

(although predominantly due to the common practise of Ottoman subjects adopting foreign nationality) and stipulated that any foreigner arriving with the intent of settling down in Ottoman lands should take on Ottoman nationality.[52] Also any foreigner on Ottoman soil who had forfeited his or her homeland's nationality (which mostly occurred if they had neglected to reregister with their consulate over a longer period of time) was considered a naturalized subject by default. However, the state's possibilities to implement these stipulations were limited.

The capitulatory powers put great emphasis on their subjects' rights on Ottoman soil and additionally tried to harness their loyalties and shape them into "storm troops" for their imperial interests.[53] Creating an aura of respectability also meant that individuals or groups that cast a bad light on the mother country were urged by the consulates to leave the Levant or at least its major cities, or in rare cases were forcibly extradited to the motherland. In the port cities, the model to integrate the immigrants was the "colony." This term was widely used to denote a rather hierarchic institution of people originating from and identifying with the same country. They accepted the authority of the consul as their representative as well as the privileged position of certain notables assuming responsibility in community affairs. These "colonies" were often ruled by rigid notions of respectability, and the patronizing attitude toward nonconformists or people of little social capital was often more oppressive than in the respective motherlands. Working-class countrymen could be integrated, but would rarely be considered equal to their middle-class compatriots. Loose moral conduct was considered damaging to the "colony's" corporate identity and was not tolerated.[54] The alternative to integrate into was "port city society," the heterogeneous amalgam of people of different origins present in the ports.

Did the late nineteenth-century lower-class immigrants of European origin choose to identify with the powerful imperialist states or did they give in to the Ottoman state's pressure to naturalize themselves? Did they associate themselves to the expatriate "colonies" or did the local ties they had established prove more powerful? In assessing the responses of the local "Europeans" of modest assets to the identities on

---

[52] BOA, İrade Meclis-i Mahsus 9/373, 1273.
[53] Schmitt, *Levantiner*, 337, 338; Fuhrmann, *Traum vom deutschen Orient*, 270–280.
[54] Smyrnelis, *Une société hors de soi*, 57–69; Fuhrmann, *Traum vom deutschen Orient*, 356–366.

offer, the different case studies come to a variety of results. Especially the conclusions drawn by analyses of foreign members of the Ottoman working class stand in stark contrast to one another. In his older works, Donald Quataert does not differentiate between foreign capital and foreign workers. He characterizes the latter as a labor aristocracy in league with the former.

In sum, although 90 percent of all persons employed by the [Anatolian, MF] railroads were Ottoman subjects, Europeans (especially Germans) occupied the highest and most lucrative posts. They held the middle-level positions in about equal numbers with the Ottoman Christians. Mostly Muslim Turks held the lowest categories of work ... The intrusion of the Europeans was a disruptive, divisive force that fractured the Ottoman polity both horizontally and vertically.[55]

In contrast, Anthony Gorman believes that

Far from being a labour elite or members of privileged and insular communities more concerned with their own affairs and developments abroad, many foreign workers in Egypt sought to organize on the basis of class affiliation and were committed to the improvement in the conditions of all workers, both foreign and Egyptian.[56]

Individual articulations found in consular archives are no less contradictory. As stated previously, Smyrnelis and Schmitt have claimed that the loyalties by many foreign passport holders (of both high and low social rank) to their respective consulates were given as part of a rational choice, a calculated means to an end, in exchange for a foreign passport or protection, or for economic and social standing, and could be reversed if the benefits of having a certain nationality faded.

At the core of the Ottoman Empire, the individuals and families did not actually attempt to have several identities through their incorporation into different institutional groups. Their identity is constructed precisely by their belonging to systems of different relationships, implying all the particular obligations and constraints, which they never perceived as absolutes; the attachment, without reservation or hesitation, to a specific institutional group, never appeared to them as a given.[57]

---

[55] Quataert, *Social Disintegration and Popular Resistance*, 71–93, 148.
[56] Gorman, "Foreign Workers in Egypt," 255.
[57] Smyrnelis, *Une société hors de soi*, 122.

The port city working class immigrants of Central European origin can serve as examples of all of these strategies – partaking in the superiority complex of their countries of origin and rejecting it, in solidarity and in rivalry with the polyethnic workforce – as I will demonstrate by a look at macro-level sources. However, by demonstrating their changing or contradictory stance, I can only add a slight nuance to what has already been said. To take the discussion on foreign origin port city residents and their possible sense of identity and identification further, I will in a second step turn to a new quality of sources. Both Schmitt's and Smyrnelis's conclusions as well as Quataert's and Gorman's ideas about allegiances and identities are mainly grounded on actions and their documentation in official sources. While reading the actions of historical agents as texts is a necessary method for any historian engaged in non-elitist history, that is, history of people who were not primarily engaged in creating texts, the complete absence of explicit articulations on matters of subjectivity by the historical agents leaves a sense of uneasiness. Is the historian simply injecting his or her own sentiments into a particular material? To tackle this problem, I have selected a sample of sources that are more explicit than usual on the subjective positioning of the nineteenth-century lower-class European immigrants into the Ottoman Empire. The purpose of this endeavor is of course not to represent the feelings of belonging of this immigrant class as a whole, but to make visible what kind of different subjective positionings could arise in this milieu.

In order to assess these documents correctly it is of great importance to take into account the communicative nature of the documents involved. Whether filing an appeal to the consulate, attracting the authorities' attention by nonconformist behavior, or writing a travelog, the agents are driven by particular needs that can be of a material kind, but can also include the necessity to inform others of the particularities of their life situation. But first to the more classic approach to working-class immigrants as a whole.

A Cosmopolitan Proletariat? Working-Class Loyalties in Hamidian Times

Toward the end of the nineteenth century, the long lasting alienation between arriving Central European artisans and the Habsburg and

Hohenzollern states changed, as the dissidents and the migrants from the periphery were no longer alone. The railway and infrastructure workers who arrived mostly from the 1890s onward originated from a different social stratum than their predecessors. Especially Salonica had not seen many non-Habsburg Germans at all until the city became connected to the Oriental Railway network.[58] These younger workers showed no particular animosity toward their state of origin, which had provided them with a fair education. Naturally, big differences remained between the workers and the bourgeois German residents of Salonica, and the consular and church officials. In Salonica like elsewhere, the European Great Powers vied for influence, and the expatriate communities saw it as their patriotic duty to support their motherlands' prestige. Church processions, balls, and school education were but a few of the tools employed to increase the community's reputation in the urban public sphere. In places where the national subjects were not so numerous, such as Salonica, however, the community was in need of support by the rank-and-file countrymen in order to reach a critical mass that could be noticed besides the much larger expatriate communities, such as the Italians, French, or British. This led to a degree of intimacy across social borders that was not known in Germany or Austria: Workers would reportedly turn to local conational businessmen or their superiors if they were in need, and be granted loans. The first German Protestant reverend Martin Braunschweig saw in this a rather paternalistic social system. The railway workers supposedly adopted the bourgeois Germans' imperialist supremacism vis-à-vis local society, even though they worked together intimately with Ottoman colleagues.[59] Despite their social docility, the workers were a cause of concern for the reverend. Braunschweig thought the workers too strongly adapted to the supposedly decadent morals of their surroundings, particularly to adultery. He deplored the fact that they had married local, often Greek women. He also criticized the railway workers for excessive drinking, an admittedly Central European vice that he believed had even worse effects under local climatic conditions, especially on those who rode the trains from

---

[58] In 1874 a line was put into service to Kosovska Mitrovica; in 1888 a branch was opened unto the Serbian border.

[59] Fuhrmann, *Traum vom deutschen Orient*, 270–280, 304–315, 337–338.

temperate Aegean Macedonia up the Vardar to the mountainous Serbian border and back.⁶⁰

Had German railway workers really adopted notions of German imperialist supremacy to the extent that Braunschweig describes? Some evidence supports this. The aforementioned Moritz Müller tried to impose German as the only language of the house on his wife and children, all of whom spoke mostly Greek, but also Judeo-Spanish and Turkish, in addition to French and Italian. An isolated father, however, who spent most of the day at work, had little chance to establish a rather exotic language in a multilingual city.⁶¹

Were Austrian railway workers enticed to support their country's corporate identity and its predominant denomination, Catholicism, vis-à-vis the port city public as well? There is less evidence of this. The Austrian state furthered Catholic schools aimed at Ottoman subjects at large and later intended to turn Bosnia and Herzegovina into a model Balkan colony with appeal both to Christian Orthodox and Muslim subjects.⁶² Individual cases though show that renouncing one's denomination could also be equated with treason in the Austrian mindset.⁶³

Foreign Workers in the Ottoman Short Summer of Radicalism, 1908 and After

The question of what place the foreign workers occupied in the framework of their countries of origin and in late Ottoman port city society can of course not be satisfactorily answered by a few comments from

---

⁶⁰ Ezab 5/1949, 3: Braunschweig, Annual Report 1900, 11 Jan. 1901.
⁶¹ Fuhrmann, *Traum vom deutschen Orient*, 362–363.
⁶² Kolm, *Die Ambitionen Österreich-Ungarns*.
⁶³ Franz Durst was stationmaster in the small town of Gevgelija. He had married a local Bulgarian, Katerina Adžiova. In an incident in 1887, Katerina was charged with inciting Bulgarian railway workers to kill a Turkish thief. Through the incident, Franz learnt that his wife had had affairs with other men. He sought a divorce that was denied by the consular staff. Even years after her release, the bureaucratic Habsburg laws on marriage did not allow for a divorce. Finally, Franz sought out the Greek Orthodox bishop who agreed to divorce him and marry him to his new partner on the condition that Franz converted. The length and bitterness of Durst's letter of justification signals that, had the extreme circumstances not forced him, this step would have seemed akin to treason to him; HHStA GK Sal, 425/Catharina Durst. See also the case of Martha Fehnl in Chapter 16, pp. 260–261.

the pastor, who had rather limited insights into their lives. Nonetheless the fact that until 1908 the consular sources remain largely silent on this matter justifies the assumption that this was an unproblematic constellation.

Like most other residents of the Ottoman Empire, German, Austrian, and Hungarian workers welcomed the end of Abdülhamid II's neo-absolute rule and made use of the new possibilities of free speech and fraternization. In Salonica, the workers were willing to forfeit their affiliation to their state of origin for the benefit of class-based solidarities.[64] In 1908, the social peace among the Germans of Macedonia broke. The German Protestant parish council split into two rival camps, each leveling heavy accusations against the other. All civic German institutions such as the school, the club, and the consulate were rendered dysfunctional by the row. The former reverend Braunschweig was sent back to Salonica, which he had left in 1902, to offer arbitration. When the bourgeois notables took steps to have the new reverend Langhoff removed, the working class parish members rebelled. They opposed the notables' arrogance in running community affairs without so much as consulting the workers. Langhoff had reached out to involve them in community affairs. But the grassroots rebellion continued to gain momentum even after the reverend had been pushed aside: The renegades took steps to constitute themselves as the parish of the Hungarian or Transylvanian Protestant church, thus threatening to rob the German cultural presence in Salonica of all critical mass. Braunschweig was the first to correctly assess the conflict as predominantly social in nature. He attributed the agitation in large part to the new political climate in the empire. The end of Hamidian neo-absolutism had opened the door to social movements and led to the first railway strike, thus momentarily overcoming older supremacist notions among the foreign workers. This had encouraged the workers to act up against being patronized in other spheres as well. Braunschweig managed to convince the notables that they would have to concede some of their exclusive power to the parish assembly. Likewise, he found his way into the renegades' houses in the railway workers' quarter of Bara. The dissident movement gave up soon thereafter.[65]

[64] Quataert, "The Industrial Working Class," 194–211.
[65] Fuhrmann, *Traum vom deutschen Orient*, 337–340.

The foreign workers' lifeworlds had for years oscillated between following their mother countries' supremacism and integrating into local society through intermarriage and collegiality. Had the workers' assimilation into local structures finally created a new multicultural, class-based identity in opposition to the railway directors' and merchants' paternalism in all spheres? For the established foreign railway workers in Salonica, often settled in town since several decades, this might even have been the case for a short while. But in a larger survey, the picture varies greatly, depending on the capital and labor structures of the various sectors. No doubt, the workplace was a place of tension as well.

One early dispute indicates that nationality was considered a capital on the labor market even in Hamidian times and that this could result in friction between Ottoman subjects and non-Ottomans. In the summer of 1895, Heinrich Grünwald, Lazar Davidovich, Julius Boni, Ferdinand Paruta, Albert Franco, Vladimir J. Alexitch, Franz Hollosy, Jakob Sibrower, Anton Gnalo, Josef Paruta, that is, Austrian or Hungarian subjects with German, Hungarian, Slavic, and Italian names, petitioned in Italian for the Viennese Foreign Ministry to intervene into a local dispute in Constantinople. The petitioners were working as freelance dragomans – as interpreters, tour guides, and tour organizers for affluent individuals or small groups. The critical moment for finding customers was the arrival of international steamers at the port. However the Ottoman authorities purportedly hindered them from boarding the arriving steamers, whereas Ottoman subjects were not hindered. Upon the embassy's intervention, the Ottoman Ministry of Police promised to keep all "hotel dragomans," no matter what passport they carried, from boarding the ships. But this practice was apparently not kept up for long, as complaints to the Dual Moanrchy's representatives by the freelance dragomans continued until 1901. By then, they suggested to found the "International Couriers' Club" under Habsburg protection, but open for all, as an institution to promote the common interests of their profession, rather than pitting the freelancers against each other, but the embassy did not approve.[66]

The railway was a site where action for the common interest was possible. The perestroika atmosphere that initially followed the 1908

---

[66] HHStA, BK Kpl 107: Foreign Ministry to Embassy, Vienna 10 July 1895, and passim.

re-installment of constitutional rule prompted many social groups to assert their rights. The fight was truly internationalist: It spread from the Bulgarian Railways to all major Ottoman railway companies, including the Oriental Railways (in the Balkans, based in Salonica and European Constantinople), and the Anatolian Railways (with its terminus in Asian Constantinople). Foreigners who had brought experience from other labor movements were essential for its organization, as the German right-wing press noticed in disgust.[67]

However, it must be stated that in many cases during the hot phase of social movements from 1908 to 1909, latent differences between workers of different nationalities were specifically targeted to disrupt protests. In mines and ports, workers of Ottoman origin often found themselves pitted against foreign investors. The standard situation was that employers attempted to use foreign workers without local affiliations, both because they were expected not to fraternize and because the state authorities had to be more circumspect in their interventions when subjects of the capitulatory powers were involved. To promote their legitimacy, the Ottoman authorities sometimes opted for law and order, that is, backing capitalist interests, and at other times championing their subjects against the outsiders. When the management of the Paşabahçe glass factory outside of Constantinople sacked some of its unruly workers of Ottoman nationality and replaced them with Austrians, the predominantly Anatolian work force reacted by occupying the factory. In this case, the head of police decided to crack down on the picketers by applying anti-strike laws.[68]

Overall, one can find evidence to support Quataert's, Gorman's, as well as Smyrnelis's points of view. Apparently workers were willing to make up part of the "colony" and profit from its superior cultural capital and even material interclass solidarity. However, they made up part of local society as well, intermarrying and working together in a very mixed company. The railway strikes and the

[67] Quataert, *Social Disintegration and Popular Resistance*.
[68] BOA, Police Ministry (ZB) 627–686: Beykoz Head of District to Istanbul Municipality, 13 March 1325 (24 March 1909). By contrast, when an Italian company hired twenty-two Istrian lumbermen for working in the forests of Albania, the local authorities rejected the company's legally obtained concession on the grounds that only Ottoman subjects were by law allowed to work in forestry. Since the blockade lasted months, the lumbermen found themselves deserted by the company in a malaria-ridden place far from Durrazzo; HHStA Adm. Reg. F 31 – 49: Vice-Consul Halla to Aehrenthal, Durrazzo 13 Jan. 1909.

Salonica church parish row, in which the Germans even used the very local strategy of "play of identities" (*jeu d'identités*, Smyrnelis), shopping around other national parishes, stand in stark contrast to the previous docility, but at the same time, Austrian scabs were at work in Paşabahçe. Material interests, social self-affirmation, but also openness were factors in an attitude that cannot simply be subsumed under the imperialist grand scheme, nor as integration into local society. As mentioned earlier, it is worthwhile to problematize this malleable identity further by looking at the individual level and turning from actions to words about the self. In doing so however, we will also leave aside the male-dominated, respectable labor world of the railways to enter the less well-reputed domains of female domestic labor and low-key entrepreneurship as well as male unproductivity.

Amalia Ruggiero

On July 8, 1900 Amalia Ruggiero née Travniček wrote to the Salonica Consulate, "As is known to the most honorable Consulate General from the previous inspection of my documents, I was born in Moravia, am thus an Austrian national and as such I request of you to take into account the following appeal." As background information, she narrates the part of her life she has led in the Levant. She had come to the Aegean region as an educator for the children of the Kavalla tobacco merchant Foskioglu in 1888. She got to know the Italian consul's cook Nikola Vutzia, and the two of them quit their positions and left first for Salonica and then for Vodena (Edessa) where they opened a temporary shop for railway construction workers on the Salonica – Monastir line. They repeated this successful business scheme on the Salonica – Dedeağaç line and then between Alaşehir and Afyon-Karahisar. Her initial savings of 50 Turkish Pounds having been depleted in the initial months, the couple possessed 100 Pounds when leaving Vodena. By the time they were living in West Anatolia, they had two children but remained unmarried. Supposedly because of his refusal to marry her or hand out her share of their savings and because of abuse, she chose to marry the foreman Alexander Ruggiero, but he left her after just two months. She moved to Constantinople with her daughter, and later found employment in Salonica as a cook. When Vutzia demanded the return of their daughter, she turned to the consul, claiming Austrian nationality and protection for herself and her children, something she apparently had so far neglected to do.[69]

This appeal is framed as a testimony, a favorite among the historians' objectives for peeking into non-elitist lifeworlds. It takes on a narrative character and it seeks to explain an assumed reality, thus combining the reconstruction of a historical scenario with background information. In testimony, we find a dialogue between "master" and "servant": There is an element of transgression against the norms set by the "master," who may be framed as God and the Church, the rightful ruler and his loyal servants, society and the common good, the class and the party, etc. The "servants," those involved in or having witnessed the transgression, are compelled in the dialogue to frame the transgression, explain how it came about. The narrative is chosen to convince the master, and as such, will vary according to what is considered a successful discursive strategy in a given place and time; for nineteenth-century Europe, they often follow a thread of bourgeois morality.

At first sight, it seems the obvious choice to read Ruggiero's plea within the parameters established by Smyrnelis and Schmitt. The very first sentence of her appeal creates the link between nationality and using the consular authority for one's own interests. The native Moravian, by her social interactions, is an established member of local society. Her lover, her husband, her employers, and customers belong to the mixed society of the major Macedonian towns and the workforce on the railway construction sites. Her interactions with her country of origin apparently lie in the past. Having lived on Ottoman soil for twelve years, she had not bothered to renew her ties with her mother country, forfeiting her passport and now having to remind the consular agents that her place of birth still qualifies her for Austrian

---

[69] HHStA, GK Sal 443, Helene u. Dimitri Travniček – Vormundschaft: Amalie Ruggiero to Consulate General, Salonica 8 June 1900. The petition led to one of the classic legal impasses due to the black holes of capitulation legislature. Could the children of an Austrian woman and an Ottoman man born out of wedlock on Ottoman soil be considered Austrian subjects? Moreover, in Konya, in inland Anatolia, where Vutzia was now living, the Austrian diplomats could not hope to execute the boy's extraction against his father's resistance. Four years later when Ruggiero was working in an Anglo-German butcher shop in Cairo, the matter had still not been resolved.

nationality despite her lack of a valid passport. Now, when under pressure, she resorted to the consular power as a resource. For years, she had disrespected both Austria's claim to a superior culture vis-à-vis the Balkans and her home country's predominant Catholic morale by diving into an adventurous life, working "on the frontier" among railway workers, having relationships with a Greek and then an Italian, living together and having children out of wedlock, leaving the father of her children for another man. In order to mobilize the consul, she clumsily reinterprets her life, so he might see in her not a sinner and a Levantine, but an Austrian damsel in distress: Vutzia had promised her marriage from the start; in the end he had started to abuse her, so in desperation she turned to her future husband; the two men had conspired behind her back to thus cheat her of her fortunes. On the other hand, an a priori assumption of a purely instrumentalist approach by Ruggiero to her petition, that in fact resembles a confession, ignores the dynamics of testimony as an act, which, depending on circumstances, can be experienced as a painful invasion into one's lifeworld or as liberation from an environment and a self-consciousness ignorant of the transgression.[70] It is highly likely that the act of putting her life in the Levant to paper, of trying to shape a coherent teleological narrative from the day of writing by itself transformed Ruggiero's perspective, that she began to believe in this view of her life: She had "gone native" for a while and having been seriously disappointed, learned the error of her ways and returned to her mother country's flock.

It cannot be clearly established which of the two interpretations of the plea has more validity. Does the problem stem from the partisan nature of information that we find in consular personal records? If we disregarded them and turned to other information that was not given in order to induce particular actions, would the picture become clearer? Would we know more about the lower-class Central Europeans on the shores of the Aegean if more of them had written down their views on local society to communicate them to others, as so many of their bourgeois compatriots had done? The answer is most likely no, as the following example will show.

---

[70] Foucault, *History of Sexuality*, vol. I, 59; Crapanzano, "Life-Histories," 953–960; Felman and Laub, *Testimony*, 46.

Anna Forneris

Anna Forneris née Hafner, born 1789 in rural Carinthia (Kärnten), set out at adolescence to live and travel in the Levant and Persia. Having returned to her native village in 1847, she wrote her memoirs two years later. She left her home according to her narrative, because of the lure of the wide world and found initial fulfillment in the nightlife of Trieste, before setting out for the Levant and marrying the owner of a Smyrna hotel. Forneris soon realized that her husband of Venetian origin was an alcoholic and enjoyed brawling, but following her son's birth stayed on until her husband died of a wound inflicted by a customer. As a widow at the age of thirty, she tried to resettle on the Habsburg coast but following a series of disappointments set out four years later for the Ottoman shore once more. She opened an inn in Constantinople's Pera, catering mainly to Germans and Italians. The successful business ended when the fire of 1829 destroyed the inn and Forneris resettled to Persia as a trader. Several years later, she returned to Constantinople with her new Sardinian husband to open a bar. As the German workers of the arsenal were laid off upon the death of Sultan Mahmud in 1838, the couple lost their mainstay customers and following other setbacks to their business, resettled once more to Persia.[71]

Forneris begins her account stating that her partial intention in publishing her memoirs is "to restrain the one or other female compatriot with wanderlust from embarking on similar follies and self-inflicted misfortunes."[72] Distancing herself from her former lifestyle and surroundings serves a communicative strategy and takes on once more a character similar to confession. She frames the path she has chosen as a zigzag caused by a dilemma. Since her youth, she had experienced "two souls within her breast": On the one hand, she was attracted by pious Catholicism and the desire to live a simple life in her region of origin; on the other, she was driven by the need to see the world at large, take pleasure in her youth, her attractiveness to men, and her ability to dance. Since her experiences with religion took place at an early age, she missed the opportunity to become a nun; by the time she had reached a mature enough age, the world at large and

---

[71] Forneris, *Schicksale und Erlebnisse einer Kärntnerin*; see also Chapter 12, pp. 178–179.
[72] Forneris, introduction to *Schicksale*.

party life had taken control of her. In her later years, she once again opts for religiosity, undertaking the pilgrimage to Jerusalem and Rome. This interpretation of her life, although sincere, is clearly motivated by the attempt to reestablish her respectability in the bourgeois and Catholic public of her home region, where zest for life, independence, resourcefulness, and adventurousness were not characteristics that were in high esteem for women. She writes after having returned from the Orient to her native Carinthia and expected her readership to be from the local Catholic conservatives that frowned on lower-class female agency. Like her Moravian compatriot Amalia Ruggiero who fifty years later set out on a similar "folly," Forneris presents herself as weak and gullible, as giving in to temptation, although her ability to compensate for ever-changing circumstances in a variety of environments, starting all kinds of jobs and businesses, and surviving several life-threatening situations, tell a different story. She writes at the age of sixty with a sense of bitterness about the countless employments, businesses, friendships, and loves in her life that at some point became a disappointment. Accordingly she does not dwell long on her original intentions or attitudes attached to her life in the East, but more on the disappointments that forced her to move on and finally return.

As already mentioned when discussing Levantine self-narratives, the genre she chose to follow, the travelog, was shaped by upper-class men who claimed to portray the objective reality of the strange ways and people they had seen, not to describe how they themselves had been affected by what they had observed. Forneris struggles to follow this objective approach, although it becomes obvious that this cold detachment does not suit her narration. She also repeats many of the derogatory characterizations of the people of the Ottoman Empire that are common tropes of the nineteenth-century travelog and wastes much space on detailed graphic descriptions. Repetition serves to win credibility with the reader: She does not challenge bourgeois assumptions on the East; instead, by reiterating the dominant paradigms of her time, she intends to symbolically take part in the domination and thus to gain esteem in the eyes of her contemporaries back home.[73] As a woman of low social status, being very original in her points of view or choice of subjects could lead to assumptions that she did not

---

[73] Pratt, *Imperial Eyes*; see also Laqueur, "Das Osmanische Reich und seine Bewohner," 461–470.

understand what she saw or that she had simply made up her experiences. By reiterating common narratives on the Orient, she fulfills the reader's expectations and in the process avoids such possible assumptions. Appropriately, her statements on the Ottoman state and port city society are not very flattering and she highlights her personal negative experiences with them: Women are of low social esteem, the Europeans in the Levant do not treat marriage with proper seriousness, and there is no possibility of securing one's rights in court.

While this negative narration of the Orient and a laudation of the simple life in Carinthia pervade the entire narrative, in a postscript she surprisingly adds a negative reflection about her life in Austria since her return.

> I had acquired a different guise, lifestyle, and habits through all those years ... and as these discrepancies in themselves are completely harmless, I did not see a reason why I should force myself in my old days. But I was therefore observed with ambiguous eyes even in my father's house and was by tendency judged to be a useless adventurer and my narrations to be crude lies or at least gross exaggerations.[74]

Her Oriental dress and customs seem not only habit but also a form of resistance against the intolerance she feels by the villagers. Instead of making an effort to reintegrate into the modest life she had lauded throughout the book, she increases this resistance further by decorating her room in Oriental style and buying a horse carriage to, as she claims, compensate for her restlessness. On the final page of her memoirs, she seems to have given up all hope of reintegration and instead expresses the wish to return to Persia: "Honestly said, I would rather be in the Orient once more."[75] The remark leaves the reader puzzled after reading chapters of derision on the immoral Levant and laudation for rural Austria. While her failed reintegration is made explicit, there is no articulation as to what in the Orient makes her want to return. This hope seems such a gross violation of the Orientalist travelogs' common sense that the author does not find the words to explain it. Whatever positive emotions Forneris entertained for the Orient, her memoirs written in the narrative of a confession fail to give us clear insights into them.

---

[74] Forneris, *Schicksale*, 133.   [75] Ibid, 134.

This example shows the limits in trying to recreate lower-class orientations and identities from travelogs, memoirs, or other explicitly narrative texts. While the text obviously demonstrates a tension between the hegemonic norms of the place of origin and the writer's emotional attachments, they are hinted at but not made explicit. This is not really surprising, as we cannot expect the marginalized to have mastered a media that was not created for and by them, and to have created their own counter-epistemology. If we are to find their statements, we will have to delve into what they have to say about themselves. This turns our attention back to archival material and to two characters that transgress against social norms in a very different way. While Ruggiero and Forneris appear as women who are too independent, mobile, and self-sufficient for the female ideals of their times, Robert Weiss and I. Wilfried Blumberg fail to fulfill the male role because of their lack of psychic integrity and independence.

Robert Weiss

It would be a wrong assumption to believe that ethnocentrism and imperialist arrogance was a mentality that the new arrivals from west or north of the Mediterranean brought to the Ottoman port cities, and that long exposure to heterogeneous port city society tempered such attitudes or reduced them to mere lip service in order to gain the favor of the consular authorities. As the following example will show, such identity patterns were sometimes adapted by individuals who had little actual contact to their motherlands.

In the winter of 1887/1888 the Salonica resident Robert Weiss, a minor, became psychotic. He repeatedly said to his mother, "Jew, the Jews, the Jews, I do not want to become Jewish, I was born a Protestant and I will die as a Protestant ... Someone in the house must die, either you or a Jew."

Several witnesses confirmed that the young German was obsessed by the idea that he was in danger of forceful conversion to Judaism. This obsession was augmented by the fear of the accompanying circumcision, a practice which in his confused state he envisioned as a castration. The widowed mother and her son were living as the only non-Jews in an apartment house owned by a Jew in Salonica. The other residents of the house kept a fearful distance from Robert, except for Salomon Salem, the grandson of the house owner. Salem confirmed that Robert was obsessed by Christian-Jewish relations and also reported outbreaks of enthusiasm for the German emperor and nation, such as "May our Kaiser live a thousand years."[76]

Robert Weiss's need to differentiate himself from his surroundings and identify with Germany and Protestantism comes as a surprise, as his relationship to them was very limited. His mother, Augustina Lukat née Bagatella, had been born in Udine, Venetia, in 1838 and had settled in the Ottoman lands at an early age. His father's family was cited by the German Consul of Salonica as a prime example of Germans who had been almost completely assimilated to local conditions:

> ... the Weiss family. Its progenitor, a Protestant from Baden, emigrated to Smyrna around the middle of the century, both his sons moved on to Salonica and married indigenous women there. The children from both of these marriages have been baptized, some as Protestants, some as Catholics, some as Orthodox, but the children of the third generation only as Catholics. One member of this family speaks only Greek and has obtained naturalization as a Hellene on Corfu; they all though pertain to the German colony simply because they have guarded their nationality more carefully than their religion.[77]

Robert Weiss had never experienced much of the Protestantism and the glory of the German nation that he turned to in his moment of crisis. He was from the second generation of Germans being born on Ottoman soil. He did not even share his denomination with all his cousins. The preponderance of Jews in his surroundings and in Salonician public life cannot have been a new phenomenon for him, as he had grown up in the city where Sephardim were the largest ethnic group by far. And yet, at the moment of his psychic illness, he experienced this preponderance as threatening, despite the fact that there was no tangible threat. Apparently, he had been exposed to anti-Semitic agitation. This propaganda marked the Jews' social position as disproportionately high and gave Robert a focus to address his own feelings of inadequacy. After his father's death in 1881, his mother had married Gottfried Lukat, a machinist on the railways, but he had died only four years later in an accident. The widow made ends meet

---

[76] PA-AA GK Sal, box 32 (Robert Weiss).
[77] Ezab 5/1948, 134–137: Mordtmann to Hohenlohe-Schillingsfürst, Salonica 24 July 1897.

by washing and ironing.[78] In these dismal circumstances, anti-Semitism and German imperialism combined to promise Robert something of a better life: A world, where he, due to his descent, would not be living at the bottom end of the social scales, while people of a supposedly inferior race were his landlord and more well-off neighbors.

Although obviously in a state of psychosis, Robert Weiss managed to convince the German consular authorities that the threat he perceived to be under was genuine, and that he needed solidarity from his overseas countrymen. The examining doctor wrote:

The aforementioned individual is of morally good predisposition and is full of a vibrant sentiment for his Protestant belief from his father's side. The intentional or accidental injury to these religious feelings was the cause that Mr. Weiss was seized by various delusions.[79]

He concluded that the most important thing was to remove Robert from his malicious Jewish surroundings where the insults had been inflicted. As a result, Weiss was sent to psychiatric institutions in the Reich.[80] The example shows in what roundabout ways imperialist chauvinism could manifest itself, far from the simple diffusion by consular agents or colonial activists. Robert Weiss had through some indiscernible channels been touched by their propaganda and had made use of it for his deluded personal revolt against his living circumstances. By adapting this aggressive worldview, he managed to procure the imperial solidarity that he had not received as a nondescript sane man.

I. Wilfried Blumberg

Would all lower-class port city residents of foreign origin agree with Forneris in condemning life in the Eastern Mediterranean as a source of malaise for them or worse, as in Weiss's case, unbearable to the point of mental disorder? Or did any of the lower-class European immigrants refuse to take sides in the confrontation between the Levant and the metropolis? Was there a voice that reclaimed the right to blend both worlds, which together shaped the lives of the expatriates

---

[78] PA-AA GK Sal, box 14 (Pass und Polizei), 27.
[79] PA-AA GK Sal, box 32 (Robert Weiss).
[80] PA-AA GK Sal, box 14 (Pass und Polizei), 27. Upon release he remained unemployed.

on the shores of the Eastern Mediterranean? Do any of the personal documents reflect the attitude of the song about the *shalvar* from the beginning of this discussion on identities, a song that shows pleasure in living in surroundings where identities blurred, blended, and produced unprecedented variances? Renouncing both the dominant trope of imperial supremacy and the powerful ideologies that favored local integration such as socialism, Ottoman constitutionalism, or local patriotism and instead carving out a third path with such a feat at first glance appears to be beyond the intellectual capacities of people with a limited degree of educational and social capital. One would expect such feats from exceptional intellectuals, such as the Austromarxist Otto Bauer, but not from the shopkeepers, railway or entertainment workers of Constantinople's Galata district, or the *Frangomahalla* of Smyrna or Salonica. And yet one document has survived in which a German resident of Constantinople outlines such a worldview. As in the case of Robert Weiss however, it is once again a figure on the margins that makes these bold statements.

I. Wilfried Blumberg visited the German Consulate of Salonica on October 4, 1905. As he did not succeed in seeing the Acting Consul Dr. Hesse, he wrote a letter to him. Blumberg, a resident of the Ottoman Empire of German nationality, had been sent to Germany in the summer of 1903 to cure his addiction to alcohol. He had first been in an institution near Halle, then near Fürstenwalde in Brandenburg. In the end, homesickness had caused him to end the therapy and set out for the Southeast once more. While the trip to Germany had been arranged with the help and possibly the finances of the German consulate, Blumberg claims that his return trip (also apparently undertaken by railway) was financed mostly by "my consulates," meaning the Ottoman consulates in Germany. This means that he must have proven to them or at least led them to believe that he was an Ottoman subject. Blumberg felt attached to Germany mainly through his worldview: He considered himself a member of the free or liberal religious (*freireligiös*) movement, a loose association based on humanist concepts and opposition to dogmas and ecclesiastical hierarchies. Surprisingly, he considered Wilhelm II the patron of the movement, despite the emperor's tendency toward a somewhat crude and medieval Protestantism.[81] Otherwise, Blumberg thanked for "all kindness, but also

[81] Benner, *Die Strahlen der Krone*.

for some lessons" the authorities had taught him (a hint that some of his time in Germany was apparently spent outside of the institutions and in conflict with the law) and included in his letter "long live the Emperor, the Empress, and all good Germans." However, he made it clear that he did not consider himself part of the nation, instead taking his "leave from the good German people in Germany." Whether such detachment from his place of origin resulted from his stay in Central Europe or whether he had felt equally distant to it prior to leaving the Eastern Mediterranean is not clear. However, his identity is clearly inspired by his place of residence: His homesickness results from the fact that "I am a Constantinopolitan"; his plans for the future, besides staying sober, were "to become a useful human being in the ranks of my Turkish nation, be they of what confession whatsoever (as I am of free religion)." He immediately added that this was not meant as chauvinism against non-Ottomans, but included in his good wishes "those who have done good to me and protected me outside of the Turkish Empire."[82]

Blumberg stated that he would continue to Smyrna where he had family to take care of. Unfortunately, the documents make no further mention of him, so it is not possible to see whether he managed to pursue his good intentions and cosmopolitan ideals, or whether he reverted to alcoholism and complacency. However, his statements stand out as the most explicit identification with local society by any nominal foreigner that has come to light in the consular archives.

These four documents show some possible positions of the lower-class foreigners residing in the Ottoman Empire. A merely instrumental attitude toward their original nationality as a means to pursue one's rights, or a back-and-forth motion between going native and confessing for the sins against the norms of the motherland and asking to return to the flock; identifying the motherland with piety and stability versus the adventurousness and instability of the Orient and feeling torn between the two; feeling rejected because the motherland does not accept divergent lifestyles, whereas the diversity of the Eastern Mediterranean absorbs difference more easily; using the imperialist claims to superiority to rebel against one's embeddedness in local society at a

---

[82] PA-AA GK Sal, box 14: Auskunftsgesuche, 168: I. Wilfried Blumberg to Hesse, Salonica 5 Oct. 1905.

socially low position; or, upon having experienced the homeland state, politely severing the ties to the motherland in order to commit oneself to making the dream of a truly cosmopolitan society in the framework of the Ottoman Empire come true – these are the reactions we can gather from the heterogeneous sources on four individuals. Although their stories mark them as extraordinary, their ways of mediating between the different identities on offer reflect common themes that possibly were employed under less spectacular life circumstances as well. Although they all exhibit the desire to guard their particular interests, their communicative strategies are no mere means to an end, but portray a sincere desire to explain the circumstances and the choices they took in their lives. It is this multilayered nature of migrant identities and their manifestations that we should take into account when dealing with the difficult task of portraying the lifeworlds of European migrants on Ottoman soil.

Conclusion

Around the Eastern Mediterranean and to various degrees around Europe and much of the rest of the globe, the nineteenth century and its rapid expansion of information, mobility, and quests for innovation complicated the search for both an individual and a collective sense of belonging. The especially high degree of input in the port cities coincided with the lack of a state-produced doctrine that convinced the majority of the population to orient their lives according to that state's prerequisites. This turned cities such as Smyrna, Salonica, and Constantinople into highly polyvalent sites for personal identities. As mentioned in the introduction to this section, this situation had been subject of reflection among many writers of the time. Friedrich Nietzsche summarized the dilemma:

Among today's Europeans, there is no lack of people who have the right to call themselves in an aloof and honorable sense displaced [heimatlos; literally without a homestead; MF] ... For their lot is harsh, their hopes uncertain, it is an art to grant them solace – but what's the use! We children of the future, how *could* we be at home in today's world! We are resentful of all ideals based on which someone could even feel at home in this fragile, broken transitional period. Concerning their "realities," we do not believe that they will be of any *duration* ... yes! But we want to exploit the *advantages* of our situation and, far from perishing in it, benefit from the free air and the masses of light.[83]

With these words, the German author put into words a sentiment that was shared by many contemporaries in different locales. We find it in the bachelor debate, in which both male and female readers of the *Journal de Salonique* agreed that their generation and their city were void of any ideals. But how did the seaside residents cope with their situation? At best, they could as Nietzsche suggested, concentrate on its advantages. It could be turned into a "cosmopolitan gods-, morals-, and arts-carnival."[84] The diversity of identities available on the market could be used without falling for any of the contemporary ideologies that Nietzsche warned of, such as conservatism, liberalism, socialism, capitalism, or worse, nationalism and racism.

Apparently quite a number of residents of the port cities lived and acted according to this Nietzschean maxim and intended to make the most of the confusion of identities prevalent in their cities. The song *To Salvari* expresses this attitude best, celebrating the confusion of national identities and concomitant gender roles one could be confronted with in the streets of Smyrna. In a similar vein, Naum Duhani and Willy Sperco, rather than attempting to define their identity as post-imperial Levantine authors would, celebrated the space that allowed them to live a life of diversity, emerging from the smoky bars of Pera at daybreak to take in the grand skyline of the imperial mosques beyond the Golden Horn. The super-Westernized likewise joined in the carnival spirit by flaunting the narrow-minded conservative and national demands on the dress code, as Halil Halid or Osman Hamdi Bey did to the dismay of the rank-and-file bureaucracy. Mehmed Effendi's combination of *antari* and *Homburg* was even provocative enough to have him dismissed from public service. The half-naked bodybuilders were a comparable provocation in the eyes of many Armenian community members. The doctor Rıza Nur found modern medical discourse a welcome opportunity to flaunt the

---

[83] Nietzsche, *Digitale Kritische Gesamtausgabe: Werke und Briefe*, eKGWB/FW-377 – Die fröhliche Wissenschaft: § 377; and eKGWB/NF-1885,2[196] – Nachgelassene Fragmente Herbst 1885 – Herbst 1886, www.nietzschesource.org.

[84] Friedrich Nietzsche, quoted in Prange, "Cosmopolitan Roads to Culture," 269–286.

contemporary silence on the topic of sex in good society. Those who managed to visit the foreign-language schools without succumbing to their rhetoric of imperialist supremacy gained access to a wide variety of possibilities, a *décloisonnement* when compared to community- and state-based windows into the wider world. While the young Osman Hamdi and Leon Sciaky made the mistake to believe they would have to choose the overseas identity over their origins, they both learned to more productively mix the two in later years. Newspapers such as the *Moniteur Oriental* managed to successfully play at expressing local sentiment and gaining international attention, if they played the game well. Even the half-German, half-Ottoman cured alcoholic Wilfried Blumberg seems to have attempted to make the most of his polyvalent situation.

And yet, it seems many residents of the port cities were not as free-minded or happy about the adaptation of different identities, styles, or perspectives according to the situation. While the editor in chief Vitalis Cohen was probably highly amused about the debate his rather predictable mix of Paris-trained writing skills, panache, and knowledge of local society had produced, the readers of *Journal de Salonique* poured their hearts out about the difficulties of coping with the boredom of middle-class life in Salonica and their inability to transgress it, even during a leisurely bicycle ride to the White Tower Garden Café. It is certainly true that many contemporaries experienced their situation as a malaise and like Bihruz Bey, Oblomov, or Ulrich (*The Man without Qualities*), were well aware of the possibilities of the modern, interconnected world, but failed to make much practical use of them when it came to their own lives. The Ottoman seaside bourgeoisie was embarrassed for the low cushions and divan they could not forfeit for the Louis XV furniture they had acquired, or if their conversational skills would not fit perfectly with Parisian parlance.

Even those who appeared successful in mastering the ways of the modern world and expanding their possibilities beyond the shallow pursuits of the commercial and bureaucratic bourgeoisie, based on an exceptional amount of leverage due to private fortunes, a tolerant family climate, or simply through circumstance, often claimed that they found their path one of suffering. This goes both for the milieus of Armenian and German actresses as well as for the artist Mihri Hanım, all of whom at least in retrospect claimed that they were afflicted by a malaise, which in Şerif Mardin's terminology translates into the Bihruz Bey Syndrome. The malaise did not leave the writer Demetra Vaka even decades after emigrating from the Ottoman world; instead she realized its universal dimensions, just as the highly mobile entrepreneur Anna Forneris realized that remigration to Austria did not cure her sense of dislocation. In the worst case, knowledge of the discrepancy between the possibilities of the wider world and one's own personal insufficiency or the feeling that contemporary society fell short of one's hopes could transmute from a latent malaise into acute psychic illness, as in the case of Robert Weiss or in his later years Friedrich Nietzsche.

Nietzsche had warned of the growing spread of nationalism and racism, which seemed to him inadequate responses to modern diversity and especially for his imagined we-group of "the displaced," who he claimed were too racially mixed and too "good Europeans" to fall for such simple answers.[85] And yet, a large segment of society thought the dilemma of modern polyvalent society was best addressed by creating normative chains to prevent contemporaries from exploiting the full range of possibilities modern society had on offer. Nationalism, often in combination with a rather conservative or minimalist reformist view of societal roles, dominated much of the advice literature and even informed much of the fiction writing that treated more diverse subjects. Women should educate themselves and manage the household and the progeny efficiently, but refrain from smoking, bicycle riding, or reading morally precarious novels. Men should wear a fresh collar every day, work hard at the office and at home, and spend their leisure time together with the family. Society balls, revealing dress, liberal exchange with the other sex, coquetry were all dismissed as they did not conform to "our" established norms of behavior, while infatuation, polygamy, lengthy socializing with friends, and excess were all condemned on the grounds that they did not convene with modern rules of society. In this way, a Procrustean bed was designed that had no room for the egoisms, eccentricities, and indeterminate stances that were so characteristic of late-Ottoman port city society. The highly polyvalent nature of the port cities in this way precipitated its own counter-discourses, and in the long run its dissolution.

---

[85] Nietzsche, *Digitale Kritische Gesamtausgabe*, eKGWB/FW-377 – Die fröhliche Wissenschaft: § 377; see also Prange, "Cosmopolitan Roads to Culture."

PART V

The End of the European Dream

20 The Lack of an Anti-European Perspective

The horizons of the West may be bound with walls of steel,
But my borders are guarded by the mighty bosom of a believer.
Let it bellow out, do not be afraid! And think:
How can this fiery faith ever be killed,
By that battered, single-fanged monster you call "civilization?"[1]

Following the reinstitution of the Ottoman constitution in 1908, port city residents made ample use of their newly found freedoms, including discussing politics in public, and in particular in the cafés. *Journal de Salonique* mocked this new practice, as it did not consider its participants competent. To show its readers how ridiculous such conversations could be, it published a summary of one conversation overheard in Nionio's (the Brasserie d'Angleterre) by, as the newspaper sarcastically wrote, "budding diplomats" under the headline "Coffeehouse Politics." The two interlocutors were discussing the ramifications of Bulgaria's declaration of independence from the Ottoman Empire and of Austria-Hungary's annexation of Bosnia and Hercegovina. They predicted a domino effect for militant nationalist movements and irredentist states. What if Hungary would now separate from Austria? Would then not Italy decide to annex Trieste with the backing of Great Britain and France? This would result in a catastrophe of historic dimensions; they claimed "And the old Europe will be torn apart, rendered powerless for all times. And it will be a new world that will be built upon the old. We are really experiencing a historical moment!"[2]

The savvy newspaper editors considered such speculation nonsense. Was Bosnia's and Bulgaria's separation from the Empire not a long-established fait accompli? What possibly could change through such a

---

[1] Mehmet Akıf Ersoy, *İstiklâl Marşı*, English translation according to wikipedia; https://en.wikipedia.org/wiki/%C4%B0stiklal_Mar%C5%9F%C4%B1#ref_n88.
[2] *Journal de Salonique*, 26. Nov. 1908.

nominal change of status on Europe's periphery? And yet, the two anonymous coffeehouse diplomats proved to be completely right in their forecast of events. Within ten years, their prediction of a chain reaction of nationalist action, Great Power retaliation, separatism, and the decline of Europe's world dominance had become reality, possibly in a more catastrophic dimension than even they had imagined.

Posterity has wondered time and again about the inability of Belle Époque society to see the coming storm.[3] Few publications before 1914 described the future as anything but peaceful and a constant unraveling of progress for all, albeit with some minor hiccups. However, the ridiculed Salonica coffeehouse world politics analysis of 1908 shows us that pessimistic scenarios, dissident voices, and diverging practices existed. They rarely made it into the "serious press," however.[4] To some extent, one might draw a parallel to the dominance of pre-2008 neoliberal discourse that was dismissive of any fears of economic overstretch, the destabilizing effects of a growing prosperity gap, and the possibility of a general rebellion against or refusal of the prevailing global order. Taking a look at early twenty-first-century predicaments can open our eyes for those of the early twentieth, and vice versa.

Idolizing Baal – A Paradigm for the Nineteenth Century

In an attempt to adequately describe the theocratic-nihilist organization Islamic State, Pankaj Mishra draws parallels to the nineteenth and early twentieth century and the period's particular hopes and frustrations that eventually led a considerable number of young men to join radical movements and perpetrate acts of mass violence and cruelty for seemingly distant political ideals. Mishra challenges the widespread liberal assumption that such acts constitute an atavistic defense against progress and outsiders. Instead he claims that such phenomena attest to the very "success" of the liberal model. According to Mishra, at the

---

[3] Clark, *Sleepwalkers*.
[4] A rare exception was the *Stamboul* chastising Great Power governments for their excessive arms expenditure despite the global aspirations for a lasting peace in 1910; *Stamboul*, 5 Jan. 1911. Hristo Brâzitsov in retrospect recalls an apocalyptic fear during the passing of Haley's Comet in spring 1910, leading to suicides, hedonist lifestyle, and corruption of values; Brızitsov, *İstanbul'dan Mektuplar*, 98.

beginning of the nineteenth century, Great Britain had emerged as the dominant economic, political, and intellectual power of the globe. Its combination of diplomacy, war, and sheer economic success led to the quick erosion of almost all other sociopolitical systems and to the global spread of attempts to conform to the British model of capitalist progress, reason, and civil rights.[5]

From the beginning of the nineteenth century and even in England itself there had been criticism of the preponderance of materialism as the foremost maxim in determining social relations. Mishra cites Percy B. Shelley, Samuel T. Coleridge, Charles Dickens, and David H. Lawrence as writers critical of this development. The spread of capitalist and reason-based worldviews met further resistance as it progressed, first in Western and Central Europe and then further afield. Following the defeat of the Paris Commune's romantic ambitions, even the young Arthur Rimbaud demonstrate a similar revolt against "reasonable" society as well as the readiness to follow even obscure political movements in the hope of deliverance from ubiquitous materialism:

The inferior race has covered all – the people, as one says, and Reason; the Nation and Science ...

Science, the new nobility! Progress. The world marches on! Why does it not turn? ...

Whom should I rent myself out to? Which beast must one worship? Which holy image is one to attack? Which hearts shall I break? Which lie must I upkeep? – Through whose blood shall I wade?[6]

Mishra lists Friedrich Schiller, Novalis, and Franz Grillparzer as German and Austrian critics of materialism. As the spread of capitalist and liberal modes progressed and managed to provide a certain degree of prosperity, anti-materialist criticism was increasingly sidelined. Nevertheless, in the regions that hardly managed to profit from the British paradigm, criticism remained more widespread and eloquent. This was the case in some regions confronted with colonialism, such as China or India, but also Russia. Mishra points out Fyodor Dostoevsky's writings as among the most analytically sharp and eloquent critiques of nineteenth-century zeitgeist.[7] In his description of the World

---

[5] Mishra, "How to Think about Islamic State"; see also Mishra, *Age of Anger*.
[6] Rimbaud, "Mauvais Sang."   [7] Mishra, "How to Think about Islamic State."

Exhibition of 1862 and London, which he considered the prototypical city of the new order, the author claims,

> You feel that something final has been accomplished here, accomplished and concluded. It is some kind of biblical image, something out of Babylon, a kind of prophecy from the Apocalypse, being fulfilled before your very eyes. You feel that a great deal of eternal spiritual resistance and denial is needed so as not to submit, not to succumb to the impression, not to worship fact and idolize Baal, in other words not to accept as your ideal that which already exists.[8]

And yet, the base for the necessary "spiritual resistance" was eroded. No genuinely premodern authorities remained to provide orientation not tainted by the ubiquitous materialist worldview. A good example is the declaration of papal infallibility as a dogma in 1870. What had been a pillar of Catholic hegemony for centuries now had to be transformed into a dogma in defiance of materialism. Thus the papacy became equated with backwardness in the mind frame of many progress advocates.[9] Christian orthodoxy, Jewish orthodoxy, Islam, Hinduism, and Buddhism did not fair much better, as they were also confronted with the question whether to dogmatically harden their stances or subject themselves to a worldview that ran contrary to many of their believers' essentials.

Recruiting Ottoman Raskolnikovs

Nonetheless, the failure of the British model of spreading prosperity to deliver to anyone beyond a rather narrow stratum of society led to a high level of frustration, especially among those who had undertaken the effort to master the skills of the modern world, but found that their personal situation or their corner of the world did not allow for the individual success that British liberal capitalism seemed to promise. This is where a generation of angry young men that Dostoevsky described as a phenomenon of the new world order came in. These Raskolnikovs were not only well educated, but also frustrated in their efforts to carve out their share of the cake; they were void of moral scruples and ready to legitimize their egoistic actions in the framework

---

[8] Fyodor Dostoevsky, quoted from Hudspith, *Dostoevsky and the Idea of Russianness*, 51.
[9] Borutta, *Antikatholizismus*, 54–56, 102–107.

of the utilitarian logic they had been taught. While many of these frustrated and potentially violent men turned to supposedly time-proven spiritual bases such as religion, the nation, or the race for orientation, these ideological sources were inevitably transformed by adapting them to the nineteenth century and degrading them to counter-discourses to the spread of materialism.[10]

When considering the Eastern Mediterranean in the framework of Dostoevsky's scenario and the accompanying dilemma Mishra describes, one must note both important similarities and differences. What Mishra calls utilitarian materialism obviously corresponds to the European Dream sketched in the opening chapters of this book. Many residents of the port cities believed they could join a world on the move and earn their place among the "cultured nations," as Western rhetoric seemed to indicate. However, their expectations were ultimately frustrated: The standard of living only saw a limited increase; rule of law, an impartial administration, sustainable peace and stability remained unattainable for most. There are several cases of angry young men who were willing to risk their own lives, callously killing or slaughtering others and justifying their acts by some aloof ideological goals. Gavrilo Princip and most especially Enver Pasha are the most famous of those born on Ottoman soil. If one relates their personal history to the partially sophisticated, contradictory, and confusing paradigms that characterized the Eastern Mediterranean port cities as sketched in this book up to this point, it should be clear that it is an unjustified simplification to consider such men country bumpkins who did not understand the ways of the city-dwellers and therefore set out to destroy them. Both the Serb juvenile nationalist from a Hercegovinian village and the Ottoman Minister of War who had grown up in upcountry Macedonia had excelled at their respective schools and could have found their way into the commercial, administrative, or political elitist circles of urban, cosmopolitan society, as many talented migrants from small towns had before.[11] It was rather a deliberate choice in concordance with a zeitgeist current to reject this path and embark on one more akin to angry young men who wished not for a slice of the cake, but to own the whole bakery (or else see it go up in flames).

[10] Mishra, "How to Think about Islamic State."
[11] Kechriotis, "On the Margins of National Historiography."

Ottoman Anti-Westernism: A Practice without a Manifesto

While identifying Ottoman Raskolnikovs is not a problem, when looking for an Ottoman Dostoevsky, one is at a loss. Anti-Westernism as a sentiment certainly existed, but no one on the Eastern Mediterranean shores matched the fundamental radicalism and observant eloquence of the Slavophiles.[12]

In the 1820s, the Austrian advocate of old regime autocracy, Anton Prokesch von Osten, and his French Smyrniote friend Alexandre Blacque had done their best to provide development aid in the tropes and rhetoric of anti-Westernism to counter the threat of a "humanitarian intervention" by the Great Powers in the Greco-Ottoman conflict. French aspirations to end "Oriental despotism" by supporting the Greeks were countered by reminding the France-based readers of the ravages of the Inquisition and recommending Catholic and Protestant missionaries to relocate to South America and leave the Orientals alone.[13] The anonymous letter-writer in the *Courrier de Smyrne*, presumably Prokesch von Osten, claimed the French public wanted to civilize the whole world "à la parisienne," equating liberty with elegant ladies, operas, and promenades. To this end, according to Prokesch, the West was willing to violate all its own rules of justice and humanity.[14] Those who identified the Greek insurrection with the reestablishment of ancient Greek democracy were declared a case for the nuthouse.[15] Criticism of the Ottoman practice of slavery was renounced by evoking the slavery practice on the plantations in the Antillean colonies. By comparison, the *Courrier de Smyrne* stated, Oriental slavery was more like the much revered ancient Hellenic one, another word for domestic servants and concubines.[16] Tactically clever – even though possibly not convincing – were the many disclaimers the *Courrier* would publish when faced with counterattacks. When the Greek president Ioannis Kapodistrias claimed the *Courrier* wanted to create a hostile atmosphere against him in Europe, the paper

---

[12] Aydın, *The Politics of Anti-Westernism in Asia*.
[13] *Courrier de Smyrne*, 15 March 1829.
[14] *Courrier de Smyrne*, 19 April, 7 June 1829.
[15] *Courrier de Smyrne*, 28 Dec. 1828.
[16] *Courrier de Smyrne*, 15 Feb. 1829. See also 19 and 26 April, 7 June 1829 for similar articles.

denied the charge.[17] When accused of being on the payroll of Metternich and Austrian autocratism, the editor wrote that the newspaper embraced French values of freedom.[18] At least Prokesch and his friend and mentor Friedrich von Gentz were privately very much amused that masquerading as Frenchmen and liberals, they could make claim to the very principles they despised, such as freedom of the press and universal human rights, in order to facilitate their propaganda and spread it via Smyrna to France.[19]

And yet, Prokesch von Osten's and Blacque's venomous writings failed to set a pattern for literature in the Ottoman Empire. While there was no lack of writers feeling reservations about the changes happening in their lifetime, most expressed them in a more parochial, defensive style. They failed to produce a true counter-vision of how the world should be organized. Examples from the earlier chapter on the bourgeoisie are typical of Ottoman anti-Westernism: Go to a modern school, but come home before the evening ball; study in Paris to improve your education, but remember to wear your fez and say your prayers.[20] The court and the bureaucracy, after "the apogee of occidentitis" around the mid-nineteenth century had passed, believed that Western technology was useful, but Western morals were corrosive. Such a worldview however did not allow for a more fundamental critique of the West. Figuratively speaking, the Ottoman intellectual answer to their particular predicament was to let "the poisonous seeds of social dissipation and corruption which we euphemistically call European civilization"[21] wreak havoc on the Well-Protected Domains, then send in a cleanup task force, made up of imams, rabbis, and clergymen, to tell the infected Ottoman subjects to forget half of what they had learned. Ottoman anti-Westernism remained intellectually challenged.

The difference becomes most obvious when one compares Ottoman travelogs of journeys to Paris, London, and the World Exhibition to

---

[17] *Courrier de Smyrne*, 4 Oct. 1828. [18] *Courrier de Smyrne*, 15 Feb. 1829.
[19] HHStA, Prokesch-Osten Papers, box 27-1, 38–42: Gentz to Prokesch von Osten, 19 Aug. 1828, and HHStA, Prokesch-Osten Papers, box 27-1, 55–58: Gentz to Prokesch-Osten, 1 Dec. 1828.
[20] See Chapter 17, pp. 267–286. Typical of such a "yes, but" position on Europeanization is the short story by Ahmet Hikmet Müftüoğlu discussed in Mende, "'Europäisierungsmißstände' um 1900."
[21] *Pharos tis Makedonias*, quoted in Anastassiadou, *Salonique*, 174–175; Mazower, *Salonica City of Ghosts*, 251–252.

Dostoevsky's comments. Ahmed Midhat, in his description of an encounter with Russian intellectuals at the Stockholm Orientalist Congress of 1899, tries to formulate a common stance against Western society, but in the end simply reiterates the Ottoman common sense of materialist affirmation versus moral condemnation.[22] When visiting the world exhibition, he does not turn to fundamental critique such as Dostoyevsky's, but sees it as "a Social Darwinist yardstick for measuring Europe's progress and the Ottomans' standing compared to it."[23] The Egyptians at the same exhibition were likewise only disturbed by the depiction of their homeland vis-à-vis the rest of the world.[24] Earlier Ottoman visitors to world fairs had not been any more critical.[25]

Interestingly, Christian-Orthodox authors from the Well-Protected Domains do not do much better at formulating an independent stance vis-à-vis the Western materialist paradigm beyond condemning school balls. This is all the more puzzling as the Eastern churches had a long history of polemics against the West, aimed initially at the Catholic Church's aspiration toward supremacy and later at the plunder and exploitation by Frankish crusaders. Elsewhere, such as with the Serbian-Orthodox Church in the Habsburg Empire, the anti-modern polemics discursively piggybacked onto the older anti-Catholic ones. However, this did not become a dominant trope among Ottoman Christians, nor did they follow the contemporary Russian trend toward anti-Western arguments.[26]

Reverse Orientalism: The Result of a Frustrated Love Affair

Toward the end of the Belle Époque, the Europe-wide feeling of tedium when faced with established customs can occasionally be witnessed. For example, the *Stamboul*'s editorial for New Year 1911, rather than considering the holiday a joyous event or pondering the prospects of progress to be achieved in the coming year, reflects on the mendacity of New Year's greetings and resolutions (ironically paired with a whole page ad by *Maison Baker* for all kinds of gilded household objects –

---

[22] Findley, "An Ottoman Orientalist in Europe," 30–31.   [23] Ibid., 38.
[24] Mitchell, *Colonising Egypt*, chapter 1.   [25] Wagner, *Imagologie der Fremde*.
[26] Aleksov, "History Taught Us," 31–46; Daskalov, "Pro- und antiwestliche Diskurse in Bulgarien," 77–86; Demacopoulos and Papanikolaou, "Orthodox Naming of the Other," 1–22.

trays, pens, chandeliers, vases – as gifts).[27] But such sparks of a more deeply felt ennui did not develop into a full-fledged critique of the civilization paradigm, even though Oswald Spengler was at the time already busy in Munich writing *The Decline of the West* in an attempt to decenter the triumphant Western master narrative.

Muslim writers such as Halil Halid, Mustafa Kamil, or Abdürreşid İbrahim did declare their disillusionment with the European Dream. However, these declarations all share the tone of a disappointed love affair and desperate plea for the absconding lover to return and for a happy end to the indeterminate promise of happiness for all who would join the world on the move. Some of them, such as Halil Halid and Ahmed Rıza, having spent long years in London or Paris, can even be considered former super-Westernized turned frustrated lovers.[28] When they attempt to formulate an Eastern spirituality as a counter-vision, this often sounds extremely hollow, in essence an incoherent amalgam of primacy of religion, tolerance, and family values. Evoking the glories of the Islamic world was not so much an act of conviction, but an ersatz ideology for these writers, as often they had no habitual attachment to practiced religion, and they chastised other Islamic countries for their lack of modernization.[29] Since their education and interests had been so Occidentocentric, they never cited any Turkish, Arabic, or Persian writers older than Namık Kemal in their writings, with the exception of the Koran or some *hadith*s.[30] Their stance did not develop into a counter-utopia such as Lev Tolstoj's or Mohandas K. Gandhi's practices of anti-modernity. Erdal Kaynar has therefore named this type or writings "reverse Orientalism" (*orientalisme à l'envers*) rather than (anti-)Occidentalism.[31]

The Eastern Mediterranean world, with its close ties and fairly rapid access to the rest of Europe, its uncertain promise that it could one day be among the winners of the world order, and its intimate intertwining of what was local and what was overseas European, failed to come up with a convincing intellectual response once it became increasingly obvious that it was not wanted among the exclusive club of triumphant

---

[27] *Stamboul*, 1 Jan. 1911.   [28] Kaynar, "Les jeunes Turques et l'Occident," 31.
[29] Aydın, *The Politics of Anti-Westernism in Asia*, 60–89. Selim Deringil even sees educated and patriotic Ottomans in a continuous "desperate struggle not to become 'Orientalized'" throughout the long nineteenth century; Deringil, "The West within and the West Without," 118–120.
[30] Kaynar, "Les jeunes Turques et l'Occident," 33.   [31] Ibid., 47.

Europe. Despite this intellectual inability, it would be wrong to believe that the Eastern Mediterranean world did not come up with a practical reply to its growing marginalization. In fact, these replies, while devoid of a distinctive manifesto or an impressive toll in bloodshed, either one of which would have made a noticeable impact in traditional historiography, were all the more effective, and possibly more developed in the Ottoman Empire than among Russian, Chinese, or Indian dissidents to the nineteenth-century world order. The answer inhabitants of the Eastern Mediterranean shores developed lay in subverting or one might say deconstructing Western superiority. Perhaps the very intimacy and lack of distance to the rest of Europe prevalent in the major port cities enabled those discontent with Western and Central European dominance to identify the weak spots in the materialist and imperialist self-image and utilize them. In this, the Ottoman population in its way was much more successful than the Chinese Boxers or the Russian Slavophiles. But to understand the Ottoman subversive practice, we must first answer the question of what violent challenges there were to the port city socioeconomic order and why they did not climax in a Boxer Rebellion.

21 | *Economies of Violence and Challenges to the Thalassocentric Order*

While intellectual challenges to the socioeconomic order oriented toward the overseas European neighbor states were limited in their scope, challenges through open violence were at almost all times present, but mostly remained of a scope that could not seriously threaten, but only curtail it. The spatial dimension is rather obvious. As has become apparent from earlier chapters, many of the worldviews, practices, and fashions described here did not reach far beyond the large cities and the Mediterranean shores. Without standing on deck of a steamer, aloof and apart from Ottoman soil, it was difficult to maintain the dichotomizing, distancing perspective of the West. The landlocked cities of the Well-Protected Domains also vied for well-paved, gas-illuminated, broad, and regular streets. However, without a quay as main point of arrival and first impression of the cities, it was not viable for these towns to transform themselves into Potemkin villages of modernity, as the Mediterranean port cities successfully had. A stranger approaching the city on horseback, in a carriage, or even by train could still survey the city's less glamorous sights in the outskirts. Attitudes differed too: A *Homburg* hat, an inconspicuous object on the quays of Smyrna, was considered scandalous in Ezine; and beer never became too popular in the souks and bazaars of Aleppo or Malatya. It is in the logic of a liberal capitalist order that it spreads unequally and the degree of participation in it is subject to large differences according to class, locality, and ethnicity. Unlike a statist order, a liberal order cherry-picks what can be easily adapted to its uses and disregards the rest as well as the damage such an imbalance can cause. But in the case of the socioeconomic order of the Eastern Mediterranean port cities, this unbalance had serious repercussions both in the short and in the long run.

Adapting the world system approach to a more differentiated state of research, Cem Emrence has stated that the Ottoman Empire of the nineteenth century was drifting apart. While the coastal development was determined by "market-based contention," it was "patrimonial politics, and discourses of autonomy and religious revival that operated as the ideological and material bases of claim-making in the Ottoman Middle East."[1] Compelling as such a narrative seems, late Ottoman social and ideological topography was more complex, overlapping, and contradictory.

When thinking of their wider surroundings, it would be a mistake to conceive of the port cities as isolated pockets situated adjacent to a hostile no-go hinterland. In fact, the maritime trade and interaction with overseas necessitated an intense exchange with the wider hinterland for the products sought on the international markets and these exchanges were by no means limited to terse and superficial market transactions. Raisins, figs, cotton, opium, tobacco, carpets – most of the preferred export goods of Western Anatolia and the Balkans were produced dozens or hundreds of kilometers from the respective ports and necessitated journeys by businessmen, caravan guides, and laborers. The cities' business districts, the markets, and ports and train stations became meeting places for the heterogeneous population of the wider region, and townspeople likewise traveled to the hinterland. Such relations were not business only, but were accompanied by amicable relationships, mutual support, and hospitality.[2] But nonetheless security regimes were not the same in the well-policed cities and in the countryside. And while the Thalassocentric order was hegemonic in the port cities, it was highly contested in the countryside, having to compete not only with the two alternatives mentioned by Emrence, but most especially with the "economies of violence."[3]

Crime, Fear, and the Hinterland

In the mid- to upper-class Saloniquenos', Smyrniotes', and Stambouliotes' mind frame and practice, not only business, but also the city's

---

[1] Emrence, *Remapping the Ottoman Middle East*.
[2] Sciaky, *Farewell to Ottoman Salonica*, 34–42.
[3] For early modern economies of banditry see Esmer, "Economies of Violence." This is not the place to deliberate whether or to what degree the scenarios described for the early nineteenth century apply to the times shortly before World War I. Suffice it to say that banditry was still widely practiced and partly supported by the rural population. For a brief discussion of late Ottoman banditry-cum-national liberation insurgencies in Macedonia, see Mazower, *Salonica City of Ghosts*, 260–264.

pleasures were complemented by those of the surrounding countryside. The inhabitants of the capital flocked to the Sweet Waters of Europe and Asia, while the Macedonian urban residents would climb the Hortaç (Hortiatis) and for Western Anatolian city dwellers, the ancient aqueducts of St. Anne's Valley (Yeşildere) were preferred picnic spots. Those more affluent would have summer houses in Constantinople's Bosporus fishing villages or on the Princes' Isles, or in Smyrna's Buca or Burnabad villages and live there for up to seven months a year, depending on the weather. But while the capital's surroundings seem to have been fairly safe to wander about in, Western Anatolia and more so strife-torn Macedonia and Thrace were far from well-protected.

City-dwellers and non-Ottoman subjects were repeatedly victims of brigand violence and kidnapping, perhaps much more rarely than up-country residents, but nonetheless, such incidents would be cause for widespread alarm.[4] A few random incidences from consular files and newspapers illustrate this. The Austrian subject Stefan Buck, for example, was robbed and killed near Karasuli (Polykastro) not far from Salonica in 1894.[5] Assaults on construction workers of the Uşak extension of the Smyrna-Kasaba Railway Line allegedly by Kurdish gangs were so numerous and violent – the consulate cites thirty-eight cases in eight months of robbery, injury, and murder – that the Habsburg Embassy urged the Ottoman army to take action.[6] The Austrian newspaper correspondent Milan Kohn Davidović was abducted, held, and mistreated by Albanian brigands on a journey from Salonica to Prizren in 1901, until the governor of Üsküp paid the ransom.[7]

The country estates of the rich Levantines and other upper-class city-dwellers, symbols of their power and influence, were far from safe havens. The Frenchman Alfons Mille was abducted from his seaside house two hours from downtown Smyrna in 1901. He was later freed against a ransom of 1,500 Turkish Pounds provided by the *vali*.[8] On the night of March 26, 1907, Robert Abbott, son of the rich and influential merchant family of British descent and nationality and Greek-Orthodox denomination native to Salonica for over a century,

---

[4] HHStA PA XXXVIII 235: Montlong to Haymerle, Sal. 24 Feb. 1880.
[5] HHStA Adm. Reg. F 52 – 105: Räuber: Clara Buck.
[6] HHStA BK Kpl 93: Smyrna Consulate General to Calice, Smyrna 19 July 1896.
[7] HHStA Adm. Reg. F 52 – 105: Räuber: Braun (Embassy) to Goluchowski (Foreign Ministry), (?) 1901.
[8] HHStA Adm. Reg. F 52 – 105: Räuber: 17 Jan. 1901.

returned to the family estate in Campagna. After passing the main gate, he was attacked, but defended himself, until more assailants entered the gate and managed to drug him and carry him off. He remained locked away in a village house, mostly blindfolded, for over thirty days until a large ransom was paid. The family believed that the estate's gardener had informed the gang of Robert's movements. A trial against the alleged kidnappers in winter of the same year saw the majority of the eighteen accused sentenced to prison between 7 and 18 years.[9] Not always did such kidnappings end without loss of life: To free the Salonician clothier Simon Simotta, abducted in 1900 during his summer stay near Klisura, Monastir, several *zaptiye* and brigands died in a firefight, before a ransom was finally paid. Simotta's sister, a female servant, and a servant's child had already been killed by the Greek, Bulgarian, and Wallachian brigands during the initial kidnapping.[10]

Arbitrary Conduct of Provincial Authorities

Following the Young Turk Revolution, the authorities were less scrupulous in their pursuit of crimes committed against foreigners in the countryside. When the visiting German engineer Edwart Richter set out in May 1911 to climb the Thessalian Olympus, a gang of Greeks abducted him and killed his escort of two Ottoman gendarmes. The Porte in its correspondence with the German Embassy pointed out that the Ottoman state's obligation to pay ransom for abducted foreigners was an obsolete element of the capitulations they did not feel obliged to fulfill. In the end, the consulate negotiated the exchange and the victim's family and the embassy provided the sum.[11]

The case would lead one to believe in the "good old times" under Abdülhamid, versus the misanthropic practice thereafter. However, this was by far not the first time the Ottoman authorities, at least at the provincial level, had been negligent or even detrimental to the liberation of a hostage. Already in 1896, the case of Dimitriaki Zlatko had given reason for serious charges by the Habsburg consulates. Initially, internal consular papers had blamed the victim himself: His

---

[9] *Examiner*, 18 June 1907; *Journal de Salonique*, 21, 25 Nov., 9 Dec. 1907.
[10] HHStA Adm. Reg. F 52 – 105: Räuber.
[11] Fuhrmann, *Traum vom deutschen Orient*, 374, 375.

claim to Austrian nationality seemed outdated, as it was based on a document from 1861. And what was an Austrian subject doing in such a dangerous region as Serres anyway? But more informed consular staff knew him to be the brother of the Habsburg consul there. According to the diplomatic claims, the release of the abducted Dimitriaki Zlatko had already been negotiated, most of the ransom installments paid by the *vali*, and the hostages (besides Zlatko there were another Christian and five Muslims) and brigands were together dancing a *horo* to celebrate the peaceful resolution of the kidnapping, when a company of soldiers attacked, killing the outlaws, but forfeiting the lives of the hostages as well. A second interpretation gave an even harsher account. Supposedly the soldiers had let the bandits run off, shot dead the two Christians despite their pleas in Turkish, and liberated only the Muslim hostages.[12]

Serres had a long established bad reputation with the Austro-Hungarian consulates. The Habsburg subject Anton Parihsi, a locally well-established resident, had been beaten for having entered the promenade on a Sunday, when it was purportedly reserved for women of all religions. According to the Salonica consulate, there had been no Muslim women present and the non-Muslim women ran when the two *zaptiye* violently protected their honor. However, following this 1877 incident, the *mutasarrıf* (district administrator) promised to detain the two culprits for as long as the consul saw fit. The Consul General of Salonica, Chiari, found this a good solution, as he deemed the local *kadı* too biased to speak a just sentence and the lack of Muslim witnesses would have posed a problem.[13]

While the 1877 incident presented a mixed picture of a provincial administration from the consular point of view – abusive policemen, an obliging administrator, an unpredictable judge – in some cases, the Ottoman authorities, not accustomed to the checks and balances the consuls provided in the maritime cities, demonstrated their rejection of Western influence outright. A spectacular example was the 1891 Church Bell Affair. In Üsküp, a few hours' train ride from Salonica, the Catholic Church had replaced its old bell with a new one. However, the police chief Yusuf Effendi, a convert; former

---

[12] HHStA BK Kpl 93: "Räuberanfälle," Demeter (Dimitraki) Zlatko in Serres.
[13] HHStA Adm. Reg. F 52 – 105: Mißhandlungen, Chiari (CG Sal) to Andrassy, Salonica 23 July, 11 Aug. 1877.

Habsburg subject named Gladić; and a fugitive from Austro-Hungarian justice, entered the church, destroyed the children's schoolbooks, and had the bell demolished to the jeers of a gathered crowd. Following the intervention of the Habsburg Embassy, the chief of police and the *vali* who had failed to intervene were transferred.[14] Such a demonstrative act would hardly have been thinkable in the large Mediterranean port cities.

Can we consider such practices a challenge to the port city socioeconomic order? Yes and no. If we look to the kidnappings and ransom bargaining, it is more fitting to consider them an attempt to be included in the materialist order, just as the frustrated modernists' "reverse Orientalism." Richter's kidnappers for example bartered vigorously for the ransom to include a gold watch for ever member of the gang, and such modern status symbols were common as part of the ransom demands.[15] We can therefore, without overromanticizing the practice, speak of a rural group asking for its share of the pie. These agents had been marginalized all the more since transport had shifted toward the sea and railways and since the Porte clamped down on the *zeybek* practice of demanding "coffee money" on the highways, an eighteenth-century custom somewhere in between security services and extortion.[16]

And yet, there is another dimension to the provincial violence. If we regard its excesses – the cruelty and infliction of terror, for example during the attacks on the railway construction workers by the brigands near Uşak or the slaughter of members of Simotta's household – it must be stated that these go beyond the "materialist" or economic necessity of brigands to make their victims comply with their orders or convince ransom payers that the threat to a hostage's life is genuine. Taken together with the cases of misconduct by provincial authorities, these must be seen as acts to limit the influence of and deter strangers from the authorities' or brigands' sphere of influence. One should not automatically surmise that such actions were by necessity directed against foreign subjects: The Kurdish brigands of Uşak also attacked Ottoman and Muslim workers with impunity. But whether strictly anti-Western or more generally xenophobic, such actions seriously

---

[14] HHStA PA XII Türkei 269, Liasse XVI (Glockenaffäre).
[15] Mazower, *Salonica City of Ghosts*, 261.
[16] Kontente, *Smyrne et l'Occident*, 400–402.

limited the sphere of influence of the Thalassocentric order: Goods could not move freely outside of certain corridors, and wealthy people could not reap the fruits of their capital to their full satisfaction. However, such circumstances delimitated the impact of the port city way of life, without seriously challenging it. The failure of violent challenges to the port city order becomes more evident when scrutinizing the Eastern Mediterranean's mini-Boxer Rebellion.

22 | The Anti-Western Rebellion on the Eve of the Belle Époque

In retrospect, historians following world system or other materialist approaches to history have wondered how a few thousand consuls, merchants, trade agents, advisors, officials, and workers plus the occasional gunboat could install an order so clearly detrimental to the objective material interests of the vast majority of Ottoman subjects.[1] They have searched for an Ottoman version of the Herero War, the Indian Mutiny, or the Boxer Rebellion, but have found only fairly isolated incidents of this sort. The reason for this is partially to be found in the question of European identity vis-à-vis the Eastern Mediterranean. A brief exemplary look at the most spectacular anti-European event in this area will show why no broad and stable anti-imperial movement could arise here.

Salonica, Saint George's Day 1876: An Attack against "Europe"

The year 1876 saw a heightened tension in all of the Ottoman Balkans due to the uprisings in Bosnia and Eastern Rumelia. The foreshadowing of Russian intervention and the danger of British or Austrian military action against the Ottomans led to a political climate in which many Ottoman Muslims were convinced that all Ottoman non-Muslims and the Great Powers were conspiring to bring the empire to an end. This friction led to several incidents of assault on and even murder of European foreigners, both in the countryside and the cities. The Salonica resident Abraham Fernandez of Austrian nationality for example, had sheltered a Jew from his three Muslim assailants and was gravely attacked by them in turn.[2] The Asseo family, Salonica locals of

---

[1] Quataert, *Social Disintegration and Popular Resistance*, 148–149.
[2] HHStA Adm. Reg. F 52 – 105: Embassy to Andrassy, Constantinople 1 Dec. 1876.

a higher social standing with Austrian passports, also became victims of such violence. A twenty-year-old member of the family had intervened when several policemen were beating a Sephardic moneychanger in the bazaar simply for not having the small change they had demanded. To punish the young Asseo's chutzpa the officials then assaulted him. When he claimed capitulatory immunity as an Austrian, the policemen reacted by increasing their violence. He had thus confirmed the cliché of the non-Muslim – Great Power conspiracy against the Ottoman order.[3] Anti–Great Power protest mixed with interreligious strife: In Kavalla, the Habsburg subject Elias Schelasi was beaten up by three *softa*s (theology students). While the assailants were arrested, so was Schelasi on the charge of blasphemy. Under the circumstances, the local vice-consul believed it best to settle for reconciliation and the release of all four, as he feared a mass reaction by other *softa*s.[4] The situation was worse in turbulent Bosnia: The mason and Austrian subject Ivan Bakotić, returning to his native Split after constructing a house for a local Muslim in Ottoman Banja Luka, was even shot dead in the countryside.[5] However, on Saint George's Day, fighting between Orthodox Christians and Muslims broke out in downtown Salonica, and the next day saw the lynching of the French Consul and German Honorary Consul.

This attack had targeted "Europe" as a community of all Christians. In fact, this is how the Muslim mob had seen the consuls' role in the preceding days. A Christian girl seeking to be converted in order to marry her Muslim fiancé had been seized and abducted by a Christian-Orthodox crowd in a public skirmish with Muslims at the train station, where the girl had arrived from up-country Macedonia. Periklis Hadjilazaros, both member of one of the wealthiest local families and consul of the USA, had supported the Christians by sheltering the abducted girl. The German and French Consuls, although not as proactively involved in the dispute, resembled their American colleague in several ways. They were representatives of Western powers and at least the German officeholder, Henri Abbott, was Greek-Orthodox

---

[3] Despite the arrival of several Asseo family members all present in the bazaar, they could not stop the aggressive officials; HHStA Adm. Reg. F 52 – 105: Räuber, Misshandlungen, passim.
[4] HHStA Adm. Reg. F 52 – 105: Mißhandlungen, Kavalla 1876.
[5] HHStA Adm. Reg. F 52 – 105: Graf Zichy, Mord an Johann Bakotic, Constantinople 15 Feb. 1876.

and a member of the aforementioned rich merchant family. When, the next day, the two made their way to the governor to demand more security for the Christians, they were seized and murdered in the courtyard of the Saatli Cami adjacent to the Konak.

The Frangomahalla's shops had closed and the quarter's inhabitants hid in their houses. The Austrian Vice-Consul Friedrich Schwan recalls that especially young Albanian men who had originally come to town for market business now occupied the streets of the Frangomahalla and were perceived as a mortal threat. The consulate itself prepared for its defense with the inadequate handful of weapons its employees could gather. Later, ten Ottoman soldiers were posted to defend the consulate, but Schwan believed they could not or would not have withstood the gangs gathered in the streets should these have attacked.[6] The anti-Western and anti-Christian riots found a quick end when gunboats from practically all major European states reached Salonica. They refrained from shelling the city after several high officials had been removed from office, indemnities were paid, an honorary funeral for the Consuls had taken place, and a number of wantonly chosen riot "ringleaders" had been hung.[7]

Beyond the immediate effect of striking fear into foreigners in the Levant for several months,[8] this event failed to erode European superiority. Instead, it strengthened it. The Great Powers were forced to demonstrate that they actually had the power and resolve to destroy Salonica, and gunboats showed an increased presence for years to come; Germany and France had to overcome their hostilities and find a common line toward the Porte; and the foreigners were driven to identify with the local Greeks, which in others cases they often did not. Thus, violent protest, when directed against either the indigenous Christians or the resident Western foreigners, caused the two sides to move together and see themselves as a community.

Anti-Western Riots Followed by Occupation: The Case of Alexandria

The prospects of grassroots violent resolution to European domination must have diminished even further following the developments of the

---

[6] Schwan, *Erinnerungen eines Konsuls*, 54–63.
[7] Anastassiadou, *Salonique 1830–1912*, 395–398.
[8] Fuhrmann, *Traum vom deutschen Orient*, 369–371.

subsequent years. Following the Russo-Turkish War, during which the Russian army had with relative ease reached the Constantinople suburbs, and its settlement in one of those suburbs at San Stefano (Agios Stefanos, now Yeşilköy), Salonica would have been reduced to a city immediately bordering Greater Bulgaria, isolated from the rest of the Ottoman Empire and dependent on the new principality. Only the return to disunity among the Great Powers and the Treaty of Berlin saved it from these prospects. Moreover, the fate of another Eastern Mediterranean port city that dared to conjure up the wrath of the Great Powers could give an indication of what they were capable of. When on June 11, 1882 a dispute over the fare between an Arab coachman and the Maltese passenger outside the shady cafés of Alexandria's port during which the coachman was killed led an already tense situation to escalate, riots broke out that resulted in the deaths of hundreds. Although order was restored by Egyptian forces, the British Navy laid the city to waste, including the modern waterfront and its own consulate, and caused the death of thousands.[9]

Once again, the threat of an anti-Christian, anti-Western mob had prompted non-Muslims, foreigners, and Great Powers to act in unison, despite the large differences and animosities between them. Only a year before, Alexandria's Jews had been the object of Greek violence due to a charge of blood libel and the British and French consulates had to shelter them. Under the common threat of an Arab Egyptian nationalist mob however, a Maltese, a native of the Eastern Mediterranean who only because of the strategic importance of his native islands for the British Empire profited from the capitulations and who under different circumstances was on the lowest rank of the pecking order both for the British and the wider port city society, had received an unprecedented (although for reasons of Great Power economic interest not unwelcome) solidarity.[10]

Besides these two ports, Jeddah in the Hedjaz was known for violent attacks on consular staff in 1846, 1851, 1856, 1858, and finally 1895. However it lay far away from the Mediterranean commercial port cities, was known mainly as the port for Hadj pilgrims, and therefore

---

[9] Mansel, *Levant*, 114–126; Mitchell, *Colonising Egypt*, 128–132.
[10] Berchthold, *Recht und Gerechtigkeit*; Clancy-Smith, *Mediterraneans*; Smith, *Colonial Memory and Postcolonial Europe*.

did not figure prominently in the mental map of the Eastern Mediterranean port city residents.[11]

Propaganda of the Deed: The Salonica Boatmen Crying for Intervention

Of the incidents following the Saint George's Day riots and the fall of Alexandria to British occupation, one case of collective violence in particular stands out, as it especially targeted symbols of European-style modernity. In 1903, the *Gemidži* (Boatmen), a radical faction of the Inner Macedonian Revolutionary Organization, an organization claiming to represent the suppressed Slavic (or Bulgarian) population of the Central Balkan provinces, targeted Salonica. They followed a course of action that had become popular among radical movements across the continent and beyond, not only among anarchists, but also Russian social and other national revolutionaries.[12] The Boatmen's direct actions against institutions and persons representing state oppression were to function as propaganda of the deed sparking off more acts of liberation violence. In following this path, they demonstrated the disrespect for life so typical of the angry young Raskolnikovs of the early twentieth century: The lives they were willing to forfeit included not only the intended and coincidental victims and their own, but also those of local Bulgarians who would invariably suffer the retaliation by police, soldiers, and the mob, as the more senior and cautious IMRO members warned them.

The Boatmen began by detonating a bomb aboard a French passenger steamship as it left the port (but in a manner that allowed the passengers to escape). The following night, they tried but failed to blow up the incoming train from Constantinople; blew up the pipe from the local gas factory, thus extinguishing all street lights; blew up the Ottoman Bank and the adjacent German Club; threw several handmade bombs at other targets, such as the German school, the Ottoman Post Office, the hotels Colombo and d'Angleterre, and the Brasserie Noubo on or near the quays. While some of these targets were of practical advantage, it seems the overall strategy of the Boatmen was

---

[11] Freitag, *History of Jeddah*, 61–64, 72.
[12] Lemmes, "Der anarchistische Terrorismus."

to show to the Saloniquenos how quickly their city could be stripped of its modernity.[13]

While the message to their fellow Ottoman subjects was that the Boatmen had the capacity in modern parlance to "bomb them back to the stone age," the message to the Great Powers was a different one. Attacks within the city were rather indiscriminate and resulted in deaths of foreigners among others, but the more measured attack on the *Guadalquivir* steamer was calculated to be a strong enough reminder that the European neighbor states could not ignore the fate of Slavic Macedonians, while a more deadly explosion would have forced the Great Powers to take a stance against IMRO. The Boatmen were thus urging the interested imperialist parties to once again take a proactive stance in spreading their so-called values in the Ottoman sphere and no longer sit aside, as they had resolved to do during the anti-Armenian massacres in Constantinople in 1895.[14] This was possibly a well-calculated decision, as an intervention into the world that connected the overseas European states with the Ottoman Empire could not be as easily ignored as the killing of Armenians in Constantinople's streets, let alone the massacres during the suppression of mainstream IMRO's later uprising in remote Ilinden.

Violence and the Embeddedness of the European Paradigm

Europe, all appearances to the contrary, was not a detached, omnipotent Other onto whom protest could easily be projected. Europe also lay within the Ottoman Empire, and the renegotiation of who was within and who was without on a day-to-day basis was important for the internal power struggle. Europeanness was a vital resource of symbolic capital. Only very few groups in the inner-Ottoman struggle for social supremacy would dare to renounce it outright. The adherents

---

[13] *Makedonija i Trakija v borba za svoboda*, 189, 190: Šopov (commercial agent) to Gešov (envoy), Salonica 17 April 1903 (Julian calendar). As one eyewitness put it, "Concessions, industrial enterprises, gold: that was the fabric of that much vaunted civilization of the West, and at that very core they would hit savagely." (Sciaky, *Farewell to Ottoman Salonica*, 74). Unfortunately the memoirs of the surviving Gemidži activist Pavel Šatev do not make their particular philosophy clear; Šatev, *V Makedonija pod robstvo*.

[14] Sefer, "Class Formation on the Modern Waterfront"; Riedler, "Armenian Labour Migration"; Quataert, *Social Disintegration and Popular Resistance*, 97–99.

of the *Tanzimat* reforms tried to prove their Europeanness by their exemplary adaptation of modern principles of administration; the citizens of Smyrna flaunted their new part of town built imitating French street grids; Greek nationalists tried to stress their affinity to ancient civilization, while Bulgarian separatists appealed to Christian solidarity. Gaining symbolic capital by being accepted as European also meant proving that one's neighbor or rival – the Old Turks, the Muslims, the unenlightened peasantry, etc. – were not qualified to be labeled in this way. Thus, due to this competition to reap the benefits of recognition as European, people who actually interacted regularly or lived in close proximity to each other found themselves pouring derogatory rhetoric on each other's collectivities as if they were from different continents, separated by unsurpassable chasms of difference. This situation, which to a certain point reproduced itself in the 1990s, has aptly been termed "nesting orientalisms."[15]

While the appeal of possibly attaining superior status for one's particular collectivity and the danger of uniting one's potential enemies into a coalition prevented the formation of large and stable anti-European alliances, the uncertain macroeconomic and macro-political situation favored individual local claims to Europeanness, and these claims managed to adapt legitimizing strategies that lent them a certain degree of credibility in Western eyes. Nonetheless, especially toward the end of the long nineteenth century, the Great Powers certainly attempted to install in the Ottoman sphere the more hypertrophic and exclusivist meanings "Europe" had acquired in outright colonial settings, and to distance themselves more strongly from local society. Much of the aforementioned travel literature attests to this effort. Despite the foreigners' partial success, local actors enviously countered the Westerners' attempts to set themselves apart from them, realizing that this would detach them from an important source of symbolic capital. But the degree of embeddedness in European discourse prevalent in the Ottoman Empire – while amounting to a weakness and disadvantage for rebelling against the West outright – for creating an Ottoman Boxer Rebellion, proved advantageous in other ways.

---

[15] Bakić-Hayden, "Nesting Orientalisms"; Bakić-Hayden and Hayden, "Orientalist Variations on the Theme 'Balkans'"; Müller, *Staatsbürger auf Widerruf*.

23 Deconstructing the European Female

It is in this context that strategies to undermine European superiority other than massive collective violence were far subtler and apparently more effective in the long run. It has been claimed that the analysis of (semi-)colonialism as a set of intentions that met with success or failure, obedience or resistance must be enhanced beyond simple action-reaction scenarios. Actions should also be tested for their spill-over into other, seemingly unrelated arenas as well as for unwanted and unpredicted effects; changes in discursive inclusions and exclusions and shifts in social emphasis from one field to another. The value of such an approach is most obvious in the Eastern Mediterranean space, where almost all of the players from among the Ottoman center, its regional contenders, and the extra-regional intruders fell short of the farfetched plans that they had set for themselves.[1] It is this function – to change what is visible and what becomes invisible in the Ottoman public sphere – that agents usually considered marginal both in the Western and Central European context and around the Eastern Mediterranean came to play a vital role. They were the easy prey, providing a back door to crack Western pretensions of superiority. They were not subject to a centrally planned policy, but to a diffuse practice that because of its success was repeated, copied, and reinforced. It was based on the basic instinct to challenge an enemy by attacking his or her weakest points, and to divide one's opponents rather than to scare them into unifying. In the aforementioned struggle – the imperial powers trying to assert their superiority and the local institutions trying to hinder this – the marginalized subjects of the imperialist centers became important because their very presence could tarnish the glory of the West.

---

[1] Fritz Klein, quoted in Gencer, *Bildungspolitik, Modernisierung und kulturelle Interaktion*, 187–188.

As already discussed in the chapter on the immigrant working-class population, Western and Central European residents of the port cities in general were the designated agents to advertise European civilization. For if the Great Powers tried to impose their notions of exclusivism and superiority in the Ottoman realm, the Westerners who could be seen locally would have to exemplify these qualities. To this extent, the respective European motherlands tried to focus the loyalties of their expatriate communities in the Ottoman lands toward promoting their civilization's purportedly superior culture vis-à-vis the locals; in short they promoted identity politics based on empire. Whether the inauguration of a church or a consulate; the visit of a renowned scholar or an impressive navy ship from the motherland; a rich merchant's or a school's annual ball; hardly any occasion in urban public life was missed to promote this superiority. But what if the lifestyle, profession, and sense of belonging of a noticeable segment of the self-proclaimed "colony" did not exemplify superior qualities, but were a source of disgrace and shame instead?

From Czernowitz to Galata and Beyond

Prostitution in the Levantine context was used to describe a number of different phenomena – from the highly professional, well-off, and well-connected traffickers to the poor and clumsy efforts to follow in their footsteps; from coercion and force to voluntary subjugation to its system, or simply immoral conduct. However, professional international networks played an important role, and Constantinople was at their center. The sex market of the Ottoman capital itself was considerable. The number of prostitutes of Habsburg origin working there is hard to ascertain. The largest crackdown on this group in particular resulted in only nineteen arrests; in 1913 fifteen women were deported, but probably a larger number had been arrested during the crackdown; finally in 1915 ten Austrian human traffickers and pimps were arrested, but apparently by then most "white slavers" of Habsburg origin had adapted a different nationality. Knowing the difficulties involved in such operations though, it is safe to assume that the number was higher. A local Habsburg resident petitioning his consulate to take sterner action in this matter claimed the number of

Austrian and Hungarian women serving Constantinople's sex trade to be as high as 300.[2]

The main place of origin for these women was the Eastern Habsburg provinces of Galicia and Bukovina. Names figuring prominently in the Foreign Ministry's dossiers are both German-Jewish and Slavonic. A much smaller but also prominent group encompasses women from Southern Hungary with predominantly Slavonic names.[3] They originated from families living under conditions of extreme poverty. The road to prostitution could take different forms. Most had already engaged in sex work in Austria. Others had run away from home and, while on the road, had been contacted by human traffickers who proposed prostitution outright or promised employment as waitresses or stage performers. Several routes led to Constantinople. For those who had strayed from home, the initial step was often crossing the border – from Neusatz (Novi Sad/Uj Vidék) to Belgrade, from Transylvania to Romania. For those who had already acquainted a trafficker in the Monarchy, the path often led directly to the steamers leaving Trieste. Once in Constantinople, the greater part of new arrivals was escorted to the local houses in Galata and Pera.[4] While some traffickers served merely as couriers, many operated on their own initiative, were contacted on arrival by intermediates or made their way independently to bars that served as "marketplaces."[5] The brothels were divided according to price range and supposedly beauty between uptown and downtown, Pera and Galata. Women who had not accepted prostitution were tortured here until they submitted. To

---

[2] HHStA Adm. Reg. F 52 – 46: Sicherheit/Prostitution, 4) Türkei: "Menschenfreund," Constantinople 19 Dec. 1896. Constantinople was however exceptional, as sources pertaining to the city far outweigh all other recorded sites of Habsburg subjects practicing prostitution in the Ottoman Empire or its vicinity. However, in Salonica, where the European foreign community was comparatively small and the Jewish community large, Galician and Bukovinian pimps or prostitutes with a Jewish background sometimes managed to integrate inconspicuously into the Jewish community claiming to be refugees from Galicia or Russia and thus went unnoticed by the consulate (HHStA GK Sal 420, Nachlaß Nathan Hermann Ball false Weismann, Israelite Community to Consulate General, Salonica 19 March 1909).

[3] See for example the list of deported prostitutes in HHStA Adm. Reg. F 52 – 46: Sicherheit/Prostitution, 2) 15/23 Dec. 1913.

[4] HHStA Adm. Reg. F 52 – 46: Sicherheit/Prostitution, passim.

[5] HHStA Adm. Reg. F 52 – 46: Sicherheit/Prostitution, 4) *Osmanische Post*, no date (before 28 Dec. 1896).

perpetuate their dependency, they were presented inflated bills for transport and clothes that had to be paid off.[6]

But as mentioned, the role of human trafficking in this city went far beyond serving local demand. Constantinople was an international hub for supplying sex workers. The recruitment for Latin American brothels was negotiated here;[7] at the same time, the Constantinople-based traffickers' reach and business journeys also extended eastward, from the Bosporus to Alexandria and Port Said, and they even supplied Bombay and Calcutta with "white" sex workers.[8] The traffickers and pimps were almost exclusively German Jews from Galicia and Bukovina, mostly men, but also some women.[9]

The predominance of Ashkenazi human traffickers and pimps in Constantinople was believed to have originated during the Crimean War in 1854, when due to the presence of countless soldiers in the city, destitute Russian Jewish former prisoners of war had established the trade, but due to the harsh living conditions in Romania, Russia, and Austria for most Jews, a steady trail of emigrants swelled their ranks.[10]

To a certain degree, these "white slavers" built on an older form of slave trade between the Ottoman core territories and the areas to its north. For centuries, slaves had been "imported" into the Ottoman markets from Ruthenia or other adjacent lands, especially as a result of military campaigns. Documents have shown their names to be predominantly of Slavonic and Christian origin. The most prominent such slave is Roxelana (Hürrem Sultan), who entered Süleyman I's harem and was later raised by him to the status of wife and mother of his heirs, in breach of conventions and purportedly because of his loving devotion to her.

A keen and persistent desire for unfree women from the North seems to have pervaded a considerable number of Ottoman male subjects, both in Süleyman's times and subsequent centuries. Female slaves of

---

[6] HHStA BK Kpl 107: Guido Panfili (Consul) to Embassy, Constantinople 2 Feb. 1911.

[7] HHStA Adm. Reg. F 52 – 46: Sicherheit/Prostitution, passim.

[8] Ringdal, *Love for Sale*, 313–319; Fischer-Tiné, "White Women Degrading Themselves," 163–190; Banerjee, *Dangerous Outcast*, 173–175; Chandravakar, *Imperial Power and Popular Politics*, 195–196.

[9] For a more detailed account of "white slave trade" immigration to Constantinople as seen through the documents of foreign Jewish aid organizations, see Bali, *Devlet'in Yahudileri ve "Öteki" Yahudi*, 323–368.

[10] Bali, *Prostitution*, 19, 20.

mostly Slavic origin, often referred to in court records as fair-haired and with light-colored eyes, seem to have formed a common feature of both demand and supply for Muslim as well as Jewish customers. Rabbinic sources claim that holding such slaves served among other purposes to fulfill their owners' desires for extramarital intercourse.[11]

There is however no sign that nineteenth- and early twentieth-century contemporaries, who were witnesses to the so-called white slave trade of their times, saw the continuity of this human trafficking with the official slave trade of past centuries. The discourses they chose to frame the "white slave trade" were nation, race, as well as empire and Western civilization.

The Changing Policies of the Habsburg Consulates on Prostitution

Originally, the Habsburg consulates' attitude toward Austrian and Hungarian prostitutes abroad was one of "live and let live," inspired by the consular officials' desire not to overburden themselves with interventions into their subjects' lifeworlds. Due to their complacency, but also due to their greater exposure to the clientele concerned, they in part even championed deviant lifestyles. Faced with charges of inaptitude in one newspaper article in 1875, the Alexandria and Cairo consulates responded that no measures could stop the immigration to Egypt of women willingly dedicating themselves to prostitution and that such measures would possibly even be illegal. The immoral lifestyle these women would adhere to there would probably be no different to the one they would have chosen in the Monarchy. The girl reported as kidnapped on a steamer and sold into prostitution in Alexandria in the newspaper article was, according to the consular officials, actually a lively girl from Gorizia ("eine lebenslustige Görzerin"). Having been disgraced there, she had left her hometown with her mother's consent and now lived a life of loose morals, but was in good spirits.[12] When pimps and involuntary prostitutes fell into the hands of the consular authorities, the consulates often avoided long

---

[11] Ben-Naeh, "Blond, Tall, with Honey-Colored Eyes."
[12] HHStA Adm. Reg. F 52 – 46: Sicherheit/Prostitution, 1) GK to Andrássy, Cairo 27 Nov. 1875.

and potentially complicated prosecution by fining the pimps no more than the expenses for the women to travel home.[13]

In 1876, the year of the aforementioned anti-Western riot on Saint George's Day and mounting tensions because of the threat of Great Power intervention, the "white" prostitutes of Constantinople even experienced the outright solidarity of their motherlands' embassies. The Ottoman authorities assumed a law and order policy, trying to clamp down on foreign prostitution. On orders of the Ministry of Justice, the district of Galata was "cleansed" of foreign prostitutes, the rounded up women detained on two ships that were to be used for their deportation. Confronted with the decision whether to turn a blind eye to a direct transgression against the capitulations or whether to champion the civic rights of a marginal group of ill repute, the Great Powers chose the latter. In a concerted action of diplomatic pressure, their embassies forced the Ottoman government to abandon its plans and set the arrested women free.[14]

But such indifference to matters of imperial prestige was not to survive for long. European women forced to engage in sex work outside of the "civilized" world became a major international concern toward the end of the nineteenth century. Although the proportion of this phenomenon to overall prostitution was not very large, and on the spot officials often observed the predominance of voluntary prostitution, several well-financed societies formed to combat it and to push European governments to take action, with success.[15] In Constantinople, the Ashkenazi Jewish community lamented the presence of its coreligionists in the nearby brothels of Galata: "Located on a long strip, in a tightly packed row, those houses are a dark spot that stain the reputation of our German community."[16] It admitted that impoverishment following the deterioration of working conditions at the Tobacco Régie had also caused Ashkenazi girls from local families to take up the trade. The community tried to distance itself from the traffickers by banning them from its synagogues, but the "white slave traders" erected their own place of worship in the middle of the red-light district, at the corner of Alageyik Yokuşu and Zürafa Sokağı.

---

[13] HHStA Adm. Reg. F 52 – 46: Sicherheit/Prostitution, 1) Sax (Consul) to Andrássy, Adrianople 5 Dec. 1878.
[14] Bali, *Prostitution*, 30.
[15] Fischer-Tiné, "White Women Degrading Themselves," 167–171.
[16] Aron Halevi, 3 Jan. 1890, quoted in Bali, *Devlet'in Yahudileri*, 341–342.

Despite protests by the Ashkenazi community, the grand rabbi tolerated this synagogue's existence.[17]

In particular, private pleas by Habsburg subjects living in the city played a vital role in prompting the consulate to take a more proactive role since the beginning of the 1890s. In their petitions, they claimed that the Austrian and Hungarian women were being held against their will. If the consulates did not take action promptly, they would petition the Viennese Foreign Ministry or even the Emperor and claim that the consular employees were corrupt or inept. They would appeal to the sense of imperialist rivalry among the European capitulatory powers:

> I thus had the opportunity to see how an Imperial German dragoman protects and represents his subjects, what kind of appearance, as if he was the owner and ruler of Turkey, and what respect and esteem he was shown by the Turkish court authorities.[18]

Germans also served as an example for prominent figures getting involved in the combat against "white slavery" in Constantinople. In 1896, a local branch of the Union Internationale des Amies de la Jeune Fille was founded under the auspices of the ambassador's wife, Baroness Marschall von Bieberstein. The Union opened a local shelter in İskender Sokağı, catering mostly to destitute female educators and servants from European countries in order to prevent prostitution or immoral behavior. During her visit in 1898, the German Empress Augusta Victoria met with the board of the Union.[19]

So suppressing prostitution became a matter of imperial prestige. Krassay, the Dual Monarchy's consul in Constantinople in the early 1890s, attempted to take more rigorous steps. After securing promises of support from a society under the protection of Lady Rothschild, he convinced the governor general Mecid Bey to aid him in arresting all

---

[17] Bali, *Prostitution*, 29. According to police reports, at the time of its dissolution in 1915, it simply served as a cover for an illegal brothel; ibid., 54, 55.

[18] HHStA Adm. Reg. F 52 – 46: Sicherheit/Prostitution, 4/Eindämmung) Armbruch to MdA, Constantinople 28 March 1891; see also diverse other petitions in the same subfolder.

[19] Radt, *Geschichte der Teutonia*, 130. Although a *Yiddish österreichischer Verein* in Constantinople is mentioned in 1886, it seems not to have combated prostitution, but rather to have collected donations from Austrian Jewish prostitutes and used them for more destitute coreligionists; Bali, *Prostitution*, 18, 19. Of the *Österreichischer Hilfsverein* in Salonica, despite its many influential Jewish members, there is no record of any activities against "white slave trade"; Brunau, *Deutschtum in Mazedonien*.

prostitutes from the Monarchy they could get their hands on. Lacking other facilities, Krassay detained them on an Austrian Lloyd steamer anchored in the port. Hoping to free them from any pressure by the pimps this way, he offered them material support while reintegrating into society. However, all but one refused. They did not trust the support to open long-term perspectives for them, believed it impossible and undesirable to work in other professions, and stated that if forcibly sent home, they would return to Constantinople at first chance. They also claimed to have no home in the Monarchy; they had either no relatives or none they wished to return to, fearing shame and contempt, and supposedly could not describe their places of origin accurately. They lauded the Constantinople brothels as a place where they were materially better off, socially integrated, and protected.

Krassay finally sent only six of them to Trieste, and restricted himself to making more low-level offers, which however did not prove much more fruitful.[20] The consulate basically limited its interventions to helping women who explicitly asked for help. But even this proved difficult, because the pimps discovered faked letters by prostitutes (or their mothers) asking for release to be a means to rid themselves of their competition.

The authorities in the Monarchy abandoned their efforts even more after receiving Sara Friedmann's petition. It is the most extensive complaint against repatriation that has survived in the Austrian State Archives and an exceptional source about the life world of a subject of human trafficking from the Habsburg to the Ottoman Empire. She was seized in a Constantinople brothel and taken by force to the Austro-Hungarian consulate in Pera in December 1895. To secure her own release she showed her Ottoman papers under the name of "Sury Fischel." Her Austrian nationality had actually expired, so the Ottoman police at first declined to turn Sara over to the Habsburg Consul, and intended to release her. In response, the embassy exacted political pressure, and when she was delivered to the Austro-Hungarian authorities, Friedmann railed at an astonished consul and insisted upon her release. A letter, apparently written in her name to her mother complaining about ill-treatment that had caused the consulate to take

---

[20] HHStA Adm. Reg. F 52 – 46: Sicherheit/Prostitution, 4/Eindämmung) Krassay to Embassy, Constantinople 25 Sept. 1891; Krassay to Lemberg Police, Constantinople 29 March 1890.

action, was a fake, she claimed. Subsequently, the consul believed her, but since she was still a minor, the wishes of her mother to have her repatriated were given precedence, and she was extradited to Cieszanów, where she sought out the county officials and eloquently gave testimony to her refusal to renew her loyalty to the Dual Monarchy. The statement in Polish was subsequently translated into German and sent to the Ministry of the Interior.

Sara Friedmann was raised by a widow burdened with six young children. Six years earlier, Sara had left home to work as a prostitute in various small towns in Galicia. One day N. Goldstaub approached her and offered employment in Constantinople. She followed him there of her own volition, and was turned over to Moishe Gottmann. Friedmann considered her life with Gottmann luxurious in contrast to the misery she had known when living with her mother. She received good clothes and her own money. The trafficker Goldstaub, not content with his initial payment, continuously pressured her for more money and when refused, sent a forged letter to Sara's mother begging for her liberation. Friedmann ended her testimony by declaring that she would at the first opportunity leave Galicia to take up her employment in Constantinople again.[21] Cases like Friedmann's, liberating a woman from the impositions of pimps and the police – to then discover that she did not desire her liberty – made the consulate officials directly concerned with such cases despair, "The tales of slavery and the dark cellar belong to the realm of legends."[22]

Krassay's failure and Friedmann's statement combined to teach the concerned authorities a bitter lesson about the Dual Monarchy's failure to meet the promises of empire. Austria had annexed Galicia and Bukovina in the 1770s, claiming to end Polish anarchy in the former and Turkish despotism in the latter. While in the beginning some initiatives had been started to integrate these Eastern outposts by replacing Polish aristocratic rule with centralized administration and unification, Vienna remained undecided as to whether to see Galicia as a province on a par with the others, as a backwater to be exploited by the central regions of the Monarchy, or as a temporary protectorate.[23] But through the Constantinople affair they learned that more than

---

[21] HHStA Adm. Reg. F 52 – 46: Min. of Interior to Min. of the House, Vienna, 29 March 1896, ff.
[22] Ibid.   [23] Maner, "Zum Problem der Kolonisierung Galiziens," 153–154.

100 years later, some of the locals still shared with the Viennese neither a language, nor a sense of geography, let alone reverence for the monarch. The limited degree of home rule in these provinces after 1868 only confounded local grievances with nationalisms.[24] The living conditions in these forgotten outposts remained so miserable that some women preferred indentured sex work in the Orient.

The Habsburg Predicament and Ottoman Reactions

The Austro-Hungarian predicament did not escape the attention of the general population of Constantinople or the authorities. Samuel Cohen, sent to Constantinople in 1914 by the Jewish Association for the Protection of Girls and Women, felt that the city's Muslim men embraced double moral standards. While being outright protective of their own community's women, they did not feel any inhibitions to tolerate or make use of the Austrian prostitutes' services, because these women were governed by foreign laws and religious codes.[25]

The prostitutes provided a convenient field to challenge claims to European superiority on the grounds of gender. The popular assumption that Muslim and Christian Orthodox societies are more restrictive on sexuality per se than Western Christianity does not hold true, as historical studies on particular periods and milieus have shown.[26] However, controlling sexuality took on an important role in the context of colonial and semi-colonial struggles for hegemony. The subjugation of women's sexuality metaphorically represented the subjugation of their country. Restrictions on women's presence in the public sphere were in many cases enforced by local communities as a reaction to nineteenth-century European expansionism and justified with recourse to reputed indigenous morals.[27] As the restriction of women's sexual availability fell under the family's right to privacy, the "public" women, whose sexuality could not be controlled through these channels, became a particular topic of debate. This concerned both sides involved: protecting the public women of one's own collectivity from foreign invaders,[28] but also protecting the women originating from the wannabe colonial rulers' motherland from the hands of

---

[24] Ibid.   [25] Samuel Cohen quoted in Bali, *Devlet'in Yahudileri*, 336–337.
[26] Rogan (ed.), *Outside In*.   [27] Yeğenoğlu, *Colonial Fantasies*, 39–67.
[28] Mehmed Ali's order in 1834 to ban prostitution from Lower Egypt must be read in this light: "prostitutes bore the brunt of hostility that was directed not

the colonial subjects. If Austria's and Hungary's women were not impeccable but could be bought and sold in the streets of Constantinople and were thus subject to the rules of free trade that supplied any local holding the necessary cash with European knives, pocket watches, and bicycles, their men had symbolically lost their potency to govern over Constantinople affairs. It was of no consequence for this scenario that the women concerned usually did not originate from the Monarchy's core regions based around Vienna and Budapest, but from its peripheral population – Serbs from Bačka, Jews and Poles from Galicia –[29] or that the Dual Monarchy had adopted a policy of regulation rather than prohibition toward its internal prostitution.[30] Habsburg subjects as a whole had to be objects of respect in the Ottoman sphere if the Monarchy was to maintain its stakes in the Eastern Question.

The increased visibility of indecent European women led to generalizations about Western decadence. Women from Germany, Austria, France, Switzerland, etc. played a vital role in education in the Ottoman Empire. Institutions were in danger of losing their prestige if they came to be associated with prostitution, as was the case in 1895 when one of the charges of the Prussian Deaconesses in Smyrna was found to be working in a local brothel.[31] But more importantly, West European women staffed the more prestigious schools, whether as nuns, deaconesses, or secular teachers. If their morality came to be doubted, the institutions themselves were affected.

The discussion of female gender roles as described earlier provided the backdrop for this second variety of attacking the notion of Western

---

necessarily against themselves or their trade but at an explicitly European-accommodating policy of the Pasha." Fahmy, "Prostitution in Egypt," 80, 81.

[29] In the colonial setting and its explicit basis of hegemony on race, the Galician prostitutes even seemed to threaten the British Empire: "The prestige of the ruling race is affected by the degradation of its members, especially if they are females. It matters not that the Austrian, Poles and Russian Jewesses who are the victims of the trade are wholly alien to the British race. In the eyes of the general population, the distinction is not recognized. These women with their white skins come from the West, whence come the rulers of this country, and the whole European community has to bear the shame of their presence in the prostitutes chakla." Punjab Government, quoted in Fischer-Tiné, "White Women Degrading Themselves," 183.

[30] Jušek, *Auf der Suche nach der Verlorenen.*

[31] PA-AA GK Sal 32 (Vormundschaft Sörgels Kinder), 62: Ebeling to GK Sal, Smyrna 6 Aug. 1895.

supremacy. While Catholic and Protestant and later other foreign-based schools had helped to spread the idea that women in the Ottoman port cities should participate in modern learning, the trope of Western loose female morality provided the welcome excuse to reaffirm traditional hierarchies and rein in too liberal an access to other models besides those of the port city religious communities. Authors such as Ahmed Midhat, a typical representative of the "Western tech yes, Western attitudes no" minimalist modernism in late Ottoman society, described the lack of chastity among European women at length.[32]

The impact of inner-Ottoman discussions about Western female decency becomes most apparent with regard to domestic educators. Many upper-middle and upper-class families hired women from France, Switzerland, Austria, or Germany to teach their children European languages and customs from a young age onward. But this custom came under strong criticism. As early as 1888, the Salonica newspaper *Pharos tis Makedonias* warned that the newly established railway link between that city and Austria-Hungary would inundate Macedonia with women of loose morals, seducing the helpless local male youth to their "Western perversions" and "the poisonous seeds of social dissipation and corruption which we euphemistically call European civilization."[33] The strong anti-European language that is induced by the mere fear of the arrival of Austrian women is noteworthy for a newspaper that in other contexts did not hesitate to portray Salonica and its Greeks in particular as exemplary of European refinement. In the course of the next decades, the newspapers elaborated several times on the moral dangers of the young women the upper class entrusted their children to. The foreigners wore very revealing clothing and were too unashamed in the presence of the other sex by local standards. Although these articles are clearly influenced by their authors' petit bourgeois envy of high society's access to education, in 1901, the Ottoman government considered measures for the removal of foreign women considered indecent from private employment as wet nurses, dry nurses, and educators. It took particular offense to the domestic employee's immodest or obscene way of dressing that was

---

[32] Sagaster, "Zum Bild der Europäerin," 64–68; Tüccarzâde İbrahim Hilmi, *Avrupalılaşmak*, 64–71.

[33] Anastassiadou, *Salonique*, 174–175; Mazower, *Salonica City of Ghosts*, 251–252.

supposedly incompatible with Islamic morals and influenced the children in their care, especially the girls, negatively.[34]

In 1904, the Smyrniote German protestant reverend noticed a trend in local society to replace Western educators with indigenous ones versed in French or German.[35] Indeed, the inspector of Salonica schools, Ziyaeddin Bey, in 1907 tried to establish preparatory classes for Muslim female educators to replace non-Muslim and foreign women in this profession. His plan was to recruit these women from the lower classes, to provide them with a high-standard scientific education in combination with Koran teachings.[36] Already the year before, Grand Vizier Avlonyalı Mehmed Ferid Paşa deplored the fact that the "confusion and excitement of the minds" brought on by foreign education caused "some youths to end up marrying foreign women," thus daring "to act against Islam."[37] The Council of Ministers recommended a more rigorous moral indoctrination in Muslim schools against such behavior. There was a certain degree of hypocrisy to this, as at least one member of the council, Foreign Minister Tevfik Pasha, had at the age of forty married the blond and blue-eyed twenty-three-year-old Swiss citizen Elisabeth Tschumi, who at the time had been educator to the British envoy's children in Athens.[38]

The Empire Strikes Back in Vain: Measures against Human Trafficking

The reputation of European (and in particular Austrian) women's chastity was at stake, and so was Western predominance in the Ottoman educational field, if Habsburg subjects publicly practiced prostitution in the streets of Pera and Galata. If these spheres were to be protected, the pimps and prostitutes would have to disappear outright or at least keep a low profile. To succeed in this endeavor, the diplomats were obliged to clamp down hard on their compatriots' activities. An inter-consular working group in Constantinople compiled a

---

[34] BOA İ.HUS. 89/1319.Ra.36, 22 Ra 1319 (9 July 1901).
[35] Steinwald, *Beiträge zur Geschichte*, 86.
[36] *Journal de Salonique*, 9 Dec. 1907.
[37] Deringil, *The Well-Protected Domains*, 117–118.
[38] Okday, *Der letzte Großwesir und seine preußischen Söhne*, 27–33, 43.
According to Tevfik's testimony, because of his wife's refusal to convert to Islam, he forfeited his chance to become grand vizier under Abdülhamid II; ibid., 33.

blacklist of "slavers." They repeatedly reminded Vienna to pressure the Monarchy's municipalities to be more scrupulous when issuing passports. They cooperated with police authorities in Galicia and Bukovina to clamp down on itinerant traffickers.

Despite the disappointments suffered after Krassay's mass arrests and Friedmann's testimony, the Habsburg authorities had occasionally managed to deal the "slave trade" some serious blows. In 1892, twenty-seven traffickers were convicted in a trial held in Lemberg (Lviv/Lvov).[39] Some of them had been extradited from the Ottoman Empire, but the local authorities had prohibited the extradition of other suspects. The crown witness was Feige Aufscher, a fourteen-year-old who had been liberated from a Constantinople brothel. In 1899, Samuel Bahr was arrested in Budapest as he was boarding a train to Constantinople accompanied by twenty-five young women.[40]

To escape the consulate's pressure, many pimps and some prostitutes took on Ottoman passports. Within little time, with local help, the Galician pimps started to beat the consulates at their own game. While claiming to protect the rights of their subjects, the foreign consulates attempted to have a word in Ottoman affairs, thus giving their subjects a strong resource to call on in their social interactions in the Ottoman sphere. When however the actions of Habsburg subjects were clearly detrimental to the Dual Monarchy's image, they managed to escape persecution by defecting to the enemy camp, that is, claiming Ottoman nationality. In a total reversal of the failed Ottoman deportation of 1876, after the turn of the century, a mixture of corruption by lower-level policemen and immigration officers; the stalemate of the two authorities trying to assert their executive competence against each other; and a nationalist glee at seeing the Austrians and Hungarians helpless to stop their pimps from walking freely through the streets of Constantinople or to save their women from being bought and sold in the local brothels, combined to create a carefree atmosphere for Austrian pimps on the shores of the Bosporus.

Needless to say, this confrontation worsened after the declaration of constitutional rule and the annexation crisis in 1908. Not only were the local authorities scrupulous to protect the rights of their newly won

---

[39] Stauter-Halsted, "A Generation of Monsters," 25–35; Wingfield, *World of Prostitution*.
[40] Bali, *Prostitution*, 21, 22.

Galicia-born citizens. They also declined to arrest foreigners on their embassy's request. In 1911, the Pera police's refusal to arrest two Austrians sparked a note by the European powers to the Porte threatening to make such arrests by means of a mob recruited from the embassies' staffs in future. The Viennese ministry had to remind the Constantinople embassy of the futility of such threats.[41]

The situation continued to deteriorate, as did the reputation of the "Europeans" in the Ottoman public's view. But while the Westerners were no longer considered models to be mimicked, the situation was worse for Ashkenazi Jews. The Polish-born David Ben-Gurion (born David Grün) remembered that during his studies in Salonica (1911), he denied his heritage to his Sephardic landlady, "because in Salonica the word Ashkenazi was synonymous with 'white slaver' (*soher nashim*)." His biographer even claims the neighbors shunned Ben-Gurion because "among Salonika's Jews it was common knowledge that all Askenazim earned their living as pimps or white slavers."[42]

The Constantinople consulate now attempted a much more rigorous policy of deportations of prostitutes and punishment of pimps, while especially the latter had almost completely adopted Ottoman citizenship. The consulate had forgotten the bitter lessons learned from the 1890s and claimed that any hindrance toward clamping down on prostitution stemmed from the constitutionalist regime.[43] On December 15, 1913, the Habsburgs diplomats deported fifteen prostitutes by ship to Trieste.[44] The same steamer was intended to deport several Austrian pimps to be tried in the Monarchy for deprivation of liberty. On December 12, 1913, two well-known pimps of Austrian nationality were to be escorted to the Galata police office for paperwork before they could be brought on board the steamer. But as the carriage approached the police station, one of the arrested called out to the crowd on the street that he was an Ottoman subject being illegally imprisoned by foreigners. An angry mob attacked the consulate

---

[41] HHStA BK Kpl 107: 1) MdA to Pallavicini, Vienna 4 Nov. 1911.
[42] Bali, *Prostitution*, 12. Once again, we can notice hypocrisy in this attitude, as historically the Sephardic Jews had been active both as traders and "consumers" of the Ottoman market in female slaves from Ruthenia; see Ben-Naeh, "Blond, Tall."
[43] HHStA BK Kpl 107: Guido Panfili (Consul) to Embassy, Constantinople 2 Feb. 1911.
[44] HHStA Adm. Reg. F 52 – 46: 2) 15/23 Dec. 1913.

carriage and liberated the pimp, and the policemen joined in the fun by landing a few blows on the heads of the astonished consulate *kavas*es, Duplica and Mustafa.[45]

To overcome the stalemate created by the foreign diplomats insisting on their extraterritorial rights and the Ottoman protection of the "white slave trade," a solution was needed that allowed all sides to keep face. During her visit in 1911, the German feminist Bertha Pappenheim suggested to the governor of Pera the founding of a *Ligue Ottomane* against white slavery, thus setting up a national agenda for the problem. But the German embassy told her frankly that they would not endanger the capitulatory rights for the handful of prostitutes of German nationality.[46]

It was finally another Ashkenazi Jew with greater authority who succeeded where Pappenheim had failed. The US ambassador Henry Morgenthau on March 12, 1914 hosted a gathering of most ambassadors and a number of mid-range Ottoman politicians and members of the local police authorities who solemnly founded the Association for the Protection of Young Girls. The Association was careful to bestow numerous chairmanships, vice-chairmanships, and honorary chairmanships on representatives of the Ottoman executive and Ottoman religious functionaries, although Morgenthau and nondiplomatic foreigners such as Israel Auerbach, representative of the *Hilfsverein der deutschen Juden*, were the main actors of the endeavor.

As the association had to maneuver carefully in order not to reawaken the nationalist passions that had led to the earlier confrontations, little progress was made before the outbreak of war.[47] However, it seems to have prompted the Ottoman administration to once again change its practice from undermining the capitulations by ignoring prostitution to undermining them by taking a law and order stance. In a harsh note dated March 26, it demanded free access for medical inspectors to all brothels operated by Habsburg subjects, whether official or illegal.[48] The Habsburg embassy responded with a carefully worded note that permission would be granted on the condition that

---

[45] HHStA BK Kpl 107: GK to Embassy, Constantinople 13 Dec. 1913.
[46] Bali, *Prostitution*, 39, 40.   [47] Ibid., 46–53.
[48] HHStA Adm. Reg. F 52 – 46: 4) Sublime Porte to Austro-Hungarian Embassy, Constantinople 26 March 1914 (copy).

the Porte submit a list of all houses that would be affected by the measure.[49] Thus, for the first time the Austro-Hungarian authorities accepted a potential infringement on the capitulations in order to restrict the trade that had so severely damaged their reputation.

The Ottoman state's entrance into hostilities against the Entente offered the long-awaited occasion for the empire to unanimously declare its full sovereignty and the abolishment of the capitulations. Its allies, Germany and Austria-Hungary, had to accept the move. But the Ottoman authorities soon had to realize that the genie could not be put back into the bottle at their leisure. They had been willing to turn a blind eye or even be protective of traffickers' and pimps' networks in their capital because of their corrosive effects on European supremacy. They had actively encouraged the pimps' and prostitutes' willingness to casually forfeit king and country. However, when at the outbreak of the World War the geopolitical situation changed and the Council of Ministers entered into an uneasy alliance with the German and Habsburg Empire, the underworld networks and their potential disloyalty continued to cause anxiety, now for all three governments involved. The foreign diplomats and their allies suspected the underworld of siding with the enemy. International counter-espionage investigations were launched against them. The association of pimps and prostitutes with the acclaimed foreign and internal archenemies of the alliance – Russia, Armenians, and Greeks – demonstrates the degree of fear felt in face of nongovernmental international networks, indentured sexuality, and disloyalty, all of which had flourished due to the previous Austro-Ottoman confrontation.[50]

In 1915, finally, utilizing the nigh limitless powers bestowed unto the police chief due to martial law, the Ottoman authorities clamped down on the "white slave trade" in the capital. The chief of police Osman

---

[49] HHStA Adm. Reg. F 52 – 46: 4) Austro-Hungarian Embassy to Sublime Porte, Constantinople 9 June 1914 (draft).

[50] According to the German navy intelligence service, the Berlin pimp Ernst Gras, aka Hans, had traveled to Constantinople to work in a garden bar as a cover for espionage for Russia. He had used Armenians, Greeks, and prostitutes to create an intelligence network. Although neither the search of Gras' Berlin apartment, nor that of Cäti Gross' – his alleged lover in the Hotel *Grand Bretagne* in Constantinople – nor the continued surveillance of her presumed other lover Konstantin Phokinos resulted in any evidence, the German and Ottoman side continued to believe that they constituted a spy network; BA-MA RM 40/733, 21 ff., 82–85.

Bedri Bey had 168 traffickers arrested and their synagogue closed. Of those arrested, 100 claimed Russian nationality, 23 Romanian, 10 Austrian, and 18 Ottoman. It is difficult to ascertain whether this comparatively low number of Austrians is due to the fact that, as Morgenthau claims, the Russians had ousted the previously dominant Galician networks or whether the "white slavers" simply claimed Russian nationality knowing that deportation to that country was impossible because of the war.[51] The crackdown was clearly motivated by security concerns and did not even claim to be a humanitarian intervention. The women who had been unexpectedly deprived of their livelihood were left to fend for themselves. However, such self-help was more efficient than the clumsy activities of the philanthropists and states concerned. The two former prostitutes known as Rosie and Freimund converted the small Ashkenazi synagogue in Galata known as *Schneidertempel* into an asylum for former sex workers.[52]

Deconstruction and the Waning of Europe's Appeal

Europe, in its imperialist self-image of the late nineteenth century, claimed to represent a superior civilization, which supposedly had a positive effect on its classes, genders, and dependent ethnicities. In the prominent port cities of the Eastern Mediterranean, these claims to superiority were challenged by various internal social groups that also desired to be called European in order to profit from the positive connotation of the word, just as the Western and Central Europeans did. While these internal groups had neither the unity, nor the resolve, nor the power basis to oppose the implementation of foreign notions of "Europe" as a whole, they nevertheless had the capabilities to sabotage it to some extent. In their challenge, they focused on the weakest link in the reasoning of Western superiority that they could physically get their hands on, namely the underworld pimps and prostitutes present in their cities. By increasing these marginal agents' visibility through public debate in newspapers, by criminalization or toleration, by impeding or expediting their movements, the indigenous social groups

---

[51] Bali, *Prostitution*, 53, 57; the putative mastermind of "white slave trade" in Constantinople, Michael Moses Salamovitz, aka Michel Pasha, whose extradition had been demanded by the Austrian authorities in 1892, still appears as Ottoman in the 1915 crackdown; ibid., 21.
[52] Bali, *Prostitution*, 29, 30.

hoped to focus attention on these less glorious subjects of the Great Powers and through them counter the European self-congratulatory image.[53] The prostitutes were used to erode the reputation of European women as educators possessing superior knowledge and morals.

The targeted groups soon realized that the new attention they drew opened windows of opportunities for them. The pimps and prostitutes could change nationalities with ease, offering their loyalty to whoever would let them carry on their business in peace. The affected European empires and their local representatives were aware of the detrimental effect the presence of their marginalized subjects could have on their role in the Mediterranean port cities from an early point onward, and tried to control them through repression or accommodation, but in the end failed. After resigning themselves to tolerating the prostitutes, the beginning of the twentieth century with its heightened anxiety to issues of nation and empire brought a new confrontation, as the new constitutional regime discovered the citizens' rights of its Galicia-born pimps. The Habsburg and other diplomats countered by clamping down on their countries' pimps and prostitutes.

Needless to say, this fight over identities and loyalties of groups that had arranged themselves to a life in between the European and the Ottoman and profiting from that position, was, despite the short-term benefits they could reap by being championed by the one or other side, detrimental to the freedoms necessary for such an in-between lifestyle. As the self-declared partisans of anti-Westernism failed to tackle the hypertrophic meaning of "Europe" itself and focused instead on those who fell short of living up to it, several distinct life patterns that crossed the theoretically so impressive boundary between the metropolis and the Eastern Mediterranean were eliminated at the dawn of the age of saturated nation-states.

---

[53] Fuhrmann, "Vagrants, Prostitutes, and Bosnians."

24 The "Unraveling" of Port City Society

The malleable identities of late Ottoman port cities that had caused pleasure, anguish, and moral condemnation had entered the political arena. Thus began the age of the Raskolnikovs; the Oblomovs, Ulrichs, and Bihruz Beys seemed outdated. Through the discourse on the marginal European foreigners, Western supremacy and the Eastern Mediterranean urban order that had been based on this presupposition had been eroded five to ten years before the political end of Western European dominance along the shores of the Aegean. The nationalist rhetoric in the construction of gender and class identities, which had previously stood in competition to the rather open and experimental practice of fashioning the self, now took on a more aggressive tone. For example, in Smyrna, movies had from their beginning in 1908 been shown with Greek captions added to the original language. Although the Greek captions were abandoned in favor of the French, English, or Italian original in 1913 in order to save money and time, Turkish nationalists demonstrated for the introduction of captions in Ottoman Turkish.[1] The colorful mix of headgear on the waterfront was also no longer considered a sign of the city's importance in the world, but as an aberration. Turkish nationalists forcefully removed the fezzes of non-Muslims, while Greek nationalists would provoke by stepping on fezzes.[2] As during earlier crises, the foreigners, the nonbelievers, and the super-Westernized were conflated into a single image, the image of a world that deserved destruction. Ziya Gökalp for example could now use "imperialism" and "cosmopolitanism" in one sentence as synonymous pejoratives. This cosmopolitan type was contrasted with an imagined ethnically pure and virtuous peasant free of the port city's corruption.[3] Symptomatic of this development is the fate of the song

---

[1] Georgelin, *Fin de Smyrne*, 132–134; DH.KMS 15/5_3, in *Arşiv Belgelerine göre Osmanlı'da Gösteri Sanatları*, 378–380.
[2] Georgelin, *Fin de Smyrne*, 182, 183.
[3] Vakkasoğlu, *Tarih Aynasında Ziya Gökalp*.

"To Salvari," which had celebrated diversity and indeterminateness. After 1922, the lyrics were adapted to the new mentality: The male singer no longer asks whether the girl is Greek, Turkish, French, or English. He limits his question to whether she is from the Smyrna suburb of Kordelio or from Karataş, which no longer hints at ethnic, but only social difference within a space now imagined to be exclusively Greek. There is no mention of a *shalvar* either (this seems too Oriental a dress), instead the song alludes to the forced migration from Asia Minor to Greece.[4]

First Dividing Lines across the Aegean and Mediterranean

And yet, it was a long way from discrediting the Occidentocentric, "cosmopolitan" order to actually toppling it and erasing its influences. The general rehearsal for the "unraveling" of port city society was the Italo-Turkish War. Outright expansionist and without even the pretense of furthering universal or liberal values, such as civilization, human rights, or the international capitalist and financial order, the Italian aggression confirmed the suspicions of all who believed that the European Dream was a lie.[5] In addition, the numerous Eastern Mediterranean port city residents of Italian nationality were to find out that foreign passports were not only a talisman against the excesses of the Ottoman state or an advantage for business and employment opportunities, but also a liability in times of war. In spring of 1912 the Ottoman government ordered all Italian subjects who were fit to travel to leave the country within two weeks, an order affecting approximately 5,500 residents of Smyrna alone. Some had already succeeded in attaining Greek nationality in the months before to avoid deportation, but were in turn affected by the outbreak of hostilities with Greece soon after, while the expelled Italians were able to return.[6] The time for the success model of flexible identities was over.

Greece managed to have the capitulations repealed for Salonica and its other territories conquered in 1912, and the Ottoman Empire

---

[4] Compare the lyrics as sung by Stefanos Vetsos in the 1950s with more modern versions, such as Glykeria's; on the post-1922 lyrics see Zelepos, "Städte als Projektionsflächen," 71–72.
[5] Borutta and Gekas, "A Colonial Sea," 1–13; Yale, Ernst Jäckh Papers, Box 1, Folder 4: H. Humann to Jäckh, Constantinople, undated (mid-Jan. 1914).
[6] Humbert, *Konstantinopel-London-Smyrna*, 63–69.

unilaterally declared them null and void in summer of 1914. And yet, change was slow and while port city society was discredited, nobody undertook decisive steps to homogenize the three maritime cities' populations before or during the war, although such plans already existed. A treaty on an exchange of populations between Greece and the Ottoman Empire had been on the table as early as 1914, but was not completed. Even when the city was occupied by French and British soldiers during World War I, Turkish, Austro-Hungarian, and German inhabitants of Salonica were not systematically interned. Even the otherwise systematic genocide perpetrated against the Armenians of Anatolia was less thorough in Constantinople and Smyrna, where "only" a few hundred were deported. The *vali* of Aydın, Mustafa Rahmi Evranos Bey, except for short spells, left the Entente nationals unhindered and apparently even protected their illicit trade with enemy countries. Due to this comparatively carefree atmosphere in Smyrna, civilities and ambiguous identities managed to survive even in wartimes. A particularly vivid expression of this is the German Navy spy in the city, Lutz, often visiting his alleged British counterpart, MacVittie, for tea, keeping in mind that MacVittie was the brother-in-law of the German Constantinople consular official and later consul general of Smyrna, Theodor Weber.[7]

The Short but Hollow Triumph of the West

For a while at least, if one only observed one's immediate surroundings and ignored the news and rumors from the countryside and the wider world, it must have seemed to the Saloniquenos, Stambouliotes, and Smyrniotes as if the prewar order was simply suspended and would return once fighting was over. And at first sight, this must have seemed the case with the defeat of the Ottoman Empire. France and Great Britain once again claimed the right to hegemony in the Eastern Mediterranean based on their civilizing missions. France was to bring good governance to Syria: The League of Nations entrusted to it the task to "take into account the rights, interests, and wishes of all the population inhabiting the said territory" and "to facilitate the progressive development of Syria and the Lebanon as independent states."[8] Great

[7] Fuhrmann, "Spies, Victims, Collaborators."
[8] League of Nations, "French Mandate for Syria and Lebanon."

Britain with its experience of managing multiethnic societies was to turn Palestine into a peaceful, just, and well-governed country for locals and Jewish colonists alike.[9] Apparently many locals were eager to believe this would also be the case in Smyrna and Constantinople under Allied occupation. According to Willy Sperco, this period was the apogee of Eastern Mediterranean cosmopolitanism, epitomized by the colorful mishmash on Constantinople streets: British, Italian, French, military uniforms (some worn by Senegalese servicemen) intermingled with Cossack military attire and the costumes of the fugitive Russian aristocrats.[10] In a similar vein, the Greek Giorgios Theotokas praises the incessant nightlife and celebrations.[11]

And yet, nothing was as before. Despite the Enlightenment rhetoric, the two powers' intention to use their mandates for imperial expansion was obvious.[12] Despite the Entente's triumph, they were actually war-weary and not able to maintain more than a short and rather passive occupation of Constantinople and parts of Anatolia. Rather than risk overstretch, they concentrated on their spoils in the Arab-dominated half of the Ottoman Empire. Therefore, while Constantinople was enjoying its unprecedented lively nightlife, the Thalassocentric order was actually on the eve of its destruction.

The occupation forces in Smyrna and Constantinople were far from impartial and disinterested administrators. The friend-foe scheme of wartimes, dividing the local population into potentially hostile Turks versus collaborating Armenians and Greeks, continued to dominate and confirmed the nationalists' fears as well as their resolve to destroy the urban order. Leading members of the Turkish nationalist movement such as Halide Edib and Mustafa Kemal narrate the occupation as the crystallizing moment for their awareness of the necessity of armed resistance.[13] This mentality canonized in Turkish national historiography – the Turks alone against a world out to harm them, a grand conspiracy of foreign powers, resident nonnationals, and all

---

[9] League of Nations, "Palestine Mandate."
[10] Sperco, quoted from Pannuti, *Les italiens d'Istanbul*, 253.
[11] Mansel, *Constantinople*, 384, 385; see also MacArthur-Seal, "Intoxication and Imperialism."
[12] The colonialist legacy in present-day Middle Eastern conflicts has been stressed in recent publications; see for example Fildiş, "The Troubles in Syria."
[13] Mansel, *Constantinople*, 389.

non-Muslim parts of the population – found its justification and birthright in this time.

Nationalist and Imperialist Blood Toll and the Withdrawal of the West

However, collaboration between local sympathizers of the Entente and the Great Powers was not as far-reaching as these initial impressions implied. Classic gunboat policy was at an end. Once the Great Powers had resigned themselves to the Arab provinces and the islands, leaving Anatolia to the Turkish nationalist forces, neither the Armenian nor the Greek nationalist cause could hope for the slightest support. When the Turkish nationalist troops had taken control of Smyrna and fire erupted on September 13, 1922, the bay was full of more than a dozen British, French, and Italian warships, all of which, once they realized their initial help at firefighting was not welcome, concentrated their men on board and only reluctantly accepted refugees fleeing from the fire on board.[14] The degree of contempt those onboard felt for the desperate refugees on the quays is best exemplified by Ernest Hemingway's cynical short story, based on reports by foreign soldiers present in Smyrna. He begins,

> The strange thing was, he said, how they screamed every night at midnight. I do not know why they screamed at that time. We were in the harbor and they were all on the pier and at midnight they started screaming. We used to turn the searchlight on them to quiet them. That always did the trick.[15]

As Hervé Georgelin points out, the fire also marked the end of Great Power influence in the Eastern Mediterranean in its nineteenth-century incarnation of capitulatory privileges, consuls, and gunboats, as well as foreign expertise and lifestyle. Foreign subjects painfully noticed the confounding of all nonbelievers as a common enemy from the perspective of militant Muslims, as French, Swiss, Italian, or British subjects were not exempt from plundering of their property or even murder in several cases.[16]

While the Smyrna Catastrophe was certainly the turning point in the "unraveling" of port city society, it was not its end. It fell to yet

---

[14] Georgelin, *Fin de Smyrne*, 201–224; Milton, *Paradise Lost*, 319–326.
[15] Hemingway, "On the Quai at Smyrna."
[16] Georgelin, *Fin de Smyrne*, 201–224.

another Great Power, Germany, to introduce to the Eastern Mediterranean bureaucratic, industrialized genocide. By sending 46,000 Salonica Jews to the death camps of Poland in 1943, it dealt the penultimate blow to pre–nation-state port city society, the second largest atrocity in the cities under study here after the cleansing of Smyrna 1922. Unlike the Greco-Turkish struggle though, where nationalisms competed for the same territory and were caught up in the illusion that this was a matter of life and death for the group concerned, even the most hardened German anti-Semites admitted that they did not have a particular issue with Southeast European Sephardim, but exterminated them nonetheless for the establishment of German extreme imperialist order in Europe.[17]

Space: Making the Nation City

Entering Constantinople in 1918, the British officer Harold Armstrong, after an initial positive impression, declared the city's modernity superficial: "a medieval dungeon fitted with one crown of modern civilization, electricity as light."[18] Already in 1912, an officer of the army annexing Salonica to Greece had written to his wife in a similar vein, "Salonica doesn't excite me [despite its] beautiful park by the sea with a cinema, music, *café chantant* and restaurant." Within a few days after this initial balanced statement appreciating the Saloniquenos' urban seaside facade of modernity, Hippokrates Pappavasileiou radicalized his opinion: "How can one like a city with this cosmopolitan society, nine-tenths of it Jews. It has nothing Greek about it, nor European. It has nothing at all."[19] Other writers of the following decades repeated Pappavasileiou's way of showing contempt for the stars of the Eastern Mediterranean: to discredit the city's previous wave of nonnational modernization (demanding a new nation-driven one), and to confound its cosmopolitanism with Orientalism (if not outright anti-Semitism) and contrast it with the supposed national purity of an imaginary heartland. This set the pattern for discursive othering, as "rootless" or "without heritage," a justification for neglect and "urban renewal."[20]

[17] Hilberg, *Vernichtung der europäischen Juden*, vol. II, 737–745.
[18] Armstrong, quoted from MacArthur-Seal, "Intoxication and Imperialism," 300.
[19] Pappavasileiou, quoted from Mazower, *Salonica City of Ghosts*, 295.
[20] Ersoy, "Melezliğe Övgü," 62–67.

The authorities were intent on imposing a new identity on the port cities. Fire was the not completely unwelcomed accessory of the transformation process, as it had been for the big thoroughfares and regularized grids introduced since the mid-nineteenth century, but on a much larger scale. Downtown Salonica saw a devastating fire in 1917 while under French and British occupation, destroying much of the inner districts and many of its prime sites of modernity. Prime Minister Eleftherios Venizelos is reported to have in retrospect regarded the fire "almost as a gift of divine providence."[21] The Greek state appointed a committee with the task to design a completely new Thessaloniki based on twentieth-century urbanist visions. The city in the nation-state was to appear as a holistic entity and not as the regulated, but highly competitive juxtaposition of capitalist, foreign, local community, and central state institutions all struggling to make their impact, nor did the twentieth century look warmly on the quirky individual tastes of investors, resulting in a mix of neo-Orientalist, neo-Goth, and pseudo-Classicist facades. Ernest Hébrard, on site as an officer of the French army, was assigned the task of drafting the urban master plan. The new urban order accentuated Greekness (by highlighting vistas of former Eastern Roman churches and ancient monuments and eclipsing Ottoman period buildings). The city's new central square, what is now known as Plateia Aristotelous, half open to the sea, is flanked by large colonnaded buildings featuring many arched windows, a style that was dubbed neo-Byzantine, but in fact greatly resembles other contemporary designs for modern housing in colonies, such as Hébrard's later work in Hanoi and Casablanca, but also the Cairo modern suburb of Heliopolis.[22] The square must be seen as the antithesis to the former quays. While they had stood for internationalist pluralism, Plateia Aristotelous was to symbolize the unity of the city, state, and nation.[23]

In Smyrna, following the devastating fire of 1922 that had destroyed especially the predominantly Greek and Armenian quarters and the central quays, but had spared much of the bazaar, the predominantly Sephardic and Turkish areas, and the northern lower-class immigrant neighborhood of La Punta, a principal reordering of the urban space of

---

[21] Eleftherios Venizelos, quoted from Mazower, *City of Ghosts*, 324.
[22] Yerolympos, *Urban Transformations in the Balkans*, 102–122.
[23] Fuhrmann, "Vom stadtpolitischen Umgang."

a similar scope took place. The 1924 plan by Henri Prost and the Danger Brothers also included wide axes and radials to replace or superimpose upon the classic checkerboard pattern that the late Ottoman authorities had introduced to the city.[24] The Turkish nation-state inscribed itself into the former heart of Smyrna's Eurocentric waterfront just as forcefully as the Greek one into its Macedonian port city by the creation of what was to become Republic Square (Cumhuriyet Meydanı), a more or less lifeless semi-circle at the focal point of several radiant thoroughfares. Its only highlight is the oversized equestrian statue of Atatürk erected by Pietro Canonica in 1932 (a nationalist marker of space similar to his Republican Monument on Taksim Square and King Constantine on Democracy Square, all in the heart of the former *Frangomahalla*s).

Both Salonica and Smyrna also used the massive destruction in the city center to erect a green belt, not only to supply downtown with air and recreation areas, but also to allow for disparate placing of new institutions considered essential to twentieth centuries: universities and fair grounds. The erection of a university in Salonica (and before in Greek-occupied Smyrna) and the fair grounds in Smyrna both in the nigh-immediate aftermath of the nationalization of the cities testify to the national importance of the message: The Greeks no longer needed the foreigners to provide institutions of higher learning, and the Turks would turn Smyrna once more into a hub of trade without prominent foreign help.

Constantinople remained the odd one out. It was not hastily overwritten with contemporary urban planning, as the new national capital Ankara was to be developed into the imperial capital's antithesis. Galata-Pera stood largely intact. However, with the embassies devoid of their power to intervene into the country's politics and finally forced to move to Ankara, the area did not boast the importance of the past. Galata-Pera had been slandered no less than the other two cities' *Frangomahalla*s. Paul Bonatz, who had come to Turkey to introduce "new German architecture" in the late 1930s, spoke of "the abominable hodgepodge of houses in Pera."[25] In this, he simply echoed the

---

[24] Serçe, Yılmaz and Yetkin, *Küllerinden Doğan Şehir*, 61–123.
[25] Paul Bonatz, quoted in Bohle and Dimog, *Architekturführer Istanbul*, 11; on Bonatz, see Bozdoğan and Akcan, *Turkey: Modern Architectures in History*, 73–79.

discourse contemporary Turkish architects employed, who spoke of "cosmopolitan piles of stone and marble."[26]

Only toward the end of the 1930s did the development of a new state-propelled urbanity commence here in earnest. It disregarded the *Frangomahalla* and developed Tanzimat Valley and the adjacent axis Taksim – Şişli instead in accordance to plans by Henri Prost. The royal stables at the bottom of Maçka Gorge were replaced by a huge stadium, signifying the new state's stress on development of the citizens' bodies. The abundance of military institutions around the valley's top was modified by converting and redeveloping several of them. Taşkışla, Maçka Armory, and the Guardhouse were turned over to the evolving Istanbul Technical University, thus belatedly bringing Abdülmecid's vision of a state-driven, balanced development of the country to at least symbolic fruition. The ruined Taksim Barracks were demolished and turned into a park as centerpiece of the Taksim – Şişli Axis.[27] Further down, the state broadcasting company and the congress center added to the intended impression of modernity.

Not only was the inner makeup of the port cities rewritten in accordance with the twentieth century; the importance of the ports was to dwindle and they were no longer to provide the main point of the city's identity. Although all three cities continue to have large, busy ports, these are now zones cut off from the city proper.[28] Infrastructure diversified and rather than boat rides that made the cities' residents set out on a sea that connected them to the farther reaches of the Mediterranean, the main transport ways shifted inland. Already by 1918, Salonica was linked by rail with Athens. Landlocked Ankara became the center of an "iron spider's web" of railway lines that were to systematically exploit the country's natural resources. It was linked to the existing network between Smyrna and its hinterland. Intercity roads and airports developed later, all the more eclipsing the ports as gateways to the wider world.

Purging Entertainment of the Other

Just as the urban space, popular culture had to be purged of nonnational elements and especially of the former overseas *Leitkultur*.

---

[26] Özlü, "Republican Response to Levantine Architectural Heritage."
[27] Batuman, "Contesting Political Imaginaries on Taksim Square."
[28] Schubert, "Seaport Cities," 54–69.

In expelling Western elements from the entertainment sector, the nationalists took two opposing approaches. The one was to nationalize the industry, the other to replace it altogether by austerity. The bon vivant Willy Sperco in 1935 deplored the excessive nationalization of names of all public places. Not only had the Grand Rue de Péra become İstiklal Caddesi (Independence Avenue) and the non-Muslim neighborhood of Tatavla Kurtuluş (Liberation) to commemorate the Greco-Turkish War over Anatolia; the Pâtisserie Parisienne had taken down its name sign, while the dance bar Rose Noire had put up the sign Siyah Gül; what had been London Beerhouse had been renamed Türk Birahanesi, the former Strasbourg was now Istanbul Birahanesi, the Artistic Cinema was renamed Sümer Sineması (as the official history theory had declared the ancient Sumerians the Turks' forefathers).[29] While nineteenth-century Pera had attempted to let its customers believe they were having their croissant on the Champs Elysées or their pint off Leicester Square, the new atmosphere disparaged the yearning for being part of a wider world and insisted repetitively on the omnipresence of the nation.

But perhaps simply renaming establishments was a less aggressive act than actually enforcing the dominance of Turks as proprietors and employees of the entertainment sector. In the same 1935 passage, Sperco deplores the fact that the ample dancing venues of the 1920s had disappeared and now the only one was the Park Hotel, one of the first major ventures owned by Turks in the entertainment sector. The proprietors, Ali Nuri and İsmail Hakkı Okday, sons of the longtime Foreign Minister Ahmed Tevfik, had built on the grounds of their father's residence what was to be the city's most prestigious hotel until the 1950s. They were in turn threatened for employing predominantly Armenian waiters.[30]

The series of wars between 1911 and 1923 that tore apart the Ottoman Empire had also separated the previously wider markets of the port city breweries. After Salonica's annexation, the Olympos Brewery was eventually taken over by its Athens rival Fix. Wartime also reinforced the *rakı* – beer opposition. Conspicuous consumption

---

[29] Willy Sperco, quoted from Pannuti, *Les italiens d'Istanbul*, 255; Eren, *Geçmişten Günümüze Anadolu'da Bira*, 107, 115; Brızitsov, *İstanbul'dan Mektuplar*, 49–52.
[30] Okday, *Der letzte Großwesir*, 129–132.

of the assumed national drink increased.³¹ On his first day in Smyrna after the Turkish National Army's capture of the city in 1922, Mustafa Kemal rode up to the Café Kraemer and ordered a *rakı*.³²

Like many other aspects of social life, beer was subjected to the predominance of national hegemony. Following the US example, the breakaway national assembly in Ankara in one of its first laws declared a total ban on alcohol and fines and imprisonment for those who sold or consumed it. When in 1924 Mustafa Kemal and the hedonists had the upper hand again, the law was repealed.³³ The national monopoly for alcoholic drinks (*İçki Tekeli*) was organized in 1926. A 1928 law demanded that all producers of alcoholic beverages in Turkey had to be registered as joint stock companies in the country. The Swiss-registered Bomonti-Nektar thus had to sell out for 8 million Swiss Francs to a company founded by Turkish citizens awaiting this opportunity. This new Bomonti-Nektar Company received a license for beer production for ten years. In 1938 the national monopoly administration took over the production directly, which continued among others for several more decades on site at the Bomonti Factory.³⁴ The first brand was initially called *Türk Birası* (Turkish Beer).³⁵ Beer had thus come under direct state control, which was now used to purge the cosmopolitan flair the beverage had enjoyed.

The Ethnically Cleansed City – A New Babylon

Just as beer had to be nationalized in the Turkish Republic, so did the music of the Anatolian refugees in Greece. *Smyrneika*, sometimes with Turkish, sometimes with Greek lyrics, and often a mix of the two, amalgamated with waltz influences, was initially seen as an impediment to Greek national culture and faced oppression. This however led the immigrants to develop it further into their music subculture, *Rebetiko*. Only later did it become absorbed into the mainstream and separated from its initial context.³⁶

---

³¹ Rahmi Bey would publicly drink *rakı* at the time when the British shelling the city were presumably having their afternoon tea; Milton, *Paradise Lost*, 81, 82.
³² Milton, *Paradise Lost*, 284, 347; Mansel, *Levant*, 214. Kraemer's and all other waterfront brasseries were destroyed in the fire a few days later.
³³ Eren, *Geçmişten Günümüze Anadolu'da Bira*, 118.   ³⁴ Ibid., 118–128.
³⁵ Zat, "Bomonti Bira Fabrikası," 296, 297.   ³⁶ Zelepos, *Rebetiko*.

The clashes over *Rebetiko* are indicative of a wider cultural dilemma. While statistically homogeneity seemed achieved following the Exchange of Populations, Smyrna and Salonica entered their perhaps most heterogeneous phases. Displaced populations with no or little prior experience with their new city of residence settled there.[37] Far from resembling the perfect unspoiled community with uniform religion, language, and loyalty that the nationalists had clamored for, the new Greek subjects knew no Greek, the Turkish citizens no Turkish, and often they adhered to customs, attitudes, and worldviews that did not conform to the rest of society. It would take two generations of indoctrination and pressure to produce homogenized society. As Fredrick de Cramer recalls based on family accounts,

The Muslim population expelled from Greece during the Exodus and settled in Izmir all spoke Greek – in fact, they couldn't speak Turkish. We had a helper in the house; I remember as a kid, our communication language with her was Greek. Whenever you went to the baker's, you would speak Greek. My grandmother spoke French and Greek until she died, she never spoke one word of Turkish. I think the last generation in Izmir to enjoy this cultural variety was my father's, until the 1950s and 60s mainly. And then, as they faded out, younger generations went to Turkish schools, like I did.[38]

Constantinople's population was less radically changed. Returning to the city of his youth in the 1930s, the Bulgarian journalist Hristo Brâzitsov claims that even twenty-five years after the Balkan Wars, many Stambouliotes still had more a sense of urban than national identity:

Many women here do not know what they are. "What do you mean? I am Stambouliote." For example, Kalliopi's mother is Greek, her father Armenian. Her mother's mother's parents from the Caucasus, originally from Syria, her father on the other hand a baptized Jew and daughter of a Salonica Macedonian woman.[39]

Turkifying the imperial city, as well as imposing Turkish identity on the port cities, would take several more decades.

---

[37] Morack, "Refugees, Locals and 'the' State."
[38] *Levantine Heritage*, "Fredrick de Cramer."
[39] Brızitsov, *İstanbul'dan Mektuplar*, 44.

Conclusion

Keeping yesterday's decaying world on its feet a little longer, they stay seated at the dinner table, while everyone else has got up to leave; for food and drink, they name things as they please and call themselves modern. These are vain and diseased pursuits.[40]

The image evoked by Halide Edip seems a fitting description of the situation at the dawn of the twentieth century: Following continuous attacks on the charm of the West, its claim to the moral high ground eroded by focusing on its prostitutes, many residents of the Eastern Mediterranean cities felt the historical transition they had grown up with was coming to an end, albeit not a happy one. Their world was in decay, and the best thing they believed was to hasten it. Disenchanted with the West, they got up and left the party. Those who did not see the signs of the time such as the editors of *Journal de Salonique*, were still busy eating up the scraps from the table. And yet, some such as Said Naum Duhani, at least in retrospect, deplored the dissolution of *Pax Levantina*. In the introduction to his *Quand Beyoğlu s'appelait Pera*, he claims that when watching the newsreel of the 1911 Italian invasion in a Paris cinema, Duhani saw Cutturi, former first officer of the Italian embassy boat and Duhani's friend, hoist the Italian flag in Tripoli. Duhani addresses him, "No, Cutturi, not you, who has drunk of the waters of 'Taxim' ... Leave this task to another."[41] His reprimand toward the Italian officer stands pars pro toto for the elitist foreign officers and diplomats Duhani had socialized with at the *Cercle d'Orient* and elsewhere in Pera, and who later seemingly without hesitation carried out their orders to dismember the Ottoman Empire, thus precipitating the chain of wars, ethnic strife, and related calamities that shook and changed the Eastern Mediterranean.

In the end, the Raskolnikovs, the angry young men and women who wanted to see Belle Époque society go up in flames, got their way. Although few of them would have envisioned the results of their actions to be as catastrophic as the events between 1911 and 1923 turned out to be, when situations escalated, the various nationalist, irredentist, and imperialist agents did not hesitate to raise the stakes

---

[40] Halide Edip, quoted from Önertoy, "Halide Edip Adıvar'ın Romanlarında Toplumsal Eleştiri," 40.
[41] Duhani, *Quand Beyoğlu s'appelait Pera*, 23.

and jeopardize the spoils they were fighting for (such as international trade, the built urban environment, or the lives of the segment of population they claimed to defend). During this confrontation, many who had previously entertained more ambiguous identities or even qualified as super-Westernized opted for one of the opposing camps.[42]

Nonetheless, the legacy of the European Dream and its impact on the Eastern Mediterranean port cities did not end by incorporation into a nation-state in 1912/1922/1923, respectively. It took long work that involved ethnic cleansing, discriminatory legislation, and economic initiative, but also education, manipulation of public memory, a new entertainment culture, and mass-scale urban planning. Seeing these cities today it remains difficult to access the complex, colorful, well-connected, and yet particularly local cultures that were at home here until roughly 100 years ago.

---

[42] As late as 1922, Ahmed Rıza published *La Faillite morale de la politique occidentale en Orient* to explain how the West had failed the people of the East; Kaynar, "Les jeunes Turques et l'Occident," 27.

PART VI

Europe and the Eastern Mediterranean Revisited

Historians have abandoned the notion that they could educate society as a whole to learn from the mistakes of the past and thus stand more or less powerless in the face of present day developments. If anything can be learned from the study of the past, it is that periods of intense economic, cultural, and personal interactions across borders and long distances will be followed by moments of contraction, conflict, and essentialism. While external threats might play an important role, it is the degree of saturation, the discontent among the marginalized and more importantly the second-class elites and their aspirants, and the psychic stress of maintaining identity, labor, and cultural flexibility that help to erode complex globally interconnected constellations. This rather simple rule is already described in a nutshell in the late medieval historian Ibn Khaldun's deliberations on the rise and fall of cities.[1] What we might add based on the study of the nineteenth century is that the new beginning following the collapse of globally complex orders does not take place from a tabula rasa or status quo ante. While claiming to reinstate a previous natural order, neither the Greek Kingdom nor the Turkish Republic nor any other post–World War I states in the region were the product of such innocence. Their identities, economies, urban planning, and other aspects of public life were very much based on the knowledge and experience of the nineteenth century. These new entities sought to either fulfill what their predecessors had only partly achieved or to avoid what were perceived as aberrations at all costs. The role the nineteenth-century order plays for our times, while dependent on the 1923 conjuncture, is rather different.

---

[1] Ibn Khaldun, *The Muqadimmah*, especially IV, 11–18.

Nostalgia for the Quays: A Political Manifesto?

Just as many other bygone sites of history, Eastern Mediterranean port cities have served as sites of projection for contemporary desires, fears, and political agendas. Demonized as the loci of imperialism and praised as exemplary places of peaceful coexistence between people of different language, religion, or origin at other historical moments, they are the object of late twentieth and early twenty-first-century discussions of whether to welcome or combat the profusion of global flows of capital, diversified culture and identity, and people. After the aforementioned periods of neglect and amnesia, the nineteenth century, its hybridity, and its Europhilia, have once again become hip around the Eastern Mediterranean. While school textbooks might still follow nationalist narratives, the cities themselves offer different readings. The Thessaloniki municipality depicts this chapter in the city's history on its website as a golden age of development, culture, and cosmopolitanism.[2] Likewise, Izmir's municipality, its archive, and moreover, the Chamber of Commerce, and individuals have in the last two decades engaged in a number of activities to honor the nineteenth century as the period when the city had been the "Star of the Mediterranean."[3] This is a reflection of nostalgia, accompanied by a huge commercial sector that peddles out commodified images of the nineteenth century in gastronomy, walking tours, and entertainment. One might see in this nostalgia a late triumph of alternative, less rigid national identities that were on offer in mid-twentieth century, such as those of Angèle Loreley or post-1912 Jewish Saloniquenos, or simply an imaginary landscape projected onto cities that were never the harmonious cosmopolis they are now often portrayed as.[4] But the nostalgia reflects a struggle that is very much relevant today.

The port cities of the nineteenth century might be gone and their particular culture written out of mainstream history, but they are in many ways still present. It is no coincidence that one of the most successful novels of the early twenty-first century, Jeffrey Eugenides' *Middlesex*, uses the early twentieth-century Eastern Mediterranean setting and Smyrna as points of departure for its story of a present-

---

[2] Thessaloniki Municipality, "Monuments."
[3] See the work of the Ahmet Pirişina City Archive and *İzmir Tarih*.
[4] Naar, *Jewish Salonica*, 277–294; Eldem, "Ottoman Galata and Pera," 18–36; Mills, *Streets of Memory*; Starr, *Remembering Cosmopolitan Egypt*.

day hermaphrodite; the state of ambivalence that challenged pre–World War I Mediterranean residents in their quests for individual identity is today further complicated by a growing range of socially conceivable gendered and sexual identities.[5]

Are we therefore as critical historians to support the image of Belle Époque Eastern Mediterranean cities as a better place, a fallen utopia that can set an example for a post-nationalist society? I would like to answer that question both with a "yes" and a "no." Nineteenth-century Mediterranean society was not a just society, nor was it color-blind to where people came from, or did it offer equal opportunities to all. Many of the grievances uttered by those in opposition to this social order must therefore be considered legitimate, although their specific aims and methods applied are less so. Port city society did not produce better people, as is best illustrated by a look at the personalities they bequeathed upon the twentieth century. For Alexandria, Philip Mansel has identified as diverse characters as Eric Hobsbawm, the British Marxist historian of Eastern European Jewish family roots; Rudolf Heß, the son of a leading Alexandrine Christian merchant of Franconian origin, who later became the German deputy *Führer*; the Egyptian president Gamal Abdel Nasser; Georges Moustaki, the French Jewish songwriter with family roots in Corfu; and Omar Sharif, the internationally active film actor of Syrian Christian origin.[6] It is telling that besides Nasser and Heß, all of the aforementioned at some point had their names changed or modified. When looking for similar prominent figures stemming from the cities under study here, the list is no less colorful. There is the rather obvious spectrum of political influential figures, especially of early twentieth-century Turkish politics, such as the Saloniqueno Mustafa Kemal, his wife, the Smyrniote Latîfe Uşakî, or the Constantinople-born national revolutionary writer, Halide Edib. Of those who emigrated to overseas, the survivor of the 1922 fire and Greek and Argentinean businessman Aristotelis Onassis is probably best known, due to his fortune, his social escapades, and his endowment dedicated to the promotion of Greek culture and sciences (and who, just as some of the key characters in *Middlesex*, manipulated his personal data after the Smyrna Fire). Among the survivors and emigrants of Smyrna 1922, the engineer responsible for the design of the *Mini* in 1956, Alec Issigonis, perhaps best reflects the

---

[5] Eugenides, *Middlesex*.   [6] Mansel, *Levant*, 133.

complicated family history of former Eastern Mediterranean ports. His grandfather Demosthenis had served in the construction of the Smyrna-Aydın Railway and had thus gathered enough favor with the local consular authorities to be granted British nationality. Demosthenis' son Konstantin married the German subject Hulda Prokopp, a granddaughter of Gottfried and Clara Prokopp, the German immigrants who had founded Smyrna's first large-scale brewery.[7] Likewise, Roza Eskenazi was born in Constantinople as Sarah Skinazi and having grown up in Salonica, changed her name, before becoming one of the musical stars of post–World War I Greece. The French Prime Minister Nicolas Sarkozy's maternal grandfather was born in Salonica into a family of local Sephardim, while his father's family originated in Hungary.

These examples as well as this book in general have hopefully illustrated that Eastern Mediterranean quays were neither hell on earth, nor utopia. They were, if anything, more colorful and more contradictory than what earlier interpretations have led us to believe, and that very contradictory nature is what makes it so complicated to ascertain their historical role, but also to judge them politically. Nineteenth-century Eastern Mediterranean port cities are not a model that one could emulate in toto. What remains impressive is the Eastern Mediterranean urbanity as a site of ambivalence. As demonstrated in the chapter on Levantine identity, it was not a binding cosmopolitan culture, but rather a space that was founded on ambivalence and that in turn continued to produce ambivalence, providing a stage for the multitude of identities. Neither clearly European nor its Other; within reach of joining the "family of cultured nations," but unsure whether that day would ever come; its residents speaking at least half a dozen languages or mélanges or pidgin versions thereof; a population that at least during some phases of the nineteenth century believed it could carve out its path to modernity on its own terms and according to its own prerogatives; politics still Ottoman, but with a heavy dose of Great Power consular meddling and various factions representing local *Eigen-Sinn* conniving with them; a stalemate that did not allow for radical change, except when imposed by global capitalism – all these unresolved constellations combined to impact on the private lives of individuals who grew accustomed to in-betweenness, seeing it as a

---

[7] Levantine Heritage, "Prokopp."

burden, an opportunity, or a state in need of radical resolution. It is this tension and state of in-betweenness that can justifiably be seen as preferable to the straitjackets that the nation-state and its supporters have sought and continue to seek to disseminate as a cure for ambivalence. Therefore, rather than lauding nineteenth-century society, one should see it as an arrangement faute de mieux, a constellation that allowed for variety, but did not champion it. To illustrate this point, it is once again helpful to recall Nietzsche, one of the harshest critics of contemporary zeitgeist and its tendencies toward conformity and mediocrity. Realizing that this constellation would not change for the better in the short run, he advised likeminded contemporaries to make the most out of the unsatisfying situation and to reap the benefits to be had from ambiguity.

Mixing the Past with the Present

The previous lines have already touched on the fact that our current debates are inevitably intertwined with bygone ages or rather our images of them. A historian's perspective is not just informed by her or his degree of insight into the past, but by the time he or she lives in. While this has long been deemed a handicap, in recent decades, its practitioners have started considering it an asset, as certain experiences help to reveal dynamics in the past that have previously not been noticed. This is very much the case for my study of urban Thalassocentric practices, experiences, identities, and their downfall in the nineteenth-century Eastern Mediterranean region. When I first started dabbling into the topic around 2005, the region witnessed a decisive revival of Europhoria. Greece had adapted the Euro currency a few years earlier, experiencing several succinct years of decisive economic growth. Likewise, Turkey's start of European Union accession talks marked the height of a wave of interest in the country's Western neighbors. Turco-Greek rapprochement had already decisively gathered pace since 1999. The September 2001 attacks on civilians and state representatives in the United States in the name of Islam and the subsequent declaration of a "War on Terror" and especially its extension to Iraq in 2003, were seen as foreboding signs, as was the outbreak of the second Intifada. But at the time they were deemed not to have immediate impact on a region that, following the end of hostilities in former Yugoslavia, the simmering down of Kurdish separatist incursions, and the end of the Israeli occupation of Southern Lebanon, seemed by majority on the path toward integration, intellectual curiosity across borders, and the reconciliation of differences within the framework of European Union membership or partnership.

In this situation, it became fashionable to open European Studies programs at Turkish universities, which were believed to prepare for in-demand knowhow for decades to come. Academic cooperation and exchange blossomed, as they did in various fields of the arts, and even the tourist industry began to realize that the Eastern Mediterranean had more to offer than just beaches and antiquities. City trips and cruises to Thessaloniki, Istanbul, and Izmir multiplied rapidly and in part now aimed at discovering the city of the present, its spaces, its culinary, music, dance, art, drama and movie scenes. It is this atmosphere that sensitized me to the lure the European Dream held for residents of Eastern Mediterranean cities in the nineteenth century.

Naturally, the situation could not be more different as I finish this book in the winter of 2019/2020. The Euro, which had seemed to be the key to Greece's prosperity, has become the country's nemesis. Local mismanagement and the imposition of austerity measures have impoverished the country's population for decades to come. In Turkey, the ruling powers have abandoned peaceful reconciliation, rule of law, and societal pluralism to replace them with an unending "War on Terror" of their own, arbitrary and politicized public institutions, and imprisonment for dissenters. While the Justice and Development Party had in its initial years of rule appealed to the non-nationalist public – claiming to be the driving force of European integration – in recent years its leaders have invoked a Eurasian strategic orientation, Islamic civilization, or simply the nation as interchangeable counter-models. The disastrous wars in Syria and Iraq no longer seem distant to observers in Turkey and the rest of Europe, but to have a direct impact on everyone's lives, in part because several of these countries have become involved in the hostilities, and in part due to the numerous casualties in terrorist attacks on the civilian populace of these belligerent countries. Refugees, both from these war zones and others, have become the ubiquitous scapegoats for the volatility of the global neoliberal order, and their deaths and suffering on the frontiers of Turkey, Greece, and other parts of Europe tacitly accepted across the continent. These dire developments of course echo the years preceding World War I and the failure of the European Dream, its inability to hold promise in the long run in the face of growing prosperity gaps, continued biases and discriminations, and how the wrath over unfulfilled promises inspired some to seek vengeance on whomever one chose to blame. But while nationalist self-images and imperialist supremacism became exit strategies out of a global order that many in early twentieth-century Europe and the Eastern Mediterranean had come to consider a burden, it remains to be seen whether the paradigm of "civilizations" will advance beyond its present-day corrosive influence and seriously threaten to topple the global neoliberal economic order or at least the concomitant cultural order, which to some degree resembles Nietzsche's "cosmopolitan gods-, morals-, and arts-carnival." These struggles over the hegemonic economic and cultural orders of our time of course take place in the financial and political realms, and also on the city streets. However, especially in the digital age, discursive hegemony plays a critical role, which is why cultural historians of the region, despite their sometimes seemingly exotic interests, hardly operate in an ivory tower, as the following example will illustrate.

The Specter of Weber's City and the Farce of Civilizations

On October 21, 2017, the Turkish president Recep Tayyip Erdoğan spoke at length on the topic of cities and Istanbul in particular. One passage drew special attention, as it seemingly entailed self-criticism, something Erdoğan is not known for. He said, "Istanbul is in this respect [among cities of ancient provenance, MF] really exceptional. But we had not recognized this city's significance; we betrayed this city and continue to betray it still. I am responsible for this too." The president had criticized Istanbul's transformation into a megalopolis and especially the nigh unrestrained spread of high-rises. While this extract was widely circulated, the speech as a whole received little attention, although it is highly revealing of the attitude and policy toward cities in the first quarter of the twenty-first century.

Erdoğan claimed that the world knew two distinct types of cities, the Western and the Eastern, and that they had produced two distinct types of people. While the former had evolved following the examples of Athens and Rome, the later derived from Medina. The Western type of city had evolved in struggle and conflict with itself and was therefore marked by a series of bifurcated spaces. By contrast, the Eastern city was a harmonious whole, where life and death, commerce and religion, the old and the new existed side by side in tranquility. Istanbul's exceptional status derived from the fact that here, "one can see the legacy of Western Rome and Byzantium in their full glory, while at the same time witnessing the modesty and spiritual depth of Medina." Now, as the municipality supposedly had solved the city's infrastructural problems, there was a new task: "Now the main thing is the way toward becoming a Medina in the true sense, that is, to prevail in the competition between the civilizations."[8]

It need hardly be stated that this conceptualization goes against everything I have described on the preceding pages. Cultures, conceived of as dictated by religions, are assumed to be amorphous, distinct, and omnipotent entities that shape one's identity. Individuals, so to speak, are products off an assembly line shaped by their respective culture, although some of them are perhaps more properly assembled than others. The city within this worldview of monolithic, exclusive cultures, does not vary conceptually too much from the Weberian image of the Asian and the European city. Cities and people in different parts of the world are the inevitable results of what happened there and not elsewhere. The difference between Weber's and the president's reflections lies rather in the value attached to the two types of cities. Whereas Weber sees struggle positively as a step toward progress, he finds the assumed lack of it in the Asian or Middle Eastern city a sign of stagnation. Erdoğan by contrast finds this struggle and the bifurcations it produces abhorrent, and values the supposed harmony of the Muslim city, which one assumes by default, is ruled by pious Muslim leaders. While Weber's essays on the city, written around the time of World War I, still exude European triumphalism, Erdoğan's statements must be read in the context of Samuel P. Huntington's *Clash of Civilizations*. Although writing at another moment of seeming triumph of the West, the defeat of Soviet communism, Huntington was much more pessimistic than Weber. He saw this moment in time more as an apogee and admonished the US government to prepare by means of rearmament, diplomatic divide-and-rule, and promotion of civil society overseas for future conflicts between five wantonly defined world civilizations.[9] Rather than rejecting the redefinition of real political differences and clash of interests into nigh

---

[8] Erdoğan, Speech held at Ibn Khaldun University.
[9] Huntington, "Clash of Civlizations?"

primordial cultural differences, the Turkish president sees the clash of civilizations as a chance for Islamic "civilization" to triumph.

It goes without saying that Erdoğan's harmonic Islamic city is only maintained with the help of armies of police, tear gas, an aggressive policy of "urban renewal," and a judiciary and penal system that combine to keep undesirables from too loudly claiming their place in it. But what is more noticeable than the degree of state-sanctioned physical violence and the threat thereof necessary for this operation, is its symbolic violence. To order the world of the twenty-first century neatly into Christian and Islamic "civilizations" and cities needs a high degree of ignorance. The spread of high-rises in Istanbul, far from being an imposition by the West, is to a large degree due to surplus capital from the Gulf countries being invested into the Turkish real estate sector and tourists from the same region who find the city so attractive exactly because of its mixed heritage and especially its more liberal entertainment sector, rather than it being a Medina replica. Moreover, the vibrancy of the city's modern arts, universities, and consumer culture are the result not of developing the city into "one of the bastions of Turkish-Islamic civilization,"[10] but of the intensity of Istanbul's exchange not only with the rest of the European continent, but also more distant regions in recent years.

Likewise, the nineteenth-century cities were not Turkish, Greek, or Jewish "bastions," but hubs of exchange and mobility with the wider world. The "little Parises," the "corners of Europe," the "stars of the Mediterranean" many locals and visitors now nostalgically yearn for and which they retrospectively whitewash, flourished exactly because there was no single authority or discourse that could enforce a monolithic vision on them. Ottoman imperial, foreign imperialist, irredentist national, but also a myriad of local or global agents who cannot easily be reduced to these etiquettes, shaped the port cities. We should not follow the dangerous Weberian assumption, which was vulgarized by Huntington and after him by contemporary demagogues, that ominous and omnipotent cultures created the cities of the Euro-Mediterranean region. Instead, historians who choose to engage with the archive, rather than expecting it to simply deliver a revelation upon them, can make visible the agents and forces that shaped the city. Urban planners of the *Tanzimat* bureaucracy; seaside flaneurs and clam divers; locally

---

[10] Erdoğan, speech held at Ibn Khaldun University.

based as well as overseas investors; opera stars and aficionados; beer brewers and beer revelers; vigilantes who acted up against the drink; dilettantes at the societal balls; local newspapers; overseas-based schools; writers of letters to the editor; readers of advice or erotic literature; immigrants finding work as railway or sex workers; bandits; and hot-blooded young men and women ready to tear local society apart are but some of the agents that historical research can flush out. In engaging not with a set, but with a multitude of sources, historians can demonstrate the smaller or larger parts such agents performed in shaping the cities they lived in and creating their particular variants of culture.

If culture is indeed "a dynamic communicative space, in which, by establishing or rejecting elements, of signifiers, symbols, or codes – including artefacts – social lifeworlds are constructed, constituted, represented, and reproduced continuously and performatively, individual and collective identities are created, and power relations are negotiated,"[11] then the residents of the nineteenth-century Mediterranean cited took part in a particularly complex negotiation process, but also one posing numerous opportunities. It is this perspective, revealing agency, rather than amorphous cultural determinants, but also individuals confronted with challenges, due to an unprecedented expansion of interconnectivity and due to faster media, more accessible modes of transportation, but also heightened curiosity for the world beyond their immediate horizons, which to some degree allows for parallels between the nineteenth and the early twenty-first century. Then as now, individuals are faced with the necessity to define their personality against the background of a dynamic, globalizing world. The answers they find are in no small part inspired by, but also go into shaping the urban space they live in. The process of defining the self in a world without clear finite borders is both intellectually and practically a challenge, all the more so since the process does not take place in an atmosphere of global solidarity, but is subject to and part of a global competition for resources, such as work, status, housing, and public recognition. Due to this neoliberal rivalry, concepts of clear-cut identities based on forces beyond our individual grasp, a sense of superior and inferior cultures, and the implicit or explicit call for violence to assert such a hegemony, appeal to a sizeable part of society.

[11] Csáky, *Gedächtnis der Städte*, 101.

However, at the moment, it is still unclear whether the determinist view of "cultures" and "civilizations" will prevail or whether the carnivalesque interpretation of culture is perhaps more resilient today than on the eve of World War I.

It is in this context that contributions by urban and cultural historians are of more than mere scholarly importance. The degree to which they are compatible with one of the two worldviews contributes to defining the overall discursive hegemony. Our approaches do not offer a passe-partout for explaining the world. The exploration of globalizing culture will only be complete with the study of global flows of finance, legal norms, ideologies, and technologies.[12] Likewise, the view from the city street is best complemented by the view from a ministry office window, the factory floor, and the provinces. Nonetheless, our perspectives are important for the times we live in. We therefore have the possibility to intervene more energetically into the so-called big discussions of nineteenth- and twentieth-century history, including the issue of modernity. While the relative insignificance of our subdisciplines in these debates is to a large extent due to misrepresentation or ignorance by competing perspectives on the nineteenth and twentieth centuries, it is also in part due to our readiness to abandon these more contested terrains. We have for a long time been all too acceptant of our subaltern role. As cultural historians, we should no longer be content to be considered unworldly investigators of obscure phenomena, as our findings have the potential to make visible obscured connections and worldviews from the past. And as urban historians, we should no longer treat the objects of our scrutiny as some esoteric counterworlds, separated from the arenas where the "big" questions of our times were resolved, but should reclaim them as the sites where Eastern Mediterranean modernity was forged.

---

[12] Appadurai, *Modernity at Large*; Hanley, *Identifying with Nationality*. It has rightfully been pointed out that globally active surplus capital and urbanization have been bedfellows since the nineteenth century and continue to be so in the present; Harvey, "The Right to the City." One of the lacunae left behind by this study is to paint a fuller picture of nineteenth-century Eastern Mediterranean cities by taking a precise look at the interdependencies of those cities' capital with the wider world, without presupposing a Marxist or Wallersteinian teleology; Soysal, *Ottoman Empire in the Age of Global Financial Capitalism*.

Bibliography

Archival Documents

Federal Archives, Berlin Branch (BA Berlin)

R 901/39576, R 901/52413.

Federal Archives – Military Archives, Freiburg i.Br. Branch (BA-MA)

Imperial Navy Files (Reichsmarine, RM) 40/565, 40/733.

Bibliothèque nationale de France, Paris (BnF)

Petition du Sieur Alexandre Blacque, undated (early Jan 1828).

Ottoman Archive of the State Archives Administration within the President of the Turkish Republic's Office, Istanbul (BOA)

Documents referred to and used in the statistical survey in Chapters 12 and 13:
1851–1868: HR. MKT. 54/34, 28 Ra 1267; HR.TO. 416/24; MVL 245/80, 05 Ra 1268; HR. MKT. 54/64, 01 R 1269, HR. MKT. 69/44, 12 R 1270; İ. HR. 126/6365, 06 R 1272; DH. MKT. 134/13, 16 Ca 1272; HR. MKT. 131/36, 23 R 1272; HR. MKT. 148/61, 14 L 1272; HR. MKT. 159/39, 14 M 1273; HR. MKT. 165/16, 29 S 1273; A.} MKT. NZD 293/78, 06 Ra 1274; HR. MKT. 213/74, 14 Ra 1274; A.} M. 19/19, 08 C 1275; A.} MKT. NZD. 293/77, 30 Ra 1276; A.} NZD. 299/9, 23 Ca 1276; A.} MKT. MVL. 107/78, 20 L 1275; A.} MKT. 366/8, 16 S 1276; DH. MKT. 318/7, 16 Ca 1276; A.} DVN. 157/10, 29 Ra 1277; A.} NZD. 300/57, 10 C 1276; A.} NZD. 312/62, 25 L 1276; A.} NZD. 320/72, 18 M 1277; MVL 834/112, 26 L 1276; MVL 836/26, 06 B 1276; A.} NZD. 365/75, 29 S 1278; A.} MKT. UM. 459/43, 22 Ş 1277; A.} NZD. 406/14, 07 N 1278; MVL 384/62, 06 N 1278; MVL 385/61, 14 N 1278; A.} MKT. NZD. 425/81, 20 Z 1278; MVL 426/93, 29 S 1280.

1869–1886: ŞD. 2860/42, 19 Z 1288; ŞD. 2861/34, 19 Z 1288; A.} MKT. MHM. 473/60, 17 Z 1290; HH. d. 14562, 1291; HR. TO. 461/49; HR. TO 61/47; Y. PRK. ZB. 1/68, 03 Z 1297; İ. ŞD. 53/2949, 06 S 1298; HH. d. 16596, 1299; ŞD. 694/39, 21 N 1299; TS. MA. D 3034 0001, 1299; TS. MA. D 3034 0002, 1299; TS. MA. D 3034 0003, 1299; TS. MA. D 3034 0004, 1299; TS. MA. D 3034 0005, 1299; TS. MA. D 3034 0006, 1299; ŞD. 686/8, 21 N 1299; DH. MKT. 1341/77, 12 Za 1300; HH. d. 16595, 1300; Y. PRK. HH. 11/3, 21 L 1300; Y. PRK. H. 11/21, 1300; İ. DH. 925/73334, 27 L 1301; HH. d. 16593, 1302, ŞD. 1282/21, 10 R 1302; ŞD. 1536/44, 17 B 1302; İ. ŞD 83/4907, 20 M 1304; MV. 8/11, 24 Ca 1303.

1887–1904: DH. MKT. 1399/4, 17 Ca 1304; DH. MKT. 1401/89, 03 C 1304; DH. MKT. 1407/12, 29 C 1304; DH. MKT. 1427/80, 06 L 1304; DH. MKT. 1457/71, 08 S 1305; DH. MKT. 1465/66, 06 Ra 1305; DH. MKT. 1467/21, 15 Ra 1305; İ. ŞD. 84/5020, 14 C 1304; İ. ŞD. 88/5219, 28 M 1305; MV. 22/27, 03 Za 1304; Y. A. RES 39/9, 10 Za 1304; ŞD. 714/17, 22 Ş 1305; ŞD. 720/15, 22 Ş 1305; ŞD. 727/10, 22 Ş 1305; DH. MKT. 1537/59, 21 Z 1305; DH. MKT. 1553/53, 05 S 1306; DH. MKT. 1537/59, 21 Z 1305; DH. MKT. 1553/53, 05 S 1306; Y. PRK. SH. 2/72, 29 Z 1305; DH. MKT. 1594/11, 12 C 1306; DH. MKT. 1599/88, 27 C 1306; DH. MKT. 1602/32, 05 B 1306; DH. MKT. 1604/36, 10 B 1306; DH. MKT. 1679/96, 13 R 1307; İ. DH. 1142/89117, 07 Za 1306; MV. 41/1, 03 B 1306; DH. MKT. 1735/114, 07 Za 1307; DH. MKT. 1740/78, 21 Za 1307; DH. MKT. 1748/107, 20 Z 1307; DH. MKT. 1756/10, 14 M 1308; DH. MKT. 1763/57, 07 S 1308; DH. MKT. 1765/13, 13 S 1308; DH. MKT.1782/108, 06 R 1308; DH. MKT. 1789/34, 23 R 1308; Y. PRK. MYD. 9/105, 03 R 1308; DH. MKT. 1844/113, 20 Za 1308; MF. MKT. 129/33, 13 Za 1308; ŞD. 2568/9, 21 M 1309; Y. PRK. ŞH 3/87, 17 Z 1308; Y. PRK. ZB 7/59, 04 B 1309; İ. MMS. 127/5411, 09 Ra 1309; BEO 1147/8478, 09 Ca 1310; BEO 42/3104, 07 M 1310; BEO 74/5542, 29 S 1310; BEO 88/6539, 22 Ra 1310; DH. MKT. 1921/26, 11 B 1309; DH. MKT. 1964/52, 26 Za 1309; DH. MKT. 1986/122, 20 M 1310; Y. A. HUS 256/89, 21 B 1309, Y. PRK. ML 14/34, 11 C 1310; ŞD. 1190/19, 19 C 1309; BEO 136/10173, 19 C 1310; BEO 181/13551, 21 N 1310; BEO 297/22228, 09 R 1311; DH. MKT. 114/41, 06 S 1311; DH. MKT. 2044/125, 04 B 1310; DH. MKT. 5/79, 06 Ra 1311; BEO 134/9983, 14 C 1310; BEO 181/13548, 21 N 1310; BEO 271/20290, 23 S 1311; BEO 293/21901, 01 R 1311; BEO 371/27799, 01 N 1311; BEO 423/31704, 19 Z 1311; DH. MKT. 198/92, 16 B 1311; DH. MKT. 222/15, 04 L 1311; İ. HUS. 20/1311 B-03, 03 B 1311; ŞD. 768/4, 29 R 1312; ZB. 70/14, 08 E 1310; A.} MKT. MHM. 533/8, 16 Ra 1312; BEO 443/33207, 24 M 1312; İ. RSM. 2/1311 L-5, 11 L 1311; Y. A. HUS. 297/39, 14 Za 1311; BEO 547/41005, 10 B 1312; ŞD. 2624/7, 22 Ra 1313; MF.MKT. 339/47, 10 Ca 1314; ŞD. 2969/51, 28 B 1313;

ŞD. 2970/1, 28 B 1313; DH. MKT. 2085/22, 03 C 1315; İ. ŞE. 10/1315 M-3, 11 M 1315; Y. PRK. AZJ 35/20, 22 Ca 1315; Y. PRK. AZJ. 35/20, 22 Ca 1315; DH. MKT. 2111/65, 12 Ca 1316; Y.PRK.MYD. 19/107, 24 Ra 1315; DH. MKT. 2149/13, 01 Ş 1316; BEO 1394/102519, 03 Ca 1317; DH. MKT. 2242/82, 27 R 1317; DH. MKT. 2251/166, 21 Ca 1317; DH. MKT. 2369/17, 07 Ra 1318; ZB. 350/78, 20 H 1316; DH. MKT. 2401/88, 16 Ca 1318; ZB. 350/78, 20 H 1316; BEO 478/11081, 29 Z 1317; BEO 740/13042, 17 B 1319; DH. MKT. 2512/64, 05 R 1319; DH. MKT. 2556/28, 19 B 1319; DH. MKT. 2556/28, 03 Ş 1319; DH. MKT. 2570/53, 12 N 1319; Y. PRK. ZB. 26/81, 09 Za 1318; BEO 945/14580, 02 Ş 1320; ŞD. 390/68, 01 Z 1319; DH. MKT. 722/18, 15 Ra 1321; BEO 131/15979, 10 Ca 1321; DH. MKT. 650/3, 11 Za 1320; BEO 428/18205, 04 Ş 1322; DH. MKT. 828/30, 21 Z 1321; DH. MKT. 868/10, 23 R 1322; Y. PRK. ASK. 212/22, 22 Za 1321; Y. PRK. BŞK. 73/64, 04 N 1322; DH. MKT 856/35, 16 Ra 1322; TFR. I. AS 15/1424, 16 Ra 1322; BEO 2347/175952, 22 Ra 1322; BEO 473/18135, 18 B 1322; DH. MKT. 856/35, 16 Ra 1322; TFR. I. AS. 15/1424, 16 Ra 1322.

1905–1922: İ. EV. 39/1323 L-03, 05 L 1323; ŞD. 823/12, 04 Ra 1323; ZB. 372/82, 13 A 1321; DH. MKT. 1060/59, 25 M 1324; ŞD. 62/45, 04 R 1324; Y. MTV. 288/38, 11 Ca 1324; ZB. 373/15, 16 Ma 1322; ZB. 385/11, 06 Ma 1322; ZA. 368/139, 11 T 1322; ZB. 387/41, 31 T 1322; ZB. 468/145, 03 Ni 1322; ZB. 80/49, 02 A 1322; ZB. 387/118, 02 E 1322; ŞD/ 177/49, 12 R 1325; Y. MTV. 298/159, 27 R 1325; ZB. 31/44, 21 T 1323; ZB. 375/97, 10 Şu 1322; ZB. 390/3, 01 A 1323; ZB. 479/53, 01 Te 1323; ZB. 479/56, 03 Te 1323; ZB. 53/51, 25 H 1323; ZB. 634/16, 26 H 1323; ZB. 65/112, 11 T 1323; ZB. 55/107, 05 H 1323; ZB. 65/112, 11 T 1323; DH. MKT. 1248/10, 15 Ra 1326; Y. MTV. 304/206, 28 Za 1325; Y. MTV. 307/143, 21 S 1326; Y. PRK. HH. 39/4, 06 C 1326; ZB. 328/111, 22 Ts 1324; ZB. 384/30, 20 Şu 1323; ZB. 487/97, 16 Ts 1324; ZB. 74/31, 04 A 1324; ZB. 327/61, 12 Te 1324; BEO 3434/257482, 20 L 1326; BEO 3434/257508, 19 L 1326; TFR. I. M. 22/2117, 24 B 1326; TFR. I. SL. 185/18430, 02 Ca 1326; TFR. I. SL. 194/19391, 24 B 1326; TFR. I. SL 195/19410, 27 B 1326; TFR. I. ŞKT. 151/15054, 08 R 1326; ZB. 327/61, 12 Te 1324; DH. MKT. 2766/17, 20 S 1327; DH. MKT. 2847/20, 28 Ca 1327; DH. MUİ. 24–1/59, 06 L 1327; Y. MTV. 131/91, 29 Z 1326; ZB. 314/68, 04 Ni 1325; ZB. 334/69, 18 H 1925; ZB. 335/115, 29 T 1925; ZB. 376/67, 08 N 1325; ZB. 377/18, 10 My 1325; ZB. 377/53, 25 My 1325; ZB. 601/129, 02 Şu 1324; ZB. 602/57, 02 Ni 1325; BEO 3511/263259, 21 S 1327; DH. MKT. 2816/5, 27 R 1327; TFR. I. SL. 213/21231, 26 C 1327; TFR. I. SL. 213/21269, 28 C 1327; ZB. 376/67, 08 Ni 1325; ZB. 376/91, 23 Ni 1325; ZB. 377/35, 16 My 1325; ZB. 378/4, 20 H 1325; DH. EUM. VRK. 4/12, 07 N 1328; DU. MUİ 109/29, 24 C 1328: DH. MUİ.

84–2/10, 29 R 1328; DH. MUİ. 92–1/14, 26 R 1328; MV. 136/48, 22 M 1328; DH. EUM. KADL. 21/33, 09 N 1328; DH. EUM. VRK 21/33, 09 N 1328; DH. EUM. VRK. 7/19, 17 M 1329; DH. İD. 75–1/37, 26 C 1329; DH. İD. 96/2, 27 Za 1329; DH. H. 1–1/14, 08 Z 1329; DH. EUM. THR 106/22, 08 S 1329; BEO 3496/262145, 26 M 1327; BEO 3933/294913, 05 N 1329; DH. EUM. THR. 106/22, 08 S 1329; DH. EUM. VRK. 8/32, 12 Ca 1329; DH. H. 1–1/14, 08 Z 1329; DH. İD. 117/20, 06 M 1329; DH. İD. 70 –1/28, 03 Z 1329; İ. MMS. 143/1329 Ş-19, 14 Ş 1329; ŞD. 1228/39, 13 Za 1329; ŞD. 1234/6, 13 Za 1329; ŞD. 1235/12, 13 Za 1329; ŞD. 441/17, 21 Ra 1329; BEO 4029/302138, 01 Ca 1330; BEO 4039/302919, 28 Ca 1330; DH. EUM. EMN. 108/43, 29 Z 1330; DH İD. 65/18, 21 Ca 1330; DH. İD. 83–1/48, 03 Ca 1330; DH, EUM. THR. 84/20, 14 Z 1330; ŞD. 2072/23, 18 M 1331; DH. İD. 160–1/25, 10 S 1331; MV. 173/5, 02 S 1331; ŞD. 454/6, 20 S 1331; DH. EUM. MTK. 42/25, 17 N 1332; DH. İD. 152/13, 04 L 1332; DH. İD. 218–1/22, 22 L 1332; DH. UMVM 113/17, 26 R 1332; DH. EUM. 3. Şb 3/22, 29 M 1333; DH. EUM. 3. Şb 6/73, 20 Ş 1333; DH. EUM. 5. Şb 19/43, 01 S 1334; DH. EUM. EMN. 66/64, 24 Ş 1333; DH. İ. UM 67/2 18, 15 B 1333; DH. UMVM 105/39, 04 B 1333; DH. HMŞ. 4–2/5-01, 03 L 1334; DH. İ. UM EK. 18/62; 16 L 1334; İ. DUİT 119/118, 21 Ş 1334; MV. 243/54, 20 Ş 1334; DH. EUM. KLH. 5/88, 13 L 1334; DH. EUM. 6. Şb 21/16, 28 Za 1335; DH. MB. HPS. M. 30/96, 24 Z 1335; DH. ŞFR. 552/27, 21 Ni 1333; DH. İ. UM 1 –3/7/25, 05 Ca 1336; DH. İ. UM 4–3/7/33, 16 B 1336; DH. UMVM 97/36, 23 S 1337; İ. DUİT 89/53, 15 M 1337; İ. DUİT 89/58, 19 C 1336; DH. EUM. AYŞ 16/39, 23 L 1337; DH. İ. UM. 19–09/1 /61, 17 S 1338; ŞD. 1261/37, 07 R 1338; MV. 215/59, 14 B 1337; MV. 251/28, 17 N 1337; ŞD. 1266/22, 07 R 1338; DH. EUM. AYŞ 44/12, 03 Za 1338; DH. EUM. AYŞ 45/39, 21 Z 1338; MV. 219/131, 21 L 1338; MV. 252/116, 19 M 1339; DH. EUM. AYŞ. 44/23, 05 Za 1338; DH. EUM. AYŞ. 44/23, 05 Za 1338; İ. DUİT 123/9, 25 R 1338; MV. 254/32, 20 R 1338; DH. EUM. AYŞ 57/20, 28 S 1340; DH. HMŞ. 8/2 22, 29 Ra 1340; DH. UMVM 114/7, 05 Z 1339; DH. UMVM 89/9, 17 Z 1339; ŞD. 2147/7, 02 R 1340; DH. EUM. AYŞ 61/29, 07 L 1340; DH. İ. UM 7–8/1 /16, 22 Ş 1340; DH. UMVM 117/5, 27 C 1340; DH. EUM. MH. 230/7, 11 L 1340.

Other Documents of the BOA

İ.HUS. 89/1319.Ra.36, 22 Ra 1319; İ.MMS. 9/373, 1273; ZB. 627/86, 13 Ma 1325.

Evangelical Parish Thessaloniki

Old Baptism Register.

Evangelical Central Archives, Berlin (ezab)

Ezab 5/1948; 5/1949.

Prussian Privy State Archives, Berlin (GStA)

Ministry of Foreign Affairs (MdA): III. HA II 758.

Archives of the House, Court, and State, Vienna (HHStA)

Administrative Registratur (Adm. Reg.): F 31–49; F 47–31; F 52–46; F 52–105.
Embassy and Consulate Constantinople (BK Kpl): 93; 107; 115.
Consulate General Salonica (GK Sal): 108; 117; 393; 420–450.
Political Archive (PA): XXXVIII 92, 93, 235; XII Türkei 269, Liasse XVI.
Prokesch-Osten Papers 27.

Political Archives of the Foreign Office, Berlin (PA–AA)

Consulate General Salonica (GK Sal): 14; 22; 32; 49.

Yale University Library

Ernst Jäckh Papers Box 1.

Published Documents (Archival Material, Letters, Databases)

Archives de la Planète (Albert Kahn Collection), Hauts-de-Seine Open Data, https://opendata.hauts-de-seine.fr/explore/dataset/archives-de-la-pla nete/images/ ?disjunctive.operateur&sort=identifiant_fakir&location= 2,28.34802,5.37321&basemap=jawg.streets.

Atay, Çınar, *19. Yüzyıl Izmir Fotoğrafları* (Antalya: AKMED, 1997).
  Osmanlı'dan Cumhuriyet'e İzmir Planları (Izmir: Yaşar Eğitim ve Kültür Vakfı, 1998).

Bali, Rıfat (ed.), *A Survey of Some Social Conditions in Smyrna, Asia Minor – May 1921* (Izmir: Libra, 2010).

Brızitsov, Hristo, *İstanbul'dan Mektuplar* (Istanbul: Kitap Yayınevi, 2016).

Erdoğan, Recep Tayyip, speech held at Ibn Khaldun University, 21 October 2017, on YouTube, "Erdoğan İstanbul'un kıymetini bilmedik," www.youtube.com/watch?v=Ghy3XE6VRt4.

Ersoy, Mehmet Akıf, "İstiklâl Marşı," wikipedia, https://en.wikipedia.org/wiki/%C4%B0stiklal_Mar%C5%9F%C4%B1#ref_n88.
Georgiev, Veličko and Trifonov, Stajko (eds.), *Makedonija i Trakija v borba za svoboda: Krajât na XIX – načaloto na XX vek* (Sofia: Makedonski Naučen Institut, 1995).
Köse, Resul, and Albayrak, Muzaffer (eds.), *Arşiv Belgelerine Göre Osmanlı'da Gösteri Sanatları: Geleneksel Seyir Sanatları (Kukla-Karagöz-Ortaoyunlu), Tiyatro, Sinema* (Istanbul: Osmanlı Arşivi Daire Başkanlığı, 2015).
League of Nations, "French Mandate for Syria and Lebanon," *American Journal of International Law* 17/3 (Supplement), www.ndu.edu.lb/Lerc/resources/French%20Mandate%20for%20Syria%20and%20the%20Lebanon.pdf. Last accessed 9 July 2020.
"Palestine Mandate," *Avalon Project*, http://avalon.law.yale.edu/20th_century/palmanda.asp. Last accessed 9 July 2020.
Levantine Heritage, "Frederick de Cramer," www.levantineheritage.com/testi86.htm; "Prokopp" (by Marie-Anne Marandet, Andrew Simes, and George Vassiadis), www.levantineheritage.com/prokopp.htm; "Osman Streater," www.levantineheritage.com/testi20.htm; "The van Lennep Genealogy," www.levantineheritage.com/pdf/The_Van_Lennep_Genealogy_Smyrna_Branch.pdf; "Walker," www.levantineheritage.com/walker.htm.
Mıntzuri, Hagop, *İstanbul Anıları* (Istanbul: Aras, 2017).
Nestoroff, Alka, *The Istanbul Letters of Alka Nestoroff* (Bonn: Max Weber Stiftung, 2015).
Schulte, Eduard (ed.), *Carl Humann, der Entdecker des Weltwunders von Pergamon, in Zeugnissen seiner Zeit 1839–1896 geschildert* (Dortmund, 1971).
Thessaloniki Municipality, "Monuments," https://thessaloniki.gr/i-want-to-know-the-city/discover/monuments/?lang=en.

Newspapers and Journals

Cervati, *Indicateur Oriental* 1887.
Courrier de Smyrne, Oct.–Dec. 1828; Jan.–July 1829; March, April 1830.
Demokratische Zeitung, 30 July 1872.
Examiner, 18 June 1907.
Heidelberger Jahrbücher der Literatur 30 (2/1837).
Journal de Constantinople, Jan., Nov. 1855.
Journal de Salonique, Oct.–Dec. 1895; Jan.–Nov. 1896; Nov., Dec. 1902; Jan. 1903; Nov., Dec. 1907; Nov. 1908.

Levant Herald, Jan. 1873.
Le Matin, July 1879.
Le Ménestrel, 31 Jan. 1858.
Morgenblatt für gebildete Leser 141 (14 June 1847).
Neue Zürcher Zeitung, 13 July 1919.
Österreichische Zuschauer, 28 July 1847.
Progrès d'Orient, Aug. 1874.
Revue commerciale du Levant 86 (May 1894), 95 (Feb. 1895), 99 (June 1895), 101 (Aug. 1895), 102 (Sept. 1895), 108 (March 1896), 109 (April 1896), 199 (Oct. 1903), 212 (Nov. 1904), 274 (Jan. 1910), 256 (July 1908), 294 (Sept. 1911), 306 (Sept. 1912), 256 (July 1908), 294 (Sept. 1911).
Servet-i Fünun 244, 2 Teşrinisani 1311 (14 Nov. 1895); 274, 30 Mayıs 1312 (11 June 1896); 449, 7 Teşrinevvel 1315 (19 Oct. 1899); 460, 23 Kanunevvel 1315 (4 Jan. 1900).
Smyrna Mail, Jan.–Oct. 1834; Sept., Oct. 1862; Feb. 1893; May 1895.
Spectateur Oriental, 29. Dec. 1827.
Stamboul, Jan. 1890; Jan. 1900; Jan. 1911.
Vossiche Zeitung, 28 Jan. 1848.

Old Literature (before 1960)

Please note: Dates of titles are according to their first publication. Therefore, reprints and new editions post-1960 will be found in this section, rather than under New Literature.

Aa.

Ahmet Mithat, *Bütün eserleri*, vol. VIII (Ankara: Türk Dil Kurumu, 2000).

Bb.

Baedeker, Karl, *Konstantinopel und Kleinasien (Balkanstaaten, Archipel, Cypern)* (Leipzig: Baedeker, 1914).
Bareilles, Bertrand, *Constantinople: ses cités franques et levantines (Péra – Galata – banlieue)* (Paris: Editions Bossard, 1918).
Barring, Evelyn, *Modern Egypt* (Cambridge: Hard Press, 2013).
Barth, Hans, *Unter südlichem Himmel: Bilder aus dem Orient und Italien* (Leipzig: Rengersche Buchh., 1893).
Bigart, Jaques, "Alliance Isréalite Universelle," in *Jewish Encyclopedia* (1906) www.jewishencyclopedia.com/articles/1264-alliance-israelite-universelle.

Braudel, Fernand, *The Mediterranean and the Mediterranean World in the Age of Philip II.*, vol. II (Berkeley: University of California Press, 1966).
Brunau, Max, *Das Deutschtum in Mazedonien* (Stuttgart: Ausland und Heimat, 1925).
Bülow, Hugo von, "Eine Konsular-Reise durch das General-Gouvernement Smyrna," in *Globus* 1864, vol. VI, 207–210, 243–246, 273–277, 342–347.
Busch-Zantner, Richard, *Agrarverfassung und Siedlung in Südosteuropa unter bes. Berücksichtigung der Türkenzeit* (Leipzig: Harrassowitz, 1938).

Cc.

Calligas, Paul, *Voyage à Syros, Smyrne et Constantinople* (Paris: L'Harmattan, 1997).
Çayan, Tigran, "La musique à Constantinople," *La Revue Musicale* 8 (11/June 1908), 329–331.
Chamfort, Sébastien Roch Nicolas, *Der Kaufmann von Smyrna* (Mannheim: E. F. Schwan, 1770).
Cinq auteurs, *L'aveugle de Smyrne* (Paris: Augustin Courbé, 1638).

Dd.

Deschamps, Gaston, *Sur les routes d'Asie* (Paris: Armand Colin Et Cie, 1894).
Duhani, Said N., *Quand Beyoglu s'appelait Pera: Les temps qui ne reviendront plus* (Istanbul: Édition La Turquie Moderne, 1956).

Ee.

Elias, Norbert, *On the Process of Civilisation* (Dublin: University College Dublin Press, 2012).

Ff.

Fallmerayer, Jakob Ph., *Fragmente aus dem Orient* (Munich: Bruckmann, 1963).
  Geschichte der Halbinsel Morea während des Mittelalters (Hildesheim: Olms, 1965).
Fanon, Frantz, *Black Skin, White Masks* (New York: Grove Press, 1967).

Formby, Henry, *A Visit to the East Comprising Germany, the Danube, Constantinople, Asia, Egypt and Idumea* (London: Mason Press, 1843).
Forneris, Anna, *Schicksale und Erlebnisse einer Kärtnerin während ihrer Reisen in verschiedenen Ländern und fast 30-jährigen Aufenthalts im Oriente, als: in Malta, Corfu, Constantinopel, Smyrna, Tiflis, Tauris, Jerusalem, Rom ... beschrieben von ihr selbst* (Klagenfurt: Heyn 1985).
Fröbel, Julius, *Ein Lebenslauf: Aufzeichnungen, Erinnerungen und Bekenntnisse*, vol. II. (Stuttgart: Cotta, 1891).

Gg.

Grothe, Hugo *Auf türkischer Erde: Reisebilder und Studien* (Berlin: Allgemeiner Verein für Deutsche Literatur, 1903).

Hh.

Hartmann, Martin, *Der islamische Orient: Berichte und Forschungen*, vol. III (Leipzig: Rudolf Haupt, 1910).
Hemingway, Ernest, "On the Quai at Smyrna," 1925, https://pantherfile.uwm.edu/wash/www/hemingway.htm.
Herder, Johann Gottfried, *Theoretische Schriften: Ideen zur Philosophie der Geschichte der Menschheit* (Berlin: Holzinger, 2013), www.zeno.org/Lesesaal/N/9781482559736.
Humbert Gustav, *Konstantinopel-London-Smyrna: Skizzen aus dem Leben eines kaiserlich deutschen Auslands-Beamten* (Berlin: Hochschule & Ausland, 1927).

Ii.

Ibn Khaldun, Abd-ar-Rahman Ibn-Muhammad, *The Muqadimmah: An Introduction to History*, vol. II (Princeton: Princeton University Press, 1967).

Jj.

al-Jabarti, Abd al-Rahman, *Al-Jabarti's Chronicle of the First Seven Months of the French Occupation of Egypt* (Leiden: Brill, 1975).
Jahn, August M., "Reise von Mainz nach Egypten, Jerusalem und Konstantinopel," in Barbara Kellner-Heinkele and Ingeborg Hauenschild (eds.), *Türkei: Streifzüge im Osmanischen Reich nach Reiseberichten des 18. und 19. Jahrhunderts* (Frankfurt/Main: Societäts-Verl., 1990), 29–63.

Kk.

Kastriotis, Stephanos, *Constantinople, janvier 1841, lettre de Stephanos Kastriotis à M. C. Polyeucte, sur les affaires d'Orient et la politique européenne* (Paris: Perrotin, 1841).

Kauder, E., *Reisebilder aus Persien, Turkestan und der Türkei* (Breslau: Schlesische Buchdruckerei, 1900).

Kerr, Alfred, *Die Welt im Licht*, vol. II (Berlin: Fischer, 1920).

Klötzel, Chesekiel Z., *In Saloniki* (Berlin: Jüdischer Verl., 1920).

Ll.

Lévy, Sam, *Salonique à la fin du XIXe siècle* (Istanbul: Isis Press, 2000).

Lindau, Paul, *An der Westküste Klein-Asiens* (Berlin: Allgemeiner Verein für Deutsche Literatur, 1900).

Lindenberg, Paul, *Auf deutschen Pfaden im Orient* (Berlin: Dümmler, 1902).

Mm.

MacFarlane, Charles, *Constantinople in 1828: A Residence of Sixteen Months in the Turkish Capital and Provinces. With an Account of the Present State of the Naval and Military Power, and of the Resources of the Ottoman Empire*, vol. I (London: Saunders and Otley, 1829).

Mann, Thomas, *Betrachtungen eines Unpolitischen* (Berlin: Fischer, 1920).

Meyers Reisebücher, *Griechenland und Kleinasien* (Leipzig: Bibliographisches Institut, 1901).

Balkanstaaten und Konstantinopel (Leipzig: Bibliographisches Institut, 1914).

Moltke, Helmuth, *Briefe über Zustände und Begebenheiten in der Türkei aus den Jahren 1835 bis 1839* (Berlin: Mittler, 1876).

Nn.

Nahmer, Ernst v.d., "Deutsche Kolonisationspläne und -erfolge in der Türkei vor 1870," *Schmollers Jahrbuch für Gesetzgebung* 3/4, 40, 1916.

Nietzsche, Friedrich, *Digitale Kritische Gesamtausgabe: Werke und Briefe*, eKGWB/FW-377: "Die fröhliche Wissenschaft," § 377; and eKGWB/NF-1885,2 [196]: "Nachgelassene Fragmente Herbst 1885 – Herbst 1886," www.nietzschesource.org.

Pp.

Pears, Sir Edwin, *Forty Years in Constantinople: The Recollections of Sir Edwin Pears, 1873–1915, with 16 Illustrations* (New York: D. Appleton and Company, 1916).

Rr.

Raschdau, Ludwig, *Ein sinkendes Reich: Erlebnisse eines deutschen Diplomaten im Orient* (Berlin: Mittler & Sohn, 1934).
Recaizade, Mahmut Ekrem, *Araba Sevdası* (Istanbul: İnkılap, 1985).
Rimbaud, Jean Arthur, "Mauvais Sang," in Arthur Rimbaud, *Une saison en Enfer* (Brussels, 1873), www.mag4.net/Rimbaud/poesies/Sang.html.

Ss.

Sacher-Masoch, Leopold von, *Venus im Pelz/Grausame Frauen* (Norderstedt: Books on Demand, 2010).
Scherer, Hermann, *Reisen in der Levante 1859–1865* (Frankfurt/Main: Winter, 1866).
Scherzer, Karl von, Humann, Carl, and Stöckel, J. M., *Smyrna: Mit besonderer Rücksicht auf die geographischen, wirthschaftlichen und intelectuellen Verhältnisse von Vorder-Kleinasien* (Vienna: A. Hölder, 1883).
Schulz-Labischin, Gotthold, *Die Sängerreise der Berliner Liedertafel nach dem Orient* (Berlin: Im Selbstverlage des Vereins, 1908).
Schwan, Friedrich, *Erinnerungen eines Konsuls: 1871–1887 Ägypten, Konstantinopel, Salonich, Korfu, Jassy, Venedig, Amsterdam, Ägypten* (Vienna: Braumüller, 1917).
Sciaky, Leon, *Farewell to Ottoman Salonica* (Istanbul: Isis Press, 2000).
Seetzen, U. J., "Reise-Nachrichten," *Monatliche Correspondenz zur Beförderung der Erd- und Himmels-Kunde*, Dec. 1803.
Steinwald, Ernst, *Beiträge zur Geschichte der deutschen evangelischen Gemeinde zu Smyrna 1759–1904* (Berlin: Vaterl. Verl.- u. Kunstanst., 1904).

Tt.

Tancoigne, J. M., *Voyage à Smyrne, dans l'archipel et l'ile de Candie, en 1811, 1812, 1813 et 1814; suivi d'une notice sur Péra et d'une description de la marche du Sultan*, vol. I (Paris: Nepveu, 1817).
Tüccarzâde İbrahim Hilmi, *Avrupalılaşmak* (Ankara: Gündoğan, 1997).

Uu.

Uşaklıgil, Halid Ziya, *Aşk-ı memnu* (Istanbul: İnkılap, 1974).

Ww.

Wanda, *Souvenirs Anecdotiques sur la Turquie 1820–1870* (Paris: Firmin-Didot et Cie, 1884).
Weber, Max, *Gesammelte Aufsätze zur Religionssoziologie*, vol. I (Tübingen: Mohr, 1972).
Gesamtausgabe, vol. XXII/V (Tübingen: Mohr, 1999).
Weil, Simone, *Simone Weil on Colonialism: An Ethic of the Other* (Lanham: Rowman & Littlefield, 2003).
Wenck, Wanda von, "Erfahrungen im türkischen Schuldienst," in Franz Schmidt and Otto Boelitz (eds.), *Aus deutscher Bildungsarbeit im Auslande: Erlebnisse und Erfahrungen in Selbstzeugnissen aus aller Welt*, vol. II: *Außereuropa* (Langensalza: Beltz, 1927), 94–105.

New Literature (after 1960)

Aa.

Ade, Mafalda, *Picknick mit den Paschas: Aleppo und die levantinische Handelsfirma Fratelli Poche (1853–1880)* (Würzburg: Ergon, 2013).
Akbayar, Nuri and Sakaoğlu, Necdet, *Binbir Gün Binbir Gece Osmanlı'dan Günümüze İstanbul'da Eğlence Yaşamı* (Istanbul: Denizbank, 1999).
Aksan, Virginia H., *Ottomans and Europeans: Contacts and Conflicts* (Istanbul: Isis Press, 2004).
Akyalçın Kaya, Dilek, *Les Sabbatéens saloniciens (1845–1912): Des individus pluriels dans une société urbaine en transition*, PhD thesis, Paris: EHESS, 2013.
Aleksov, Bojan, "'History Taught Us Not to Fear Anything from the East and Everything from the West': A Historical Perspective on Serbian Occidentalism," in Gabriella Schubert and Holm Sundhaussen (eds.), *Prowestliche und antiwestliche Diskurse in den Balkanländern/Südosteuropa* (Munich: Sagner, 2008), 31–46.
Allfrey, Anthony, *Edward VII and His Jewish Court* (London: Weidenfeld & Nicolson, 1991).
Alpargın, Melike Nihan, *Istanbuls theatralische Wendezeit: Die Rezeption des westlichen Theaters im 19. und frühen 20. Jahrhundert des Osmanischen Reiches* (Munich: Herbert Utz, 2013).

Altın, Hamza, "Ziya Gökalp'in Eğitim Tarihimiz Açısından Önemi," *History Studies* 2 (2/2010), 493–509.
Amenda, Lars and Fuhrmann, Malte (eds.), *Hafenstädte – Mobilität, Migration, Globalisierung, Comparativ* 17 (2/2007).
Anastassiadou, Meropi, "Les Occidentaux de la place," in Gilles Veinstein (ed.), *Salonique, 1850–1918: La ville des juifs et le réveil des Balkans* (Paris: Autrement, 1993), 143–152.
  Salonique 1830–1912: Une ville ottomane à l'âge des réformes (Leiden: Brill, 1997).
  "Sports d'élites et élites sportives a Salonique a la fin du XIXe siecle," in Paul Dumont and François Georgeon (eds.), *Vivre dans l'Empire ottoman, sociabilités et relations intercommunautaires (XVIIIe–XXe siècles)* (Paris: L'Harmattan, 1997), 145–160.
And, Metin, "Eski İstanbul'da Fransız Sahnesi," *Tiyatro Araştırmaları Dergisi* 2 (4/1971), 77–102.
Andrews, Walter G., "Speaking of Power: The 'Ottoman Kaside,'" in Stephan Sperl and Christopher Shackle (eds.), *Qasida Poetry in Islamic Asia and Africa* (Leiden: Brill, 1996), 281–300.
Antonwicz-Bauer, Lucyna, *Polonezköyü-Adampol* (Istanbul: Erler, 1992).
Appadurai, Arjun, *Modernity at Large: Cultural Dimensions of Globalization* (Minneapolis: University of Minnesota Press, 1996).
Aracı, Emre, *Naum Tiyatrosu* (Istanbul: Yapı Kredi, 2010).
Aydın, Cemil, *The Politics of Anti-Westernism in Asia: Visions of World Order in Pan-Islamic and Pan-Asian Thought* (New York: Columbia University Press, 2007).
Aymes, Marc, "The Port-City in the Fields: Investigating an Improper Urbanity in Mid-Nineteenth-Century Cyprus," *Mediterranean Historical Review* 24 (2/2009), 133–149.

Bb.

Baer, Marc David, *The Dönme: Jewish Converts, Muslim Revolutionaries, and Secular Turks* (Stanford: Stanford University Press, 2010).
Bakić-Hayden, Milica, "Nesting Orientalisms: The Case of Former Yugoslavia," *Slavic Review* 54 (4/ 1995), 917–931.
Bakić-Hayden, Milica and Hayden, Robert, "Orientalist Variations on the Theme 'Balkans': Symbolic Geography in Recent Yugoslav Cultural Politics," *Slavic Review* 51 (1992), 1–15.
Bali, Rıfat, *The Jews and Prostitution in Constantinople, 1854–1922* (Istanbul: Isis Press, 2008).
  Devlet'in Yahudileri ve 'Öteki' Yahudi (Istanbul: İletişim, 2010).

Banerjee, Sumanta, *Dangerous Outcast: The Prostitute in Nineteenth Century Bengal* (Calcutta: Seagull, 1998).
Barak, On, *Egyptian Times: Temporality, Personhood and the Techno-Political Making of Modern Egypt, 1830–1930*, PhD thesis, New York University, 2009.
— "Scraping the Surface: The Techno-Politics of Modern Streets in Turn-of-Twentieth-Century Alexandria," *Mediterranean Historical Review* 24 (4/ 2009), 187–205.
Başdaş, Begüm, *Old Buildings/New Faces: Urban and Social Change in Galata, Istanbul – Turkey*, MA thesis, University of California, 2001.
Batuman, Bülent, "Contesting Political Imaginaries on Taksim Square," lecture at Orient-Institut Istanbul, February 27, 2013.
Bayly, Christopher Alan, *The Birth of the Modern World, 1780–1914: Global Connections and Comparisons* (Malden: Blackwell, 2004).
Belge, Murat, "Istanbul Past and Future," in Ministry of Culture (ed.), *Istanbul* (Istanbul: Kültür ve Turizm Bakanlığı, 1993), 155–170.
Ben-Naeh, Yaron, "Blond, Tall, with Honey-Colored Eyes: Jewish Ownership of Slaves in the Ottoman Empire," *Jewish History* 20 (3–4/2006), 315–332.
Benner, Thomas H., *Die Strahlen der Krone: Die religiöse Dimension des Kaisertums unter Wilhelm II. vor dem Hintergrund der Orientreise 1898* (Marburg: Tectum-Verl, 2001).
Berchthold, Johannes, *Recht und Gerechtigkeit in der Konsulargerichtsbarkeit: Britische Exterritorialität im Osmanischen Reich 1825–1914* (Munich: Oldenbourg, 2009).
Berkant, Cenk, *İzmirli bir mimar: Raymond Péré*, MA thesis, Ege University, Izmir, 2005.
Berov, Ljuben, "The Course of Commodity Turnover at the Thessalonica Port and the West European Economic Cycle in 19 C. up to 1912," *Études Balkaniques* 4 (1985), 72–88.
Bertsch, Daniel, *Anton Prokesch von Osten (1795–1876): Ein Diplomat Österreichs in Athen und an der Hohen Pforte* (Munich: Oldenbourg, 2005).
Beyru, Rauf, *19. Yüzyılda İzmir'de Yaşam* (Istanbul: Literatür, 2000).
Biçer-Deveci, Elif, "The Movement of Feminist Ideas: The Case of Kadınlar Dünyası," in Liat Kozma, Cyrus Schayegh, and Avner Wishnitzer (eds.), *A Global Middle East: Mobility, Materiality, and Culture in the Modern Age, 1880–1940* (London: I. B. Tauris, 2015), 347–355.
Bohle, Hendrik and Dimog, Jan, *Architekturführer Istanbul* (Berlin: DOM, 2014).
Borutta, Manuel, *Antikatholizismus: Deutschland und Italien im Zeitalter der europäischen Kulturkämpfe* (Göttingen: Vandenhoeck & Ruprecht, 2010).

Mediterrane Verflechtungen: Frankreich und Algerien zwischen Kolonisierung und Dekolonisierung (Konstanz University, work in progress).
Borutta, Manuel and Gekas, Sakis, "A Colonial Sea: The Mediterranean 1798–1956," *European Review of History* 19 (1/2012), 1–13.
Bourdieu, Pierre, "The Forms of Capital," in J. Richardson (ed.), *Theory and Research for the Sociology of Education* (Westport: Greenwood, 1986), 241–258.
Bozdoğan, Sibel and Akcan, Esra, *Turkey: Modern Architectures in History* (London: Reaktion Books, 2012).
Burke III, Edmund, "The Deep Structures of Mediterranean Modernity," in Biray Kolluoğlu and Meltem Toksöz (eds.), *Cities of the Mediterranean: From the Ottomans to the Present Day* (London: Tauris, 2010), 198–214.

Cc.

Çelik, Zeynep, *The Remaking of Istanbul: Portrait of an Ottoman City in the Nineteenth Century* (Seattle: University of Washington Press, 1986).
Center for Asia Minor Studies (ed.), *Smyrna Metropolis of the Asia Minor Greeks* (Alimos: Ephesus, n.d.).
Cerasi, Maurice; Petruccioli, Attilio; Sarro, Adriana, and Weber, Stefan (eds.), *Multicultural Urban Fabric and Types in the South and Eastern Mediterranean* (Würzburg: Ergon, 2007).
Cezar, Mustafa, *XIX. Yüzyıl Beyoğlusu* (Istanbul: Akbank, 1991).
Chandravakar, Rajnarayan, *Imperial Power and Popular Politics: Class, Resistance and the State in India, c. 1850–1950* (Cambridge: Cambridge University Press, 1998).
Chiharu, Inaba and Esenbel, Selçuk, *The Rising Sun and the Turkish Crescent: New Perspectives on the History of Japanese Turkish Relations* (Istanbul: Boğaziçi University Pr., 2003).
Clancy-Smith, Julia Ann, *Mediterraneans: North Africa and Europe in an Age of Migration, c. 1800–1900* (Berkeley: University of California Press, 2011).
Clark, Christopher, *The Sleepwalkers: How Europe Went to War in 1914* (London: Penguin, 2013).
Clayer, Nathalie; Grandits, Hannes, and Pichler, Robert (eds.), *Conflicting Loyalties: Social (Dis-)integration and National Turn in the Late and Post-Ottoman Balkan Societies (1839–1914)* (London: I. B. Tauris, 2011).
Colonas, Vassilis, "Vitaliano Poselli: An Italian Architect in Thessaloniki," in Attilio Petruccioli (ed.), *Environmental Design 1990: Presence of*

Italy in the Architecture of the Islamic Mediterranean (Rome: Carucci Editions, 1987), 162–171.
Conrad, Sebastian, *Globalgeschichte: Eine Einführung* (Munich: C. H. Beck 2013).
Couroucli, Maria, "Se rendre chez l'autre: La visite dans la société grecque," in François Georgeon and Paul Dumont (eds.), *Vivre dans l'empire Ottoman* (Paris: L'Harmattan, 1997), 335–348.
Crapanzano, Vincent, "Life-Histories," *American Anthropologist New Series* 86 (4/1984), 953–960.
Csáky, Moritz, *Das Gedächtnis der Städte: Kulturelle Verflechtungen – Wien und die urbanen Milieus in Zentraleuropa* (Vienna: Böhlau, 2010).

Dd.

Dahmen, Wolfgang, "Pro- und antiwestliche Strömungen im rumänischen literarischen Diskurs – ein Überblick," in Gabriella Schubert and Holm Sundhaussen (eds.), *Prowestliche und antiwestliche Diskurse in den Balkanländern/Südosteuropa* (Munich: Sagner, 2008), 11–30.
Daskalov, Roumen, "Pro- und antiwestliche Diskurse in Bulgarien," in Gabriella Schubert and Holm Sundhaussen (eds.), *Prowestliche und antiwestliche Diskurse in den Balkanländern/Südosteuropa* (Munich: Sagner, 2008), 77–86.
Demacopoulos, George E. and Papanikolaou, Aristotle, "Orthodox Naming of the Other: A Postcolonial Approach," in George E. Demacopoulos and Aristotle Papanikolaou (eds.), *Orthodox Constructions of the West* (Fordham Scholarship Online: January 2014), 1–22, https://fordham.universitypressscholarship.com/view/10.5422/fordham/9780823251926.001.0001/upso-9780823251926-chapter-1.
Deringil, Selim, *The Well-Protected Domains: Ideology and the Legitimation of Power in the Ottoman Empire, 1876–1909* (London: I. B. Tauris, 1998).
"The West Within and the West Without: The 'Elite Lore' of the Ottoman Empire," in Faruk Birtek and Binnaz Toprak (eds.), *The Post-Modern Abyss and the New Politics of Islam: Assabiyah Revisited. Essays in Honor of Şerif Mardin* (İstanbul: Istanbul Bilgi Univ. Press, 2011), 112–115.
Conversion and Apostasy in the Late Ottoman Empire (Cambridge: Cambridge University Press, 2012).
Dietrich, Anne, *Deutschsein in İstanbul: Nationalisierung und Orientierung in der deutschsprachigen Community von 1843–1956* (Opladen: Leske + Budrich, 1998).

Dimitriadis, Sotirios, *The Making of an Ottoman Port-City: The State, Local Elites and Urban Space in Salonika, 1870–1912,* PhD thesis, SOAS, University of London (2013).

Diner, Dan, *Lost in the Sacred: Why the Muslim World Stood Still* (Princeton: Princeton University Press, 2009).

Dominik, Paulina, "From the Polish Times of Pera: Late Ottoman Istanbul through the Lens of Polish Emigration," in Anna Hofmann and Ayşe Öncü (eds.), *History Takes Place: Istanbul, Dynamics of Urban Change* (Berlin: Jovis, 2015), 92–103.

Dumont, Paul and Georgeon, François, *Un bourgeois d'Istanbul au début du XXe siècle* (Leuven: Peeters, 1985).

Dumont, Paul, "Le français d'abord," in Gilles Veinstein (ed.), *Salonique, 1850–1918: La ville des juifs et le réveil des Balkans* (Paris: Autrement, 1992), 208–225.

"Salonica and Beirut: The Reshaping of Two Ottoman Cities of the Eastern Meditteranean," in Eyal Ginio and Karl Kaser (eds.), *Ottoman Legacies in the Contemporary Mediterranean: The Balkans and the Middle East Compared* (Jerusalem: Hebrew University Press, 2013), 189–208.

Dura, Talat, "Interview," in Edhem Eldem (ed.), *Bankalar Caddesi: Osmanlı'dan günümüze Voyvoda Caddesi = Voyvoda Street from Ottoman Times to Today* (Istanbul: Osmanlı Bankası Bankacılık ve Finans Tarihi Araştırma ve Belge Merkezi, 2000), 247–273.

Ee.

Eğecioğlu, Ömer, "The Liszt-Listmann Incident," *Studia Musicologica Academiae Scientiarum Hungaricae* 49 (3–4/2008), 275–293.

Eldem, Edhem, "Istanbul: From Imperial to Peripheralized Capital," in Edhem Eldem, Daniel Goffmann, and Bruce Alan Masters (eds.), *The Ottoman City between East and West* (Cambridge: Cambridge University Press, 1999), 135–206.

"An Ottoman Archaeologist Caught between Two Worlds: Osman Hamdi Bey (1842–1910)," in David Shankland (ed.), *Archaeology, Anthropology and Heritage in the Balkans and Anatolia: The Life and Times of F. W. Hasluck, 1878–1920* (Istanbul: Isis Press, 2004), 121–149.

"'Levanten' Kelimesi Üzerine," in Arus Yumul and Fahri Dikkaya (eds.), *Avrupalı mı Levanten mi?* (Istanbul: Bağlam, 2006), 11–22.

"Ottoman Galata and Pera," in Ulrike Tischler (ed.), *From "milieu de mémoire" to "lieu de mémoire": The Cultural Memory of Istanbul in the 20th Century* (Munich: Martin Meidenbauer, 2006), 19–36.

"Foreigners at the Threshold of Felicity: The Reception of Foreigners in Ottoman Istanbul," in Donatella Calabi and Stephen T. Christensen (eds.), *Cultural Exchange in Early Modern Europe,* vol. II: *Cities and Cultural Exchange in Europe, 1400–1700* (Cambridge, Cambridge University Press, 2007), 114–131.

"Bir Biyografi Üzerine Düşünceler: Edhem Paşa Rum muydu?" *Toplumsal Tarih* 202 (2010), 2–12.

"A French View of the Ottoman-Turkish Wine Market, 1890–1925," paper presented at *Conference of Vines and Wines: The Production and Consumption of Wine in Anatolian Civilizations through the Ages,* Research Center for Anatolian Civilizations Istanbul, 4 Dec. 2011.

"(A Quest for) the Bourgeoisie of Istanbul: Identities, Roles, and Conflicts," in Ulrike Freitag and Nora Lafi (eds.), *Urban Governance under the Ottomans: Between Cosmopolitanism and Conflict* (London: Routledge, 2014), 159–186.

Eldem, Edhem; Goffman, Daniel, and Masters, Bruce, "Conclusion: Contexts and Characteristics," in, *The Ottoman City between East and West* (Cambridge: Cambridge University Press, 1999), 148–152.

Emrence, Cem, *Remapping the Ottoman Middle East: Modernity, Imperial Bureaucracy and the Islamic State* (London: I. B. Tauris, 2012).

Enis, Ayşe Zeren, *Everyday Lives of Ottoman Muslim Women: Hanimlara Mahsûs Gazete (Newspaper for Ladies) (1895–1908)* (Izmir: Libra, 2013).

Erenberg, Lewis A., *Steppin' Out* (Chicago: University of Chicago Press, 1984).

Eren, Ercan, *Geçmişten Günümüze Anadolu'da Bira* (Istanbul: Tarih Vakfı, 2005).

Ersoy, Ahmet, "Melezliğe Övgü: Tanzimat Dönemi Osmanlı Kimlik Politikaları ve Mimarlık," *Toplumsal Tarih* 189 (2009), 62–67.

Ersoy, Ahmet; Gorny, Maciej, and Kechriotis, Vangelis (eds.), *Discourses of Collective Identity in Central and Southeast Europe (1770–1945): Texts and Commentaries,* vol. I: *The Creation of the Nation State* (Budapest: Central European University Press, 2010).

Ertuğrul, Halit, *Azınlık ve Yabancı Okulları* (Istanbul: Nesil, 1998).

Esmer, Tolga U., "Economies of Violence, Banditry, and Governance in the Ottoman Empire Around 1800," *Past & Present* 224 (1/2014), 163–199.

Eugenides, Jeffrey, *Middlesex: A Novel* (London: Picador, 2002).

Exertzoglou, Haris, "The Cultural Uses of Consumption: Negotiating Class, Gender, and Nation in the Ottoman Urban Centers during the 19th Century," *International Journal of Middle East Studies* 35 (1/2003), 77–101.

Ff.

Fahmy, Khaled, "Prostitution in Egypt in the Nineteenth Century," in Eugene Rogan (ed.), *Outside In: On the Margins of the Modern Middle East* (London: I. B. Tauris, 2002), 77–103.

Falierou, Anastasia, "Enlightened Mothers and Scientific Housewives: Discussing Women's Social Roles in *Eurydice (Evridiki)* (1870–1873)," in Duygu Köksal and Anastasia Falierou (eds.), *A Social History of Ottoman Women: New Perspectives* (Leiden: Brill, 2013), 201–224.

Farah, Irmgard, *Die deutsche Pressepolitik und Propagandatätigkeit im Osmanischen Reich von 1908–1918 unter besonderer Berücksichtigung des "Osmanischen Lloyd"* (Halle (Saale): Universitäts- und Landesbibliothek Sachsen-Anhalt, 2016).

Faroqhi, Suraiya, *The Ottoman Empire and the World around It* (London: I. B. Tauris, 2004).

Felman, Shoshana and Laub, Dori, *Testimony: Crises of Witnessing in Literature, Psychoanalysis, and History* (New York: Routledge, 1992).

Fildiş, Ayse Tekdal, "The Troubles in Syria: Spawned by French Divide and Rule," *Middle East Policy* 18 (4/2011), 129–139.

Findley, Carter Vaughn, "An Ottoman Orientalist in Europe: Ahmed Midhat Meets Madame Gulnar, 1889," *American Historical Review* 103 (1/1998), 15–49.

  Turkey, Islam, Nationalism, and Modernity: A History, 1789–2007 (New Haven: Yale University Press, 2010).

Firges, Pascal, *French Revolutionaries in the Ottoman Empire: Diplomacy, Political Culture, and the Limits of Universal Revolution, 1792–1798* (Oxford: Oxford University Press, 2017).

Fischer-Tiné, Harald, "'White Women Degrading Themselves to the Lowest Depths': European Networks of Prostitution and Colonial Anxieties in British India and Ceylon ca. 1880–1914," *Indian Economic & Social History Review* 40 (2/2003), 163–190.

Fortna, Benjamin C., *Imperial Classroom: Islam, the State, and Education in the Late Ottoman Empire* (Oxford: Oxford University Press, 2002).

Foucault, Michel, *The History of Sexuality*, vol. I (New York: Pantheon, 1978).

  Discipline and Punish: The Birth of the Prison (New York: Vintage, 1979).

Frangakis-Syrett, Elena, *The Commerce of Smyrna in the Eighteenth Century, 1700–1820* (Athens: Centre for Asia Minor Studies, 1992).

  "The Making of an Ottoman Port: The Quay of Izmir in the Nineteenth Century," *Journal of Transport History* 22 (1/2001), 23–46.

Freitag, Ulrike, *A History of Jeddah: The Gate to Mecca in the Nineteenth and Twentieth Centuries* (Cambridge: Cambridge University Press, 2020).

Freitag, Ulrike and Oppen, Achim v. (eds.), *Translocality: The Study of Globalising Phenomena from a Southern Perspective* (Leiden: Brill, 2010).

Fuhrmann, Malte, "Visions of Germany in Turkey: Legitimizing German Imperialist Penetration of the Ottoman Empire," paper presented at *The Contours of Legitimacy in Central Europe: New Approaches in Graduate Studies*, St. Antony's College, Oxford, (May 2002), www.users.ox.ac.uk/~oaces/conference/papers/Malte_Fuhrmann.pdf.

Der Traum vom deutschen Orient: Zwei deutsche Kolonien im Osmanischen Reich 1851–1918 (Frankfurt/Main: Campus, 2006).

"Vom stadtpolitischen Umgang mit dem Erbe der Europäisierung in Istanbul, Izmir und Thessaloniki," in Ulrike Tischler and Ioannis Zelepos (Eds.), *Bilderwelten – Weltbilder: Die Gegenwart der Vergangenheit in postosmanischen Metropolen Südosteuropas. Thessaloniki, Istanbul, Izmir* (Frankfurt /Main: Peter Lang, 2009), 19–62.

"Vagrants, Prostitutes, and Bosnians: Making and Unmaking European Supremacy in Ottoman Southeast Europe," in Nathalie Clayer, Hannes Grandits, and Robert Pichler (eds.), *Conflicting Loyalties: Social (Dis-)integration and National Turn in the Late and Post-Ottoman Balkan Societies (1839–1914)* (London: I. B. Tauris, 2011), 15–45.

"Spies, Victims, Collaborators and Humanitarian Interventionists: The Germans on the Hellenic and Ottoman Shore of the Aegean," in Panikos Panayi (ed.), *Germans as Minorities during the First World War: A Global Comparative Perspective* (Farnham: Ashgate, 2014), 189–212.

Fuhrmann, Malte and Kechriotis, Vangelis, "The Late Ottoman Port Cities and Their Inhabitants: Subjectivity, Urbanity, and Conflicting Orders Editorial," *Mediterranean Historical Review* 24 (2/2009), 71–78.

Gg.

Gavrilova, Rayna, "Historische Anthropologie der Stadt," in Karl Kaser, Siegfried Gruber, and Robert Pichler (eds.), *Historische Anthropologie im südöstlichen Europa: Eine Einführung* (Vienna: Böhlau, 2003), 269–289.

Gekas, Sakis, "Class and Cosmopolitanism: The Historiographical Fortunes of Merchants in Eastern Mediterranean Ports," *Mediterranean Historical Review* 24 (2/2009), 95–114.

Gellner, Ernest, *Nations and Nationalism* (Ithaca: Cornell University Press, 2008).

Georgelin, Hervé, *La fin de Smyrne: Du cosmopolitisme aux nationalismes* (Paris: CNRS, 2005).

Georgeon, François, "Présentation," in Paul Dumont and François Georgeon (eds.), *Vivre dans l'empire ottomane: Sociabilités et relations intercommunitaires (XVIIIe–XXe siècles)* (Paris: L'Harmattan, 1997), 5–20.

"Le ramadan à Istanbul de l'Empire à la république," in Paul Dumont and François Georgeon (eds.), *Vivre dans l'empire ottomane : Sociabilités et relations intercommunitaires (XVIIIe–XXe siècles)* (Paris: L'Harmattan, 1997), 31–113.

"Ottomans and Drinkers: The Consumption of Alcohol in İstanbul in the Nineteenth Century," in Eugene Rogan (ed.), *Outside In: On the Margins of the Modern Middle East* (London: Tauris, 2002), 7–30.

Abdulhamid II: Le sultan calife (Paris: Fayard, 2003).

Geyikdağı, Vesile Necla, *Foreign Investment in the Ottoman Empire: International Trade and Relations 1854–1914* (London: Tauris Academic Studies, 2011).

Giannatou, Savina, "Smyrneiko Minore," Songs of the Mediterranean *(CD)*, sleeve notes (Boulder: Sounds True, 1998).

Ginio, Eyal, "Migrants and Workers in an Ottoman Port: Ottoman Salonica in the Eighteenth Century," in Eugene Rogan (ed.), *Outside In: On the Margins of the Modern Middle East* (London: I. B. Tauris, 2002), 126–148.

Girardelli, Paolo, "Sheltering Diversity: Levantine Architecture in Late Ottoman Istanbul," in Maurice Cerasi, Attilio Petruccioli, Adriana Sarro, and Stefan Weber (eds.), *Multicultural Urban Fabric and Types in the South and Eastern Mediterranean* (Würzburg: Ergon, 2007), 113–140.

"In & Around Lord Elgin's Palace at Pera: European, Levantine & Ottoman Intersections in Architectural Culture (ca. 1798–1831)," paper presented at *Anamed Fellows Symposium*, Research Center for Anatolian Civilizations Istanbul, 22 April 2016.

Göçek, Fatma Müge, *Rise of the Bourgeoisie, Demise of Empire: Ottoman Westernization and Social Change* (Oxford: Oxford University Press, 1996).

Goffman, Daniel, "Izmir: From Village to Colonial Port City," in Edhem Eldem, Daniel Goffman, and Bruce Masters (eds.), *The Ottoman City between East and West: Aleppo, Izmir, and Istanbul* (Cambridge: Cambridge University Press, 1999), 79–134.

The Ottoman Empire and Early Modern Europe (Cambridge: Cambridge University Press, 2002).

Gorman, Anthony, "Foreign Workers in Egypt 1882–1914: Subaltern or Labour Elite?" in Stephanie Cronin (ed.), *Subalterns and Social Protest* (London: Routledge, 2008), 213–236.

Gotter, Ulrich, "'Akkulturation' als Methodenproblem der historischen Wissenschaften," in Wolfgang Esbach (ed.), *wir/ihr/sie: Identität und Alterität in Theorie und Methode* (Würzburg: Rheinberg-Buch, 2000), 373–406.

Grindon, Gavin, "Revolutionary Romanticism: Henri Lefebvre's Revolution-as-Festival," *Third Text* 27 (2/2013), 208–220.

Guillon, Helene, *Le Journal de Salonique: Un périodique juif dans l'Empire ottoman (1895–1911)* (Paris: Presses Université Paris-Sorbonne, 2013).

Gül, Murat, *The Emergence of Modern Istanbul: Transformation and Modernisation of a City* (New York: I. B. Tauris, 2012).

Gülersoy, Çelik, *Tepebaşı: Bir Meydan Savaşı* (Istanbul: İstanbul BB Kültür A.Ş., 1993).

Gürsoy, Deniz, *Harcıalem İçki Bira* (Istanbul: Oğlak, 2004).

Gürsoy, Melih, *Bizim İzmirimiz* (Istanbul: Metis, 2013).

Hh.

Hamadeh, Shirine, *The City's Pleasures: Istanbul in the Eighteenth Century* (Seattle: University of Washington Press, 2007).

Hanley, Will, "Grieving Cosmopolitanism in Middle East Studies," *History Compass* 6 (5/2008), 1346–1367.

Identifying with Nationality: Europeans, Ottomans, and Egyptians in Alexandria (New York: Columbia University Press, 2017).

Hanssen, Jens, Philipp, Thomas, and Weber, Stefan, "Introduction: Towards a New Paradigm," in id. (eds.), *The Empire in the City: Arab Provincial Capitals in the Late Ottoman Empire* (Würzburg: Ergon, 2002), 1–28.

Harvey, David, "The Right to the City," *New Left Review* 53 (Sept.–Oct. 2008), https://newleftreview.org/II/53/david-harvey-the-right-to-the-city.

Hauser, Julia, *German Religious Women in Late Ottoman Beirut* (Leiden: Brill, 2015).

Hauser, Julia; Lindner, Christine B., and Möller, Esther, "Introduction," in id. (eds.), *Entangled Education: Foreign and Local Schools in Late Ottoman Syria and Mandate Lebanon (19th–20th Centuries)* (Würzburg: Ergon, 2016), 11–30.

Hayden, Robert M. and Naumović, Slobodan, "Imagined Commonalities: The Invention of a Late Ottoman 'Tradition' of Coexistence," *American Anthropologist* 115 (2/2013), 324–334.

Heckmann, Friedrich, "Ethnos, Demos und Nation, oder: Woher stammt die Intoleranz des Nationalstaats gegenüber ethnischen Minderheiten?" in Gerhard Seewann (ed.), *Minderheitenfragen in Südosteuropa* (Munich: Oldenbourg, 1992), 60–85.

Hein, Carola (ed.), *Port Cities: Dynamic Landscapes and Global Networks* (New York: Routledge, 2011).

Herzog, Christoph, *Geschichte und Ideologie: Mehmed Murad und Celal Nuri über die historischen Ursachen des osmanischen Niederganges* (Berlin: De Gruyter, 1996).

"Migration and the State: On Ottoman Regulations concerning Migration since the Age of Mahmud II," in Ulrike Freitag, Malte Fuhrmann, Nora Lafi, and Florian Riedler (eds.), *The City in the Ottoman Empire: Migration and the Making of Urban Modernity* (London: Routledge, 2011), 117–134.

Hilberg, Raul, *Die Vernichtung der europäischen Juden*, vol. II (Frankfurt/Main: Fischer, 1994).

Hobsbawm, Eric J., *On History* (London: Weidenfeld & Nicolson, 1997).

Nations and Nationalism since 1780: Programme, Myth, Reality (New York, 2004).

Hourani, Albert H. and Stern, Samuel M. (eds.), *The Islamic City: A Colloquium* (Philadelphia: University of Pennsylvania Press, 1970).

Huber, Valeska, *Channelling Mobilities: Migration and Globalisation in the Suez Canal Region and Beyond, 1869–1914* (Cambridge: Cambridge University Press, 2013).

"Education and Mobility: Universities in Cairo between Competition and Standardisation 1900–1950," in Liat Kozma, Cyrus Schayegh, and Avner Wishnitzer (eds.), *A Global Middle East: Mobility, Materiality and Culture in the Modern Age, 1880–1940* (London: I. B. Tauris, 2015), 81–108.

Hudspith, Sarah, *Dostoevsky and the Idea of Russianness: A New Perspective on Unity and Brotherhood* (London: Routledge, 2004).

Hughes, Edward J., "Exotic Drift: Pierre Loti between Contemporaneity and Anteriority," in Margaret Topping (ed.), *Eastern Voyages, Western Visions: French Writing and Painting of the Orient* (Berlin: Peter Lang, 2004), 241–264.

Huntington, Samuel P., "The Clash of Civilizations?" *Foreign Affairs* 72 (3/1993), 22–49.

Ii.

Ilbert, Robert and Yannakakis, Ilios (eds.), *Alexandrie 1860–1960: Un modèle éphémère de convivialité. Communautés et identité cosmopolite* (Paris: Autrement, 1992).

İnalcık, Halil, "Istanbul: An Islamic City," *Journal of Islamic Studies* 1 (1990), 1–23.

Turkey and Europe in History (Istanbul: Eren, 2006).

İslamoğlu-İnan, Huri, "Introduction: 'Oriental Despotism' in World-System Perspective," in id. (ed.), *The Ottoman Empire and The World-Economy* (Cambridge: Cambridge University Press, 1987), 1–26.

Jj.

Jana, Katja, *"Behind the Hat There Are Warships" – Nationalism, Colonialism and Masculinities in Late Ottoman and Early Turkish Republican Society and Politics*, PhD thesis, Göttingen University (2016).

Jušek, Karin J., *Auf der Suche nach der Verlorenen: die Prostitutionsdebatten im Wien der Jahrhundertwende* (Vienna: Löcker, 1995).

Kk.

Kaelble, Hartmut, "Die Debatte über Vergleich und Transfer und was jetzt?" *H-Soz-u-Kult* 8 Feb. 2005, http://hsozkult.geschichte.hu-berlin.de/forum/id=574&type=artikel.

Kandilakis, Manolis, "Xenoglosses efimerides tis Thessalonikis," *Thessaloniki* 1992, 153–165.

Karagiannis, Evangelos, "The Pomaks of Bulgaria: A Case of Ethnic Marginality," in Christian Giordano, Dobrinka Kostova, and Evelyne Lohmann Minka II (eds.), *Bulgaria: Social and Cultural Landscapes* (Fribourg: Fribourg University Press, 2000), 143–158.

Karahan, Burcu, "Repressed in Translation: Representation of Female Sexuality in Ottoman Erotica," *Journal of Turkish Literature* 9 (2012), 30–45.

Kasaba, Reşat; Keyder, Çağlar, and Tabak, Faruk, "Eastern Mediterranean Port Cities and Their Bourgeoisies: Merchants, Political Projects and Nation-States," *Review* 10 (1/1986), 121–135.

Kaschuba, Wolfgang, *Lebenswelt und Kultur der unterbürgerlichen Schichten im 19. und 20. Jahrhundert* (Munich: Oldenbourg, 1990).

Kaynar, Erdal, "Les jeunes Turques et l'Occident, histoire d'une deception programmée," in François Georgeon (ed.), *'L'ivresse de la liberté': La revolution de 1908 dans l'Empire Ottoman* (Paris: Peeters, 2012), 27–65.

Kechriotis, Vangelis, "On the Margins of National Historiography: The Greek İttihatçı Emmanouil Emmanouilidis – Opportunist or Ottoman Patriot?" in Amy Singer, Christoph K. Neumann, and S. Akşin Somel (eds.), *Untold Histories of the Middle East: Recovering Voices from the 19th and 20th Centuries* (London: Routledge, 2011), 124–142.

"Civilization and Order: Middle-Class Morality among the Greek-Orthodox in Smyrna/Izmir at the End of the Ottoman Empire," in Andreas Lyberatos (ed.), *Social Transformation and Mass Mobilization in the Balkan and Eastern Mediterranean Cities 1900–1923* (Heraklion: Panepistimio Kritis, 2013), 115–132.

"Atina'da Kapadokyalı, İzmir'de Atinalı, İstanbul'da Mebus: Pavlos Karolidis'in Farklı Kişilik ve Aidiyetleri," *Toplumsal Tarih* 257 (2015), 28–35.

Ketencioğlu, Muammer, *İzmir Hatırası*, sleeve notes (Istanbul: Kalan, 2007).

Keyder, Çağlar, *State and Class in Turkey: A Study in Capitalist Development* (London: Verso, 1987).

"Port Cities in the Belle Epoque," in Biray Kolluoğlu and Meltem Toksöz (eds.), *Cities of the Mediterranean: From the Ottomans to the Present Day* (London: Tauris, 2010), 14–22.

Keyder, Çağlar, Özveren, Eyüp, and Quataert, Donald, "Port-Cities in the Ottoman Empire: Some Theoretical and Historical Perspectives," *Review* 16 (4/1993), 519–558.

Khalapyan, Hasmik, "Theater as Career for Ottoman Armenian Women," in Duygu Köksal and Anastasia Falierou (eds.), *A Social History of Ottoman Women: New Perspectives* (Leiden: Brill, 2013), 31–46.

Khuri-Makdisi, Ilham, *The Eastern Mediterranean and the Making of Global Radicalism, 1860–1914* (Berkeley: University of California Press, 2010).

Kırlı, Cengiz, "Coffeehouses: Public Opinion in the Nineteenth Century Ottoman Empire," in Armando Salvatore and Dale F. Eickelman (eds.), *Public Islam and the Common Good* (Leiden: Brill, 2004), 75–97.

Kloosterhuis, Jürgen, *"Friedliche Imperialisten": Deutsche Auslandsvereine und auswärtige Kulturpolitik, 1906–1918* (Frankfurt/Main: Peter Lang, 1994).

Kocka, Jürgen, "Das europäische Muster und der deutsche Fall," in id. (ed.), *Bürgertum im 19. Jahrhundert* (Göttingen: Vandenhoeck & Ruprecht, 1995), vol. I, 9–84.

Koçu, Reşad Ekrem, "Bira, Birahane," in id. (ed.), *İstanbul Ansiklopedisi* (Istanbul: İstanbul Yayınevi, 1961), vol. V, 2805–2806.

"Bizans Birahanesi," in id. (ed.), *İstanbul Ansiklopedisi* (Istanbul: İstanbul Yayınevi, 1961), vol. V, 2829.

Eski İstanbul'da Meyhaneler ve Meyhane Köçekleri (Istanbul: Doğan, 2002).

Köksal, Duygu, "From a Critique of the Orient to a Critique of Modernity," in Duygu Köksal and Anastasia Falierou (eds.), *A Social History of Ottoman Women: New Perspectives* (Leiden: Brill, 2013), 225–248.

Kolluoğlu, Biray and Toksöz, Meltem, "Mapping Out the Eastern Mediterranean: Toward a Cartography of Cities of Commerce," in id. (eds.),

Cities of the Mediterranean: From the Ottomans to the Present Day (London: Tauris, 2010), 1–22.

Kolm, Evelyn, *Die Ambitionen Österreich-Ungarns im Zeitalter des Hochimperialismus* (Frankfurt/Main:Peter Lang, 2001).

Kontente, Léon, *Smyrne et l'Occident: De l'Antiquité au XXIe siècle* (Paris: Yvelinédition, 2005).

Köprülü, Tuna, *İstanbul'daki Yabancı Saraylar* (Istanbul: İbb Kültür A.,̧ S. Yayınları, 2010).

Köse, Yavuz, *Westlicher Konsum am Bosporus: Warenhäuser, Nestlé & Co. im späten Osmanischen Reich (1855–1923)* (Munich: Oldenbourg, 2010).

Kössler, Armin, *Aktionsfeld Osmanisches Reich: Die Wirtschaftsinteressen des Deutschen Kaiserreiches in der Türkei 1871–1908* (New York: Arno Press, 1981).

Krawietz, Birgit, "The Sportification and Heritagisation of Traditional Turkish Oil Wrestling," *International Journal of the History of Sport* 29 (15/ 2012), 2145–2161.

Kreiser, Klaus, "Zur inneren Gliederung der osmanischen Stadt," *Zeitschrift der Deutschen Morgenländischen Gesellschaft* Supplement 2 (1974), 198–212.

"Public Monuments in Turkey and Egypt, 1840–1916," *Muqarnas* 14 (1997), 103–117.

Kresse, Kai and Simpson, Edward (eds.), *Struggling with History: Islam and Cosmopolitanism in the Western Indian Ocean* (London: Hurst, 2007).

Ll.

Laqueur, Hans-Peter, "Das Osmanische Reich und seine Bewohner aus der Sicht eines Südtiroler Bäckermeisters (1851/52)," in Marlene Kurz, Martin Scheutz, Karl Vocelka, and Thomas Winkelbauer (eds.), *Das Osmanische Reich und die Habsburgermonarchie: Akten des internationalen Kongresses zum 150-jährigen Bestehen des Instituts für Österreichische Geschichtsforschung, Wien, 22.–25. September 2004* (Vienna: Oldenbourg, 2005), 461–470.

Lemmes, Fabian, "Der anarchistische Terrorismus des 19. Jahrhunderts und sein soziales Umfeld," in Stefan Malthaner and Peter Waldmann (eds.), *Radikale Milieus: Das soziale Umfeld terroristischer Gruppen* (Frankfurt/Main: Campus, 2012), 73–117.

Lemon, Herald, "Eastern Empires and Middle Kingdoms: Austria and China in Hoffmannsthal and Kafka's Orientalist Fictions," paper from *The*

Contours of Legitimacy in Central Europe, Oxford, May 2002, http://users.ox.ac.uk/~oaces/conference/papers/Bob_Lemon.pdf.

Lewis, Bernard, *The Emergence of Modern Turkey* (Oxford: Oxford University Press, 1961).

The Muslim Discovery of Europe (New York: W. W. Norton & Co., 2001).

What Went Wrong? The Clash between Islam and Modernity in the Middle East (London: Weidenfeld & Nicolson, 2002).

Lüdtke, Alf, "Einleitung: Herrschaft als soziale Praxis," in id. (ed.), *Herrschaft als soziale Praxis: Historische und sozial-anthropologische Studien* (Göttingen: Vandenhoeck & Ruprecht, 1991), 9–63.

Mm.

Macaraig, Nina, *Çemberlitaş Hamamı in İstanbul: The Biographical Memoir of a Turkish Bath* (Edinburgh: Edinburgh University Press, 2019).

MacArthur-Seal, Daniel-Joseph, "Intoxication and Imperialism," *Comparative Studies of South Asia, Africa and the Middle East* 37 (2/2017), 299–313.

Machtan, Lothar and Ott, Réné, "'Batzebier!' Überlegungen zur sozialen Protestbewegung in den Jahren nach der Reichsgründung am Beispiel der süddeutschen Bierkrawalle vom Frühjahr 1873," in Heinrich Volkmann and Jürgen Bergmann (eds.), *Sozialer Protest: Studien zur traditionellen Resistenz und kollektiver Gewalt in Deutschland vom Vormärz bis zur Reichsgründung* (Opladen: Westdt. Verl., 1984), 128–166.

Makal, Oğuz, "İzmir Sinemaları," in Şahin Beygu (ed.), *Üç İzmir* (Istanbul: Yapı Kredi, 1992), 387–394.

Makdisi, Ussama, *Artillery of Heaven: American Missionaries and the Failed Conversion of the Middle East* (Ithaca: Cornell University Press, 2008).

Maner, Hans-Christian, "Zum Problem der Kolonisierung Galiziens: Aus den Debatten des Ministerrates und des Reichsrates in der zweiten Hälfte des 19. Jahrhunderts," in Johannes Feichtinger, Ursula Prutsch, and Moritz Csáky (eds.), *Habsburg postcolonial: Gedächtnis – Erinnerung – Identität* (Innsbruck: Studienverl, 2003), 153–164.

Mansel, Philip, *Constantinople: City of the World's Desire 1453–1924* (London: St. Martin's Press, 1996).

Levant: Splendour and Catastrophe on the Mediterranean (London: John Murray, 2010).

Marchand, Susanne, *German Orientalism in the Age of Empire* (Cambridge: Cambridge University Press, 2009).

Mardin, Şerif, "Super-Westernisation in Urban Life in the Ottoman Empire in the Last Quarter of the Nineteenth Century," in Şerif Mardin, *Religion, Society, and Modernity in Turkey* (Syracuse: Syracuse University Press, 2006), 135–163.

"Conceptual Fracture," in Gürcan Koçan (ed.), *Transnational Concepts: Transfers and the Challenge of the Peripheries* (Istanbul: İstanbul Technical University Press, 2008), 4–18.

Masashi, Haneda (ed.), *Asian Port Cities 1600–1800: Local and Foreign Cultural Interactions* (Singapore: NUS Press, 2009).

Masters, Bruce, "Millet," in Gábor Ágoston and Bruce Masters (eds.), *Encyclopedia of the Ottoman Empire* (New York: Facts On File, 2009), 383–384.

Matthee, Rudi, "The Ambiguities of Alcohol in Iranian History: Between Excess and Abstention," in Bert G. Fragner, Ralph Kauz, and Florian Schwarz (eds.), *Wine Culture in Iran and Beyond* (Vienna: Österreichische Akademie der Wissenschaften, 2014), 239–250.

Mazower, Mark, *Salonica: City of Ghosts* (London: Harper Perennial, 2005).

McPherson, Kenneth, "Port Cities as Nodal Points of Change: The Indian Ocean, 1890s–1920s," in Leila Fawaz and Christopher Bayly (eds.), *Modernity and Culture: From the Mediterranean to the Indian Ocean* (New York: Columbia University Press, 2002), 75–95.

Mende, Leyla von, "'Europäisierungsmißstände' um 1900: Eine Kurzgeschichte des osmanischen Schriftstellers Ahmet Hikmet Müftüoğlu," *Themenportal Europäische Geschichte* (2011), www.europa.clio-online.de/essay/id/fdae-1539.

Mestyan, Adam, "*A Garden with Mellow Fruits of Refinement*": Music Theatres and Cultural Politics in Cairo and Istanbul, 1867–1892, PhD thesis, Central European University, Budapest (2011).

Arab Patriotism: The Ideology and Culture of Power in Late Ottoman Egypt (Princeton: Princeton University Press, 2017).

Middell, Matthias, "Transregional Studies: A New Approach to Global Processes," in id. (ed.), *The Routledge Handbook of Transregional Studies* (London: Routledge, 2018), 1–16.

Mills, Amy, *Streets of Memory: Landscape, Tolerance, and National Identity in Istanbul Athens* (Athens, Georgia: University of Georgia Press, 2010).

Miloradović, Jelena and Vučinić-Nešković, Vesna, "Corso as a Total Social Phenomenon: The Case of Smederevska Palanka, Serbia," in Klaus Roth and Ulf Brunnbauer (eds.), *Urban Life and Culture in*

Southeastern Europe: Anthropological and Historical Perspectives (Berlin: LIT, 2006), 229–250.

Milton, Giles, *Paradise Lost: Smyrna 1922. The Destruction of Islam's City of Tolerance* (London: John Murray, 2009).

Mimaroğlu, Reşad, "Bosfor Birahanesi," in Koçu Reşad Ekrem (ed.), *İstanbul Ansiklopedisi*, vol. VI (Istanbul: İstanbul Yayınevi, 1961), 2966–2969.

Minuti, Rolando, "Oriental Despotism," in *European History Online* 3 May 2012, http://ieg-ego.eu/en/threads/models-and-stereotypes/the-wild-and-the-civilized/rolando-minuti-oriental-despotism.

Mishra, Pankaj, "How to Think about Islamic State," in *Guardian* 24 July 2015, www.theguardian.com/books/2015/jul/24/how-to-think-about-islamic-state.

Age of Anger: A History of the Present (New York: Farrar, Straus and Giroux, 2017).

Mitchell, Timothy, *Colonising Egypt* (Berkeley: University of California Press, 1991).

Molho, Rena, *The Memoirs of Doctor Meir Yoel: An Autobiographical Source on Social Change in Salonika at the Turn of the 20th Century* (Istanbul: Isis Press, 2011).

Morack, Ellinor, "Refugees, Locals and 'the' State: Property Compensation in the Province of Izmir Following the Greco-Turkish Population Exchange of 1923," *Journal of the Ottoman and Turkish Studies Association* 2 (2015), 147–166.

Müller, Dietmar, *Staatsbürger auf Widerruf: Juden und Muslime als Alteritätspartner im rumänischen und serbischen Nationscode Ethnonationale Staatsbürgerschaftskonzepte, 1878–1941* (Wiesbaden: Harrassowitz, 2005).

Müller-Wiener, Wolfgang, *Die Häfen von Byzantion Konstantinupolis Istanbul* (Tübingen: Ernst Wasmuth, 1994).

Müns, Heike, "Migrationsstrategien der böhmischen Musikanten im 18. und 19. Jahrhundert," in Klaus Roth (ed.), *Vom Wandergesellen zum 'Green Card'-Spezialisten: Interkulturelle Aspekte der Arbeitsmigration im östlichen Mitteleuropa* (Münster: Waxmann, 2003), 63–80.

Nn.

Naar, Devin E., *Jewish Salonica: Between the Ottoman Empire and Greece* (Stanford: Stanford University Press, 2016).

Necipoğlu, Gülrü, *Architecture, Ceremonial, and Power: The Topkapı Palace in the Fifteenth and Sixteenth Centuries* (Cambridge: MIT Press, 1991).

Nowill, Sidney E. P., *Constantinople and Istanbul: 72 Years of Life in Turkey* (Leicester: Matador, 2011).

Oo.

Oberling, Pierre, "The Quays of Izmir," in Hâmit Batu and Jean-Louis Bacqué-Grammont (eds.), *L'Empire Ottoman, la Republique et la France* (Istanbul: Isis Press, 1986), 316–319.

Okday, Şefik, *Der letzte Großwesir und seine preußischen Söhne* (Göttingen: Muster-Schmidt, 1991).

Ortaylı, İlber, *İmparatorluğun En Uzun Yüzyılı* (Istanbul: Hil, 1983).

Avrupa ve Biz (Istanbul: İş Bankası, 2008).

Osterhammel, Jürgen, *Die Entzauberung Asiens: Europa und die asiatischen Reiche im 18. Jahrhundert* (Munich: Beck, 1998).

The Transformation of the World: A Global History of the Nineteenth Century (Princeton: Princeton University Press, 2015).

Osterhammel, Jürgen and Conrad, Sebastian, "Einleitung," in id. (eds.), *Das Kaiserreich transnational: Deutschland in der Welt 1871–1914* (Göttingen: Vandenhoeck & Ruprecht, 2004), 7–27.

Önertoy, Olcay, "Halide Edip Adıvar'ın Romanlarında Toplumsal Eleştiri," *Ankara Üniversitesi Dil ve Tarih-Coğrafya Fakültesi Türkoloji Dergisi* 18 (1/2011), 37–46.

Owen, Roger, *The Middle East in The World Economy, 1800–1914* (London: I. B. Tauris, 1993).

Özcan, Azmi and Buzpınar, Ş. Tufan, "Tanzimat, Islahat ve Misyonerlik: Church Missionary Society İstanbul'da 1858–1880," *İstanbul Araştırmaları* 1 (1997), 63–77.

Özgürel, Avni, "Almanya'dan işçi getirtmiştik," *Radikal*, 22 July 2007.

Özlü, Nilay, "Republican Response to Levantine Architectural Heritage: The Example of Alexandre Vallaury," paper presented at *Levantines of Beyoğlu Conference*, Casa d'Italia Istanbul, 24 Sept. 2016.

Pp.

Palairet, Michael, *The Balkan Economies, c. 1800–1914: Evolution without Development* (Cambridge: Cambridge University Press, 1997).

Pannuti, Alessandro E., *Les Italiens d'Istanbul au XXe siècle: Entre préservation identitaire et effacement* (Istanbul: Isis Press, 2008).

Pelvanoğlu, Burcu, "Painting the Late Ottoman Woman," in Duygu Köksal and Anastasia Falierou (eds.), *A Social History of Ottoman Women: New Perspectives* (Leiden: Brill, 2013), 153–171.

Pernau, Margrit, *Bürger im Turban: Muslime in Delhi im 19. Jahrhundert* (Göttingen: Vandenhoeck & Ruprecht, 2008).

Petrov, Milen V., "Everyday Forms of Compliance: Subaltern Commentaries on Ottoman Reform, 1864–1868," *Comparative Studies in Society and History* 46 (4/2004), 730–759.

Pichler, Robert, "Hirten, Söldner und Wanderarbeiter: Formen der mobilen Ökonomie in den Dörfern des südalbanischen Hochlandes," in Karl Kaser, Robert Pichler, and Stephanie Schwandner-Sievers (eds.), *Die weite Welt und das Dorf: Albanische Emigration am Ende des 20. Jahrhunderts* (Vienna: Böhlau, 2002), 133–161.

Pınar, İlhan, "Yüzyıl Sonunda Yüzyıl Başı Retrospektif Bir Gezi Denemesi," *İzmir Kent Kültürü Dergisi* 1 (5/2000), 159–161.

Polat Haydaroğlu, İlknur, *Osmanlı İmparatorluğunda Yabancı Okullar* (Ankara: Ocak, 1993).

Prange, Martine, "Cosmopolitan Roads to Culture and the Festival Road of Humanity," *Ethical Perspectives* 14 (3/2007), 269–286.

Pratt, Mary Louise, *Imperial Eyes: Travel Writing and Transculturation* (London: Routledge, 1992).

Qq.

Quataert, Donald, *Social Disintegration and Popular Resistance in the Ottoman Empire, 1881–1908* (New York: New York University Press, 1983).

"Labor History and the Ottoman Empire, c. 1700–1922," *International Labor and Working-Class History* 60 (2/2001), 93–109.

"The Industrial Working Class of Salonica, 1850–1912," in Avigdor Levy (ed.), *Jews, Turks, Ottomans: A Shared History, Fifteenth through the Twentieth Century* (Syracuse: Syracuse University Press, 2002), 194–211.

Rr.

Radt, Barbara, *Geschichte der Teutonia: Deutsches Vereinsleben in Istanbul 1847–2000* (Würzburg: Ergon, 2001).

Reinkowski, Maurus, "Hapless Imperialists and Resentful Nationalists: Trajectories of Radicalization in the Late Ottoman Empire," in Maurus Reinkowski and Gregor Thum (eds.), *Helpless Imperialists: Imperial Failure, Fear and Radicalization* (Göttingen, 2013), 47–57.

Reinwald, Brigitte, "Space on the Move: Perspectives on the Making of an Indian Ocean Seascape," in J. G. Deutsch and Brigitte Reinwald (eds.), *Space on the Move: Transformations of the Indian Ocean Seascape in the Nineteenth and Twentieth Century* (Berlin: Klaus Schwarz, 2002), 9–20.

Rekanati, David A. (ed.), *Memory of Saloniki: The Greatness and Destruction of Jerusalem of the Balkans,* vol. I (1972), chapter 14, www.jewishgen.org/yizkor/Thessalonika/thev1_014.html.

Richmond, Steven, *The Voice of England in the East: Stratford Canning and Diplomacy with the Ottoman Empire* (London: I. B. Tauris, 2017).

Riedler, Florian, "Hagop Mintzuri and the Cosmopolitan Memory of Istanbul," *EU Working Paper Mediterranean Programme Series* 13/2009; http://cadmus.eui.eu/bitstream/handle/1814/10913/EUI_RSCAS_2009_13.pdf?sequence=1.

"Armenian Labour Migration to Istanbul and the Migration Crisis of the 1890s," in Ulrike Freitag, Malte Fuhrmann, Nora Lafi, and Florian Riedler (eds.), *The City in the Ottoman Empire* (London: Routledge, 2011), 160–176.

Ringdal, Nils, *Love for Sale: A Global History of Prostitution* (New York: Grove, 2004).

Roche, Max, *Education, assistance et culture françaises dans l'Empire Ottoman* (Istanbul: Isis Press, 1989).

Rogan, Eugene (ed.), *Outside In: On the Margins of the Modern Middle East* (London: I. B. Tauris, 2002).

Rosenthal, Steven, "Foreigners and Municipal Reform in Istanbul, 1855–1865," *International Journal of Middle East Studies* 11 (2/1980), 227–245.

Rothman, E. Natalie, *Brokering Empire: Trans-Imperial Subjects between Venice and Istanbul* (Ithaca: Cornell University Press, 2013).

Rothermund, Dieter and Weigelin-Schwiedrzik, Susanne (eds.), *Der indische Ozean: Das afroasiatische Mittelmeer als Kultur- und Wirtschaftsraum* (Vienna: Promedia, 2004).

Ss.

Sagaster, Birte, "Zum Bild der Europäerin: Stereotypen in der frühen osmanisch-türkischen Literatur," *Berliner Lesezeichen* 1 (2/1996), 64–68.

Sajdi, Dana, "Decline, its Discontents and Ottoman Cultural History: By Way of Introduction," in Dana Sajdi (ed.), *Ottoman Tulips, Ottoman Coffee: Leisure and Lifestyle in the Eighteenth Century* (London: I. B. Tauris, 2007), 1–39.

Salama, Mohammad R., *Orientalism and Intellectual History: Modernity and the Politics of Exclusion since Ibn Khaldun* (London: I. B. Tauris, 2011).

Salzmann, Ariel, *Tocqueville in the Ottoman Empire: Rival Paths to the Modern State* (Leiden: Brill, 2004).

Sandalcı, Mert, "Interview" by Ayşegül Oğuz, *Radikal Hayat*, 21 March 2009, www.radikal.com.tr/Default.aspx?aType=HaberYazdir&ArticleID=927015.

Sariyannis, Marinos, "Time, Work, and Pleasure: A Preliminary Approach to Leisure in Ottoman Mentality," in *New Trends in Ottoman Studies: Papers Presented at the 20th CIÉPO Symposium*, Rethymno, 27 June–1 July 2012, 797–811.

Šatev, Pavel P., *V Makedonija pod robstvo: Solunskoto sâzakljatie (1903 g.); podgotovka i izpâlnenie* (Sofia: Bâlgarski Pisatel, 1968).

Schäbler, Birgit, "Civilizing Others: Global Modernity and the Local Boundaries (French, German, Ottoman, Arab) of Savagery," in Birgit Schäbler and Leif Stenberg (eds.), *Globalization and the Muslim World: Culture, Religion and Modernity* (New York: Syracuse University Press, 2004), 3–29.

Schick, İrvin Cemil, "Print Capitalism and Women's Sexual Agency in the Late Ottoman Empire," *Comparative Studies of South Asia, Africa and the Middle East* 31 (1/2011), 196–216.

Schmitt, Oliver Jens, *Levantiner: Lebenswelten und Identitäten einer ethnokonfessionellen Gruppe im osmanischen Reich im "langen 19. Jahrhundert"* (Munich: Oldenbourg, 2005).

Schubert, Dirk, "Seaport Cities: Phases of Spatial Restructuring and Types and Dimensions of Redevelopment," in Carola Hein (ed.), *Port Cities: Dynamic Landscapes and Global Networks* (London: Routledge, 2011), 54–69.

Sefer, Akın, "Class Formation on the Modern Waterfront: Port Workers and Their Struggles in Late Ottoman Istanbul," in M. Erdem Kabadayı and Leda Papastefanaki (eds.), *Working in Greece and Turkey: A Comparative Labour History from Empires to Nation States, 1840–1940* (New York: Berghahn, 2020).

Sellaouti, Rachida Tlili, "The Repubic and the Muslim World: For a Regenerated Mediterranean," in Alan Forrest and Matthias Middell (eds.), *The Routledge Companion to the French Revolution in World History* (London: Routledge, 2016), 97–117.

Şeni, Nora, "Les Levantins d'Istanbul à travers les récits des voyageurs du XIX siècle," in Edhem Eldem (ed.), *Première Rencontre Internationale sur L'Empire Ottoman et la Turquie Moderne* (Istanbul: Isis Press, 1991), 161–169.

Serçe, Erkan; Yılmaz, Fikret, and Yetkin, Sabri, *Küllerinden Doğan Şehir/ The City Which Rose from the Ashes* (Izmir: İzmir Büyükşehir Belediyesi, 2003).

Sevengil, Refik Ahmet, *Türk tiyatrosu tarihi*, vol. III (Ankara: Milli Eğitim, 1961).

Sevinçli, Efdal, *İzmir'de Tiyatro* (Istanbul: Ege, 1994).

Shaw, Stanford J. and Shaw, Ezel Kural, *History of the Ottoman Empire and Modern Turkey*, vol. II (Cambridge: Cambridge University Press, 1995).

Sinanlar Uslu, Seza, "Apparition et développement de la presse francophone d'Istanbul dans la seconde moitié du XIXe siècle," *Synergie* 3 (2010), 147–156.

Smyrnelis, Marie-Carmen, *Une société hors de soi: Identités et relations sociales à Smyrne aux XVIIIe et XIXe siècles* (Paris: Peeters, 2005).

Smith, Andrea L., *Colonial Memory and Postcolonial Europe: Maltese Settlers in Algeria and France* (Bloomington: Indiana University Press, 2006).

Somel, Selçuk Akşin, *The Modernization of Public Education in the Ottoman Empire 1839–1908: Islamization, Autocracy and Discipline* (Leiden: Brill, 2001).

Soysal, Funda, *Ottoman Empire in the Age of Global Financial Capitalism: The Causes and Consequences of the 1895 Stock Market Crash in Istanbul*, PhD, Boğaziçi University Istanbul (in progress).

"The Ottoman Period of Robert College," in Cem Akaş (ed.), *Bir Geleneğin Anatomisi: Robert Kolej'in 150 Yılı* (Istanbul: Suna & İnan Kıraç Araştırmaları Enstitüsü, 2013), 69–70.

Stauter-Halsted, Keely, "'A Generation of Monsters': Jews, Prostitution, and Racial Purity in the 1892 L'viv White Slavery Trial," *Austrian History Yearbook* 38 (2007), 25–35.

Staitscheva, Emilia, "Zum Europa-Diskurs in Bulgarien, exemplifiziert an literarischen Texten," in Gabriella Schubert and Holm Sundhaussen (eds.), *Prowestliche und antiwestliche Diskurse in den Balkanländern/ Südosteuropa* (Munich: Sagner, 2008), 219–230.

Starr, Deborah, *Remembering Cosmopolitan Egypt: Literature, Culture, and Empire* (London: Routledge, 2010).

Stauth, Georg, "Anatomies of the Mediterranean in Modern Theory," in Faruk Birtek and Binnaz Toprak (eds.), *The Post-Modern Abyss and the New Politics of Islam: Assabiyah Revisited. Essays in Honor of Şerif Mardin* (Istanbul: Istanbul Bilgi University Press, 2011), 55–80.

Stoklásková, Zdenka, "Wandernde Handwerksgesellen als privilegierte Gruppe: Ein Beitrag zur Geschichte des Handwerks in den böhmischen Ländern," in Klaus Roth (ed.), *Vom Wandergesellen zum 'Green*

Card'-Spezialisten: Interkulturelle Aspekte der Arbeitsmigration im östlichen Mitteleuropa (Münster: Waxmann, 2003), 29–44.

Tt.

Tabak, Faruk, "Imperial Rivalry and Port-Cities: A View from Above," *Mediterranean Historical Review* 24 (2/2009), 79–94.

Talbot, Michael, "Hanımefendis Just Wanna Have Fun: An Alcoholic Postcard from Late Ottoman Istanbul," *Ottoman History Podcast* (2014), www.docblog.ottomanhistorypodcast.com/2014/12/hanmefendis-just-wanna-have-fun.html.

Teich, Mikulás, *Bier, Wissenschaft und Wirtschaft in Deutschland 1800–1914: Ein Beitrag zur deutschen Industrialisierungsgeschichte* (Vienna: Böhlau, 2000).

Tekeli, İlhan, "Nineteenth Century Transformation of Istanbul Metropolitan Area," in Paul Dumont and François Georgeon (eds.), *Villes ottomanes à la fin de l'Empire* (Paris: L'Harmattan, 1992), 33–45.

Anadolu'da Yerleşme Sistemi ve Yerleşme Tarihi Yazıları (Istanbul: Tarih Vakfı, 2011).

Theweleit, Klaus, *Objektwahl (All You Need is Love...): Über Paarbildungsstrategien & Bruchstück einer Freudbiographie* (Frankfurt/Main: Stroemfeld/Roter Stern, 1990).

Thurston, Gary, *The Popular Theatre Movement in Russia, 1862–1919* (Evanston: Northwestern University Press, 1998).

Tuğlacı, Pars, *Osmanlı Mimarlığında Batılaşma Dönemi ve Balyan Ailesi* (Istanbul: İnkılap Aka, 1981).

Türe, Fatma, "The New Woman in Erotic Popular Literature," in Duygu Köksal and Anastasia Falierou (eds.), *A Social History of Ottoman Women: New Perspectives* (Leiden: Brill, 2013), 173–200.

Türesay, Özgür, "An Almanac for Ottoman Women: Notes on Ebüzziya Tevfik's Takvîmü'n-nisâ (1317/1899)," in Duygu Köksal and Anastasia Falierou (eds.), *A Social History of Late Ottoman Women: New Perspectives* (Leiden: Brill, 2013), 225–248.

Uu.

Ur, Aviva Ben, "'We Speak and Write This Language against Our Will': Jews, Hispanics, and the Dilemma of Ladino-Speaking Sephardim in Early Twentieth-Century New York," *American Jewish Archives Journal* 50 (1–2/1998), 131–142.

Vv.

Vakali, Anna, "A Christian Printer in Selanik under Trial in the City's Tanzimat Council in the Early 1850s: Kiriakos Darzilovitis and his Seditious Books," *Cihannüma* 1 (2/Dec. 2015), 23–38.

"Nationalism, Justice and Taxation in an Ottoman Urban Context during the Tanzimat: The Gazino-Club in Manastır," *Turkish Historical Review* 7 (2/2016), 194–223.

Vakkasoğlu, Vehbi, *Tarih Aynasında Ziya Gökalp* (Istanbul: Nesil, 2012).

Veinstein, Gilles, "Un paradoxe séculaire," in id. (ed.), *Salonique 1850–1918* (Paris: Autrement, 1992), 42–63.

Vourou, Anna, "Interview Thessaloniki 1985," in Christine Rillig (ed.), *1895–1985 – 90 Jahre Evangelische Kirche dt. Sprache in Thessaloniki* (Thessaloniki: self-published, 1985).

Ww.

Wagner, Veruschka, *Imagologie der Fremde: Das Londonbild eines osmanischen Reisenden Mitte des 19. Jahrhunderts* (Göttingen: Vandenhoeck & Ruprecht, 2016).

Weis, Eberhard, *Der Durchbruch des Bürgertums 1776–1847* (Frankfurt/Main: Ullstein, 1982).

Willson, Laura, "Operatic Battlefields, Theater of War," in Gavin Williams (ed.), *Hearing the Crimean War: Wartime Sound and the Unmaking of Sense* (Oxford: Oxford University Press, 2019), 175–195.

Wingfield, Nancy M., *The World of Prostitution in Late Imperial Austria* (Oxford: Oxford University Press, 2017).

Wishnitzer, Avner, "Eyes in the Dark: Nightlife and Visual Regimes in Late Ottoman Istanbul," *Comparative Studies of South Asia, Africa and the Middle East* 37 (2/2017), 245–261.

"Shedding New Light: Outdoor Illumination in Late Ottoman Istanbul," in Josiane Meier, Ute Hasenöhrl, Katharina Krause, and Merle Pottharst (eds.), *Urban Lighting, Light Pollution and Society* (London: Routledge, 2018), 66–88.

Wolff, Larry, *The Singing Turk* (Stanford: Stanford University Press, 2016).

Yy.

Yeğenoğlu, Meyda, *Colonial Fantasies: Towards a Feminist Reading of Orientalism* (Cambridge: Cambridge University Press, 1998).

Yeğin, Uğur, (ed.), *Evvel zaman içinde ... İzmir* (Izmir: İzmir Ticaret Odası, 2009).
Yerasimos, Stéphane, "A propos des réformes urbaines des Tanzimat," in Paul Dumont and François Georgeon (eds.), *Villes ottomanes à la fin de l'Empire* (Paris: Harmattan, 1992), 17–33.
Yerolympos, Alexandra, *Urban Transformations in the Balkans (1820–1920): Aspects of Balkan Town Planning and the Remaking of Thessaloniki* (Thessaloniki: University Studio Press, 1996).
"Conscience citadine et intérêt municipal à Salonique à la fin du XIXe siècle," in Paul Dumont and François Georgeon (eds.), *Vivre dans l'empire ottomane: Sociabilités et relations intercommunitaires (XVIIIe-XXe siècles)* (Paris: Harmattan, 1997), 123–144.
Yıldız, Murat C., "What Is a Beautiful Body?" *Middle East Journal of Culture and Communication* 8 (2015), 192–214.
Yılmaz, Seçil, "Threats to Public Order and Health: Mobile Men as Syphilis Vectors in Late Ottoman Medical Discourse and Practice," *Journal of Middle East Women's Studies* 13 (2/2017), 222–243.

Zz.

Zachs, Fruma, "'Under Eastern Eyes': East on West in the Arabic Press of the Nahda Period," *Studia Islamica New Series* 106 (1/2011), 175–180.
"Cultural and Conceptual Contributions of Beiruti Merchants to the Nahda," *Journal of the Economic and Social History of the Orient* 55 (1/2012), 153–182.
Zandi-Sayek, Sibel, "Struggles over the Shore: Building the Quay of Izmir, 1867–1875," *City and Society* 12 (1/2000), 55–78.
Ottoman Izmir: The Rise of A Cosmopolitan Port, 1840–1880 (Minneapolis: University of Minnesota Press, 2012).
Zarinebaf, Fariba, *Mediterranean Encounters: Trade and Pluralism in Early Modern Galata* (Oakland: University of California Press, 2018).
Zat, Vefa, "Bomonti Bira Fabrikası," in İlhan Tekeli (ed.), *Dünden bugüne İstanbul Ansiklopedisi* (Istanbul: Tarih Vakfı, 1995), vol. III, 296, 297.
Zelepos, Ioannis, *Rebetiko: Die Karriere einer Subkultur* (Cologne: Romiosini, 2001).
Die Ethnisierung griechischer Identität 1870–1912: Staat und private Akteure vor dem Hintergrund der "Megali Idea" (Munich: Oldenbourg, 2002).
"Städte als Projektionsflächen im griechischen Popularlied des 20. Jahrhunderts: Istanbul, Izmir, Thessaloniki," in Ulrike Tischler and Ioannis Zelepos (eds.), *Bilderwelten – Weltbilder: Die Gegenwart der Vergangenheit*

in postosmanischen Metropolen Südosteuropas. Thessaloniki, Istanbul, Izmir (Frankfurt/Main: Peter Lang 2009), 63–100.

Zerman, Ece, *Studying an Ottoman "Bourgeois" Family: Said Bey's Family Archive (1900–1930)*, MA thesis, Boğaziçi University, Istanbul (2013).

Zürcher, Erik J., *Turkey a Modern History* (London: Tauris, 2017).

Index

Abbott, Henri, 365–366
Abbott, Robert, 359–360
Abdülaziz, 84–85, 158–159
Abdülhamid II, 74, 85–86, 88, 194, 234–235, 325–326, 360–361
Abdülmecid, 63–64, 70–71, 84–85, 130–131, 157
   Dolmabahçe Theater and, 122–123
   first years of, 179
   Great Powers and, 84
   restrictive attitude of, 139
   vision of development, 398
Ade, Mafalda, 292–293
Adriatic littoral, 311–312
Adžiova, Katerina, 325
Aegean Sea, 79, 154–155, 391–392
Age of Anger (Mishra), 27–28
Age of Revivals, 32–33, 139–140, 179–180, 187, 250. *See also* Tanzimat
agricultural exports, 13
AIU. *See Alliance Isréalite Universelle*
Albanians, 269–270
Alcazar de Byzance, 131–132
Aleppo, 56, 306–307, 357
Alexandria, 115–116, 124–125, 366–368, 375–376
   British capture of (1882), 368
   French capture of (1798), 37–38
   Jews in, 367
   Place des Consuls, 84
   population of, 11
Algeciras, 30–31
Alhambra Cinema, 131–132
Âli Pasha, Mehmed Emin, Grand Vizier, 227–228
Aliye, Fatma, 249–251
alla franga clothes, 100, 273, 279
alla turca clothes, 279
Allatini (family), 113

Allatini, Moishe, 222–223, 239–240
Alliance Isréalite Universelle (AIU), 221–224, 228
Alsancak. *See* Punta
Amber Barracks (Smyrna), 84–85
American Board of Foreign Missions, 220
American Dream, 263–264
Amicis, Edmondo de, 89–90, 105
Anatolia, 394–400
Anatolian popular music, 83. *See also* Rebetiko
Annales school, 13
anti-Armenian massacres, 368–369
anti-Christian riots, 366–367
anti-European alliances, 370
anti-imperialism, 364
anti-modernity, 354–355
anti-quays, 86–92
anti-Semitism, 336–337, 394–395
anti-socialness, 204
anti-strike laws, 328
anti-Westernism, 352–354, 366–368, 376, 388–389
apartment houses, 67
Apollon Theater, 134
Arab Christians, 292–293
Arab Egyptian nationalist mobs, 367
Araba Sevdası (Ekrem), 202–203, 214
Aracı, Emre, 128–129
archived voices, 33–35
Ardot, Paul. *See* Cohen, Han Youssé
Arif'in Hilesi (Çuhacıyan), 166–167
Aristotle Square (Plateia Aristotelous), 396
armed resistance, 393–394
Armenians, 200, 243–244, 292–293, 368–369
Armstrong, Harold, 395
Arshak II (Çuhacıyan), 166–167

455

Art Nouveau, 3–5, 137
artisans, 304–308, 323–325
Ashkenazi community, 376–377, 385–386
"Asiatic cities" (Weber), 11–12
"Asiatic Mode of Production" (Marx), 11
L'Assedio di Silistria (Panizza), 153–154
Asseo family, 364–365
assimilation, 307
Association for the Protection of Young Girls (Constantinople), 386
Atatürk. *See* Kemal (Atatürk), Mustafa
Athanassoula Beer Garden, 187
Audisio, Gabriel, 22–23, 31, 296–297
Aufscher, Feige, 384
Augusta Victoria, 377
Austria. *See* Habsburg Empire
L'aveugle de Smyrne (anonymous), 138–151
Ayasoluk, 44–45
Aydın, 44–45

Bahr, Samuel, 384
Bakotić, Ivan, 364–365
Balkan Wars, 401
balls (dancing), 113–115, 118, 208, 275
Baltalimanı Treaty, 1838, 38–39
banditry, 358
Barachin, 63–64
bare feet, 273–274
Bareilles, Bertrand, 275–277, 284–285
Barère, Bertrand, 38
Barth, Hans, 177–178, 184–185, 187–188, 274, 276
Bartissol, Edmond, 74
Bauer, Otto, 337–338
Bayly, Christopher A., 20–21
Bedri Bey, Osman, 387–388
beer, 26, 174–175, 190
  at apogee, 188–192
  attitudes and spatial practices assumed vis-à-vis, 173–174
  coming to Ottoman Empire, 175–181
  cons of, 199–205
  Constantinople and, 96–97, 177, 184, 208
  cultural role of, 175
  Europeanization and, 202–203
  Islam and, 194
  pros of, 194–199
  Salonica and, 96–97, 194, 205–208
  silent rise of, 181–184
  Smyrna and, 96–97, 208
  unchallenged mass consumption and production of, 184–188
  Westernization and, 173
Beethoven, Ludwig van, 152–153
Beirut, 11, 30–31, 190–192, 221–224, 227–228
Belgrade, 373–374
Belisario (Donizetti), 161
Bellas Effendi, 184–185
Belle Époque, 17, 297, 348, 354–355, 402–403, 407–408
Benčić, Jovan, 312
Ben-Gurion, David, 385
Benliyan, Serovpe, 169–170
Bentham, Jeremy, 51, 55–56
Bernhardt, Sarah, 149–150, 163–164
Beşçınar Gardens, 135–136, 247–248
Beyoğlu. *See* Pera
Beyru, Rauf, 138–151
Bhabha, Homi, 25
bicycle races, 247–248, 255–256
Bihruz Bey, 214, 216–217, 246–247
Bihruz Bey Syndrome, 248–249, 263–264, 283–284, 342–343
bin Ali, Necep, 199–200
Bir Zambağın Hikâyesi (Rauf), 254–255
Black, Niven Kerr, 60–61
Blacks, 269–270
Blacque, Alexandre, 235–237, 300, 352–353
Blumberg, I. Wilfried, 335, 337–342
boatmen (*Gemidži*), 368–369
bodybuilders, 256–257
Bohemia, 315–316
Bohemian Orchestras, 83, 303–304, 314–320
Bolland, Charles, 184–185
Bomonti Beer Garden, 187, 189
Bomonti Brothers, 185–186
Bomonti-Nektar Company, 189–190, 400
Bonaparte, Napoleon, 40, 43–44, 49

Bonatz, Paul, 397–398
Book of Women (*Zenannâme*) (Fâzıl), 253
Borutta, Manuel, 30–31
Bosco, Giovanni Bartholomeo, 129
Bosco Theater, 129–130, 139. *See also* Naum Theater
Bosnia and Herzegovina, 325
Bosporus, 50, 63–64, 78
Boulanger, Gustave, 228–229
Bourdieu, Pierre, 25
bourgeoisie, 142–143
  class formation of, 281–287
  compradore, 298
  of Constantinople, 111
  in Eastern Mediterranean, 268
  emerging national, 271–272
  of Germany, 324–325
  internationally standardized, 267–281
  military-bureaucratic, 270–271
  morality, 330
  narratives on, 267
  obsession with, 277–281
  perspective on Europeanization, 13–14
  petit bourgeois, 272
  of Salonica, 111, 239–240
  of Smyrna, 111
  stratum of, 266–267
Boxer Rebellion, 355–356, 364, 370
Brasserie Aleko, 120–121
Brasserie Alhambra, 126
Brasserie d'Angleterre, 205–206
Braudel, François, 19–20, 22–23
Braunschweig, Martin, 323–326
Brâzitsov, Hristo, 176, 401
brigands, 358–363
British Empire, 381
British Levant Company, 55
Brunau, Max, 195–196
Buca, 102, 107–109
Buck, Stefan, 359
Buddhism, 350
Bukovina, 379–380
Bulgaria, 347
  Greater, 366–367
Bulletin des nouvelles (newspaper), 235
bureaucracy, 67, 77–78, 114–115, 168, 315, 352–353, 413–414
  Constantinople and, 228–229
  court, 122–123
  Georgeon on, 199–201
  higher schools for, 219–220
  rank-and-file, 341–342
  Turkish members of, 167
burlesque, 99–100
Burnabad, 102, 109
Büyük Sulh Brewery, 190–191
Byzantium, 89–90

cabarets, 147
Café at the White Tower, 135–136
café chantant, 126–128, 131–132, 168
Café de Paris, 126
Café des Fleurs, 131–132
Café Kraemer, 186
Cairo, 56, 375–376
Calligas, Paul, 50–51, 59–60, 87, 89–90, 109
Çamlıca Hill, 50–51, 187, 203
Cammarano Theater, 109–110, 124, 125
Canning, Stratford, 44–45, 161
Canonica, Pietro, 396–397
capitalism, 14, 62, 195, 263–264, 357
capitulatory powers. *See* Great Powers
capitulatory privileges. *See* Great Powers
Carinthia, 334
Carnival Week, 111
Catholicism, 52–53, 289–290, 325, 332–333
  adherence to, 290–291
  hegemony of, 350
  Levant and, 291
Cattaro, 309–310
Çelik, Zeynep, 64–65
censorship, 234–235
Central Europe, 10–11
Cercle d'Orient, 132–133, 293–294
Cercle Levantin, 107
Cevad, Ahmed, 48, 251, 257
Cevahircizade Abdülkerim, 196–199
Chamfort, Sébastien-Roch, 152
chastity, 383–384
Chevalier, Michel, 43–44
cholera epidemic, 308–309
Christian Ottoman subjects, 289
Christian schools, 221–222

Christian-Jewish riots, 237–238
Christians, 118, 413
church archives, 320
Church Mission Society, 220
Cité de Pera, 130–131
civil society, 70–71
civilité, 142–143
civilization
  fausse, 267
civilizationist narrative, 21–22
civilizing mission, 142–149
Civilizing Process (Elias), 142–143
clam-diving, 104
Clancy-Smith, Julia, 30–31
class formation, 266–267, 287
  of bourgeoisie, 281–287
  economic and structural components of, 267–268
  nationalism and, 390–391
clergy, 284–285
cloisonnement, 267
coffeehouses, 99–100, 131–135, 348. *See also specific establishments*
  entertainment and, 126–127
  large-scale performances in, 125
  in Smyrna, 83, 100
Cohen, Han Youssé, 164
Cohen, Samuel, 380
Cohen, Vitalis, 164, 239–240, 243–244, 319, 342
Coleridge, Samuel T., 349
collective violence, 371
Colombo, Giacomo, 135–136
colonial inferiority complex, 66
colonialism, 20–21, 31, 40, 231–232
Cominotti, Madalena Emilia, 162–163
Committee of Union and Progress, 147–148, 231–232
commuter traffic infrastructure, 79
Concordia, 126, 131–132
Concordia Theater, 135, 162–163
Confessions of an Opera Addict (Şuayip), 149–151
conspicuous consumption, 94
Constantinople, 5–6, 8–9, 21, 25, 37–38, 397–398, 411
  anti-Armenian massacres in, 368–369
  beer and, 96–97, 177, 184, 208

bourgeoisie of, 111
bureaucracy and, 228–229
Calligas and, 50–51
consulate construction in, 70
Eastern Mediterranean, Constantinople-centered hegemony and, 107
entertainment in, 119–120
French Chamber of Commerce in, 76, 87
French dramatists in, 138
Golden Horn and, 52
Habsburg Consulate in, 230
Hartmann on, 45–46
historic center of, 89–90
human trafficking and, 374
identity and, 340
Italian music scene in, 157
Jahn on, 63, 67–68
Marseille and, 54
Moltke and, 49
narrowness of streets in, 78
occupation forces in, 393–394
official planning of, 67–68
Paris and, 163–165
Pera and, 90–91
population of, 66
quays in, 74–75
railway workers of, 337–338
sex workers in, 303–304
Smyrna and, 80
Société Musicale de Constantinople, 113–114, 132–133
steamships and, 77–78
Swift (ship) arrival in, 56–57, 60–61
Ubicini and, 104–105
Wagner and, 154–155
white slave trade and, 377
constitutionalism, 337–338
Constitutionnel (newspaper), 236, 300
Corneille, Pierre, 122
corruption, 270
corso, 102–106
cosmopolitanism, 17, 26–27, 195, 208
  education and, 227
  imperialism and, 390–391
  indeterminate state of identity and, 212
  Orientalism and, 395
  working-class and, 323–325

counter-utopia, 355
Courrier de Constantinople (newspaper), 236–237
Courrier de Smyrne (newspaper), 71, 107–109, 236, 352–353
courtoisie, 142–143
Covent Garden, 130–131
Cramer, Fredrick de, 400–401
Crespi, Carlo, 213–214
Crétot, Léon, 155–156
crime, 358–360
Crimean War (1853–1856), 104–105, 133, 153–154, 306–309, 374
Il crociato in Egitto (Meyerbeer), 152–153
Csáky, Moritz, 24, 215–216
Cuban War of Independence (1895–1898), 238
Çuhacıyan, Dikran, 118–119, 166–168
cultural capital, 95, 116, 122, 208–209, 224
  contradictory sources of, 300–301
  flaunting, 267
cultural history, 21, 24
  anthropo-centric concept of, 23–24
  basic problems of, 24
cultural transfers, 23–24
culture shock, 57–59
Cumaovası, 102, 177
Cvijić, Jovan, 22–23
Czernowitz, 372–375

Damascus, 56
dancehalls, 295
Danger Brothers, 396–397
Dardanelles, 60–61
d'Arezzo, Guido, 158
Darwinism, 249–250
Davernon, Terrassor, 127
Davidović, Kohn, 359
deaconesses, 109, 221–222, 224, 381
The Decline of the West (Spengler), 354–355
décloisonnement, 47–48, 231–232, 341–342
d'Ectot, Madame de Mannoury, 254–255
demanding "coffee money," 362
demographical changes, 60–61

department stores, 89–91
Depasta Brothers, 149
Les derniers Levantins (Loreley), 295–297
d'Escorches, Marie Louis, 38, 43, 45
Dickens, Charles, 349
digital age, 410–411
diplomatic history, 19–20
district administrator (*mutasarrıf*), 361
dogs, packs of, 63–64
Dolmabahçe Palace, 70–71, 84–85, 158–159
Dolmabahçe Theater, 122–123
domestic labor, 328–329
Donaty, Louise, 259–260
Donizetti, Gaetano, 124, 129–130, 154–155, 158–159, 161
Donizetti Pasha, Giuseppe, 158–159, 161
Dostoevsky, Fyodor, 349–351, 353–354
drama writing, 151–154
dramatic arts, 95–96
Dual Monarchy. *See* Habsburg Empire
Dubrovnik. *See* Ragusa
Duchaine, A., 190–191
Dumont, Paul, 15–16, 19, 26, 116
Durst, Franz, 325
Dussaud, Frères, 73
Duterte, Armand, 161–162

Early Modern Ottoman world, 19
Eastern Mediterranean, 6–7, 52
  Belle Époque and, 407–408
  bourgeoisie in, 268
  calamities in, 402
  civilizing mission and, 145
  collective sense of belonging in, 340
  colonialism and, 40
  composers' and playwrights' interest in, 157
  Constantinople-centered hegemony and, 107
  cosmopolitanism, 26–27
  culture of, 8–9
  diversity of, 339–340
  drama scene of, 172
  entertainment in, 119–120, 138–151
  Europe and, 25–28
  European Dream and, 49, 403

Eastern Mediterranean (cont.)
  Europhilia and, 406
  family life in, 314–315
  foreign theater stars in, 162
  Great Powers influence in, 394
  gunboat policy and, 41
  historiography of, 10
  identity, 217
  Italian opera performers and, 152
  leisure practices of, 118–119
  London stock exchange and, 13
  marginalization of, 355–356
  modernity in, 415
  nation building and, 269
  nationalism in, 7–8
  opera and, 150–151
  sociabilities of, 95–96
  steamship services in, 43–44
  theater in, 95–96
  urban history of, 18, 22
  urban practices in, 17–18
  urban studies of, 20–21
  World War I and, 38–39
Eastern Rumelia, 364–365
Écôle et famille (magazine), 241–242
economies of violence, 358
Eden Theater, 136, 155–156
Edhem, İbrahim, 228–229
Edib (Adıvar), Halide, 393–394, 402, 407–408
education, 403
  Christian schools, 221–222
  cosmopolitanism and, 227
  foreign-based schools, 232–233
  imperialism and, 219–220
  influence of, 219
  Italian national schools, 221–222
  Jewish community schools, 221–222
  missionary institutions and, 220
  modern educational systems, 225–226
  in Ottoman Empire, 381
  Salonica and, 222–223
  Smyrna and, 221–222
Egypt, 144
  Africa and, 46–47
  Arab Egyptian nationalist mobs, 367
  immigration of women to, 375–376
  occupation of, 38–39

Ekrem, Recaizade Mahmut. *See* Recaizade Mahmut, Ekrem
Eksaristeron Theater, 126
Eldem, Edhem, 15–17, 291
Elias, Norbert, 142–143
elitist organizations, 112–113
Elyahari, Jakob, 180
embezzlement, 85–86
Eminönü, 74–75, 78
Emrence, Cem, 14, 357–358
England, 54
Enlightenment, 10, 55
entertainment, 26, 208, 398–400
  coffeehouses and, 126–127
  in Constantinople, 119–120
  culture of, 99
  in Eastern Mediterranean, 119–120, 138–151, 157
  new forms of, 94
  possibilities, 109–110
  in summer, 104–109, 112, 126, 133
  Western forms of, 100
  women in, 260–261
Enver Pasha, 351
La Epoca (journal), 239–240
Erdoğan, Recep Tayyip, 411–413
Eren, Ercan, 174, 176
Esad, Mahmud, 249–250
escapism, 150
Eskenazi, Roza, 407–408
ethnic prejudice, 119
ethnocentrism, 231
Étranger, 135–136
Eugenides, Jeffrey, 406–408
Eurocentrism, 232–233
Euro-Ottoman acculturation, 22
Europe, 8, 93
  arrivals to Ottoman Empire from, 302, 311–314
  cities in nineteenth-century, 66
  collective sense of belonging in, 340
  as concept and culture, 29–30
  constant evocation of, 67
  crisis in, 306–307
  decline of, 347–348
  Eastern Mediterranean and, 25–28
  imperialist self-image of, 388–389
  languages and customs of, 382–383
  lower-class immigrants from, 320–323

Ottoman Empire and, 304
quays, attributes of modern Europe embraced in, 79–80
Smyrna commercial exchange with European ports, 71
upper-class of, 302
waning appeal of, 388
European Casino, 107, 109, 119, 272–273
European cultural hegemony, 80
European Dream, 26–28, 46–47, 93, 95–96
  disillusionment with, 355, 391
  Eastern Mediterranean and, 49, 403
  Hartmann and, 269–270
  lure of, 410
  opera and, 150–151
  utilitarian materialism and, 351
European dress and etiquette, 272–273
European paradigm, 369–370
Europeanization, 8–9, 33, 208–209
  acquis communautaire of, 270–277
  beer and, 202–203
  bourgeoisie perspective on, 13–14
  cycles of acceptance of, 175
  internalizing, 277–281
  negative assessment of, 66
  Ottoman Empire and, 70–71
  process of, 28–29
  resistance against, 87
  theater and opera and, 145
  urban space and, 29, 86–87
Europeanness, 298–299, 369–370
Europhilia, 406
Europhoria, 409–410
Euterpe Theater, 109–110, 124–125
Evranos, Mustafa Rahmi. *See* Rahmi Bey
Exchange of Populations, 7–8, 400–401
exclusivism, 372
Exertzoglou, Haris, 283–284

Fallmerayer, Jakob Philipp, 152–153
family life, 314–315
family privacy, 67
Faraggi, M., 247–248
farmers, 304–308
Faroqhi, Suraiya, 19–20
Farrère, Claude, 3–5
Fatih, Ahmed, 306–307

Fâzıl, Enderûnlu, 253
Fehim, Ahmed, 170–172
Fehnl, Martha, 260–261
Ferah Theater, 134
Ferid Paşa, Avlonyalı Mehmed, 383
ferman, 128–129
Fernandez, Abraham, 364–365
Feuer, Adele, 199, 260–261
Les filles à marier (Girls to be Married Off) (Cohen, V.), 243–244
filthiness, 63
fishing villages, 78
Flaubert, Gustave, 124
foreign workers, 325–329
Formby, Henry, 50, 58–60
Forneris, Anna, 49, 57–58, 178–179, 181, 332–335
Forty Years in Constantinople (Pears), 299–300
Fossati, Gaspare, 70
Foucault, Michel, 55–56, 272
France, 54, 165
  Alexandria, French advance upon, 37–38
  colonialism and, 231–232
  fausse civilization, 267
  Syria and, 392–393
  theatrical prestige of, 155
Frangomahalla, 54–55, 62, 72–73, 106–107, 337–338, 366
Frank Street, 62–63, 67–68, 71
Frankish Quarters. *See Frangomahalla*
free or liberal religious movement, 338–339
freedom of movement, 320–321
Freitag, Ulrike, 24
French Chamber of Commerce in Constantinople, 76, 87
French language, 224–225, 246–247, 267
  mastery of, 226
  newspapers, 234–235, 238–239, (*See also specific newspapers*)
  publications, 241–242
French Revolution, 20–21
French Theater, 131–132, 142, 154–155, 166–167
Frenchness, 300
frenkhanes, 62
Friedmann, Sara, 378–379, 384

Friedrich Wilhelm IV (king), 221
Fröbel, Julius, 82–83, 270–274
Fuad Effendi, 247–248

Galata, 337–338, 372–375
  Ashkenazi community and, 376–377
  police in, 385–386
  port facilities in, 77
  prostitution in, 383–384
  quays, 76, 102–103
  stock market, 136, 243–244
  waterfront, 78
Galata-Pera, 52, 64, 74–75, 397–398
  department stores in, 89–90
  fire suffered by, 67–68
  society, 102–103
Galdi, Matteo, 38
Galicia, 310, 316, 318, 373–374, 379–381, 384–385, 388–389. *See also* Habsburg Empire
Gallipoli, 60–61
gambling, 147
Gandhi, Mohandas K., 355
Garnier, Philippe, 136
Gautier, Théophile, 105
Gavand, Eugène Henri, 78–79
Gazette Française de Constantinople (newspaper), 235
gazinos, 191–192
Gedikpaşa, 134, 141–142
Gedikpaşa Theater, 122–123, 147
Gekas, Sakis, 30–31
Gemidži (boatmen), 368–369
gender roles, 243–244, 250–252, 279–280
  discourse on, 255
  myriad of, 264
  new, 259
  Ottoman Empire and, 253
  rearranging, 257
Genoa, 82
Georgelin, Hervé, 224, 394–395
Georgeon, François, 15–16, 19, 26, 93, 116
Germany, 307, 313–314, 387
  anti-Semitism and, 394–395
  bourgeoisie of, 324–325
  Holy Roman Empire, 175–176
  imperialism and, 336–337

Gérôme, Jean-Léon, 228–229
Ghanem Efendi, Khalil, 155–156
Giraud, Ernest, 76, 79, 87, 188–189, 191–192, 194
  on fashionable dress, 273
  on underground funicular railway, 272
Girls to be Married Off (*Les filles à marier*) (Cohen, V.), 243–244
La Gitana (Pisani), 158–159
Giustiniani, Bartholomeo, 131–132
globalization, 14, 414–415
Goffman, Daniel, 15–17, 54
Gökalp, Ziya, 233, 390–391
Golden Age, 294–297
Golden Horn, 52, 74–75, 89–90
Goldoni, Carlo, 152
Goldstaub, N., 379
Goncharov, Ivan, 216–217
gonorrhea, 258
Gorman, Anthony, 321–323
Gottmann, Moishe, 379
Grand Bretagne, 316–317
Grand Champ des Morts. *See* Taksim
Grand Rue de Pera, 63–64, 102–103, 132–133
Gras, Ernst, 387
Great Britain, 38–39, 348–349
Great Powers, 45, 70, 74–75, 132–133, 364–365, 367
  Abdülmecid and, 84
  capitulations, 230, 232–233, 321, 377, 387, 394
  changing cast of, 38–39
  consular meddling by, 408–409
  exclusivism and, 372
  expansion of, 219
  humanitarian intervention by, 352–353
  imperial powers, 371
  influence in Eastern Mediterranean, 394
  national post offices of, 76
  over-identification with, 266
  politics of, 25
  retaliation, 347–348
  Salonica and, 366
  subjects of, 388–389
  Treaty of Berlin and, 366–367
  vying for influence, 323–325

Greco-Turkish War (1919-1923), 398–399
Greece, 50–51, 182–183, 391–392
Greek Casino, 107
Greek language, 227–228
Greek music, 109. *See also* Anatolian popular music; *Rebetiko*
Greek nationality, 391
Greek Philharmonic Association of Smyrna, 127–128
Greek war of secession (1820-1829), 50–51, 62, 128–129, 152–153, 352–353
Greekness, 396
Greek-Orthodox Church, 7–8, 291
Christian-Orthodox authors, 354
Greek-Orthodox population, 220
Grigorios VI (Patriarch), 284–285
Grillparzer, Franz, 349–350
Guadalquivir (ship), 368–369
Guatelli Pasha, Callisto, 133–134, 158–159
Guillon, Hélène, 239–240
Gül, Murat, 67–68
Gülhane Edict (1838). *See* Reform Charter (1838)
Güllü Agop, 142, 166–167, 169–171
gunboat diplomacy, 25, 41, 47–48, 92, 394–400
Gürsoy, Melih, 235
gymnastics, 248–249, 256

Habermas, Jürgen, 25
Habsburg Empire, 37–38, 70, 216–217, 259–260, 306–307, 311–314, 317–318, 327, 334, 347, 354, 373–374, 379–383, 387, 407–408
  Eastern provinces of, 318–319
  Foreign Ministry of, 377
  Galicia and Bukovina annexed by, 379–380
  Habsburg Consulate, 230, 307–308, 316, 375–380
  Habsburg Embassy, 139, 359, 361–362, 386–387
  Habsburg predicament, 380–383
  prostitution and, 373–374, 380
  public image of, 384
  women and, 380–381
Hacı Bey, 63

Hadj pilgrims, 367–368
Hadjilazaros, Periklis, 365–366
Halid, Halil, 287, 341–342, 355
Halid, Refik, 29–30, 118
Hamdi Bey, Osman, 228–229, 285–287, 341–342
Hamidian Era, 32, 241–242, 320, 323–325
Hamidiye Fountain, 85–86
Hamidiye Hospital, 86, 88
Hanımlara Mahsûs Gazete (newspaper), 251–253
Hanly, John L., 237–238
Hanson, J. O., 107
Hanssen, Jens, 16
Hartmann, Martin, 45–46, 88, 269–271
Hauser, Julia, 231
Hearts of the West (1910), 3–5
Hébrard, Ernest, 396
Hekimyan theater group, 168
Hellenic Kingdom. *See* Greece
Hemingway, Ernest, 394
Henderson, Nevile, 226
Herero War, 364
Hermes (newspaper), 87
Heß, Rudolf, 407–408
highlife, 120–121
Hilfsverein der deutschen Juden, 386
Hinduism, 350
hinterland, 357–360, 398
Hofmannsthal, Hugo von, 215
Holy Roman Empire. *See* Germany
Homburg hats, 357
L'homme qui assassina (Farrère), 3–5
Horden, Peregrine, 31
horse-drawn carriages, 78
hospitals, 84–86, 88
Hotel Colombo, 135–136, 195–196
Hotel d'Angleterre, 135–136, 186
Hotel Olympos Palace, 186
Hotel Royal, 135–136
Hotel Splendid, 135–136
Houquet, Henri, 140
house visits, 101–102
Hugo, Victor, 228
Hulusi Bey, 65, 88
human rights, 271–272
human trafficking, 374–375, 383–388. *See also* white slave trade

humanitarian intervention, 352–353
Humann, Carl, 101, 111–112
Humbert, Gustav, 275
Hungary. *See* Habsburg Empire
Huntington, Samuel P., 412–414
Hurşid Pasha, 180
Hüsnü Bey, 257–258
Hyde Clark, Henry, 44–45

Ibn Khaldun, Abd-Ar-Rahman bin Muhammad, 405
İbrahim, Abdürreşid, 355
İbrahim Hilmi, Tüccarzâde. *See* Tüccarzâde İbrahim Hilmi
Ice Skating Palace, 120–121
İdadiye, 86, 225–226
idealist activities, 247–248
identity, 212–213, 364. *See also* Levantine identity
  Constantinople and, 340
  contradictory sources of, 300–301
  Eastern Mediterranean, 217
  formation, 26–27
  indeterminate state of, 212
  malleable, 328–329
  non-Muslim, 224–225
  politics, 372
  of Stambouliotes, 401
  state-determined, 213
  struggle for legitimacy, 296–297
  in urban society, 302–303
  World War I and, 214
L'Impartial (newspaper), 65
Imperial, 135–136
imperial cosmology, 55–56
imperial powers. *See* Great Powers
imperialism, 406
  anti-imperialism, 364
  blood toll of, 395–400
  cosmopolitanism and, 390–391
  education and, 219–220
  Europe, imperialist self-image of, 388–389
  German, 336–337
  high, 219
  marginalized subjects of, 371
  opera and, 154–155
  two-faced nature of, 223–224
L'impresario delle Smirne (Goldoni), 152
İnalcık, Halil, 22–23

inbetweenness, 408–409
L'Indépendant (newspaper), 241–242
Indian Mutiny, 364
Indian Ocean, 18
Indicateur Ottoman Illustré (almanac), 183
infrastructure workers, 323–325
Inner Macedonian Revolutionary Organization, 368. *See also* boatmen (*Gemidži*)
Insurance Map, 89
intelligentsia, 165–166
interclass solidarity, 328–329
intercommunal reciprocity, 115
İpekçi Efendi, İsmail, 135–136
Iraq, 409–411
Islam, 7–8, 84, 115–119, 350, 413
  beer and, 194
  family privacy and, 67
  glories of Islamic world, 355
  lifestyle of, 173
  morals of, 382–383
  Muslim men, 275
  non-Muslim identity, 224–225
  Ramadan, 99–100, 114–115, 117–119
  roots of, 281–282
  upper-class Muslim women, 196–199
  War on Terror and, 409–410
  Women of Islam (*Nisvan-ı İslâm*) (Aliye), 250–251
Islamic State, 348–349
Ismail (Khedive), 46–47, 84
Issigonis, Alec, 407–408
Istanbul. *See* Constantinople
Istanbul residents. *See* Stambouliotes
Italian Charity Ball at Hotel Olympia, 113–114
Italian Melodrama Theater, 124–125
Italo-Turkish War (1911), 391
Italy, 96–97, 165, 313–314
  Constantinople, Italian music scene in, 157
  Eastern Mediterranean, Italian opera performers and, 152
  national schools, 221–222
İttihad (newspaper), 147–148
İttihad ve Terraki. *See* Committee of Union and Progress
Izmir. *See* Smyrna
Izmir residents. *See* Smyrniotes

Index

al-Jabarti, Abd al-Rahman, 37, 43
Jahn, August M., 63, 67–68
Jale, Afife, 134–135
Jameson Raid in Transvaal (1895-1896), 238
Jesuit church, 53
Jewish Association for the Protection of Girls and Women, 380
Jireček, Konstantin, 22–23
Journal de Constantinople (newspaper), 162–163
Journal de Salonique (newspaper), 64–65, 74, 88, 113, 136
  on Committee of Union and Progress, 231–232
  founding of, 239–240
  Girls to be Married Off (*Les filles à marier*), 243–244
  letter to the editor of, 247
  readers of, 252–253, 341–342
  sales of, 246–247
  theater and, 146
  von Sacher-Masoch and, 253
Journal de Smyrne (newspaper), 144, 236–237
Judaism, 220, 335–336, 374. *See also* Ashkenazi community; Sephardic Jews
  Alexandria, Jews in, 367
  Christian-Jewish riots, 237–238
  Jewish community schools, 221–222
  Jewish women in traditional dress, 274
  Jewish workers, 206
  orthodoxy, 350
  Saloniquenos, Jewish, 406
  Smyrna and, 222–223
  Southeast European Sephardim, 394–395
Jupiter Theater, 161–162

Kağıthane, 79
Kakavopoulos, Giannis, 197
Kalamaria, 86
Kamil, Mustafa, 355
Kandilakis, Maniolis, 241–242
Kapıcı, Faiz Efendi, 118–119
Kapodistrias, Ioannis, 352–353

Kara Ahmed, 256–257
Karakaşyan, Virginia, 169
Karamanlis community, 7–8
Kasap, Teodor, 234–235
Kasımpaşa neighborhood, 90–91
Kastriotis, Stephanos, 43, 46
Kataklum Variété, 120–121
Kauder, E., 75–76
kayıks, 79
Kaynar, Erdal, 355
Kemal, Namık, 234–235, 250, 355
Kemal (Atatürk), Mustafa, 187–188, 393–394, 396–397, 399–400, 407–408
kidnapping, 359–362
Kivotos Café, 125
Koçu, Reşad Ekrem, 176, 182, 201–202
Köksal, Duygu, 263–264
Kolluoğlu, Biray, 16–18
Konak (governor general's office), 72–73, 84–85, 365–366
Konak Square, 84–86
Korais, Admantios, 55
Koran, 355, 383
Köse, Yavuz, 178, 202–203
Kosmos, 176
Kosta, Hadži, 282–283
Kraemer's Theater, 126
Krassay, 377–380, 384
Kukuli Theater, 171–172
Kurayyim, Muhammad, 37–38
Kurds, 269–270, 359
Kypseli (Samartzidou), 251–252

labor, 405
  aristocracy, 321–322
  domestic, 328–329
  female, 258–259
  migration of, 312
  radicalism, 77, 207
Latîfe Hanım, 407–408
Launay, Marie de, 285–286
law-and-order, 328
Lawrence, David H., 349
League of Nations, 392–393
Leblebici Horhor Ağa (Çuhacıyan), 118–119, 166–167
Lefebvre, Henri, 25
leisure practices, 95, 118–119, 208

Leitkultur, 398–399
Lent, 111
Levant, 7, 334. *See also* Levantine identity
  Catholicism and, 291
  Eldem on, 291
  entertainment and, 157
  foreigners in, 366
  going on tour in, 318
  nineteenth-century wars in, 38–39
  prostitution in, 372–375
  theater in, 122–125
  touring, 160
  urbanity of, 11
Levant Herald (newspaper), 162–163, 226, 238–239
Levant Times and Shipping Gazette (newspaper), 237–238
Levantine identity, 288–290, 298
  malleable character of, 302
  paths to recreating, 297–301
  relative obscurity of, 292
  research on, 292–294
  self-definition of, 300–301
  Smyrna and, 293–294
Levy, Saadi, 239–240
Levy, Sam, 225–226, 287
Lewis, Bernard, 21–22
Liebermann, Moses, 317–318
Liebermann Orchestra, 317–319
Ligue Ottomane, 386
Lindau, Paul, 276
Lindenberg, Paul, 80
Lindner, Christine B., 231
linguistic confusion, 214
Liszt, Friedrich, 112
literacy, 241–242, 270
literati, 155–156
London, 45, 67
London stock exchange, 13
Loreley, Angèle, 295–297, 406
Lorraine, Aimée, *see* Lüttgens, Amanda
Loti, Pierre, 89–90
Lotti, Marcella, 146–147
Louis XIV, 170–171
lower-class, 335
  actresses and actors, 171–172
  contempt against, 281
  lower middle classes, 94
  migration, 305, 311, 320–323, 339–340
  quays and, 82–83
  residential areas, 74–75
  upper-class and, 92
Lukat, Augustina, 336
Lukat, Gottfried, 336–337
Lumpenproletariat, 270–271
Lüttgens, Amanda, 171–172, 259, 261–262
Lüttgens, Anna, 259–260

Macedonia, 309–310, 382–383
  Slavic-speaking population thereof, 368–369
MacFarlane, Charles, 56–57, 62
Mačić, Savo Đuro, 312
Maçka Gorge, 70–71, 92, 398
Magakyan, Bedros, 169–170
Maghreb, 30–31
Mahmud II (Sultan), 60–61, 66–67, 158, 272–273, 281–282, 332
Makdisi, Ilham, 213
Malatya, 357
male body, 255–258
Malfer, Natale, 312–313
Malpassuto, G., 135
Malpassuto, Lisa, 135
Man without Qualities (Musil), 216–217, 246–247
Manasse, Seraphine, 142, 168
Mansel, Philip, 281, 407–408
Maometto II (Rossini), 152–153
Le Marchand de Smyrne (Chamfort), 152
Marche de l'Exposition Ottomane (Guatelli), 158–159
Marche Impériale (Guatelli), 158–159
Marcopoli-Poche family, 300–301
Mardin, Şerif, 12–13, 214, 216–217, 283–284, 342–343
Mareček, Rudolf, 317
marginalization, 23–24, 27–28, 355–356, 371
Mariani, Angelo, 160
maritime culture, 24
maritime exchange, 18
market liberalism, 179–180
Marlo, Alessandro, 158–159

Marmara, Rinaldo, 297
Marmara Sea, 50–51, 78
marriage, 244–245, 261
Marschall von Bieberstein, Adolf, 377
Marseille, 45, 54, 65, 82
Marx, Karl, 11
mass transit, 272
Masters, Bruce, 15–17
materialism, 349–350
  spread of, 350–351
  utilitarian, 351
Mecid Bey, 377–378
Meclis-i Vâlâ-yı Ahkâm-ı Adliyye, 139–140
meddâh (traditional storytellers), 99–100
Mediterranean. *See* Eastern Mediterranean
La Méditerranée et le monde méditeranèen à l'époque de Philippe II (Braudel), 22–23
Mehmed Ali. *See* Muhammad Ali
Mehmed IV, 122
Mekteb-i Sultânî, 225–226
Mele, Gaetano, 129
memoir, 297–301
Menasse, Seraphine, 154–155
Mesopotamians, 50–51
Messageries Maritimes (shipping company), 76
Mestyan, Adam, 130–131, 154–155, 159–160
meta-region, 30–31
Meyer, Leopold de, 161
Meyerbeer, Giacomo, 152–155
meyhane, 206–207
Middell, Matthias, 24
Middle Ages, 11–12
middle-class, 119–120, 277, 280–281, 358–359
  life in Salonica, 246–247
  lower middle classes, 94
  of Ottoman Empire, 284–285
  Ottoman Sephardic youth, 230–231
  sense of tranquility of, 146–147
  Smyrniotes, 71
Middlesex (Eugenides), 406–408
Midhat, Ahmed, 204, 250, 278, 282, 353–354, 381–382

migration, 208, 305
  of labor, 312
  long-distance, 302
  lower-class, 311, 320–323, 339–340
  north-to-south, 308–311
  to Ottoman Empire, 305
  of women to Egypt, 375–376
Mihri (Müşfik) Hanım, 262–263, 342–343
The Miller's Daughter (Manasse), 168
Ministry of Pious Endowments, 71
Mintzuri, Hagop, 199–201
Mishra, Pankaj, 27–28, 348–351
Mission Laïque Française, 228
missionary institutions, 220
The Misunderstood Civilization (Vojnikov), 282–283
Mitchell, Timothy, 55–56, 65–66
Mınakyan, Mardiros, 170–171
Mızıka-yı Hümâyun, 122–123, 141–142, 157–158
modernists, 19–20
modernity, 25, 33, 89–90
  anti-modernity, 355
  Eastern Mediterranean, 415
  producing, 273
  quays and, 86–87
modernization, 21–22, 33
Modiano, Fernandez and Co., 185–186
Modiano, Leon, 228
Modiano family, 112–113
Mollah, Aaron, 230
Möller, Esther, 231
Moltke, Heinrich von, 49, 57–58
Monaco Palais de Cristal, 126
Moniteur Oriental (newspaper), 341–342
Monte, Lenora, 133–134
Moravia, 309–310
Moustaki, Georges, 407–408
Mozart, Wolfgang Amadeus, 152–153
Mubarak, Ali Pasha, 65
Muhammad Ali, 38–39, 84
Muhtar, Mahmud, 275–276
Müller, Moritz, 314, 325
multiculturalism, 17
Musa Bey, 147
Musa Pasha, 153–154
Musil, Robert, 8, 26–27, 215–217, 246–247, 295–297

Mustafa Bey, 255–256
Mütalaa (magazine), 247–248
mutasarrıf (district administrator), 361

1908, events of, 155–156
Naar, Devin E., 16–17
narodno kolo, 282
Nasser, Gamal Abdel, 407–408
nation building, 269
national drinking culture (*rakı*),
    188–189, 194–195, 200–201,
    399–400
  benefit of, 205–206
  sociability of, 204
National Theater, 134
nationalism, 341–342
  Arab Egyptian nationalist mobs, 367
  blood toll of, 395–400
  class formation and, 390–391
  in Eastern Mediterranean, 7–8
  separatist, 228
  spread of, 343
  surge of, 241–242
  Turkish, 233, 247–248, 394–400
Naum Duhani, Michel, 128, 130–131,
    142, 293–294
Naum Duhani, Said, 148–149, 176,
    182–183, 195–196, 293–294,
    341–342, 402
Naum Theater, 110–111, 122–124,
    141, 293–294
  fire damage to, 139–140
  French Theater and, 154–155
  gap left behind by, 131–135
  internal regulations of,
    147
  Lotti and, 146–147
  Parisian press on, 145
  splendor of, 128–131
Nava, M., 132–133
Nea Skene, 126
neo-absolutism, 325–326
neoclassical buildings, 70
Nerval, Gérard de, 276
Nestlé, 91
Nestorova, Alka, 92
Netherlands, 54, 70
New French Theater, 131–132
New Jerusalem, 52–55
Nicola, Papa, 129–130

Nicomède (Corneille), 122
Nietzsche, Friedrich, 8, 215, 340–343,
    408–409
Nigar Hanım, Şair, 262
Nişantaşı, 92
Nisvan-ı İslâm (*Women of Islam*)
    (Aliye), 250–251
nonconformist behavior, 323
Novalis, 349–350
Nur, Rıza, 341–342
Nûri, Celâl, 251

Oblomov (Goncharov), 216–217
Occident, 91
Occidentocentric pastimes, 116
Odeon Theater, 138, 161–162
oil wrestling, 256–257
Okday, Ali Nuri, 399
Okday, İsmail Hakkı, 399
oligarchy, 67
Olympia Cinema, 137, 317
Olympia theater, 3–5
Olympos Beer, 206–207
Olympos Brewery, 206–208
Olympos Palace, 135–136
Onassis, Aristotelis, 407–408
opera, 95–96, 126, 315
  addiction to, 149–151
  civilizing mission and, 142–145
  consumers of, 149–151
  difficult travel conditions and,
    154–155
  Eastern Mediterranean and, 150–152
  European Dream and, 150–151
  Europeanization and, 145
  imperialism and, 154–155
  interest in, 172
  Paris, 130–131
  salutary nature of, 139
  Smyrna and, 122–125
  Turkish characters in, 152–153
Opera at Place d'Opéra. *See*
    Cammarano Theater
Oppen, Achim von, 24
Ore Mountains, 315–316
Orient Theater, 134
Oriental Railway Company, 313–314,
    323–325
Oriental Theater Company,
    170–171

Orientalism, 10–11, 21–22, 283–284, 299–300
  cosmopolitanism and, 395
  nesting, 369–370
  reverse, 27–28, 354–356, 362
  rigid notions of, 46
Orientbummler, 303–304
Ortaylı, İlber, 33
Osman Hamdi Bey. *See* Hamdi Bey, Osman
Osmanische Lloyd (newspaper), 238–239
Osterhammel, Jürgen, 20–21
Other, 142–143
The Ottoman City between East and West (Masters, Goffman and Eldem), 15
Ottoman Empire, 8, 13, 308–309, 370, 402
  Arab-dominated half of, 393
  Balkan provinces of, 364–365
  beer coming to, 175–181
  Bulgaria declaration of independence from, 347
  Christian Ottoman subjects, 289
  Christian schools in, 221–222
  crisis in, 243–244
  defeat of, 392–393
  derogatory characterizations of, 333–334
  Early Modern Ottoman world, 19
  economy of, 188–189
  education in, 381
  Europe and, 304
  European arrivals to, 302, 311–314
  Europeanization and, 70–71
  forced integration of, 43
  freedom of movement and, 320–321
  gender roles and, 253
  Greece and, 391–392
  human trafficking and, 383–388
  imperial cosmology, 55–56
  improving cities in, 69
  intelligentsia of, 165–166
  late Ottoman society, 14
  legacy, 30–31
  lower-class emigration to, 305, 339–340
  mastery of French language and, 226
  middle-class of, 284–285
  middle-class Sephardic youth, 230–231
  migration to, 305, 323
  navy of, 90–91
  Pax Ottomana, 37–38, 51
  reforms and modernization attempts, 16
  relations to, 290
  Salonica and, 366–367
  Second Constitutional Period of (1908-1924), 241–242
  Smyrna and, 84–85
  state bankruptcy of, 183–184
  theater and, 159–163, 165–166
  unregistered residents of, 313
  urban public of, 47
  Well-Protected Domains, 180, 189–190
  Westernization and, 48
The Ottoman Empire and the World Around It (Faroqhi), 19–20
Ottoman framework, 30
Ottoman Joint-Stock Company, 190–191
Ottoman Theater, 127
Ottoman Theater Company, 169
Owen, Roger, 12–13

packs of dogs, 63–64
Pagos, 138–151
Palais de Cristal, 131–132
Palamas, Kostis, 239–240
Palestine, 80, 392–393
Pangalti Theater, 134
Pangaltı, 69
Panizza, Giacomo, 153–154
Pannuti, Alessandro E., 295
Panopticon, 51, 55–56
Papadopoulos, Kostaki, 190–191
Pappavasileiou, Hippokrates, 395
Pappenheim, Bertha, 386
Paris
  apartment houses in, 67
  Constantinople and, 163–165
  literati of, 155–156
  Naum Theater, Parisian press on, 145
  opera, 130–131
  Salonica and, 163–165
Paris Commune, 106
Passage de Hönischer, 89

passport controls, 74
Pasteur, Louis, 182
Pâtisserie Parisienne, 398–399
patriarchical system, 250, 264
Pax Levantina, 402
Pax Ottomana, 37–38, 51
Pears, Edwin, 299–300
peasant emancipation, 304–305
Pelvanoğlu, Burcu, 262–263
Pentziki Brothers, 205–206
Pera, 74–75, 91, 117, 133, 373–374
   Austro-Hungarian Consulate in, 378–379
   contemporary art and theater scene, 239
   dancehalls of, 295
   entertainment culture of, 99
   fire, 70, 128
   Istanbul and, 90–91
   Naum Theater, 122–123, 128–131
   police in, 384–385
   prostitution in, 383–384
   theater and, 134–135
peripheralization, 15
personal hygiene, 280–281
Persoviz, Louis, 133
Peschken, Elise, 113–114
Petek, Franz, 313
petit bourgeois, 272
Petit Champ des Morts, 195
   outdoor consumption of beer at, 103, 133, 186
Petit Champ Theater, 113–114, 120–123, 133, 148, 161–162
   Bernhardt and, 164
Petit Lycée (Salonica), 224–225, 228–230
Pharos tis Makedonias (newspaper), 382–383
Philipp, Thomas, 16
Picciotto, Moïse, 292–293
picnics, 102–106
Pisani, Bartolomeo, 158–159, 167
Place Muhammad Ali, 84
Plateia Aristotelous, 396
Plathy of Nagypalugyar, 213–214
Poche, Josephe, 292–293
Poche-Marcopoli family, 293–294
The Poet's Marriage (Sacy), 166
police, 147, 384–386

policemen (*zaptiye*), 238, 359–361
polygyny, 249–251
Polynesians, 230–231
Pomaks, 7–8
Portugal, 29–30
Potokar, Anton, 313
poverty, 304
Princip, Gavrilo, 351
Prinkipos Island, 203
process sociology, 28–29
Le Progrès de Salonique (newspaper), 241–242
Progrès d'Orient (newspaper), 237–238
Prokesch von Osten, Anton, 107, 236, 352–353
Prokopp, Clara, 213–214, 407–408
Prokopp, Fanny Bertha, 213–214
Prokopp, Gottfried, 176–178, 189, 213–214
Prokopp, Hulda, 407–408
promenades, 102–104
Prost, Henri, 396–398
prostitution, 255–258, 372–375, 389.
   See also human trafficking
   Austria and, 380
   British Empire and, 381
   Habsburg Consulate on, 375–380
   Habsburg Empire and, 373–374
   involuntary, 375–376
   in Pera and Galata, 383–384
Protestantism, 284–285, 291, 336–339
provincial authorities, 360–363
provincial violence, 362–363
Public Debt Administration, 89–90
public memory, 403
public space, 65
Punta, 44–45, 396–397
Purcell, Nicholas, 31

Qardahi, Sulayman, 144
Quagliardi, Tobias, 124
Quais Anglais, 89, 102–103
Quataert, Donald, 321–323
quays, 71–75
   anti-quays, 86–92
   attributes of modern Europe embraced in, 79–80
   in Galata, Constantinople, 74–76, 102–103

lower-class and, 82–83
modernity and, 86–87
nostalgia for, 406–409
public property along, 85–86
in Salonica, 3–5, 8–9, 78
in Smyrna, 3–4, 8–9, 21, 25, 75, 78
Quays Theater, 126

Ragusa, 309–310
Rahmi Bey, 277–278, 391–392
railways, 44–45, 327–328
 Oriental Railway Company, 313–314, 323–325
 Salonica and, 398
 Smyrna-Kasaba Railway Line, 359
 underground funicular railway of Constantinople (*Tünel*), 272
 workers, 327, 337–338
rakı (national drinking culture), 188–189, 194–195, 200–201, 399–400
 benefit of, 205–206
 sociability of, 204
Ramadan, 99–100, 114–115, 117–119
ransom, 359–360
Rasim, Ahmed, 200–202
Raskolnikov, 350–352, 368, 390–391, 402–403
Rauf, Mehmed, 251, 254–255
Rebellio (theater company), 123–124
Rebetiko, 400–401. *See also* Anatolian popular music; Greek music
Recaizade Mahmut, Ekrem, 202–203, 214
recreation, 205–206
Reform Charter (1838), 64–65
reforms. *See* reorderings (*Tanzimat*)
refugees, 410–411
Reinach, Salomon, 219–220
Reinwald, Brigitte, 24
renaming popular culture, 398–399
Renan, Ernest, 308–309
reorderings (*Tanzimat*), 32, 233, 257
 adherents of, 369–370
 planners of, 413–414
Republic Square (Izmir), 396–397
Reşid Pasha, Mehmed, 44–47, 63–67
Reşid Pasha, Mustafa, 86–87, 140
La revue commerciale du Levant (digest), 87

Revue Musicale (journal), 146
Rhinelanders, 50–51
Richter, Edwart, 360
Rimbaud, Arthur, 349
Ristori, Adelaide, 124–125
Rıza, Ahmed, 355
Robert College, 227–228
Rodosto, 60–61
Roma, 269–270
Roman Catholic Church. *See* Catholicism
Roman de Violette (d'Ectot), 254–255
Romanticism, 55–56
Rosenkranz Orchestra, 316–317
Rossini, Gioachino, 152–155
Rothschild (Lady), 377–378
Rougon, François, 184–185
Rougon-Macquart (Zola), 276
Roux, M., 235
row houses, 67
Rue Parallèle, 73
Ruggiero, Amalia, 329–333
Ruhr Region, 101
rule of law, 270–272
Rumeli Theater, 131–132
Rumelia, 88
rural population, 115–116
Rüşdiye, 219–220
Russia, 37–38, 70, 73–74, 235, 349–350, 364–365, 374, 387–388
 anti-Westernism and, 354
 campaign against, 308–309
 Crimean War and, 306–307
 fugitive aristocrats from, 392–393
 influence of, 236
 revolutionaries from, 368
Russo-Turkish War (1876), 167, 170, 366–367

Sabah (newspaper), 117–118
Sabri Pasha, 73–74, 135–136
Sabri Pasha Boulevard, 86, 88
Sacher-Masoch, Leopold von, 239–240, 253
Sacy, Samuel Silvestre de, 166
Saïd, Edward, 29–30
Said Bey, 116–118
Saint George's Day riots of 1876, 27–28, 364–366, 368, 376
Saint-Simonianism, 43–44

Sajdi, Dana, 21–22
Salla, Edouard, 131–132
Salon de Variété, 135–136
Salonica, 21, 25
  beer and, 96–97, 194, 205–208
  bourgeoisie of, 111, 239–240
  capitulations repealed for, 391–392
  coffeehouse world politics analysis in, 348
  downtown, 396
  education and, 222–223
  entertainment culture of, 99
  female cyclists in, 247
  Germans in, 323–325
  Great Powers and, 366
  Hartmann on, 45–46
  heterogeneous phases of, 400–401
  İdadiye, 225–226
  identity and, 340
  Jupiter Theater, 161–162
  massive destruction in city center, 397
  middle-class life in, 246–247
  Muslim Quarter, 88
  Ottoman Empire and, 366–367
  Paris and, 163–165
  population of, 11, 66
  promenades in, 103–104
  public buildings in, 85–86
  quays in, 3–5, 8–9, 78
  railway workers in, 327
  railways and, 398
  residential uptown areas of, 89–90
  Saint George's Day 1876, 27–28, 364–366, 368, 376
  Sciaky and, 61, 91
  Sephardic Jews of, 219–220, 224–225
  Smyrna and, 52–55
  state institutions in, 86
  theater and, 135–137
  use of guns during theater performances in, 146–147
  volta of, 82
  women in, 244
Saloniquenas, 244–246
Saloniquenos, 52–53, 245, 392–393
  Jewish, 406
  lifeworlds of, 82
salons, 248–249

To Salvari (song), 341–342
Samartzidou, Euphrosyne, 251–252
Sami, Şemseddin, 250
San Stefano Treaty (1878), 366–367
Sansoni, Basilio, 129–130, 139
Sardinia-Piedmont, 153–154
Sarigiannis, Marios, 93–94
Sarkozy, Nicolas, 407–408
Schäbler, Birgit, 46–47
Schelasi, Elias, 364–365
Schick, İrvin Cemil, 250, 254
Schiller, Friedrich, 349–350
Schmitt, Oliver, 289–291, 300–301, 323, 330–331
Schwan, Friedrich, 366
Sciaky, Leon, 48, 61, 91
  memoirs of, 278
  Petit Lycée and, 224–225, 228–230
Scognamillo, Giovanni, 297–299
Second Constitutional Period of the Ottoman Empire (1908–1924), 241–242
Şehzade Mosque, 134
self-censorship, 234–235
self-fulfillment, 264–265
self-refinement, 146
Selim III (sultan), 122–123
Sent'Agata, Jacob, 312–313
separatism, 304–308, 347–348, 369–370
Sephardic Jews, 112–113, 170–171, 212–213, 225, 336–337
  middle class Ottoman Sephardic youth, 230–231
  from Salonica, 219–220, 224–225
  Southeast European Sephardim, 394–395
  Spanish-speaking Jews, 52–53
September 2001 attacks, 409–410
Serbian-Orthodox Church, 354
Servet-i Fünun (journal), 147–149, 164–165
  Bomonti Beer Garden and, 187
  readers of, 149–150
sex market, 372–373
sex work. *See* prostitution
sex workers, 303–304, 373–374
sexual fulfillment, 244–245, 251, 254, 257

Index 473

sexually transmitted diseases, 257–258
Seydiköy, 102
Şeyh-ül islam, 194
shadow theater, 99–100
Sharif, Omar, 407–408
Sharuf, Yaqub, 282–283
Shelley, Percy B., 349
shishas, 91, 93–94, 99–100, 117, 147–148
Le siège de Corinthe (Rossini), 152–153
Sienkiewicz, Henryk, 239–240
Simotta, Simon, 359–360
Şinasi, İbrahim, 166, 168
Singer, 91
Şirket-i Hayriye, 77–78
slaves, 374–375
Slavic Macedonians, 368–369
Slavophiles, 352, 355–356
Smith, William, 130–131
Smyrna, 25, 65
   Barth and, 187–188
   beer and, 96–97, 208
   Blumberg and, 339
   Bomonti-Nektar Company and, 189–190
   bourgeoisie of, 111
   Calligas and, 50–51
   clam-diving and, 104
   cleansing of, 394–395
   coffeehouses in, 83, 100
   commercial exchange with European ports, 71
   Constantinople and, 80
   corso of, 82
   deaconesses in, 221
   disaster of 1797, 107
   diversity of, 127
   downtown, 109
   entertainment culture of, 99
   fires suffered by, 68–69
   first railway station in, 44–45
   foreign soldiers in, 394–400
   German Consul to, 82–83, 274–275
   heterogeneous phases of, 400–401
   identity and, 340
   Insurance Map, 89
   Judaism and, 222–223
   Kauder on, 75–76
   Levantine identity and, 293–294
   massive destruction in city center, 397
   occupation forces in, 393–394
   opera and, 122–125
   Ottoman Empire and, 84–85
   passport controls in, 74
   population of, 11, 66
   promenades in, 103–104
   quays in, 3–4, 8–9, 21, 25, 75, 78
   residential uptown areas of, 89–90
   Salonica and, 52–55
   street grids of, 369–370
   travelers arriving in, 58
   travelers' comments about, 80
   as trendsetter, 110–111
   Trieste and, 62
   vali in, 63
Smyrna Mail (newspaper), 102, 109–110, 124–125, 177, 238–239
Smyrna Theater, 127–128
Smyrna-Kasaba Railway Line, 359
Smyrneea (newspaper), 235
Smyrnelis, Marie-Carmen, 290, 323, 330–331
Smyrniotes, 123–124, 392–393
   lifeworlds of, 82
   middle-class, 71
sociabilities, 15–16, 26, 101–102, 267, 275, 293–294
   concept of, 93
   creating new, 95–96
   of Eastern Mediterranean, 95–96
   forms of, 93–94
   of nineteenth century socio-cultural order, 94
   women and, 252–253
social capital, 208–209
social mobility, 261
social obligations, 112
social self-affirmation, 328–329
social success, 81
socialism, 337–338
Società operaia Italiana di Mutuo Soccorso, 113–114, 132–133
Société de Bienfaisance des Adolescentes israélites, 113–114
Société des Quais, 72–73

Société Musicale de Constantinople, 113–114, 132–133
Sœurs de la Charité, 221
softas (theology students), 364–365
Sörgel, Georg, 314
Spectateur Oriental (newspaper), 235
Spengler, Oswald, 354–355
Sperco, Willi, 295, 297–300, 341–342, 392–393, 398–399
spiritual resistance, 350
Sporting Club, 81, 112–113, 118–119, 127–128
Stamboul (newspaper), 117–118, 127, 164–165, 237–239
Stambouliotes, 43, 392–393, 401
steam engine, 20–21
steam power, 78–79
steamships
  Constantinople and, 77–78
  revolution of perception, 56–62
  services, 43–44
Steeg, Camille Louis, 229–230
Stengel, Clara, 177–178
Stockholm Orientalist Congress of 1899, 353–354
Storari, Luigi, 124
Şuayip, Ahmed, 144, 149–151, 155, 165–166
Sublime Porte, 70, 89–90
suburbanization, 105–106
Süleyman I (sultan), 374
Sultanic privileges, 38–39
summer retreats to the countryside, 109, 112, 358–360
Swift (ship), 56–57, 60–62
symbolic capital, 369–370
symbolic violence, 288
syphilis, 257–258
Syria, 306–307, 392–393, 410–411
Syrian Protestant College, 227–228
Széchenyi (Count), 131–132

Tabak, Faruk, 14–15, 40
Taksim, 69, 91, 102–105, 397, 402
Taksim Barracks, 105
Taksim Gardens, 129
Taksim – Şişli Axis, 398
Talbot, Michael, 196–199
Tallyerand, Charles de, 38

Tancoigne, J. M., 110–111
Tangiers, 30–31
Tanzimat (reorderings), 32, 233, 257
  adherents of, 369–370
  planners of, 413–414
Tanzimat Valley, 398
tariffs, 38–39
Tavşan Adası, 63–64
Teatro Opera Italiana, 317
technical progress, 43–44
Teutonia, 132–133
Tevfik, Ahmed, 399
Tevfik Bey, Osman, 247–248
Tevfik Pasha, 383
Thalassocentric order, 27–28, 48
  backdrop for, 39
  destruction of, 393
  general framework for, 40
  hegemonic nature of, 357–358
  integration into, 47
  rearrangement of urban space and, 84
  sphere of influence of, 362–363
theater, 26
  amateur, 107–108
  consumers of, 172
  critics, 170–171
  in Eastern Mediterranean, 95–96
  escapism and, 150
  Europeanization and, 145
  France, theatrical prestige of, 155
  history of modern, 165–166
  Journal de Salonique and, 146
  in Levant, 122–125
  Ottoman Empire and, 159–163, 165–166
  Pera and, 134–135
  Rebellio (theater company), 123–124
  Salonica, use of guns during theater performances in, 146–147
  Salonica and, 135–137
  shadow, 99–100
  shishas banned from, 147–148
  traveling troupes, 126–127
  volatility of careers in, 138
  women and, 258–262
Théâtre de Marseille, 126
Théâtre de Petit Champ. *See* Petit Champ Theater

Theatro Evterpo. *See* Euterpe Theater
theology students (*softas*), 364–365
Theotokas, Giorgios, 392–393
Thessaloniki. *See* Salonica
Thessaloniki residents. *See* Saloniquenas; Saloniquenos
Tobacco Régie, 91
Toksöz, Meltem, 16–18
Tolstoj, Lev, 355
Topkapı Palace, 55–56
   Tower of Justice in, 55–56, 60
Tošić, Đuro, 307–308
Tošić, Jovan, 307–308
traditional storytellers (*meddâh*), 99–100
Trakalis, Antonis, 135–136
Translocality, 24
Transregionality, 24
Transylvania, 373–374
Transylvanian Protestant church, 325–326
travelogs, 315
Treaty of Berlin (1878), 366–367
Tricon, Charles, 235
Trieste, 30–31, 259, 309–310, 347, 378
   Calligas and, 50–51
   Smyrna and, 62
Tschumi, Elisabeth, 383
Tüccarzâde İbrahim Hilmi, 279–280, 281–282
Turkey, 298, 410–411
Turkish language, 7–8, 165–168, 170, 227–228
Turkish National Army, 399–400
Turkish nationalism, 233, 247–248, 394–400
Turoczdivek, Loerinz Joseph Peter Mehmed, 213–214
La Turquie (newspaper), 236–237

Ubicini, Jean Henri Abdolonim, 104–105, 154–155, 182
under-class practices, 82–83
Union et Progrès ou La Nouvelle Turquie (Crétot), 155–156
Union Française, 113–114, 132–133
Union Internationale des Amies de la Jeune Fille, 377
Unkapanı (Salonica), 64

upper-class, 110–111, 119–120, 333–334, 358–359
   country settlements, 78
   of Europe, 302
   leisure and shopping, 74–75
   lower-class and, 92
   Muslim women, 196–199
   sociability, 293–294
   women, 254–255, 262–265
urban beautification, 93
urban change, 67
urban history, 15–18, 20–22
urban infrastructure, 101–102
urban perspective, 28–32
urban renewal, 67–68
urban society, 302–303
urban space, 29, 84, 86–87
urbanism, 8–9, 15–16
urbanity, 19
urbanization, 415
Uşakî, Latîfe. *See* Latîfe Hanım
Uşaklıgil, Halid Ziya, 91, 126, 169, 225
Usko, Johannes, 55
Uslu, Seza Sinanlar, 235

Vaka, Demetra, 263–264, 342–343
vali, 63, 361–362
Variété Theater, 131–132
Veinstein, Gilles, 32–33
Veneto-Ottoman wars, 37–38
Venice, 54, 64, 152
Venizelos, Eleftherios, 396
Verdi, Giuseppe, 149, 154–155
Verdi Theater, 131–132
Veuve Prokopp. *See* Prokopp, Clara
vilayet, 74
Vilmot-Medori, Giuseppina, 146–147
violence
   collective, 371
   economies of, 358
   provincial, 362–363
   symbolic, 288
   against women, 250
Vivre dans l'empire ottomane (Georgeon and Dumont), 15–16, 19
Vojnikov, Dobri, 282–283
Voyvoda Caddesi, 76–77, 90–91
Vutzia, Nikola, 329–330

Wagner, Richard, 149, 154–155
Wallachia, 282–283
Wallerstein, Immanuel, 13–15, 17 (*See also* world system theory)
  Braudel and, 19–20
Walthard, Friedrich R., 213–214
Walthard, Gustav Rudolf Hermann Macedonius, 213–214
War on Terror (2001 ff.), 409–410
Weber, Max, 11–13, 29–30, 273, 284–285
Weber, Stefan, 16
Weber, Theodor, 391–392
Weil, Simone, 219–220, 230–231
Weiss, Robert, 335–337, 342–343
Well-Protected Domains. *See* Ottoman Empire
Wenck, Wanda von, 277–278
Werwer, Marie Louise, 101
West-Eastern reconciliation, 92
Western decadence, 381
Westernization, 48
  beer and, 173
  dichotomy of, 64–65
  ideas of, 48
  majority of historians on, 66–67
  narratives of, 165
  super-, 287
Westphalia, 101–102
white slave trade, 377. *See also* human trafficking
  campaigns against, 27–28
  clamp down on, 387–388
  framing of, 375
  protection of, 386
white slavers, 374
  of Habsburg origin, 372–373
  nationality of, 372–373
Winter Garden, 120–121
Winter Theater, 148–149, 163–164
Witt, Ludwig, 308–309
Wolff, Larry, 138–151
women, 196–199, 211–213, 245–246, 343
  Austria and, 380–381
  Bohemian Orchestras and, 314–320
  chastity of, 383–384
  domestic labor by, 328–329
  emancipation of, 271–272
  in entertainment, 260–261
  female labor, 258–259
  female variety of Bihruz Bey Syndrome, 263–264
  Hungary and, 373–374, 380–381
  independent, 260–265
  Jewish women in traditional dress, 274
  migration to Egypt by, 375–376
  at mixed sociabilities, 252–253
  newspapers by women for women, 251–252
  pleasure-seeking, 255
  restriction of sexual availability of, 380–381
  Salonica, female cyclists in, 247
  in Salonica, 244
  theater and, 258–262
  trope of Western loose female morality, 381–382
  unfree, 374–375
  unmarried, 244–245
  upper-class, 254–255, 262–265
  violence against, 250
  young and middle-aged, 254
Women of Islam (*Nisvan-ı İslâm*) (Aliye), 250–251
working-class, 323–325
World Fair in Vienna (1873), 285–286
world system theory, 13–17, 21 (*See also* Wallerstein, Immanuel)
  cultural dimension dismissed by, 21–22
World War I, 38–39, 45–46, 61–62
  cleavage erupting around, 298
  eve of, 170, 414–415
  identity and, 214
  years preceding, 410–411
wrestling, 256–257

Yaver Bey, 141–142
Yenibahçe Theater, 170–171
Yıldız Palace, 122–123
Yılmaz, Seçil, 257–258
Young Turk Revolution (1908), 77, 204–205, 227–228, 360
Young Turks, 63–64
Yugoslavia, 409–410
Yürüks, 269–270
Yusuf Efendi, 361–362
Yusuf Pasha, 118

Zaman (newspaper), 205–206
zaptiye (policemen), 238, 359–361
"Zemire" (Çuhacıyan), 166–167
Zenannâme (*Book of Women*) (Fâzıl), 253
Zionism, 247–248

Ziya, Halid. *See* Uşaklıgil, Halid Ziya
Ziyaeddin Bey, 383
Zlatko, Dimitriaki, 360–361
Zola, Emile, 276
Zonaro, Fausto, 262
Zunkel, Hedwig, 113–114

Lightning Source UK Ltd.
Milton Keynes UK
UKHW031015101120
373118UK00006B/61